Civic Center

Dearest Sam:

I was still in boot-camp when I heard of your father's death. It was bitter news. I thought how you would receive it, alone in some dingy English city. I lay on my sack in the barracks and thought about it. I couldn't write you. Any letter I wrote while at Sheepshead would not have lightened your burden. I simply took it for granted that you would know how I felt. We are so linked that neither of us ever faces a crisis without thinking of the other. I did at Sheepshead as you did at Blanding. Whenever some new horror rose I invariably told myself that you had faced the very same one and doubtlessly many far worse.

I didn't ship in the regular service. After three weeks on a fuel training ship based on Baltimore I was transferred to administrative duty in Atlantic Headquarters. So I was stationed in New York until I secured a release last week.

I'm going to Chicago, but not to stay. I will probably move East. My job with Britannica ends on January 1st. I'm going to make my way Rosenfeld-style, as a free-lance.

Last week I saw Kappy + Elmer Diehl. Neither of them knew what you were doing, how you were living.

I'll see Rochelle and Judy and your mother next week. Write me c/o Vanguard Press, 424 Madison Ave. N.Y. 17.

Love,
Saul.

SAUL BELLOW

Letters

EDITED BY
BENJAMIN TAYLOR

VIKING

VIKING
Published by the Penguin Group
Penguin Group (USA) Inc., 375 Hudson Street,
New York, New York 10014, U.S.A.
Penguin Group (Canada), 90 Eglinton Avenue East, Suite 700,
Toronto, Ontario, Canada M4P 2Y3 (a division of Pearson Penguin Canada Inc.)
Penguin Books Ltd, 80 Strand, London WC2R 0RL, England
Penguin Ireland, 25 St. Stephen's Green, Dublin 2, Ireland
(a division of Penguin Books Ltd)
Penguin Books Australia Ltd, 250 Camberwell Road, Camberwell,
Victoria 3124, Australia (a division of Pearson Australia Group Pty Ltd)
Penguin Books India Pvt Ltd, 11 Community Centre,
Panchsheel Park, New Delhi–110 017, India
Penguin Group (NZ), 67 Apollo Drive, Rosedale, North Shore 0632,
New Zealand (a division of Pearson New Zealand Ltd)
Penguin Books (South Africa) (Pty) Ltd, 24 Sturdee Avenue,
Rosebank, Johannesburg 2196, South Africa

Penguin Books Ltd, Registered Offices: 80 Strand, London WC2R 0RL, England

First published in 2010 by Viking Penguin, a member of Penguin Group (USA) Inc.

1 3 5 7 9 10 8 6 4 2

Copyright © Janis Bellow, 2010
Introduction copyright © Benjamin Taylor, 2010
All rights reserved

A small portion of the Introduction and a number of the letters first appeared in *The New Yorker*.

Photograph credits
INSERT ONE:
Pages 1 (all), *3* (bottom), *5* (bottom): Courtesy of Janis Bellow; *2* (top), *4* (bottom), *8* (top): Courtesy of Nathan Tarcov; *2* (bottom), *3* (top left and right, middle): Courtesy of Sylvia Tumin; *5* (top): Photograph by Polly Forbes-Johnson Storey; *6* (top right): Fred W. McDarrah/Getty Images; *6* (bottom): © Walker Evans Archive, The Metropolitan Museum of Art; *7* (top): AP Photo; *7* (middle): Courtesy of Kentucky Library and Museum, Western Kentucky University; *7* (bottom): Photograph by Evalyn Shapiro, used by permission of Harold Ober Associates Incorporated; *8* (bottom): © 2010 Nancy Crampton
INSERT TWO:
Pages 1 (top): Joan M. Elkin; *1* (bottom), *2* (top): © 2010 Nancy Crampton; *2* (bottom), *7* (top), *8* (bottom): Courtesy of Janis Bellow; *3* (top): AP Photo/Greg Marinovich; *3* (middle): Estate of Evelyn Hofer; *3* (bottom): Courtesy of Smadar Auerbach-Barber; *4* (top): Paul Buckowski/Times Union (Albany); *4* (bottom): The University of Chicago; *5* (top), *8* (top): Nancy Lehrer; *5* (bottom): © Cella Manea, by permission of Cella Manea and The Wylie Agency; *6* (top): Boston University Photography; *6* (bottom): Marco Fedele di Catrano; *7* (bottom): Rachael Madore

ISBN: 978-0-670-02221-2
LIBRARY OF CONGRESS CATALOGING IN PUBLICATION DATA AVAILABLE

Printed in the United States of America
Set in Adobe Garamond Pro
Designed by Francesca Belanger

CONTENTS

Introduction: *"This Caring or Believing or Love Alone Matters"*   vii

Chronology   xvii

PART ONE: *1932–1949*   I

PART TWO: *1950–1959*   95

PART THREE: *1960–1969*   187

PART FOUR: *1970–1982*   291

PART FIVE: *1983–1989*   403

PART SIX: *1990–2005*   463

Editor's Note and Acknowledgments   553

Index   559

Sections of photographs follow pages 156 and 380.

INTRODUCTION

"This Caring or Believing or Love Alone Matters"

W hen urged to write his autobiography, Saul Bellow used to say there was nothing to tell except that he'd been unbearably busy ever since getting circumcised. Busy with the making of novels, stories and the occasional essay; with romance, marriage, fatherhood, divorce, friendship, enmity, grief; with the large-scale events of history and small-scale events of literary life; with the prodigious reading habit and dedication to teaching that saw him into his later eighties. Busy, not least, corresponding. The great authors are not all so good at letters; indeed, you could make a considerable list of figures of the first rank who were perfunctory correspondents. It would seem to be a separate gift, as mysterious as the artistic one. Looking over the best letter writers in our language of the last century—Virginia Woolf, D. H. Lawrence, Hart Crane, Katherine Anne Porter, Evelyn Waugh, Samuel Beckett, John Cheever, William Maxwell, Elizabeth Bishop, Robert Lowell, Flannery O'Connor, James Merrill—one finds every sort of personality and no common denominator. Some kept diaries, others did not. Some were prolific, others produced relatively little. The most one can say is that each led a rich additional life in his or her correspondence, rich enough to have become a part of literature itself.

Four generations—the one before him, his own, and the two following—are addressed in Bellow's tremendous outflow, an exhaustive self-portrait that is, as well, the portrait of an age. His correspondents are a vast company including wives, sons, friends from childhood, fellow writers, current and former lovers, current and former students, admiring and disadmiring readers, acolytes asking him to read what they'd written (he nearly always did, it seems), religious crackpots, autograph hounds (hundreds), obsessive adulators, graphomaniacs and seriously insane people.

It will come as no surprise to readers of Bellow's novels and stories that he can in his letters be instantly dramatic as well as very funny. Here are a few instances from the Alfred Kazin file. First, Paris, January of 1950: "And of this I am sure: that he [Stendhal] would do as I do with his copy of *Les Temps Modernes*, that is, scan the latest *sottises*, observe with brutal contempt the newest wrinkle in anguish, and then feed Simone's articles on sex to the cat to cure her of her heat and give the remainder to little G[regory] to cut dollies from; he can't read yet and lives happily in nature." And from Martha's Vineyard, summer 1964: "We've seen a bit of Island Society. Styron is our leader, here in little Fitzgeraldville. Then there is Lillian Hellman, in whom I produce symptoms of *shyness*. And Phil Rahv who keeps alive the traditions of Karl Marx. I'm very fond of Philip—he's *mishpokhe*—and he gives us a kind of private Chatauqua course in *Hochpolitik* from which I get great pleasure. Why can't we forgive each other before we become harmless?" And from West Brattleboro, Vermont, summer 1983: "That I've become an unforthcoming correspondent is perfectly true; I take no pleasure in these silences of mine; rather, I'm trying to discover the reasons why I so seldom reply. It may be that I'm always out with a butterfly net trying to capture my mature and perfected form, which is just about to settle (once and for all) on a flower. It never does settle, it hasn't yet found its flower. That *may* be the full explanation."

Despite the comradely tenor of these excerpts, relations with Kazin were far from easy. Reading the file through, one encounters Bellow as often outraged as affectionate. Yet in the aftermath of renewed hostilities between them, he dispatched this in the summer of 1982:

Dear Alfred,
A happy birthday to you, and admiration and love and long life—everything. Never mind this and that, this and that don't matter much in the summing up.
Love from your junior by five days,

With others of his generation, relations were less volatile. John Cheever he loved, delighting in their differences of style and heritage. On both sides the letters are courtly, of the great-man-to-great-man kind, yet abundantly tender. Here is Bellow's reply to Cheever, who had asked him to read page proofs of *Falconer*: "Will I read your book? Would I accept a free trip to Xanadu with Helen of Troy as my valet? [. . .] I have to go to New York this weekend, and also to Princeton to see my son Adam playing Antonio, the heavy in *The Tempest*. [. . .] I would like to see you too, but don't know when I will be free from this mixture of glory and horror." (He had just won the Nobel.) Or his riposte, two years later, to Cheever's solicitation of names of writers to be honored by the American Academy of Arts and Letters: "I perish of greed and envy at the sight of all these awards which didn't exist when we were young and mooching around New York." To Cheever's specific request for names of critics to honor, Bellow responds: "There are no critics I could nominate for anything but crucifixion." And this, finally, written in December 1981, after he learned how gravely ill Cheever was: "Since we spoke on the phone I've been thinking incessantly about you. Many things might be said, but I won't say them, you can probably do without them. What I would like to tell you is this: We didn't spend much time together but there is a significant attachment between us. I suppose it's in part because we practiced the same self-taught trade. Let me try to say it better—we put our souls to the same kind of schooling, and it's this esoteric training which we had the gall, under the hostile stare of exoteric America to persist in, that brings us together. Yes, there are other, deeper sympathies but I'm too clumsy to get at them. Just now I can offer only what's available. [. . .] When I read your collected stories I was moved to see the transformation taking place on the printed page. There's nothing that counts really except this transforming action of the soul. I loved you for this. I loved you anyway, but for this especially."

Writing to Ralph Ellison, with whom he shared digs and the early struggle for recognition, he is larky, freewheeling. Here he writes from the University of Puerto Rico, where he was spending the spring term of 1961: "I keep going [. . .] and drift with the stray dogs and the lizards and wonder how many ways a banana leaf can split. The dog population is Asiatic—wandering tribes of mongrels. They turn up in all the fashionable places, and in the modern university buildings, the cafeterias—there're always a few hounds sleeping in a cool classroom, and at night they howl and fight. But with one another, not with the rats, another huge population, reddish brown and fearless. You see them in vacant lots downtown, and at the exclusive tennis club at the seashore. I won't be surprised to see them at the crap table, watching the game. Then there is the mongoose clan. They eliminated the snakes, but now no one knows what to do about their raids on the chickens. So much for the zoology of this place. The island is beautiful. The towns stink. The crowds are aimless, cheerful, curious and gaudy. Drivers read at the wheel, they eat and they screw while driving."

Letters to John Berryman sound a different note. Fragility of life and arduousness of art are the preoccupations. In October 1963, with unforeseeable national tragedy waiting in the wings, Bellow's mood is already dark: "I can't say that all is well with us. My lifelong friend Oscar Tarcov was carried off by a heart attack on Wednesday. I feel I'd rather die myself than endure these deaths, one after another, of all my dearest friends. It wears out your heart. Eventually survival feels degrading. As long as death is our ultimate reality, it *is* degrading. Only waiting until Cyclops finds us." Their friendship was rooted in literary fellow feeling; such pleasure as there is comes from mutual awe. Bellow writes in the spring of 1966: "You have extended my lease on life with these poems. Nothing more stable than inspired dizziness. The poet's answer to the speed of light and the Brownian motion of matter. We have no holy cities, maybe, but we do have Dream Songs."

In letters to the next generation—to Philip Roth, Cynthia Ozick, and Stanley Elkin among others—one encounters a man reluctantly accepting the role of senior eminence, though scarcely at home with it. What's most striking is how differently he responds to each of the three. To Roth in December 1969, thanking him for a letter about *Mr. Sammler's Planet*: "Your note did me a lot of good, though I haven't known what or how to answer. Of course the so-called fabricators will be grinding their knives. They have none of that ingenuous, possibly childish love of literature you and I have. [. . .] There aren't many people in the trade for whom I have any use. But I knew when I hit Chicago (was it twelve years ago?) and read your stories that you were the real thing. When I was a little kid, there were still blacksmiths around, and I've never forgotten the ring of a real hammer on a real anvil."

And in the autumn of 1974, responding to Roth's essay "Imagining Jews": "I was highly entertained by your piece in the *New York Review*. I didn't quite agree—that's too much to expect—but I shall slowly think over what you said. My anaconda method. I go into a long digestive stupor. Of course I am not a Freudian. For one fierce moment I was a Reichian. At this moment I have no handle of any sort. I can neither be picked up nor put down." Finally this, twelve years later: "I want to thank you again for looking after me in London. As you realized, I was in the dumps. [. . .] The Shostakovich quartets did me a world of good. There's almost enough art to cover the deadly griefs with. Not quite though. There always are gaps."

Writing to Ozick, Bellow's theme is history, as here in the summer of 1987: "I was too busy becoming a novelist to take note of what was happening in the Forties. I was involved with 'literature' and given over to preoccupations with art, with language, with my struggle on the American scene, with claims for the recognition of my talent or, like my pals of the *Partisan Review*, with modernism, Marxism, New Criticism, with Eliot, Yeats, Proust, etc.—with anything except the terrible events in Poland. Growing slowly aware of this unspeakable evasion I didn't even know how to begin to admit it into my inner life. Not a particle of this can be denied. And can I really say—can anyone say—what was to be done, how this 'thing' *ought* to have been met? Since the late Forties I have been brooding about it and sometimes I imagine that I *can* see something. But what such broodings amount to is probably insignificant. [. . .] I can't even begin to say what responsibility any of us may bear in such a matter, in a crime so vast that it brings all Being into Judgment."

With Stanley Elkin, he is more intimately reminiscent, more deeply revealing. This from spring 1992: "When I was young I used to correspond actively with Isaac Rosenfeld and other friends. He died in 1956, and several more went in the same decade, and somehow I lost the habit of writing long personal letters—a sad fact I only now begin to understand. It wasn't that I ran out of friendships altogether. But habits changed. No more romantic outpourings. We were so *Russian*, as adolescents, and perhaps we were practicing to be writers. Isaac himself made me conscious of this. When he moved to New York I wrote almost weekly from Chicago. Then, years later, he told me one day, 'I hope you don't mind. But when we moved from the West Side' (to the Village, naturally) 'I threw away all your letters.' And he made it clear that he meant to shock me, implying that I would feel this to be a great loss to literary history. I felt nothing of the sort. I was rid of a future embarrassment.

"But it wasn't a good thing to be cured of—the habit of correspondence, I mean. I'm aware that important ground was lost. One way or another it happened to most of the people I knew—a dying back into private consciousness and a kind of miserliness."

But the formidable letters written in maturity and old age belie Bellow's reiterated claim to have lost the art. The disappearance of those young letters to Rosenfeld is a misfortune for which there are hundreds of compensations, early and late. "It is extraordinarily moving to find the inmost track of a man's life and to decipher the signs he has left us," Bellow wrote. Herein are seven hundred and eight letters charting his inmost track and granting the nearest view we shall have of him.

"He had pledged himself to a great destiny," his old friend and enemy Kazin wrote. "He was going to take on more than the rest of us were." Bellow's career, among the longest in American literary history, does indeed seem outsize—in ambition, learning, vision, bravura, fulfillment. In freedom. The letters collected here bear witness to all he was, but the autobiographical narrative they sketch is overwhelmingly an artist's story. His struggle to write the next page of fiction is, for better or worse, what matters most on any given day. A journey through the Bellow archive reveals how much was taken on, and how much accomplished. The hundred and forty linear feet at Regenstein Library, University of Chicago, include manuscripts, notebooks, address books, appointment books, incoming mail, carbons and (later) photocopies of outgoing mail, photographs, newspaper and magazine clippings, personal objects and so on. Some items: A hectoring letter from his aged immigrant father, dated September 23, 1953, the month in which Bellow's early masterpiece *The Adventures of Augie March* was published: "Wright me. A Ledder. Still I am The Head of all of U. Signed, Pa." A letter from John F. Kennedy dated September 8, 1961: "I am hopeful that this collaboration between government and the arts will continue and prosper. Mrs. Kennedy and I would be particularly interested in any suggestions . . ." etc. A legal instrument certifying that one Saul Bellow, being duly sworn on oath, deposes and says that his naturalization as a U.S. citizen was effective on August 3, 1943, at Chicago, Illinois, as attested by Certificate of Naturalization No. 5689081. (He had arrived from Quebec with his family on July 4, 1924. In other words, the leading American novelist of his generation, who dramatized like no one else American low-street cunning and highbrow foolery, who sought to itemize every particular of the American urban clamor, was not officially American till he was close to thirty years old.)

Also, from the early 1980s, an old-fashioned calling card on which is written, in a spidery hand, "Shall call at your hotel tomorrow Friday at 5:00 P.M. in the hope of seeing you. Sincerely, Sam Beckett." They did indeed meet the following afternoon in the bar of the Hôtel Pont Royal, 7 rue de Montalembert, Saint-Germain-des-Prés. The living embodiment of modernism was eager to meet the great quarreler with modernism. In the event, little was said. Their encounter resembled Proust's famous meeting with Joyce. After the halting exchange of civilities, Proust had asked Joyce's opinion of truffles, and Joyce allowed as he liked them and so on, miserably. A number of versions of the meeting were later reported, most of which sound embroidered. Whatever was said, one thing is clear: Those mighty opposites had no wish to meet again.

Nor did Bellow and Beckett. Had he read *Dangling Man*, Bellow's first published novel, Beckett would have come upon this quick bit of dialogue—

"If you could see, what do you think you would see?"

"I'm not sure. Perhaps that we were the feeble-minded children of angels."

—and might have wondered if he, Beckett, had written the lines, for they could as well have been spoken by Vladimir to Estragon in *Waiting for Godot* or by Nag to Nell in *Endgame*. But Beckett, that good and generous man, was likely responding to everything in Bellow antithetical to himself: an unfazed humanistic faith and, beyond that, a faith in things beyond the grave. The last ditch, the final straw, the end of the line, the *fin de partie*—all these ways of thinking, all these metaphors for nullity, were anathema to Bellow's fundamentally buoyant, bright-hearted imagination.

A photo from his bar-mitzvah year shows a handsome, compact boy in knickerbockers, kneesocks and spectators, smiling mildly into the camera. The day is sunny, the season leafy. In one hand he holds an open book. Harder to see, tucked under an arm, is a second book. No time to waste, what with all there was to read: Tocqueville, Stendhal, Balzac, Dostoyevsky, Marx, Flaubert, Durkheim, Tolstoy, Weber, Conrad, Frazer, Dreiser, Malinowski, Boas, Wyndham Lewis, D. H. Lawrence. This "superior life," as he calls it in *Humboldt's Gift*, this insatiable book-hunger, was from childhood the necessary complement to "bread-and-butter, meat-and-potatoes, dollars-and-cents, cash-and-carry Chicago." Alongside the Division Street world of peddlers, tailors, greengrocers, fishmongers, butchers, *ganzer machers,* touts and *shnorrers* was this lavish invitation to otherness, this superabundant hospitality of books. "I had a heart full of something. I studied my favorite authors. I rode the bobbling el cars reading Shakespeare or the Russians or Conrad or Freud or Marx or Nietzsche, unsystematic, longing to be passionately stirred."

Bellow's bookishness has inclined critics to sum him up as a novelist of ideas. True, his protagonists are intellectuals—but intellectuals who discover how feeble their learning is once real life has barged in. He shows the comic inefficacy of ideas when brought to the test of experience. Scratch these intellectuals and you find flesh-and-blood, struggling, bewildered human beings. In *Herzog*, for example, Bellow dramatizes the sad hilarity of a scholar no more able to finish his magnum opus, *The Roots of Romanticism,* than Mr. Casaubon in George Eliot's *Middlemarch* could finish his *Key to All Mythologies.* But when Moses Herzog undergoes the additional humiliation of being cuckolded by his best friend, the block lifts. He finds he can write—not, however, about Romanticism. What he manically scribbles is letters. Not the stamped-and-mailed kind collected here. No, it's unsent letters that save Herzog, epistolary furor transmuting the failed Romantic scholar—by one of Bellow's beautiful reversals—into the article itself, a genuine Romantic. Let others dabble in nihilism as they please; for Herzog life remains what it had been for Keats—the vale of soul-making. The thing he'd attempted to tackle at second hand Herzog now knows *originally*, without mediation, as a birthright. His humiliation becomes the groundwork for revelations of the Sublime. Letters are dispatched to an ever more sacred company. Here, for example, is Herzog writing to his childhood friend Shapiro: "But we mustn't forget how quickly the visions of genius become the canned goods of intellectuals. The canned sauerkraut of Spengler's 'Prussian Socialism,' the commonplaces of the Wasteland outlook, the cheap mental stimulants of alienation, the cant and rant of pipsqueaks about Inauthenticity and Forlornness. I can't accept this foolish dreariness. We are talking about the whole life of mankind. The subject is too great, too deep for such weakness, cowardice—too deep, too great, Shapiro." And to Morgenfruh, a social scientist fondly remembered from graduate-school days: "Dear Dr. Morgenfruh, Latest evidence from the Olduvai Gorge in East Africa gives grounds to suppose that man did not descend from a peaceful arboreal ape, but from a carnivorous, terrestrial type, a beast that hunted in packs and crushed the skulls of prey with a club or femoral bone. It sounds bad, Morgenfruh, for the optimists, for the lenient hopeful view of human nature." And here to God, in whom Herzog (like his maker) involuntarily believes when he feels life beating against its boundaries: "How my mind has struggled to make coherent sense. I have not been too good at it. But I have desired to do your unknowable will, taking it, and you, without symbols. Everything of intensest significance, especially if divested of me." Finally, and most movingly, to his long-dead mother: "The life you gave me has been curious, and perhaps the death I must inherit will turn out to be even more profoundly curious. I have sometimes wished it would hurry up, longed for it to come soon. But I am still on the same side of eternity as ever. It's just as well, for I still have certain things to do. And without noise, I hope. Some of my oldest aims seem to have slid away."

You love Moses Herzog for blindness, for haplessness, for thrashing around. At length, you love the feeble-minded child of angels for having come into his own. All that letter writing has delivered him to silence. At the book's climax, while a hermit thrush sings his evening song, Herzog's self and soul chat amiably, inwardly: "But what do you want, Herzog?" "But that's just it—not a solitary thing. I am pretty well satisfied to be, to be just as it is willed, and for as long as I may remain in occupancy." He fills his hat with flowers: rambler roses, day lilies, peonies. "At this time he had no messages for anyone. Nothing. Not a single word." Resentment, rage, hatred, jealousy, self-pity—all are transfigured into natural piety. And such piety, in Bellow's mimetic art, has the last word, however bad the news from Olduvai Gorge.

Novels and stories draw their strength from the humility of the emotions, not from the grandeur of big ideas. Their abiding power is a belief—always difficult to sustain—in the existence of others. "This caring," says Bellow, "or believing or love alone matters." Let one instance, taken from *Humboldt*, stand here for hundreds. The scene is the old Russian Bath on Division Street: "Mickey who keeps the food concession fries slabs of meat and potato pancakes, and, with enormous knives, he hacks up cabbages for coleslaw and he quarters grapefruits (to be eaten by hand). The stout old men mounting in their bed sheets from the blasting heat have a strong appetite. Below, Franush the attendant makes steam by sloshing water on the white-hot boulders. These lie in a pile like Roman ballistic ammunition. To keep his brains from baking Franush wears a wet felt hat with the brim torn off. Otherwise he is naked. He crawls up like a red salamander with a stick to tip the latch of the furnace, which is too hot to touch, and then on all fours, with testicles swinging on a long sinew and the clean anus staring out, he backs away groping for the bucket. He pitches in the water and the boulders flash and sizzle. There may be no village in the Carpathians where such practices still prevail."

Franush appears and vanishes, yet he is immortal, a datum nothing can unmake.

From the Fifties, the population of what Bellow called "my Dead" steadily grows, of course. Inevitable in the collected letters of a long life: more and more loved ones nowhere certainly but in the safekeeping of memory. After seventy-five, you look in vain for survivors from the older generation; after eighty-five, only remnants of your own remain. Like Rob Rexler in "By the Saint Lawrence," his last story, written at the age of eighty, Bellow no longer sees death as the ugly intruder. The metaphor has changed. Now death is the universal magnetic field, irresistible, gathering us in. Yet now, as never before, the ecstatic sense of being alive—and the hallucinatory vividness of those who are gone—bear down on Rexler with blessings. He recalls his earliest encounter with death: In Lachine, at the level crossing of the Grand Trunk, a man has been killed by an oncoming train. Standing up on the running board of Cousin Albert's Model T for a better look, Robby sees organs in the roadbed. Aunt Rozzy, when Albert and Robby come home to tell her, lowers her voice and mutters something devout. Remembered in old age, the long-ago day is suddenly possessed as much more than a memory. Everything that happened then seems also to be happening now. Elderly Rob Rexler *becomes* young Robby stroking Cousin Albert's close rows of wavy hair, as Albert fiercely pushes the hand away. "These observations, Rexler was to learn, were his whole life—his being—and love was what produced them."

A sentence of fiction like that is art of the highest order. Bellow's letters are the other side of the tapestry, hitherto unseen: tangled, knotty, loose threads hanging, reverse of the radiant design. He called his novels and stories "letters-in-general of an occult personality." The letters-in-particular here collected reveal the combats, the delights, the longings—the will, the heroic self-tasking—that gave birth to such lasting things.

—Benjamin Taylor

CHRONOLOGY

1912–13 Abram Belo forced to flee Russia following trial in which he is convicted of conducting business on false papers. ("In Petersburg Pa had made a handsome living. He dealt in produce and traveled widely. He was the largest importer of Egyptian onions and Spanish fruit.") Immigrates to Lachine, Quebec, a village on the Saint Lawrence River. Wife Lescha (Liza) Gordin Belo and their three children—Zelda (Jane), born 1906; Movscha (Moishe, Maurice), born 1908; and Schmule (Samuel), born 1911—follow once he is settled. Abram variously works as a baker, junk dealer and small-scale importer of dry goods. Family name is changed to Bellows.

1915 A fourth child, Solomon (later Saul), born on June 10 at 130 Eighth Avenue, Lachine.

1918–19 Family moves from Lachine to Montreal. ("We lived on Saint Dominique's Street, which is a good clerical name, but in addition you had old Reuben, who could barely walk, going to shul or coming from shul—and you had all kinds of people. Very strange people, most of them Yiddish speaking, in this neighborhood.") Abram fails repeatedly at various enterprises. Solomon begins religious training. ("We were near the waterfront, on a long hill, and I used to go across the street to my rabbi. His name was Shikka Stein and he had a very Chinese look. [. . .] He taught me my *Aleph Beis* and then we began to read *Breishis* and it was wonderful. For one thing, these were all my relatives. Abrahams and Isaacs and Chavas and so forth. So yes, it was like a homecoming for me. I was four years old and my head was in a spin. I would come out of Shikka Stein's apartment and sit on the curb and think it all over in front of my house.") Speaks French in the street, Yiddish at home.

1923 Following U.S. enactment of the Volstead Act banning sale of alcoholic beverages, Abram supports family by bootlegging liquor across the Canadian-American border. Aged eight, Solomon falls ill with peritonitis and pneumonia; six months of convalescence at Royal Victoria Hospital. ("I started to read in the hospital, where I spent a lot of time. They would come around with a cart [. . .] and you would pick some books; mostly they were foolish fairy tales, but sometimes there was a real book.")

1924 Abram goes to Chicago to work in bakery of cousin Louis Dworkin. Rest of family illegally enter U. S. to join him, arriving at Chicago on July 4. Residence in Humboldt Park. Family name now Bellow. (In subsequent years, brothers Maurice and Sam will again add the final *s*.) Sol is enrolled in Lafayette School and Columbus Elementary. Abram widely entrepreneurial. ("My father owned various businesses, always very strange businesses. For instance, he sold wood to the Jewish bakeries of Chicago, as fuel. He had this bakery experience so he knew all the Jewish bakers in Chicago. Of course they wanted to buy from him. But for my father this involved going to the lumber mills in Michigan and Wisconsin and buying up the scrap wood, the reject wood, and bringing it to Chicago in freight cars and then selling it to his bakeries.")

1928 With Isaac Rosenfeld, Sol composes Yiddish send-up of "The Love Song of J. Alfred Prufrock." ("I had a very close friend in Chicago when I was about thirteen. He and I were very mischievous and we used to translate—or parody—famous poems into Yiddish, just for fun. That's why we did T. S. Eliot. So: *In dem zimmer / vu die waibers zinnen / redt men fun Karl Marx und Lenin . . .*") Both parents inculcate early love of nineteenth-century Russian literature.

1930 Following graduation from Sabin Junior High, enters Tuley High School, where, in addition to Rosenfeld, friends include Oscar Tarcov, Louis Sidran, Abe Kaufman, Sam Freifeld, David Peltz, Hymen Slate, Louis Lasco, Stuart Brent, Rosalyn Tureck, George Reedy, Nathan Gould, Herbert Passin, Yetta Barshevsky and Zita Cogan. ("The children of Chicago bakers, tailors, peddlers, insurance agents, pressers, cutters, grocers, the sons of families on relief, were reading buckram-bound books from the public library and were in a state of enthusiasm, having found themselves on the shore of a novelistic land to which they really belonged, discovering their birthright, hearing incredible news from the great world of culture, talking to one another about the mind, society, art, religion, epistemology, and doing all this in Chicago.") Collaborates with childhood friend Sydney J. Harris—later well-known columnist at *Chicago Daily News*—on novel. Sydney brings book to New York; is taken up by John Dos Passos and Pascal Covici among others. ("In the opinion of the New York experts who had read our manuscript, Sydney was an obvious winner. Covici the publisher had commissioned a book on Chicago's revolutionary youth and paid Sydney an advance of two hundred dollars. In the judgment of the publishing illuminati, I would do well to enter my father's business.")

1931–32 Abram's fortunes improve, despite Depression. Family moves from West to East Humboldt Park. ("We belonged to the heart of the country. We were at home in the streets, in the bleachers. I remember portly sonorous Mr. Sugerman, the *schochet* on Division Street, singing out the names of the states during the Democratic roll call, broadcast on the radio, that nominated FDR. He did this in cantorial Jewish style, as though he were standing at the prayer desk, proud of knowing the correct order from A to W, an American patriot who wore a black rabbinical beard.")

1933 In January, graduates from Tuley and enrolls at Crane Junior College in Chicago Loop. At home, frequent political arguments between father and son. ("For some reason Trotsky took a very powerful hold in certain American cities and Chicago was one of them. To read Trotsky's *History of the Revolution* was an eye-opener—even though most of it was party-line; we didn't know that at the time. And this caused conflict at home because my father didn't want me reading Lenin. He was very shrewd about such things, and he knew a lot about what was going on in the Soviet Union in the Twenties, and he knew much more about it than I did. I would have done well and saved myself a lot of trouble if I had listened to him, because he had it straight from the very beginning.") Mother dies after long battle with breast cancer. In autumn Sol enrolls at University of Chicago, following Rosenfeld's lead. ("[Isaac's] color was generally poor, yellowish. At the University of Chicago during the Thirties, this was the preferred intellectual complexion.") Rents furnished room at Hyde Park boardinghouse.

1934 Abram, now owner and manager of the Carroll Coal Company, remarries. Sol and friend Herb Passin ride the rails as far as New York and Montreal. Both briefly arrested in Detroit.

1935 Family faces financial reversals. Abram can no longer send Sol to University of Chicago. Transfers to Northwestern; studies English literature; also anthropology under Melville J. Herskovits, influential social scientist of the day. ("I learned that what was right among the African Masai was wrong with the Eskimos. Later I saw that this was a treacherous doctrine—morality should be made of sterner stuff. But in my youth my head was turned by the study of erratic—or goofy—customs. In my early twenties I was a cultural relativist.")

1936 Publishes pieces in *The Daily Northwestern*, signing himself "Saul Bellow."

1937 Named associate editor of *The Beacon*, a monthly for which he writes. James T. Farrell, famed author of *Studs Lonigan*, befriends him. Bellow graduates from Northwestern with B.A. in anthropology. Awarded graduate fellowship in Department of Sociology and Anthropology at University of Wisconsin, Madison; Rosenfeld already a doctoral student there.

1938 After two semesters, abandons graduate study and returns to Chicago. Works briefly for the WPA, writing biographies of Midwestern writers. Marries Anita Goshkin of Lafayette, Indiana, prominent in Northwestern radical circles, daughter of immigrant Jews from Crimea, "straightforward, big-bosomed, and very assertive," as Herb Passin would recall her. Bellow takes job at Pestalozzi-Froebel Teachers College on South Michigan Avenue, teaching courses in anthropology and English. Works of literature he assigns include novels by Flaubert, Dostoyevsky, Dreiser and Lawrence.

1939 Sets to work on *Ruben Whitfield*, first attempt at a novel. "I met on the street a professor who put a difficult question to me. He, Dr. L, was a European scholar, immensely learned. Growing bald, he had shaved his head; he knew the great world; he was severe, smiling primarily because he had occasion to smile, not because anything amused him. He read books while walking rapidly through traffic, taking notes in Latin shorthand, using a system of his own devising. In his round, gold-rimmed specs, with rising wrinkles of polite inquiry, he asked, 'Ah? And how is the *romancier*?' The *romancier* was not so hot. The *romancier*'s ill-educated senses made love to the world, but he was as powerfully attached to silliness and squalor as to grandeur. His unwelcome singularity made his heart ache. He was, so far as he knew, the only full-time *romancier* in Chicago (apart from Nelson Algren), and he felt the queerness (sometimes he thought it the amputation) of his condition. [. . .] I am bound to point out that the market man, the furniture mover, the steamfitter, the tool-and-diemaker, had easier lives. They were spared the labor of explaining themselves."

1940 Reads Stendhal. Also D. H. Lawrence's *Mornings in Mexico*. Travels to Mexico City with Passin. ("We had an appointment with Trotsky and we came to the door of the house: an unusual amount of excitement. We asked for Trotsky and they said who are you, and we said we were newspapermen. They said Trotsky's in the hospital. So we went to the hospital and we asked to see Trotsky and they opened the door and said, he's in there, so we went in and there was Trotsky. He had just died. He had been assassinated that morning. He was covered in blood and bloody bandages and his white beard was full of blood.")

1941 Short story "Two Morning Monologues" accepted by Philip Rahv for publication in *Partisan Review*.

1942 *Ruben Whitfield* evidently abandoned. Completed draft of another novel, *The Very Dark Trees*, accepted by William Roth of Colt Press; payment is one hundred fifty dollars. In New York, Bellow stays with Rosenfeld. ("On Seventy-sixth Street there sometimes were cockroaches springing from the toaster with the slices of bread. Smoky, the rakish little short-legged brown dog, was only partly housebroken and chewed books; the shades were always drawn (harmful sunlight!), the ashtrays spilled over.") Engages literary agent Maxim Lieber and meets Alfred Kazin and Delmore Schwartz. Draft board defers Bellow twice owing to hernia. Forced to suspend operations at Colt Press. William Roth sends fifty-dollar consolation fee. Bellow burns manuscript of *The Very Dark Trees*. Reads and is influenced by Rilke's *Notebooks of Malte Laurids Brigge*. ("When I find a writer like that he generally turns into a kind of underground song whose voice I hear all the time, day and night.") Begins work on novel *The Notebook of a Dangling Man*.

1943 Fails to win Guggenheim Fellowship. Whittaker Chambers rejects his application for employment as film reviewer at *Time*. Gets part-time job at *Encyclopaedia Britannica*. ("Isaac Rosenfeld said that it cost less than a thousand dollars a year to be poor—you could make it on seven or eight hundred.") Excerpt from novel in progress appears in *Partisan Review*. Is draft-deferred a third time.

1944 *Dangling Man* published by James Henle at Vanguard Press on March 23, 1944; praised by Edmund Wilson in *The New Yorker* as "one of the most honest pieces of testimony on the psychology of a whole generation who have grown up during the Depression and the war." Anita gives birth to son Gregory in April. Henry Volkening, co-founder of literary agency Russell & Volkening, acting now as Bellow's agent.

1945 Accepted into Merchant Marine. Posted to Atlantic headquarters at Sheepshead Bay, Brooklyn. Following Japanese surrender, released to inactive status. Begins work on next novel, *The Victim*, "a story of guilt," as he proposes it.

1946 Second application for Guggenheim Fellowship unsuccessful. University of Minnesota, Minneapolis, hires him as assistant professor of English. Among senior colleagues is Robert Penn Warren, who will be lifelong friend. Also comes to know Hubert Humphrey, then mayor of Minneapolis.

1947 First trip to Europe: Paris, Barcelona, Madrid, Málaga, Granada. *The Victim* published in November by Vanguard. ("In writing *The Victim* I accepted a Flaubertian standard. Not a bad standard, to be sure, but one which, in the end, I found repressive [. . .] A writer should be able to express himself easily, naturally, copiously in a form which frees his mind, his energies. Why should he hobble himself with formalities? With a borrowed sensibility? With the desire to be 'correct'? Why should I force myself to write like an Englishman or a contributor to *The New Yorker*? I soon saw that it was simply not in me to be a mandarin.")

1948–49 Receives Guggenheim Fellowship. Publishes "Spanish Letter" in *Partisan Review*. Breaking with Vanguard Press, goes to Viking; Monroe Engel is his editor. Journeys with Anita and Gregory to Paris, their home for next two years. American friends and acquaintances there include Mary McCarthy, Lionel Abel, William Phillips, Herbert Gold, James Baldwin and Harold "Kappy" Kaplan, friend from early Chicago days. Through Kappy, meets Georges Bataille, Maurice Merleau-Ponty, Albert Camus, Arthur Koestler, Czeslaw Milosz and Nicola Chiaromonte. Develops strong distaste for French intellectual life: "One of the things that was clear to me when I went to Paris on a Guggenheim grant was that *Les Temps Modernes* understood less about Marxism and left-wing politics than I had understood as a high-school boy." Embarks on new work, *The Crab and the Butterfly*, then stalls. One spring morning while watching sanitation sweepers opening hydrants and sunlit water sparkling in gutters, resolves to write different sort of novel. ("I had walked away from the street-washing crew saying under my breath, 'I am an American—Chicago-born.' The 'I' in this case was not autobiographical. I had in mind a boyhood friend from Augusta Street in Chicago of the mid-Twenties. I hadn't seen Augie since the late Twenties; the Forties were now ending. What had become of my friend, I couldn't say. It struck me that a fictional biography of this impulsive, handsome, intelligent, spirited boy would certainly be worth writing. Augie had introduced me to the American language and the charm of that language was one of the charms of his personality. From him I had unwittingly learned to go at things free-style, making the record in my own way—first to knock, first admitted.") In March 1949, publishes "Sermon by Dr. Pep" in *Partisan Review*. In October publishes "The Jewish Writer and the English Literary Tradition" in *Commentary*. In Rome, meets Ignazio Silone, Alberto Moravia and Elsa Morante. Evenings at Antico Caffè Greco. Story "Dora" appears in *Harper's Bazaar*. In December visits London; in addition to publisher John Lehmann, meets Cyril Connolly, Henry Green and Stephen Spender.

1950 Lectures in April at Salzburg Seminars. Visits Venice, Florence, Rome, Positano and Capri. Returns to America in September and settles with family in Queens, New York. "Italian Fiction: Without Hope" in *The New Leader*; "Trip to Galena" in *Partisan Review*.

1951 "Dreiser and the Triumph of Art" (review of F. O. Matthiessen's *Theodore Dreiser*) in *Commentary*. Story "By the Rock Wall" in *Harper's Bazaar*. In New York begins course of Reichian therapy with Dr. Chester Raphael. ("I turned into a fol-lower of Wilhelm Reich and, for two years, I had this nude therapy on the couch, being my animal self. Which was a ridiculous thing for me to have done, but I was always attracted by these ridiculous activities.") "Gide as Autobiographer" (review of André Gide's *The Counterfeiters*) in *New Leader*. "Address by Gooley MacDowell to the Hasbeens Club of Chicago" in *Hudson Review* (reprinted in *Algren's Book of Lonesome Monsters*, edited by Nelson Algren). Second visit to Salzburg.

1952 In spring term, lectures at Reed College and the Universities of Oregon and Washington. Meets Theodore Roethke and Dylan Thomas. Translates I. B. Singer's "Gimpel the Fool" for *Partisan*, Singer's first appearance in English. Bellow's "Laugh-ter in the Ghetto" (review of Sholem Aleichem's *The Adventures of Mottel the Cantor's Son*) in *Saturday Review of Literature*. Reviews Ralph Ellison's *Invisible Man* for *Commentary*; Ellison and wife Fanny will be lifelong friends. In June, first residency at Yaddo, artists' colony in Saratoga Springs, New York. In autumn, takes post at Princeton as Delmore Schwartz's assistant and comes to know John Berryman, who will be among his greatest friends. ("What he mainly had on his mind was literature. When he saw me coming, he often said, 'Ah?' meaning that a literary discussion was about to begin. It might be *The Tempest* that he was considering that day, or *Don Quixote*; it might be Graham Greene or John O'Hara; or [Maurice] Goguel on Jesus, or Freud on dreams. [. . .] There was only one important topic. We had no small talk.") "Interval in a Lifeboat," extract from *Augie March,* published in *The New Yorker*. Meets Sondra Tschacbasov, newly graduated from Bennington College and working as receptionist at *Partisan*. ("I could have gone out with Philip Rahv or Saul," she would later recall. "I chose Saul.")

1953 "Hemingway and the Image of Man" (review of Philip Young's *Ernest Hemingway*) in *Partisan*. Bellow begins teaching at Bard College, Annandale-on-Hudson, New York. Lives in nearby Barrytown on the estate of Chanler Chapman, son of eminent American man of letters John Jay Chapman. In July, second residency at Yaddo. In September, publishes *The Adventures of Augie March* to tremendous critical acclaim. ("My earlier books had been straight and respectable. As if I had to satisfy the demands of H. W. Fowler. But in *Augie March* I wanted to invent a new sort of American sentence. Something like a fusion of colloquialism and elegance. What you find in the best English writing of the twentieth century—in Joyce or E. E. Cummings. Street language combined with a high style. [. . .] I think *The Adventures of Augie March* represented a rebellion against small-public art and the inhibitions it imposed. My real desire was to reach 'everybody.' I had found—or believed I had found—a new way to *flow*. For better or for worse, this set me apart. Or so I wished to think. It may not have been a good thing to stand apart, but my character demanded it. It was inevitable—and the best way to treat the inevitable is to regard it as a good thing.") At Bard, comes to know Irma Brandeis, Heinrich Blücher, Hannah Arendt, Theodore Hoffman, Anthony Hecht, Theodore Weiss, Keith Botsford and Jack Ludwig.

1954 "The Gonzaga Manuscripts" in *Discover.* "How I Wrote Augie March's Story" in *The New York Times Book Review.* "A Personal Record" (review of Joyce Cary's *Except the Lord*) in *The New Republic.* Receives National Book Award for *Augie.* Separates from Anita and resigns position at Bard. Spends summer at Wellfleet, Massachusetts, where friends and acquaintances include Alfred Kazin, Mary McCarthy and Harvard professor Harry Levin.

1955 Abram Bellow dies of aneurysm. ("[W]hen I wept at the funeral, my eldest brother said to me, 'Don't carry on like an immigrant!' He had business friends there and he was ashamed of all this open emotionalism.") Story "A Father-to-Be" in *The New Yorker.* Interviews "Yellow Kid" Weil, legendary Chicago con man, for *The Reporter.* Receives second Guggenheim Fellowship. "The French as Dostoyevsky Saw Them" in *The New Republic.* Establishes residence at Reno, Nevada, awaiting divorce.

1956 In Reno, marries Sondra in February. Arthur Miller, awaiting his own divorce, settles into nearby bungalow with Marilyn Monroe. "Rabbi's Boy in Edinburgh" (review of *Two Worlds* by David Daiches) in *Saturday Review of Literature.* At Yaddo in September, meets John Cheever, whom he will rank highest among contemporary American writers of fiction. With eight-thousand-dollar inheritance from father, buys ramshackle residence at Tivoli, New York. Teaches at the New School for Social Research. *Seize the Day* published in *Partisan Review* in November. ("I think that for old-time Chicagoans the New Yorkers of *Seize the Day* are emotionally thinner, or one-dimensional. We had fuller or, if you prefer, richer emotions in the Middle West. I think I congratulated myself on having been able to deal with New York, but I never won any of my struggles there, and I never responded with full human warmth to anything that happened there.") "The University as Villain" in *The Nation*.

1957 Sondra gives birth to son Adam in January. Bellow at work on new novel based freely on former Barrytown landlord Chanler Chapman. Teaches spring term at University of Minnesota, where Berryman is on faculty. In the Bellows' absence, Ralph and Fanny Ellison living at Tivoli house. In May, visits Richard Stern's writing seminar at University of Chicago where he meets twenty-four-year-old Philip Roth, instructor of English and author of unpublished story "The Conversion of the Jews," which Bellow admires. Fourth and final residency at Yaddo. Autumn semester at Northwestern.

1958 Continues work on novel based on Chapman, now called *Henderson the Rain King*. In Minneapolis again for autumn term.

1959 "Deep Readers of the World, Beware!" in *The New York Times Book Review*. *Henderson the Rain King* published in March. ("I was much criticized by reviewers for yielding to anarchic or mad impulses, and abandoning urban settings and Jewish themes. But I continue to insist that my subject ultimately was America.") "The Swamp of Prosperity" (review of Philip Roth's *Goodbye, Columbus*) in *Commentary*. Comes to know young fiction writer Alice Adams. At work on play variously entitled *Bummidge, The Upper Depths, Scenes from Humanitis* and, ultimately, *The Last Analysis*. Separates from Sondra.

1960 Sondra asks for divorce. Bellow does State Department lecture tour of Poland and Yugoslavia; Mary McCarthy also on tour. ("Saul and I parted good friends," McCarthy afterward writes to Hannah Arendt, "though he is too wary and raw-nerved to be friends, really, even with people he decides to like. He is in better shape than he was in Poland, yet I felt very sorry for him when I saw him go off yesterday, all alone on his way to Italy, like Augie with a cocky sad smile disappearing into the distance.") In Israel, meets S. Y. Agnon, greatest of modern Hebrew prose writers. Journeys to Naples, Rome, Paris, Edinburgh and Manchester. In London, meets his new publisher, George Weidenfeld; reception in Bellow's honor attended by Stephen Spender, Anthony Powell, Louis MacNeice,

Karl Miller, J. B. Priestley and others. "The Sealed Treasure" in *Times Literary Supplement*. Begins work on novel *Herzog*. Founds *The Noble Savage*, quarterly magazine coedited with Keith Botsford and Jack Ludwig; contributors will include Ralph Ellison, Arthur Miller, Nelson Algren, Josephine Herbst, Harold Rosenberg, John Berryman, Howard Nemerov, Herbert Gold, Harvey Swados, Thomas Pynchon, Robert Coover, Jules Feiffer, Edward Hoagland, B. H. Friedman, Dan Wakefield, Cynthia Ozick, John Hollander, Donald Finkel, Seymour Krim, Thomas Berger, Marjorie Farber and Louis Gallo. Realizes Sondra has been having affair for more than a year with his colleague (and obsessive emulator) Jack Ludwig. Divorce from Sondra final in June. Bellow falls in love with Susan Glassman, daughter of prominent Chicago physician.

1961 Teaches spring term at the University of Puerto Rico. "Literary Notes on Khrushchev" in *Esquire*. Marries Susan Glassman in November and teaches autumn term at University of Chicago.

1962 "Facts That Put Fancy to Flight" in *The New York Times Book Review*. With other leading American writers and cultural figures, attends White House dinner to honor André Malraux. (President Kennedy, Bellow later remarks, "could be on good terms with the intellectuals because, thank God, he didn't have to be one himself.") Writes foreword to *An Age of Enormity*, Theodore Solotaroff's collection of essays by Rosenfeld. Northwestern awards Bellow honorary doctorate. "Scenes from Humanitis—A Farce," early version of *The Last Analysis*, appears in *Partisan Review*. Bellow receives five-year appointment as professor in Committee on Social Thought at University of Chicago, where colleagues include sociologist Edward Shils, historian of religions Mircea Eliade and classicist David Grene. Death of William Faulkner. Co-teaches seminar, first of many, with Grene. In English department, novelist Richard Stern will be another close associate and friend. "Where Do We Go from Here? The Future of Fiction" in *Michigan Quarterly Review*. Writes movie reviews for Cyril Connolly's *Horizon*.

1963 Childhood friend Oscar Tarcov dies of heart attack, aged forty-eight. Bellow publishes "The Writer as Moralist" in *Atlantic Monthly*. Honorary doctorate from Bard. Edits and provides introduction for anthology *Great Jewish Short Stories*. ("We do not make up history and culture. We simply appear, not by our own choice. We make what we can of our condition with the means available. We must accept the mixture as we find it—the impurity of it, the tragedy of it, the hope of it.") Reviews *Beatrice Webb's American Diary* in *The Nation*.

1964 Susan gives birth to son Daniel in March. Bellows spend summer on Martha's Vineyard, where friends and acquaintances include Lillian Hellman, William and Rose Styron and Robert Brustein; Herbert Berghof and Uta Hagen are houseguests. *Herzog* published in September. ("Herzog says, 'What do you propose to do now that your wife has taken a lover? Pull Spinoza from the shelf and look into what he says about adultery? About human bondage?' You discover, in other words, the inapplicability of your higher learning, the absurdity of the culture it cost you so much to acquire.") Forty-two weeks on best-seller lists; one hundred forty-two thousand copies in hardcover. *The Last Analysis* premieres on Broadway in October at Belasco Theater. ("In *The Last Analysis* a clown is driven to thought, and, like modern painters, poets, and musicians before him, turns into a theoretician. I have always had a weakness for autodidacts and amateur philosophers and scientists, and enjoy observing the democratic diffusion of high culture.") Reviews negative; closes after twenty-eight performances. In October, Pascal Covici, trusted editor at Viking after Engel's departure, dies of heart attack. Bellow donates Tivoli house to Bard College.

1965 Catharine Carver now Bellow's editor at Viking. "A Wen," one-act play, appears in *Esquire*. Awarded National Book Award for *Herzog*; accepting it, says: "Without the common world the novelist is nothing but a curiosity and will find himself in a glass case along some dull museum corridor of the future." Mayor Richard J. Daley confers five-hundred-dollar prize on behalf of Society of Midland Authors. (Bellow later remarks: "Art is not the mayor's dish. Indeed, why should it be? I much prefer his neglect to the kind of interest Stalin took in poetry.") In June, attends White House festival of the arts, boycotted by Edmund Wilson, Robert Lowell and others. In the East Room, reads aloud from *Herzog*; John Hersey reads from *Hiroshima*; Dwight Macdonald circulates antiwar petition among festival participants. (President Johnson says afterward: "They insult me by comin', they insult me by stayin' away.") Bellow spends second summer on Martha', Vineyard. Receives Formentor Prize. "Orange Soufflé," another one-act play, in *Esquire*.

1966 Lengthy *Paris Review* interview, conducted by Gordon Lloyd Harper. Dramatized version of *Seize the Day*, directed by Herbert Berghof and starring Mike Nichols as Tommy Wilhelm, performed in workshop at Theatre of Ideas. Bellow accepts assignment from *Life* to write profile of Robert F. Kennedy, then candidate for Senate from New York; abandons project after discouraging week in Kennedy's entourage. Delivers ill-received keynote at PEN Congress in New York:

"We have at present a large literary community and something we can call, *faute de mieux*, a literary culture, in my opinion a very bad one." Meets Margaret Staats. Evening of one-acts, *Under the Weather*, premieres at Fortune Theatre, London, to generally favorable reviews. Delmore Schwartz dies in July. *Under the Weather* on Broadway in October at Cort Theater, starring Shelley Winters; reviews savage; closes in less than two weeks. Separates from wife Susan. Begins work on novel *Mr. Sammler's Planet*. Upon departure of Catharine Carver, Denver Lindley becomes his editor at Viking.

1967 Travels to Middle East to cover Six-Day War for *Newsday*. ("Many of the dead are barefooted, having thrown off their shoes in flight. Only a few have helmets. Some wear the headdress. After leaving Gaza, I saw no live Egyptians except for a group of captured snipers lying bound and blindfolded in a truck. The tent dwellers had run off. Their shelters of old sacking and tatters of plastic were unoccupied, with only a few dogs sniffing about and the flies, of course, in great prosperity.") Balance of summer at East Hampton, New York, where Saul Steinberg and Harold Rosenberg are among his friends. Delivers "Skepticism and the Depth of Life" at various American colleges and universities.

1968 Spring in Oaxaca with Maggie Staats; summer in East Hampton. In September at Villa Serbelloni, Rockefeller Foundation retreat at Lake Como, where he befriends young poet Louise Glück. Childhood friend Louis Sidran dies of cancer. *Mosby's Memoirs*, collection of stories, published in October. Divorce from Susan. Aaron Asher succeeds Denver Lindley as Bellow's editor at Viking. In London, confers with George Weidenfeld, his British publisher. Chance meeting with Graham Greene. Death of John Steinbeck in December.

1969 In January, Josephine Herbst dies. Bellow enters treatment with Heinz Kohut, Chicago-based founder of influential "self-psychology" school of psychoanalysis. Returns in June to Villa Serbelloni, Bellagio; August on Nantucket. *Mr. Sammler's Planet* published in back-to-back issues of *Atlantic Monthly*.

1970 S. Y. Agnon dies. *Mr. Sammler's Planet* published in book form. Bellow visits Nairobi and Addis Ababa. At Purdue University, delivers "Culture Now: Some Animadversions, Some Laughs," assault on fashionable avant-gardism of, among other publications, *Partisan Review* under editorship of William Phillips and Richard Poirier. Receives honorary doctorate from New York University. June at Jerusalem artists' colony Mishkenot Sha'ananim.

1971 "Culture Now" printed in *Modern Occasions,* quarterly magazine edited by Philip Rahv. Bellow wins National Book Award for *Mr. Sammler's Planet.* Off-Broadway revival of *The Last Analysis* at Circle in the Square; reviews more favorable; closes after five weeks.

1972 John Berryman leaps to his death from Washington Avenue Bridge in Minneapolis. ("Faith against despair, love versus nihilism, had been the themes of his struggles and his poems. What he needed for his art had been supplied by his own person, by his mind, his wit. He drew it out of his vital organs, out of his very skin. At last there was no more.") Harvard and Yale award Bellow honorary degrees. Edmund Wilson dies in June. Bellow travels to Japan. Nicola Chiaromonte dies. Henry Volkening dies; Bellow engages Harriet Wasserman, Volkening's protégée, as new literary agent. Death of Harvey Swados. In November, delivers "Literature in the Age of Technology" at Smithsonian Institution.

1973 Attends meetings of the Chicago Anthroposophical Society. In April, begins six-week residency in Rodmell, East Sussex, at country house of Virginia and Leonard Woolf. Through Mircea and Christinel Eliade, meets Alexandra Ionescu Tulcea, Romanian-born professor of mathematics at Northwestern. At Viking, Elisabeth Niebuhr Sifton now Bellow's editor. In December, Philip Rahv dies.

1974 "Humboldt's Gift," excerpt from novel in progress of the same name, appears in *Playboy.* Growing enthusiasm for Anthroposophy and writings of founder Rudolf Steiner. ("I do admit to being intrigued with Steiner. I do not know enough to call myself a Steinerian. The college professor in me wants to administer a quick quiz to those who knock him, to see whether they have done their homework.") In November, marries Alexandra Ionescu Tulcea. "Burdens of a Lone Survivor," a second excerpt from *Humboldt's Gift,* in *Esquire.*

1975 Attends White House dinner in honor of Prime Minister Harold Wilson. Travels to England to speak with Owen Barfield, barrister-philosopher and devoted Steinerian, whose book *Saving the Appearances* is source of Bellow's Anthroposophical interests. *Humboldt's Gift* published in August. In October, begins three-month stay in Israel to collect material for work of nonfiction; interviews A. B. Yehoshua, Amos Oz, Abba Eban, Jerusalem mayor Teddy Kollek and Prime Minister Yitzhak Rabin. Alexandra lectures on probability theory at Hebrew University. In November Lionel Trilling dies; in December, Hannah Arendt.

1976 Wins Pulitzer Prize for *Humboldt's Gift*. Nonfiction work *To Jerusalem and Back* appears in back-to-back issues of *The New Yorker*; published as book in October. In December, Bellow awarded Nobel Prize "for the human understanding and subtle analysis of contemporary culture that are combined in his work." At Stockholm, sounds familiar theme of previous addresses: "We must not permit intellectuals to become our bosses. And we do them no good by allowing them to run the arts. Should they, when they read novels, find in them only the endorsement of their own opinions? Are we here to play such games?"

1977 First District Court of Chicago nullifies property settlement in 1968 divorce from Susan, ruling that Bellow had underestimated current and future royalties, and orders him to pay increased alimony and child support. In March, delivers Jefferson Lectures in the Humanities in Washington, D.C., two long reflections on Chicago. ("I was taken aback on my first trip to New York in the Thirties to find the tracks of the Third Avenue El so close to the parlor windows of the tenements. There was always plenty of space in Chicago; it was ugly but roomy, plenty of opportunity to see masses of things, a large view, a never entirely trustworthy vacancy; ample grayness, ample brownness, big clouds. The train used to make rickety speed through the violet evenings of summer over the clean steel rails (nothing else was clean) through the backyards of Chicago with their gray wooden porches, the soiled gray stairs, the clumsy lumber of the trusses, the pulley clotheslines. On the South Side you rode straight into the stockyard fumes. The frightful stink seemed to infect the sun itself, so that it was reeking as well as shining.") In May, awarded Gold Medal for Fiction of American Academy and Institute of Arts and Letters; John Cheever makes presentation. In September, Cook County Circuit Court holds Bellow in contempt for failure to pay alimony and child support to Susan; sentenced to ten days in jail; sentence subsequently overturned. In Cambridge, Massachusetts, for autumn. Teaches at Brandeis, as does Alexandra. Befriends Leon Wieseltier, graduate student in Jewish history and philosophy at Harvard. Begins five-year appointment as member of Prize Fellows Committee charged with selecting recipients of MacArthur "genius" grants.

1978 Leaves Viking for Harper & Row where his new editor is Harvey Ginsberg. In July, Harold Rosenberg dies; in August, Ignazio Silone. Travels with Alexandra to Romania to see her dying mother, Florica Bagdasar, former Romanian minister of health. Illinois Court of Appeals orders defendant Saul Bellow to pay plaintiff Susan Glassman Bellow half a million dollars in settlement of property dispute stemming from their 1968 divorce.

1979 In March, Jean Stafford dies. Bellow spends summer at West Halifax, Vermont. Works steadily through autumn on new novel *The Dean's December*.

1980 Co-teaches seminar, the first of many, with Allan Bloom, colleague in the Committee on Social Thought. (Authors covered over the years include Shakespeare, Rousseau, Stendhal, Dostoyevsky, Dickens, Joyce, Proust, Tolstoy and Shakespeare.) David Grene also sometimes in attendance. Harvey Ginsberg leaves Harper & Row; Edward Burlingame now Bellow's editor.

1981 Attends reunion of Tuley High School. Speaks in May at Brasenose College, Oxford. In June, visits Barley Allison at Almería, Spain. Nelson Algren dies. In Paris, meeting with Samuel Beckett.

1982 *The Dean's December* published in February. John Cheever dies in June. ("I think that the differences between John and me endeared us to each other more than the affinities. He was a Yankee; I, from Chicago, was the son of Jewish immigrants. His voice, his style, his humor were different from mine. His manner was reticent, mine was . . . something else. It fell to John to resolve these differences. He did this without the slightest difficulty, simply by putting human essences in first place; first the persons—himself, myself—and after that the other stuff—class origins, social history. A fairly experienced observer, I have never seen the thing done as he did it—done, I mean, as if it were not done at all.") Bellow and Alexandra again in rented house in West Halifax, Vermont. They begin building new house on nearby acreage Bellow has purchased. Story "Him with His Foot in His Mouth" in *Atlantic Monthly*.

1983 Summer in newly completed house. "In the Days of Mr. Roosevelt" appears in *Esquire* in December.

1984 Long story "What Kind of Day Did You Have?" in *Vanity Fair* in February. Collection of stories *Him with His Foot in His Mouth* published in May. Lachine Public Library renamed Saul Bellow Public Library. Revisits birthplace at 130 Eighth Avenue. In June, Lillian Hellman dies. Bellow on Capri to receive Malaparte Prize; Moravia in attendance. Bellow asks resident author Shirley Hazzard to take him to ruins of Villa Jovis, palace of Roman emperor Tiberius, which he'd last visited in 1950. ("Probably my final chance.") At the end of August, hosts five-day international symposium in Wilmington, Vermont, that includes Czesław Miłosz, Heinrich Böll, Andrei Sinyavski, Alain Besançon, Pierre Hassner, Leszek Kołakowski, Allan Bloom, Ruth Prawer Jhabvala, Werner Dannhauser and others.

1985 Anita, first wife, dies in March. Brother Maurice dies in May, brother Sam in June. Alexandra asks for divorce. Bellow leaves North End, moves to Hyde Park. Observes seventieth birthday quietly in Vermont. Elsa Morante dies. Bellow addresses Ethical Culture Society in New York.

1986 Leaves Harper & Row for William Morrow & Company; Harvey Ginsberg once again his editor. Participates in PEN International Conference in New York. Addresses PEN in London. In March, Bernard Malamud dies; in April, Mircea Eliade. Deepening love for Janis Freedman. They begin their life together at 5825 Dorchester, Hyde Park. Sydney J. Harris dies in December.

1987 Contributes introduction to Allan Bloom's *The Closing of the American Mind*. ("A style of this sort will seem to modern readers marred by classical stiffness—'Truth,' 'Knowers,' 'the Good,' 'Man'—but we can by no means deny that behind our objection to such language is a guilty consciousness of the flimsiness, and not infrequently the trashiness, of our modern talk.") With Janis, travels to Lugano, Milan, Aix-en-Provence, Lyon and Jerusalem. Writers' Conference at Haifa; Bloom, Martin Amis and A. B. Yehoshua in attendance. *More Die of Heartbreak* published by Morrow. Lectures at Amherst College. Reads at Trenton College.

1988 Receives Medal of Freedom from Ronald Reagan. ("I never saw anybody in public life who was so at ease and who played his role so well, with the vitality of an artist.") In April, Paolo Milano dies. Bellow leaves William Morrow and returns to Viking. In Philadelphia, delivers "A Jewish Writer in America" to Jewish Publication Society. In spring term, lectures at Dartmouth College, then travels to Italy with Janis. Receives Scanno Prize in Abruzzo. In Paris, Bellow and Janis on holiday with Allan Bloom and Michael Z. Wu at Hôtel Crillon.

1989 Begins work on two major novels, *All Marbles Still Accounted For* and *A Case of Love* (both unfinished at his death). Malcolm Cowley dies. In March, Bellow publishes *A Theft*. In June, Barley Alison dies. On August 25, in Wilmington, Vermont, marries Janis Freedman. On leave from Chicago, teaches autumn term at Boston University and gives BU's Convocation Lecture. Speaks also at Harvard. In September, Robert Penn Warren dies; in October, Mary McCarthy. Bellow travels to Washington to receive PEN/Malamud Award. In Bartlesville, Oklahoma, receives P. V. Helmerich Distinguished Authors Award. Novella *The Bellarosa Connection* published in December. Death of Samuel Beckett.

1990 "Something to Remember Me By" published in *Esquire*. Bellow speaks at celebration for Vaclav Havel in New York. In May, he and Janis go to Amsterdam and London. Warm friendship with Martin Amis. Delivers Romanes Lecture at Oxford. In London, tea with Margaret Thatcher at 10 Downing Street. ("She didn't need me. She answered her questions herself.") With Janis, belated honeymoon at Sidmouth in the south of England. On June 10, John Auerbach, Al Glotzer, Zita Cogan, Saul Steinberg, Eleanor Clark, Rosanna Warren, Keith Botsford, William Arrowsmith, Philip Roth, Claire Bloom and others gather for surprise seventy-fifth birthday party thrown by Janis at Betty Hillman's Petit Chef in Wilmington, Vermont. ("It was very Chekhovian," Roth recalled. "People got up and burst into tears and sat down.") In New York, receives Medal for Distinguished Contribution to American Letters. Takes up study of Latin; reads Caesar's *Commentaries*. Alberto Moravia dies in September. In October, at Art Institute of Chicago, Mayor Richard M. Daley hosts a second birthday celebration. Travels with Janis for lectures and readings in Montreal, San Antonio, Miami and Cincinnati.

1991 Continues with *All Marbles Still Accounted For* and *A Case of Love*. Winter trip to Italy and Israel with Janis. At invitation of Bruno Bartoletti, lectures on Mozart in Florence. For *Travel Holiday*, writes "Winter in Tuscany." Visits friends John and Nola Auerbach at Kibbutz S'dot Yam in Caesarea. Attends Tuley High School reunion. In July, Isaac Bashevis Singer dies. Allan Bloom seriously ill; Bellow and Janis attend to him daily.

1992 In April, dinner at Robie House to celebrate fiftieth anniversary of Committee on Social Thought. Bloom in attendance; dies in October of complications from AIDS. ("What did the people who reproached him for his elitism want him to do about his evident and—I might add—benevolent superiority?") Death of William Barrett.

1993 William Arrowsmith dies. Beena Kamlani now Bellow's editor at Viking. *It All Adds Up*, collection of nonfiction pieces, published. With Janis in Paris from March through May; teaches at Raymond Aron Institute at invitation of historian François Furet. Lectures in Portugal and Hungary in April. Chancellor John Silber invites Bellow to teach at Boston University; he accepts and, ending three decades at University of Chicago, moves with Janis to Boston. ("I gave Chicago the best years of my life, as they say in divorce court. [. . .] When people asked me, why are you leaving, I said because I can't walk down the street any more without thinking of my Dead, and it was time. I had a girlfriend here or went to a party there or attended a meeting there and so forth. Most of the people whom I had known so well and loved so well were gone.") In November, travels to University of Iowa, where he guest-lectures at Frank Conroy's writing workshop. Delivers convocation address at University of Toronto.

1994 George Sarant, son of Isaac and Vasiliki Rosenfeld, dies. In March, Bellow honored at Boston Public Library dinner. Lectures at Adelphi University and, in April, at Harvard. Travels to Portland, Oregon, and Seattle on speaking engagements. In November, while on working holiday on Caribbean island of Saint Martin, falls dangerously ill from ciguatera poisoning after eating contaminated fish. Back in Boston, hospitalized from Thanksgiving until the New Year.

1995 In January, Edward Shils dies. Bellow resumes teaching duties at Boston University; still convalescent, holds classes at home on Bay State Road. Again able to travel, returns to Hyde Park to address capacity crowd at Mandel Hall of the University of Chicago on "Literature in a Democracy." Visits friend Werner Dannhauser at Michigan State University and delivers lecture there. Ralph Ellison dies in April. Stanley Elkin dies in June. In July, Bellow's last short story, "By the Saint Lawrence," appears in *Esquire*. With Keith Botsford, founds new literary journal, *News from the Republic of Letters*. Gallbladder surgery in December.

1996 Bellows leave Bay State Road apartment and relocate to house in Brookline. Death of Eleanor Clark in February. In preparation for seminar called "Young Men on the Make: Ambitious Young Men in the Novel," Bellow re-reads Dostoyevsky's *Crime and Punishment*. ("[T]he Russians have an immediate charismatic appeal—excuse the Max Weberism. Their conventions allow them to express freely their feelings about nature and human beings. We have inherited a more restricted and imprisoning attitude toward the emotions. We have to work around puritanical and stoical restraints. We lack the Russian openness. Our path is narrower.") Other readings for course include *Père Goriot*, *The Red and the Black*, *Great Expectations*, *Sister Carrie* and *The Great Gatsby*. Gives University Professors lecture at Boston University. Readings at Harvard and Queens College. Begins work on *Ravelstein*, novel based on life and death of Allan Bloom. After twenty-five years, severs professional ties with Harriet Wasserman and engages Andrew Wylie as literary agent. Meyer Schapiro dies in March. In December, Bellow's former wife Susan dies of aneurysm, aged sixty-three.

Chronology

1997 Novella *The Actual* published in April. In July, François Furet suddenly dies. Bellow in Washington, D.C., for unveiling of his portrait at National Portrait Gallery. As always, Bellows spend most of spring, summer and fall in Vermont. Owen Barfield dies in December, aged ninety-nine.

1998 In New York, Bellow participates in tribute to Ralph Ellison at 92nd Street Y. Lectures at Northeastern University, Boston College and Landmark College. Interviewed by Martin Amis for BBC television documentary. In Boston, attends dinner parties and outings with friends new and old, including Ruth and Len Wisse, Stephanie Nelson, Keith and Nathalie Botsford, Rosanna Warren, Judith and Christopher Ricks and Monroe and Brenda Engel. Death in April of Wright Morris. In June, Alfred Kazin dies. In Vermont, dinners and parties with Walter Pozen, Herb and Libby Hillman, Arthur and Lynda Copeland and Frank Maltese; Philip Roth, Norman and Cella Manea, Joan and Jonathan Kleinbard, Sonya and Harvey Freedman, Wendy Freedman, Robert Freedman, and Martin and Isabel Amis make frequent visits.

1999 Death in May of Saul Steinberg. In June, J. F. Powers dies. Bellow sits for long reflective interview with Romanian novelist Norman Manea, later published in *Salmagundi*. Continues work on *Ravelstein*. Alice Adams dies. In September, Bellow lectures at Montreal. A very pregnant Janis travels with him to Lachine to visit The Saul Bellow Library. Bellow sits for series of interviews with Philip Roth. On December 23 in Boston, Janis gives birth to Naomi Rose Bellow. ("I'm sure no child living will have a better mother than my new child is going to have.")

2000 *Ravelstein* published. Publication party at Lotos Club in New York. Karl Shapiro dies. At Harvard, Bellow reads from *Ravelstein*. Receives New England Library Award. Summer visitors to Vermont include Philip Roth, Maneas, Kleinbards and Amises. In October, Bellow, Janis and Rosie visit the Kleinbards in St. Louis.

2001 *Collected Stories* published, with preface by Janis Freedman Bellow and introduction by James Wood.

2002 Though ill, Bellow continues at Boston University, inviting James Wood to co-teach seminar. Death of John Auerbach.

2003 Library of America begins publishing collected works of Saul Bellow in five uniform volumes. Janis asks Roger Kaplan, Martin Amis, Keith Botsford,

James Wood and others to co-teach weekly seminar with Bellow. Rosalyn Tureck dies. Death of sister Jane Bellow Kauffman at ninety-seven.

2004 Bellow receives honorary doctorate from Boston University. Prolonged illness. David Grene dies in September. Bellow, Janis and Rosie still wintering in Brookline, summering in Vermont.

2005 Saul Bellow dies at home in Brookline on April 5 and—after traditional Jewish rites—is interred in Brattleboro Cemetery, Brattleboro, Vermont.

PART ONE

1932–1949

On winter afternoons when the soil was frozen to a depth of five feet and the Chicago cold seemed to have the headhunter's power of shrinking your face, you felt in the salt-whitened streets and amid the spattered car bodies the characteristic mixture of tedium and excitement, of narrowness of life together with a strong intimation of scope, a simultaneous expansion and constriction in the soul, a clumsy sense of inadequacy, poverty of means, desperate limitation, and, at the same time, a craving for more, which demanded that "impractical" measures be taken. There was literally nothing to be done about this. Expansion toward what? What form would a higher development take? All you could say was that you accepted this condition as a gambler would accept absurd odds, as a patient accepted his rare disease. In a city of four million people, no more than a dozen had caught it. The only remedy for it was to read and write stories and novels.

—"The Jefferson Lectures"

1932

To Yetta Barshevsky

May 28, 1932   South Harvey, Michigan

RESOLUTION [scrawled on back of envelope]

My dear Yetta:

I know this letter will be unexpected, less unexpected of course than my impromptu departure, but nonetheless unexpected. Even I had not anticipated it. I had only time enough to snatch my bathing suit and several sheets of paper. The day's events have left my mind in turmoil, but I take this opportunity to write to you, Yetta, to tell you that which has for weeks been gathering, fermenting in my breast, that which has been seething and boiling in me, and finding no expression in spontaneity. It is something, Yetta, that more through uncertainty and cowardice than anything else I have not been able to broach to you. True, I am a self-confessed coward. Cowards we are all intrinsically, but the justification of cowardice lies in the confession.

It is dark now and the lonely wind is making the trees softly whisper and rustle. Somewhere in the night a bird cries out to the wind. My brother in the next room snores softly, insistently. The country sleeps. The waves surge angrily at the house, they cannot reach it, they snarl and pull back. Over me the light swings up and back, up and back. It throws shadows on the paper, on my face. I am thinking, thinking, Yetta, drifting with night, with infinity, and all my thoughts are of you. But my thoughts of you are not altogether kind, they sting, they lash. Or shall we talk business?

You will think, perhaps, "Phrase-monger." For yours is a Young Communist League mind. Or: "What can have gotten into solid, bovine Bellow?"

But all the time you will have a presentiment, and all the time you will pray. (For you are devout, Yetta.)

"Why does he write, why does not the fool wait until he comes back so I can intimidate him?"

I hate melodrama. The only thing that I hate more intensely than melodrama and spinach is myself. You think perhaps that I am insane? I am. But I have my pen; I am in my element and I defy you. (Here there is a lengthy pause, a gusty sigh, and the indomitable Bellow rolls on in all his fullness and strength.)

As of late there has been a noticeable rift between us. It seems that the incorrigible [Nathan] Goldstein is uneasy. It seems that in the presence of others you are too lavish in your affection toward him. The situation indeed is critical. (By the way, Yetta, make it a point to show this to Goldstein.) Mind you, I make no sacrifice, no secret of giving you up. I abhor sacrifice and martyrdom—they are hypocrisy within hypocrisy—an expression of barbaric dogma and fanaticism—their motive, their masked motive, is a disgusting one—it is merely the hiding of the egoism of individualism.

So it is through mutual consent that we part. You to listen to Goldstein's Marxian harangues with a half-feigned interest; I to loll on the bosoms of voluptuous time and space and stifle desire and hope. The Oriental, you know, is a fatalist. It is perhaps atavism that prompts me to say, "What is to be will be." And so I am content. I have no regrets. For some time I will shroud myself in an injured reserve. Maybe I will find solace in the philosophic calm of the ascetic. Man ever seeks to justify his acts. To be a recluse is a justification of the wrongness of a right. In several weeks with a cynical droop to the lip and a weary eye on a sordid world, I the young idealist will lay his woes and his heart at Pearl's feet. If she spurns them I will go home and write heart-rending poetry and play the violin. If not, I will lapse into a lethargic contentment that will last only as long as the love lasts. For love stupefies.

So I sever relations with you.

We may still be casual friends. But some day when I am in my dotage and you are many chinned and obese we may be reconciled. In the Interim be happy—if my notorious skepticism allows me, I too will endeavor to find contentment with Pearl.

So Yetta,

It is Good-bye—

You are at liberty to do as you like with this letter.

Evidently on holiday with one of his brothers, Bellow has just turned seventeen when he writes this, his earliest surviving letter. Nathan Goldstein would shortly marry Yetta. Following their divorce in the 1940s, Yetta would marry Max Shachtman. Pearl's identity is untraced.

1937

To James T. Farrell

[n. d.]   [Chicago]

Dear Mr. Farrell:

It may surprise you that the associate editor of the *Beacon* should be politically of a mind with you, but that is the case. I have asked Al Glotzer several times to write to you for me. I'm tired of asking him; I am quite sure he hasn't written. And perhaps it would be a shame if he dissipated his Machiavellian genius in trivial correspondence.

If you will tell me why you have taken up with the magazine, and what you have gathered of [Sydney] Harris from his letters, and what your opinion is of the role of the magazine, and whether you think it can be useful, I for my part will undertake a long narrative of the whole venture and try to explain my position on it. I will try to give you an inkling of it now: Editorially I can't push the magazine to the left because Harris is a shrewd, opportunistic bastard who won't permit it. However, if we load the magazine with Bolshevik writers of national reputation, we can have Harris hanging on a ledge before long.

Already the Stalinites have excommunicated him and pronounced the magazine anathema. Jack Martin, local educational director of the C.P., wrote Harris a letter calling him a fascist record, agent of the Gestapo and a few other unoriginal things. It is peculiar how the Stalinites have lost central discipline by spreading themselves through liberal groups. They are scattered so widely that Martin's dicta have not yet come to the ears of the ranks, and every day little fresh-faced YCL boy scouts come to ask space for the American Youth Congress or United Christian Youth meetings, space which Harris freely, even prodigally, gives.

Of course we have not yet lost the CP. For the liberals swarm around us, and as inevitably as fruit flies gather on lush bananas, so do [Earl] Browder's minions flock to liberals. If Harris thinks it profitable there may be reconciliation. Harris thinks nothing of assassinating a scruple or knifing a principle if thereby he can profit.

I would like very much to hear from you.

Sincerely,

Bellow was working as associate editor of The Beacon, *a monthly founded by his childhood friend Sydney J. Harris that advertised itself as "Chicago's Liberal Magazine," an editorial stance uncongenial to Bellow's youthful Bolshevist sympathies. In this letter he attempts to make common cause with the Trotskyist Farrell, author of the Studs Lonigan trilogy. Earl Browder had become chairman of the American Communist Party in 1932. During his term as general secretary, he supported the Popular Front, a Stalin-sanctioned policy of friendly outreach to liberals and support for New Deal policies. Running as Communist candidate for President in the 1936 election, Browder won 80,195 votes. Albert Glotzer (1908–99), a founder of the Trotskyist movement in America, had been the first Westerner to visit Trotsky in exile on the Turkish island of Prinkipo, in the Sea of Marmara; there Glotzer was briefly his secretary and bodyguard. In 1937 he served in Mexico City as stenographer for the John Dewey–led commission that exposed the fraudulence of Stalin's charges against Trotsky. Glotzer would be a lifelong friend of Bellow's.*

To Oscar Tarcov

September 29, 1937   Madison

Dear Oscar:

I've had a real letter fest this evening, four letters. I'm not a little worn out with transmitting news, or rather manufacturing it, for there has been no real temporal or spatial news of importance, with the exception of the renaissance of Isaac [Rosenfeld]. Isaac is beginning to spring a little gristle in his marrow. Who knows, he may develop bone if he continues. He's a serious scholar now, and if he doesn't break down into his characteristic monodic delivery he'll be a gent of substance when the year is out. He reads earnestly and constantly. He is suddenly grave, and for the past week he has given no sign of surrealism.

It is all too easy to be righteously critical. It is impossible to condone my jumping at you that Saturday. By doing so I laid myself open to as much blame as was owing you, and shared your weakness evenly with you. Besides, without knowing, without being sure of what moved you to act as you did, I really answered the promptings of my own secret and unconscious life.

But you were goddamned trying. And although I shouldn't have been so impatient, the squabble had a long genesis. I think you had it coming. Your elaborate, desperate rakishness and airiness was more than I could take. It went back beyond New York, beyond your mother, beyond Pearl too; it went

Saul Bellow: Letters

back to an obscure but nevertheless bitter self-understanding, and the pressure of that half-understanding and the crush of a welter of the other things I have mentioned, you fought off with that wild pose. In all this I am not altogether correct, but I am not altogether wrong either. There is more than a germ of truth, or my life has been unique.

I suppose Isaac has told you of my illness. I'm still weaker than a rabbit's belly. Now I lay me down.

Yours,

Oscar Tarcov (1915–63) had been, along with Isaac Rosenfeld, Bellow's closest childhood friend; the three grew up within a few blocks of one another in the Humboldt Park district of Chicago. In the spring of 1937 Bellow graduated from Northwestern with a B.A. in anthropology, and was awarded a graduate fellowship in the Department of Sociology and Anthropology at the University of Wisconsin, Madison, where Rosenfeld was already a doctoral student.

To Oscar Tarcov

October 2, 1937 Madison

Dear Oscar:

First about my family: Of course there was an awful blowout before I left. My father, spongy soul, cannot give freely. His business conscience pursues him into private life, and he plagues those he loves with the scruples he has learned in that world I so detest. He started giving me a Polonius, berating all my friends, warning me, adjuring me, doing everything short of damning me. Of course he damned all the things I stood for, which was the equivalent of damning me also. The night before he had made perfectly hideous for me. Art Behrstock had been over, and no sooner did the old man discover Art had been in Russia than he withered him with arguments and insults. When he started on me, on the instant of my leaving, I blew up and told him precisely the place he occupied in my category of character, what I thought of his advice, and that I intended to live as I saw fit. I told him all this as you may expect without faltering, and I didn't do it in subdued terms. I told the old man that if he didn't want to give me his measly allowance in Madison I would just as lief stay in Chicago and get a job and a wife and live independent of the family forevermore. The coalbins resounded with my shouts and imprecations, till the old man as a defense-measure decided that he was needed somewhere and swam off into the gloom. The next I hear of this is that the old man is heartbroken because I have not written to him. Did he expect a manifesto of love after such a clash? That is why the old woman [Bellow's stepmother] called you up; to discover if I had made any disclosures to you.

I had a letter from Sam (my brother) this morning, in which he urged me to write, and I think I shall now. But what have I to say to him? He sees me as quite a different creature than I really am. To him I am a perverse child growing into manhood with no prospects or bourgeois ambitions, utterly unequipped to meet his world. (He is wrong, am not unequipped but unwilling.) My father and probably all fathers like him have an extremely naïve idea of education. They think it is something formal, apart from actual living, and that it should give one an air of highbrow eminence coupled with material substance (money). They do not expect it to have an effect on the moral life, on the intellectual life, and I doubt whether they have ever heard of an esthetic life. They are good folk, when they are not neurotic, and what after all can we expect? Such conflicts must come if we are to honestly follow out the concepts we learn or teach ourselves. What nexus have I with the old man? What shall I say to him? In his way he is a curio. For instance: He boasts of having read the complete works of Pushkin, Lermontov, Chekhov, Tolstoy, Turgenev, and Dostoyevsky. I believe him. But how has he been able to look open-eyed at these men and act as he has shown himself capable of acting? [. . .]

So much for the family.

So you're going into anthropology; sweet Jesus! It's a hell of a lot better than the English department. And if you are not going to train yourself in a money-making technique you could choose no better field. It is the liveliest, by far, of all the social sciences. Since it is your intention to go to school, I think it is the best discipline, the one that will aid you most. Of course, you will have to learn to keep your balance, but that should be easier in anthropology than in English. As for satisfying the finance corporation that is putting you through—*Rien n'est plus simple* [*]. For the good student there are scholarships and fellowships galore. You have no notion how naïve socially many writers are. The tendency of our time, anyhow, is to rate the moral excellence over the esthetic. I don't think any of us are pure estheticians. Closest is Isaac, who also falls short. There will be a little awkwardness in anthropology—prehistory and physical anthropology and parts of descriptive anthropology. But after all, these are the least important parts of

* French: Nothing is simpler.

anthropology. I regard them as necessary implements, the tools of social philosophy. With a little effort and application you can brush them out of the way. Moreover, if you are good at rationalizing, you can find certain charms in even the tools.

You ought to meet [Alexander] Goldenweiser. Even Isaac is completely won by the man. A perfect cosmopolite, a perfect intellect. He knows as much Picasso as he does Tshimshiam religion, he knows Mozart as well as Bastian, and Thomism as well as Polynesia. You ought to see the books that line his shelves. Next to [Alfred L.] Kroeber stands Sidney Hook, and Lenin, and of course many of Trotsky's pamphlets. He can open up in a seminar and discuss for an hour the anthropological thinking of Elisée Reclus, the anarchist geographer, the great friend of Kropotkin. He is a piano virtuoso, an esthetician, a Bolshevik, a deeply cultured man.

I am taking a seminar with the great Kimball Young, in advanced social psychology, a class with friend [Eliseo] Vivas, about whom Isaac will be delighted to write you. A course in the classical economists, and one in European prehistory.

I guess you have a good half-hour's reading in the above. Leave you to digest it.

Alexander Alexandrovich Goldenweiser (1880–1940), a Ukrainian-born social scientist and disciple of Franz Boas, was greatly esteemed for his groundbreaking research in totemism as well as for his charismatic teaching style. He was in residence at University of Wisconsin, Madison, for the academic year 1937–38.

To Oscar Tarcov

[Postmarked Madison, Wisconsin, 13 October 1937]

Dear Oscar:

How shall I help you? What can I do? Whatever I could I would do with all my heart. If I were lying next to you in hell I would help you with all my power. But hell is for our ancestors. For us, nothing so simple. I can give you no advice because I am so different from you for one thing, and because, for another, my own problems are by no means settled.

I am a strange dog, Oscar. Strange things occur in me that I cannot account for. Just now I am deeply in love, and I think I shall continue in love, because it is my salvation. You, on the other side, could not find salvation in love. You see how different we are? Even our capacities for love are different.

You'll have to settle your problems by yourself. You'll have to wrestle with your own devil because, though I am at present sitting on mine, he is kicking and undefeated.

However, I think you are on the right track. Stick to anthropology; I wish I could accept it wholly. It will bring you closer to truth perhaps, make you happier, perhaps. If you discover a province in it to make yours, you are sure at least to be freer. If any discipline can do it, it is anthropology. You will see what I mean if you read the *Autobiography of a Papago Woman, Memoirs of the A.A.A.*, a monograph published by the American Anthropological Association. You can doubtless find it in the periodical room. It was published only last year. When you read it you will see how many universes there are. That there are other lives, the color of clay, narrow as cave walls but still broad as rock and free and fierce as wolves.

Read it and write back.

Yours,

To Oscar Tarcov

[Postmarked Madison, Wisconsin, 7 December 1937]

Dear Oscar:

I'm tearing this off in cruel haste; it's a shame to treat you this way. But this is the period preceding the period of paper-writing. I have several on my hands, more than I should perhaps have undertaken. The result is, of course, that I bear more than my normal load of fretting. I know I waste more time fuming and bustling than I spend in work. But I can't break the habit.

Ever since he began his paper on the Absolute as conceived by Josiah Royce, Isaac has been intolerable. If they hand out laurels for sheer evasiveness and careful and reserved ambiguities in the Philosophy Department, Isaac should get the juiciest they have on hand. If the paper is well received by [Max C.] Otto, Isaac will stay. If not he will return. In process of writing his paper he has suddenly discovered, however, that he gets along swimmingly without Chicago when he has something to do. One can predict even less for Isaac than for me.

I didn't get around to pumping you about your feeling towards anthropology. If you want to volunteer some information I shall be glad to get it, because if it is necessary for me to unconvince you of something it is best for me to begin preparing now.

Yours,

After two semesters, Bellow abandoned graduate study, returned to Chicago, and married Anita Goshkin of Lafayette, Indiana, a daughter of immigrant Jews from the Crimea who was prominent in Northwestern radical circles— "straightforward, big-bosomed, and very assertive," as Bellow's high-school friend Herb Passin remembered her.

1939

To Oscar Tarcov

October [?], 1939   [Chicago]

Dear Oscar:

You are perfectly right. We should have had a talking-out before you went away. But to be perfectly frank too, I didn't care, at the time that you left, to talk to you. I was neither angry nor disgusted, but "disaffected," alienated to the point of indifference. I needed nothing from you and it was of small consequence to see you and talk to you. Whether you stayed or left was all one to me. In fact I felt the air was a little clearer after you had gone. Now I am being as open as I can, telling you how I felt and what I felt. I think you could make about the same confession. There are many reasons on both sides.

I haven't the same attitude now, so you can put at least one salutary gain to your departure.

I'm glad you won't have to come back to Chicago the way Isaac did, sour and sick but prepared to resume his twenty-second straight year on the same set. He's trying to get on the *Yiddish Courier*.

I know you'll be tickled to hear that Passin is joining the F.O.R. (Fellowship of Reconciliation), a Christian Pacifist outfit, and has renounced Marxism *in toto*. I knew that he could play the "Christianized" role temporarily under the influence of Cora and his father-in-law, the terrible Doctor. But to see him undertake it in lieu of a political career surprises and disgusts. Somehow I think it could be all overlooked if it were done for political reasons. The real reasons turn his whole action cold and greasy.

He got hold of Isaac and he too now touts some of Passin's views without, I think, realizing how completely they were formed by wishes first and deliberation last.

Ask him in your next letter. Anita sends her regards—

To Oscar Tarcov

[Postmarked Chicago, Ill., 5 December 1939]

Dear Oscar:

I hear you became offended by the mention of "cleared air" in the last and only letter I sent you. Perhaps I was, as they say around here, semantically maladroit. I think I can explain what I meant. I am anxious there should be no misunderstanding about such an innocuous phrase; it appears to me that it has swollen out of all proportion into an insult.

You have no idea (or maybe you have now) what a condition our circle was in. Marriage kept me aside, apart, or more accurately involved me in a different way, so that I think I really saw what was coming off. You and Isaac and a few others were gummed into a very disagreeable relationship. By definition—social placing—the group was a friendly one. But there was very little friendship in it actually and more jealousy, covert rage, detestation and in fact a need to use one's friends as one should use one's enemies. For instance, there were evenings when there could be no doubt about the fact that you detested me. That was evident from the way in which you needled me.

In the next scene of this tender little drama there occurred a polarization. I was shot into the [Sam] Freifeld camp; you and Isaac drew together into a new nucleus. And when that happened your interdependence intensified. What one did supplemented the others' acts. So also with what one thought, one hoped, desired, wrote, admired, etc. To me that seemed ridiculously, childishly feeble. Two such creative (for that is what you hoped to be and even set yourselves up to be) individuals should not cleave together so closely. Well, so far as I could see you were stuck together in helplessness. Together you fulminated against the others, against yourselves, and if I looked ridiculous to you at some moments during that time, have a good goggle at yourself. You were stagnating and in no picturesque or admirable way.

The attachment you two evolved for [Abe] Kaufman had a different reason than the one you found. I did not object to Kaufman at all but to the reason. It was very simple. He acted strong while you were weak. He was bold and adventurous and careless and you were really very timid. A lot of disagreeable buffoonery came off. It put you in no better odor than anyone else. I saw pathology not passionate friendship and of course immediately I became a boor. I hate the kind of worship you two worked up for an individual who was remarkable, yes, but as full of error as anybody else. In that deification you looked preposterous to me: taken in, self-deceived, hectically involved and reliant and, Jesus, the whole thing looked idiotic to me. It showed your helplessness up so baldly. It was pitiful.

I made mistakes, of course. But with this qualification, I made mistakes, *too*. But I saw yours as easily as you saw mine and I could have told them to you on the spot, at any time. That night at Isaac's when I would not produce humbug humility, I wasn't prepared for it whereas you, you had staged the whole thing and therefore could turn your cheek in the best Dostoyevsky style. The whole thing was nasty. It didn't do Kaufman any credit. It didn't do you any good either. You had set him off against me on the basis of a very feeble sort of thing that you didn't completely understand yourself. The whole thing was simply asinine. What it revealed clearly even to the stupidest of us that night was that you, Isaac, Kaufman regarded yourselves as a sort of aristocracy with a permanent patent for stepping on the fingers of others. But how readily you howled when your own fingers were under the sole.

If you saw the present Kaufman-Rosenfeld arrangement you would know what I mean, maybe . . .

Since that sort of thing stopped when you went away the air *did* clear. I don't want to kid myself. We were *not* friends this last summer. You chose me out as a deadly enemy. You can't deny that. Therefore why should I have attempted falsely to keep a relationship going. I saw viciousness more often than friendliness. Think what you were like then and see if you can honestly blame me. It's too bad that you, a devotee of the truth, can't stand it sometimes.

I said the same thing in my first letter only not so elaborately. In the last five months or so there has been time for the harder feelings to fall away and be replaced by some of my former affection for you. I hate like all hell to have you estranged for the worst of all possible reasons: attempt at honest analysis. I hope you will accept my explanation. And I hope you reply because I don't think it will be possible to write again otherwise. I suppose Isaac has already told you that I will probably go to Mexico this February.

Regards to Ruthie and Sid,

Yours,

Abe Kaufman was another of Bellow's high-school classmates.

1940

To Oscar Tarcov

[n.d.]   [Chicago]

Dear Oscar:

Let's drop writing in that line. That's what you suggested in the first place; that we shouldn't try to at this distance. And you were right, I think. There is another distance I might mention and that is the one between me and realization (and realization and action, too). A good deal of what you say about Anita I couldn't dream of denying. I have had a great deal of trouble lately over her and several times in the last two months we have been on the verge of separating. We have had quarrels which really originate not out of trivial things but out of the fact that in numerous ways we are strongly disagreeable to each other. And for another thing the principal reasons for marriage have no existence any longer. But I have been breaking myself in two to reconcile because I don't want another failure added to an already long list.

Chuck that for the moment. From what I hear I will soon be able to talk to you and that will be much better.

I have missed you—tremendously. Not as much as Isaac, perhaps; I have many more tasks and preoccupations. But still I share strongly his opinion that you should stay in New York. [. . .] If you can hold out, stay where you are at least for a while.

It is likely that I will go to Mexico in spring. I have already given notice at Pestalozzi[-Froebel Teachers College]—[. . .] I think I can get you the job there. So that if no war breaks out I believe you can look forward to a very good job that will give you independence and leisure; an independence and leisure that I have used to my good advantage in the last year.

I have almost finished *Ruben Whitfield*. I'll be done with it by spring. I don't think it's as good a book as I can write. But then it's really a subject for a much better-developed writer and a more fully developed individual. It wasn't really my project. My views and interests changed so often in the course of the writing that every month I wanted to go back and do the whole thing over in a new way. I have re-written some parts as many as four times and the result shows great inconsistencies. What I am planning now is more personal and not so smart and tough and I am so eager to begin the new thing that I am hustling *Ruben* along. It has become painful and sometimes even obnoxious and frequently the whole *shmeer* seems so transparent and fatuous that I want to abandon it. But I am going to finish it.

This idea of "finish it" is present not only in *Ruben* and in my marriage but also in the movement. I was alienated before the factional fight but now the whole affair has become nauseous—the Old Man's attempt to knife [James] Burnham and cast him out of the movement, the excruciating hysteria of the old timers [. . .], the stupidity of the polemics—all this has made me resolve that if the minority capitulates and yields Burnham a few more, I am finished.

I have begun to read in order to re-evaluate the principles of bolshevism, or better, to learn them for the first time—[Franz] Borkenau, [Arthur] Rosenberg, Rosa Luxemburg's attitudes to Leninism. It's a goddam crime that at the time that the war is on us the only revolutionary party in the country falls to pieces. We'll be crushed too, I think.

Isaac has quit already. How do you feel about it?

I don't intend to drop out immediately. I'm waiting (and plenty of others are also) to see what happens at the convention. I may hold on. I don't want to leave just when it is becoming dangerous. For that very reason.

Give my regards to Ruthie and Sid,

Yours,

No trace remains of Ruben Whitfield, *Bellow's tentative first novel. The political party Bellow and Tarcov still belonged to, and which Rosenfeld had left, was the Socialist Workers Party, a Trotskyist affiliation opposing the Stalinist orthodoxy of the American Communist Party. By the autumn of 1939, however, the SWP had itself broken into two factions, a majority headed by James P. Cannon and blessed by Trotsky ("the Old Man") from his Mexican exile, and a minority led by Max Shachtman and James Burnham, who, following the Molotov-Ribbentrop pact and the Soviet invasions of Poland, Latvia, Lithuania and Finland, declared the USSR an imperialist aggressor and enemy to the socialist movement. At the SWP's third national convention, in April 1940—to which Bellow is referring here—the Cannon faction would prevail, and Burnham and Shachtman left the party along with forty percent of its membership, including Bellow and Tarcov.*

To Oscar Tarcov

[Postmarked Chicago, Ill., 9 December 1940]

Dear Oscar:

You remember, don't you, that I didn't know what my draft-number was? Well I got my papers yesterday and you need feel "singled out" no longer. My local order no. is 282 and with every possible deferment I can't hope to stay out of a uniform longer than a year. My citizenship is in the hands of the Immigration Department and the man handling my case there gives me his assurance that I will have my first papers by the middle of January at the latest. And since first papers and no more are required I don't see how I can possibly get out. At best I can only make class two.

I'm very glad I didn't know what my number was. It gave me ease of mind, a certain Damoclean peace. Not that I'm terribly disturbed now. It harasses and upsets my friends much more than it does me. I don't even have to try to comfort myself. Nothing has been changed.

Isaac feels he is being discriminated against. He doesn't want to stay home alone. He even speaks now of volunteering and claims it isn't proper to remain behind when everything he values is in training camp.

Of course it's no joke but, frankly, I was surprised that I personally had been getting away with it so long. With every individual in the Western World and a great part of the Eastern either in arms or beneath them it seems incredible that we should go free long. It's a sort of luck which isn't designed for me. It's designed for the Herb Passins of the world, not for me. You remember how you felt about getting and holding a job? Well, I feel the same way about getting out from under. It just isn't for me—for us, I should say.

That we got away, free so long, is merely accidental. It's rather a heavy-footed irony that I who hate so much and fear so much anything of a "kill" or "crush" connection should be drawn into army service so quickly.

See you Christmas,

Saul Bellow: Letters

1941

To Oscar Tarcov

February 8, 1941   [Chicago]

Dear Oscar:

I expected you to call me when you were in. I thought perhaps you had tried to get me while I was out of town from Wednesday night to Friday. That's probably the way it was.

I'm completely legalized now [as a Canadian residing in the U. S.] and there is no danger for me as long as aliens are not touched, and even then it is safe to suppose that Canadian aliens will have relative immunity when they start filling the camps (for I believe there will be camps). So far indications are that since I am a non-citizen I am not draftable and, while I don't feel exactly comfortable and secure, it is reasonably permissible for me to make some plans for next year.

The story you heard when you were here last has been cut in half and in that form *Partisan Review* is going to publish it in the next issue. It's very peculiar. I'm tickled, of course, but at the same time I don't know what to make of it. [Dwight] Macdonald wrote me asking if he could print the first two monologues; the other two, he said, weakened the total effect and should be left out. Well, the ones he chose are the bulk of the manuscript, about three-fourths. He asked if I would care to revise "Lover" and "Politics" but I didn't know what he meant and I specifically had no idea what he meant by a weakened total effect and so, rather dazed and not very sure that the two alone would do me any credit, I let it go. I'm flattered, happy and doubtful all at the same time. I hope he knows what he's doing.

I saw Passin just before leaving for Canada. We didn't have a great deal to say. A confidential conversation was out of the question while there were others around and we made no definite appointments for the future. I have no objection to him as long as there is no falsefacing on either side. I refuse absolutely to be used as a vaunting post and I dislike very much playing an accommodating and fraudulent *entre nous* (*nous* standing for the putatively great). I don't mind doing a friend the favor of giving therapeutic assistance but in Herb's case it's too difficult and costs too much in compromise. [. . .]

Isaac came back refreshed, chipper and hopeful from Champaign. There have been a lot of changes in him recently—all of them good. Whether Vasiliki [Isaac's wife] is responsible for them or not I don't know. But he works very hard and apparently with benefits in sight. In the last two weeks—I suppose you know—he wrote a couple of sonnets which I think are the best things he ever did. *Er vert a mensch, bislechvise* [*].

Yours,

I hope the address is right. What the hell is the idea of *two* towns [Champaign and Urbana]?

To Oscar Tarcov

February 20, 1941   Chicago

Dear Oscar:

For a long time now I have been wondering how to answer your letter. To begin with it was, paradoxically, just the sort of letter I have been awaiting from you; one in which you would be a little more recognizable than the Oscar of "cons" and cold-owl trips to see a girl who fucks. Now you are as much Oscar in those situations as in the letter, but I prefer the variety of Oscar I find there. At least he is more congenial to me and more real, by which I mean once more attracted by the concerns through which I knew him. I lost track for a long time of this more desirable individual and, I may suppose, so did you and it is a natural satisfaction to have rediscovered him.

In a way your enthusiasm reminds me that I have always been a sort of combination vanguard and experimental rabbit in the trio that includes both of us and Isaac. The function was not a too-pleasurable one and not an extremely beneficial one; it put a greater responsibility of performance on me than I wanted. But when Isaac became a philosopher and you a sociologist and my position went into decline I was not relieved, I was dissatisfied instead. I was especially dissatisfied with you, not because you had become a "sociologist," you hadn't; we discussed that last time you were here. It was not a matter of ceasing to write, either. Or that was only incidental. For lack of a better way to put it, you no longer showed either the sensibility or even the desire for a certain sort of sensibility which all of us had long ago agreed was a great value, perhaps the greatest of all values. Isaac hadn't lost it and I was hammer-and-tongs after it but in you, for reasons which I could better understand than accept, it often seemed entirely absent. The things you did in Champaign could never successfully supplant it and you knew it but there were cogent and plausible reasons for postponement and reasons also for

* Yiddish: Bit by bit, he's coming into his own.

fatalism—you had had bad years, you would be in the army soon, etc. But I doubt whether those reasons were more important than the absence of a fundamental need for remembering or writing or perceiving.

The letter proves you still capable and that alone gives me more pleasure in you than anything you have done in the last two years. But of course I cannot write merely saying "I am pleased."

Publication in *Partisan Review* flatters me greatly, but I cannot honestly say that I am too proud of what I have done. I got galley-proofs today and cannot look at them long enough to make the needed corrections. This is no exaggeration. I would much rather have published something else. Maybe I am too demanding and exacting; maybe I lack what is essential: the careless attitude of journalism which teaches you to throw into print anything you scribble off; maybe it is wrong to be too painstakingly careful and perhaps I might have been in print long ago but for that scrupulous observance of standards. But with the galleys on the table, now that it is too late I still feel that I was right.

You and Isaac and Sam [Freifeld] and Louie [Sidran] and one or two others were the only people who were honestly and legitimately unenvious and happy to hear that *P.R.* had accepted me. I got a shock from Kappy and especially from Celia [Kappy's wife]. You see, Kappy had sent that story of his away at the same time and he got it back with an encouraging note of rejection which made just about the same criticism of the first part that we made. The next day I got a letter of acceptance and it was quite understandably hard for him to swallow. But what set me up a little was Kappy's attitude that he is after all the more qualified *littérateur* and that I am a sort of skillful but not too serious operator or literary light cavalryman. Well no doubt he knows more about literature, but I am, well, *myself* and *myself* hates to see what I do called inconsequential or trivial. But he continues friendly and so do I. It is Celia who is so difficult and who when she does see us does not have the open and free manner without which intimacy falls flat on its face. It is pretty transparent that she is nettled.

I drank beer with Herb [Passin] all last Wednesday afternoon and got exactly what I expected but in a much more polished and able performance. Since breaking down the act and getting him to let down his hair would have taken more beers than you suspect and since even if that had been my goal there would have been a great risk of being sick all the next day, I went home at five. But I had taken a lot of punishment for three hours and I didn't feel any too good that evening. I think he was badly in need of someone more imaginative than his wife and less official than people like [Fay-Cooper] Cole or [Melville J.] Herskovits to talk to. But sometimes—often—the devices he uses with them come out and clasp you like a pair of ice tongs. God damn it, how I hate to feel that I am being used! I don't mind giving myself but being taken is rotten and makes me feel literally, sexually, buggered. I hate like the devil to say it. If Herb is successful I am glad but (and I detest this in myself almost as much as in others) why does he carry a pocket-sized lithograph ready-inked to stamp the behinds of his friends with? It is bad behavior and bad esthetics, as all lies are bad esthetics.

I send Isaac's regards. He is very busy and hardly sees anyone. I don't get to visit home more than once a week.

Yours,

"Kappy" is Harold Kaplan, a great friend and sparring partner of Bellow's, particularly in these early days, who after the war went to Paris, where he continues to live. Fay-Cooper Cole and Melville J. Herskovits were influential anthropologists at the University of Chicago and Northwestern respectively.

1942

To Melvin Tumin

[n.d.] [Chicago]

Dearest Mel:

I think this letter would be best begun with the news, so that you won't have to scramble around for it over miles and miles of prose. It is now more than a week since I returned. I accomplished a great deal in New York, though I did not find any takers for the novel. Some publishers told me frankly that they were upholders of bourgeois morality; others that it was simply not commercial. Two offered me advances. Dial Press wanted me to do a book on the Army, any sort of book, even day-to-day autobiography, not fiction at all. The fate of the novel now rests with Dwight Macdonald. He has no great hopes for it and neither have I. Parts of it will probably appear in *PR* and then it will be forgotten until it crops up posthumously, and thank God I won't be there to see it. But wait, there is more. First, I have an agent. His name is Maxim Lieber, he operates in a cold, dim cell on Fifth Avenue near 44th St., he represents such talents as Erskine Caldwell and Albert Halper, etc. It is his opinion that I will be a success if only I learn to be suppler, more compromising, less adamantly set in my purposes. What more is there to say about Maxim Lieber? He is one of those people who is constantly characterizing himself. The least of his acts is a giveaway. "Balzac wrote for money," he says. "Oh, don't sneer. So did Shakespeare and so did Beethoven. And you'll either come around or remain obscure. We'll see whether you sneer when you're forty." I assured him it was an ineradicable trait and that I would sneer till eighty, if I lived that long. I did not add that contact with the likes of Lieber would undoubtedly shorten my span. Be that as it may, now that we have each other I may start appearing in print a little more often, providing, of course, that I have the leisure and power to write in the Army. It will have to be power, leisure or no leisure. I work better under stress anyhow.

Both Isaac and myself have recently done reviews for the *New Republic* where Vasiliki is now employed [. . .]. Strategically her position is invaluable for us and we—Isaac especially—have been getting all kinds of leads from our contact with various editors. For instance, through one of his leads Isaac has become a radio writer for the Jewish People's Committee and I was to have begun working for *Time* when I was recalled by my draft board. I am again 1-A; last week I took a second blood test and if my virtue is vindicated I shall be inducted within the next two weeks.

Freifeld is rising ever higher in the bureaucratic realm; there seems to be no limit to that boy's enterprise. But he *works*; as a rule doesn't get home until eight in the evening. Often he is up half the night on some investigation or other. Saturdays until six and seven, Sundays and holidays he spends at the office. So don't be piqued because he hasn't written. It is difficult for him. He adopts, as you will learn, a very special tone in his letters and is at great pains to write them. It takes a long time and the process is inconceivably punctilious—the epigrams have to be thoroughly thought out and before any step is taken the proper mode has to be established. As a matter of fact he has written a letter designed for you but hasn't had time to get it typed, or so he said when I registered your complaint with him.

Kap begins working for the OWI [Office for War Information] in a few days. For a while he had an extraordinary streak of extraordinarily bad luck. He was supposed to go to work for the Department of Justice. He had been accepted, approved by the FBI, and so on. And then he found, when all the tests were over, that the post had been abolished some time before. He immediately left for New York and after a ten-day wait got the other appointment.

There are two births to report. The Grosses have had a girl, the Passins a boy—Thomas Britt (I think there are two tees; I wouldn't like to be caught in error). And oh yes, the Ithiel Pools have produced a Jonathan Pool, middle name of Robert. That's all the parturition for the present. Other announcements as they become necessary will be made, and much more fittingly, by the womenfolk.

Herbert came back after a month in Dallas which he spent with Susie. She came down from the hills to meet him. What happened will forever remain in the files of Eros. [. . .] I hate to make fun of anyone's passions. The struggles from which they proceed are always real even when their manifestations are ridiculous. Perhaps I shall have to become accustomed to the idea that there is always what my austere-critical mind will designate as ridiculous. Perhaps what I deplore in Passin is the succession [of loves]. Perhaps if he had one or two only to show for his entire life I would feel more charitable towards him. I mean this only with regard to Susie. Almost everything else about Passin I respect. I say almost because I make several important reservations. While I am entirely in sympathy with his attitude towards Cora [Passin's then wife] and the child, I am out of sympathy with that trait of stubbornness which makes it impossible for him to be wrong up to the moment when the fissure opens underfoot and drags him in. To the last instant he will deny there is a fissure. He will deny it with such assurance that you will look again in perplexity. Sure enough, there it is, yawning. You throw a couple of rocks into it to show him. See? But he still denies it. Only when he is hurtling down do you hear him cry, "It's true." Then also there is something I distrust in Passin's view of the world. It has intelligence, it has practical shrewdness, but it is deplorably narrow too, I am afraid. Give Passin a problem and he will solve it; give him a fortress he will reduce it; give him a clue and he will elaborate it. But he has failed to discover in the world any principles but the ones that serve him. His outlook, to reduce it to a phrase, is technical, not poetic. He loves one object with such great fervor simply because his fund of love is not more generally expended. Nevertheless, I do respect Passin, I do honor him. If I see in him the miscarriage of great capacities I see also their success. Passin is admirable.

Right now he is treed. He doesn't know what to do about Cora. He is no good with her. You know how rapidly his organs submit to his psyche. He can't succeed with her though he wants to, and badly. Meanwhile he doesn't know what to do about Susie. And Sammy . . . You ought to do something about him, you really ought. He doesn't have a chance and he's giving himself a hell of a deal. Besides he torments Passin, still treating him as his confidant. Herb can't stand it. And I believe for once Herb is jealous when Sammy talks to him. He doesn't mind her having slept with him but it's merely that other kinds of intimacy which he describes, which are simple not carnal, hurt him far more. Why don't you try to do something? Do whatever you can.

Now for you, divine and goat-eared boy, as Kappy calls you, I give you advice as an elder statesman in love and in the knowledge that you must have winced when I poked fun at Passin and his inamorata. You know I have been led to take rather a light attitude towards your affairs by the very way in which you conducted them. And I am not the only one. I have not met your Shirley yet. If the Army doesn't rush me I will, though. I don't know what to expect in advance. I have hunches. But I do know that at a distance of several thousand miles she is apt to be magnificently appetizing, whereas if you slept with her on Irving Park Road tomorrow you might not give a damn for her on Saturday. I'll stretch it to two bangs, three as an extra concession to your constancy; but no more. I haven't forgotten the Russian and one or two other items of your love life. So before you make any move to import her across leagues of desert, snow, mountain, etc. be sure you know what you're up to. You must admit that your record gives me no choice but to say this to you. Certainly you cannot have failed to think of it yourself. You have. But in the unreality of bananas, dysentery, bad whiskey, waddly *muchachas*, hills, lizards and the rest of the bizarre, over-colored, hellish, romantic *cauchemar* [*], you may not be capable of sensible resolutions. If I were you I wouldn't undertake any commitments at such a distance. I am afraid, however, that you are marked for fatality by your testicles as surely as the cat by its curiosity. Far be it from me to stand in the way of Destiny. I'll visit Her some time next week. [. . .]

The East was a good thing for me. I went around receiving my accolades. It was such a relief to come out of the Chicago basin where two or three friends had me subsist on their estimates and to find in the larger world of New York that I was regarded as an up-and-comer. Bertram D. Wolfe said my story was one of the finest he had ever seen an American writer do on Mexico. Clement Greenberg said . . . I don't want to quote all these testimonials myself, it would seem like so much self-gilding. I will simply name the names: Mary McCarthy, Nigel Dennis, Alfred Kazin, *ad regurgitam*.

* French: nightmare

And don't think your letter, which Anita forwarded, was not important to me.

I have worn myself out batting it around with you this morning. I will close now with all my love. My next will be a theoretical letter treating of some of the points you have raised and which I am too tired to try my intellectual muscles on just now.

Hasta luego,

You're lucky the censor is not somebody from the Hays Office. My, what swearing. Let's hope it isn't a lady-censor.

Melvin Marvin Tumin (1919–94), later a professor of sociology at Princeton well known for his work on race relations, was at this time doing doctoral field research in Guatemala.

To Melvin Tumin

[n.d.]   [Chicago]

Dearest Moish:

It's very unfair of me, I know, not to have written so long. You must think that someone who is constantly with a typewriter must be reminded daily of the letters he owes. That is true. I am reminded of them, but sometimes I simply cannot write them. Should I begin in detail to tell you how things have until lately been with me you would quickly understand why. But since I would be engaged night and day for two months in so doing and you are quick at inference, we'll jump over that. I was greatly affected by your last letter and if I had answered it at once, as I originally planned to do, our correspondence would be one letter ahead. But only one. In the last six weeks I have sent Isaac a single letter and Kappy a single apologetic note, and that has been the total extent of my epistling. So you need not feel neglected. You have not been neglected, really. I mention you so often that Anita with her psychoanalytic smile says, "Ah? Your boyfriend again." The joke has become one of her staples. She knows how desperately I miss you and says it wistfully because no woman likes to feel she is not her husband's or lover's all-in-all. Women as a rule cannot make adequate qualitative distinctions when it comes to love.

I have watched the mailbox anxiously for your story. (You see the mailbox has not lost its potency; it is still the little cold tin womb in which the world makes me a little present from time to time of another installment of my life.)

Anita showed me her letter [from you] last week. I see she has told you about my new book. I quite deserve the eulogy. It is good, as far as it has come. And it has been important to me in that it has partially revived me. I had been *fartroymt* [*] in the worst, most narcotic sense until I began it. Suddenly, out of base *merde*, I began to manufacture gold. Thank God for such alchemical powers in the greatest feat of human engineering. It is not very much nowadays to make gardens out of literal shit but to transmute spiritual shit, that is something!

Only with my present short perspective, I shall never be able to finish what I started. No one is untouched, nowadays. Each of us in his way is a casualty of the war. If I were to begin to tell you what has happened to me . . . Everything from being disappointed in my job-quest with machine-like regularity to being reduced to a charity case. My father has had to give me money, to my shame. You know how full of ugly, bastardly pride I am. It really has embittered me. I have felt myself wholly abandoned. I have had no one to talk to. Isaac and Kappy are doing fairly well in New York. Sam, poor bureaucrat, has been engulfed, his human qualities swallowed. He has not time for them except on weekends and even then resents having his rest disturbed. Tarcov? No. Only with Abe Kaufman have I been able to maintain some halfway decent human intercourse and that has been nearly all in the realm of ideas, and mainly esthetic ideas. In all other ways our outlook is too different for the most essential kind of communication. And I have been spectator to my own victimization, have watched the terrific beating and endured it bodily too. Until three weeks ago when I began to write I wanted the Army to take me. The sooner the better.

And now perhaps you will be better able to judge why I did not write. I did not intend to tell you this, but the instant the typewriter began to jiggle a little more rapidly it started coming out. I cannot prevent it. I am so full of it that everything I touch is by a reverse Midas process turned somber. I have taken the first round of pummeling in my maturity and it has been dreadful. There have been more sideshows in the arcade of contumely than I can remember. Family. Even former students. Even Passin. Even *Hersky* [Melville J. Herskovits, Bellow's former teacher at Northwestern] has aimed his little boot at me. Last week he called me up at two thirty in the afternoon. It seems

* Yiddish: in a fugue state, spaced-out

I had used him as a reference in connection with the national roster of scientific and specialized personnel. He had phoned to tell me how much trouble it was to fill out the forms. He was a busy man, a busy man! In some detail he insulted me on each of the following: 1. The fact that I am unemployed and at home at 2:30 P.M. 2. My lack of qualification as an applicant for any consideration from the national roster. 3. The fate of my novel. (He had anticipated what would happen, he gave me to understand.) And last, *in algemein* [*], my wasted life. Perhaps that will help enliven for you the whole idea of the transmutation of shit. If I can turn from that to writing within the space of half a day (that's all it took me to recover) it is I and not Squibbs who have found the Priceless Ingredient.

Hijo de la chinga madre! [**] Do you see what I mean? At four o'clock I can tell myself I am immune. At four fifteen I am lost again. Man's happiness is largely a product of the stability of his prospects. Mine are pfffft!

The organization which has sent you so many hundreds of miles away to study aborigines might more profitably have engaged you at home. Goosing-relationships between the wives of siblings have fewer mysteries than the operation of a single draft board. In two months my status has changed three times and so far as I can tell will change again within the next two weeks or so. Was it any wonder that I *longed* to be called? Is it strange to prefer no future to an uncertain one? *Juges en toi-même* [***].

A further and more reasonable word about "no future." I find the prospect of enjoying the benefits of a peace without having contributed to the peace (of whatever sort; I am hoping for the best) intensely disagreeable. I realize that as an artist I have the principled right to claim exemption. It would be just, but in all conscience I could not plead for it. Besides it would be foolish, don't you think so? Like filing an appeal to be released from an epidemic on the grounds that someone should live to record it. No. You may remember the advice of the old German in *Lord Jim:* "In the destructive element immerse." It is for the world to pull the artist from the destructive element and not for him to ask it to. Cervantes lost an arm fighting the Moors, Calderon, I think it was, wrote one of his plays sitting in the hull of one of the ships of the Armada. And Socrates. If I pull out of this with a whole skin I will write a book called "Socrates was a Hoplite."

* Yiddish: in general
** Spanish: fucking son of a bitch
*** French: Judge for yourself.

Saul Bellow: Letters

Voilà, dear Mel, the picture.

We are moving, shortly. Anita has a new job out in Dunning and we shall have to go to the North Side. I will send the new address as soon as I know what it is.

Please write.

Love,

To Melvin Tumin

Dearest Moissay:

[. . .] Somehow I have not clicked with editors. About two months ago I wrote a story called "Juif!" which carried in it all the sting and tragedy I could impart. It is immeasurably above "The Dead James." Never have I had such letters of apology from editors refusing to take it. By their own standards it is as well-tailored as any of the sweet little nostalgic pieces they print, but it is liable to awaken too much feeling. So out it goes. [. . .]

Permit me to give you a second example. You remember "The Car"? Last summer Whit Burnett [editor of *Story*] was interested in it. "Tell Bellow to bring the last few pages up to par," he said to my agent, "and we'll probably be able to use it." I was in terrible need at the time, so I doctored it up and sent it in. Three months later it was returned to me. No explanation, no comment, only a brief note. "Sorry this failed to get my final OK, W.B." When I picked up the current issue of *Story* it was full of a coarse-grained piece of shit by WB himself, a fictional version of the life of Robert Burns with lumps of half-digested haggis in it. *Je m'en fous de tous les WB et les autres enfants chiennes. Que tu pierde sus miembros en un dia de sangre, W.B.* [*]

There is nothing new with me. I am a recluse, I am a bear. I bite people's heads off when they cross me. I have known one hundred sixty-nine brands of humiliation.

Two weeks ago I stopped work on my novel—it was not direct enough—and have since solaced myself with a book called *The Notebook of a Dangling Man*. It has taken possession of me. I have written twenty-thousand words already and have not come one third of the whole way. It is the complete wartime swansong of a "righteous man" who strove with all his heart not to be an undergroundling but who now sees himself forced to the pavement and

---

* French, then Spanish: To hell with the Whit Burnetts and other little bitches. May you lose your pecker one bloody day, W[hit] B[urnett].

begins to realize that he may have to be a telluric creature after all because the age *requires* it. I don't know myself what the QED will be because I have not finished the demonstration. It will have to be the end-product of its own logic. I think it will end with questions not answers. But then, the work of the artist cannot be expected to comprehend that of the scientist and the philosopher as well. It sets up the hypotheses and tests them in various ways, and it gives answers, but these are not definitive. However, they need not be definitive; they sing about the human situation. It is a kind of truth these answers give, the truth of sorrow and of celebration, the truth that we are stamped with immortality and the truth that we live meanly.

I shall be finished in a month, for certain and perhaps sooner.

Now for some news. Kappy is leaving the country on a mission. I don't know whither; North Africa is the most likely spot for him. They don't speak French on Guadalcanal.

Edith [Tarcov] has had a little girl Miriam Jean; Rochelle [Freifeld] ought to yield any day now. *Voici tout le but humain.* [*]

Don't pull my leg about fighting off your adorers like Gauguin in the movies. [. . .] You ought to be starting home soon, no? Pack up your papers and come. Leave something in Guatemala for the next anthropologist. Don't hog it all. However, I don't think you ought to leave the country without meeting three officials of higher rank than the ones Herb boasts of knowing in Mexico. If possible, meet the President. I want to be present when you tell him, "Señor X and I discussed the Indian problem. I handed him an eighty-five-page memorandum in Spanish and six of the principal varieties of Chibchan on the teaching of Kant in the Sixth Form. He rewarded me with the Order of El Caiman Gordo, third-degree, and said that after the war he would authorize a grant for me to go all through the country teaching the natives contraception and that I would naturally travel overland in his Buick which is decorated fore and aft with the Seal of State. And, Herb, you won't believe this, *er ret mich a shidukh mit sein tochter* [**]. She carries a dowry of eighty thousand milreis or pesos or whatever the coin of the realm is, and a bi-annual world cruise. I was made a chief of the Prtchiwai tribe for successfully dosing the elder of the shamans with castor oil on the first occasion of his tasting salami. I was initiated"—here bend to show the clan cicatrices—"and when I left was accompanied fifty miles by singing, weeping villagers. When

* French: There's life's purpose.
** Yiddish: He proposes to fix me up with his daughter.

I reached the coast I sent each of them an alarm clock and five Coca-Cola bottle-caps in token of *Bruderschaft* [*]."

Write soon,

Love,

To William Roth

February 23, 1942 Chicago

Dear Mr. Roth:

I am sending the uncorrected mss. at Rahv's insistence. The whole novel is about two hundred pages long, i.e. between sixty and seventy thousand words.

Only the first chapter has been rewritten—the rest is first-draft.

If you will be kind enough to attend to *The Very Dark Trees* speedily (for better or for worse) I will be infinitely grateful, because the Army is hot on my heels and I should like to have the fate of the book decided before I leave.

Yours very truly,

Bellow had submitted The Very Dark Trees, *his next novel after* Ruben Whitfield, *to William Roth, editor in chief of the Colt Press.*

To William Roth

April 2, 1942 Chicago

Dear Mr. Roth:

The Army has just notified me that I will be inducted on June 15th.

With this hanging over me I would like to clear up all my business, and especially *The Very Dark Trees,* as quickly as possible. Please let me know how I stand at your earliest opportunity.

Very truly yours,

P.S. Are you interested in novelettes? I have several which I am very eager to publish.

* German: brotherhood

To William Roth

Dear Mr. Roth:

Your letter bowled me over; I am neither too shy nor too hardened to admit it freely, and I wish I could frame a very special kind of "thank you." The occasion certainly calls for it.

I do not mind waiting until November, and your terms are entirely satisfactory. Just now, it happens, I have no pressing need for an advance. I have money enough and time enough to complete and polish the novel. You see, I am teaching part-time in a local normal school. The draft board has deferred me to permit me to finish the term there.

The other copy of the novel was farmed out and is still wandering around somewhere in the desolate sticks of the industry. I have been trying to call it in for some time. If I get it within the next few days I shall notify you and there will be no need for you to send your copy. But if it does not come in I shall have to ask you to send me it for I have none with me. Thank you again. I shall be waiting for some further word from you and a contract.

Appreciatively yours,

Bellow's letter of April 2 had evidently crossed in the mail with Roth's acceptance.

To William Roth

June 24, 1942   Chicago

Dear Mr. Roth:

After rushing like the devil to get through in time I was turned back temporarily at the induction station on a technicality. I'll be free now till mid-July. Since I didn't expect to be here this summer I gave up my teaching job and I will have an incomeless month unless you can see your way clear to advancing me something.

It would be a bad time to go over the mss. for errors. My friends and I read it in a hell of a hurry the night before I was to have been snatched.

I don't know where I'll be when the proofs come. I've arranged to have a friend here read them for me. But that will be only in the last extremity (i.e. in case I should happen to be in China or Australia).

Sincerely,

To William Roth

[Postmarked Chicago, Ill., 29 July 1942]

Dear Roth:

I owe myself a kick for inconsiderateness. I should have thought to ask you what your plans were and whether you had some sort of war immunity. Instead I took it for granted that you were deifically remote from any such concerns. This coordinator business has a promising sound and I hope you prosper at it.

Your faith in me is bracing. You haven't seen the novelette and you have only my word that it is good. It will be as good as I can make it, so much I can promise. I'll send it on in a few weeks and hope with fervor that you won't be disappointed in it.

Now as to the book, I have no hopes for quick results and no particular anxiety, just the usual, rather remote, niggling uneasiness. I have not sent the carbon-copy out and I have no intention of doing so until you get some replies from the East. Then if the results are disappointing I shall simply send both copies to Macdonald and go off to the Army and let the law of probabilities take care of the rest.

Yours, etc.

To William Roth

[n.d.] [Chicago]

Dear Roth:

I was terribly hard hit by the bad news, as you might expect. I had thought that the book at least was something I need no longer worry about. Your own situation, as I gather it, makes me feel equally bad. I hope you can salvage more than you imply you can. There is no need to send more money. I would return the fifty if I did not need it so badly, myself having gotten myself in debt.

About the disposition of the manuscript: Do you think you can find another publisher for it? I hate to bother you with difficulties you might be spared. If you haven't the heart to trouble with it just send it back collect. I'll do what I can to dispose of it. It does seem to me that you ought to do something to hold your gains together for the post-war period, encyst yourself, somehow, until the trouble is over. I'm sure most of the people you've been dealing with would want to go along. Perhaps you can continue. It should be something to hope for, at any rate.

But to sum up in the matter of the manuscript: If you don't think you can find someone to take it I should like you to send it back so that I can offer it to a few more publishers before the war snuffs out all my chances.

Condolences and all my best wishes,

Upon being drafted himself, William Roth had suspended operations at Colt Press.

To William Roth

[n.d.] [Chicago]

Dear Roth:

I haven't tried anyone yet. Rahv wrote in Macdonald's name that he would undertake to peddle the novel for me. What's your opinion? Is that a good idea? I don't want to put you to a lot of trouble; you've been much fairer to me already than you need have been. But if you want to continue handling this for me I shall not expect you to exert yourself for nothing, and if a miracle should come to pass I insist you get an agent's percentage—(it is so figmentary that I hesitate to speak of it). Please be guided by your own interests in this and not by any feelings of obligation.

One of my friends suggests that I get three or four more copies typed and send them around. If you think that's a good idea and want to handle this for me I will raise the necessary money and send it on. There would be no sense in having it done here.

Don't bother with [James] Laughlin [at New Directions]. He read the first six or seven chapters and after an equal number of months decided that he didn't want the book. I don't like the way he does things. He's spoiled; if it occurs to him to clear up a bit of business he may do it, haphazardly, or he may let it hang until he gets around to it, forgetting meanwhile that there are others involved to whom the time means much more.

I should like to explain that I feel I am miles and centuries away from *The Very Dark Trees*—whole developmental heights. Oh, I still feel it deserves publication, in fact since I will never have time to finish any of the long things I have started I am determined it *must* be published, for it is to give me the right (in the postwar period, if we have one) to continue as a writer. But in a sense it is business, not literature. I am taking you at your word and am working over a novelette which is, well, fifty times better than the novel. (I should amend that to "ten times" for the sake of objectivity.) I hope you will be able to persuade your partner to go on publishing, even if it is only small things that you bring out.

By all means let's understand each other clearly on this agent business, and that as soon as possible.

Luck,

Try a last stab at your partner.

To William Roth

Dear Roth:

Evil days. My old gray head no longer goes up with pride when someone says, "My boy, you are promising." But then, too, I am inured to some extent. I have so often been kicked in the shins I have ceased to think that there is any personal malignancy in it. It's just the general lot, that's all. I need no one to tell me your shins are in bad shape also.

It's too bad we shan't meet until and unless we last out the war. The disposition of a book is not as important as that. There will be more books, if God sees fit to let me come through, and undoubtedly you will publish them if you are similarly protected. But meantime I would like to verify my idea of you.

Stay away from Dutch Harbor [in the Aleutians]. If you are inclined, and, if your location is no military secret, write. I don't know what will happen to me. What information I have is all indefinite. But we may both want correspondents in the Army, or in remote places.

Don't worry about the mss., you've done far more than your share already. I'll have a friend in New York pick it up and peddle it around as well as he can—perhaps turn it over to Macdonald.

I don't know, and I can't continue to care intensely and still function. I have to take this attitude, you see.

All best luck in Alaska and God be with you. Try to write, but unless you really are impelled to, don't.

Praschai [*],

* Russian: Farewell.

1943

To Dwight Macdonald

[n.d.]   [Chicago]

Dear Dwight:

If you wrote stories, you would find that editors sowed criticisms with a liberal hand and very carelessly. My reply, if I were to bother to make one, would in most cases be simply "Bah!" But I find yours very just in the case of "The Car," and I am only too delighted to be able to offer an editor a posy, for once. The "centreless facility which destroys the form by excess elaboration" is not quite right, but it is sufficiently close. The greatest difficulty, after one has conceived a story, is to keep the conception always in clear focus. It is not because I write too easily that I sometimes fail. I would be more successful, perhaps, if I did write with more careless dash. But what I find heartbreakingly difficult in these times is fathoming the reader's imagination. If he and I were both of a piece, it would not be so hard. But as it is I am ringed around with uncertainties and I often fail to pull myself together properly, banishing distraction and anxiety. And so I find myself perpetually asking, "How far shall I take this character? Have I made such and such a point clear? Will the actions of X be understood? Shall I destroy a subtlety by hammering it?" Etc.

Besides, being the local draft-board freak is not an unmixed boon. I do not know from day to day what to expect and, as a 1A, cannot go back to teaching. It's impossible to make the best use of one's capacities at such a time, and it is nearly as crippling to know that one's talents are being kept hobbled. And there you are.

I [. . .] am now nearing the end of *Notes of a Dangling Man*, a short, semi-autobiographical novel which rather pleases me. I am going to have to peddle this one on my own, too. Max Lieber, my agent, is a patriot, and the *Notes* is not exactly a sweet little bundle of V's.

Max expects me to become a moneymaker, someday. At present, however, he thinks me still a little wild and when I send him a mss. he doesn't try very hard to market it.

Last December I sent him a story called "Juif!" that I think you would like. If you phone him I am sure he will not object to sending it to you, although I suspect that he is a bit of a Stalinist.

If you want to run it I will send a corrected copy from Chicago. There are a few slips and rough spots that I overlooked in the draft Lieber has.

Yrs,

Less than a "patriot" and more than "a bit of a Stalinist," Maxim Lieber (1897–1993) was in fact a covert agent of the Soviet Union. In 1951, realizing he would either have to testify before the House Un-American Activities Committee against Alger Hiss, with whom he had spied in the 1930s, or else refuse to cooperate and go to prison, Lieber fled with his wife, Minna, to Cuernavaca, Mexico. Thereafter they made their way to Warsaw, where housing, along with a teaching post for Minna, were provided by the Polish government.

1944

To David Bazelon

January 25, 1944   [Chicago]

Dear David:

I too am sorry we didn't arrive at a more solid understanding. Whatever it is that thrusts itself between us is a very potent thing. I can't pretend to understand it and, in fact, I have made the most negligible effort. I tell you this with no attempt to mitigate my slackness, but you must not interpret this as a lack of interest in you. Far from it. I am greatly interested; but I have given myself over wholly to those matters that you limit to inner dialogues and those are my politics, too. Can I be wrong in assuming that politics are one function of a person's humanity? I think you would not say so. This is not egotism in me, nor, as you call it, tiredness, evidence of defeat. None of that. The principal difference between us, if I guess correctly, is that I hold that the forms outside do not assure the manhood of the man. We can ask of them that they should not impede it, as they now do, but we are not safe in assuming the assurance. The right political belief, in other words, in itself secures nothing.

It is necessary to be a revolutionist. But I would deny that I was less one because I do not participate in a political movement. Perhaps your criticism would be juster if I saw, but refused to enter, the right one.

I think I could have shown you a great deal about *my* kind of politics; I would have been glad to do so, regarding it as a privilege.

Sorry about the delay, I had proofs to read. Write to me.

Yrs,

David Bazelon (1923–96) was a contributor to leading literary and political journals and the author of, among other works, Power in America: The Politics of the New Class *(1967).*

To David Bazelon

March 20, 1944   [Chicago]

Dear Dave:

Oscar told me last week that *politics* was going to print your story. I'm glad of it. I shall be sure to send you an opinion as soon as I've read it. I don't think it makes much difference where a story appears just so it reaches the people you want it to reach, and *politics* is read by pretty much the same public as *PR*. Besides, I think you're a writer and that you should write and publish and make yourself known. It's best to get an early start. You'll be writing much more maturely at twenty-eight than I am because of it. You get used to declaring yourself publicly and you save a lot of time and effort and spare yourself a long fight for confidence. Macdonald [editor in chief of *politics*], though on the whole I don't care for his literary opinions, knows what writing is, and his endorsement verifies Isaac's opinion of you, and Oscar's and mine. It's all to the good. I'd like to advise you, by the way, to avoid making a mistake of mine, the mistake of taking criticisms of a single story too seriously. One doesn't stand or fall by a single story or a single book of stories.

I'd like to say this about your last remarks: I don't advise others to follow the Dangling Man into regimentation. That was not advice. When you read Dangling Man you will see that I was only making an ironic statement about the plight of the Josephs. I don't encourage surrender. I'm speaking of wretchedness and saying that no man by his own effort finds his way out of it. To some extent the artist does. But the moral man, the citizen, doesn't. He can't. As to what I would advise Johnny to do, concretely I can't say. In general I would say, "Be a revolutionist. Nothing we have politically deserves to be saved."

And I would include the U[niversity] of C[hicago] and the Great Books Project in nothing. Did you see that Education for Freedom article in *PM*? I think Dwight ought to run a piece about it. The information in *PM* is mostly wrong, but it's right in spirit. [Robert Maynard] Hutchins' anti-mammalianism deserves some grand, public derision. Some reliable man in Teacher's College ought to be invited to try. [. . .]

I have an idea Dwight's not fond of me anymore because I didn't agree with him about the war. However, I'd be happy to be found wrong.

Write.

Yours,

To Alfred Kazin

March 25, 1944   [Chicago]

Dear Alfred:

Splendid! You're a lucky Jew-boy. I congratulate and envy you. I'd like to come down to New York to see you off in style, with a great celebration. After all, you're something like a personal emissary for Isaac and me and dozens of our sort, going to see what our prospects are and whether *homo sap.* offers more hope in England than here. It's about time we heard not from newspapermen and politicos but from people we can trust. And of course it's a wonderful thing for you, personally. *Immenso jubilo!*

My book, as you suspect, gives me *veytig* [*]. I wish you would tell me what you think; I can have only misgivings at this stage. Clearly, the book is not what it should be, not what I can write. A more resolute character would have refused to have it published. But, alas! I fancy that even now I can give a pretty fair estimate of it. The writing is sound, the idea—of the impossibility of working out one's own destiny freely in such a world—is a genuine one. The rest is a hash, a mishmash for which I deserve to be mercilessly handled. But it's so hard now to find a way to use one's best powers. What can be done? Isaac labors with the same difficulty. He has not reached the level where he can thunder. Like myself he is still somewhere in the trees. In the trees one rustles. You know whence thunder comes. I venture to say it's not as bad as that for a critic. He finds his drama ready for him; the novelist has to assemble it from the materials he bumps blindly, fish-like, with his nose. And he has to change it, arrange it, set it in motion. And he has to be prepared to face inspection at his nakedest. I wouldn't say that the critic doesn't. Before I go too far, in my present wild state, let me end with this: that the critic, say

* Yiddish: pain or woe

[Edmund] Wilson (you painted this art yourself), has choicer, richer, subtler characters at his disposal. It's a great advantage and a safer game.

There are other advantages. Most good writing in this century is of the cognitive type. Necessarily. Instead of a typical drama of man you have millions of disparate tendencies much easier to discuss than to represent or dramatize. But that's a long *geshikhte* [*].

I suppose I shall have to take my pannings mercifully.

I'm terribly pleased, by the way, at your leaving *Fortune*. Not for you. You're not a high-pressure boy. You belong in our camp.

This has been on my conscience, too. I should have liked to speak frankly about certain matters on our last meeting in Rockefeller Center, but I couldn't without playing hob with the private affairs of other people. Mine I wouldn't have cared about, I'd have spilled. After it's blown over I shan't keep anything back.

Let's both write oftener.

Yours,

To Jean Stafford

[n.d.]   [Chicago]

Dear Miss Stafford:

You remember me, I think. Bellow, the man who never called you back because he was desperately busy elsewhere. My purpose in coming forward now is to tell you how very happy I am to find you a fine writer. I haven't read the book, just the chapter in *PR*. It is heartening to read such writing. I reserve the right to criticize on some heads, but the writing, the writing I acknowledge with all my heart. I say it who should know by virtue of having slaved at it, if by no other.

I've had no occasion to use Pepto-Bismol again, but I own a large bottle. It was all I had to remind me of you until the last *PR* arrived.

Best wishes,

Stafford's formidable debut novel, Boston Adventure, *had been excerpted in* Partisan Review.

---

* Yiddish: story

Saul Bellow: Letters

To David Bazelon

November 20, 1944 Chicago

Dear David:

I'm glad you decided to pick up the fallen correspondence, though how satisfactory you will find me as a correspondent is hard to say. I don't write letters often. My correspondence with Isaac, for instance, has quite died, but that, perhaps, is owing to our bearishness. He in his cave and I in mine. I think, however, that we are not of the same species. I am a black not a grizzly, and in my mature years not characteristically unsocial.

Oscar has told me about your troubles. Those are serious things and you might have guessed that I would not neglect this opportunity to tie them to politics. Fail with yourself and you fail everywhere. That lesson I have learned at such cost. You must win in yourself: with the psychiatrist's help, with love's help, with reason's help, with the help of social action. But the revolutionary moment cannot help because it is no seat of sanity, there is no ethic in it to respect, it is baneful to reason because it is wholly deterministic. I could go on. This will make you mad. But I beg you to consider without giving in to anger what it can do for you as a *mensch*. For a writer it is poison.

I am writing away, for better or worse. I tried to finish a novelette in time for the *PR* contest but I'll never be through throwing out twenty-page chunks.

I know you will write soon. I am braced and waiting.

Best,

1945

To Samuel Freifeld

[n.d.]

Dear Sam:

I was still in boot-camp when I heard of your father's death. It was bitter news. I thought how you would receive it, alone in some dingy English city. I lay on my sack in the barracks and thought about it. I couldn't write you. Any letter I wrote while at Sheepshead would not have lightened your burden. I simply took it for granted that you would know how I felt. We are so linked that neither of us ever faces a crisis without thinking of the other. I did at Sheepshead as you did at Blanding. Whenever some new horror rose I invariably told myself that you had faced the very same one and doubtless many far worse.

I didn't ship in the regular service. After three weeks on a foul training ship based at Baltimore I was transferred to administrative duty in Atlantic Headquarters. So I was stationed in New York until I secured a release last week.

I'm going to Chicago, but not to stay. Will probably move East. My job with *Britannica* ends on January 1st. I'm going to make my way Rosenfeld-style, as a free lance.

Love,

In early spring, after a third deferment from the Army, Bellow had enlisted in the Merchant Marine and been posted to Atlantic headquarters at Sheepshead Bay, Brooklyn. Following the Japanese surrender in August, he had been released to inactive status.

To James T. Farrell

September 15, 1945   [Chicago]

Dear Jim:

I'm putting in for a Guggenheim (Jim Henle [Bellow's editor at Vanguard Press, who had published *Dangling Man* the previous year] says my chances are better this time) and I'd appreciate it greatly if you would once more consent to sponsor me. I'm putting on one of my annual drives to get out of Chicago. It grows more like Siberia all the time. I come in, petition the Czar to free me from banishment, he refuses and I get into the Pacemaker with the other condemned and return. Seriously, Chicago oppresses me in a way only another Chicagoan can understand. It terrifies outsiders—[Edmund] Wilson, for instance, in his piece on Jane Addams in "Travels in Two Democracies"—but it haunts the natives.

I don't know what you thought of my first book. I hesitated to ask you to back my Guggenheim application if you thought I was a ham. I asked Jim Henle about it and he said you thought I was a good writer. I didn't expect you to like *Dangling Man* but I would have been disturbed to learn that I was in your opinion a bum and ought to take up finger painting.

Sincerely,

1946

To Edmund Wilson

April 22, 1946   [Chicago]

Dear Mr. Wilson:

I want to thank you for supporting my Guggenheim application. I didn't get a fellowship, as you perhaps know if you have seen the announcements. It occurs to me that one aspect or another of [my prospectus for] *The Victim* offended, antagonized or even frightened some of the people on the committee. In the nakedness of outline some of its ironies were disagreeable, I suspect. I'm inclined to think that they aroused someone's dislike.

But who can guess anything about the motives and ways of institutions? You woo them like Ixion and clasp a cloud.

The Victim is nearly finished and is scheduled by Vanguard for spring, 1947. I like it better than my first book, myself. In spite of its theme it doesn't—I think—have the tone of *souffre-douleur*. [*]

I very much appreciate your having gone to the trouble of recommending me.

Sincerely yours,

To Henry Volkening

February 4, 1946   Minneapolis

Dear Henry:

A man named George Auerbach who heads a group called the American Creative Theatre at 12 Minetta St. wrote this week to ask whether I would be interested in dramatizing *The Victim*. I asked Eric Bentley about Auerbach and he reported very favorably, not on Auerbach, whom he doesn't know personally, but on the groups (the Actor's Lab, Hollywood, etc.) with which he is connected. So I wrote Auerbach that I was interested. I made the whole thing rather noncommittal, however. Meanwhile it occurred to Bentley that since one theatre-man had found the book dramatically promising others might also and he suggested getting in touch with someone like Elia Kazan. Which I pass on to you. Did "Dora" arrive? The more I ponder its saleability, the less saleable it seems.

Best,

* French: punching bag; fall guy

Henry Volkening (1902–72) was co-founder of Russell & Volkening, the leading literary agency of its time. Volkening would remain Bellow's agent from 1944 until his death in 1972.

To David Bazelon

[n.d.]   [Minneapolis]

Dear Dave:

You should have come. We were disappointed when you wrote that you couldn't. Though we learn to do without a great number of friends, up in the prairies, still we don't become ascetic on principle. I did want to see you. Besides, you could have inspected the town (both towns) and the university. It would have helped you in your decision.

I agree that you could profit by a few years at school. Living on serious work is impossible now. Something has to be thrown to the wolves: to the *New Leader* or *New Republic* if not to the University. I teach two hours a day, or less. The rest of the time is mine—three weeks or so between quarters and all of the summer quarter. There are many irritants, of course, but they are not—[Seymour] Krim and Isaac to the contrary notwithstanding—crippling. I don't think a writer could permanently stay at a university unless, like Warren, he was also a scholar or critic. Teaching often gravels me, but I'm confident that I can liberate myself from it in two or three years. Sooner, if *The Victim* goes as well as I expect it to. Moreover, in your case, you've had an invaluable immunization against universititis. [. . .]

I'm half way through the second draft. Warren has read it and seems to feel that it'll sell. He liked it. I sent Henle a copy of the first draft. He disapproved of Mr. Schlossberg and thought the restaurant scene was a set-piece—wrongly. Otherwise he approved highly of it. Last week he sent me a copy of Calder [Willingham]'s novel, of which I've read about two hundred pages. Calder hits savagely beside the mark. He's very nervous. Very capable in some ways, a fine ear, but on the whole more vehement than imaginative. I don't know what makes so many of the Southern writers gratuitously violent. Faulkner has come closest to harnessing violence to tragedy, but the off-horse pulls harder with him, too.

My feeling is that you should keep your hand in at fiction regardless. It may well be that you have a biographical talent. You should of course find the kind of writing in which your pliancy is greatest and your imagination freest.

We all look for that. But it's too early to give up fiction. How many novelists have shown their powers during their twenties?

Let me hear.

Love,

Calder Willingham's novel, soon to be published by Vanguard, was End as a Man.

1947

To Samuel Freifeld

[Postmarked Madrid, date illegible; postcard of *El Bufón Don Sebastián de Morra* by Velázquez, Museo del Prado]

Dear Sam—

Thomas à Becket, your friend and mine, would be without note here where the people are the martyrs, every man his own, and the blood of saints and poets would be gratuitously shed—if offered at all. Besides which, the poets own Fiats and eat ten courses at dinner.

To Edmund Wilson

October 3, 1947   Minneapolis

Dear Mr. Wilson:

Two years ago you sponsored my application for a Guggenheim. I wonder if you would do so a second time. I have a new book coming in November, *The Victim,* and I rather think I'll be luckier this year. I know this sort of thing is a great bother to you, but the powers will have it so.

Sincerely yours,

To Robert Penn Warren

October 5, 1947   Minneapolis

Dear Red—

I'm sorry we missed seeing you and Cinina (Anita came to New York to meet me). Lambert Davis said he was expecting you daily. I would have liked nothing better than to hang around another week, but as it was I came back to Mpls. three days after the start of the quarter, arrived with a congestion of Spanish and Midwestern scenes in my head and my blood overcharged by a week of gluttony. Americans *can* remain fat in Spain; I, for some reason, lost about twenty pounds there and took steps to recover some of them in New York, but went too fast. No doubt there was an ideological reason for eating so much—we may not be strong in Phoenician ruins but we *do* have steamed clams. At all events, I'm living on milk and eggs, principally.

Meanwhile I've unpacked my papers and am gradually coaxing myself back to work. I have a number of stories to do; after that, a novel. I'm applying for a Guggenheim, and I'd greatly appreciate it if you'd permit me to give you as a reference.

[. . .] I expect you'll put off sailing until *All the King's Men* opens. You must be having a wonderful time with [Erwin] Piscator and his assistant.

Anita asks to be remembered to you and Cinina.

All the best,

That spring, German émigré director Erwin Piscator was rehearsing Warren's stage version of All the King's Men *at the Dramatic Workshop of The New School for Social Research in New York. By "assistant," Bellow presumably refers to Piscator's wife and collaborator, the dancer Maria Ley.*

To Henry Volkening

[n.d.]   [Minneapolis]

Dear Henry:

This is a copy of my reply to the enclosed and little enough to relieve my swollen feelings. I definitely do not want Henle to publish my next novel. You may say what you please about hard times in the publishing business. They're not so hard but that a book like *Eagle at My Eyes* [by Norman Katkov] can't go through three printings in its first month with no more (to say the least) to recommend it than my book. Henle gave me an advance of seven hundred fifty. I still owe him money. And doesn't he seem pleased in his letter. Small wonder!

Yours,

Glad you like "Dora." I don't think the *New Yorker* will.

To Robert Penn Warren

[Postmarked Minneapolis, Minn., 17 November 1947]

Dear Red:

Thank you very much for being so agreeable about that Guggenheim business. I am terribly superstitious about formal letters. It's harder for me to write the insurance company than to do a story; why, an analyst may some-day be able to tell me. Anyhow, I appreciate it enormously.

I do like the [Leonard] Ungers very much. So far we've met in company only—the social whirl this fall has been dazzling—but I think Leonard and I have sized each other up as people from the same layer of the upper air (or lower depths; whichever you like). And of course Sam Monk is wonderful as you probably well know. And the Hivnors: Bob got married last summer. We're very lucky, in short. As far as the place itself is concerned, well, I understand what Augustine meant when he said "the devil hath established his cities in the north." I've lived in Montreal and in Chicago. [. . .]

My friend Isaac Rosenfeld, by the way, doesn't call gossip gossip anymore; he calls it social history. I think that's very good, don't you?

I wish I had a good excuse for going to New York during Christmas. I'd love to see *All the King's Men*, but I have no such excuse and I'll have to read about it in my two-day-old *Times*. [. . .]

Best to Cinina,

Yours,

To Melvin Tumin

[n.d.]   [Minneapolis]

Dear Mel—

[. . .] Anita's family is utterly wretched. Her mother, who last year lost her eldest son, is full of hurt and, at seventy-three, only her black eyes have animation, the rest of her is rigid. The sister-in-law (married to Anita's brother Max) had her wave of talent about twenty-five years ago, at seventeen or so, and was sent to Italy and Germany to "complete her musical studies," came home and flopped and now teaches piano to kids who come with hockey-sticks and baseball mitts. She is very cultural *haut monde* with me and because I would rather play with Herschel's [Gregory's] trains than enter her cultural *haut monde*, she is vengeful and digs at me, saying to Catherine, Anita's eldest sister, "Please buy me *The Axe of Wandsbek*, a *good* novel, at your librarian's discount. I want to send it to my brother Raoul." This poor Raoul, formerly a violinist who played in a good chamber group, is now a lawyer in the alien-property-custodian's office in Washington. And then Catherine, at fifty years, has colitis and bad temper and washes herself with fifty lotions a day. So much for Anita's family. If I were to tell you of mine—Lordy! My father spoke for an hour at a dinner given for my brother, when he turned forty, on the significance of the name Moses. *Shtel sikh for!* [*]

On Saturday Herschel became ill and I had to return to Minneapolis alone. He's still sick—in protest, I'm sure, if we're made alike, at the horrors of Chicago, *Yemach ha shem.* [**]

Freifeld is in a really bad way, trapped, Melvin. His father died while he was in Germany and when he returned he had to keep the business in order to pay off debts and support his mother, who has turned into an incubus in revenge for thirty years of servitude to the paralyzed old man. Rochelle holds one arm, Mama the other and fortune pummels all three. Rochelle is still punishing Sam for his German infidelities, which he was foolish enough to confess. Because she was virtuous she won't forgive him.

You ought to write. Sam feels bypassed and abandoned. He's in danger of losing his great gift of life in drought. I hate to see it happen to Sam who was so full and overfull.

Well, enough woe. There are still beauty, fucking, little children and friendships in this world.

Best love,

To Henry Volkening

[n.d.]   [Minneapolis]

Dear Mr. Volkening:

Here are some extracts from the letter I was about to send [to Henle]:

"I have had the disappointment in the last two weeks of receiving letters from friends and acquaintances in various parts of the country who had seen reviews of *The Victim* and tried to buy it only to be told by local booksellers that they had never heard of it. Knowing nothing of the mysteries of book distribution, I had always assumed, innocently, that the leading stores in every city automatically received a few copies. It rather shocked me to learn that the University of Chicago bookstore and Woolworth's didn't even know I had published a new book. As a Chicagoan and a Hyde Parker, I feel hurt

* Yiddish: Just imagine!
** Hebrew: May the name be blotted out!

by this. Until Red Warren's review was printed, only a handful of people knew *The Victim* had appeared, and those who missed the *Daily News* of Dec. 3rd have had no further opportunity to learn of it. Since I have been tolerably well reviewed, I can't understand why that should be.

"I know you will accuse me again of putting off the philosopher's robe and of being too impatient, and that you will repeat that before I have published five or six books I can't expect to live by writing. But as I write slowly I will be forty or so before my fifth book is ready and I don't think it is unreasonable of me to expect that the most should be made of what I do produce. When I see my chances for a year or two of uninterrupted work going down the drain I can't help protesting the injustice of it. This year I have been ill and teaching leaves me no energy for writing. I had hoped that I would be able to ask for a year's leave but I shall have nothing to live on if I do, and I see next year and the next and the one after that fribbled away at the university. My grievance is a legitimate one, I think. I don't want to be a commercial writer or to be taken up with money. I have never discussed money matters with you in four years, not even when I signed contracts, except for the letter I wrote you last spring about the new book. You were annoyed with me; you said it was impossible to speak of plans five months in advance of publication. But now the book is out, it hasn't been badly received and already it seems to be going the way of *Dangling Man* . . ."

I don't think it immoderate to ask why the book hasn't been advertised in Chicago, at least. Henle has taken only three ads. One in *PR* before publication, one in the Sunday *Times* and one in the *Saturday Review*. I don't ask him to make me a millionaire, Lord no! But he seems to be satisfied with very little as a small publisher, and I have to be content with even less. *Dangling Man* sold less than two thousand copies the first year and about a hundred a year since then. The advance sale of *The Victim* was twenty-two hundred; I shall be greatly surprised if it totals five thousand copies in all. If it were to bring me enough to live on for a year I wouldn't think of trying to sell it to the movies for sure butchery. It will be no pleasure to me, I assure you, if the book is sold. I simply need the money to put Minneapolis behind me.

What provoked me to write in this fashion was a note I received in which Henle said he expected the Progressive Book Club to have *The Victim* as its March choice. At seventy-five cents. It seems to me that this is tantamount to remaindering the book and getting shut of it. The Progressive Club has as members people who might normally be expected to buy a book like mine.

If it does dispose of something like two thousand copies, I will receive something under two hundred bucks and half-saturate the market, or whatever they call it.

I've been writing stories. I have quite a packet of them that I am working over, health and leisure permitting. Recently I sold a travel letter to *Partisan Review* at the new rates. [. . .]

I'm making plans, together with Ed McGehee (already represented by you and Mr. Russell), to get together a travel anthology and to expand the article into a preface. I'd greatly appreciate it if you'd take this matter over for us. The anthology will be called *Spanish Travelers* or something like that and will be made up of accounts by 18th-, 19th-, and 20th-century travelers in Spain, many great writers among them from Casanova to Roger Fry. Random House has already expressed interest in this, and if you like we can get up an outline.

Please read this overwrought document charitably.

Yours sincerely,

PS I'm going to write Henle only that I'm resuming relations with you—a by-the-way note. I'm depending on your discretion in this matter, acting on your advice not to send the letter to Henle. It would be disastrous if he were to learn circuitously about my dissatisfaction.

To David Bazelon

December 1, 1947   Minneapolis

Dear Dave:

I'm still down in the neighborhood of a hundred sixty lbs. but apart from a certain understandable nervousness I'm not in bad condition, merely mindful of old age and death more than I should normally be. Which probably accounts for my inscription in the *Charterhouse*—"fly, Fleance . . . !" [*] And then, too, my battles (the two books) have tired me out. I feel I have one foot on the right path and another somewhere else: I don't know where that is but perhaps it is a better place than what I have always considered the "right" one. Anyway, the feet aren't together.

Commentary's foolishness is very annoying. I thought the Hammett piece was one of your best. I never saw the idea of the *job* treated in just that

---

* In *Macbeth,* when Banquo and Fleance are ambushed, Banquo holds off the assailants and cries, "Fly, good Fleance, fly, fly, fly! / Thou mayst revenge."

way. And *Partisan*'s conventionality is of course exasperating. If it's pip-squeaks they're guarding against someone ought to tip them off about the pipsqueaks they've been publishing. It's just that they consider *Partisan* a very classy magazine and feel, like the managers of concert halls who have Beethoven's name painted on the proscenium and would feel the dignity of the establishment lowered by Louie Armstrong's at the other end, a connection between culture and incantation.

About school: I think you must accept it as Raskolnikov did Siberia: indispensable punishment. Soon I fancy you'll be able to arrange to write articles as term papers. There's no reason, for instance, why the Hammett piece shouldn't be a perfectly acceptable term paper. When you get the requirements out of the way, you'll be much happier. Universities are full of fools, naturally, but so are all establishments. Brains and talent are the *raison d'être* for the university, however, and can't be entirely repudiated. Not *entirely*. You can always invoke the *raison d'être*. Besides, when you've got Tennyson behind you you can't be kept from Hardy, etc. But you know all this. [. . .]

I spent Thanksgiving Day in Chicago with Oscar and Vic and Johnny, eating goose and thinking up schemes to make a million dollars. My father offered to make me a mine superintendant at ten thousand. The fact that I was a celebrity last week made no difference to him. A mine's a mine, but *Time* is a mere striving with wind. I smiled at the offer but in the old heart of hearts I had to admit that he made sense. His instinct is sound. He doesn't read my reviews, only looks at them. Again, high wisdom. The reviews are incredibly vulgar, so why read them?

I'm glad [Elizabeth] Hardwick didn't take the axe to me. She's very formidable.

Write me.

Love,

1948

To James Henle

[n.d.]

Dear Jim:

Surely you don't mean that the total sales of the book come to two thousand! Why, you wrote last November that it had an advance sale of twenty three hundred. Is the two thousand you speak of in addition to the advance sale? That would be little enough for a novel that has been reviewed like mine. And if you mean that the *total* sale is two thousand I hardly know what to say after two years of wringing to pay bills and fighting for scraps of time in which to do my writing. Have I nothing to look forward to but two years of the same sort and a sale of barely two thousand for the next novel I write? And can it be worth your while to continue publishing books which sell only two thousand copies? I don't understand this at all; I feel black and bitter about it, merely.

Best,

To David Bazelon

January 5, 1948   Minneapolis

Dear Dave:

I agree with you entirely about *The Victim* that it is not so successful as it might have been and does not grow to the fullest size. Compared to what is published nowadays between boards, it is an accomplishment. Judged by my own standards, however, it is promissory. It took hold of my mind and imagination very deeply but I know that somehow I failed to write it *freely*, with all the stops out from beginning to end. They were out in a few places. I could name them. And I must admit that in spite of the great amount of energy I brought to the book at certain times, I was at others, for some reason, content to fall back on lesser resources. For instance, it would not have been difficult to make Leventhal on the same scale as I did Allbee but I thought it would be seen that they were aspects of one another. As though it wouldn't have been evident if I had allowed Leventhal a bit more room. But there is a certain diffidence about me, not very obvious socially, to my own mind, that prevents me from going all out, as you call it. I assemble the dynamite but I am not ready to touch off the fuse. Why? Because I am working toward something and have not yet arrived. I once mentioned to you, I think, that one of the things that made life difficult for me was that I wanted to write before I had sufficient maturity to write as "high" as I wished and so I had a very arduous and painful apprenticeship and still am undergoing it. This journeyman idea has its drawbacks as well as its advantages. It makes me a craftsman—and few writers now are that—but it gives me a refuge from the peril of final accomplishment. "Lord, pardon me, I'm still preparing, not fully a man as yet." I'm like the young man in the Gospels, or have been till lately. "Give all thou hast and follow me," says Christ. The young man goes away to think it over and so is lost. There's a limit to thinking it over, even if grace isn't immediate. But there must be something I'm afraid to give up. It isn't through not wanting.

I do think that [Greenwich] Village-sensibility has peculiar dangers. In the Village where so much desire is fixed on so few ends, and those constantly narrowing ends, there is a gain in intensity and a leak and loss in the respect of solidity. The Village is too unfriendly to the common, much too gnostic. Besides, the novelist labors in character, not in psychology, which is easier and swifter; the psychology of a man comes from many different sources, a theory that is shared; the vision of him as a character comes from the imagination of one man. The Villagers are poetic theorists in psychology and consider a vision of character naïve when it fails to satisfy their hunger for extremes. One could not write a novel in Village psychology because that is a group-product. I don't think I make myself clear.

But I'm writing a novelette which may surprise you. It's called "Who Breathes Overhead." From Schiller's "Diver"—"Who breathes overhead in the rose-tinted air may be glad." It's about the *amor fati*, the vein of enjoyment that runs through our deepest suffering, and it centers about a man who is rotting to death in a hospital room. His stink offends the other patients. The hero of the story defends him because nothing is, for him, more valuable than life or more sacred than the struggle to remain alive. Here I know what I'm doing. The apprenticeship is in its last days. [. . .]

I had hoped that you would show up in Chicago, a deserving scholar taking a Christmas rest, like myself.

Love,

To Henry Volkening

February 18, 1948   Minneapolis

Dear Henry:

That was a nice letter of Mrs. [Katharine] White's. She's right not to ask for revisions, though I feel she would ask for them if she were genuinely after the story, because I wouldn't, I couldn't start nipping, creasing or deleting to suit the policy of a magazine. The policy of a magazine ought to be to publish good stories, and the blitheness that seeks to ward off boredom above everything else runs inevitably into thin squeaking—as the New Yorker does. Have you seen E. Wilson's remarks on it in *Commentary*? They went right to the button. But does this mean he has broken off with the magazine?

Henle answered me at great length and he said that in the long run I couldn't miss (but how long is long?) and that Farrell and every other serious writer in America had the same bad row to weed. I answered him, more mildly than the first time, that Farrell's books started to come out during the Depression and that these are fat years. What is fundamentally wrong, it seems to me, is that Henle has too small an organization to push a book to the retailers. Arthur Bergholz explained the whole thing very sensibly from the seller's standpoint. A good many firms have been fishing after me with hints of gold and spinners of silver. Of course I hear that Leviathan Viking swallowed Lionel Trilling up whole and stilled the prophet's voice pretty damn effectively. Still, the come-ons are attractive. I can understand your reluctance to try to break Vanguard's option. But I can tell you that when my next novel is ready it'll take a lot of hauling to harness me to Vanguard's wagon again. However, I'll think of measures to take when the time is ripe.

Meanwhile, it may be a sound idea to get up an outline of that Spanish Travelers book I mentioned before. My piece in *Partisan* (have you seen it?) might do as an introduction. I could easily lengthen it. McGehee and I have gone a little into the literature and believe we could get up a fascinating anthology. These big houses need grist, don't they? For their standing mills. Publishing may be slack now but it would be worth it to any house to invest a couple of thousand dollars and have a book ready when the wave returns. Could you perhaps sound out old Mr. [Pascal] Covici? We need money in the worst way. [. . .]

As ever (as you see),

To Melvin Tumin

[n.d.]   [Minneapolis]

Dear Moish:

A little destiny is a treacherous thing. Once again I am doing things that I only half understand because something commands me to do them. I went in and asked Zozo [Joseph Warren Beach, chairman of the Department of English at the University of Minnesota] for a year's leave, terming it so— though it's perfectly clear to us both that I won't be returning. And after all I am a family man now; I have more gray hairs than black. This may not appear to be an excess in view of the fact that I have just published a book which has been well received. But that book, now past its sales prime, has sold in the neighborhood of twenty-two hundred copies.

Anyway, I had sworn not to stay. We have a little money and I have applied for a Guggenheim, but I have been so often rejected by Guggenheim I have no right to look for anything but still another *no*. Isaac's is really the first

Saul Bellow: Letters

case I know of a needy writer and a deserving one getting the prize. Ordinarily it goes to people who have enough of a reputation to have acquired money by means of it. Them as has, gets. The executors of a vast estate could never find it in their hearts to be disloyal to that grand principle.

Of course I am aware that I have much to be grateful for. More than ever aware since coming back from Europe. At least I write on my own terms, and on my own terms have two thousand readers. The price is pretty high, but I (we) am (are) still in a position to pay it. [Whereas] in Spain the terms are dictated by Francisco [Franco] and the Church.

Freyt mir zeyr [*] that [R. P.] Blackmur thinks well of me. I hope he hasn't seen the piece on novelists and critics that I had in *The New Leader* some time back. I had it in mind to exempt him personally, for I really learned a great deal from *The Double Agent* and *The Expense of Greatness,* but as you had put an iron for me in his fire I couldn't very well do it.

I hear hopeful things about your book from sociologists who have wind of it. Phil Selznick wanted to use it in California, I know.

Speaking of social science, who should turn up on the faculty here but Joe Greenberg, as unbevelled as ever. Hersky was here for Convocation, arms laden with African, Haitian and jazz records and his old *spiel*. Neither of us looked the other up. But I said to the disciple, "Is this the Science of Anthropology?" Stoutly he answered yes, whereupon I beat up on him without mercy.

We hear nothing from Passin. Cora, who has gone out to be with him, occasionally writes. Do you correspond with him? Do you think he has given us up as part of the degenerate West?

I hope to hear from you very soon. Don't wait until you have "news."

Love,

To David Bazelon

March 8, 1948   Minneapolis

Dear Dave:

[. . .] I haven't read *Don Juan* since my course in the Romantics, circa 1936. There you have the advantage of taking six years or so to mature before beginning to study. Principally I recall "hail Muse, etc." and Juan and Haidee. It's shameful. The poem is one of the things I mean to read again. One never recovers from the attacks of pedantry made in weak and impres-

* Yiddish: It pleases me

sionable times. And my list of books to re-read is getting incredibly long. There isn't time enough in this life even to get enough sleep, says Old Man Karamazov, so how can you have time enough to repent and be saved? [. . .] Among the things I've judged of utmost importance to get back to are music and Hebrew before it is too late to recover them. On Tuesdays I translate one chapter of Job and on Wednesday nights play duets with a political scientist named Sandstrom. I still manage to keep my morning free for writing and the result is that I'm not less than a month or so behind in my duties at the university, may its name be erased (there's the Hebrew). In all crises there I call on temperament to get me by. All the same, I haven't got the time I need for writing and don't get nearly enough of it done. Since October I've done nothing but a novelette of about thirty thousand words—a dazzlingly white elephant, too short for a book and too long for a magazine. That's the only new thing. I did take out one of my stories, shine it up and sent it to Russell and Volkening who sold it to *Harper's Bazaar*. Which is a hopeful sign; I have a drawerful of stories in the first draft. They'd better be marketable, for I've asked for a year's leave of absence—three years of teaching straight is more than flesh and blood can endure—and while I've applied for a Guggenheim I don't feel I'm really, in Guggenheim's eyes, the Guggenheim type.

Anyway, I'm not teaching next year. Our plans aren't definite. We wanted to go to Europe, but the putsch in Czechoslovakia makes war seem too close and the next long night (the final?) about to start. We thought of going to New Mexico but they test atom bombs there. Let me not breathe neutrons. Or the West Indies. Have you any ideas? Will furnish our own light. [. . .]

I regret that your friend [Philip] Rieff's magazine went on the rocks. Now I have a long review of Bernanos's *Joy* to dispose of. I can't send it out as a review at this late date, so I must run it into an article or let it moulder.

Please go on feeling epistolary.

Love,

In February, Czech Communists backed by the Soviet Union had seized political and military power in Czechoslovakia, sending shock waves throughout Western Europe, Great Britain and the United States.

To the John Simon Guggenheim Memorial Foundation

March 26, 1948   Minneapolis

Dear Mr. [Henry Allen] Moe:

During the past year I earned about four thousand dollars, five hundred of which came from writing. My wife and I used almost all of this money— we have a child of four—although I imagine we could have managed on thirty-five hundred.

I knew of course when I applied for a Guggenheim Fellowship that the stipend was twenty-five hundred and I was, and am still, ready to accept that amount in order to be free from academic duties to write. I have no certain resources for the coming year. I believe that from the sale of things I have already written I could earn five hundred and perhaps a little more.

If I receive the Fellowship, I would prefer it begin in October, 1948. I contemplate leaving Minneapolis and doing my work in New York State.

Sincerely yours,

The Guggenheim Foundation customarily asks successful candidates to submit a budget for the coming year prior to awarding the fellowship. Henry Allen Moe was executive director of the foundation.

To Melvin Tumin

April 21, 1948   Minneapolis

Dear Moishe:

Yes, I turned out after all to be a Guggenheim type. Who would have thought, as the Macbeths said, the old man had so much blood in him? Somehow, under deep layers, the old irremovable feeling lurks that I am a born slightee and that no one can really take very seriously the marks I set on paper. In Chicago last week my father looked, when I told him of the award, as he had looked at the gold star in my third-grade copybook. Yes, very fine, but there is still life with its markets, alleyways and bedrooms where such as you are conceived between a glass of schnapps and a dish of cucumbers and cream. So where is grandeur? Not in Guggenheims, he is perfectly right. Nevertheless, there is grandeur. Little does he *really* know. When I say slightee, I do not mean slighted in the gift of life, which is never negligible; I merely mean slighted in the award of badges and distinctions. And even that is no longer true. Lucky the Guggenheim came along when it did. I was about to accept an offer at Bard College, Annandale on Hudson (with two hyphens). If I do what Isaac has done with the Fellowship, namely, rest, I may have to go there the year after. I can very well understand why Isaac has done that; I'm tempted to do likewise. One works so hard to become eligible that one really needs an opportunity to cancel the grind. Besides, it is a very desirable thing to go fallow and wait for a second growth. It's a kind of return to the natural self before the tilling of discipline and the nervousness of the first tries which bring about a disfigurement of the original bent or a cast in the pure eye of the original endowment—don't mind my abuse of metaphors. It's a harassing life, in short, for writers as for professors of sociology; they have a way of slighting the real end. I must say, here, that sociologists are the greater offenders. I listen to them around here with every effort to be fair and understanding but I can't make out their Man. Surely that's not *homo sapiens, mon semblable*! The creature the theologians write about is far closer to me.

I got a like complaint about Kappy from [Herbert] McCloskey and from Isaac. Isaac and I are, of course, in a slightly different category: Chicagoans and writers. Whereas you're from Newark and knew the Ur-Kaplan. That's very important, for Kappy has made himself after his own image, has chosen to be the Parisian Kaplan and has put behind him the part of his history that doesn't fit the image. This self-incubation is a fascinating thing. Having re-explored the boundaries of freedom under God's law (Faust) the next move logically tempts man to free himself from the definition other men give him. That's the Nietzschean "Grand Style." A man's birth and all the primitive facts about him are accidental and not free. Why should he be the Kaplan his mother bore and Newark stamped when he has the power to be the Kaplan of his choice? You have felt that, I have, Passin has. Only some of us have had the sense to realize that the man we bring forth has no richness compared with the man who really exists, thickened, fed and fattened by *all* the facts about him, all of his history. Besides, the image can never be *reyn* [*] and it is especially impure when money and power are part of its outfit. Kappy is an official. In justice to him, however, it must be said that it would be hard to resist exploiting such great gifts, it would be hard for anyone. It's the best, the strongest, the most talented whose lives miscarry in this way. I deeply hope, for Kappy, that he recovers before the damage to his power to feel goes any further. I thought when I heard him last summer discoursing on concentration-camps that only tragedies of that magnitude had the power to

* Yiddish: pure, clean

Saul Bellow: Letters

touch him, the catastrophe in gross. So many of the lovers of humanity in bulk have no feeling for persons. They only obey a compulsory healthy-mindedness for mankind in general, for sufferers in numbers. [. . .]

I got a rather disagreeable letter from Kurt [Wolff] about *The Victim*. I didn't mind his criticisms of specific things but I disliked extremely his telling me "you aren't there *yet*" and all his didactics, his tacking me down with neat clips. He meant less well than he thought he did. You yourself have always objected to the opinion I give of myself. But even if it were not just it would still be necessary, as you would understand if you were subjected to as much scaling down and leveling by dozens of means, from historical comparison to personal attack. *The Victim* has its share of faults but so do many other universally and deservedly admired books. This equalitarianism of men who do not care for themselves and therefore cannot allow others to give great value to human personality is extremely dangerous to writers who are after all devoted to a belief in the importance of human actions. The Gods, the saints, the heroes, these are human pictures of human qualities; the citizen, the man in the street, the man of the mass have become their antithesis. I am against the triumph of this antithesis and Kurt in his letter put himself on the side of the enemy, the envious Casca. *The Victim* where it is successful is a powerful book. I take my own due for it. There aren't many recent books that come close to it and I can't take seriously any opinion that doesn't begin by acknowledging that. There you have it. I'm not modest. Whether I'm truly aware of my shortcomings will be apparent in my next books. It will be apparent for I'm very thoroughly aware of a large number.

Genug [*].

We haven't decided where to go next year. Have you any ideas? I'm waiting to hear from you. I feel a very great warmth toward you, Moishe, and I don't want it to lapse again. You and Isaac are the only friends to whom I write at such length.

Love,

Political scientist Herbert McCloskey and his wife, Mitzie, had become close friends of Bellow's at the University of Minnesota.

* Yiddish: Enough.

To Henry Volkening

[n.d.]   [Minneapolis]

Dear Henry:

[. . .] I'm teaching, not too conscientiously, three courses and though I have assistants (two of them) to grade papers I cannot rule from afar. My presence is indispensable. I took a day off last week to go to Chicago and hear [Arthur] Koestler and I'm paying for it now in heavier toil.

I haven't written to Henle yet. I've just received his congratulations on the Guggenheim, so how can I? But I got a jog today from some friends in Philadelphia who couldn't obtain *The Victim*. They wrote to friends in Passaic, and they couldn't get it. The results in Rochester were no better. Finally they wrote New York. But that's discouraging. I haven't even been banned in Philadelphia. It seems I have a D rating among booksellers. God stiffen them!

I didn't know [J. F.] Powers was on your list. I'd like to meet him. Why don't you suggest to him that he call me next time he's in Minneapolis?

And maybe you know of a good place for me to go next year. Anywhere, within reason, in the western hemisphere.

I'll send the novelette (it'll be ready soon) to [Philip] Rahv and tell him that I do business through you. [. . .]

Best,

To Henry Volkening

April [?], 1948   Minneapolis

Dear Henry:

Last time I wrote to Henle I said that I thought I had a right to devote all my time to writing. He replied that I had indeed. No more. Other publishers have offered me the opportunity. One wanted to give me enough money for a year. I know you favor my staying with Vanguard. At least you don't want to be the instrument of divorce. But I can't see why I should stay. I think I'd be better off with another house.

Do you think Henle would release me if I asked him to?

As ever,

To Melvin Tumin

[n.d.]   [Minneapolis]

Anita is fast winning her campaign to go to Europe. I have been opposing her. I don't like to hazard a year of writing, and France or Italy may be too exciting and disturbing. I came back last fall exhausted and sick and for two

58   Saul Bellow: Letters

or three months was good for nothing. Instead of going to Europe I have been proposing that we settle in the East, settle for good in the country outside New York. I'm sure I can have the Bard job in '49 and I've thought of buying a house in that part of the state. I'm weary of milling around, living in a different house each year, getting accustomed to strange beds, new rooms, curious furniture and the peculiarities and grievances of landladies. Formerly Anita agreed with me. In fact I didn't get her out of Chicago initially without a great deal of *veytig*. But she's got the migratory habit now, apparently. She promises to settle down when we return from abroad. And she's winning, as I've said. If everything were to go well in Europe . . . well, there are attractions. I continue to hesitate because Anita did so badly in Mexico with the language; she was terrified and clung with all her weight to me; I couldn't tolerate that. The results, though I haven't said so before—perhaps didn't really understand—were disastrous. Nearly fatal. But she promises to behave differently in France. Kappy and Celia are very actively agitating and I am, this week, for the first time really tempted. When we leave Minneapolis in July we'll be homeless again. Rich DPs, that's what it comes to. So it seems we won't be living in the same vicinity, you and I, for another year at least.

I'm never, as you know, without some kind of *kopdreyenish* [*]. And recently the chief *dreynish* has been publishing. We were hard hit by the failure of *The Victim*. For it was, financially, a failure. Vanguard sold less than twenty-five hundred copies. It was hard not to blame Henle for that. The flop he made of it has been the scandal of publishers' row for months. [. . .]

Just at present I'm working on a novelette called *The Crab and the Butterfly* which maybe *Partisan* will publish. Rahv has an idea that something should be done for the novella and has written to say that he plans to run one a year—in imitation of *Horizon*, let it be added. The crab is human tenaciousness to life, the butterfly is the gift of existence which the crab stalks. The crab cannot leap or chase but stands with open claws while the creature flaps over him. This is, for a while, I hope, the last of the "heavies." I should like to write a purely comic book next in a spirit of *le gai savoir*, Nietzsche's *gaya scienza*, ringing comedy, not the centerless irony of the *New Yorker* which takes the name nowadays. I'm much attracted by a subject to which you would have no objections, I'm sure—I wouldn't write or publish any such thing—: the high fun of the weeks after you returned from Guatemala. The

* Yiddish: mental aggravation

comic side of it, of which I'm sure you're aware, appeals to me tremendously. Naturally, I wouldn't undertake it without a *nil obstat* from you though what I have in mind is not a copy of the original. Someone altogether different drawn from a very few elements that are yours and totally transformed.

Write me,

Love,

To Henry Volkening

[n.d.]   [Minneapolis]

Dear Henry:

Henle has released me. Not without anger and reproach, but he has let me off. I'm tingling with distress over the whole thing and I'm also relieved; the relief definitely outweighs the other. Clearly there was no pleasant way to do it, though I tried very hard to be moderate. [. . .]

The word's been going around New York for weeks now that I was going to break away; I'm sure he must have heard it and expected me to ask to be let off.

I hope you don't come in for any reproaches. None of this was your doing though Henle will almost certainly feel that the recent renewal of our connection has something to do with the break. I apologize in advance for any bad feeling between you that I may cause.

But now the way's open and we can begin to consider proposals. Or do you think I ought not to negotiate a contract with anyone until I have a book ready?

Best,

To Alfred Kazin

May 2, 1948   Minneapolis

Dear Alfred:

There's universal lamentation because you're not coming. Sam Monk, who is the Department's new head, was deeply disappointed and the lady instructors and female assistants set up a cry like Milton's Syrian damsels over the limbs of Osiris. It's perfectly decorous to report this to a man on the threshold of fatherhood, isn't it? And the McCloskeys ask me to say that your decision saddens them. But on the whole I think you're wise to stick to your book; there aren't many members of the English Department who wouldn't gladly change places with you.

I went to hear Purcell's *Dido and Aeneas* yesterday and sat next to Herr

Doktor Allen, the philologist, who did his best to ruin the concert for me utterly. First, were you coming? He regretted that you weren't (even he!) and recalled a trip he and MacDowell had arranged for visiting professors to the north of the state when you were here. Then, "The man who reviews Mr. [Allen] Seager's new book in the *Saturday Review of Literature* says he is the best of the professor-novelists—better than Warren. What do you think of that?" I hoped Mr. Seager wouldn't get a swelled head and fall from first position. Next we started on the writing of books and the shafts began to zip past. All I could think of was, "See what a rent the envious Casca made!" How they hate all writers who don't appear in the *PMLA* or the *Post*! And there was the chorus singing, "Great Minds Against Themselves Conspire." Yes, by becoming professors, not satisfied to remain mere writers.

So I think you've chosen wisely.

Needless to say, your liking *The Victim* made me very happy—grateful, to qualify further. I think of the conversation between Cummings and interlocutor, in this connection, on the preface to *The Enormous Room*:

"Mr. Cummings, don't you want to be read more widely?"

"Widely? Not deeply?"

Of course the proud novelist assumes that there is a depth. There's a great deal of truth in your remark that the book is harshly conceived. If I thought this harshness were a result of character or temperament I should be extremely disquieted. I understand it, however, as the result of an incomplete assimilation of suffering and cruelty and an underdevelopment of the elements that make for harmony. I sense them but I don't see them as plainly as the others and haven't mastered them as elements of fiction. I could simply invoke them, state them flatly, but I'd feel false if I did. I think the bonds of naturalism were too strong for me in *The Victim*. I didn't want to go beyond probabilities for the two men. I drove myself to be faithful to them, not sufficiently aware that *The Victim* was in a substantial sense a fantasy, too. I ought to have given Leventhal greater gifts. I'm trying to understand why I showered so many on Allbee instead. It's a perverse kind of favoritism toward outsiders and strictness with the beloved children—which originates, I think, with my father.

It's very gratifying for me to be able to discuss this with you. We don't get enough of this kind of discussion, you and I.

We haven't decided where to go next year. Anita is all for Europe. I'm not convinced, though my mind isn't shut to it. Did you enjoy Italy, and can you make any recommendations? I asked Paolo [Milano] for some a few months ago, but he hasn't answered.

Love to both of you and best regards to Pearl,

[. . .] Henle and I have as of last week broken off. He bungled both books awfully.

In Act III of Dido and Aeneas *the chorus sings: "Great minds against themselves conspire, / and shun the cure they most desire." Paolo Milano (1905–1988), editor of* The Portable Dante *(1947) and later chief literary critic for* L'Espresso, *would be among Bellow's close friends for forty years.*

To David Bazelon

May 27, 1948   Minneapolis

Dear Dave—

[. . .] The trouble with anthropology is that it doesn't consider people at full depth. Anti-poetic, therefore basically unfaithful. Mere botanizing.

Spring is fabulously beautiful here in the wilderness.

Love,

To the John Simon Guggenheim Memorial Foundation

June 4, 1948   Minneapolis

Dear Mr. Moe:

The house we had been promised in New York is not forthcoming and, as we have received an invitation from friends in Paris to join them and have been assured of living quarters by them, I should like to know if the Guggenheim Foundation would have any objection to our going abroad in October.

Sincerely yours,

To Henry Volkening

June 10, 1948   Minneapolis

Dear Henry:

I have a short vacation between terms, and I'm typing out one of the stories I told you about. I'll send you a copy—rough—so that you can gather some idea of what it is I have in the trunk. This is fairly representative. I have a feeling that you'll see it as little-mag material, but maybe I'm wrong.

I've met Jim Powers twice and I like him tremendously. His wife is so abnormally quiet that there's little you can say about her save that she *is* quiet. We hope to know her better.

Alvin Schwartz, a friend of mine whose book *The Blowtop* was published and murdered by Dial, has sent me eighty pages of a new novel which I think better than the first and very, very good. I've advised him to get in touch with you and you'll probably hear from him soon.

Thanks for the tear-sheets from *PW*. [Monroe] Engel [at Viking Press] sent me a copy of the Graham Greene [*The Heart of the Matter*]. I think it's his best though I have plenty of reservations about it. Why don't religious writers *benefit* by faith? They're so timid and tangential about it. In their place I'd want to roar like a lion. That's the lion of Judah, I suppose. Whereas Mr. Greene takes his Christian lamb to school with him and lets the teacher—i.e., the strength of the secular—put it out. I'd like to see a little more extravagance.

Best,

To Henry Volkening

September 27, 1948   Paris

Dear Henry:

I seem to be unable to accustom myself to ships. A very light sea made me sick the second day out and it wasn't till we were nearly on the other side before the feeling left me that my sweetbreads had changed places with my brain. But everything has been very peaceful save for the robberies we've been subjected to. Prices are doubled as soon as one opens one's mouth, though one were to have two heads and a beret on each.

Next Monday we get into the apartment we've rented from an old English gentleman who used to race automobiles and who still writes articles for the racing magazines in London and carries on an international correspondence with Greek and Portuguese fans. He's crazy about the new typewriter I had to bring for a bribe and he's taking it to Cannes to write a book, leaving me to struggle with mine in his, I hope, not too cold study. [. . .]

Best,

To the John Simon Guggenheim Memorial Foundation

October 20, 1948   Paris

Dear Mr. Moe:

We are for the time being settled at 24 Rue Marbeuf, Paris VIII, in a flat belonging to a man who may come back from Nice in a month's time or stay there till April. The coal strike will induce him to remain, I think. Should he come back sooner than we expect we may move on to Italy where life is reputedly simpler.

With best wishes,

To Samuel and Rochelle Freifeld

[Postmark illegible; postcard of Le Jardin et Palais du Luxembourg, Paris]

Dear Sam and Rochelle,

We're here and all and not Frenchified. I at least—Jamesian American—more stubbornly barbarian than ever. How are you and when are you going to write your stout friend?

To Monroe Engel

October 25, 1948   Paris

Dear Monroe:

I'm sorry we had all that mix-up before sailing, but I'm sure you've experienced the harassment of traveling *en famille*, no one more reliable than yourself to take care of tickets, trunks, bags, boxes and sacks, etcetera. A few friends came to the hotel to see us over the last humps and we somehow got the trunks shut and ready.

We've been in Paris nearly a month, rather well settled in an apartment and I've already been at work for two weeks and now, if it weren't for an occasional fusillade of French under the window or at the back of the house, I'd be able to imagine, without the least trouble, that I was in Minneapolis. Except that Minneapolis houses are much better heated. I don't get out very often now and when I think of it resent this voluntary encapsulation and damn writing as an occupation.

I have a strong suspicion that we won't be able to remain in France long. The country hasn't begun to feel the effect of the recent strikes. But three million tons of coal were lost and everyone expects cuts in electric power and gas. In some parts of the city the electric *coupures* have already started and Paris pitch black is no place for us.

Through Paolo Milano I am in correspondence with people in Rome and we are thinking of heading there. I may go there alone to find a place within a week or two.

I'd be glad to hear that everything is going well with you. Will you send me a note so that I'll know the lines of communication are up? I enjoyed the Auden reader very much though I was rather horrified at the pieces on Sophocles and Euripides. Everyone to his own form of daring—or outrage.

Best,

Viking had just published The Portable Greek Reader, *edited and introduced by W. H. Auden.*

To Oscar and Edith Tarcov

[Postmarked Paris, 1 December 1948;
postcard of the Champs-Élysées]

Dear Oscar and Edith:

You know what it is for me to write a letter unless directly inspired from Sinai. But I must confess that I am wanted by Sinai for disobedience and various other infractions. I have put off writing till I got my bearings. Now that I have them, I'm going to Italy to lose them. Full explanations soon.

Love,

To Henry Volkening

December 17, 1948   Paris

Dear Henry:

Don't be too concerned about "Dr. Pep"; it's a production of impulse and may well be unclear to everyone. It appears to be a sermon on diet; it is really one on our failing connection to reality. Things are increasingly *done out of sight* in an increasingly false milieu and we are encouraged to forget our debt to the rest of the creation, to labor and suffering. This is done in order that we may be able to perform the complicated tasks of a civilization. The whole emphasis of our civilization, viewed on the ideological side, has been on love and gentleness. Now what is the relation between this and the blood shed out of sight? Why, you have revolutionaries who are going to shed blood once and for all, for the gentlest of reasons (Robespierre). You can't have an omelet without breaking eggs, they say. That is, the secret underlying their gentleness is their ferocity. A humanized and cultivated environment, like an apparently gentle man, often similarly overlays ferocity. The pruning that makes Fontainebleau harmonious gives an idea to the revolutionary. Dr. Pep goes on to say that the true gentleness is to be found in the man whose sacrifice is personal. And that's the main line of reasoning. As for the manner of writing, I do not find it hard to justify. It gives me great pleasure to jump over the difficulties of required form—required, that is, by the readers trained by editors to look for a sort of strict little dance in fiction. Consequently there is a sort of richness in writing which is supposed to be not for us: the honey in the lion's mouth. It's not so much considered daring to go into the lion's mouth as it is thought bad form. One doesn't go into anybody's mouth.

I am surprised that you don't mention the story called "Looking for Mr. Green" which I mailed to you some time before "Dr. Pep." I was rather expecting you to blow your top over it—as A[lvin] Schwartz would say—and am beginning to think how to reproach the postal bureaucracy for its loss. It may still arrive. Luckily there are copies. I have one and one was sent to my friend Paolo Milano. I don't believe the copy will be fit to send round—you may not think the contents fit, either. In that case, please have the mss. retyped at my expense. This kind of delay makes me see purple. And on going through my things I learned that I had lost the mss. of a story, "The Rock Wall," that I had counted on getting off to you next. I suspect it may have gone with a lot of stuff I burned before leaving Minneapolis.

So is it. Anyhow, I'm working, and eventually something ought to come in that will reward your patience.

We're going to Nice to spend Christmas and in January I'm going on to Italy for a month. Next April we'll move there together but at present I want to get off and think through a novel, or novels, for there are several in my mind. I came across a hundred pages of one I began three years ago. Still eminently printable but not the step forward I should like to make.

If the mss. of "Mr. Green" hasn't arrived, please phone Milano.

Best wishes and Merry Xmas,

To J. F. Powers

December 18, 1948   Paris

Dear Jim:

Congratulations on the baby. It's an excellent thing to have daughters, once one has accepted fatherhood in principle, and to be spared the Oedipal struggle. Sons don't light your cigar and bring your slippers. As for the pious beggars at Notre Dame, I don't know if they'd be willing to intercede for you in a thing like this. For that matter, I haven't even seen pious beggars near the church. All that neighborhood is full of peddlers of twenty-French-poses and you can't get into the cathedral without being solicited by half a dozen sinners under the feet of the apostles. It's interesting psychologically and I suppose there's a providential purpose around, too, as usual.

We haven't had any snow, but Paris has been terribly gray and somber and I'd give a great deal to see sunshine. Theoretically, I oughtn't to mind the weather; I should be working. But there's some kind of doom, apparently, about the Guggenheim. Rosenfeld and Lionel Trilling and several others in New York told me that I'd better not try to buck it. I've written two stories here, but not a word of the novel so far. I haven't even been able to think of it and I'm planning to go to Italy for a change of luck.

I've seen excellent reviews of *Prince of Darkness* in the *Statesman* and the *Spectator* and several good ads for it. [John] Lehmann is doing very well for you. I'll look out for Italian notices when I go to Rome and send them to you. Swedish is the only language my book has been translated into. I haven't seen a copy of the translation and I have an idea I'd be shocked by the look of it. I'm hoping to meet Carlo Levi through a friend, Nick Chiaromonte. It must have been I who recommended *Christ Stopped at Eboli*; I was urging everyone to read it in my missionary zeal. Probably trying to earn my professorial pay by disseminating good books. [. . .]

You ought to look up Red Warren. He's an awfully good guy. [. . .]

Don't stop writing.

Yrs,

James Farl Powers (1917–1999), regarded by Bellow as one of the most gifted American writers, was the author of Prince of Darkness and Other Stories *(1947). In 1962 he would win a National Book Award for his novel* Morte d'Urban.

To Henry Volkening

[n.d.]   Freiburger Hof, Freiburg

Dear Henry:

Please forgive me for having made you such a poor return for your fine letters. I haven't been too busy to write, and I have had plenty of time for it. I have two very long, unfinished letters to you stuffed in among my junk. The reason I didn't send them was that I couldn't finish them—they would have each been ten million words long [. . .]. Your last letter came with a batch of mail from Paris last night; it contained the news of the *New York Times* item, etc. The only way I'll ever be able to tell you about these last four months, Henry, is to talk to (not *with*) you—and I long to do this, although I do not know how long it will be before I have that happiness. You must prepare yourself for the ordeal in whatever far-off future: clasp a bottle of your bootlegger's finest brew in your right hand and endure until the tidal wave shall have spent its force.

I am at length in the Black Forest. I arrived here a few days ago by a kind of intuition—the inside of me was like a Black Forest and I think the name kept having its unconscious effect on me. It is a very beautiful place—a landscape of rich dark melancholy, a place with a Gothic soul, and I am glad that I have come here. These people with all that is bestial, savage, super-natural, and also all that is rich, profound, kindly and simple, move me more deeply than I can tell you: France at the present time has completely ceased to give me anything. That is no doubt my fault, but their books, their art, their cities, their people, their conversation—nothing but their food at the present time means anything to me. The Americans in Paris would probably sneer at this—I mean these Americans who know all about it and are perfectly sure what French literature and French civilization stand for, although they read no French books, speak little of the language, and are never alone with French people.

I cannot tell you much at the present about these last four months. I will tell you that I have had some of the worst moments of my life during them, and also some of the best. All told, it has been a pretty hard time, but I am going to be all right now. I don't know if you have ever stayed by yourself for so long a time (few people have and I do not recommend it) but if you are at all a thoughtful person, you are bound to come out of it with some of your basic ore—you'll sweat it out of your brain and heart and spirit. The thing I have done is one of the cruelest forms of surgery in the world, but I knew that for me it was right. I can give you some idea of the way I have cut myself off from people I knew when I tell you that only once in the past six weeks have I seen anyone I knew—that was Mr. F. Scott Fitzgerald the master of the human heart and I came upon him unavoidably in Geneva, a week or two ago. I can tell you briefly what my movements have been: I went to Paris from New York and, outside of a short trip to Rouen and a few places near Paris, stayed there for almost two months. I think this was the worst time of all. I was in a kind of stupor and unfit to see anyone, but I ran into people I knew from time to time and went to dinner or the theatre with them. My publisher came over from England and was very kind. He is a very fine fellow—he took me out and I met some of the celebrities—Mr. Michael Arlen, and some of the Left Bank People. This lasted little over a day, I was no good with people, and I did not go back to see them. I began to work out of desperation in that noisy, sultry, uncomfortable city of Paris and I got a good deal done. Finally I got out of it and went to Switzerland. I found a very quiet comfortable hotel in Montreux—I had a good room with a balcony overlooking the lake—and in the weeks that followed I got a great deal accomplished. I knew no one there at all—the place was filled with itinerant English and American spinsters buying post cards of the Lake of Geneva— but one night I ran into the aforesaid Mr. Fitzgerald, your old-time college pal and fellow Princetonian. I had written Mr. F. a note in Paris—because Perkins is very fond of him and told me for all his faults he's a fine fellow— and Mr. F. had had me to his sumptuous ap't. near the Bois for lunch and three or four gallons of wine, cognac, whiskey, etc. I finally departed from his company at ten that night in the Ritz Bar where he was entirely surrounded by Princeton boys, all nineteen years old, all drunk, and all half-raw. He was carrying on a spirited conversation with them about why Joe Zinzendorff did not get taken into the Triple-Gazzaza Club. I heard one of the lads say, "Joe's a good boy, Scotty, but you know he's a fellow that ain't got much background." [. . .]

I had not seen Mr. F. since that evening until I ran into him at the Casino at Montreux. That was the beginning of the end of my stay at that beautiful spot. I must explain to you that Mr. F. had discovered the day I saw him in Paris that I knew a very notorious young lady, now resident in Paris getting her second divorce, and by her first marriage connected to one of those famous American families who cheated drunken Indians out of their furs seventy yrs. ago and are thus at the top of the estab. aristocracy now. Mr. F. immediately broke a sweat on finding I knew the lady and damned near broke his neck getting around there. He insisted that I come ("Every writer," this gr't philosopher said, "is a social climber") and when I told him very positively I would not go to see the lady, this poet of the passions at once began to see all the elements of a romance—the cruel and dissolute society beauty playing with the tortured heart of the sensitive young writer, etc. He eagerly demanded my reasons for staying away. I told him the lady had cabled to America for my address, had written me a half dozen notes and sent her servants to my hotel when I first came to Paris, and that having been told of her kind heart I gratefully accepted her hospitality, went to her apt. for lunch, returned once or twice, and found that I was being paraded before a crowd of worthless people, palmed off as someone who was madly in love with her, and exhibited with a young French soda jerker with greased hair who was on her payroll and, she boasted to me, slept with her every night ("I like his bod-dy," she hoarsely whispered, "I must have some bod-dy whose bod-dy I like to sleep with," etc.). The end finally came when she began to call me at my hotel in the morning saying she'd had four pipes of opium the night before and was "all shot to pieces" and what in God's name would she do, she had not seen Raymond or Roland or Louis or whatever his name was for four hrs., he had disappeared, she was sure something had happened to him, that I must do something at once, that I was such a comfort she was coming to the hotel at once, I must hold her hand, etc. It was too much. I didn't care whether Louis had been absent three or thirty hrs. or whether she had smoked four or forty pipes, since nothing ever happens to these people anyhow—they make a show of recklessness, but they take excellent care that they don't get hurt in the end—and for a man trying very hard to save his own life I did not think it wise to try to live for these other people and let them feed upon me.

So I told Mr. F. the great analyst of the soul to tell the woman nothing about me, to give no information at all about me or what I was doing or where I was. I told him this in Paris; I told him again in Switzerland and on both occasions the man got shut of her as fast as he could—that ended Montreux for me. She immediately sent all the information back to America. Heartrending letters, cables, etc. with threats of coming to find me, going mad, dying. Then began to come directly to my hotel. I wanted to batter the walls down—the hotel people, who had been very kind to me, charged me three francs extra because I had brought a bottle of wine from outside into the hotel (they have a right in Switzerland to do this) but I took my rage out on them, told them I was leaving the next day, went on a spree, broke windows, plumbing fixtures, etc. in the town, and came back to the hotel at 2:00 AM, pounded on the door of the director and on the doors of two English spinsters, rushed howling with laughter up and down the halls, cursing and singing—and in short *had* to leave.

I went to Geneva where I stayed a week or so. Meanwhile my book came out in England—I wrote beforehand and asked the publisher not to send reviews because I was working on the new one and did not want to be bothered. He wrote back a very jubilant letter and said the book was a big success and said, "Read these reviews—you have nothing to be afraid of." I read them, they were very fine, I got in a state of great excitement. He sent me great batches of reviews then—most of them very good ones, some bad. I foolishly read them and got in a very excited condition about a book I should have left behind me months ago. On top of this, and the cables and the letters from New York, I got in Geneva two very bad reviews—cruel, unfair, bitterly personal. I was fed up with everything. I wrote Perkins a brief note telling him goodbye, please send my money, I would never write again, etc. I wrote the English publisher another, I cut off all mail by telegraph to Paris, I packed up, rushed to the aviation field and took the first airplane to Lyons.

It was my first flight, it was magnificent, there is nothing like flying to ease a distressed spirit. The beautiful little farms of the Rhone valley appeared below me, I saw a little dot shoveling manure in a field and recognized a critic, I got to Lyons, ate some good food (there are good restaurants there) and immediately got to work again. A week later I flew to Marseilles. Then I went up to Arles in Provence (God it was hot) then back to Marseilles. Then I flew back over the southern Alps to Geneva where I had left most of my baggage.

It was a grand trip, lasted three weeks and did me an infinite amount of good. All the time I scrawled, wrote, scribbled. I have written a great deal—my book is one immense long book made up of four average-sized ones, each complete in itself, but each part of the whole. I stayed in Geneva one day and of course Mr. F. was on the job, although he had been at Vevey and then at Caux—his wife he says has been very near madness in a sanatorium at Geneva, but is now getting better. (It turned out that she was a good half hour by fast train from Geneva. When I told him I was leaving Geneva and coming to the Black Forest he immediately decided to return to Caux. I was with him the night before I left Geneva, he got very drunk and bitter, he wanted me to go and stay with his friends Dorothy Parker and some people named Murphy in Switzerland nearby. When I made no answer to this invitation he was quite annoyed, said that I got away from people because I was afraid of them, etc. (which is quite true, and which I think, in view of my experiences with Mr. F. *et al.*, shows damned good sense). I wonder how long Mr. F. could last by himself, with no more Ritz Bar, no more Princeton boys, no more Mrs. F. At any rate I came to Basel and F. rode part way with me on his way back to Caux. A final word about him: I am sorry I ever met him, he has caused me trouble and cost me time; but he has good stuff in him yet. His conduct to me was mixed with malice and generosity—he read my book and was very fine about it; then his bitterness began to qualify him. He is sterile and impotent and alcoholic now, and unable to finish his book, and I think he wanted to injure my own work—this is base but the man has been up against it, he really loves his wife and I suppose helped get her into this terrible fix. I hold nothing against him now. Of course he can't hurt me in the end, but I trusted him and I think he played a shabby trick by telling lies on me.

At any rate, I got over my dumps very quickly, sweated it out in Provence, and here I am, trying to finish up one section of the book before I leave here. I may get to England where Reeves my publisher assures me I can be quiet and work in peace. I like him intensely and there are also two or three other people there I can talk to. I have never been so full of writing in my life—if I can do the thing, I want to believe it will be good.

I found a great batch of letters and telegrams when I got back from exile. Reeves was very upset by my letter, and was wiring everywhere—he sent me a wonderful letter, he said the book had had a magnificent reception and not to be a damned fool about a few reviews. And Perkins wrote me two wonderful letters—he is a grand man, and I believe in him with all my heart. All the others at Scribner's have written me, and I am ashamed of my foolish letters and have resolved not to let them down.

I know it's going to be all right now. I believe I'm out of the woods at last. Nobody is going to die on account of me, nobody is going to suffer any more than I have suffered—the force of these dire threats gets a little weaker after a while, and I know now, no matter what anyone may ever say, that in one situation I have acted fairly and kept my head up. I am a little bitter at rich people at present, I am a little bitter at people who live in comfort and luxury surrounded by friends and amusement, and yet are not willing to give an even chance to a young man living alone in a foreign country and trying to get work done. I did all that was asked of me, I came away here when I did not want to come, I have fought it out alone, and now I am done with it. I do not think it will be possible for me to live in New York for a year or two, and when I come back I may go elsewhere to live. As for the incredible passion that possessed me when I was twenty-five years old and that brought me to madness and, I think, almost to destruction—that is over, that fire can never be kindled again.

A pure fantasy, of course. Fitzgerald had been dead for nearly a decade.

1949

To David Bazelon

Dear Dave:

Without a prod I had sent you, I swear, a note before your letter came. It's true that I hadn't written to anyone. Last summer, there were so many knives drawn round me that it's taken several months to get the dazzle of them out of my eyes. I've been silent to knifers and non-knifers alike. The only exception was for Isaac; to an old friend—it's nearly twenty years that we've known each other—one goes on writing. Seven times seven. Apparently I'll never get it through my stupid head that it's no use.

The man to address at Minn.—if you really mean to go there—is Samuel Monk, Falwell Hall, the new head of the Dep't., replacing Beach, and a very decent, generous and intelligent guy. Say that you're writing at my suggestion, explain what you've been doing the last five years and why you think you'd be happy in a university. The less bull the better. How? That's your *tsores* [*]. Myself, I recently mailed in my resignation. I will probably—it's not settled—stay in Europe another year.

So Oscar has a car! I'll be damned! Everybody is becoming so serious.

Paris *is* savage. Wonderfully beautiful but savage in an unexpected quarter; in its calculating heart. The secret of the whole affair—it's revealed in Balzac, but no one seems to read him seriously—is a certain grotesque arithmetic. The wit of the city is a branch of addition and subtraction. Every American boy brought up in a good bourgeois atmosphere breathes the air of home in Paris. *And in addition, it is Paris.* Terribly important. It is now blameless to be a bourgeois. So what can be more delightful for an American? No, I must confess that's excessively hard on Americans. It's often said that Americans are less materialistic than Europeans. My feeling is that Americans are attached *in principle* to things. They seem to own them for symbolic reasons. With the French, on the other hand, there is no metaphysical universe about it—it's the things they want, the more hereditary the lovelier for snobbish rather than sentimental or innate reasons. And that is a kind of symbolism, I admit, but it's limited. More briefly, and with all that it

* Yiddish: problem or trouble

spiritually implies, the Frenchman is always turned homeward, to his cozy, shutter-drawn nest, and the American is always running away from home. But each home, after its kind, is perfect. Italy's a much healthier country than either, relatively free of budget-fever, pride and American chase.

I've done some work, but I haven't been killing myself. It takes time, you know, to accustom oneself to, etc. I have a mild case of copper-curse. Isaac and Trilling warned me against it. Neither did a lick of work last year. [. . .]

Love,

To Henry Volkening

January 2, 1949   Paris

Dear Henry:

The letter from Mrs. [Katharine] White is very gratifying to an old ego-maniac like me. Also to an old mold-shatterer. Sooner or later people are bound to reach an adult state with respect to writing and permit the common use of words already in most common use in family magazines. And it's salutary now and then to admit that one does *not* print the things one thinks well of, freely and always. *Mais passons* [*].

Rahv always pays when the piece is set up, at the rate of two-and-one-half-cents-a-word. That, as an old stoic of my tribe says, is better than nothing. To which you will reply, but still not much. However, I am very pleased and thankful to you for sending "Dr. Pep" out. I will write to Phil in a day or so—you must forgive his laconic manner; that, from him, was high praise; usually he says, "I have accepted yr. piece for near pub."—and ask him to send the proofs to me and the check to you. I may even begin to bargain for a special rate. After all, I hear he gives one to Gide.

We've had a very pleasant holiday on the Riviera, at Nice and San Remo, and I am beginning to think of getting back to the mill and pile together my grist for a novel. Meanwhile, I'll continue to putter with stories. The mss. of one on which I had counted has disappeared and I may try to do it again from memory.

Happy New Year to you and your family and to Mr. Russell.

Best,

Maybe you ought to try "Mr. Green" in the *Kenyon* or *PR*?

* French: But let's move on.

Saul Bellow: Letters

Katharine Sergeant Angell White (1892–1972), a founder of The New Yorker *in 1925, was for many years its chief fiction editor.*

To Henry Volkening

January 5, 1949   Paris

Dear Henry,

[. . .] So far my fishing has been rewarded by only one nibble, from Harvard. I believe I could get a job there, but I'd have to teach English for one thing and live in Cambridge for another. Is it not better to stay in Paris, you ask? Well, perhaps it is; for some, for most, perhaps, it would be a fatuous question to put to oneself. Monroe Engel wants to know what the devil I want to return for. Well, the fact is that foreign residence becomes rather emptying after a while. You do your work and see your few friends, read French books, admire the Seine and the Tuileries, get to know hidden squares and unavailable (to the Many) restaurants and bistros. Presently you find yourself with fewer human contacts than you had in Minnesota. Next, "What human contacts will there be in Cambridge?" God spare us! Cambridge!! So, I'm stalling Cambridge for a while. Till I've felt around a little more, anyway. Do you think I could get the thin end of myself in Queens where they're starting a "creative writing" program? There's a man called—I think—Robertson who runs the English Dept. NYU is out, I guess—my friend Rosenfeld teaches there and I don't want to horn in on him; he's got troubles enough. Maybe I ought to start a nightclub, or become a press agent.

Do you ever see Alfred Kazin? He may have some ideas, he always does. And then, of course, I do have about ten untried stories in my kit, and parts of *Augie* and the novel I put by are quite publishable. What I need is time. And a *pied-à-terre*, which is where Mr. [Harold] Guinzburg [owner of The Viking Press] comes in. But for the time being I think it best to stall, stall everyone except Augie.

I'm sending about six chapters of the latter in to Mr. Moe at the Guggenheim Foundation, and I'll ask him to send them on to you and Monroe Engel. They're first-draft, but very full, and I think will enable you to answer my previous questions about one installment or two for Viking.

I don't think Moe likes me well enough to come across with a second fellowship. Here, again, Alfred would know, and if you have an opportunity soon I'd take it very kindly if you'd ask him.

All the very best *voeux* for the New Year,

To Oscar, Edith, Miriam, and Nathan Tarcov

[Postmark illegible; postcard of Michelangelo's *Pietà*]

Dearest Oscar, Edith, Miriam, Nathan—and may the list grow even longer:

I'm convinced from my experience that Rome is exactly what everyone in Chicago needs. Italy, anyhow, since Rome would overflow. One year's fellowship for every Chicagoan would bring a bloodless and happy revolution. As it is, I'm a lone beneficiary. Anita is in Paris.

Love,

To Samuel Freifeld

[Postmark illegible; postcard of Chiesa di Santa Maria in Cosmedin, Rome]

Dear Sam'l—

The temple on the right was once the temple of the Vestals. Near the Tiber, a few yards away, was the Greek district in the days of Augustus. I'm telling you this because Rome reminded me that you were a historian. As for me, I'm no longer a professor, whatever else I may be, having resigned from Minn. Chances are I won't come back to the U.S. in a hurry. Not because I don't miss you, but a year's exposure is incomplete.

Love to Rochelle and Judy,

To David Bazelon

January 25, 1949   [Rome]

Dear Dave:

Ecco Roma! I don't think one should settle in the Village without first making the Grand Tour for perspective. For example, Eddie's Aurora of W. 4th St. makes better spaghetti than any restaurant I've tried in Italy. Also, the San Remo is socially more stimulating than the original S.R.—and so on. I'll be properly grateful when I come back.

Here is magnificent Rome—a much more kindly, open, accessible and humane place than Paris. I can't however really say I'm homesick. Particularly not for Minneapolis. What I do miss is friendly intimacy. Imagine what it would be like in N.Y. with ten words of English and very few acquaintances. I'm here alone; Anita is in Paris. So what I get is a species of lonely-mute's view of the great city. A condition not without its interest. And you? *Qu'est-ce que tu fais? Tout est bon?* [*]

* French: What are you up to? All's well?

Love,

You should see [Lionel] Abel in Paris!! *C'est assez cocasse* [*].
Dress coat, monocle. Works the restaurants.

Lionel Abel (1911–2001) was a playwright, critic and member of the Partisan
Review *circle who published numerous books including a memoir,* The Intellectual Follies *(1984).*

To Henry Volkening

February 27, 1949   Paris

Dear Henry:

I wrote to you about a month ago and you haven't answered so I reckon
the letter must be lost. That occasionally happens. I haven't heard from Rahv
either; I imagine he must be licking some of the wounds from that unjust story
of Mary McCarthy's that won Mr. Connolly's *Horizon* prize. [. . .] I read
the story last night; there'll be an awful wailing in the Village when it gets
to the States; it's an utterly cold wind of a story. I think that Mary McCarthy,
amazingly enough, doesn't know how cold.

I've rented a room on Rue des Saints-Pères—Hôtel de l'Académie—and
am scribbling away at a book. I don't know how good it is—will be—but it's
a book, and it's my vocation to write books and I follow it with the restlessness of true egomania. I'm preparing the full outline of another, one that I
have confidence in but don't feel quite prepared to begin, since it has to do
with Americans abroad. So I'm occupied for the time being with the aforementioned. It will be not of the best but, in these dreadful times of low
standards, good enough. I hope.

The communications of Guy Henle apropos of the Italian translation are
terser and terser. If it pleases God, I've seen the last. As for Smith College,
I've said neither yes nor no and I'm waiting to see what's offered. [. . .]

All the best,

Mary McCarthy's brief novel The Oasis, *in which Philip Rahv and others are
satirized, had been published in* Horizon.

* French: It's rather funny, in a comic-operatic way.

To Henry Volkening

Dear Henry:

No, I have no sardonic comments for Mr. [John Crowe] Ransom for whom my fiery spirit usually makes an allowance of respect. I don't expect him to stop being an editor for my sake and I think he behaves far more honorably than Rahv, that Commissar of Grumps, since I've never heard him represent himself as a snorting radical straight in the line of Prometheus, whereas Mr. Rahv is supposed to handle the Promethean fire as though it were no hotter than liniment, and is a charter-rebel from way back. I'm sending to ask why he didn't tell me his reasons for rejecting the story. He's owed me a letter for about two months and I think I now see why. He'll say, of course, that it is a good story. (He's printed *only* good stories these many, many years and mine falls below the *niveau général* [*].) But I'm going to make things as hard as possible for him because he's too long believed that the *avant-garde* (what a damning idea *avant-garde* is anyhow) has made its home with him. Like an aunt who once knew Lenin. When a story comes that tears out the nice old borders of sleepy sweet-williams the aunt snaps that of course she wants something wilder, tiger lilies, lilies of Mr. Joyce's breed, such as you see in the conservatory, and prefers the real thing in sweet-williams to impostures in tigers.

I'm telling him also that I observed with dissatisfaction in somebody else's *PR*—my sub. has been cut off—that "Dr. Pep" is announced as a story. "Dr. Pep" is *not* a story. It's something else, *sui generis*; I don't know what.

Since I want to see "Mr. Green" published and would like to see it published in *Kenyon Review*, I'd consent to have dashes in place of that terrible word in most common use all over the English speaking world and the great coagulate verb-noun-adjective of school, bar, factory and army which dominates most conversations. Even Truman allows his use of "son of a bitch" to be quoted. What circumspect dogs we are, compared to the chief executive. *He* knows times have changed. So since my ambition to be President is fruitless anyhow, because I'm Canadian-born, let there be dashes. And then, if Ransom doesn't want it, I think you might give over torturing editors with their limitations and send "Mr. Green" to the showers. I'd like if possible to have Lionel Trilling see it, with the note attached that I'd hoped he'd be able to read it in *PR*.

I hope by summer to be done with a mss. of about two hundred pages

* French: the general level

which Viking might be willing to bring out, not as the contract novel, which I'll begin as soon as this first thing is out of the way. Again, in this present book, the subject is not cheery but the matter, page to page, is very comic and perhaps *Kenyon* would like the first chapter of thirty pages since it is—*je le dis moi-même* [*]—rather funny. The subsequent book will be, according to my lights (and you may think them dark lights), altogether a comedy. [. . .]

Please remember me to Mr. Russell and Mrs. Volkening.

Best,

To J. F. Powers

March 30, 1949   Paris

Dear Jim:

About two months ago I came back from the magnificence of Rome to the impressiveness of Paris, felt myself all over, found I was just about the same, except perhaps a little more spoiled and lazy, and have been on a strict regime ever since, writing daily. I'm about half done with a book; the subject's a gloomy one but the book is funny, a combination I can trust you to understand. The title I've chosen for it is *The Crab and the Butterfly*, which I think does the tendency justice, and if I don't go anywhere—it isn't likely; the slack has just about been run out of Mr. Guggenheim's bounty—I ought to be done with it in the summer. A bad time, as everyone knows, to finish a book. A book ought to be finished in the spring. [. . .]

I read Mr. Waugh's review of your book [*Prince of Darkness and Other Stories*], and seeing a statement he made to *Time* (which runs after him with basins) I was able to understand it. He told the interviewer that his favorite American writer was Earl Biggers, or something like that. What I most disliked in his review was his failure to make it implicit (I didn't expect him to put it in so many words) that you were a better writer than he. As for [John] Lehmann, he's the best of publishers but he is a publisher and is bound to give the wrong reason; and what sort of review is it that starts out with the publisher's claims? I loathe that. I loathe snobs and Waugh is one of the worst sort. I've met a good number of snobs here; the best of them redeem themselves with profligacy. It shows they have a rather generous, helpless side. But snobbery *and* piousness? I have an Old Testament eye for abominations, a little reddened by this one.

---

* French: I say it myself.

[. . .]

You ought to do the piece for *Partisan*. *Partisan* has been kind of lean since it became a monthly. That's partly *Partisan's* fault. I'm sure that *PR*, *Kenyon* and some of the branch publications of the *Journal of Philology* like the *Hudson* or *Sewanee* turn down enough good material every month to make one fine number. But it is partly our fault, too. There ought to be more doing, more kinds of things written. A little guild life. [Leslie] Fiedler has the right idea, don't you think so? He does all kinds of writing. Well, perhaps it's because he's in Montana. Substitute for social life. [. . .]

Let's hear from you,

To David Bazelon

April 10, 1949   Paris

Dear Dave:

Yah, I'll write to Huntington Brown [of the Minnesota English Department] for you. I hope it does good, for Huntington and I had difficult times with each other. He's the archetype of the learned idiot. He's a Harvard Ph.D., conservative to the flap of his long underwear, collects pornographic poetry, has a pistol range in his basement, knows how to mend a dog sled in driving snow and is an Admiral Peary *manqué*, is president of the burial society of Minneapolis, and takes vitamin B1 all summer long on the belief that mosquitoes will not bite a man whose perspiration is saturated with it. And that's not all. But the man I'm going to send the hottest plug to is Sam'l Monk himself, a very sweet and intelligent guy who is head of the department and one of the dozen or so people in Minneapolis that I miss. [. . .]

Of course, one sees a number of collapsed Americans here, but their inflation could not have been very high at home. There's Jimmy Baldwin, for instance, who seems to be down and out and is sponging mercilessly. He hasn't applied his sponge to me yet. He doesn't do a great deal. Whenever I pass the Flore and the Deux Magots he's in company, drinking beer. Then there's [Milton] Klonsky, who is *verschwunden, spurlos, versenkt* [*]. He hated Paris, like every good American—that's practically the litmus test; said he was driving off to Nice with some creep. He may be in Nice, he may be in Italy. Who knows? He was very low in spirits. I was a little low myself when he arrived, but in the Empyrean by comparison; hence no company for him.

* German: vanished, sunk without a trace

Besides, I was working. Do I say "besides"? That was the ray that blights, for Milton. Anyway, he's gone and I haven't heard from him. As for [Lionel] Abel, he's in the Vaterland and thinks of Eighth St. as the *verfluchte Kameroons*. [*] [. . .]

What news? What are you really going to do next year? How is my friend Rosenfeld? Since starting with the [Wilhelm] Reich he has nothing to say to me. Coldness of the happy cured to their sinful and sickly old friends.

Love,

Milton Klonsky (1921–1981) was an essayist, historian and William Blake scholar best known for The Fabulous Ego *(1974).*

To Henry Volkening

April 13, 1949   Paris

Dear Henry:

I've just about touched the halfway mark in this book (called *The Crab and the Butterfly*, tentatively). It's writing itself very quickly and it's certainly full of astonishing things—I mean things that astonish me. I'm hunting for point of view with a long gun and shoot at anything that moves, especially Henry James. The first draft ought to be finished in June, the final one early in the fall. I won't have done so badly, then, my first year out of the professoriate. The six months it took me to get started perhaps make me step all the livelier.

Smith College was a bubble. It's just as well because Anita has got a very fine job as medical social worker with an American agency for DPs and there's no special hurry about my becoming employed. With a book to show, I can apply in 1950 for a Guggenheim renewal; my chances will be better. Jim Powers was turned down on his application for a second ride. Too many meritorious applications. But if he had had a large amount of work to show I think Moe wouldn't have refused him. Poor Jim is *au pied du mur* [**] with two kids to support.

Monroe Engel sent me a huffy-sounding note saying that he was going to Florence and I could conduct future business with Covici. Did he mean that

* German: the damnable Cameroons; fig., the boondocks
** French: lit., at the foot of the wall; impoverished, up against it

I could go to hell? I'm sorry I haven't written more to him but if he thinks I'm going to tell him over my shoulder every so often what I'm going to do in the next chapter, he's crazy.

Comment ça va? How is beautiful South Bend?

Best,

Monroe Engel (born 1921) was Bellow's editor at Viking, with which he'd signed after breaking ties with James Henle at Vanguard.

To Henry Volkening

[n.d.]   [Paris]

Dear Henry:

Note the new address. Another. We had to leave Marbeuf about a week ago; the old auto-racer and his wife came back from the Côte d'Azur and we had to go into a small hotel. Now we have the Rue de V[erneuil] until the first of October when we will have to find other landlords who want their long holiday in the Riviera paid for. The people from the Rue de V. are going to Biarritz for the season. But sufficient unto the day. Meanwhile the two concierges have done their best to lose our mail for us. I know of three letters that have been sent back to the States, and one of them may have been yours. If one was, I hope no good news of the sort that can't wait was in it.

The first writing of *The Crab* should end in June, as I predicted. It has been a little slow these last two weeks for various reasons, one of them being that I have been unable to hold back from *The Life of Augie March*, a very good thing indeed. I've done a considerable piece of it, a piece good enough to be published as it is. I'm very enthusiastic about it, and though I will finish *The Crab* because I hate to have unfinished novels on the table, it might not be a wrong plan to publish *Augie* first. It will be quite long, but worth the delay. In any case, I'll be returning with two books, *ce qui me plaît beaucoup* [*].

I did a short piece for my friend Lionel Abel who has (had, rather) a little periodical called *Instead*. Do you recall? Well, *Instead* has had its back broken by the times and I sent the thing to John Lehmann who had been asking me for something. Lehmann's going to print it in *New Writing #35*. What he aims to do about the money—it will be insignificant—I know not. If he sends it

* French: which pleases me very much

to me, I'll tell you the amount. But since he knows you represent me, he'll probably know what to do.

As for the Viking installments, I have a feeling that I ought to take them while the taking's good. True, Anita has a job now, but living in Paris abolishes every cent of it and we'll be coming back to New York pauperized as well as homeless. [. . .] What do you think? Shouldn't we ask Viking to turn on the cornucopia? [. . .]

We hear nothing but bad news from the States. You'd be doing me a great favor by sending some good.

All the best,

Nothing from Ransom? *If* he still wants "Mr. Green," I'd like to re-write the last three pages before he sets it up.

To Henry Volkening

June 10, 1949   Paris

Dear Henry:

The explanation of the John Lehmann mix-up is as follows: I wrote you last winter that my friend Lionel Abel had asked me for a piece; he was editing a magazine called *Instead,* and his pay was all that was supporting him in Paris. Since he's a good sort of guy and the cause worthy, I re-wrote a speech, something on the order of "Dr. Pep" and gave it to him. Then I sent a copy of same to Lehmann, who accepted it. But *Instead,* by a caprice of the lady who was paying for its publication, folded and Lionel is now out of a job and the last state is worse than the first. So "The Thoughts of Sgt. George Flavin," as this thing is called, won't be published in America. Unless Phil Rahv, who liked "Dr. Pep" *à outrance* [*], doesn't mind publishing it from *New Writing #38.* I don't think—the old song—any other magazine would care for something not-a-story, not-an-essay or anything recognizable.

In a letter that may have been lost en route, I asked you not to pass around "Mr. Green" anymore because I've re-read it and decided to re-write it. I have a fresh idea about it. When this overhauling will take place I can't say, because my hands are full at the moment with the two books. One is almost done—the first draft—and another is in the first stages. I feel that the second, *From the Life of Augie March,* is the best thing I've ever written. The

---

* French: extravagantly

first is a book such as I might have done two, three or five years ago—a good book but nothing transcendent. Also a very grim book. This is why I've had the notion that it would be better to publish *Augie* first. I'm writing it very rapidly and can easily meet Viking's deadline of June 1950 with enough material for a book. I have the feeling that it'll turn out long enough for two volumes, but of this I'm not positive. Anyhow, I'll send you the first chapter shortly. It may be publishable separately.

Monroe has signaled me from his hilltop villa in Florence. I'll say nothing to him about two books, as you advise. Perhaps I'll return to Italy in August to visit him and other people. [. . .]

I don't hear much about literary life in America, except the Pound controversy. I haven't seen a *Times* book section since December and can't say I feel privation. Is Harvey [Breit] still on the job? Give him my kindest regards, please.

[. . .]

Best,

Owing to Ezra Pound's treasonable and anti-Semitic broadcasts from Rome during the Second World War, a number of writers, including Bellow, were furious when he received the first Bollingen Prize from the Library of Congress in 1949.

To Henry Volkening

July 27, 1949   [Paris]

Dear Henry:

The heat is slaughterous in Paris. People ask me whether it's hotter in the States. Since it seems to give deep satisfaction, I always say yes. Generally I let them come out ahead and believe the beans are better, the beer hoppier, the soap more lathery *und so weiter* [*] in Europe. By the front page of the *Tribune*, I know what sort of summer's day you've had and can always be sure, whatever the comparative temperatures, that yours was grittier and sootier. But it's with no sort of pleasure.

The mornings are cool enough, and I manage to do my stint before the worst of the day. How it reads, ask not, however, because I can't see and won't be able to until the fall.

Mme. Wm. A. Bradley who acts for Vanguard has "sold"—the quotes are

* German: and so on

for effort—my two books to Gallimard (NRF), which also asks an option on the next three. How lovely and divine is confidence. It's all right with me, since Gallimard is the best publisher in France. But is it all right with you, with Viking? I am going to see Mme. Bradley on Friday in her elegant house at 18 Quai de Béthune; I shall tell her what I think and ask her to stand by for word from you.

We're not going to Italy this summer, as planned. It's awful of me to say so, I know, given what Italy is and what I am, but I haven't got the time. Besides it's too damned hot.

All the best,

To Monroe Engel

October 24, 1949   Paris

Dear Monroe:

Except for a short vacation in Spain, in August, I'd been working faithfully and hard, and had reason to be cheerful when I saw Guinzburg, for I'd done a good deal. But then I read over carefully what I'd done and saw that the book I'd been rather confident of was not what I thought it was. I'd opened something new and, I think, infinitely better in the last part of it; the first was simply not of the same order and had to be raised or scrapped. I didn't have it in me at this time to attempt this, so I've dived into something else I had started. On this, I've for some reason been able to work much faster than I've ever been able to work before. I do one fairly long chapter a week, and I expect to have the length of a book in first draft by Christmas. By the length of a book, I mean something like a hundred thousand words, not by any means the full length of what I plan. In any case, the first chapter is coming out in *PR* presently (November, they tell me), and if you'd like to see more I can send you carbons.

How's your own work going? I trust you've had better luck. I was in a state when I read over what I had written. All my cherished pride in being a steady performer took a belly-whop.

Do you see Isaac and Alfred? Please give them my love.

Best,

November 20, 1949   Paris

Dear Dave:

I know you're a loyal friend of mine, none more, and that you speak up for me whenever the axe is unsheathed. Therefore you'll understand what difficulties you put me in by writing as you did about Margaret [Bazelon's woman friend, living in Paris], also a friend of mine, though by no means so near. But I do like her; she's in some ways irresistible, as you know. You shouldn't have spoken as you did about her even if you felt what you said to be true, and I'm not sure you did. Because such is not the way to speak of anyone, so despisingly; it's the ruin of intercourse, that sort of bolshevism. One wry grin and you throw away the subject as Nedick's do a squeezed orange. You were speaking of a person and a not inconsiderable one; moreover, someone who admired and loved you a good deal. For I'm sure Margaret wanted to marry you and gave you as much opportunity to ask her to as she could. Since you didn't, all that you have to blame her for is wishing to get married. Now if you think marriage is an abject state for anyone, man or woman, and have something more *digne* [*] to propose than the black and hypocritical rags of matrimony, you can preach and publish your gospel in Hebron. But if you will agree to see anything at all normal in the human couple, it'll be hard to make a wrathful case against Margaret, some thirty years old, tired of living alone or with other women and of mere sleeping around.

Anyhow, I observed some protocol. I didn't go to her wedding for reasons of loyalty, but I did go to dinner, accepting a *fait accompli*. Frankly, I couldn't figure out, for the life of me, what conduct you would have laid on me and saw nothing treasonable in a plate of borscht, anyhow. Her husband is a reasonably good guy, sturdy, of apparently nice temper, Norwegian, of northern equableness.

This may be as good a place as any to say that I approved very much of your article on women in *Commentary*.

Now to speak of more *freylikh* [**] things: What have you been doing? Do you like your job, and does teaching agree with you? I trust you'll have something good to say for it, since it looks as if I'm going to have to put my-

* French: worthy, meritorious
** Yiddish: happy

self under the pedagogue's yoke again next year. I suppose I could stay in Europe for another year. But a third! Nay. I have to come back to the States, if for no other reason than I feel myself more and more an *Amerikaner*, and the place of such is more or less in *Amerika*. I badly miss American energy, even that of Minneapolis where hardly anybody at all is cultured. Here most everybody knows the year of Molière's birth and what François I said to Henry VIII on the Field of Cloth of Gold, but it's a weary satisfaction. Really weary. The working class round the Place de la Bastille has life, but it's not greatly different from what you find in Gary and Whiting, take away the berets and substitute beer for wine and television for concertinas. The rest is increasingly like museum custodianship, it appears to me.

You'll be seeing Klonsky again, soon. He hath fled and no doubt will louse me around, for we ended in collision; but I could tell you some pretty stories too. Which I won't, for reasons adumbrated in paragraph one.

Let's hear from you soon.

Best,

About the [D. H.] Lawrence *Tales*: They're pretty expensive and I'm somewhat strapped, so will you enclose a ten-dollar bill in your next? I think that'll do for two copies. If there's a surplus I'll buy you something else of his you can't get in N.Y.

To David Bazelon

December 3, 1949   Paris

Dear Dave:

I'm answering you somewhat against my inclination, for your letter was horrible and wolfish, and ought not to be answered. But having set off your stuff you appear to feel, at the end, that everything can now be as before, which decidedly it can't.

Of course I don't know what went on between you and Margaret, but I don't remember having taken any airs of *expertise*. I know your letter on her marriage made her wretched, while what you wrote to me about it was what I called it. When you say of a woman I know, or indeed any woman, that she has a stripe of white paint where her cunt ought to be, I think it is wrong; it is what I call bolshevik, not unjustifiably. Though I have often put up with your thinking me so, I am not stupid; when I say bolshevik I am thinking of a certain kind of destructiveness of which I have had some personal experience and of which I have also read a good deal in the polemical literature of Lenin, Trotsky and the Stalinists. I have a fairly well developed ear for tones and years' experience of manners of a different kind for contrast.

Now as for the wedding, it's true that I needn't have stayed away. But because, as you say, I didn't know a great deal about your relations with Margaret I had to depend on her to a large extent to furnish clues to your feelings. I gathered from her attitude that you might feel it unfriendly of me to attend. But this is all trifling. The important thing is that after nearly ten years of friendship you should discharge such a load against me for a rebuke that wasn't unjustified and in any event wasn't harshly made.

Did I say to you that you loyally defended me from literary attacks? You're completely mistaken. I was thinking of what Alvin had often told me, that you spoke well of me when others spoke unkindly. In general. Now you tell me "it isn't worth the effort" and you are speaking entirely of my writing. Had our friendship rested, childishly, on "literary loyalty" we'd have been through long before this. You must think me an idiot if you believe I haven't known for years what attitude you took toward it. I shouldn't say that you had ever covered me with laurels, and you've all too obviously spared me your opinion of what I've published since *The Victim*. Any writer naturally likes to have the things he does appreciated, but when have I ever twisted your arm for this? Now you "reveal" something that you think will crush me, as though you had spared me long enough, whereas in fact I had long ago come to terms with your estimate of my work, your reasons for it and the right and wrong of it, because I felt there were sympathies and attachments of greater importance than either the writing or your criticism. I don't try for salvation through writing. From lack of foresight, I have no better profession. I'll apply elsewhere for salvation, when I find the right place.

No, you don't belong to polite society, but you belong to a society all the same and have more of a membership in it than I have in any. It hasn't inculcated very good things in you. There's no need to describe these. I want no part of them, that's all I want to say.

Sincerely,

To Oscar Tarcov

December 5, 1949   Paris

Dear Oscar:

[. . .] I was overjoyed at your thick letter. In the first place, we hadn't heard from anyone in weeks and were beginning to feel really in *goles* [*]. And in the second, with it there came plenty of others, but what others! Junk, madness, haughtiness, injury. Enough to provoke a man to abjure all intimacy and withdraw to a tent as far as possible from sea-level, whence life came, and live on snow and hawkshit. Presently I'll tell you about this. But you can see that something sane and kind, in the nick of time, saved me from absolute despair.

Speaking generally, I'm in an enviable position. *On n'a pas lieu de se plaindre* [**]. I'm in France, comfortable, comfortably employed, and want for nothing except some extremely necessary things which nearly everyone else lacks too. When I come back from seeing Spanish cities or speak with deportees and survivors, I know there's nothing in my private existence that justifies complaint, or melancholy for myself, and that *Hamlet* is a luxury item in the life of mankind and adumbrates the difficulties we will all face after bread is plentiful. Save in America and this small fringe of Europe, it isn't. After all, we're incredibly wealthy, and if we look for a parallel to our problems I think we can find it, historically, in the annoyances of the surfeited rich. Or in Hamlets who have everything except what they really require of others and themselves. It's a horrible thing to be Hamlet and not born a prince, Jean Genet says. I'd say, answering with the voice of the middle class, that the first is a misfortune which makes the second insignificant. Frankly, I'm sick and tired of all that sort of melancholy and boredom. France has given me a bellyful of it, France alone, not counting Chicago and New York. I'm out for *sursum corda*. Lift up the heart. Still, the bad tidings keep coming in and that makes it a kind of Quixotic job. There's no other worth taking, however.

I'll tell you specifically what things are like. I get up, have breakfast, read the papers; Herschel goes off to school, Anita to her office, the maid puts up a lunch for me, I stick it in my briefcase and walk about a mile to my room, past the Russian embassy and curiosity shops. The weather is generally dark and gray, but the spirit only balks at it once in a while. In my room, 33 Rue

* Yiddish: exile
** French: One has no business complaining.

Vaneau, I light the woodstove with ancient copies of *Le Rire*, pausing to look at some of the smutty cartoons of 1906. Then I fiddle around a bit and go to work. Late in the afternoon I come out again. This is the difficult part of the day, especially if it's raining. I go home, shave, play with the kid awhile, go out along the Seine, read in a café, etc. Twice a week I play casino with an American painter at the Rouquet and drink cocoa. I have almost no friendly, that is, really intimate, intercourse with anyone except Anita. We see the Kaplans, Nick Chiaromonte and his wife and several other people. We have few French acquaintances because you have to make an enormous effort to justify yourself to the French and prove that you're not a barbarian at best and pain in the ass at worst. So far as my observation goes, there are two kinds of people in France, the workers and the other French. The workers are infinitely superior and are, really, what we at home have always considered *French*, the others what we meant by bourgeois. You see then what it's like. In many ways, it's the best sort of life you can arrange, nowadays, given what things are, but it's anything but warm. That's why what I hear from you and others at home is so important—the source of first connection—and Anita and I take great pleasure in talking about you. In what goes on, you and Edith are not only your own "switzerland," as you say, but ours, too. Well, then, when you write of Sam [Freifeld] it's terribly disappointing. Isaac was even less charitable about him, describing his visit to New York. But then Isaac is probably not far from thinking the same things of me. I don't know how you stand with him these days. Better, I hope. I'm entirely in the dog-house, I feel.

In some ways it's having chosen to become a writer that places me in this position. Anyhow it seems the more I write and publish, the more "public" things become, the less *first* contacts live. People draw off into coldness and enmity who'd have kinder feelings toward me if I were a photographer of dogs or a fish-expert. I hope with all my heart that your experience and Edith's will be different.

For instance, I got a hideous letter from Bazelon, full of rage; really one of those doggish, clawing things that want to go snarling straight into your inmost spirit and destroy you. I assure you I'm not exaggerating. He says, "I don't speak up for you" (when my writing is criticized) "because it naturally isn't worth the effort, first. Secondly, some people just don't care for your writing for literary reasons of their own. And third, I didn't understand that our friendship rested on literary loyalty." The cause of this? One of

Dave's girl friends, to whom he was much attached, got married recently in Paris. I had gotten to know her well and consider her a friend of mine. Just before her wedding, Dave sent me a perfectly nauseating letter about her, attacking her sexually, etc. I answered that it was bolshevistic of him to express himself so about anyone. That since he had always been a loyal friend to me, he might understand my being loyal to her. That, however, I hadn't gone to her wedding because he might not have liked it, etc. A perfectly inoffensive letter in which I said not a single thing about "literary loyalty"—as though by now it weren't perfectly clear what opinion his Hudson Street friends had of my writing. I shan't say that I don't care at all, but I don't, effectively, care. I've never policed any of my friends on this score or twisted any arms. I've never quarreled with Sam or Isaac on this subject, their attitude has never essentially affected my feelings toward them. *Ecco!* My first contacts! Evidently Dave had been getting this ready for a long time and I had only to mention something so foolish as loyalty to have him gush it into my face.

Where does this bring me? To coming back to the States. Ay, the happy day. Probably I could remain in Europe, if I wanted to work out a deal. But just now I want to come back. At least for a year. I don't any longer have my job at Minnesota, but I've written to apply to other places.

[William] Phillips of *PR* is here. Better acquaintance with him shows me what you're up against with editors. As we used to say in Tuley, "His taste is in his mout." They don't believe there can be writing, he and his mob, and know from nothin'.

Best love, and write soon,

Write to 33 Vaneau. We have to move again.

Nicola Chiaromonte (1904–1972) was a leading essayist and theater critic both in America at The New Republic *and* Partisan Review *and in Italy at* L'Espresso *and* La Stampa. *With Ignazio Silone, he founded the magazine* Tempo Presente.

To Herbert and Mitzie McCloskey

[n.d.]   [Paris]

Dearest Herb and Mitzie,

After a year and a half in Paris, *bien isolé*, a very mysterious and above all friendless life, letters like yours are in the most literal sense from another world where I have friends from whom, inexplicably it sometimes seems, I have separated myself. But of course such separations are the characteristic ones, now, and *sans le savoir* [*] I get into the path—*put* myself there, I mean—of the characteristic. I can't say why I left Mpls. any more than I could explain why, when it happened, I pulled out of Chicago. I submitted to an intuition, and later understood that I had (for me) done right. There are things you can't comprehend by staying with them. But many of these moves are heavy. They are Jonah journeys.

So I needn't say "frankly" in preface to the following: that I don't really know where I ought to be. You must be as well aware of it as I am. My intuitions are more made up than my mind.

I wrote to Sam Monk because both Gug. and Viking money will have run out by March, to ask *whether* he knew of any jobs for me. He was very solicitous, and he inquired at Harvard. I've not definitely turned anything down. It's still possible that I may go to Harvard. Meanwhile I've applied for a Gug. renewal. My difficulty is explained by the fact that I worked eight months at a book I've decided to put aside. Since October, I've finished about two-thirds of *Augie March*—an on the whole much better performance. If I'm to live by my writing I can't afford such eight-month losses.

So I don't know what we'll be doing. Economically, it might be just us well to stay in Europe, though we're coming home for a visit in September. Europe is not the Great Good Place for me, though with all my dissatisfaction it has taught me a great deal about what and who I am. That is, really, what and who *others* are. These discoveries are not true when condensed, so that I'll leave to wait till fall to tell you of them, and to hear yours and see you again, a pleasure I often have in daydreams.

Yes, I'd like to be in Mpls. again; I need a *pied-à-terre*. But I know it would be temporary again. I am very hostile, I tell you once more what you surely know, to "literary culture." I think of it as an enemy. I am not thinking only

---

* French: without knowing it

of *des gisants funestes* [*] like H[untington] Brown and a host of others who have made literature originate in itself, for whom even *belief* is literature.

And, along with "literary culture," the other vanities of "culture" that have no meeting with chaos. If there's anything that dwelling in this French park has shown me it is the blindness that a great cultural inheritance bequeaths. The idea of a university, as Ortega says, is in classicism; the true life of poetry, as he also tells us, is in shipwreck.

That's been the teaching of my intuitions, too, and that's why I spoke of Jonah. I haven't been able to resist safety, and I haven't been able to rest in it. I know that if I don't get the Guggenheim, I'll jump at the chance to be at Mpls. The greatest charm of it would be living with you once more. But I know also that I'll jump again; that I couldn't permanently stay.

Because I understand that the best of me has formed in the jumps.

The theory of it apart, I'm moved at being wanted by people who know I disagree with them and disapprove of what they do, people like Leonard [Unger] and [William Van] O'Connor.

We're going to Salzburg in April, in May to Venice, in June to Rome, and we're sailing at the end of August. Will you be in the East around Labor Day? If you could be, what great pleasure to see you in New York.

Tumin is conducting a tour from Princeton and I expect him here in July. He's written kindly to me, but we've had a sort of quarrel over I[rving] Howe.

Best love to all of you,

* French: sculpted funereal figures, lying supine

PART TWO

1950–1959

——————◆•◆•◆——————

And now here's the thing. It takes a time like this for you to find out how sore your heart has been, and, moreover, all the while you thought you were going around idle terribly hard work was taking place. Hard, hard work, excavation and digging, mining, moling through tunnels, heaving, pushing, moving rock, working, working, working, working, working, panting, hauling, hoisting. And none of this work is seen from the outside. It's internally done. It happens because you are powerless and unable to get anywhere, to obtain justice or have requital, and therefore in yourself you labor, you wage and combat, settle scores, remember insults, fight, reply, deny, blab, denounce, triumph, outwit, overcome, vindicate, cry, persist, absolve, die and rise again. All by yourself! Where is everybody? Inside your breast and skin, the entire cast.

—The Adventures of Augie March

1950

To Robert Hivnor

[n.d.]   [Paris]

Dear Bob:

I wish I had stayed in a temperance hotel with the temperate. Although I don't judge the inverted with harshness, still it is rather difficult to go to London thinking of Dickens and Hardy, to say nothing of Milton and Marx, and land in the midst of fairies. My publisher is one; all the guests at his cocktail party were ones; all the *Horizon* people, with the single exception of a man who apparently suffered from satyriasis, likewise at their cocktail party. This single exception was chasing Sonia Brownell Orwell, who didn't appear to have a husband on the point of death. It was confounding. Modern life is too much for me. *Bien, je m'en fous* [*]. I enjoyed London anyway. There was a fire in the Covent Garden basement, carol-singing in Trafalgar Square led by a spontaneous girl who stood on the base of a statue. And the Channel was rough both passages, but the second time I came off dull but victorious at Dieppe.

[Paolo] Milano writes from Rome that [Eric] Bentley has become a Titoist. He wants to know why, but without being able to say, I feel it's very natural. That's all the news I have for you about the theatrical world. Except that I went to Camus's new play which was grievously bad. Also to *Le Bossu* at the Marigny, which just couldn't resolve to be corny enough and so lost its opportunity for redemption by fun. [. . .]

Incidentally, Dick Ellmann is trying to get me a Briggs-Copeland fellowship there [at Harvard]; I have no job for next year, not much money, and if I fail to get a Guggenheim (not competing with you; I'm among the applicants for renewal) I'll be in a rather bad spot.

Anita leaves her job in April and we go to Salzburg for a month. Afterwards, Italy. After that (early September) home. Everything's very indefinite and *déraciné*. Except *Augie March*, which I work on with great satisfaction every day. I'm very pleased that you liked chapter 1. Hope you will the next. [. . .]

The snapshot was a *succès fou* with Gregory and the rest of us. Your son's very handsome.

All the best to you both (all three),

* French: So I shrug it off.

Robert Hivnor had been a colleague and friend of Bellow's at the University of Minnesota. Eric Bentley (born 1916), playwright, critic, cabaret performer, translator, has been for fifty years the preeminent historian of modern European drama; he and Bellow were also colleagues at University of Minnesota. Albert Camus's "grievously bad" play was Les Justes.

To Monroe Engel

January 12, 1950 Paris

Dear Monroe:

I have just sent out a stack of mss. with my Guggenheim application and asked H. A. Moe to forward it to you when his committee have done feeding their spirits on it. Part of the *Crab and the Butterfly,* which I put aside for *Augie March* is in the bundle, four or five chapters out of the middle of it; when you've seen them you'll perhaps feel easier about my having given over—for the time being. As for *Augie March,* I'm having such an enthusiastic labor with it that it hadn't occurred to me—in my daily stump-bombings—how a reader might feel about risking limbs in the clearing. No, I don't believe it has dropped or changed its pace in the fifty thousand words of it I've done so far. You judge for yourself, but please remember you'll read it *exactly* as first written, without a single alteration. Ch. 1 in *PR* was re-written once.

There are reasons of all sorts for coming back, not all of them financial, but the financial in themselves weigh a good deal. I've put in for a Guggenheim. I don't think Mr. Moe cares much for me (Alfred, perhaps, may be in a position to put in a word) and I don't feel that I'm going to get anything from him. I have written to Prof. Ball at Queens College to ask for a job and shall have to wait for his answer before I can ask you to do anything about an apartment. The only other prospect I have is, queerly enough, at Harvard—the Briggs-Copeland Fellowship. There's nothing else. And life in Paris is not cheap; I'd have to go to work for UNESCO or something like that if we wanted to stay.

I'm going to Salzburg in April. By that time the first draft of *Augie* will be ready, please God, and I can start the grinding—provided the noise of Germans cheering for Thomas Wolfe isn't too loud. [. . .]

What's Isaac doing, by the way? I never hear from him at all. Is it the sad lot of the boyhood friends of analysands coming to me? Well, when you see him tell him that we love him and think of him often. Is he writing a novel? Have you seen what he's doing? What is it like?

Best to everyone,

To Alfred Kazin

January 28, 1950 Paris

Dear Alfred:

A little list of disloyal people who are astonished at my wanting to come back to America will be just the thing, just the thing. It's also rather interesting that people don't believe Balzac, Flaubert and Stendhal when they write of French life and of Paris—much less Dostoyevsky in that queer little book called *Le Bourgeois de Paris*. They prefer to trust Henry James, or Henry Miller or even Carl Van Vechten and all that happy American throng that lived around the Montagne Ste. Geneviève. But if Stendhal were alive today, he might very conceivably choose to live in Washington, D.C.—considering what has become of his beloved Milan. And of this I am sure: that he would do as I do with his copy of *Les Temps Modernes*, that is scan the latest *sottises*, observe with brutal contempt the newest wrinkle in anguish and then feed Simone's articles on sex to the cat to cure her of her heat and give the remainder to little G[regory] to cut dollies from; he can't read yet and lives happily in nature.

But, a few lines of business. My news has reached you in a confused and debased state. I merely asked Monroe and/or Henry to inquire of you what the situation was. I didn't mean for them to shake you with a storm of demands in my name. I *don't* think you ought to write to Moe. I've already sent him a batch of mss., and if merit has anything to do with his decision—which I understand is not strictly the case—there ought to be no question about the decision. I know J. F. Powers was refused a renewal recently, however, and Jean Stafford told me last summer that Moe had called her in to discuss Powers with her. Her praise didn't help. But this reveals that there is some sort of Prague Arcana in use along 5th Ave., and I thought you might know something about it. As for the teaching, that too came to you with more hot and urgent sweat than it originally issued with. *Ça n'est pas tellement grave* [*]. I'll try Sarah Lawrence, but it would give no joy. What I principally need is a shack wherein to finish a book. After it's done, I'd as lief

* French: That's not so serious.

work in a factory as remain in what are called intellectual milieux—my heart's abhorrence, they're coming to be. Wherever there are people who still *desire* something, even if they are after false gods. Perhaps you know a kind of industrialist who would give a writer still in fair physical condition a job in a cannery or mattress factory. I'm not joking.

I still hope I'll soon be able to read your book. Preparatory to going to Salzburg (April) I have picked up *On Native Grounds* and read large parts of it again with great pleasure. Also, I thought your piece in *PR* superb—the one on Melville. It ought to be compulsory reading in all graduate schools. Apparently [Richard] Chase and [Cleanth] Brooks (*Understanding Fiction*— Warren is to blame too, alas, who should know better) are convinced that to write a story is to manipulate symbols. What are they going to make young writers in the colleges think but that they daren't their most natural step but must learn "mythic" footwork? This is what happens when literature itself becomes the basis for literature and classics become crushers.

Eh, bien . . . write me some good news.

Yours,

To Monroe Engel

March 26, 1950   Paris

Dear Monroe:

My prophetic heart has stolen all the bases; I didn't get a Guggenheim, for reasons best understood somewhere else. I shall have to make do without, but energetically, and I suppose one can't expect to have first lick, always, at fortune's spoon. Had I gotten the Guggenheim we'd have moved to a cheap town on the Côte d'Azur, for the Fellowship money wouldn't have been enough to live on in the expensive States. But now it seems to me that I'd better move into New York, and I'd consider it a great favor if you'd inquire of Mr. Guinzburg about a flat: the location doesn't matter too much, and I understand, furthermore, that it had better not matter—one'd better not be too particular. Large and cheap; I'm used to having a room off to one side. Perhaps we could get something in Isaac's neck of the woods. That would be a considerable advantage to wives and children, since I'm told the Rosenfelds feel their exile from the Village very keenly.

I've decided on New York because odd jobs can be found there teaching, and you can't get reviews to do unless you show your face in editors' offices. I'm not at all worried about making out; I have quite a few stories that may be saleable and, if you have no objections, I can try to get a few chapters of *Augie March* published in *Commentary*.

The great annoyance about the Guggenheim rejection is that it will slow up work on my novel.

Before I leave Paris, on Friday of this week—to go to Salzburg for a month—I will send you a few more chapters of it. It is, as you'll see, an episodic book. I have done about a hundred thousand words and, when I come to a natural resting point, I plan to take a pause and consider the maturer part of it. Do you think the book could be published up to that resting point, the remainder to follow in a year or so? Of course, it remains to be seen whether you like it at all. I'll be waiting, a little uneasily, at Schloss Leopoldskron, Salzburg, for your opinion. Please remember, as you read it, that I generally put everything that strikes me as relevant into a first draft and shrink it afterwards; I wouldn't have sent the mss. out in such rough condition if it hadn't been necessary to support my Guggenheim application.

I've written another letter to Harold Taylor [president of Sarah Lawrence] explaining that I had already sent him, last January, a *curriculum vitae*. Of course he doesn't want to hire people he's never seen. Unfortunately, he won't be able to see me until the first week of September, when I come back. I've asked him, however, to consider me for some part-time work next fall. He will have made all his full-time appointments long before then. I'm very grateful to you, Monroe, for the trouble you've taken for me. And hope to show that my gratitude is made of pretty durable material.

All the best,

To Henry Volkening

March 26, 1950   Paris

Dear Henry:

[. . .] And now I'll have to unstrap that batch of stories. I didn't want to do that because to work them over would take time from *Augie March*. But, on a whisper from my prophetic heart, I started a new one even before the refusal from Guggenheim arrived. Another query: a letter from prison (in Paris) written by an Italian black marketeer and con man to a rich American he had been steering around the night clubs, explaining why he is in jail. Rather curious. But perhaps the *New Yorker* will one of these days break precedent and publish something bizarre. I've gotten quite a lot of comment about the story in *Harper's* [*Bazaar*] from people who think more of it than I ever did.

In writing to Monroe, I've set afoot a campaign to have the first large part of *Augie March* (about a hundred twenty thousand words) published as the contracted novel. It is an episodic book. The first half of it stands by itself. And I thought I had better unmask my motives now, since it is obvious that these hundred twenty thousand represent only one half of the total. I could never put over this half as the whole, saying nothing about the rest. If Viking wants to wait for the whole quarter of a million words, perhaps it will extend my subsidy for another six months. Probably would see me dead first, common sense says to me, speaking low. [. . .]

All the best,

The story in Harper's Bazaar *was "By the Rock Wall," which Bellow apparently lost and had rewritten.*

To Monroe Engel

April 30, 1950   Paris

Dear Monroe:

I'm very pleased, very happy, about your response. While I didn't exactly take the Guggenheim rejection as literary criticism—how can such an organization *criticize*—I couldn't help, nevertheless, feeling uneasy . . . on the side where my judgments sometimes fail me, the helpless side. But then there's the stronger side, and there I knew that the course I'd been following for a long time was at last producing results, that I'd put my hand strongly to a good thing and was making it resound. Or, putting it another way, I believe I'm beginning to make some real excavations. I'm delighted that you agree. *Ad n[auseam]*, I've notified you that you were going to see the raw mass. You hear that far too often, I'm sure. And I must say that although I have some kind of instinctive sense of what the finished thing will be, I've never had such a mass to knead and shape either, and I don't know how I'll fare with it. The abundance gives me confidence, however, and wherever that and the life, the feeling of the book, are connected there'll be no pruning. But I haven't read over what I've done, consecutively. When I do, I may very well share your objections. My own figure for the shape of the book is that of a widening spiral that begins in the parish, ghetto, slum and spreads into the greater world, and there Augie comes to the fore because of the multiplication of people around him and the greater difficulty of experience. In childhood one naturally lives as an observer. And it may be that Augie doesn't sufficiently come forward at first; but in my eyes, the general plan of the book—its length—justified this. I have a further part in mind for almost all the characters so far introduced, even the ones like Kreines and Five Properties. And Sylvester will be a considerable Machiavellian too.

Another two hundred pages, and the design will be almost entirely visible; and there will be *still* more—the second part will be again as long, with sections on the war and the life of a black-marketeer in Europe and a final, tragic one on the life of the greatest Machiavellian of them all, Augie's brother Simon. Sometimes I'm not sure that Augie will bear so much traffic, and again think that he *must* bear it, be sent through the bitterest of contemporary experience if my purpose is to have its real test. In any case, publishing a first volume would give me a breather in which to mature the sequel. But we can discuss this, as you propose, in September, when I'll have a good deal more to show.

[. . .]

Anyway, it looks as though we'll be coming to New York to live. I don't know what rents are now, but I wouldn't like to pay much more than sixty or seventy. Eighty, if I must. As for the size of the flat, that depends on the section we move into. In a neighborhood where I could find a room to write in, we wouldn't need six rooms. Four to six, let's say, then. The bigger the better. We have furniture and household stuff in Chicago, so they needn't be furnished. [. . .]

Thank you for your letter.

Best,

To Henry Volkening

June 7, 1950   Rome

Dear Henry:

I thought, immodestly, that you would like *Augie*, and I'm delighted. Mountainous sales? I'd be satisfied with moderately hilly ones. But one never knows, for it'll be a large book, and I have an idea that there's something saleable about sheer bulk; people feel they're not being cheated. As for your objections, I haven't yet read what I've done, and I've worked at some speed, carelessly. It may be, when I read, that I'll agree with you and with Monroe. Just now, I feel the booklearning is indispensable for its dimensions. It isn't hard to explain. For that matter, it may not need any explanation; it represents a kind of Midwestern culture common enough, and left out by a harmful convention. Writers are altogether too tame about what they may assume; they need to take more license.

If you think there are chapters that might interest magazine editors, show the mss. around. I do have a copy with me and the first, handwritten one is in Paris. We can't lose all three. At worst, the written one would have to be typed off again. If anyone will take a chapter, I can polish it up; not printable as is. [. . .]

On the 15th, we're going to Positano, near Sorrento, and we'll be there until the 20th of July. I've been asked to a conference of the most lofty anti-Stalinists, in Berlin at the end of June. I haven't decided yet whether I'm going. I'm not too keen about it, but five lotus-eating weeks I'm afraid would not agree with me.

Yours,

To the Tarcovs

June 26, 1950

Dear Tarcovs—

Just now we're in Positano, on the gulf of Salerno, in the midst of the mountains and hanging over the sea. The fishermen have no motors and plant their own lobster traps, the women make lace on bolsters, simply with pins and bobbins, and on holy days the Saints are taken for a walk by a procession. It would seem incredible for the gods never to see the sun, and they are shown it on Sunday.

And we're coming home in Sept. I expect things will be much altered. I read the papers with revulsion, when I get them. The only papers here are the Italian and catastrophe's an old story to them—they prefer gossip.

So we'll be in Chicago for a week or two in Sept., and then to New York. I have evening work at NYU. Fear Isaac doesn't like that. He sent me a sore, and rather nasty note about it, as though I had done something behind his back. What's wrong with people at home, anyway, and what's the snarling for? Isaac knows perfectly well that if my being at NYU would be doing him the least harm I'd turn down the job. I've told him so, and the truth of it doesn't need any protestation. But he'd rather dislike me than converse about it and for my part I can't continue to care many damns as the years accumulate on my head.

That's Bazelon and Isaac, one or two others, and leaves me and thee. Rather old-fashioned. Similarities in our families account for it maybe.

Saul Bellow: Letters

Though you may not like the comparison just now, with Morrie's sins [Bellow's brother Maurice, who'd fathered a child out of wedlock and faced a paternity suit] tumbling from the closet. I knew something about them, of course, but wasn't abreast of them all and hadn't heard about the suit till you wrote me of it. I'd like to know more. It moves me to think of my father in this, and of the kids. It'll do the rest of the family good if they're not beyond remedies.

This is turning out to be a sad letter, and that's peculiar because I've been feeling the opposite of sad. Just went down to the harbor with Herschel, lecturing him on the geology of mountains. Sins of the father. I *tried* to tell you and Isaac about the Illinois limestone.

It did us much good to get your letter with some evidence of happiness in it and word of the kids and of your writing. You seem more gallant about the last than I am. I'm beginning to think of bricklaying.

Best love,

Till July 20—Pensione Vittoria, Positano (Salerno), Italia.

Spring Ode

Thunder brings the end of winter,
Rinsing the yellow snow from the gutter;
Calico spots flare at the window;
I lie in my bathrobe, eating butter.
Grease on my cheeks—the fat of the season
Now dead and sealed, now dead and waxy.
Foxes yap on the tenement stairs;
Hope arrives in a Checker taxi.
His clever face is now surveying
The hallway with its sooty tatters,
The playing-card banners overhead,
The cymbals, scales and other matters.
My bathrobe sleeves are stiff with yolks,
Speckled with crumbs of my winter's eating;
Bottles and eggshells on the floor
Lie between us at our meeting.
He falls into my arms, we kiss,

We cry like reunited brothers.
He tells me how he searched for me
Among the others.
My cheeks are fat, my eyes are wet,
His hand rests sadly on my shoulder;
We cannot help but see how much
Each has grown older.

—Bellow

To Samuel Freifeld

July 12, 1950   Positano

Dear Sam'l:

Probably was silly to talk about exile. I merely meant that, abroad, one wants to feel abroad *from* a place; for Europeans do have such home places, and if their friends do not support them, there are other things that do, so that one doesn't have to look into one's consciousness or memory for proof that existence isn't accidental. Anyway, if I'm in exile so are you, from me. Exile in your own parlor, among appearances of substance.

And then, you see, I'm a kind of connections-keeper. For instance, your papa and a few other relatives are very lively daily preoccupations of mine. Personages *like* them appear in *Augie March*. You don't, and needn't, look for yourself (the way I have of scrambling things); someone else is in your place. Most ways you'll be pleased by this monument; it's an honorable one; and you know your pa was too rich to be held by oblivion. And you're free enough a man to be pleased rather than offended.

Why we're coming back? Well, one doesn't form intimacies here, and I have a strong societal sense. The French are not the people to encourage intimacy. The Italians, yes; or apparently, but you come to a place with them beyond which you cannot go, possibly because they don't, for themselves, go beyond it either. On the other hand, you may say: "Who wants your stinking intimacy anyhow?" and "Stand off, you and your intimacy"—with some justice. But then one is surrounded by signs of the great mutuality of this past, great *relation*, and wants to get off the egocycle and go home to see what can be done.

Much love to you all [. . .]

To Monroe Engel

July 15, 1950   [Positano]

Dear Monroe—

Is Isaac's nose out of joint about NYU? Mine is a little. He makes me feel that I've undermined him there. I can still drop out, if he's affected. How can I know whether he is? I have no way of telling what's at stake for him. For me there's nothing. I simply don't want to get in his way. Not from friendly feeling—there's not much lost between us now; he'd like to become strangers, and I'm not so opposed to that as I formerly was—but because I'd prefer, if I have to struggle with someone for survival, that it be a person I never struggled with before.

We're about to leave Positano. Do you know it? Near Amalfi. Four thousand feet of mountain descending to the Gulf in a width of about eight hundred yards. We have the Siren Islands on one side and the Calabrian Mts. on the other. The islands now are owned by Léonide Massine and there are occasionally Russian women landing in Positano and demanding pen and paper at Giacomino's coffee-house to write long somethings.

By rising early to beat the heat I've written a long lot of *Augie March*; at four hundred pages it's nothing like finished. It may be again as long. And then what: *che cosa faremo?* [*]

I know [Herbert] Gold well, and like him; some of his things that I've read, the most recent, are very good; the very last thing he sent me was well-nigh perfect. One of a series, he says, I believe he's going to call it *The Economic Life*. You ought to ask him for it.

Good to hear about Jean Stafford, Mrs. Oliver Something. She sent me a wedding announcement. Heroic to marry so soon after a divorce. Mrs. Oliver *Jensen*! I just remembered. I'll be grateful to you if you'll congratulate her, thank her for me and tell her I haven't forgotten that she gave me two bucks when she went to Germany. Is she writing anything now? She could be very good. I'm in favor of her.

Quoi d'ailleurs? [**] I still arrive homeless. In Paris: 33 Rue de Vaneau will still do, after Aug. 1st.

Best,

* Italian: What will we do?
** French: What besides?

To Henry Volkening

Dear Henry—

This is Monday. We're leaving Positano on Thursday, the 20th—for Rome, Siena, Florence, Turin, Grenoble and Paris. Paris on August 1st. On the 29th we're supposed to sail. I add the provisional word because reading about Korea in this little town in a five-day-old newspaper, I don't know but what we'll be in an internment camp on the 29th [. . .]

Our address in Paris will be 33 Rue Vaneau, again.

I hope your summer is approximately as good as mine. It can't be exactly as good because of the age of the papers when I see them, whereas you read the *Times* and all the truth that's fit to print as soon as it's discovered.

I'll be reading mine in a barrel, I think, by flashlight.

All the best,

On June 25 North Korean forces had crossed the thirty-eighth parallel into South Korea, precipitating an international crisis that would lead to three years of war.

To Henry Volkening

August 21, 1950   [Paris]

Dear Henry—

This is the 21st *août*; on the 29th we sail, arriving in New York on Sept. 4, *environ*. Anita and the kid will go on to Chicago, and I'll follow them a couple of days later to visit home briefly.

Paris improves when viewed with *les yeux passagers* [*] of a tourist. Off and on, I've been writing, and I'll have some four hundred pages of mss. to show Viking. I still think it would be a good idea to stop at some natural place in the narrative and publish a volume. I have an immense plan for the rest, and who knows whether there'll be time for it all before we're swamped.

The Russians can have Europe now *à l'oeil*, for nothing—for the shouting. I don't think they'll let the opportunity escape—*à bientôt*.

* French: the roving eyes

1951

To Herbert McCloskey

[n.d.]   [Queens, New York]

Dear Herb—

I get news of you from Jenny who is a cheerful interpreter and whom I like to believe. You are going to California, building a house, finishing your book, and Mitz and the kids are well. You sound very lucky to me.

The only thing simple in my life is *Augie M.* Everything else is wickedly complicated and perhaps the one accounts for the other. Even *Augie* goes slowly now, and speed was the reason for his success before. I am near the end of Book 1. Did I tell you that Viking is thinking of publishing it in two parts?

I saw Sam Monk at the MLA convention. He said there'd be nothing for me at the U. for a while. Have you had a real falling out about Fiedler? You ought not. Sam is rightly down on Fiedler for some of the things he's published.

Sam, by the way, will be teaching at Columbia this summer.

Not a word from Tumin. I saw him last in Paris. Where it was a convenience for him to have friends. Here he sees only [Ralph] Ross, and has not once phoned me. Perhaps he's afraid of being asked for money. Shit! He *has* become a Princeton professor, hasn't he, and has to be careful about impecunious writers. Since he's a clandestine writer himself, maybe he believes I should pay for my brazenness. Besides, he's always had the fear that I would write about him and write ruinously. Holy and almighty God—why do the intelligent men become radiologists and the blind study humanity!? [. . .] Incidentally, my monologue on Intelligence will come out presently in the *Hudson Review.*

A few more financial hits like that from the *Hudson,* financed by the Morgan family (pays two cents a word) and I'll have to go to work in a defense plant. This morning I read Truman's manpower note. I can see myself in line at an office. Someone in front of me works at the Copacabana? Fine! Coats chicklets, colors Superman. Excellent, all exempt. Then come I:

"What are you?"

"A writer."

"For *The Reader's Digest, Red-Book, Noble Savage, Breezy Stories, Fleabite Gazette?*"

"For many a one of these."

"Then report in Pittsburgh Friday to the Hell's Hinge Corp. Bring your own shackles."

Best love,

To Herbert McCloskey

January 30, 1951   Queens, New York

Dear Herb,

Thank you for trying, and for your offer. I know I have no better friends in the world than you and Mitzie, and I wouldn't hesitate to ask for a loan if I needed the money and couldn't get it from someone who could spare it more easily. But there's my father who has a lot of it, and [Arthur] Lidov who's become rich, too, and would willingly let me have a few hundred. Really, I don't need it now, I have enough. By the middle of summer, if I don't get a break, I will need some. But then I can always do something. I've gotten by for a long time. Nearly three years I've been able to give to writing and private griefs—to say nothing of considerable happiness. And conceivably I may still get by. I've applied for a Rockefeller grant and the signs are better than fair. [. . .]

Winter diseases have begun to hit us. First there was a virus, and then the grippe. I had a bad case of the latter, aggravated by a penicillin reaction. I'm only one day out of bed—flat for nearly a week, and during the breather between semesters, too, when I had planned to do so much. And then I've been forbidden to smoke, too. Permanently; I can never again have a pipe or a cigar; not even a cigarette. So I'm sending you some of my pipes, dividing them between you and Paolo. [. . .]

I suppose, damn it! that nearly everybody is some kind of writer and thus your writing has to be judged by these crypto-novelists wrapped as philosophers, sociologists, and even revolutionists. I'll give you ten to one that Max Shachtman has written a novel on the Bridgman convention, or something like that [. . .]

To John Lehmann

[n.d.]   [Queens]

Damn, what a letter! It surpasses anything I've ever seen. Not a word about the quality of the novel. If you can find nothing better to say upon reading *Augie March* than that you all "think very highly" of me, I don't think I want you to publish it at all. I'm not selling you a commodity. Your attitude infuriates me. Either you are entirely lacking in taste and judgment or you are being terribly prudent about the advance. Well, permit me to make it clear once and for all that it doesn't make a damned bit of difference to me whether you publish the novel or not. You have read two-thirds of it, and I refuse absolutely to send you another page. Return the manuscript to Viking if you don't want to take the book.

Poet-publisher John Lehmann (1907–1987) brought out the extremely influential magazine New Writing *(subsequently* Penguin New Writing*) as well as founding, in 1946, John Lehmann Limited, under which imprint Bellow, Thom Gunn, Laurie Lee, Elizabeth David and others were published.*

To John Lehmann

July 19, 1951 [Queens]

Dear John:

I have your letter before me.

In one place, it reads: "You say . . . that you are still amenable to doing the great work in two parts . . ."; and in another: "You have indeed posed us a very tricky problem, but as you know we all think highly of you and very much hope that in the end the job won't be beyond our means."

Now, I know you haven't seen anything like my book among recent novels. I've been reviewing them; I know what they are. They're for the most part phony, or empty-hearted, banal and bungling. I should have thought it would do something to you to see *Augie*. By your own admission you had almost finished reading the manuscript, and yet you had nothing to say about it. You were cool; businesslike, merely; you were terribly patronizing and you put me in a rage. In London you had made me feel—or tried to make me feel—that you had done me an immense favor in publishing my novels. I will *not* be made to feel that about *Augie March*. It damned well isn't necessary.

I have discussed this matter with Guinzburg, and he has left the decision to me. I think that, having blown my top, I have, for my part, cleared the air. If you still want to publish the book, I shall be glad to see it appear under your imprint. The manuscript is now six hundred pages long and at the present reckoning I have another two hundred to go. There is no break in the narrative, really. Any break would be arbitrary. Certainly the fifty pages you ask for would not bring the volume to a close; they begin a new action which continues for another two hundred pages.

I know this presents you with some difficult problems, but I don't want to hear about the difficulties exclusively. As to your being treated as a salesman, I think you're under a misapprehension. It wouldn't have made any difference to me what a salesman thought of my book.

Yours,

To Herbert McCloskey

[n.d.]   [Queens]

Dear Herb:

For many reasons, your letter made me happy. I keep it with various necessary talismans on my desk and read it often. I *knew* I could reach you and Mitzie, because of your generosity toward me. I shall have such readers.

I know how steeped in impatience people are and how little capable of giving attention. You ought to have seen the letter I received from Tumin after he had read *Augie*. Perhaps you heard something about his feelings in Princeton. Too much sociological and literary analysis, I suppose, crippled him as they do many others in reading. I was amazed. But it is really too much to expect people to come out of their feelings. Though I intended it as one of the revolutionary effects of the book that they should be forced, torn away from them and the sickness of the habitual diagnosed—not cured, that is not the work of literature. Freifeld reacted somewhat as Mel did. I should have thought people would desire a world to be brought to life of which we have felt the mass and trouble mostly—going elsewhere for superber being or beauty (to the Old World) and therefore putting ourselves in a false position, for our feeling hearts of course stay with our own experience. But some people do not seem to wish it.

I go on, though. I work with great speed as I think must be apparent. But the book is extremely long. On some days it lays a great strain on me. I think that a long book ought not to be so dense; it will be tiring. But I have a great deal for Augie to face and can't let up. The mss. is already about four hundred pages and I believe that's only half the work. Viking wants me to publish half of it and I've been tempted. For one thing the war [in Korea] may capsize everything. But if that'd been a real factor I would probably never have undertaken to write such a book. Anyhow, I will have a good deal to show you, Herb, when you come East, as I hope you will do.

I have reason to be grateful for my job at NYU. It leaves my days free. If after taxes I got a little more than two thousand, I'd have no complaint. I expect to earn about a thousand more by writing. *PR* and *Commentary* have helped, so far. But I wonder whether I could get into Minnesota for the summer sessions with a creative writing course. For one term, two years ago, they paid me something like eight hundred. Do you think, now that I'm older, they'd give me a little more? [. . .] Queens is a terribly expensive place. Little G. has a half-scholarship at school, but still the tuition is what it used to be at Chicago in 1933. I'm fairly sure I could go to Ohio for the summer, but I'd far rather spend it with you. If you will be there, that is. What do you plan to do? Will you be reading proofs of your Russian book by that time? [. . .]

Red Warren's settled in Manhattan for the year; we see him and Isaac and Paolo and the Partisaners. Isaac's even more strapped than I am and he's looking for work outside New York too. Maybe Ross will give him a job if he goes to Minn.

[. . .] I've asked *Commentary* to send you a copy of my story ["Looking for Mr. Green"].

Best love to you all,

1952

To Elizabeth Ames

[n.d.]

Dear Miss Ames—

On various occasions I have recommended writers to you. This time I am writing on my own behalf. I should very much like to come to Yaddo for a couple of weeks this summer and would be infinitely obliged to you if you could give me a quiet room in which to finish a novel I've been working on for quite a long time. It's nearly done now.

I'd like to come on June 15th and stay for two weeks. Perhaps my application comes too late. I hope not.

As sponsors I can offer Mssrs. Granville Hicks, Alfred Kazin and Paolo Milano.

Sincerely yours,

Elizabeth Ames (1885—1977) was from 1926 until 1971 director of Yaddo, the famed artists' colony at Saratoga Springs, New York.

To Herbert McCloskey

March 20, 1952   [New York City]

Dear Herb:

[. . .] Perhaps we could meet in Chicago too. I won't, of course, be spending all my time with my father. How can I? After ten minutes, there's alas nothing more to say. After which I have to stand by, for he gets angry if I desert this silence. But I start to crumble under it and have to save myself.

In fewer words, I'll be in Chicago on the 4th (Friday). I have to leave on the evening thereof in order to make Seattle by Sunday night (I have to check all the schedules). So if you leave Minneapolis on the 3rd, Chicago will make a pleasant stopover for you, and then I'll see you also in Minneapolis on April 30th.

Love to Mitzie and the kids,

I don't know how serious 17 Minetta St. is; I'm in the process of finding out. But have to find out. In November when I moved here I considered myself divorced. Now I simply consider myself calm. I suggest you revisit Anita and Greg while you're in the East, if you can find time.

To Lionel Trilling

June 23, 1952   Saratoga Springs, N. Y.

Dear Lionel:

[. . .] I rarely read the *Times*. It's enough for me to know that it exists, and every day, and especially on Sunday, appears. But on your recommendation, I read Diana's piece. And then [John] Aldridge's sequel. You'd need no Swami powers, I'm sure, to divine the fact that I disagree most violently. Are most novels poor today? Undoubtedly. But that is like saying mutilation exists, a broken world exists. More mutilated and broken than before? That's perhaps the world's own secret. Really, things are now what they always were, and to be disappointed in them is extremely shallow. We may not be strong enough to live in the present. But to be *disappointed* in it! To identify oneself with a better past! No, no!

I spoke of boredom in my Ellison piece ["Man Underground" in *Commentary*]. Yes, there's a great disease, an ancient disease now greatly magnified by our numbers. Man is sick of man; man declares man superfluous, and says in his heart that he himself is superfluous. "But," some say, "there is no society which gives us our value and creates importance for us." And this is to argue that a man's heart is not itself the origin and seat of importance. But to assert that it *is* so and to prove and proclaim it with all one's powers—that is the work and duty of a writer now; it ought to be the work and duty of critics, too.

As though Sunday weren't rugged enough without the *Times* and the Aldridges.

Best wishes,

To Elizabeth Ames

July 28, 1952   [New York City]

Dear Miss Ames—

Once more I want to thank you for Yaddo's hospitality and for your kindness.

I badly needed those two weeks in order to turn myself round and find the proper direction.

The city's hot. Though there're hotter places (they tell me) this one's hot enough for my taste.

Gratefully yours,

To Bernard Malamud

July 28, 1952   New York

Dear Bernard Malamud,

I read *The Natural* with great pleasure. Every page of it shows the mind and the touch of a real writer. The signs are unmistakable, and it's always a thrill to discover them.

Your story "The Loan" made a deep impression on me, too. It has a Hardyesque turn that I particularly approve of.

All best wishes for your success.

To Herbert and Mitzie McCloskey

[Postmarked Princeton, N.J., 10 September 1952]

How are you, all of you? All the Bellows live and flourish. Ask Isaac. Me, this week I turn the cap shut on *Augie* in his pickling mason jar and am ready to play peek-a-boo again with the universe.

State of the soul much better. *Very* sorry two days were all.

Love,

To Robert Penn Warren

[Postmarked Princeton, N.J., 27 October 1952]

Dear Red:

It would be nice to see you sometime. I'm a lot more free now, having all but finished *Augie*. It won't be published for a while. I've missed the spring list. But it is done.

So if you do any weekend socializing in New York, may I call you somewhere?

I look for announcements of your long poem. Have you finished it? When's it coming out?

Augie was very difficult for me in the last half. I suppose I succumbed to the dreadful thing I warn everyone against—seriousness. I had to throw away about two hundred pages at the end and re-write them. My slogan was, "Easily or not at all," but I forgot it. Too much of a temptation to speak the last word. Either it's already inscribed on our brows or it isn't. I speak of my own brow, natch, and of Augie's.

Hope you had a wonderful summer,

Warren's long poem was Brother to Dragons: A Tale in Verse and Voices, *which would be published the following year.*

To Henry Volkening

November 10, 1952   Princeton

Dear Henry:

I mailed the mss. to Mrs. White [at *The New Yorker*] by special delivery last Thursday, so if she's in New York she received it on Friday and you should be hearing from her any day.

I'm up to Ch. XXI in the revision of *Augie*. There are, in all, XXVI. Thus the Liberation comes this month. And then there's one section that I'll do over especially for you, and Viking won't get any of *that*. I suppose I could get a better deal if I told Pat [Covici] of my situation, but then I'd have to discuss it with him. Than which nothing could suit me less.

The Vanguard check came, thank you very much. You know what makes everything happen? Love, Henry. You ought to know that by now. Only Love is married to Hate, isn't it! You know, a new mythology ought to go good. Ambivalence is their little daughter who lives on the shores of the Superego, etc.

Vale,

Following Monroe Engel's departure from Viking, Pascal Avram Covici (1885–1964), who had edited John Steinbeck's The Grapes of Wrath *and* East of Eden, *became Bellow's editor.*

To Samuel Freifeld

December 28, 1952 Princeton

Dear Sam:

Thanks for answering. I ordered those records on Dec. 1st, and they should have arrived long ago. I've sent a tracer after them, and they should be coming in one of these days. The reason I bought them is that I want to observe your birthday. You shouldn't reproach me, since it means something when one is suffering suddenly to remember that since childhood a certain love has existed without changing. The love I have for you is something literal brotherhood never gave me.

I have written to Oscar; it's terrible luck. Is he better? Is he still in the hospital?

I've just gotten out of the hospital myself. I had virus pneumonitis, or some such damned thing. My strength is very low. The book took it out of me, and what this book didn't take Anita did.

The situation is bad. Her rigid unlovingness has driven me out—that and nothing else. I've done my best to stay and often I've felt that either going or staying threatened me with death. So I tried to choose the braver and at least less ignominious death.

Happy New Near, and my love to Rochelle and my love to Judy and Susie. God bless you all,

To David Goldknopf

[n.d.] [Princeton]

Dear David:

I got a letter off to Elizabeth Ames in a hurry, and I hope she will send you an invitation. Frankly, I have a selfish interest in the success of your application. I may be—most probably will be—in Yaddo myself in July and I'd like to be sure of at least one person there. Miss Ames herself is a good and charming woman but she has creeps innumerable on her list. Perhaps it's not her fault solely but the situation in the "arts." Anyhow there are usually more phonies than deerflies on the estate, getting into your hair.

I would like to see you sometime soon. I get into New York on weekends, and I spend those mostly with my son. We often go to the zoo, or to the Museum of Natural History. If you have wild animals or stuffed Indians at your house he'd be delighted to come and I'd be glad to bring him.

Best wishes,

1953

To Robert Penn Warren

January 7, 1953   Princeton

Dear Red—

I wish you both long life and all the happiness in the world.

It'd be nice to see you, one of these days. I suppose you'll be going to Europe soon. Perhaps we can have one drink before you leave.

Albert [Erskine] tells me your poem's done. I hope to read it soon. *Augie's* finished, thank God.

Best wishes,

Warren had just married the writer Eleanor Clark. Albert Erskine was his editor at Random House.

To the John Simon Guggenheim Memorial Foundation

January 20, 1953   Princeton, N.J.

CONFIDENTIAL REPORT ON CANDIDATE FOR FELLOWSHIP

Name of Candidate: Bernard Malamud

Mr. Bernard Malamud is, to my mind, one of the very few writers of the first order to appear since the debut of J. F. Powers. I am perfectly sure that he will become a major novelist. He has every prerequisite: the personal, definite style, the emotional resources, the understanding of character, the dramatic sense and the intelligence. He understands what the tasks of an imaginative writer of today are. Not to be appalled by these tasks is in and of itself a piece of heroism. Imagination has been steadily losing prestige in American life, it seems to me, for a long time. I am speaking of the poetic imagination. Inferior kinds of imagination have prospered, but the poetic has less credit than ever before. Perhaps that is because there is less room than ever for the personal, spacious, unanxious and free, for the unprepared, unorganized and spontaneous elements from which poetic imagination springs. It is upon writers like Mr. Malamud that the future of literature in America depends, writers who have not sought to protect themselves by joining schools or by identification with prevailing tastes and tendencies. The greatest threat to writing today is the threat of conformism. Art is the speech of an artist, of an individual, and it testifies to the power of individuals to speak and to the power of other individuals to listen and understand.

Literal-minded critics of Mr. Malamud's novel, *The Natural*, complained that it was not about true-to-life baseball players and failed entirely to see that it was a parable of the man of great endowments, or myth of the champion. I have immense faith in Mr. Malamud's power to make himself understood. I should be very happy to hear that he had become a Guggenheim fellow.

To Oscar Tarcov

March 9, 1953   Princeton

Dear Oscar:

I had heard about your good news and was very happy for you. If I hadn't been so utterly flattened out I'd have written at once to tell you so. But I'm sure you knew how I'd feel about an event like this and I know also that you understand how at times one needs every ounce of strength to get over the daily obstacles and can only have daily perspectives. Now I am better; I can admit I was very desperate, that I was very nearly dead. Things have improved greatly. I can now sleep, eat and function normally, and I seem to be making it.

I was planning to come to Chicago during spring vacation, at the beginning of April, but my old man isn't going to be there then so I'll probably arrive in June, toward the end of the month, with Gregory. This may be my last visit to Chicago for some time to come, because people will be taking the axe to me when *Augie* is published. Publication date is set for after Labor Day. If I had the dough I'd go to Europe and stay out of the way altogether. But I haven't. I may be teaching at Bennington College, therefore, when Sept. comes.

Gregory is not so disturbed as you might imagine. He knows how strong his parents' love for him is. He does not feel abandoned by me, in fact we have never been closer. I have never loved him more.

I'll most certainly want to write a piece about your book when it comes out. It's great news, Oscar. It made me very glad.

My best love to you all,

Tarcov's first novel, Bravo My Monster, *had been scheduled for publication in the autumn by Regnery.*

To James H. Case, Jr.

June 6, 1953

Dear President Case:

I shall be happy to accept appointment as Assistant Professor of English at Bard College for the year 1953–1954 at an annual salary of four thousand five hundred dollars.

I plan to come up to Bard sometime next week to make housing arrangements and to arrange the details of my schedule with the Registrar.

Sincerely,

To Henry Volkening

August 25, 1953

Dear Henry—

What know I about such matters? Doesn't Diarmuid [Russell] know more than I could if I studied? When *Augie* is published, there will be a big bang and even the British will hear it. I don't think we ought to act in dread of the workhouse. Were [André] Deutsch a British Vanguard I'd say no. But if the Deutsches will publish a sizeable first printing, will produce a neat book and will advertise, why, I won't object.

Henry, look! Would you marry your daughter off to her first suitor? This book, old man, is a child of mine.

Let's have not simply a figure but some notion of the Deutsch intentions. Heavens! *You* should know *this*!!!

Yrs. from the midst of night,

To Katharine Sergeant Angell White

September 25, 1953   Barrytown, N.Y.

Dear Mrs. White:

I wish to point out to you, an editor of the *New Yorker*, that Mr. [Anthony] West's review of *Augie March* is disgraceful. Mr. West is at liberty to dislike my book; that is a prerogative no sane author would deny a critic. But Mr. West, without any warrant whatever, has made me out to be a disciple of the New Criticism and has constructed, and attacked, a mad symbolical novel that bears no resemblance to the one he was given. In writing the book

I was aware of no symbolic aims. Out of his own turbulence, thoughtlessness and pedantry Mr. West has attributed to me things as remote from me as the moon. "Simon" and "simony," eagles and "virility," "sex" and "culture"—really, it is simply too much! I feel I must write to you for the sake of my mental health. Let us hope that it is only my mental health that is endangered and not that of your readers as well.

Sincerely yours,

To Pascal Covici

September 25, 1953   Barrytown

Dear Pat—

Thanks for the [Harvey] Swados review. I'm glad to see he feels as we do about things. A. West is a *mamzer* [*] of a different color. I thought it only reasonable that I should protest such a horrible misrepresentation of *Augie* and wrote to Mrs. White explaining that I was not a New Critic and Symbolist and that West had invented this lurid and foolish book that he was attacking in his own foolish and disorderly mind. [. . .]

Love,

The ad in the *Times* was beautiful.

To Lionel Trilling

October 11, 1953   Barrytown, N.Y.

Dear Lionel,

I've more than once wanted to write you a letter of thanks. I know that you have contributed more than a little to the success of my book. I'm in your debt also for mental support—for the intelligence of your reading. Though I'm not, perhaps, the most objective judge to be found, I thought your essay brilliant. The many criticisms of *Augie* I've seen since have made me appreciate yours all the more; I appreciate above all your sense of justice, for I know the book must have offended you in some ways.

Reading Emerson's "Transcendentalist" the other day while getting ready for class, I ran across a passage on the remoteness of the high-minded transcendentalist from worldly activities which made me think of one of our differences. It goes like this:

* Yiddish: bastard

"We are miserable with inaction. We perish of rest and rust: but we do not like your work."

"Then," says the world, "show me your own."

"We have none."

"What will you do, then?" cries the world.

"We will wait."

"How long?"

"Until the universe beckons and calls us to work."

"But whilst you wait, you grow old and useless."

"Be it so; I can sit in a corner and *perish* (as you call it) but I will not move until I have the highest command . . . your virtuous projects, so called, do not cheer me. If I cannot work at least I need not lie . . ."

So it runs. And this attitude (would you call it "inner-directedness"?) is what seeped into my comedy. It isn't that *Augie* resists every function—that would make him a tramp; and while I would not hesitate to write about tramps if I were called to it, *Augie* is something different. I was constantly thinking of some of the best young men I have known. Some of the very finest and best intentioned, best endowed, found nothing better to do with themselves than Augie. The majority, whether as chasers, parasites, bigamists, forgers and worse lacked his fairly innocent singleness of purpose. They had reached the place where they fixedly doubted that Society had any use for their abilities. I think if you had been aware of their great negativism you might have taken another view of my "propaganda." To love another, genuinely to love, is the inception of a function, I wished to say. I suppose I didn't quite make [my point] convincingly. It may be that for this a kind of intelligence is required that I'm not able to exercise. I'm satisfied with the other kind—the intelligence of imagining. I would be satisfied, that is, but for the fact that you sometimes can't imagine very far without crossing the border into the other kinds of intelligence.

Not the least of my surprises, as reviews come in, is my surprise at the chaotic disagreement as to what constitutes normalcy. This is picturesque! Writers on the fiftieth floor of the Time building speak confidently with the *vox populi*, telling us what is normative in American life. The scene couldn't be more bizarre. An anarchy of views upon normalcy. We might get some sociological principle out of this: When the daily life of a people is full of astonishments, miracles and wonders, the lives of individuals are duller (a natural reaction to the disorganizing hyperaesthesia resulting from overstimulation) and the greater the disorder and lack of agreement the larger the number of spokesmen for "normalcy." [. . .]

Your discussion of my treatment of the hero was full of brilliant perceptions (the eagle as anti-hero I had not thought of) but I was myself more conscious of satirizing this disagreement over the normative.

On the whole, however, I was fairly free of deliberate intentions. I could scarcely follow Mr. West's review with its system of symbols. I had forgotten, since leaving Great Books Inc., what "simony" meant.

Well, it's all very interesting and what fascinates me most is the book's sale. *That* I had never anticipated. The world's a mysterious place.

Yours faithfully,

"A Triumph of the Comic View," Trilling's very favorable assessment of Augie, *had appeared in* The Griffin, *the Readers' Subscription newsletter.*

To Samuel Freifeld

October 19, 1953   Barrytown

Dear Sam,

You did exactly right in your conversation with my father. I don't know what anyone can do about my father except to change his character and that lies within the power of no one. Therefore, whatever you said, you said on your own account or in the name of justice, but practical effect I think there should be none. Myself, I have tried to hold no grudge and I had already answered his letter before yours arrived. I see no reason why I should not be faithful to whatever was, in the past, venerable in my father and I do my best to make allowances for the rest. I wouldn't be uneasy about any of this if I were you. It's just like my father to begin to be generous long after the rest of the world has begun. He's impressed by my new fame and even more by the sales of the book and so now he feels uneasy and wants, too late, to go on record as a good parent. I try to make him feel that there is plenty of time.

I can well imagine how you feel about *Augie*. I myself feel happier about this book than about anything I have ever done in the line of books because I have a sense of how much of it is just, and that you who know so much about the matter are also pleased with it is a great satisfaction to me. I feel that I have kept things from obscurity which should not sink and for that reason the book is as much intended for you as myself. The personal identification is altogether warranted. If you didn't make it I'd feel that I had missed the mark. [. . .]

As for Oscar's book, I have written it up for the *Saturday Review*. I hope that will do some good.

Love,

To Alfred Kazin

October 22, 1953   Barrytown

Dear Alfred—

[. . .] I don't know what to make of the reviews either. What is there to say except that the reviewers have been Augie Marchean reviewers? They have led me to coin a phrase: "low seriousness." Comedy is illegal—it isn't even seen—it *isn't*. In low seriousness no one laughs until the cue is given; one then asks gravely, "Now, why was it appropriate to laugh?" Enter hereupon Bergson, Freud, Dante and Charlie Chaplin, each bearing a basket of rocks. The rocks are piled on our breast in a huge cairn and so goes it.

A. West is simply a bad novelist and re-wrote *Augie* unspeakably—a horror. Stendhal says bad taste leads to crimes. Who can doubt it? Mrs. White and Wm. Shawn are aghast. But whose baby after all is A. West?

I feel I am at the point of growing wicked, so I stop, with much love,

To Leslie Fiedler

October 25, 1953   Barrytown, N.Y.

Dear Leslie,

It is a little weird to think that we have never exchanged a single letter. A fair share of the responsibility for this (if responsibility there be) is mine. I often wonder why I balk so at letter writing. I used to accuse myself of lacking energy, but it is too late for that now. I think it is because I talk to myself so much, a habit which has no virtue whatever to redeem it. Now that I've begun, I find that I can write quite easily to you. You may be one of my God-appointed correspondents.

I'm very glad *Augie* pleased you. The writing of it gave me considerable pleasure; it was wonderful to feel I had the gift of amusement. Of course not everyone is amused. The book has many faults; and so has almost everyone. Though I was always of the opinion that people were hard to give pleasure to, it was nonetheless a shock to see how many suffered from low seriousness— my new favorite description of the "earnestness" of deep readers. What makes people so sober? We've sunk a great depth if the funnyman also finds it necessary to be a prophet. I have my own share of low seriousness, of course, but I think of it as a curse. I am not a born prophet.

The last third of the book was written under terrible difficulties. I suffered, and still do suffer, terrible pains after the separation. I found no alternative. I could not spend the rest of my life with [Anita]. Nor was it good for her to live with me. As for Gregory, I doubt that he will suffer as much from our divorce as I suffered from my parents' "good" family life. I love Gregory and I know how to make him feel my love. He is injured, but not really seriously injured, and his position also has its advantages. At Princeton last year I nearly went down, and Anita's troubles were as terrible to me as my own. We are both infinitely better than we were.

I can imagine how hard it is to face Missoula after Rome. I was uneasy even in New York when I came back—and I had *hated* Paris for having defeated my aspirations, both the good and the bad. I said *even* New York. I don't know. I'm sure Missoula has it over New York.

My very best to Margaret and the kids.

Yours,

Leslie Fiedler (1917–2003), influential American critic, is best remembered for Love and Death in the American Novel *(1960). His other books include the essay collections* An End to Innocence *(1955) and* Waiting for the End *(1964), as well as a collection of stories,* The Last Jew in America *(1966).*

To Katharine Sergeant Angell White

October 27, 1953   Barrytown, N.Y.

Dear Mrs. White:

I am grateful to Mr. Shawn for having taken the trouble to read *Augie March* and I greatly appreciate your precedent-breaking offer [to allow a printed response in *The New Yorker* to Anthony West's unfavorable review]. That Mr. Shawn agrees with me that I have been done an injustice satisfies me completely. I cannot see what would be gained by answering Mr. West, whether sweetly or hotly. The confusion is so vast, involved and peculiar that I don't feel brave enough or capable enough to deal with it. There are some misunderstandings that simply weaken you when you contemplate their complexity. In some odd sense Mr. West's review is not a piece of criticism but a piece of fiction; it is a very bad short story or something of that kind. For after all Mr. West invented what did not exist; he wrote what he thought to be my novel, and as he is a bad artist he produced a disfigured something. One cannot show the error of such a "something." I don't mean to try. What would be the good of it?

It is very reassuring, however, to know that you feel the review falsified and misrepresented the book. That really is more than enough for me.

Sincerely yours,

To Edith Tarcov

[n.d.]   [Barrytown]

Dear Edith—

Thanksgiving Day! I have Gregory with me, and for the first time in months I can enjoy a leisurely afternoon. Never have I worked so hard at teaching. Small colleges demand infinitely more of you, and it is a thankless and poorly paid labor. On Fridays I generally have to go to New York to have my teeth—preserved. They are in that stage. And when I have finished running around the City and have returned from my visit to Forest Hills I reach Barrytown on Sunday in a state of exhaustion. And you know what Mondays are. Moreover, there are the *difficulties*. I know I have no right to complain to you, with your trouble, so much more real and visible than mine.

Sometimes I think that man, for hundreds of centuries weakened by parasites—lice, fleas, tapeworms, fungi, etc.—has replaced them with parasitic anxieties which deplete him. Because he is used to feeling depleted and it does not seem to him right that he should be well.

But this is very like me, to start out to thank you for your letter on my book and fall instead into dismal theories. I owe you my deepest gratitude. Yours was the sort of letter one expects from a friend. For whom is a book written, after all?

I'm glad you observed, as no one else has, Augie's bent for the illicit. I have often felt that the effort to lead a normal, respectable American life would make an outlaw of me. Stores and offices I have always found intolerable. Better knowledge of history might teach me the difference between impatience and freedom, but I do feel that the world asks an undue degree of control over us. At any rate, I am constitutionally unable to accept so much control and have passed this inability on to Augie. The devil's disobedience is from pride, but Augie misses the love, harmony and safety that should compensate our obedience. People have accused me of asociality, and Trilling asserts Augie is "wrong" i.e. unprincipled. To me Augie is the embodiment of willingness to serve, who says "For God's sake, make use of me, only do not use me to no purpose. Use me."

I can say it comically, not otherwise. Squeezed into "functions" in which all higher capacities die of disuse, we are considered unprincipled if we comment on the situation by so much as a laugh. Can Augie be anything but, in his mild way, an outlaw? Only, instead of being outside, as a Cain or Ishmael are outside, his desire is to be an Augie. Surely the greatest human desire—not the deepest but the widest—is to be used. If there were no will to be used the social process would be pleasureless, wholly pleasureless. Augie's is the most reluctant *non serviam* [*] ever heard.

Enough of *Augie* though. There is a lot to be complained of in the book.

The news of Oscar's operation has depressed me. I hope he will be seeing the last of hospitals. You must be very gloomy about it. It is a shame. Is there any other possible therapy? Forgive my foolish questions, but I feel this in my bones.

The review in *Saturday Review* [of Oscar's novel] *had* to be done as I did it because I was in the position of having asked for the book. I could not review it in the tone I would have taken had the book come unsolicited. They would not have accepted from me a review they considered obviously written for a friend. The political problem was a delicate one. I say this only because I have intimations of Oscar's dissatisfaction with the piece I wrote. You have my assurance that I did my utmost.

I won't be coming to Chicago for a long time, so won't you please write? Regards to everyone.

Love,

To Samuel Freifeld

November 30, 1953   Barrytown

Dear Sam—

People *will* feel exposed, ridiculed, no matter how you deal with them. *Any* mention causes them shame. They can't think that perhaps it was my aim to love not shame them. If you wanted to think about and find meaning in *my* existence I would thank you for it, not curse you.

A few years ago when my brother thought he had cancer he cried out, "I pissed my life away!" And *now* look at him. That's all forgotten. But I didn't forget the great pain of hearing a man condemn himself. Forty-five years of life must contain some meaning.

Of course, so long as our misery is secret our honor is whole.

Well, I never dreamed that I could be an uncursed prophet, so I accept the curses. I agree that I am an outlaw. In outlaw bravado I have no interest. I only meant that I wish to obey better laws.

* Latin: I will not serve.

Well, I haven't much news to tell you. I am fairly happy. I do a lot of thinking. As yet, to no great purpose.

Love to everyone,

To Bernard Malamud

[n.d.]   [Barrytown]

Dear Bernard:

I don't get many letters about *Augie* that I feel like answering. By pressure of numbers, society can make a specialist of you, if in no other way. *Augie* threatens to become my specialty as flying the Atlantic became the Lindberghs'—allow me one more immodest analogy: as jumping from the bridge became Steve Brodie's.

With this preface, let me say that I thought your letter one of the best, a terribly acute criticism. I'm not at all inclined to counter your criticisms. You're a writer yourself, a real one; you know that self-defense is not what we ought to be thinking of. I made many mistakes; I must plead guilty to several of your charges. Yes, Augie is too passive, perhaps. Yes, the episodes do not have enough variety; the pressure of language is too constant and uniform. That he is too august I think I might dispute. At least I felt his suffering sharply—maybe I didn't get it across. He isn't, to me, an Olympian. Only, he's engaged in a War of Independence and the odds are vastly against him. It is devaluation of the person that he fights with. No doubt this war, like any war, produces exaggerations. Our passivity often is so deep that we do not recognize that the active spirit underneath has meanwhile organized an opposition, an opposition that wears the face of passivity. Some of the trouble is Augie's; some of it the world's. That is no excuse in literature, though it may be one in history. But I can't claim that I was trying for perfection. There are times when I think how nice it would be to edit a new and better novel out of it. But I can't allow myself to forget that I took a position in writing this book. I declared against what you call the constructivist approach. A novel, like a letter, should be loose, cover much ground, run swiftly, take risk of mortality and decay. I backed away from Flaubert, in the direction of Walter Scott, Balzac and Dickens. Having brought off my effort as well as I could, I must now pay the price. You let the errors come. Let them remain in the book like our sins remaining in our lives. I hope some of them may be remitted. I'll do what I can; the rest is in God's hands.

Two things about the book please me still: the comedy and the characters. Many people have missed what, to me, is the fun of the book. They suffer from culture-gravity. They say "picaresque" and don't laugh. The baseball experts landing on your *Natural* with both feet are in the same league: sinners against imagination and the spirit of comedy.

I'm very grateful to you for writing.

Yours,

New York bookmaker Steve Brodie claimed to have survived a daredevil leap from the Brooklyn Bridge on July 23, 1886. (Whether he actually did so or not is unknown.) To "pull a Brodie" or "do a Steve Brodie" entered the American language as terms for doing something spectacular and dangerous.

1954

To Alfred Kazin

January 7, 1954   Barrytown

Dear Alfred:

I wouldn't have taken the Bard job last June if I hadn't been very hard up. Not that the school is so bad—it has much to recommend it, the students are bright and those that are earnest are terribly earnest in every sense of the term. If you want to teach, Bard is the place for you. But it you want to write also, *méfie-toi*! [*] The lit. faculty is good. Heinrich Blücher is *good*, some of the arts people are good, too. The large majority are mediocre and cantankerous types who couldn't make it at Bryn Mawr, Antioch, Bennington, Black Mtn., etc.

Myself, I have no clear plans. I am trying to recover a state of mind lost unawares about a year ago.

I'll tell A. Wanning that you're perhaps interested in Bard. Maybe you could arrange to work with Heinrich. That would make Bard worth your while. [. . .]

Love to you both,

The name of the new Bard *zaddik* [**] is James H. Case, Jr.

* French: Beware!
** Hebrew: holy man or righteous man

Heinrich Blücher, husband of Hannah Arendt and like her a refugee from Nazi Germany, taught for many years at Bard.

To the John Simon Guggenheim Memorial Foundation

February 1, 1954   Barrytown, N.Y.

CONFIDENTIAL REPORT ON CANDIDATE FOR FELLOWSHIP

Name of Candidate: James Baldwin

Mr. Baldwin's outline is more eloquent than anything I could write in support of his application. I do not see how it can fail to impress the Committee, with its wisdom and its talent. For the most part, the Whites have hitherto dealt with individual Negroes as representatives of their race— as social types. Mr. Baldwin makes a special bid to be considered as an individual—to have all men considered so. He approaches the matter as an artist and social historian; first as an artist, however. Social scientists and professional historians have unjustly been given preference to artists in this field of writing.

Baldwin's successful proposal to the foundation was for work on an essay collection that would appear in 1955, the epoch-making Notes of a Native Son.

To Robert Penn Warren

March 27, 1954   Barrytown, N.Y.

Dear Red:

That's awful, about the leg! I hope it was only a Tennysonian and poetic fracture that will give you an opportunity to dream, and not one of those rough Hemingway-type broken legs. You sound cheerful about it, but then you have an enviable way of referring to your troubles. I wish I had it. As the youngest child I learned to make the most of mine.

I expected you to get the poetry award; you should have gotten it. But I'm sure this is not an injustice that excites you, and though it would have made me feel better to have you on the platform I can only congratulate you on your missing the whole thing. It was an *auto-da-fé*, with poor [Bruce] Catton, an awfully nice guy, catching hell, and me in my button-down *sanbenito* [*] boiling in the face.

* Spanish: penitential garment worn to the stake

Now everything is nice and quiet once again; I'm writing and I'm in very good spirits.

You could write an ode on that cast and turn the whole thing to profit. Always for bearing off fortune under the very nose of calamity.

Very best wishes,

Bellow had received the National Book Award for Augie March. *Bruce Catton had won in the nonfiction category for* A Stillness at Appomattox. *Warren's* Brother to Dragons *had been a finalist in poetry, but lost to Conrad Aiken's* Collected Poems.

To Oscar Tarcov

[n.d.]   [Barrytown]

Dear Oscar:

I'm very glad the operation went off well and that you have your health again. Now for heaven's sake, let hospitals alone.

Your letter gave me a stir. Yours isn't a happy condition, though it's better than the former one. I wonder what adjustment can be made in our friendship. I was never willing to give it up. You must know that. I realized you were down on your luck and had no margin for patience with me. But I was suffering too, and all I could do was withdraw from your harsh judgments. Had either of us been a little happier we would have done better by the other. But our miseries were anti-symbiotic, or something like that. I was in the strange condition of being envied while I lay at the bottom of hell. This being the case, I had no alternative but to close my mind.

It does no good to rake these things over now. I am as eager to bury them as you probably are.

My ideas about the future are vague. Bard College is pretty shaky right now, and anyway I think I may try to make a living at writing. It will have to be a sizable income, and it puts me in a strange position to be, in the ridiculous term people have imported, an *avant-garde* writer with a slick writer's requirements. For one year it may be possible, and after that—who knows?

Merry Pesach, and love to everyone,

To John Berryman

[n.d.]   [Barrytown]

Dear John—

Forgive silence. These days letters come hard for me. I attach much consequence to my inability to write them. It means my heart is lazy, and I am very tired. Also, it may mean that I am loath to say what I think, and that is miserable.

There was no rush about the money. I am being stripped anyway [by divorce], and the value of money is exaggerated. With twice as much I am half as well off, but thank you anyway for sending it. Courtesy of poets. I never repay what I borrow from businessmen.

Your bad health is a nuisance. You should really decide to improve it, John. God knows, I'm a prey to too many weaknesses myself not to understand how it is. But there is a difference between being prey and *agreeing* to be prey. I do *not* agree. My defects will kill me, but they'll have to fight me first, and they will lose a few battles before they win the war.

Things are not good, but they are better with me. Slowly, I'm beginning to get my strength back, though Anita B. has not let up in her campaign to get me crucified. It's a good many miles to Golgotha yet.

Sasha [Sondra Tschacbasov] is infinitely more happy than she's been in her life, I think. A poor book by Arnold Bennett I read this A.M.—*Lillian*—had one good thing in it. A young girl requires making. A man makes her into a woman. Whither then? I hope she'll become my wife, but it is a great thing to have waked someone into life, and Sasha is a very considerable human being. [. . .]

We must have a conversation about health and disease. Meantime, old man, for the love of Mike stop knocking yourself out.

All the best,

To Samuel Freifeld

[Postmarked New York, N.Y., 25 April 1954]

Dear Pal—

Got record. Very enjoyable—I thank you. Separate thank-occasions are hardly the thing between blood-brothers. I have more gratitude in me than separate thank-grains can ever measure.

So you met my strange delightful buddy Delmore [Schwartz]. And Elizabeth? I hope you hit it off. I am very fond of them. Has Berryman come around? I took the liberty of giving him your address, too. [Peter] Viereck I don't much care for. Are you still so "conservative"? I called it a phase and let it go at that. Strange you should argue with me as though I were a *Nation* liberal. Me?!!! So I refused to compound error by thinking you a McCarthy. Was I right?

About Eliot—I forgive you because you haven't seen *The Confidential Clerk*. Wait! I don't know what I'm protesting too much about. Do you mean that he's a mighty Niagara and I a mere squirt? Possibly. But someone has to stand up for Jews and democrats, and when better champions are lacking, squirts must do what they can.

Thank (again!) you for your kindness. Just know I still have about enough dough to get by for a while. I considered calling on you for a loan when I found a house to buy. I need a place of my own very, very badly. I am nearly ready to *sit* and be Columbus's chronicle, not one of his crew. It would do Gregory good, too; he loves to be with me, and it makes him happy to come to me in a settled place.

Anita keeps me fairly strapped. She always took far more than she gave. I don't reproach her with anything; her nature is its own reproach. I am genuinely sorry for her but I can feel more compassion as an ex-husband. [. . .]

Best love,

To Theodore Weiss

[n.d.]   [Barrytown]

Dear Ted:

I see you've made out something about my character by reading *Augie*. It's true. Since I had to be there, I ended by rejoicing in Bard. It was quite something. We must have a full-dress discussion of it when you come back. I'd have made some compromise and stayed if I were a tougher character. But you've got to have stability *somewhere* to survive this *pays de merveilles* [*], cloud-cuckoo, monkey-on-the-back, *avant-garde* booby cosmos, and I'm afraid I just don't have it—grit, gumption, spunk, stick-to-itiveness, values founded on rock. With all my heart I enjoyed the sight of a skinny pallid little boy arriving in a chauffeur-driven Cadillac and a lot of other things, more numerous than the daffodils. I took walks and fiddled with fiddling [Emil] Hauser and had excellent conversations. But I couldn't survive meetings and in the end stopped attending. And if I had to choose between trichinosis and talking an hour with F[elix] Hirsch I'd—you know! Where's that

* French: wonderland

raw pork? And [James H.] Case—an Ivy League *shlimazl* [*]! I say little of the rest of the administration, and of the trustees I have only to speak the name. They are wonderful! Giants of deformity. They could stand with Sobakevitch or any other giant in *Dead Souls*.

I'm going to miss Jack Ludwig and Ted Hoffman and Heinrich [Blücher] and Andy and you. You and I are, I think, the slowly but durably acquainted type and I have a pleasant expectation of knowing you better. I'll be around in the spring. Europe, alas, is not in my plans. My son can't do without my help this year. It is also somewhat the other way around. But he's starting at another school; I'm beginning another book, and barring the unbarrable unforeseen you'll find me here in the spring when you arrive.

Isn't it amazing how little truth about English weather there is in English poetry? I wonder why that is. They knew no better, perhaps.

Sondra and I send all three of you (I assume Roz is still with you) our very best.

Theodore Weiss (1917–2003), poet and longtime editor of the Quartely Review of Literature, *was at Oxford for the year.*

To John Berryman

December 7, 1954   [New York City]

How are you, John?

We begin to look for you now, as Xmas comes on, you melancholy Santa Claus. Last night in solemn conversation, when near looped, your name came up. Spoken by me, in fact. It was something nice, and so tonight I make wig-wags through the dark of night towards Minnesota. Minneapolis *is* beautiful, I agree, and I was happy there, after a fashion. Part of those sixteen years before the fortieth year. Which is the very next. I don't fear it very much however. I'm growing so lazy, John, it appalls me. I don't even worry. My anxieties are like old dogs. They no longer run after rabbits. They only dream and whine, asleep.

Am writing a handsome new book, which is so far highly satisfactory. It's called *Memoirs of a Bootlegger's Son, or The Song of the Oedipus Complex*. I do not worry about that either. Do you know, though, as I creep near the

* Yiddish: loser

Saul Bellow: Letters

deepest secrets of my life, I drop off like a lotus-eater. I am being extremely lazy.

It's probably all to the good that you left Iowa, since they didn't appreciate you. I'd be happy to know you were friendly with Herbert McCloskey and his wife [in Minneapolis]. They are my very good friends, and I have written them about you. [. . .]

Write well, and remember me to everyone.

Love,

And Sondra's love.

1955

To the John Simon Guggenheim Memorial Foundation

March 27, 1955   333 Riverside Drive, New York

Dear Mr. Moe:

In response to your inquiry I am able to say that my estimated income from writing for the year beginning in September, 1955 is about three thousand dollars. As you will perhaps recall, I have two dependents. There may be other money coming but I can't be sure of it.

My plans for work during the coming year (September '55 to September '56) will take me to Rome for at least half of that time and I estimate my own traveling expenses at about five hundred; living expenses for myself and my family during the entire period of the Fellowship would run to about three thousand. About three thousand more would cover the clerical and other smaller expenses. I am therefore asking the Guggenheim Foundation to consider my request for a Fellowship grant of approximately thirty-eight hundred dollars. This should enable me to finish my novel now in progress.

Sincerely yours,

To Sherry Mangan

June 3, 1955   [New York City]

Dear Mangan—

Thank you very much. My spirit, at least, was sober and I remember and stand by what I said. I couldn't agree more about Manhattan and its miseries, and I will get out of here soon. But before I (or we) come to Spain, a short stay in Nevada is required of me, divorce laws being of a near-Spanish backwardness. So we should be arriving in Europe in February of '56. A Guggenheim makes matters easier for me this year.

What are your plans? Will you be staying long in Málaga? I'd hate to put you to the trouble of describing it if you were not going to be there. In 1947 I spent a week there and saw it a little.

Yours with best wishes,

John Joseph Sherry Mangan (1904–61) was an editor, poet, novelist and leading journalist at Time, Life, *and* Fortune *in the 1940s. A dedicated Trotskyist long after the cause had faded, Mangan would find himself more and more isolated, dying alone and impoverished in Rome.*

To Malcolm Cowley

June 5, 1955   Barrytown

Dear Malcolm—

Thank you for your most generous Guggenheim letter. The news of the award came at about the same time as my father's death and I have been in a confused and incompetent state these last six weeks. I'm only now beginning to come out of it a bit. I'm sure your letter had great weight with the committee and I'm very grateful.

Sincerely,

To Leslie Fiedler

June 14, 1955   333 Riverside Drive, New York

Dear Leslie—

Since my father's death last month I've been slow at everything. Not that I was ever prompt in anything, but life is particularly difficult in all departments just now. If I knew where I was going to be at Xmas I would be glad to help you bring up engines against the New Orthodoxy, as you name it. But as I have a Guggenheim and can travel, how do I know where the old spirit in my feet is going to lead me? *Not* to Paris, that I can tell you. But neither is it likely to take me to Chicago. Many thanks just the same.

I'm grateful for the kind mention you gave me in the *N[ew] R[epublic]* piece, although I don't consider myself part of the *Partisan* group. Not those dying beasts. (They posed as Phoenixes but were Dodos.) I always knew it. I have ever been unideological. I have sophisticated skin and naïve bones.

As for the sales of *Augie*, Viking denies *Pop. Library* figure, but who says it's bad to be a Jew in America? Is it better in Israel?

Shalom, and greetings to Margaret et al.,

Perhaps you'd like to try Wright Morris? His address is 501 Beechtree Lane, Wayne, Pa.

To Alfred Kazin

June 29, 1955   Barrytown

Dear Alfred:

Last night Sondra dreamed that Anne had given birth to a daughter (hurray) and that her friend Anita Maximillian had given birth to another, and that you were the father of both, and everyone was supremely pleased— as why shouldn't everybody be? I congratulate everybody. This dream indicates that in Sondra's eyes you have become the Father personified. For you this is honor, and for me it is hope. We are both well. Sondra has lost her job, to great delight. First she was affronted, and then it made her, as it should have done, happy. [. . .]

My own spirits, as may show forth, are not at all low. I'm not doing the sort of thing I want to do. Not yet. But God lets me practice my trade for several hours of the day, so what have I to complain of? And I read a good many books and wait for matters to straighten themselves out, and I am confident that they will. The other day, enjoyed [Jacob] Bronowski's book on Blake; it did me good to read a Marxian again. I'm told he's an engineer and member of the Coal Board.

Well, *molti saluti*, and don't be too nervous. I'm sure Anne can do this thing quite easily.

All the best,

Thanks for the wine!

To Ruth Miller

July 27, 1955   Barrytown

Dear Ruth:

"May I say something?" Somewhere in Italian comedy there's a man who prefaces everything with this; I forget the place, but it is very funny. Well, then, this is what I want to say. Your essay has many peculiarities, all of them first-rate. My mind follows yours, and Ralph [Ellison]'s, too, through the hoops, up the ropes, into the trapezes, down in the net and all around the three rings. This was exhilarating and good, every minute of it. There's nothing that brightens the mind more than this sort of exercise. You are a good woman, you have every talent you need, talent to burn, and you are wise, too, and I take great pride and happiness in being your old friend. But may I say something?

It is this: Your explication [of *Invisible Man*] is too dense, too detailed. It needs some divorce from the text. Perhaps it is too much like laboratory analysis, but I don't hope to capture the difficulty in simile. Let me ask you, Do you think that all portions of the book have equal merit? I speak of literary merit. And do you think all the parts are equally necessary to the structure of the book? You see, you have left out the literary side of the matter almost entirely and that, to my mind, is a mistake. I myself distinguish between the parts of the novel that were *written* and those that were constructed as part of the argument; they are not alike in quality. The first third of the book is beautiful, whereas the Brotherhood portion is ordinary. The sweet-potato seller, the eviction, the riot can't be compared with the mechanical symbols, the hospital, the seduction. The former are in full cry after the Meaning and your interest is in Opinion rather than in Creation.

I think this is a fault of all American books, including my own. They pant so after meaning. They are earnestly moral, didactic; they build them ever more stately mansions, and they exhort and plead and refine, and they are, insofar, books of error. A work of art should rest on perception. "Here" in other words, "is my vision, be meaning what it may." The rest doesn't count a bit. Ralph is wrong to think that it did. I tell him so often.

And I can't understand the passion for adding meaning to meaning in a work of art, and *making* meaning proliferate from ordinary incidents. The original guilty parties are perhaps Proust and James. Let us assume that Proust at least could not help himself. But this is a hanging matter with James, and with the rest of us. Aren't there jungles enough—personal, racial, national, historical? Must we make more snakes, grow more lianas, more leaves, cause more heat, sting and cause more scratching? May I say one last thing? Writing should derive from the Creation, and not attempt to add to it. We should require things to be simpler and simpler, greater and greater.

Anyway, with your permission, I will send your essay to Delmore S[chwartz]. He may want it in shorter form. Do you mind? I'll phone you when I'm in town next weekend to discuss your visit to Bard. I think you'd like it here. Meanwhile, curse me if you must; forgive if you can, your old and faithful pal,

Bellow first met Ruth Miller in 1938 at Pestalozzi-Froebel Teachers College, where she was his student. Delmore Schwartz was at this time an editor at Partisan Review. *In 1991 Miller would publish* Saul Bellow: The Biography of an Imagination, *which ended their long association.*

To Pascal Covici

[n.d.]   [Barrytown]

Dear Pat:

Have done most of Wilhelm over *de novo*. What do you think of *Seize the Day* as a title?

Plus a few words from Flaubert to the effect that tears are to the heart what water is to fishes.

Can you send me (ominous words) a copy of A. Miller's last play or plays?

The 15th, your deadline, is a Sunday. So let's make it the week of the 15th. Don't forget that in addition to everything else I have to entertain a friend of yours who is arriving the day after tomorrow. I am working like a miner, so there's no lack of earnestness, only a certain aged slowness of the mind and fingers.

Love and kisses,

To Henry Volkening

October 19, 1955   Sutcliffe Star Route, Reno, Nevada

Dear Henry:

I've simmered down, by slow degrees. As you have guessed, it isn't easy to follow this course. I'm living alone, thirty miles from anywhere, in the desert. The ranch proved too expensive, and I have taken this cabin, or shack, decent and pleasant in its way, but its isolation is beyond anything you've ever seen. I thought it would be better to live like this for a while and study my soul, and I still think it is the wise course for me. I have even begun to work again, after weeks of idleness. But there are times when I must, and literally do, howl.

In answer to your question, this is my permanent address in Nevada. How long I will stay here depends on my wife. And henceforth, that is all that does depend on her wish. After six weeks, I will be free under the laws of Nevada to move about as I wish, and I will keep my cabin and spend a good deal of my time in San Francisco, where I have friends. Nevada divorces are valid everywhere after a year.

Sondra is in Los Angeles. We both felt it to be wiser for her to be there. I have no intention of bouncing from divorce into marriage. When I have lived for a year or so freed from my burden and still feel as I do about Sondra we will begin to think about marrying.

I have not forgotten the Illinois piece. It's about half done now, and should be ready about the middle of November.

Thanks for your patience, Henry. I value your friendship.

Best,

To Pascal Covici

November 1, 1955   Sutcliffe Star Route, Reno, Nevada

Dear Pat:

Sand and poison, eh?

Look, Pat, let's not make baby talk. I am not one of your money-mad writers, and whatever you and Henry decide upon will be acceptable to me. You know perfectly well why I was sore. But I'll spell it out for you, so that you can't possibly avoid my meaning.

I am not Andrea del Bellow the faultless writer; I am a sinner like the rest. I can't expect to please everyone, I know, least of all some of your editorial colleagues. They, I realize, are indispensable to you, whereas I am not. But you are my editor, aren't you? Now when they grumble about me, I hear the echo from you, and should I deny my own hearing? And should I be pleased about it when complaints about my unpleasantness come down to me? And should I be happy when it is necessary to submit my stories, like any lousy beginner, before a contract can be drawn? The stories should have come to me for reworking, and when I was satisfied with them it is my opinion that Viking should have received them and published them without a single damn syllable of protest.

If you don't want these stories you needn't take them. I won't get my sand and poison up and bolt Viking. I love you too much for that and I don't want my books to be published by a canning concern. But stand by me honorably, and don't give me any Madison Ave. double-talk, but consider my pride as a workman. I am not unqualifiedly enthusiastic about everything I write.

When I have read through them, I myself may not want to publish these things. But that should rest with me.

As for the advance, I am not one of your four-star generals weighted to the balls with medals and prestige; nevertheless you haven't lost much dough on me yet.

You old bat, if I didn't love you like a parent I'd never get so worked up.

Yours,

To Ruth Miller

November 5, 1955   Reno

Dear Ruth:

I sit here drinking Ming Cha tea and eating Belgian biscuits and looking at Irving's picture. You've done a good thing, the two of you, you've made me very happy. Because it is so good to be remembered, especially when you are absolutely, unconditionally and almost astrally alone. After several weeks at a place for dudes, I took a cabin in the desert. Solitude isn't so difficult; I've developed a taste for it. But it is rather dangerous in its own fashion, and it's part of your good deed to have recalled me from this one-man lotus banquet.

I found that I had acquired such a charge during the last few years in New York that it gave me a case of the bends to change pressure. I've been here now for almost six weeks and have almost fulfilled the minimum residence requirement. Of course, unless Anita is converted I shall have to be here a good while longer; and if she is on some Road to Damascus it's odd she hasn't [arrived] yet, for she's been around the earth several times, in miles. I don't expect her to stop persecuting me. All the same, she's in for a bit of a shock herself. Sometimes it strikes me funny, and when I laugh no one hears. I can whoop my head off out here; it startles only the coyotes.

Next week I'm going down to San Francisco for a while, to see how civilization will affect me. I'm horribly excited by it, and can hardly sleep. I can scarcely adjust myself to Reno, with its slot machines. What will I do in San Francisco where I have friends, and where I'm to meet Sondra? She has been in Los Angeles all this while.

It was wonderful of Irv to send me the picture; I sit and admire it, and perhaps my judgment isn't altogether artistic; the thing has values of sentiment for me. I thank you both with all my heart.

Do I get a letter too?

Love,

To Samuel Freifeld

November 5, 1955   Reno

Dear Sam'l:

Here I sit in the desert. I took a very remote place, by preference. I needed such a place, and it has served its purpose—though no purpose is ever served as fully as the words would have it. But it's been fair enough. You will be astonished not to hear complaints, but I haven't any. Oh yes, now and then it's gone a little hard with me, but nothing mortal has happened. And now the first six weeks are almost out, and I find myself almost regretting that they've gone so quickly. This sort of life suits me more than I would have thought possible. I fish and ride, and walk and read and write; at moments I even think. On Columbus Day I lit a little candle, for isn't this what America was supposed to have been? Wasn't one supposed to think a bit here?

Next Wednesday I'm going down to visit the McCloskeys. Aren't you surprised to hear that they're in Palo Alto? Herb is with an outfit called The Center for Advanced Study in the Behavioral Sciences, an Institute like the one in Princeton but for social scientists. I found him out there and now I'm about to visit, and I'm in a state of rare excitement, for Sasha is going to meet me there, after many weeks alone in L.A.

I've been getting carbons of your letters to Covici. You're far too good to the old bat, believe me. I shall have him do something very special for you, something I haven't conceived of yet, but something.

I shall throw myself down and cry, "Gentlemen, study my behavior, if you please!" I'll show them behavior!

I presume you haven't heard from my brother [Sam]. I've sent him a few postcards, and have had a single letter from him. I'm growing fond of my brother again.

The Illinois piece is almost done. It's scandalous here and there; I mean there are ironies in it that permit a complex reading. I would have been a great legalist, I bet you. Incidentally, Anita should soon be served with my complaint. I *love* that.

Send me a little note, old pal. Remember you occupy one of the top compartments of my heart.

Regards,

"Illinois Journey," commissioned by Holiday, *would initially be rejected for publication, then printed two years later.*

To Alfred Kazin

[n.d.]   [Reno]

Hurrah, hurray, hurray!
For Adams, Donald J.
He stands for the best of everything
In his column on Sunday.
Ah, Fielding and Tolstoy
He loves like an old boy.
But give a boost to Joyce or Proust
And he straightaway cries out "Oy!"
"Give me a yarn to read.
I ask for nothing subtle.
The best is what I understand—
The rest you can damn well scuttle."

L'envoi: "My brow is as high as yours, buddy.
It's only my green eyeshade that makes it seem lower."

J. Donald Adams was a regular (and much despised) book reviewer for The New York Times.

To Alfred Kazin

[n.d.]   [Reno]

Dear Alfred:

In this wilderness, and that is no figure of speech, I haven't seen your book yet. But I did chance to see the review in the *Times*, which I thought so foul that I wanted to bang [Cleanth] Brooks on the head. Eastern white-collar? Why, he might as well have come out flatly with "Jew." What vileness! How I detest these "rooted" Southerners among us poor deracinated Hebes of the north. I notice that they teach at Yale, though, or Minnesota. If they are not missionaries from Southern culture they are liars and cowards. Christly heavens, what *chutzpah*!

Accept my double congratulations, on book and baby, and never mind these hookworm victims.

Love,

Brooks had reviewed Kazin's essay collection The Inmost Leaf *in* The New York Times Book Review.

1956

To William Faulkner

Dear Mr. Faulkner,

The first three proposals seem fair enough although, with the exception of the recommendation on the McCarran Act, rather vague. Of course I agree that it would be a good thing to bring people from Bulgaria and Poland and Hungary here to see America provided that they are not harmed by the police of those countries when they return.

But I am writing this letter in order to give you my views on your suggestion (made, I assume, after I left the meeting) that we ask for the release of Ezra Pound. "While the Chairman of this Committee," you say, "was awarded a prize by the Swedish Government and was given a decoration by the French Government, the American Government locks up one of its best poets." This is a truly astonishing piece of reasoning. You, Mr. Faulkner, were deservedly honored by these governments. But you did not, to my knowledge, try to overthrow or undermine either of them. Besides, Pound is not in prison but in an insane asylum. If sane he should be tried again as a traitor; if insane he ought not to be released merely because he is a poet. Pound advocated in his poems and in his broadcasts enmity to the Jews and preached hatred and murder. Do you mean to ask me to join you in honoring a man who called for the destruction of my kinsmen? I can take no part in such a thing even if it makes effective propaganda abroad, which I doubt. Europeans will take it instead as a symptom of reaction. In France, Pound would have been shot. Free him because he is a poet? Why, better poets than he were exterminated perhaps. Shall we say nothing in their behalf?

America has dealt mercifully with Pound in recognizing his insanity and sparing his life. To release him is a foolish and feeble idea. It would identify this program in the eyes of the world with Hitler and Himmler and Mussolini and genocide. But I am not so much concerned with the practical side of the matter here. What staggers me is that you and Mr. Steinbeck who have dealt for so many years in words should fail to understand the import of Ezra Pound's plain and brutal statements about the "kikes" leading the "goy" to slaughter. Is this—from *The Pisan Cantos*—the stuff of poetry? It is a call to murder. If it were spoken by a farmer or a shoemaker we would call him mad. The whole world conspires to ignore what has happened, the giant wars, the colossal hatreds, the unimaginable murders, the destruction of the very image of man. And we—"a representative group of American writers"—is this what we come out for, too? A fine mess!

Sincerely yours,

Bellow had been tapped by New York Times *journalist Harvey Breit to participate in "People to People," a committee of writers and publishers established to counter Soviet propaganda and to promote pro-American values abroad. President Dwight Eisenhower had appointed Faulkner as chairman.*

To Philip Rahv

[n.d.]   [Reno]

Dear Phil:

I have been rewriting Wilhelm, and he's lengthened a little. Not a great deal. A few thousand words, perhaps, which is proportionately not much. I'm supposed to turn the manuscript over to Viking, soon, and as I hear from Volkening that you don't need copy until the first of June I have asked Covici to send you galleys. I hope everything works out smoothly. I've been so long in this desert banishment, I've lost all sense of civilized processes. But we'll be coming out of this soon. I'm calling this story *Seize the Day*. Maybe Tamkin ought to say it in Latin: *Carpe Diem*. That isn't plausible, however. Anyway, until later in the year, Hail and Farewell. (You can see what a Roman I've become in Nevada.)

Best wishes, and many thanks for accepting the story.

To Ruth Miller

[n.d.]   [Reno]

Well, honeychild, from first to last, from beginning to end your story is an unbroken and brilliant success. For once you will hear no criticism, nothing but praise and admiration and words of happy pride. Everything you do advances the excitement, the pity, the knowledge. This is what we live for, and when we have suffered and labored for our faults, finally it is given us to say something necessary, and in a world which threatens us with extinction through superfluity, the saying of something necessary is an act of heroic virtue. And this is how I feel towards your story. In order to get the gift and achieve the power you've had to go to the hospital more than once. I am sorry for the price. But you've well repaid yourself.

The progress of the thing is continual. [. . .] Many a wreck takes place before our eyes. Husbands go down. Children. As we swim away from the wreckage we count our blessings.

Kid, God bless you. Take it from me, you have fully deserved his blessings.

Now, comes the practical question: Where will you print it? Have you given it to Henry V[olkening]? I am sure he can place it. Try him with it. Should you be disappointed in him we will try some magazine editors I know.

Have you gotten the wedding announcement? Probably. I shan't be beside myself twice in the same letter. I shall let a Yiddish word speak for me: *glucklikh* [*].

When can I come back? I wish I knew. Anita still wields her wicked power. She wants money, money, money, money, or failing money, blood. Now she wants to insure my life, too, with a term policy. This is her way of telling me that she is betting I will die soon. No man knows. But not even my death would improve her. The boy writes to me, and I to him. The separation is a bad business.

Do you need the mss. or may I keep it?

And thanks for the pickles.

And tell Irv I take great comfort from his print, and thank him once more.

Love,

I had the h[emorrhoid]ectomy myself, once, and you have my active sympathy. Hope the worst of it is over.

Love from Sondra.

Bellow had married Sondra Tschacbasov in February.

* lucky

To Granville Hicks

Dear Granville Hicks:

An excellent idea. I have been giving it serious thought and I am very much in favor of such a book and I think no one is better fitted than yourself for the job. I can, however, understand Wright Morris's hesitation. I too am working at a new novel, as Henry may have mentioned, and it is rather like enjoying the girl and defending her from attackers at the same moment—difficult, very difficult!

Of course we are continually aware, while working, that we are under attack, and so perhaps it is wiser not to pretend that we are a species without enemies. I am familiar with Lionel Trilling's attitude, of course. It is one of the historical blessings of Jewish birth that one is used to flourish in the face of hostile opinion. I hinted at this last year when Francis Brown of the *Times Book Review* asked me to write a piece. The attitude I took then was that the modern world is full of people who declare that other people are obsolete. Stalin and the Kulaks, Hitler and the Jews and Slavs and gypsies, and Trilling and T. S. Eliot and several others have decided that novels are done for historically. So that one Hegelian posse or another is always riding hard on the heels of practically everyone. Possibly college professors are excepted.

Anyway, Francis Brown would not print [my essay]. He said it was not "vintage Bellow." The quote is direct.

Afterwards I thought it over and decided that there is only one way to defeat the enemy, and that is to write as well as one can. The best argument is an undeniably good book. If that doesn't convince 'em, and it may not for the spirit of denial is very strong, one has at least labored to some purpose in having reached less arbitrary and opinionated souls who have not yet learned of the lamentable obsolescence of fiction. Arguments will be met by further arguments, and victory will always fall to the critics.

But I have no objection to framing my views on the writing of fiction and on the situation of the writer. I do have strong views and there is no use in trying to conceal them. I am entirely willing, even eager, to air them in your anthology. But I greatly fear the enemy will say, "These vanishing Americans deny that they are vanishing." Or, "These lizards presume to call themselves still dinosaurs." Of course, lizards are far less extinct than many men I know (like Trilling). But you see it *is* a little awkward to *insist*, and possibly this is what Wright has in mind.

Have you thought of Thornton Wilder as possible contributor?

I should very much like to know what you think of my points. Soon my wife and I are returning; we expect to be in New York by mid-June. Perhaps we can have a conversation about this. Henry knows my whereabouts, usually, and he can arrange a meeting.

With very best wishes,

Granville Hicks (1901–82) was a literary critic, teacher, and editor who published, among other books, Figures of Transition: A Study of British Literature at the End of the Nineteenth Century *(1939) and, in an early Communist phase,* John Reed: The Making of a Revolutionary *(1936). He had proposed that Bellow write an essay on the current state of fiction for an anthology,* The Living Novel: A Symposium, *scheduled for 1957. Bellow's contribution was "Distractions of a Fiction Writer."*

To Pascal Covici

March 16, 1956   Reno

Dear Pat:

You got me into this [*San Francisco*] *Examiner* bother. The Hearst Press, no less! I know you're an old cynic to whom these things are as the clouds that pass. I myself am beginning to feel like that. Disgusting! Here Nixons, there Eisenhowers, Kefauvers. Bah! Harding was at least funny. But there were people to make fun of him. Now everybody is respectful and fish-headed and utterly, piously stupid. And I'm supposed to go to SF for this piously created cultural occasion. I am a promising writer who wrote a shocking but powerful book and I learned about writing from the New Testament. Me! [. . .] I am sure I said that having been brought up to regard the Old Testament as truth, the New Testament looked to me to be fiction. It still does. So now this irony has been turned about for the readers of the *Examiner* so that I sound no brainier than a stove pipe. But pious, pious, pious. Mmm! I pray, I love Jesus and Eisenhower and kiss everyone's backside with patriotic and worshipful humility. Note: They aren't even paying me a fee for it. All of this ass-kissing is philanthropic; I do it for culture, for Ike and for you, and for Hearst and beautiful San Francisco, and for book sales.

This little trip will cause a short delay in the delivery of those stories. I have written another new, long one. Now in Henry's hands. It looks like a piece of my Joshua novel, the bootlegger's son's memoirs, and it represents my first real effort to create a heroine. I seem to have done it. I've at least convinced myself. I'm hoping the *New Yorker* will buy it. For since the *Holiday* fiasco (it turns out that I wasn't pious enough about Carl Sandburg and Marshall Field or somebody) I'm rather short of money. Though, like a well-heeled writer I'm donating my services to the *San Francisco Examiner* together with Ilka Chase and Irving Stone—note well those names, dearest Covici!—yes, just like a penniless Polish baron who has nothing but his moustache and his pride.

Africa [i.e., *Henderson the Rain King*] is about half completed. Shall I send you five or six chapters for safekeeping? I have the carbons. It may be a good idea. But I must ask you not to show the stuff to anyone.

I must be in one of those hornet's moods of mine. I always manifest them to people I love. Others would bat me down. But, you see, I have to monkey with my old stories; I have to speak in San Francisco. And I have to wait here until my settlement is completed. None of these things do I want to do. Hence the temper. Please forgive me.

One serious remark: I have a feeling that the African thing is going to be very good.

Best to Dorothy and the children.

Love,

To Ralph Ellison

April 2, 1956 Reno

Dear Ralph:

How goes your—I am on the point of saying exile, but it's I who am exiled, while you're in the middle of everything. Was there so much to be apprehensive about? A good long look back to this side is probably what you've needed for some time. God knows it doesn't bear too much looking at when it's right on top of you. One close look a month is about enough for me, when I buy *Life* and see that Faulkner is threatening a second Civil War, and if one of the best has become such a damned fool, imagine what the worst are like. I began to miss the great world after a few months here in the desert, and then some real or pretended GI sold me a subscription to *Newsweek* and conned me out of nine bucks. The thing has never come, and perhaps I've made a double gain. In three weeks of desert any city boy can become hayseed green.

I hope it's been a good year for you and Fanny; for Sondra and me it's been a remarkable one. You wouldn't have known me, Ralph, with my casting outfit and a new reel pulling in rainbow trout. Sitting a horse, too. But this doesn't mean any Hemingway conversion. I like fish, but after you've pitted your brain against theirs for an afternoon, the interest begins to give out. I'm fonder of horses. But you can't kid yourself. The jets go over the sky with a clap of air after them, and there goes your primitive moment.

My interest in literature is beginning to revive. I hate it less now than I did last year. God knows how my back ever came to be under *this* cross. To do something once in a while is a thrill, if you don't have the money-spectre waiting on the throne for you to perform and grovel like a damn clown. It hasn't become easier; it's that I care less. The small legacy helped. I don't like to hand my father's money over to Anita, since they hated each other, but I tell myself that it does something for Greg. I can't specifically say what that is. It ensures a bourgeois upbringing. Poverty would be better, but it isn't to be found anyhow.

We'll be back in the East this summer to spend August with the kid, and we'll probably stay there. We're very nearly broke, and I'm trying to arrange some part-time teaching. A book of stories is coming out this fall, but that won't bring in very much. Besides, all stories seem to me yesteryear's ghosts. All that scaffolding, and then you're lucky to mount one little Christmas star. There's comfort in the fact that one of the stories is a small novel— almost. It's the one I wrote at Bard last summer, and there's a good deal of excitement in it.

Let me have some good news of yourself and your labors and your six months of Rome.

Love to you both,

In February, Life *had published Faulkner's "A Letter to the North" in which, responding to those "who would compel immediate and unconditional integration," he had warned, "Go slow now. Stop for a time, a moment."*

To Samuel S. Goldberg

[n.d.]   [Reno]

Cher Samuel:

I have a brief pause in my occupations, having recently completed and sent off my long story or novelette, *Seize the Day*, to Viking. It'll appear with several other pieces in the fall, and let's hope it will bring some revenue. The hope is rather flimsy. Stories, even mine, can't expect much of a sale. The

Guggenheim is coming to an end, and I had a disappointing bust-up with *Holiday*. The editors told me first to write the Illinois piece in my own way and then were appalled by my long discussion of boredom in the Midwest. They wanted me to cheer things up a little, like a true native son. But I couldn't do that. Like Lincoln, I was a lousy immigrant.

Without my Pa's small legacy, in other words, I could never make do. But I've had a valuable illumination about money, thanks to *Seize the Day*. I've learned the true value of a dollar. It's about two cents, on my scale. We need money on account of our vices. But after all, vice isn't everything. There are also cheaper vices, and I am remodeling Walden mentally for modern habitation. I'll explain this to you in person some time in June when we return.

I've never seen Sondra so well. You wouldn't know her. I can't congratulate myself often enough. Do you still wander round the bookstores? If you should see a copy of R. F. Burton's *A Mission to Gelele, King of Dahome*, please capture it for me and send it out. I'm in the midst of a long novella about an explorer and need it for some of the details. God will bless you for sending it air-express. I will pay all charges. It's more important to me than the next election.

Love,

To John Berryman

May 16, 1956   [Reno]

Dear Mr. Berrimon:

Vous m'excuserez, j'espère, quelques fautes menues. Je n'ai pas le don suprême de la politesse.

I 'ave *souvent* theenk of your conference *sur* I-do-and-do-not-wish-to-be-cast-upon-your-shore. It is a *titre sublime. Et sérieusement, vous avez peint* ze human situation more better than J.-P. Sartre *avec une seule* strook. I do and do not wish. *Voici la question! Elle est toute là, là, là!*

My own mind has amended it as follows. I do and do not wish to acknowledge that I have been wrestling at close quarters with a grizzly bear. I have been buying and selling, earning and spending, peeling potatoes, drinking seltzer, and this brown pelt before my dizzy eyes belongs to . . . to . . . an acquaintance. *Mais n'en parlons plus.* A further step might be taken. Father, forgive them, they know and do not know what they do.

Focus is all.

I begin again:

Dear John:

My focus has improved remarkably. I now get an image and a half instead of two.

I am always delighted to hear from you, whether the news is good or not. How much—how infinitely better when I sense a tranquil spirit, as I now do. New York is not good for us. No, nor Princeton neither. John, you give me great satisfaction. I think of the three of us—you and I and [Tom] Riggs composing that damn Xmas poem and I feel, some four years later, at least two of us are making it.

Your letter gives me the first good opinion I've had of [T. S.] Eliot in some time. I'm delighted! Let us exchange copies. I have a sort of zany book coming in November. It isn't exactly worthy of us, perhaps. *C'est pour gagner la vie.* But in addition I have accomplished something *vraiment pas mal. Sans blague,* Berrimon. I think you will be pleased. We shall have a private reading when we reach Minneapolis early in June.

Can you really put us up for a day or two? You will make us divinely happy.

We leave here on the 1st of June. Possibly earlier. We drive to Boulder, Colo. first for one day. And then to Mpls. We shall wire or write from the road to give the exact time of our arrival.

Much love, from the intense inane which surrounds me today,

To Ralph Ellison

[n.d.]   [Saratoga Springs, N.Y.]

Dear Ralph:

I've never enjoyed writing letters. Vasiliki says that Isaac, whose journals she took after his death, had some uncomplimentary things to say about the way I answered letters. I deserve them. There is some wickedness hidden here and I ought to root it up, even if it should mean going to an analyst. It's part of some disagreeable reticence in me—laziness; worse; something very nasty.

Anyway, there's a lot to tell. I don't know where to start—Sondra is going to have a baby in February: that's the best of the news. Then, in rapidly descending order, we've bought ourselves a wreck of a house in Tivoli [New York]. I wanted to be near Greg for some of the time at least, and I had a little money that my father willed me, which I was spending anyway, and to keep it all from trickling away we put it into a large building. We can't even live in the place yet, because there's no water, and I'm writing to you now from Yaddo where I've taken refuge. At a hundred seventy-five feet the drillers did strike some veins but I don't know yet whether they give enough water. A couple of beguiling fairies sold us the place and lied about the water, the roof—not sure I'll have enough money to keep things going. Plaster, paint, carpentry, taxes, fuel. But I'm not supposed to worry about these problems here. I came to work on my book. It isn't the bootlegger but something entirely different. Which will greatly surprise you. My hero is just now hunting lions in East Africa with a native king, an inspired king who is opening my hero's eyes. These are great eyes, and they were thickly shut, and I'm making the most of it all. I try to read books of African travel but I become very impatient with them. I find the travelers didn't know how to write about Africa. And since I was once an anthropology student I find it easier to invent my own tribes, customs and all. There are two tribes. One is wicked, the other is good, more or less Essene, Children of Light. My traveler respects the children of light, but he learns much more from the children of darkness. That's hardly a surprise, and I can't find it in my heart to be satisfied with anything so obvious. This is why I have taken to hunting lions. Something may come of the lions. If I can't touch the heart of the great mystery (this time) I may as well spin a yarn.

You will see, anyway, that I haven't been idle. I've covered the country, East and West. If only I could be a little more idle, and think of the things I've seen. But I permit myself little rest; I fuss. All the old, tiresome sins. You know me, Al.

It was thoughtful of you to write about the Fulbright. I suppose you're well into your book now, and that Fanny has entirely recovered. These suppositions are hopes. We miss you here. I could use some of those long conversations we used to have. Even a meditative hour on Riverside Drive. It isn't the Tiber, but it's not worthless.

New York is as ever. Gregory is five foot two and physically a man at the age of twelve. One of these days he's going to stop thinking about the Dodgers. He's a great success. I'm very proud of him.

Love to you both,

Fanny and Ralph Ellison were in Rome for the year.

To Gertrude Buckman

August 2, 1956   Tivoli, N.Y.

Dear Gertrude:

This is more like it. You see, I need your good opinion, yours and that of people like you. It isn't that my detractors won't let me live, etc. One must appreciate detractors, too. It's merely that when you've tried to make a little more reality, or tried to reclaim a little of infinite unreality, you like to hear from your brothers and sisters that it hasn't been one more illusion.

Besides, I had been thrown millions of light years by Isaac Rosenfeld's death. He died while writing something and it's something of a comfort to feel that writing something perhaps matters. Perhaps it does.

My best thanks,

Gertrude Buckman was Delmore Schwartz's former wife. Schwartz would serve as the model for Von Humboldt Fleischer, Bellow's figure of early brilliance and subsequent crackup in Humboldt's Gift. *Isaac Rosenfeld had died at his desk on July 14, 1956, at the age of thirty-eight.*

To Ruth Miller

August 23, 1956   Tivoli, N.Y.

Dear Ruth:

Sondra was too unwell to travel to Poughkeepsie. I myself have been none too hot, either, since Isaac's death. I've had to sit at home and pull myself together. The house has been a great headache. It interfered so with all the vital processes that at last I had to turn the matter over to Sondra—no business woman, let it be said. You're lucky to be married to a painter. They understand plastering, wiring, etc. My attitude towards these things has always been that I should know enough about them to write of them confidently. Anyway, I phoned today to Vassar and learned that school had ended on the 19th. I was disappointed. I thought it would continue till Labor Day. I guess I don't listen when you tell me things.

As this is being written I imagine you're in the air between La Guardia and Chicago, either going or returning. If the house were in better repair I'd ask you up for Labor Day. But now the well has given out. We may have to drill a new one (another thousand down the hole, literally). Oh well, Pa didn't *really* think I could hold on to his legacy.

So, we'll meet in NY when the New School season on me opens. The sharpshooters are oiling their guns. My days and nights are immersed in literature, but when it comes to holding class I am progressively less articulate and I make a fool of myself.

I'm going on with *Henderson the Rain King*. We shall make a three-way trade, soon: Irv's movie, your novel and mine exchanging hands.

Don't be angry with us; we wanted to come. But Sondra was in bed, and Vasiliki Rosenfeld who was here was in no condition to be left alone.

Love,

To Josephine Herbst

[n.d.]   [Tivoli]

Dear Josie:

I went through Pennsylvania on a fast train yesterday, and I thought of getting off to thank you for your letter. It was only fantasy, because I was going from Washington to New York, and wasn't even on the right line. But I'm very grateful to you for that letter. I felt it through and through. We lose a lot of our humanity, struggling. The challenge is not to lose, rather to regain, to refine. What, if not that, are we for? When I see you or get a note from you I am aware how honorably you meet difficulties. I see in you a winner. If you think *Seize the Day* was good, I am satisfied that I'm doing all right. It's hard for me to know, because so much of the time I'm deaf, dumb and blind, the slave of unknown masters.

I'm glad you're going to Greece to write. Greece, somehow, seems appropriate. But before you go let's have a conversation. Why don't we meet in town? Better yet, why don't you come out and stay here with us for a while? What about Thanksgiving? [. . .]

Thanks for your kindness.

Josephine Herbst (1892–1969) was the author of Pity Is Not Enough *(1933),* The Executioner Waits *(1934), and* Rope of Gold *(1939). She wrote from Germany for the* New York Post *in 1935 and went on to report from Spain and Latin America for various magazines.*

To John Berryman

Dear John:

I feel you are acting in your own best interest. This may sound forbidding, like too much prudence, but there are prudences and prudences and growing older we learn to respect the higher branch of the family. My love to you both, *carte blanche*.

Your Isaac poem came. Surprising how much of it I had remembered from the telephone—"half through, he crampt dead." You do the right thing to keep the mark drawn high when one of us dies. It's the only sort of answer we have got. Negative capability, isn't that what Keats called it? I think and think about Isaac, and my recollections are endless—twenty-six years, of which I've forgotten very little. Isaac himself began to have doubts about thinking, and he passed them on to me. Now I feel more than ever what a strange activity thinking is. Anyway, since his going my life has been far less my own, and there are days when I care less. I have to recover my negative capability.

Meanwhile, *Anne Bradstreet* has given comfort. When I read it in Princeton there were a lot of competing excitements. Later I saw it better, and now very clearly. [Edmund] Wilson is right and more than right. He usually is; a sound man. You seem just now to have poetry practically to yourself. Yes, [Robert] Lowell is very fine but he hasn't built himself as much freedom as you have—this power to bring elements together which gives the greatest release. There's plenty of talent; we're all talented, but it's this further strength we're a little short of.

The *Bradstreet* is wonderful. I take nothing from it if I say that your more recent poems are written in something more like my tongue. I think *Bradstreet* is a triumph in modern poetry, but there are formal properties in modern poetry and fiction, too, which are only there for us to overcome. All the formal properties have to be cracked and the simplicities released—like, "Torture me Father lest I be not thine." So much has fallen away from our lives, we really think most barely when the truth is with us; ". . . he enjoyed despair/ did wrong . . ."; that is more like it. That's a brother's insight.

I don't do very much. Every once in a while I put *Henderson* on me like a plumber's level. The bubble is usually in the wrong place, so I sigh and knock off for the day. But Sondra is a beautiful mother-to-be, and Greg gave me much pleasure last month, so my life is far from barren. Too many awful

SB and Sam, seated, Jane and Maurice, standing

SB, Liza, Jane, Abram, Maurice, and Sam

Brother Sam and SB

Oscar Tarcov

SB, Celia and Harold "Kappy"
Kaplan

SB and Anita, Chicago, 1942

SB and Melvin Tumin, Chicago, 1942

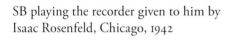

SB playing the recorder given to him by
Isaac Rosenfeld, Chicago, 1942

SB in Spain, 1947

Ralph and Fanny Ellison, ca. 1948

Edith, Nathan, Oscar, and
Miriam Tarcov, ca. 1948

Delmore Schwartz

SB in the Fifties

John Berryman

Josephine Herbst

Lionel Trilling

John Cheever

Robert Penn Warren,
Eleanor Clark and family

Karl Shapiro

SB with Daniel, Adam and Gregory

Alfred Kazin

distractions, however, big gloomy houses, money, alimony problems, friends low in spirits, and ghosts, large numbers of highly individual ghosts.

Anyhow, will we be seeing you and A[nne] soon? Give the ladies an opportunity, make common cause, give us all a big boost. What say? Come one, come all.

Love,

To John Berryman

December 14, 1956   Tivoli

Dear John:

No, I'm not taking it too hard. It's only that manipulations are so foolish. I hate to be manipulated and jockeyed, you know. It's the pale shadow of diabolism. In this world of ghosts who administer funds and keep up a faint life still by the aid of gossip and politics, it's the pallor of the devilment that gets me. [. . .] I never do realize it in time. I'll be, till death, a dummy. And probably one in Hades, too. That seems to be the point of Orpheus. He simply couldn't cope with hell. Our education is all wrong!

Your name is not at all mud in N.Y. The whole idea of mud is an absurdity. In some quarters we are always necessarily mud, but not where thoughts are thought and feelings are felt. Everything will soon be forgotten. The rate of scandal, like every other thing, is stepped up. Three years ago *I* was involved in the big one. Now I'd have to remind people of it elaborately, give them a refresher, they've so thoroughly forgotten. Anyway these are questions of the conduct of life which we settled for ourselves some few years ago. In my eagerness to ensure your getting the grant I tipped myself over. I meant to do you good, but it seems to have come out harm. It's as inevitable as shoelaces, since I don't know the first thing about prudence. I have to admire it from a distance. You haven't settled into other people's affairs because you shun idleness. Now for God's sake, let's let all these things go slide down the flume. We have some twenty or thirty years of work lying before us.

The *Job* is very, very good. Mpls. seems to be tuned in on it. When I was there I had the good fortune to find a rabbi at Hillel who was willing to put me through the Hebrew. I didn't get far enough, and one of these days I will go forward. I don't know a great deal about metrics but yours sound very right to me.

As for the Freud lecture, I don't believe I ought to try it. It would make me very nervous to prepare it and ball Henderson up. He's thriving now, so why put his poor soul in hazard? Thanks anyway, greatly.

I'm sorry you won't be coming East. Come back with us in June, anyway.

Love and best Xmas greetings,

Berryman had embarked on a modern version of the Book of Job, never to be completed.

To Alfred Kazin

December 17, 1956   Tivoli

Dear Alfred:

Eight-months-pregnant Sasha lies on the couch holding Greg's dog. (It sounds like Ch. 1 of a proletarian novel). I say, "Where's Alfred's letter?" And she says, jaunty, "In the folder where I put all the letters." *À la bonne heure!* [*] I open the folder and ransack it. I find a box top that says, "Mail This to Ivory Snow and Get a Free Rand McNally Map of the US." Thanks, I've already been there. What would you get, I wonder, if you mailed in the top of Pandora's Box?

Did I see your review [of *Seize the Day*] in the *Times*? Of course. It pleased me enormously. H'm, I thought, most people don't even have friends, much less friends who approve of what they do. Bellow, you're a very lucky (young) man. But as everybody knows, ingratitude begins with luck and so I didn't send you a note, as I should have done. I count on you to realize that I am having a time of it with all these changes—house, child, book, money, relatives, trains and cars, New York, Hungary—and to forgive me.

Suddenly it occurs to me that the last we were all together was at the time of Ann's pregnancy, and now you have (by all reports) a beautiful daughter, and we haven't even had a glass of tea. What do you say to our exchanging calendars so that we can look for each other in New York? Our house is splendid and manorial but has no beds, and unless you own sleeping bags we can't ask you to come here.

Now, for instance—Sasha and I plan to be in New York on Jan. 4th, 5th, 6th and 7th, possibly even the 8th. Do you think you'll be in on any of those days? We'll probably be staying with Covici on Morningside Drive. I'm in the city on Thursdays, usually. Don't tell me you spend all your time in Amherst. I refuse to believe it.

Love to you both (all three, all four of you),

* French: well and good

To Samuel Freifeld

December 27, 1956   Tivoli

Dear Sam'l:

[. . .] I am working, not at my best, but working nevertheless at my *métier* [*]. Because I have to. Because, once, I chose it, and it's just as well that I be faithful somewhere. We are comfortable here, and nothing is lacking except some money, and that not too sharply. I'm coming to Chicago to give a lecture on the 22nd. I shall arrive a day sooner, and if Sasha is well I shall stay over a day after. The lecture pays five hundred and I couldn't conscientiously refuse.

The business in hand, I don't understand very well. But I've signed where it was indicated that I should, and have made a statement which ought to satisfy my brother or his lawyer. Last summer Sam told me he was not going to share in the remainder of our father's money. He seems to have changed his mind, the privilege of women, businessmen, and brothers.

I think our ancient experience in love affairs, going back to Oakley Blvd. and Irving St., probably taught us some valuable lessons and in particular prepared us for moments of disappointment. The more I think of what happened the more reason I have to be pleased that the thing [Freifeld's marriage] ended before more harm was done. To you this is a cold comfort, but I have great confidence in our power to recover from everything. Except death, of course. But who's talking about *that*! Maybe we'll recover even from death, if it comes to a pinch. But in the meantime I'm confident of your earthly resurrection.

I hope to find you in a state of calm and patience.

With love,

1957

To Granville Hicks

[n.d.]   [Minneapolis]

Dear Granville:

[. . .] Your remarks on Brendan Gill tickled me. I'm sure he wasn't mortified, he doesn't mortify easily. But that *New Yorker* outfit is a strange one. First they give me a chance to beat up on A. West which, like a gent, I refuse.

* French: profession

Then they give my next book to Gill knowing full well (Wm. Maxwell was present) that Gill and I have had a hassle. Strange people. But I tell you this, I have no desire to understand them.

Spring has been weird enough here. For my money, the reasons are all atomic.

We'll be back in Tivoli by mid-June, and we hope you will visit us again. Best,

Brendan Gill had panned Seize the Day *in* The New Yorker.

To Ralph Ellison

May 27, 1957   Minneapolis

Dear Ralph—

I won't discuss with you in a letter any of the things suggested by your last. It isn't a good idea. I'm writing now simply to say that the house in Tivoli is open to you for as long a time as you like or need.

Sasha and I have been in Minneapolis since March. It was just what we needed. On the farm the year round we'd both go nuts. And NYC is out. Too rough, too choking. It wins by a decision over me. No knockout but I'll never be the same.

I'll send the book you asked for when I get to New York in about two weeks. We'll be passing through only. I find the Midwest agrees with me. Here I recognize things. And I'm near Chicago, which is not unimportant. I've been there several times this year, and next winter I'll be teaching for ten weeks at Northwestern and hanging around the joints with Sasha's bookie uncle.

The new kid is beginning to sit up and take notice. He seems to have a sense of humor. Having survived the birth trauma he finds life a laughing matter.

So should we all.

I hope your book is going well.

Good luck and love to you both from Sasha and me,

To James Laughlin

Dear J,

Thanks for the German article. I had already seen it but another copy is gratefully received. Not that I read German.

About Delmore, I'm just as depressed as you are. He's got it in his mind that I'm one of his ill-wishers, detractors, slanderers—who knows, and he phoned me in the middle of the night using techniques the GPU might have envied, threatening to sue me for slander and frightening my poor wife. With Katie [Carver's] assistance I did try to look after him. I made an effort to get rid of the private detective he had hired at enormous cost, but the guy wouldn't be shaken and in the end prevailed with Delmore. God knows he found plenty of purchase inside Delmore's head. We raised a little dough to help him, not necessarily for psychiatric care, since I wasn't absolutely sure that he needed it, but for his general care while he was being weaned from pills and gin. But he broke loose and I can be of no further use to him now. I imagine the detective, [Vincent] Stanzioni, is still sucking around him, and anybody who wants to do Delmore a good turn will push this guy into the Hudson. Evidently there is more to these sleuth characters than meets the public eye.

With best wishes,

James Laughlin (1914–1997), founder and director of New Directions, the leading house for modernist literature in America, had published Delmore Schwartz's books, notable among them In Dreams Begin Responsibilities *(1938) and* The World Is a Wedding *(1948). During his stay at the mental ward of Bellevue Hospital in New York, Schwartz had been paranoically convinced that his wife, Elizabeth, was adulterously involved with art critic Hilton Kramer, and hired a private detective, Vincent Stanzioni, to investigate. Catharine DeFrance Carver (1921–1997) would become Bellow's editor at Viking after Covici's death in 1964. Earlier at Reynal & Hitchcock, Harcourt Brace and Lippincott, she had edited Katherine Anne Porter, E. E. Cummings, Elizabeth Bishop, John Berryman, Lionel Trilling, Leon Edel, Bernard Malamud, Leslie Fiedler and Richard Ellmann. In the later Sixties, disgusted by America's involvement in Southeast Asia, she moved to London, where she would work for Chatto & Windus, Victor Gollancz and Oxford University Press.*

To the John Simon Guggenheim Memorial Foundation

December 26, 1957   Tivoli, New York

CONFIDENTIAL REPORT ON CANDIDATE FOR FELLOWSHIP

Name of Candidate: Bernard Malamud

I am an admirer of Mr. Malamud's work, and I don't lack for company. Mr. M. deserves the cheers the critics have given him (an exceptional case). His excellent qualities speak clearly for themselves. Among writers of Jewish descent he is distinguished by a fine and delicate sense of traditions. There is a coarse customary way of dealing with the Jew in the Anglo-Saxon world. [Israel] Zangwill started it, and Michael Gold almost ended it. I wish he had done it in for good. Alas, it hangs on. Mr. Malamud happily has no truck with it. I think his merits will be no less plain to the gentlemen of the committee than they are to me.

To Philip Roth

December 26, 1957   Tivoli, N.Y.

Dear Philip Roth—

Manuscripts around here shift and wander in huge piles, like the dunes. Yours turned up today, and I apologize to you for my disorder. It hurts me more.

My reaction to your story was on the positive side of the scale, strongly. But mixed, too. I liked the straightness of it, the plainness about biology. That kind of thing suits me to the ground. I thought Moe was excellent; Pa, too. A company of Japanese committing hari-kari, though, I wasn't sure about. A great idea, but palpably *Idea*. I have a thing about *Ideas* in stories. Camus' *The Plague* was an *IDEA*. Good or bad? Not so hot, in my opinion. With you the *Idea* gains ground fast, easily. It conquers. What of Moe?

Look, try Henry Volkening at 522 Fifth Ave. My agent. A very good one, too. Best of luck. And forgive my having the mss. so long. I should have read it at once. But I don't live right.

Yrs,

The story Bellow was responding to was a draft of "Expect the Vandals," published the following year in Esquire.

1958

To Ralph Ellison

February 14, 1958   Evanston

Dear Ralph—

Drop me a line sometime to say how things are coming. It doesn't have to be a full-scale letter. I'm incapable myself of writing one. It's been years since I could.

Chicago is—is something, I guess. No point in blaming the place. Some inward struggle no matter where you are. I suppose you experienced the same in Rome.

Anyhow, Adam is walking, and that's nearly something. Life is just one long country fair for that kid. He's medicinal to me. Sasha's okay now; we all had pneumonia more or less, on arriving.

On the 1st of April we'll be back. Come up and help me put in garden vegetables. Bring manuscript.

All the best,

To John Berryman

February 19, 1958   Evanston

Dear John—

For months now I have been lost in the remotest bush of Africa with Henderson. On Labor Day I started *de nouveau* and have written about five hundred pages since. Almost done now. The last fantasy is taking place in the neighborhood of Newfoundland. Crash fire—crash ice. I need to cool things off. Anyway, Eugene H. Henderson will give you a run for your money. And I believe he comes out sane, though he goes in mad. And that's news.

Adam is one year old today. Paul, too, soon. We should bring them together; and their decrepit parents as well. How is it that we haven't bumped into each other in nearly a year?

Love to Anne. *Ton ami très distrait* [*],

You owe me copies of poems. Do you remember? I don't see them in magazines. Do I rate a private subscription?

* French: your addled friend

To Pascal Covici

[n.d.]   [San Francisco]

Dear Pat:

Marshall [Best]'s information comes from a note sent to Tom [Guinzburg] who had some pleasant things to say about *Henderson*. I've finished the book (longhand) and this morning I am about to begin on the typewriter. There are three final chapters and although the written manuscript numbers more than five hundred pages I don't feel that this should be such a long book. You're right, I mustn't trample and hurry; I've got to work it out at leisure, now that I've got all the facts down. Leisure, I said. Not to be confused with idleness. I've worked too hard moving it to allow idle winds to blow it all away. Except in two or three places, I anticipate no deep difficulty. But those two or three places (towards the end) do exist. (The King and the lion, mostly.) The ideas have to be absorbed into the comedy. I've got to take a short breather before I try this. Five hundred pages since Labor Day, and most of them the right pages. I'm bushed. Between Evanston and *Henderson*, I've worn myself out, but I recover quickly and I should be fit to start the final campaign after a couple of weeks of sleep in Tivoli. San Francisco is all right, I guess, although it makes you feel that after a journey of three thousand miles you might at least have gotten out of America.

Best regards to everyone—the born, the reborn, the newborn.

Schreck dich nicht [*].

Love,

To John Berryman

July 24, 1958   [Tivoli]

Dear John,

Many thanks, dear pal, for your handsome note. When it's you who tells me something I rely utterly on it, and what you tell me does me infinite amounts of good. Fun comes hard—like, alas, its parents, pleasure and happiness, whom we have to pursue. I know whom to chase, but sometimes it makes me very grim. And I do love old Henderson, but not steadfastly, as he deserves. At least the book is finished, or almost. I suspect that in the middle I was maybe too business-like and earnest. But I'm trying to give earnestness the sack. I think I'm going to be able to do it. Laying down the law too much. A bad trait, ever since Moses started it.

* German: Don't be scared.

The *Don [Quixote]* is as handsome as any book I've ever seen. It's going to make me take up my Spanish again; meanwhile I gloat over the plates and read the scholarly notes.

When may we see you and Anne and Paul? Tivoli stands open.

Yours, no bunk,

To Leslie Fielder

[n.d.]   [Tivoli]

Dear Leslie—

I didn't intend to sound mean. Of course, friendship (*manqué?*) or old acquaintance; it never ripened into friendship.

In some ways, I understand and sympathize with your position. Only I think positions *emerge* in a work of art, and you seem to think they're imposed. It makes small difference what the artist says he thinks, and a "prepared" attitude is an invitation to disaster. Perhaps you'll think this more "misology" (hard word). I only complain that intelligence has become so naked. Ideology is of no use to us in refurnishing the empty house.

Anyway, to be a "misologist," if I am indeed one, is almost as subversive as possible. Only humanists are more subversive—the most subversive of all—and I am a humanist. *Henderson* is not Reichian confusion, but comedy. I shun doctrine. I am willing if I must to be a destroyer, but not on a doctrinaire basis.

Where is Goshen, Vt.? Far from Tivoli, N.Y.? [. . .]

Best to Margaret.

Yours,

To Pascal Covici

October 2, 1958   Minneapolis

Dear Pat—

[. . .] I haven't written my Columbia speech, and I don't know what to say, I'm so bewildered, but I'll arrive by plane on the 9th or 10th to say it, and I'll probably seem self-assured and confident on the platform. God has given me that gift in exchange for what he has taken away in content.

Dr. Neuhl, after a month of conversations, believes I'm normal after all. It makes me sorry for the rest of you guys. So this is life? What I've got? And normal life, too? How sad for everybody! But it has been considerate of me, I declare, to defend human ideals by separating myself from the happy many. I must be a sporting type.

Sondra is well. She reads med[ieval] history sixteen hours a day and has little time for anything else. A kind sort of woman looks after Adam from 9:00 to 3:30 daily. It costs a little, but then I don't know how to enjoy money, anyway. Haven't a clue, and never have had. What do you do with it? If *Henderson* earns a lot, maybe Harold G[uinzburg] will agree to give me a course of private lessons.

Can you read my hand?

Give my love to Dorothy, and make sure she's the right Dorothy, and ask if she will be my guest at Granada's on Sat. of next weekend. You come, too. I'm inviting my mother-in-law as well.

Your dear friend,

But I haven't been able to write anything. I'm still swimming towards the life-raft.

To Ralph Ellison

[n.d.]   [Minneapolis]

Dear Ralph:

What's the news? The proofs [of *Henderson the Rain King*] are in and I'm trying to make a rest cure of this University teaching. The administration fights back. I'm being worked comparatively hard but I try to sleep through most of it, and victory seems to be on my side. Meanwhile Sasha reads vast volumes of Byzantine history. I swear she's going to end up in Coptic church history. Boring subjects delight her. I take a deep interest in them (fast asleep). But we do manage to have a good time often. The political rallies have been pretty hot, and tonight's election night and I'm off for D7C HQ with a clutch of beer bottles to whoop it up for my candidates. [Adlai] Stevenson was here last week, as funny as Mort Sahl.

Luckily there's nothing here like Madison Sq. Garden or the Coliseum and you get a chance to kid with the politicians.

Adam has most of his teeth now, and a considerable vocabulary—some of it unfortunate. He's caught us unprepared by the speed of his learning-power before we could remember to stop saying shit. However, a little honest shit does no harm.

Anything I say next will be compromised by the above.

Any leaks?

And can we save that pine tree? It's getting serious.

Tanti saluti. What do they say?—*Auguri!*
Love,

1959

To Josephine Herbst

January 31, 1959   Minneapolis

Dear Josie:

You know what hard luck is and therefore I shan't be impressing you with the following—I offer it only in explanation of my failure to answer your letter.

Sondra and I had a blowup last June and she took the kid and went to the city. I had to hold together the house and my impossible book and take care of my older son who came to spend the summer with me. We had one of those struggles, Sondra and I, that you've probably seen before. No account of them can be given without full details and that is a hopeless job. She was working in an art gallery while I was re-writing *Henderson* by dictating the text, revising as I went, to a typist. Eight, ten, twelve and fourteen hours a day for six weeks. By mid-August I was near suicide.

A nephew of mine, my sister's son, had this even more seriously in mind. Toward the end of the month, in his Army barracks in San Francisco, being in great trouble and seeing no way out, he killed himself.

I drove to Chicago for the funeral.

Then I came on to Minneapolis. Sondra and I patched things up. Which means just about as much as it says. Patches, for two or three months, were all we had to bless ourselves with. More recently we've done better. It turned out that Sondra has a nervous disorder, in itself not too serious. It doesn't affect her health but it does account for our marital disorders to a considerable extent. Anyway, life has brightened, if it doesn't glitter downright. But then there isn't enough glitter in half a lifetime to dunk your toast in. The baby is handsome and quick, and Sondra has enrolled in graduate school where she's doing extremely well.

I don't tell you this to have it weigh on your heart ("Man's trouble!") but only because it will seem loutish of me not to have answered. Josie, I couldn't do it. I've had enough in the last year to justify a decade of paralyzed silence but I claim no special privilege that way. I'm fond of you, more than a little, and I want to hear from you. Can you spare me a few lines?

How is your book? May I see some of it? I'll send you a copy of *Henderson* very soon. [. . .]

Affectionately,

Bellow's nephew Lawrence Kauffman had hanged himself in his barracks at the Presidio while awaiting military trial on a charge of theft.

To Pascal Covici

[n.d.]   [Minneapolis]

Dear Pat:

The liquor was hidden, the light left burning. Was everything in good order when you returned? I'd be desolated if it wasn't. I hope you and Dorothy had a tall old time in the South. After you left the weather [in New York] became deadly cold.

What's there to report? Lillian H[ellman] and I had a good talk as a result of which I've made fine progress with the Tragedy of Bummidge the self-analyst. Next week I plunge into Act II. I go and go—write and write. Oh: Meridian Press is wildly eager to publish a magazine, on very good terms to editors and contributors.

Also the Ford Foundation has been heard from. Today I received forms to fill with details of my financial history. It seems I don't earn enough annually to ship a goat to Guatemala from next door in Honduras.

Any news about *Henderson*? If it isn't very very good, please spare me.

Were the pictures frightful? I'm sure they must have been.

The Hebrew dictionary and the records arrived. Many thanks.

Remember me with love to Dorothy.

Yr. devoted friend,

No check for Jan.?

To Elizabeth Ames

February 5, 1959   Minneapolis

Dear Elizabeth:

I hope you've had a good year.

Mine has been very mixed. Luckily, as I slowly discover, my character is a tough one. Here I'd gone around thinking that I was the flower of fragility. What a misconception! Well, we'd better be sturdy. They're getting the machines ready to carry us body and bones to the moon. Just imagine Yaddo on Mars and Venus. It's a very sobering idea.

I am asking Viking Press to send you a copy of *Henderson the Rain King*. It might have originated in the Mars Yaddo and not at Saratoga Springs where it actually had its birth. You may find it a poor return for your hospitality. And then again you may like it. I hope so.

Love,

To Josephine Herbst

February 18, 1959   Minneapolis

Dearest Josie:

In haste: You bet there's a magazine. It's coming out in September. Meridian Press is publishing it and I'm one of the editors, *primus inter pares*. I'm anxious to read some of your things, particularly the memoirs. I have a feeling they must be extraordinarily hot. Do you have a copy to spare me? I'd be very grateful. The editors of this thing are very eager to stay away from the typical literary magazine. To some extent it will of course be literary, but we want to avoid overemphasis on literature. There'll be no criticism in it, or very little. It should be topical, too, and writers ought to be encouraged to do reportage, familiar essays, social comment and all of that. To get away from the notion that literature is about itself. Such bunk.

I'll write in more detail soon. I don't generally. But I feel drawn to you. Why? Perhaps you understand this better than I. I've come to love you. There's something about you that brings out that feeling in me, very strongly. [. . .]

To Pascal Covici

February 19, 1959   Minneapolis

Dear Pat:

We seem to be making a splash [with *Henderson*], and I know that doesn't displease you. I haven't read any reviews except the ones you send, and those after Sondra has looked them over. She feels that I shouldn't have to lick any more wounds than I received last summer, and I suppose she's right. Anyway, I think there's every reason to be satisfied with what I have seen. The rest can't count for much; besides, I can't allow myself to brood over any of it, good or bad. I've seen more than one writer stop his work to concern himself for a year or two or three with the fate of a particular book, then to discover that he had lost the thread. I'm writing the second act of a farce, and that's what I shall try to think about.

Before the Ford [Foundation] fortune came through, I had accepted invitations to give a couple of talks, one at Illinois and another at Chicago in April. After April 24th I aim to take a short holiday. At the beginning of June, we're coming East *en famille*. I realize that you're wondering what the grant amounts to. Well, it's eight thousand a year for two years, and that's nothing to complain about. The Foundation assumes that with this base, I can earn what more I need and suffer no undue anxiety. That's true. But I'll need to do the play, now, and I can't see what objection there is to the magazine. It *excites* me. Isn't that as good as money? And since I won't be teaching it'll be highly beneficial because I need some other kind of interest even when I'm writing.

Naturally, we'll be in Minneapolis for part of next year so that the psychiatry and the neurology can go on. They tell me I'm making great speed, and Sondra too is much better. All's well in the sack, unusually well, and we've begun to feel much affection for each other. So it'd be ridiculous to depart for long from this base. I'll be in and out, next year.

I think the *Times* piece stirred up quite a lot of hornets. That's fine. They've been quietly chewing paper for a long time, undisturbed.

Love to Dorothy.

Yours as always,

Bellow had just published "Deep Readers of the World, Beware!" in The New York Times Book Review.

To Ralph Ellison

[n.d.]   [Minneapolis]

Dear Ralph:

I've been tightly wound up for a few months. It would have done me some good to take the advice I gave you so freely a few years ago and remain above the battle. The fighting about poor *Henderson* has been fierce and wild, and to make matters worse I'm not quite sure where I myself stand. For I'm not in possession of my head and don't know what parts of the book originate in gaiety and which in desperation. It's easy enough to see through the prejudices of critics and to assess their vindictiveness against the new and the unexpected but it's not as though the book occurred as a pure act of the imagination. The worry and the struggle and confusion of mind and feeling of the last two years have muddied it. I know what answer I'd like to give but what bothers me is the strong will to give it and I'm not sure but that the attitude is stronger than all the other elements in *Henderson* together. From this you'll conclude that your friend is badly mixed-up; we must be besotted ere we can become wise, Montaigne says. Yes, but how long, O Lord! And then too the mixture of success and failure is bewildering; it keeps you from being properly besotted, although the moving down that took place last summer should satisfy the most exacting moralist. I'm inclined to set the whole of *Henderson* down to dizziness and begin to think of a new start. [. . .]

I'd like to have something from you in the first issue, part of the novel, if the seacook isn't ready. Maybe you could spare a few pages of the boy preacher. That would be fine. It would give you the advantage also of seeing a little of it in hard print. For me, anyway, that's always valuable; you may feel otherwise.

I hope the house hasn't been troubling you. [. . .] I gathered that the oil bills bothered you. I don't really mind paying them. The expense of the house is altogether pretty small. I get a few hundred dollars a year from my father's estate which just about covers the fuel costs and makes me feel that my old man still gives me shelter. I guess everyone figures these arrangements out according to his own fetishistic devices. A few details: If [Jack] Sarda [the handyman] hasn't cleaned the leaves out of the gutters, he ought to. Also, he and I arranged to have the front stairs and the shutters painted (it should have been done before winter), so would you remind him of that, and also of the aluminum door we discussed for the kitchen? Why do I always connect "artistic temperament" like his with poor performance? I'm beginning to think also of the garden. The strawberry plants must need a little cultivating, and the garden ought to be disked up as soon as the ground dries. The guy at Ed Smith's Service Station (Elmer) always does that for me. The peat and the fertilizer ought to be spread around first, though if you're busy it's no great deal, I enjoy doing that sort of thing, and can look after it in June when we come up.

For the magazine, which we call *The Noble Savage*, we have a few excellent pieces. One by John Berryman on India, one by a young fellow named [Edward] Hoagland (he wrote a book called *Cat Man*) which is very fine, a short thing by Wright Morris, etc. You're listed as a contributing editor. If you have no objection to that would you mind sending to me, or to Aaron Asher at Meridian Books, a little statement giving your consent?

Saw Malamud in Chicago. Unquestionably the right choice for the award. All the best from the queen of the Middle Ages. From me too.

Bernard Malamud's novel The Assistant *had just received the National Book Award for Fiction.*

To Pascal Covici

April 6, 1959   Minneapolis

Dear Dr. Covici:

I'm referring the enclosed letter to you in the faint hope of getting you to heed my will for once. Will you kindly instruct the lady to send not one of those dead-goose pictures which make me look like the Fred Allen of Nicaragua but the laughing photograph which you said you liked but never used? That's a long question because it's so rhetorical. I expect the same old photo to go to Chicago. My prediction is thus on record and the rest is up to you.

The trip to Puerto Rico has had to be called off for psychiatric reasons. Illness in the family. Someone near to me. Myself. No, summer's coming, and we'll be off from Mpls, and next winter we'll probably be in Europe or Asia, so it doesn't make sense to have a holiday now. Anyway, I must get through the play although I haven't much energy to bring to it at this moment. I'm doing my weak best with life on every front. If only the barbarians won't push. Since I speak in Chicago on the 24th and at Pittsburgh on the 29th of this month, I plan to come to NYC directly after the Chicago talk. I'll try to leave the same night so that I can spend Sat., Sun. and Mon. in New York, flying to Pittsburgh on Tuesday and proceeding to Purdue on Thursday, earning seven hundred en route. It'll be very restful to watch the best-seller list no longer. Three weeks. Not much. Still, last letter to me was somewhat puzzling for you said it wouldn't sell a hundred fifty thousand copies. Of course not. But forty? Thirty? Even thirty would be very good. It would pay the mortgage at Tivoli. Best place in the world for suffering. I'll keep it for old age or insanity.

Then is it all right with Dorothy if I appear for a few days towards the end of the month? I promise to make no trouble. I want to see Greg and Lillian Hellman, and perhaps we could spend a day in the country with Ralph Ellison if I can borrow a car or rent one. Samuel S. Goldberg would lend me his Cadillac convertible.

Best regards and love,

To Pascal Covici

[n.d.] [Chicago]

Dear Pat—

I think that Elizabeth Ames and Josephine Herbst, both at Yaddo, never received copies of *Henderson*. Would you ask Rita to check?

Last night I had dinner with Marilyn [Monroe] and her friends at the Pump Room. Today the news sleuths are pumping me. Marilyn seemed genuinely glad to see a familiar face. I have yet to see anything in Marilyn that isn't genuine. Surrounded by thousands she conducts herself like a philosopher.

I heard from Greg this morning. He passed a difficult examination and was admitted to Bronx Science High School. How do you like that!

Yours,

About Marilyn Monroe Bellow would later say, "She was connected with a very powerful current but she couldn't disconnect herself from it. [. . .] She had a kind of curious incandescence under the skin."

To Harvey Swados

April 9, 1959   Minneapolis

Dear Harvey,

Your review of *Henderson* made me happy. There's such a chaos of misunderstanding surrounding it that I feel like cheering when the main points are made out—spirited comedy, here and there edged black with earnestness. I can't agree that it's sentimental at the end—but then, how could I?

Last, I want you to consider writing something for a semi-annual magazine of which I'll be one of the editors. Meridian will publish it and pay contributors five cents a word. I want to make it possible to let off some steam, to write in the good old ranging way that was natural to novelists in the Twenties—in the spirit of *Dial* and the *Mercury, The Enormous Room* or *The American Jitters* (while Wilson yet lived, and before he became the great blimp of *The New Yorker*).

Would it appeal to you to cover the [Floyd] Patterson [–Ingemar Johansson] fight and/or other Garden events? I understand that Cuss Amato, P.'s manager, is a psychologist, so I was told at least. He was described to me as having taught Patterson (fascinating idea) the necessity to feel fear in the ring. I assume P. is naturally free from it.

You'd have a ball. Meridian would buy you tickets and pay for your fare and dinners. Other contributors will be Ellison, Wright Morris, John Berryman, myself, D. H. Lawrence (over his dead body) and other friends of yours. Possibly Arthur Miller. What do you say? I want to see stories, too, of course, but I'm particularly keen about getting writers into the world again. Literature has for too long been their whole life. I hope the book is going well.

All best,

Harvey Swados (1920–72) was a fiction writer best known for Out Went the Candle *(1955) and* Nights in the Gardens of Brooklyn *(1960). His September 1959* Esquire *essay "Why Resign from the Human Race?" is said to have inspired the founding of the Peace Corps. Swados's review of* Henderson the Rain King *had appeared in* The New Leader.

To Fanny Ellison

April 14, 1959   Minneapolis

Dear Fanny,

You're very kind about *Henderson*. Here and there it's as close to frenzy as a man can get while continuing (somehow) to laugh, and it contains elements I hope I've seen the last of. One of these days I'm going to enter the little inner room where my best humanity has been locked up for a long time. Not just yet.

We're all much better than we were. I think it did us nearly as much good to get away from Tivoli as you say it's done Ralph to be there.

I wish you, in all ways, the best of everything.

Your friend,

To Alice Adams

[n.d.]   [Minneapolis]

Dear Alice:

Your story is much better, if no less grim. (*I* should talk.) The spirit in which you wrote makes it very hard to discuss. It's so obviously a last cry of the heart that I don't like to make any technical points. And nevertheless, the story is very "technical," too; both in the good sense and the not-so-good. You are much more of an American than I. There are signs of it all over the place. You do a job of work on the edge of panic. Of your work itself, the writing, I haven't a bad word to say. And I really can't say anything against the story either. Of its kind it is wonderful. There's nothing left to discuss except the kind; which brings us back to the beginning of the paragraph. I don't want to drive tractors into the center of your soul. I think I may be very stupid about this matter, and I must ask you in advance to forgive me.

It's the smallness of the compass that bothers me. The story is cut off from life at one stroke. There's something too breathless about it, and there isn't enough space or air for the emotions. They can't expand and therefore grow painful. Does that make sense? Or let me put it in the old-fashioned and possibly—to you—pompous esthetic terms of unity and diversity. The story lacks diversity, and its very virtues make it intolerable by holding you tightly. Besides, you don't have to write like all the sisterhood since Virginia Woolf. You ought to give up some of the conventions of feminine sensibility.

This may not sound kind, but I assure you all the unkindness is in the sound. For a long time I allowed myself to be pushed into these small spaces, too. I am only urging you to utter the magic syllable "Whoosh" in the face of psychological oppression. The nineteenth century drove writers into attics. The twentieth shuts them in nutshells. The only remedy is to declare yourself king, or queen, of infinite space. There is a word for that too, megalomania, but you have taught me (that's an excellent touch, the fervor with which the girl takes unto herself the various mental diseases) not to worry about that.

I think Sasha and I will blow the West pretty soon. I have to get back East. Not that I look forward to any of it—always excepting my son. Because of a deadline I had to decline Berkeley's invitation to lecture. So we shan't be getting back to San Francisco, alas. How I wish we could.

It was very good of you to try to fix me up with a job. Money is awfully tight these days. Anita is a devil at finance. I, on the other hand, am a damn fool at it. I realize—too late—that I might have had a thousand more out of my Guggenheim if my timidity hadn't prevented. But what'sa use'a talk?

Sure I knew Bill Brown in Paris. I recall that he was fine, jolly and nutty. Whenever he grows serious he wears a look of intensest anguish—right? That's the same guy.

I don't know about [Norman] Mailer. I like him, but he's such an ideologist. I do everything the hard way.

Love,

Alice Adams (1926–99) was an American fiction writer best known for her short stories, collected in After You've Gone *(1989) and* The Last Lovely City *(1999), and for her novel* Superior Women *(1984).*

To Ralph Ellison

[n.d.]   [Minneapolis}

Dear Ralph,

I counted on the two little old dolls to plant the garden, but I suppose spring cleaning was too much for them, those moth-flakes. So I'm going to ask you to go to the Farmer's Coop in Red Hook and buy sweet corn, cucumber and squash seed and plant a few rows, please, reading from left to right tomatoes, about six or eight hills of cucumbers, five or six rows of corn (six should be an even number) and about five hills of squash where the tomatoes used to sit. The rail in the middle of the garden is the worst, as you'll see. There I put in beans last summer to enrich the ground. You can do all this in a few hours and oblige me greatly. It'll keep us all in produce this summer, and give Sasha and me a good reason to go out in the sun.

The mower will never do, I suppose. They're cheaper now, and I may go to Montgomery Ward [. . .] and get one with a guarantee. Money? Somehow it turns up when it's needed, and I've learned to stop thinking about it in excess.

Lettuce, carrots, etc. are raided by rabbits and woodchucks, and to plant them in the open is no use.

If Sarda has pooped out we'd better begin to get bids from others for regular yearly care. We'll close out old randy Jack fairly but inexorably unless he wakes from that long sleep.

I'll be along soon to attack the hares. Hope the garden isn't too demanding. Put in whatever you like, but I'd feel crazy to live in the country without corn and tomatoes. It's bad enough not to have a cow.

Love,

To Bernard Malamud

May 10, 1959   Minneapolis

Dear Bern,

I shy away from all writers' organizations. The PEN is about my limit, and I have doubts about that. No doubt the [Authors] League is fine, but the publisher and the agent aren't the enemy. The enemy (and I'm not horribly hostile towards them, either) is a hundred sixty million people who read nothing. What's the League going to do about them, about Orville Prescott, about TV and Hollywood? It may increase my income by six hundred per annum. I don't care about increasing my income by six hundred per annum. It isn't worth joining an organization for. [. . .]

Best,

To Richard V. Chase

May 27, 1959   [Tivoli]

Dear Mr. Chase:

I find myself in the strange position of one who provokes comment on his behavior and then tries to avoid hearing it. Ordinarily I can't read what people have to say about my writing. But I read your essay with particular satisfaction and agreed with many of your points. Freedom for what? This is the philosophical or religious question I seem to have failed to satisfy. It's a strange thing to be a "cognitive" writer without the will or the capacity to continue to a definite conclusion. I sometimes think the comedy in my books is a satire on this inconclusiveness.

Of course, mere writers of fiction have never been burdened with such responsibilities before, and I doubt that much good art can result from this striving for useful or intellectually acceptable opinion.

Anyway, you've done a good thing for me and I'm very grateful.

Sincerely yours,

Richard V. Chase (1914–62), Columbia University professor of English, was best known for The American Novel and Its Tradition *(1957). His essay "The Adventures of Saul Bellow" had just appeared in* Commentary.

To William Phillips

July 13, 1959   Tivoli, N. Y.

Dear William—

Every few months in *PR* your rats gnaw at my toes. It would be unnatural if I did not notice.

Yrs,

To John Berryman

August 12, 1959   Tivoli

Dear John:

Splendid! Gorgeous! This is the way to reply to the disintegrating fates. I've sent poems and Taj to Meridian, and you shall be rewarded (not in just measure); we are trying to spread our funds to pay all our honorable contributors. Perhaps we ought to publish more Dream Songs—say a dozen. Five will stun—ten would awe. That's as you see fit. I merely ask you to revolve it in your mind.

About the editing: I thought you might like it. As you're a contrib. ed. you won't want to see unworthy poetry in the magazine. There is some good taste on the masthead, but not your authority. At least we can do the screening and obtain your opinion. Wouldn't think of laying a burden on your frail back (frail as whips!).

You will be pleased with most of *Savage*.

Paul and Adam had a great life in the sunshine, both boys naked, tottering after dachshunds and butterflies.

Stay intacto and thrive for the sake of your devoted,

To Josephine Herbst

August 15, 1959   Tivoli

Dear Josie:

Wonderful to get a letter from you. It always brings back my balance, if that should happen to be out, and it often is. You've got more stuff in you than ten ingénues.

Well, I too have stuff, and I get worn out by the dreary people it's somehow become my business to see for whom Despair is shoptalk, like Rinse for the housewife. Damn them all! At a party a few weeks ago, worn out by all the talk, I allowed myself to say something to the man next to me about the human instinct for truthfulness, and he laughed in my face. So I reminded him of Pilate, and then his feelings were hurt. His *feelings*! Phooey!

I never imagined that *Henderson* could be ultimately successful. My state when I wrote it was too bad, going round and round like a centrifuge. Some of it is all right—the language, mostly, and the physical imagination, but I'm aware that it gets mixed up between comedy and earnestness, which is another way of saying that I've got literature mixed up with lots of other matters. That's bad. Out of our greatest needs we've made a big chunk, or ball, and we push, push. Sisyphus was no such damn fool. He was a sinner, but at least he wasn't the author of his own rock. Though psychoanalysis would probably knit its brows and say, But of course he was. What amazes me most about H[enderson] is its reception. It beats me that I should be accused of cunningly willing the whole thing into being. Do these people who are called (but why?) Critics suppose that anyone would *want* to feel as I did? It utterly beats me. I can't imagine what the hell they're up to. *They* are the mystery. Because if they're in outer darkness how did they happen to bring their typewriters with them?

Basta! You seem in good spirits. I'm aware that you have your troubles, but it must be something of a dignity for the troubles to have you. Because, Josie, you are *something*. I love you dearly. I'm waiting to see what you have for us. There may be a little money in it for you, which I'm certain the business people will let you have in advance (before publication). Authority on the *Savage* is shared by three of us, but I holler most. Anyway, I shall be looking in Box 185 every morning for your manuscript.

With love,

To Josephine Herbst

September 5, 1959   Minneapolis

Dear Josie:

I read your piece immediately and wouldn't put it down for any inducement. It's the sort of thing that gives the world a new spin. I see the ants running on the bark with different eyes as I read and know I've fallen in with the real thing. Your piece goes along at first in a plain, truthful fashion and suddenly, without effort or engineering, becomes beautiful.

Here and there I've marked some passages which pleased me less—and they're very few. Perhaps the piece should start with a more dry attack. It takes a little too long. That's probably a result of excision from the book. But everything is supported by feeling, and never in excess, and you're beautifully clear about Hemingway and Dos Passos, and even lesser characters like [Rafael] Alberti. As for the self that comes through, it's the one I fell in love with in Yaddo's plutocratic dining room, *coup de foudre* [*].

I'm sending the manuscript out to the other eds. There are two, and I think I can promise you they'll agree with me.

Much love,

* French: at first sight; lit., thunderbolt

Herbst had submitted "The Starched Blue Sky of Spain," her memoir of the Spanish Civil War. Considered today among the best accounts of that conflict, it would run in the inaugural issue of The Noble Savage.

To John Berryman

[Postmarked Minneapolis, Minn., 8 September 1959]

Dear Pal—

Take it from a well-known lover of beauty—you have the goods.

As for poem-reading—simply append yr note to the editors so that they choose with your consultation. Simple.

As for money—not knowing what funds we command but standing ready to share all, I have asked Meridian to send you in partial payment two hundred fifty dollars.

See you soon.

Nil desperandum [*],

To Ralph and Fanny Ellison

October [?], 1959   Minneapolis

Dear Ralph and Fanny—

Sash and I are no longer together—not by my choice. You saw us together all summer, so you probably understand her decision as well as I. She has no complaint to make of me this time. All she has is a decision. She says she likes me, respects me, enjoys going to bed with me—and no longer wants to be my wife. I have no explanations to offer, only the facts. I don't know what she may have to say. I have to say only that I'm in misery, and especially over Adam.

Please don't speak of this to anyone. She has filed for divorce and I have reason to be glad I'm going away, now. I'll be in Yugoslavia when the divorce becomes final, and I'm grateful to be spared the public part of this, anyway.

Love,

* Latin: Do not despair.

To Keith Botsford

October 15, 1959   Minneapolis

Dear Keith—

By now you'll have heard from Jack [Ludwig]. I have something to tell you with the understanding that it remain *entre nous*. No one here knows that Sash and I have been going through another very bad—a desperate—period. I tell you this because I owe you the truth. You're understandably depressed and you deserve an explanation of my silence. Just now I can't think about the *NS*, nor about writing, mine, yrs, anyone's.

We don't understand each other well, but we can come to understand each other, and deeply. The capacity is there, and so is the desire. You must not think of Jack and me as a faction. We agree upon very little. Personal relations between us are virtually nonexistent. As for Jewishness, Jack calls what he is Jewish and that makes me un-Jewish by definition. For the first time I am trying to ascertain what my Jewish parentage and upbringing really signify. But that, too, is for future discussion, and there will be many discussions. I have great hopes for our friendship.

Yesterday Sash cut her hand so badly with a coffee can that I thought her finger was severed and phoned an ambulance. The gash went to the bone. Five stitches and insanely painful. I'm taking care of Adam now. The [illegible] is not yet. Please forgive me for this note, and please say nothing even to Ann.

Much love,

To Pascal Covici

November 1, 1959   Minneapolis

Dear Pat:

She may not have loved me at all. She certainly doesn't love me now, and perhaps even hates me. When I was weaker there was some satisfaction for her in being the strong one. But when I recovered confidence and loved her more than before, even sexually, she couldn't bear it. So last summer when things seemed at their best they were really, for her, at their worst. Because now she was the sick one. I don't know why she waited until we were settled down in Minneapolis, holding a lease, etc. I guess she leaned somewhat on her psychiatrist. With his support, she was able to tell me she didn't and couldn't love me, and perhaps had never loved anyone except as a child. The psychiatrist doesn't approve of what she's doing, but he's bound to help her and so she's able to make use of him. Anyway she walked into the living room with icy control about three weeks ago and told me she wanted a divorce. There's no one else involved. There doesn't need to be. She does everything on principle, a perfect ideologist. The divorce papers are signed. I'm to pay a hundred fifty a month for the baby, and till the end of the year I'll maintain the house, since it was rented for a year. If she were to change her mind again, I wouldn't change mine. It isn't that I don't love her. I do. But she'd only take the rest of my life, and I'm not ready to part with that. Not yet, even though I've lost her, lost the boy, lost almost everything.

I'm leaving Minneapolis the week of the 15th, and I'll be in New York Thanksgiving week. I expect to fly to England right after the holiday. Due in Warsaw on the 11th of Dec. There I may see misery enough to take my mind off my own grief. It may as well be made useful.

Love to Dorothy—

Yours,

To Richard Stern

November 3, 1959   Minneapolis

Dear Dick—

Delighted with your review, which at last—at first—establishes that it was my aim to make ideas and actions interchangeable. As to whether *Henderson* works, your view is as good as mine. Last night reading Blake, the lost children and especially "A Little Girl Lost," I began to suspect he must have sunk deeply into my unconscious. Add innocence (the second innocence) per experience, passing by way of lions. But really only one book is worth writing now. If we have only to say "humanity stinks in our nostrils" then silence is better, because we have heard *that* news. Our own bones have broadcast it. If we have more than this to say, we may try but never require ourselves to *prove* "—oh, no, that is not shit but the musk of the civet; it smells bad because it's so concentrated. Diluted, it's the base of beautiful perfumes." No amount of assertion will make an ounce of art. So I took a chance with *Henderson*. I can tell you what I wished it to be, but I can't say what it *is*. Every ability was brought to it except one—the talent for self-candor which so far I have been able to invest only in the *language* of what I've written. I should be able to do better than that. People are waiting. My own soul is waiting.

Anyway, I love your review. It comes very, very near the real issues, and it's written in the style I approve of (Biedermeier of ideas).

Now a personal note: I'm having an ugly time—suffering no end. Sondra and I are both in despair over the course things have taken and I *don't* expect a happy ending. This is private. For your eyes only. There are no frigidities, impotencies, adulteries, only miseries. Poor little Adam doesn't know he's about to be sentenced. I can't help him because it has nothing at all to do with me. I love Sash and respect her. But she has drawn the sword, and is just *meshuggah* enough to swing it. And perish by it, maybe. I trust you to say nothing of this anywhere. It would be terrible to have the families drawn into it. [. . .]

I take off for Poland in mid Nov. May stop in Chicago.

Eternellement,

Born in 1928, Richard Stern is the author of many novels including Golk *(1960),* Europe or Up and Down with Baggish and Schreiber *(1961),* Stitch *(1965),* Natural Shocks *(1978),* A Father's Words *(1986) and* Pacific Tremors *(2001). His review of* Henderson the Rain King *had appered in* The Kenyon Review.

To Keith Botsford

November 5, 1959   Minneapolis

Dear Keith—

No, there's really nothing I can do—no remedy that pride prevents me from applying. Nothing can change Sasha's mind. It's she who's doing this, cutting me off, taking away Adam. I can't say for what failures of mine. Not the ordinary ones like money, sex, rivals or any of that. But maybe *because* there have been no such failures. If I were miserably weak, she would pity and protect me. It's what I am that's unbearable to her. The essence of me. So there's no hope. For if my wife doesn't want *that*, what am I to do? Sasha is an absolutist. I think I've loved even *that*, in her. I believe I learned with her to love a woman, and I can't see where or how my heartsickness will end.

Perhaps I could name other subtler failures—I failed to master my own freedom or to interpret the world to the satisfaction of her mind. But for such inadequacies a husband might reasonably expect compassion from his wife. If she loved him. But she doesn't love me.

Your letter made me feel, not for the first time, the bond between us. If I need you, I'll come without hesitation. If you should ever need me (never in this way, I hope) you'll find me reliable.

Much love,

And to Ann. She's silent but I'm aware of her feelings.

To Pascal Covici

November 10, 1959   Minneapolis

Dear Pat—

I wanted to phone, and perhaps I will yet. You know what a thorough sufferer I can be. I not only hit bottom, I walk for miles and miles on it. Instead of growing less my capacity for staying below increases as I grow older. I try very hard to hate Sondra, and I have good grounds, many, many wounds to hate her for. But I'm not very good at it, and I succeed best when I think of her as her father's daughter. For she is Tschacbasov. She has a Tschacbasov heart—an insect heart. But really I love her too much and understand her too well to feel the murderous hatred that would help me (therapeutically). And there's the child. There's no therapy for that. To recover a little happiness will never help me. I need a big victory. It's not inconceivable that I will win—all the small bridges behind me have been burnt.

I'm leaving here Sat. the 14th, and I have to spend a few days in Pittsburgh with Ted Hoffman—to speed through the rest of the play. Must get that over with. I have a book to write, and I must clear the decks. [. . .]

Please hold whatever mail you get for me. I've given your address. And send the new Act I to Hellman. Did you receive it?

Thank God, I'll be out of this by Sat., teeth filled, pockets empty.

Much love,

To Richard Stern

December 15, 1959   [Bonn, W. Germany]

Dear Dick—

I've blown into Bonn with wind and snow. It's colder than Poland, more comfortable than Chicago, richer than Croesus and prouder than Sondra. In fact, my travels in totalitarian lands have taught me more about marriage and "love" than Franz Alexander could. I go to round out my studies in Yugoslavia and Italy. Then I'm going to have a two-week holiday in Israel.

Is life treating you? *Bitte vergessen Sie mich nicht* [*].
Yours,

Franz Alexander (1891–1964) was a prominent psychoanalyst at the University of Chicago.

To John Berryman

December 17, 1959
[Postcard from Bristol Hotel Kempinski
Berlin W15—Kurfürstendamm 57]

Dear John—

[. . .] Greet my friends and check on mine enemies. Lecturing is for the birds. St. Francis understood.

Love,

* German: Please don't forget me.

PART THREE

1960–1969

————◆•◆•◆►————

Because, you see, intelligence is free now (he said), and it can start anywhere or go anywhere. And it is possible that he lost his head, and that he was carried away by his ideas. This is because he was no mere dreamer but one of those dreamer-doers, a guy with a program. And when I say that he lost his head, what I mean is not that his judgment abandoned him but that his enthusiasms and visions swept him far out.

—Henderson the Rain King

1960

To Pascal Covici

January 18, 1960   Belgrade

Dear Pat—

Yesterday when I arrived in Yugoslavia, there was no mail at all. Can it be that Sondra hasn't forwarded it, or that you've got my schedule mixed up? I'll be in Yugoslavia until about Feb 1st. And I have a feeling there's something very wrong in Minneapolis. I've written separately to four people, one of them the psychiatrist, asking for news but haven't had a single answer. From Jack Ludwig I received a letter in Warsaw one-sentence-long saying only that Adam was well—as of Dec 28th or so. Can you find out for me what the situation is? Air mail to Belgrade takes only four days. This universal silence makes me afraid. The news must be awful. Jack would tell you, if you phone him, whether I ought to come back.

Yours,

To Ralph Ellison

January 20, 1960   Belgrade

Dear Ralph,

I'm much better. I'm beginning to sit up and take solid nourishment, and I'd enjoy my convalescence greatly if I didn't have to do this cultural functionary bullshit. But even that has its compensations. I wouldn't have minded Poland—particularly Poland—for all the meetings and lectures and teas and whisky I had to wade through. Eastern Europe has told me a lot about my family—myself, even. It's made a Slavophile of me.

About Adam I never hear. I phoned Minneapolis finally, and spoke to the psychiatrist. From Macedonia. This was Macedonia's first call to Mpls. Adam's all right. He'll even out—he's built for it. [. . .]

How's the book? How's Fanny?

My love to the three of you.

To Pascal Covici

January 22, 1960   Belgrade

Dear Pat—

The reason for the wire was that no bills had been forwarded and I didn't want Ralph to have an awkward time with the oil company. But the stuff arrived today. Never a word about Adam. Never. I had to phone Minneapolis—the psychiatrist—from Skopje in Macedonia (very near Romania). Adam's fine.

There was so little room for deterioration when I left New York that it's easy now to say I'm better. I really am. I've even begun to sleep again, without drugs. And I met a young lady in Poland—well, not so young, but lovely—who comforted me well. I thought also she had given me the clap, and I was very proud but the doctor in Warsaw said it was only a trifling infection. The clap *can* be arranged, I suppose, if a man has a serious ambition to get it. I'm just a dilettante.

As for work, I've been doing a little, picking at the play and writing a story. My stories aren't very successful. They always turn into novels, because one thing leads to another. I suppose I lack a sense of form. Well, now that I realize, perhaps I can begin to study the matter. If a critic were to say it, I'd ignore him. The story *is* about Sondra, and it may be a trial run, who knows? First I must stop in my travels. I'd better come home, I think, and file my taxes and move East and complete the play and start the book. And begin my life. More and more I feel that I haven't yet got under weigh. When, O Lord?

Next week I dash through Italy. Write me c/o Cultural Affairs U.S. Embassy, Rome. I haven't the time to shop for trinkets. Yugoslav tableware is awful. Would Dorothy like some Serbian embroidery? Good, I'll get her some. On Feb. 15th I sail to Haifa (U.S. Embassy, Jerusalem) and on March 3rd, Rome and on March 18th London again and on March 22nd or so home.

Love,

To Ralph Ross

February 4, 1960   [en route]

Dear Ralph—

On the train from Ljubljana to Venice I am suddenly struck by a motive of prudence—the first in several years. You advised me to get a lawyer in Mpls. and I think you were absolutely right. I can't trust Jonas Schwartz

[Sondra's lawyer], and I don't know what arrangements he will think just. No reason why I should allow him to do any thinking for me.

This is a major pain in the neck to you, I know; this is the price you must pay for being the most reliable friend I have in Mpls.

Can you get a lawyer to look after my interests? The case is simple to describe: 1.) Sondra has abandoned me but 2.) I am willing to let her have a divorce on two conditions: a.) that I pay no more than a hundred fifty a month for Adam and b.) that I have the right to visit Adam regularly and to have him with me during his holidays. Should the lawyer need more information he can reach me c/o Cultural Affairs U.S. Embassy, Rome till Feb. 1st, or Tel Aviv till March 1st. After March 1st, I'll be in Rome again for a week. Then London, then home.

Have you become parents yet? I hope everything is going well. In the first days of your fatherhood I hesitate to bring upon you my post-graduate tribulations. But life is pushing at my back. And I suppose it's a good sign that I've decided to defend myself, finally. I can tell you without the distortion of optimism that I'm very well. Now. Since Poland.

The train is bucking its way into Trieste.

Goodbye,

Love,

I was greatly comforted in Warsaw.

Ralph Ross was a philosopher and much-loved teacher at New York University and, subsequently, at the University of Minnesota.

To Richard Stern

[Postmark illegible; postcard from Venice—Piazza San Marco] Today—special for Bellow—Venice has a snowstorm. God salts my every bite. Just the same it *is* Italy. Even the irrigation ditches are dug with sensitivity.

Be all my sins remembered,

To Pascal Covici

March 4, 1960   Tel Aviv

Dear Boss—

I'm flying out of here today, filled with impressions and tired out. Stranger pilgrimages have been made, but few so fatiguing. I'm down about twenty lbs. and ready to go back to my business, which is to be fatter and to write books. I've had too much of sights and flights, and girls. Still I wanted to wear myself out, and I'm well satisfied with the results I've gotten.

There's hardly anything I do as well as I know I can and that includes traveling. I'm still waiting for my life to begin. However, I'm nearer to a beginning than I've ever been. [. . .]

Is everything well with you? Do you want regards from Billy Rose (Ben Hecht's friend)? Everyone comes to Israel. You should, too. Get a real Romanian meal.

Remember me to Dorothy,

With love,

Bellow had evidently seen the impresario Billy Rose in Israel. Thirty years later, Rose would turn up in the Jerusalem sequence of The Bellarosa Connection.

To Ralph Ellison

March 8, 1960   Rome

Dear Ralph—

While you were being blasted by snow, I was in the Red Sea staring at tropical fish through the glass bottom of a boat. Have you had a rough time at Tivoli this winter? I read that this has been another blizzard of '88, and I have visions of you and Rufus [the Ellisons' dog] snowbound and Bill Lensing heading a rescue party.

But these events are always worse in the papers.

Is the *Savage* out? Is the book going again? Is Fanny well? I hope the answers are all of the best.

I'm away again tomorrow. Paris, London and on the 22nd NYC. Two days to see Greg and I go to Washington and Chicago and Mpls. There I expect to stay a month (six weeks!), get divorced, kiss Adam, and towards the end of May join you in Tivoli.

Perhaps Jack Wheeler can do the bedrooms upstairs while you're away in Chicago. What are your dates there?

Best love,

To Marshall Best

March 16, 1960   London

Dear Marshall:

[. . .] As to my own writing and the Ford Foundation—I've been writing while traveling. I always manage to keep at it. Besides, if I hadn't gone off in November I might now be in the loony bin and not in London. This has a metaphorical sound but I mean it literally. You might as well hear from me what I assume you've heard from Pat [Covici] or Harold [Guinzburg]. In October, my wife asked me for a divorce and I almost cracked. It was entirely unexpected. Then I decided almost instinctively that I'd better get away and for that reason accepted the offer of this trip, and I'm anything but sorry, for I'm fit again. It's not certain that I'd have done much writing in Mpls. Probably I'd have mouldered at my desk, trying. You know that I'm not reckless and irresponsible and that I wouldn't go off on a toot abandoning all work and responsibility. An emergency arose and I met it as well as I could.

Many thanks for your letter.

See you soon,

Marshall A. Best (1901–82) was editor and later chairman of the executive committee at the Viking Press.

To Marshall Best

March 17, 1960   London

Dear Marshall:

Brooding about your letter, I can see the whole thing clear. You recommend me to the Ford Foundation, and my gay lark in Europe puts you in a tough position. But suppose it hasn't been a gay lark? Suppose I have been dutifully suffering my way from country to country, thinking about Fate and Death? Will that do as an explanation? And if, here and there, I gave a talk in Poland and Yugoslavia, did I violate the by-laws?

All jokes aside, what I saw between Auschwitz and Jerusalem made a change in me. To say the least. And that ought not to distress the Ford Foundation. I'm sorry to cause you any embarrassment, but there ought not to be any in my going to Europe and the Middle East for a few months. Now I'm coming back to write a book, and I see nothing wrong anywhere. I might have written a thousand pages in Minneapolis and thrown them all away. I know I've done the necessary and proper thing and it annoys me to be criticized for it.

All best,

To Alice Adams

April 9, 1960   Tivoli

Dear Alice—

They held your letter for me till I got back from Europe where I had gone for five months to get over the shock of divorce. This time it was done unto me (as I had done unto others). All this marrying and parting amounts to idiocy. Nobody will do well, nobody is well. We all prescribe suffering for ourselves as the only antidote for unreality. So—I've emptied bottles and bottles, and now I'm going to dig in at Tivoli, my *feste Burg,* my asylum, and reconsider everything all over again.

Love,

To Susan Glassman

May 5, 1960   [Tivoli]

Dear Susan:

No, I haven't forgotten to write, only I've been so pressed, harried and driven, badgered, bitched, delayed (and even—in Maryland—taken into custody by the State Police) that I haven't even had time to sit down and cross my legs. Till now, in Tivoli. Good old Tivoli. There are so many ghosts in this old joint that my own, in new sheets, are like laughable freshmen. Come, we'll cut the grass and play croquet with spooks.

Love,

To Stanley Elkin

May 13, 1960   Tivoli, N.Y.

Dear Mr. Elkin:

I approve very highly of your story and am sending it on to the other editors with the hope that they will share my admiration for it. I'll let you know their decision as soon as I know it myself.

Sincerely yours,

P.S. I particularly liked the grocery on 53rd Street and the employees and shoppers, but I was not at all sure that the last passages really bore the accumulated weight. It is too easy to float to a conclusion with the support of certain Jewish symbols. I am a little bit suspicious of the use you make of them.

Elkin's story was "Criers and Kibitzers, Kibitzers and Criers." It would appear in Perspective *rather than in* The Noble Savage.

To Herbert and Mitzie McCloskey

[n.d.]   [Tivoli]

Dear Herb and Mitzie,

I'm sure you made the right decision abt Mpls. Time to bust out. It had given you about all it could give. Anyway, change is one of my elements—money for Morgan, fire for phoenixes and salamanders, and new addresses for me. *Ergo!*

I'll spare you the sad details of my visit to Mpls. I crept back to Tivoli, where I'm by myself, with too much on my mind to fill the solitude yet. I'm winding up the play *The Last Analysis*. I am getting ready to write a novel. Now that I've been thrown out of middle-class security I can't avoid being a writer. Though I'm one of the finest avoiders in the land.

Greg and Adam are fine, and I'm not too bad. I miss all of you. I hope you're all well and have had an end of bad news. Send me a note or at least a copy of the Soviet book. Now the gov't. admits espionage, I don't see why they didn't supply you with material.

Much love to all of you.

On May 1, 1960, a U-2 spy craft had been shot down over Sverdlovsk by a Soviet surface-to-air missile. President Eisenhower initially claimed that it was a weather plane. When Khrushchev announced a week later that the pilot, Francis Gary Powers, was alive and the aircraft mostly intact, Eisenhower was forced to acknowledge that the United States had been conducting espionage flights. McCloskey and John E. Turner had just published their book The Soviet Dictatorship.

To Susan Glassman

May 31, 1960   Tivoli

Dearest Susie—

Guilt smote me when I got back. The train looked seedy. I might at least have gone on it with you. I suppose I was exercising my power of autonomy. Anyway, love is better to feel than guilt. In future, I'll try to be reasonable though human.

When I returned the Ashers arrived. They might have phoned en route!

Susie, we had a beautiful time. A beautiful time is its own reward.

Immer dein [*],

To Susan Glassman

June 9, 1960   [Tivoli]

I'm a little bit miserable today. Lillian H[ellman] admires what I've written but insists it's not a play. Well, perhaps it's not. It's a pity to have wasted so much time, but (I'm great at finding compensations—it's so Jewish) I wasn't *fit* to write anything else last year.

And then, one more reason for misery. I think Sondra is getting married [to Jack Ludwig] in October, which makes her conduct throughout even worse. She didn't have to try to demolish me in order to re-marry. Ach! It's not a great deal, but it's something and temporarily it depresses me.

You un-depress me. I feel better already, Susie. [. . .]

With kisses and only slightly sad smiles.

Yours,

Sondra Tschacbasov and Jack Lugwig would not marry in October, or ever.

To Susan Glassman

June 15, 1960   [Tivoli]

Dearest Susie:

The Burroughs [novel, *Naked Lunch*] is shocking for a few pages and then becomes laughable because it's so mechanical. Grand Guignol. It doesn't have much human content, and I think it's just the other side of all the "niceness" and "cleanliness" and "goodness" in the country. On one side the scrubbers and detergent-buyers, and on the other the dirty boys, equally

---

* German: Ever thine

anal. Black and white are the colors of paranoia, nothing in between. If I'm using clinical language, it's because *Naked Lunch* forces it on me. It's clinical. And that would be all right if it were the beginning of something. Raskolnikov must have been crazy, but he was more. Here there isn't more. But I was glad of a chance to read it. Do you want it sent back?

The trouble I have reading your letters brings me to this machine. My handwriting is nearly impossible, too.

Yes, it took me an awfully long time to grow up, but I take comfort from Vol. II of [Ernest] Jones on Freud which begins "In 1901 Freud, at the age of forty-five, had attained complete materity, a consummation of development that few people really achieve." So there, I can't even *spell* maturity. One of these days I'll tell you all about my therapeutic adventures. Of course I sat in a box. It removed the warts from my fingers.

All week I've felt like a man who is trying to fill a test tube under Niagara. It's not a bad simile. The rain has bent everything double for three days and I feel very wet and peevish. But your letter this morning was a very fine stimulant.

Immer dein,

To Leslie Fiedler

June 24, 1960   Tivoli

Dear Leslie:

I've just read your [Karl] Shapiro piece in *Poetry,* and I really think you're way out. How you got there I don't know but it's time to come back. I'm in earnest. You have a set of facts entirely your own, and you interpret people's motives most peculiarly. What is this "marketable" Jewishness you talk about? And who are these strange companions on the bandwagon that plays *Hatikvah?* It's amusing. It's utterly wrong. It's (I don't like the jargon but it can't be avoided here) Projection. What you think you see so clearly is not to be seen. It isn't there. No big situations, no connivances, no Jewish scheme produced by Jewish Minds. Nothing. What an incredible *tsimis* [*] you make of nothing! You have your own realities, no one checks you and you go on and on. You had better think matters over again, Leslie. I'm dead serious.

Fiedler had just published "On the Road; or the Adventures of Karl Shapiro" in Poetry.

* Yiddish: a sweetened dish of stewed fruits and vegetables; fig., an imbroglio

To Susan Glassman

June 29, 1960 [Tivoli]

Dearest Susie,

All present and accounted for. I think I've found the right channel and I'm feeling very cheerful. That is, I'm too busy to dwell on being cheerful, but I must be cheerful somewhere below, in the engine room. More soon.

With Sondra, I've had the regulation four-bladed duel about seeing Adam, and after being stabbed only a few times I am being allowed to have him for a week in Chicago, in August. I'm getting off easy. (She doesn't bleed except in the natural course.)

Is *Augie March* such a drone? Hmmm! I don't know, myself. I made the discovery in it about language and character from which *Henderson* arose but *Augie* itself is probably crude. My *Ur-Faust*. In the evening of life, about thirty years from now, I may amuse myself by doing it right. I still love Grandma, Einhorn, Simon, Mimi!! And Mintouchian. And the eagle.

To Susan Glassman

July 4, 1960 [Tivoli]

Dearest Susie:

No, nothing at all wrong, only the unusual usual. Toil, tears, sweat and business-wriggling: I seem to be a great operator on a small sector. That is, I've always lived like a sort of millionaire without money. Never any question of "neediness" on the one side nor of greediness on the other. Somehow I've managed to do exactly what I like. There are certain philosophers (Samuel Butler, if he is one) who say we really do get what we want. Question: Can we bear it when we get it? That's the question that's the beginning of religion.

No, darling, I'm very well. I hope you are, too, and that you look forward to the 15th as I do.

To John Berryman

July 4, 1960 Tivoli

Dear John—

Not bad, now. I'm divorced and better for it. One madness at a time. It's the least Justice can allow us. And I'm writing something, too.

Savage #2 has gone to the printer, and very good, though not as good as it would have been with the Taj, which we had to lay over till *#3*, so you'll probably appear with Vachel Lindsay and me instead of D. H. Lawrence and Louis Guilloux.

Are you really coming to visit me in Tivoli? It'd be a great event. I am not likely to be in Mpls. much. Perhaps to see Adam now and then, though if that is "played" on me, or if my veins are going to be used to string Sondra's harp, the child and I will not see much of each other.

Don't you think the Bennington alumnae association owes us both wound-stripes?

Say hello to McCloskeys. And write down those squibs for [*Savage*] #3. What did you think of #1? You've never said.

Transcontinental blessings,

To Edmund Wilson

July 30, 1960   Tivoli, N.Y.

Dear Edmund—

I understand from Monroe Engel that you like the *Noble Savage*. This encourages me to ask you for a contribution. I think you would find yourself in good company.

With best wishes,

To Susan Glassman

September 1, 1960   [Tivoli]

Baby, I know you're going through all kinds of difficulty, enough to account for all the strange phenomena. It is all the more important now that I should not lose my bearings, too, and you should not be displeased by my holding on to them. One of us must, if we're not both to be overboard. I do have myself in pretty good order, and I can help you when you come East. Much that seems very difficult to you will look fairly elementary to me, and as long as we keep this balance we needn't fear panic on all fronts. The move East is *not* so hard. Towards your parents you've always had an independent bearing but you've never been independent in naked fact. Well, that's not so difficult. What will be more formidable will be making a life of your own in a strange city, but that's not too awful either, once you've seen the world. And you *have* seen it, and it's the world you've got to cope with, not NYC or Chicago. Besides, in me you have a friend. I've never refused my friendship, now have I? I said I wasn't going to write a letter, and I've gone and done it. Shows how much I know my own mind. But I've got myself tranquil at the center, somehow. Maybe it's my convalescence. And it doesn't even bother me to be ignorant of my next moves.

Be my sweet and balanced Dolly.

To Alice Adams

[n.d.]   [Tivoli]

Dear Alice -

I'm very sorry to hear of this, and I hope you're better. I always have more to say about life when it's myself that's in trouble. The most useful thing perhaps I can say is that I've always had a great liking for you and thought you very vital, a woman evidently built to make it.

Sometimes what I'm sorriest about and most puzzled by is this feminine belief that one makes it in love, only in love, and that love is a kind of salvation. And then women, and sometimes men, too, demand of each other everything—everything! And isn't it obvious by now that no human being has the power to give what we require from one another. When I saw that, the external world began to come back. My great need had made it almost disappear.

I hope the worst of this is over for you, or will soon be: I hate to think of you suffering. Never mind what I said earlier. I said that for myself. For you I'd prefer something else.

Yours very affectionately,

To Alice Adams

September 10, 1960   [Tivoli]

Dear Alice -

The only sure cure is to write a book. I have a new one on the table and all the other misery is gone. This is the form any refusal to be unhappy takes now, and I suppose it saves me from a merely obstinate negative. Because it isn't merely for oneself that one should refuse a certain alternative. It's also because we owe life something.

Do you ever come East? I don't think I'll be in SF for a while. In January I go to Puerto Rico to teach for four months. My first assignment in more than two years.

Don't fly through these parts again without notifying me.

Yours affectionately,

To Keith Botsford

October 4, 1960   [Tivoli]

Dear Keith,

[. . .] I want the magazine to go on, want it badly, but I haven't come up to expectations, and have to go into this with myself very honestly. This is a great age for sleepers, myself snoozing with the rest, now and then sending out a call to awaken. No, it's not as bad as all that, but it's not what I had planned and hoped. But let's not quit yet. [. . .]

All the best,

Love,

To the John Simon Guggenheim Memorial Foundation

October 12, 1960   Tivoli, N.Y.

Dear Mr. Ray:

Thank you for your letter. I've seen lots of stuff since I was so rash as to become an editor—new stuff, that is. Most of it is pretty poor, of course, but there are six or eight young writers, relatively unknown, who are first-rate. James Donleavy who wrote *The Ginger Man* is to my mind one of our best writers. I don't think his book sold well, and I can't say how he supports himself. Then there's Grace Paley (*The Little Disturbances of Man*), a housewife with two or three children and a husband who earns a rather modest living. Thomas Berger who wrote *Crazy in Berlin* is very good; so is Richard G. Stern, author of *Golk*. I'm sorry you were unable to give a fellowship to Leo Litwak who applied last year. He's *got* it, I think, and he should be encouraged to apply again. I hope this list will be useful to you.

With best wishes,

Gordon Ray had succeeded Henry Allen Moe as president of The Guggenheim Foundation.

To Jonas Schwartz

October 19, 1960   Tivoli

Dear Jonas:

Wise of you to write. If I had the dough I'd be glad to accept your kind offer. But I can't have checks bouncing, and right now I'm broke. The play is no more, and I owe Viking ten grand. I'll find the dough and get it to you next month. As for Adam, he can always count on his monthly check. I love that boy, and I have a hunch that in the end that love is going to count for more in his life than the "protection" of lawyers and courts. But I don't want to get into an argument with you; I'm fond of you and I think your heart is in the right place. The thing is over, though as a father I think you may understand that against my better judgment I sometimes long for Adam. I haven't seen him since August nor have I heard about him. In October I got a wire from Sondra—SEND MONEY AT ONCE—giving me the new address. I had sent it to the old because I didn't have the new. The money goes out regularly, and so do requests for one word of news about the child. I ask also for my recorders, one of them a gift from Isaac which I have kept and used for twenty years. No answer. Jonas, is it criminal of me that she decided to divorce me? Is it nothing that I'm the child's father? Do I have to be slandered and smeared in Minneapolis? I know that you [. . .] think she's a darling girl. I happen to think differently. But I don't want to win an argument with you, vindicate myself or damn her. I want to make a deal to send the checks regularly on the 1st provided I get one postcard a month about Adam. I see no point in being unilaterally obliging. So the answer to your generous proposal is no, until such time as my feelings towards Adam are recognized. I am something more than an automatic source of checks. I am a *mensch*. I tried to be a husband to that poor castrating girl—an odd desire, but I had it. Now that I've lost it I am, on that side at least, a happier man. All right, no more infancy, no more self-pitying grief, but for every concession I make there'll have to be a concession traded from here on in.

I'm glad your children are doing so well. They're good girls, both of them, and do you [. . .] credit. Don't worry about Berryman. He's the soul of honor in everything that involves his responsibilities as a teacher, and I can assure you that Miriam [Schwartz's daughter] will be treated fairly. Poets are a strange breed. Greet the bourgeoisie of Minneapolis for me. They all come to your cellar to drink your whiskey and enjoy your emotional outbursts.

I have arthritis of the cervical spine, and headaches, but apart from that I am in good heart and working well. I see Greg often. Last week he told me he had Sondra's word for it that I am a rat but he loves me just the same.

Yours in Christ,

To Richard Stern

[n.d.] [Tivoli]

Dear Dick:

Herzog has got me down. As sometimes happens by the hundredth page, my lack of planning, or the subconscious cunning, catch up with me, and so I'm back in Montreal in 1922, trying to get a drunk to bed and I'm not sure I'll know what to do once he's sleeping. God will provide. Consider the lilies of the field—do they write books? [. . .]

Suddenly Greg, who is a junior, says he'd like to attend the U[niversity] of C[hicago]. He's got good grades in everything except trigonometry, he tells me. As soon as the Bellows have learned to add a check at Walgreen's they lose interest in mathematics. Are there any scholarships he could put in for? [...]

Yours from the perihelion of his orbit,

To Gertrude Buckman

October 22, 1960   Tivoli

Dear Gertrude,

I'm no longer in a position to give you much news of Delmore, because he now has me in his subversive files. He accuses me of slandering him and, when last heard from, was threatening me with a lawsuit. I had asked a friend of mine from the Payne Whitney Clinic to visit him at Bellevue and although Delmore received this man without hostility, he seems later to have worked it out in his mind that I had meant to railroad him. Dr. Hatterer's opinion was that Delmore was not in need of extended treatment and what he mainly needed was a period of rest. There was no need therefore for Delmore to enter Payne Whitney which never accepts patients for periods shorter than three months. Anyhow no one had authority to intervene for Delmore and he was, and so far as I know still is, at the mercy of the lawyers and detectives he has hired, and the creeps whose good offices are always free and always available. I hope with all my heart that they won't hurt him, that he will not hurt himself. He seems to have devised for himself a system for survival in the midst of crises he generates himself—the eye of the cyclone or the brink of disaster. That's a very crowded brink. My own life is usefully quiet. I suppose that means that I am out of things. I couldn't be gladder. Thanks for the book you sent; one of these days I shall certainly read it, but just now I am writing one myself which I hope you will have the charity to read when it comes out.

Best wishes,

To John Berryman

[Postmarked Tivoli, N.Y., 23 November 1960]

Dear John,

Wouldn't you like to sing an aria or two in the next *Savage*? That department is the weakest; it needs your strengthening voice. I'm contributing several pieces. The other editors are in drydock. But I myself, more barnacles than hull, go on. The younger generation rates zero; we aging writers are the whole hope of the future.

Give out.

Saw your old pal [R. P.] Blackmur at Yale last week, and he is even older. He drops lighted cigarettes in the furniture and slowly searches for them. This made good sport for the sober watchers. I was one.

Rispondi, amico! [*].

We have two weeks.

To Susan Glassman

November 30, 1960   [Tivoli]

Carissima! Washington, Wed Dec 21st at 8:40. What-what-what? Yours in frenzied speed,

Bellow the Rocket, with a rocket's love!

To Richard Stern

December 10, 1960   Tivoli

Dear Dick—

This is very good news, all of it. Congratulations! And congratulate Gay for me (if she knows that I know). I belong to the increase-and-multiply school myself, sons-of-Abraham division. As for the books, they'll give you a fixed place on the map, and in these backward times that's not so easy to obtain.

Herzog is like Old Man River, he don't say nothing. You and me we sweat and strain but he empties into the Gulf. We're close to the halfway mark. And I'm getting ready to take off for Puerto Rico. [. . .]

All the best,

To the John Simon Guggenheim Memorial Foundation

27 December 1960   Tivoli, N.Y.

CONFIDENTIAL REPORT ON FELLOWSHIP CANDIDATE

Name of Candidate: Mrs. Grace Paley

An excellent writer, fresh, original, independent, clear in her aims. She's written some stunning stories. In speaking of "fresh news" Mrs. Paley does not exaggerate. I have published one chapter from her novel in the magazine

---

* Italian: Answer, friend!

I edit. If I were a publisher I'd like to publish her book. I hope the Foundation will help her to finish it.

To Mark Harris

[n.d.]

Dear Mark—

When my father died I was for a long time *sunk*. I hope you're a wiser sufferer. My business is survival, with pain unavoidable.

By now I'm far better. Thanks for job offer. Have to say no.

All best,

1961

To Susan Glassman

[January 15, 1961]   [Rio Piedras, Puerto Rico]

Dolly: I am away, spectacles, testicles, wallet and watch. [. . .] I miss you already. I'm going out now to lunch with Keith, who just blew in.

Till tomorrow.

To Susan Glassman

January 16, 1961   [Rio Piedras]

On the plane, only I had bathed. There were three hundred passengers and six hundred children. Next to me a priest smoked cigars. He had a dozen in his upper coat pocket and said that'll be just about enough for the trip. Then came cold supper. Ham wrapped around asparagus, roast beef in red something and glazed chicken breast with a first lieutenant's stripe in red pimento. After which coffee-flavored French pastry. Everybody dying of heat and finally PR almost on time. Your absence made me take two sleeping pills, from which I haven't yet recovered. So till tomorrow your glad lover looks with dazed eyes at the mango trees. This is like nowhere else. I feel like little Gray Sambo.

Last night my pillow was you—a poor substitute. Particulars follow. Eat! Don't fret!

Love,

To Susan Glassman

January 18, 1961 [Rio Piedras]

Dolly—

I am writing on one of the consecrated pages, two Cuba libres in me at Botsfords' tennis club, tropical sunset, the Caribbean like a sublime footpath behind, and the palm trees doing their job in front. There are problems (O heavy word!). I need a car, a house, a stone, a leaf and a door. The island is marvelous. You will fall in love with it, being of an open nature. You will. It's going to be a great March. Must, however, find a place to live. Keith was too confident about the places available. Wants me to live with him forty-five minutes out and with three kids, and maid, and no car. I see now that a Vespa is suicidal. This driving makes Rome and Paris look like Wellesley and Vassar. [. . .]

The wire was signed Pres.-elect and MRS. Kennedy.

Love,

Bellow evidently refers to an invitation to John F. Kennedy's inauguration delivered by Western Union.

To Susan Glassman

January 23, 1961   [Rio Piedras]

Dolly—

I'm getting nowhere that I can see. One week in Puerto Rico and my inquiring mind's very well satisfied. I'd be happy to return, but no, the grille is down now and I must try to wake up from this pressing, beautiful heat—everlasting summer—and the depressed sense of having come out of the movies at midday. I haven't yet found a place. The Botsfords are kind, the kids lovely, the Puerto neighbors friendly and all that jazz, but I am on the turntable with no music coming forth. And I begin to miss you badly.

I've fought the good fight against the tropics. People advise me to rest more and give up the Northern tempo. I realize I adore running and dislike repose. Now I've seen bananas growing. Okay! Shall I lie under a tree with eyes shut and mouth open like a child and let the lizards chase over me?

And I really do miss you—even your earnestness; sometimes it has struck me funny, but I miss it.

Write me, Susie, I need to hear something good from you.

Love,

To Ralph Ross

Dear Ralph—

The scandal on the grapevine from Mpls. evidently isn't all contra-Bellow. Well, well—it has its amusing aspect, even. All these senseless old words like *adultery* and *infidelity* and *love honor obey*. Well, you told me I didn't understand the fabric of society and a word to the wise has made a student of me. Not a cynic, but a student.

[Ted] Hoffman tells me you were great at Carnegie [Tech]. Did you want that fancy job? I thought it no harm to put your name in the hopper.

Puerto Rico is a long way from the Jacks and Jills and Jonases. It suits me fine. I have general friends, all-purpose friends, a *dear* friend, and I'm writing a book, growing a new life the way newts grow tails.

Best to Alicia.

Yours ever,

To Ralph Ellison

[n.d.]   [Rio Piedras]

Dear Ralph:

It's great here in the tropics. I look out and see the little birds cringe in the mahogany tree as the helicopter swoops over. This is, and for once Kazin had it right, one of the most noisy places in the entire world. But one must rise above ordinary complaints. Perhaps the noise means something, and I try to tune in. Meanwhile I go on, looking for a place to live, and that's not simple here either. There's a great shortage in winter because of the vacationists from New York. And nevertheless I keep going, and drift with the stray dogs and the lizards and wonder how many ways a banana leaf can split. The dog population is Asiatic—wandering tribes of mongrels. They turn up in all the fashionable places, and in the modern university buildings, the cafeterias—there are always a few hounds sleeping in a cool classroom, and at night they howl and fight. But with one another, not with the rats, another huge population, reddish brown and fearless. You see them in vacant lots downtown, and at the exclusive tennis club at the seashore. I won't be surprised to see them at the crap table, watching the game. Then there is the mongoose clan. They eliminated the snakes, but now no one knows what to do about their raids on the chickens. So much for the zoology of this place. The island is beautiful The towns stink. The crowds are aimless, cheerful, curious and gaudy. Drivers read at the wheel, they sing, they eat and they screw while driving. Keith had an accident last week. So far, in his little Volkswagen (with ninety thousand miles on it) I've escaped. But I should get clipped soon. What else? I miss Susie, but badly. I hope she'll be able to come down soon.

Write me a note. And can you keep the Tivoli post office supplied with those large manila envelopes for forwarding?

Remember me to Fanny.

All best,

To David Peltz

February 2, 1961   Rio Piedras, Puerto Rico

Dear Dave—

Don't ask! But Division St. seems to have made us of iron, and we survive it all. But, to the point: A very good friend of mine, Hannah Arendt, at Northwestern as visiting lecturer, wants to see Chicago. Can you show her interesting things? She's great. Perhaps you've read her stuff. Well over fifty—Phyllis needn't worry.

Love,

To Susan Glassman

February 8, 1961   [Rio Piedras]

Dolly, from your nutty but devoted and adoring lover, here are a few pages more of this impossible *Herzog* whom I love like a foster brother. I'm sorry about *your* brother. I feel so very loving towards you I could take the whole thing on myself and give you a rest under the sun—lying on the sand, well loved and recovering from the snows and grief of New York. *Sacre bleu!* What a jerk I am. But since I have gone off on you, let's make the most of the climate, anyway. Let us cling to the climate and to each other.

Now sweetheart, list. The name of the woman at Dell is Elizabeth Shepherd. Thank heaven I've got that down without fucking up the spelling; never was there such a fucky-knuckled character. Tear up as many of the books as you have and give them to her, and when you come down we'll draft the introduction and it'll pay for the expensive apartment we'll have to take. But the hell with that. Money will be found. There are always more windfalls. Now the CBC has paid me an unexpected three hundred to produce [my one-act play] "The Wrecker" on TV. I should knock off a few of those little things. They earn one a lot of money over the long pull. So if one must pay two hundred fifty, one pays two hundred fifty. I'm so greedy to see you, I can't maintain the normal greed. We'll work matters out.

I've gotten a very clever and affectionate card from Greg about his grades (quite high) and I don't see how I can turn down the U. of C.—because of him. He's applied for a scholarship. So the money I'm paid there will be the least of it. As for you and me, dolly, I am not supposing that by next winter there'll be such a problem ab't Chicago as you anticipate. Boy, the ambiguity of this Bellow! But I love you very much, Susie.

To Louis Gallo

February 15, 1961   Rio Piedras, Puerto Rico

Dear Mr. Gallo:

Your letter was a little sassy but it was amusing, too, and on the whole I thought you meant well but were being awkward, and what's the good of being a writer if you must cry every time someone makes a face? I became an editor against my will, because I'm tired of enduring the nausea that comes over me when I pick up a Little Magazine or a Literary Review. I could not bring myself to believe that matters must really be so bad—that everyone was really so spoiled and lazy and opportunistic and sly and snobbish and hopeless—that educated people really must deserve to be despised by their brothers in business (I don't mean college-educated people but those who have developed hearts and intelligences)—that the people who have power over us might as well exercise it because we have well deserved their abuse by our stupid cowardice. In short, Mr. Gallo, not to spell out the cultural history of America in the Thirties, Forties or Fifties, I decided, together with some friends who felt as I did, that it was not very profitable to keep wringing one's hands over this wicked condition. And, full of illusions, we therefore started a magazine. (The first aria of *TNS #3* contains—or will when it appears in about a month—my estimate of the early returns on this venture.) There is no money in it for me or any of the others. I still go out now and again and teach school. I don't mind too much. Not to crown myself with too many flowers, more than my weak head can stand, the sacrifice is not really great. [. . .]

You have guessed my religion, Mr. Gallo—Louis, if I may. If Mr. Einstein, Albert, declined to believe that God was playing dice with the universe, I—we—can't believe, ugly as things have become, and complicated, that human life is nothing but the misery we are continually shown. I worry about Affirmation and the Life-Affirmers—the princes of the big time [New York City] across the river from where you buy your Drano [Trenton] who whoop it up for Life . . . But I'd better check myself. I have some things to add to *Seize the Day* but not in this expository style.

I hope *The Noble Savage* will work, or at least start something, and I hope to see more of your writing, a great deal more, in the magazine and elsewhere.

As for your views of what I do—well, yes, your judgment is pretty sound, I believe. When I got the idea for *Augie March*—or rather when I discovered that one could free oneself, I became so wildly excited I couldn't control the book and my hero became too disingenuous. However, I don't enjoy discussing old books.

I must now go and read the menu at the lunch counter below. It's noon, and I get hungry by the clock.

To Jack Ludwig

[n.d.]   [Rio Piedras]

Dear Jack;

I have tried very hard to avoid writing this letter, but I suppose there's nothing else to do now. Your phenomenal reply of February 4th forces me to tell you a few of the things I feel about your relations to the magazine and me, personally.

First, as regards *TNS*. I know how well you can tell yourself, within your Ludwig Disneyland, that you have done things, edited, attended to the needs of the magazine. With you, the intention is enough. A few passes of the Ludwig wand and *voilà*—a magazine! You have done nothing in months but read a few manuscripts. Others you have detained for periods up to half a year, and when asked about them have simply answered that your secretary [. . .] had stashed them away. Is that all? When I asked you to edit things, you said you couldn't, you had TV programs, lectures and other obligations. Still the manuscripts kept coming back from you, when in their own sweet time they did come back, with scrawled notes recommending editing. I have those notes, a whole collection of them. Therefore, I did the [Jara] Ribnikar [piece], and thoroughly, did this and that, and would, let me add, have continued to carry you—I think my letters of last summer made that clear, those unanswered letters which were never without friendly inquiries—if you had shown the slightest sign of commitment to the magazine. I know nothing of what you felt. Only God knows that. But I do know what your actions were.

And the "unintended slight" has nothing to do with it. What do you mean by "slight"? I can't figure that out. It's perfectly true that I was off in Poland for a time for reasons you understand as well as I do, and perhaps even better. By now I can't be sure that I *do* know more about them. And Keith [Botsford] was off in Venice, that's true too. I assumed that during my absence you two would take charge of *TNS,* and Keith assumed that we would do the same while he was gone. But I was in Warsaw and he in Venice, not in New York. You, an editor of the magazine, come to town on business of your own, and to mend your fences, and call neither me nor [Aaron] Asher, but conceal your presence, and then, after having done practically nothing since early summer, you write from Mpls. to ask me for a table of contents you might have gotten on the phone from Aaron. What can you, without hallucination, believe you have to do with *TNS*? You were looking forward to the two of us in PR handling #4! And what did you do about #3? You sent two inept and scarcely readable paragraphs for the arias which I threw out in disgust. I don't think you are a fit editor of the magazine. You have, in some departments, good judgment. I trusted your taste and thought you might be reliable as an editor, but you are too woolly, self-absorbed, rambling, ill-organized, slovenly, heedless and insensitive to get on with. And you must be in a grotesque mess, to have lost your sense of reality to the last shred. I think you never had much of it to start with, and your letter reveals that that's gone, too.

In fact it's a fantastic document and I'm thinking of framing it for my museum. You thought I'd be at the boat to greet Keith? Which boat? I've heard of no boat. You took Sondra's word for it that I was in Tivoli? Well, for several days with Adam I was there. But I was in New York a good deal of the time, and so were you, before Sondra arrived. And besides, why take Sondra's word for it? She and I exchange no personal information. How would she know where I was? Did I write her that I would be at Tivoli? Without consulting me, you phoned [my lawyer] John Goetz in Mpls. to find out whether I was giving you an accurate account of the legal situation last spring, but without a second thought you simply accept what Sondra tells you of my whereabouts. There seems to me to be a small imbalance here. Especially since we're not only colleagues but "friends," and haven't seen each other in nearly a year. Pretty odd, isn't it? And if you had phoned (and I believe you'd have had the strength to resist my invitation to Tivoli) would I have come to New York to see you? In all this there is some ugliness, something I don't want explained, though I'm sure that as a disciple of the Hasidim and believer in Dialogue and an enthusiast for [Abraham Joshua] Heschel, and a man of honor from whom I have heard and endured many lectures and reproaches and whose correction I have accepted, you have a clear and truthful explanation. All the worse for you if you are not hypocritical. The amount of internal garbage you haven't taken cognizance of must be, since you never do things on the small scale, colossal.

It wouldn't do much good to see matters clearly. With the sharpest eyes in the world I'd see nothing but the stinking fog of falsehood. And I haven't got the sharpest eyes in the world; I'm not superman but superidiot. Only a giant among idiots would marry Sondra and offer you friendship. God knows I am not stainless faultless Bellow. I leave infinities on every side to be desired. But love her as my wife? Love you as a friend? I might as well have gone to work for Ringling Brothers and been shot out of the cannon twice a day. At least they would have let me wear a costume.

Coventry, pal, is not the place.

To Richard Stern

February 27, 1961 [Rio Piedras]

Dear Dick:

Don't worry about a thing. [Jules] Feiffer has all the wit, charm and pathos you could possibly want. I think this thing is going to go. For *TNS* however—well, we have to deal with eternities. World Pub. is so slow it takes four or five months after we're done with the issue to manufacture; it's a *krikhik* [*]—the word is Yiddish—schedule; two issues a year, and awfully frustrating. Chapter 1 of the new novel is very good, but so obviously part of a longer work we can't take it.

I've been hammering at Herzog's back for months, and have several hundred pages of narrative about as steady as the moon's orbit. The whole now looks far different from what you saw, and that will look even more different in the end. It seems I used to work by adding steadily, and I now do it by adding and then boiling down. I know it sounds like cookery, but that's what Plato said poetry was, one of the arts of flattery, like hairdressing and soup-making.

I'll show up in Chicago towards the end of May, quite willing to talk. Even about Susan, if you like. I think by now I know her quite well. I can tell you more about her than most others can tell me. I shrink from marriage still, but not from Susan.

* creeping, crawling

About May 29th, I think.

Meanwhile, give my best to Gay, to Shils, and to the kids. I'm sorry you didn't get the Gug, but I think it'll come one of these years. Keep after it.

À bientôt,

To Gregory Bellow

February [?], 1961   [Rio Piedras]

Dear Greg:

Your letter amazed me. What's all this solemnity about honest men and faith and credit? I thought you were a socialist, for liberty and equality. It seems you really are a capitalist, all for the buck. Or do you think you're saving your mother from my swindles, or protecting her from bankruptcy or starvation? What sort of nonsense is this? You have two parents. Both love you. The interests of both should be close to you. *Both.*

What is it that's not rightfully mine—the alimony? Is it rightfully Anita's? By what right? Because I injured her? But I've never billed her for the pain she caused me. Or is it a one-way street? This is money I work very hard for, for I am somewhat slipshod and incompetent about my earning, and inefficient. Normally (whatever that is—what's normal with me?) I don't mind too much. But I've had a difficult time. Don't you know that? Really I'm so surprised at your failing to realize that I've had a hard time I'm tempted to laugh. After all, the difficulty and the weeping and all of it has involved you! And that's really quite funny, don't you think, that you should now be so indignant and send me boyscout messages about how a scout is honorable. But really, socialist to socialist, what's the sense of alimony rain or shine? She has a job and a guaranteed income. I haven't. She's neither sick nor in dire need whereas I can without exaggeration claim I've had a wretched time. I don't suppose you think the Sondra-Adam business was fun. And with the heartbreak of it went the expense. You can't imagine how much it all costs to lose a wife and child. I've exhausted my credit. I owe Viking ten grand, and my English publisher eighteen hundred, and Sondra's mother a thousand, and [Samuel S.] Goldberg, and taxes and so on and on and on. Wouldn't it have been nice of Anita, who knew of these hardships, to let me off a bit and say, "See here, I know it's rough. But though you've done me wrong I am not vengeful. You can start paying again when you're able"? Now that would have been something like humane. I could have sworn socialists were a little like that. I must have been reading the wrong books. You may ask why, with these views of alimony, I ever consented to pay it. Well, I did it because

Anita's lawyer wouldn't allow me to return from the West and reside in New York unless I agreed to the terms. So to be near you I agreed. And I was good about it for years and years. But now I'm on rather lean days, so you say, Take him to court. And she says, in sorrow, I can't afford it. Not quite accurate, Greg. It would have cost her nothing if she were in the right. In that event I would have to pay the court costs, too. But she and I would have to submit statements of financial condition to the court, and perhaps the alimony might be taken away altogether. For my financial condition is pretty bad. Yes, it looks palmy. I earn six thousand here for the term, but I pay more than five thousand to Anita and Sondra, so one might say that I've come here to make that money. It only takes five months or so. But what do I do in June, Greg?

If you are, as you say, making a man of yourself you might think of the condition of another man, your father. Why does he do these things? Is he a lunatic? What's the sense of those books he writes? Obviously my unreliable financial condition is related to the fact that I write books. And you might try thinking about this in terms other than the dollar. Those are blood cells in my eccentric veins, not dimes. It's odd that I should have to persuade my son that I'm human. Fallible, silly, human, not altogether a waste of time. I'll get by somehow—scrape by, steal by, squeak by. I always have. If I strike it rich, why, I'll buy ice cream and Cadillacs for everybody. And then everyone will say how honest I am and your good opinion of me will return, and your *faith* in me. It's all silly.

Your devoted

Papa

To Hymen Slate

March 1, 1961   Rio Piedras, Puerto Rico

Dear Slate—

It's funny, but I had the same feeling about you, that *you* were more accessible and open to feeling. Under the leadership of Isaac and Abe [Kaufman] that was all the thing. It took twenty years to find out how odd everyone else was; and how much alike. In many ways the same person with different faces—a little more paranoid here, a little more depressed there. But how unlike what we thought then! I who was supposed to be worldly got my first glimpse of the world only a few years ago. And even Abe has become practical. When I was in Cambridge last year Jerry Lettwin who teaches at MIT told me that Abe was thin, quite a man about town, and no longer the old loon. Too bad, if true.

Your piece is already in proof and you should be getting a copy of *TNS #3*, and a small check. I hope it will encourage you to do more. You should, you know. You have a good voice or tone, and a lot of knowledge and ability. I'm not printing "Slate's Proof" for old time's sake. And I'd be very careful ab't firing the ambitions of any man past forty if I didn't believe it would be quite a simple thing for him to do something good. I'm convinced it wouldn't be too hard for you. Think about it.

Regards to Evelyn.

Best,

Around Hyde Park, social worker Hymen Slate was for many years a much-loved chess player and Socratic talker. He and Bellow had been classmates at Tuley High School.

To Keith Opdahl

March 12, 1961 Rio Piedras, Puerto Rico

Dear Mr. Opdahl:

Those are very stiff questions. One is always tempted to give a proper answer, the answer that wins the Bible. Of course the man of will is easier to see clearly, and seeing clearly is a sort of love, I suppose. It may be that Blake meant something of this sort when he spoke of cleansing the gates of perception. And the energetic, good or bad, make themselves more clearly seen. I can confess without much difficulty that, being a man who makes up his mind with slow pain, I admire those who know their minds. They may of course be dangerous, in that their decision will be not to love. But that doesn't prevent me from loving them, or my more affectionate characters from doing so. The affectionate characters are stubborn too, and go their own way. They have powerful will, and affection suits them because it removes obstacles and resistances. They have their own will to power, I've never been in any doubt about that. If they are not obviously selfish they are nonetheless greedy. Some sense of life acts through them, and that is their passion. To me their affectionate charm often appears a disguise. However, I wouldn't *argue* any of these matters with you. I may well be wrong, but the drama and the comedy make that somewhat irrelevant. They are first, and the meanings are the comet's tail—when there is a comet.

The Crab and the Butterfly depressed me terribly. It was too heavy, and I let it go and turned to *Augie March* instead.

Sincerely yours,

Keith Opdahl is the author of The Novels of Saul Bellow: An Introduction *(1968).*

To Edward Hoagland

March 13, 1961   Rio Piedras, Puerto Rico

Dear Mr. Hoagland,

I wonder why I found it hard to answer a letter which gave me so much pleasure. Perhaps I don't know what to do with something that satisfies me so much. We all seem to be pretty poor about praise, about giving as well as receiving. Your letter shows you to be a bright exception in the giving at any rate. I hope you will be as good about taking it when your turn comes. I know from the two books and the one story I've read that it's sure to come.

On the whole I think your judgment of what I've done is the one I would give myself. Oddly enough, I do feel extraordinarily locked up, and some of my books, especially *Augie March*, are written in a jail-breaking spirit. And most prison breaks, like most revolutions, are unsuccessful. After I had written *The Victim*, I felt the limitation of conventional despair and disappointment and all the rest of it, of that romanticism which makes excessive and ridiculous demands for the individual and seems ignorant of what there really is to ask for. In the excitement of freeing myself, I think I went too far. I would go about it differently now. As for *Henderson*, I understand it least of all my books. Oh, I can tell you in detail what I was after, but I'm quite blind to the whole. I can identify the passages in which I was completing my stride, hitting home. However, it is a queer book. So is the one I'm at work on now, of which I haven't found the center. I don't seem to have connected this time either. Not as clearly as one should. I want to do the thing purely a few times before I stop. [. . .]

I hope you will have something to offer *The Noble Savage* soon. We're making up the fourth number now and we have plenty of space. Perhaps you have a story for us, or a personal essay. I'd be happy to see you write something—something personal about New York. That kind of thing is so seldom done. You could do it well.

Sincerely,

Edward Hoagland (born 1932) is an American novelist and major essayist, particularly admired for his nature writing in such collections as The Peacock's Tale *(1965) and* The Courage of Turtles *(1971).*

To Louis Gallo

April 4, 1961   [Rio Piedras]

Dear Lou—

You don't write letters easy to answer. One wants to—oh yes, indeed one does—but there's always the temptation to say, "See the collected works, vol. so and so." I'm writing a book in which I want to try my strength against some of these same questions. And argument really means nothing. That's for philosophers. Writers can only try to demonstrate in close detail without opinion. You may have the upper hand in argument. You may in fact have it in earnest truth as well. I don't know. I take you to be relentlessly kicking a way through a good many lies. The signs are there, especially in your letters and in the article on readers, which greatly impressed me.

And I suppose it doesn't greatly matter what one says in the way of position-taking. In art the real proofs are overwhelmingly factual. I wouldn't be caught dead with a Program for Life and Joy in my pocket. Or, as the new Administration has it, Energy and Fun, a Sense of Humor and all the rest of that. And the thing is mysteriously mixed with you, too, for at the same time that you say Nausea and Torture you show a knotty and bitter sense of comedy, and that, far more than the *position*, is what gets me. Yes, I know the position, of course. My God! how wouldn't I know it? I never lived in my mother's basement and used her washing machine, but that's only a detail. The rest, from direct and concentrated experience, is very familiar to me too. I've never known what it was to lead an accepted life. But the non-accepted life has its own terrible dangers, and horrible corruptions as you know lie in wait for the solitary resister. A writer has his choice in America of a grand variety of hells. Yours happens to suit my own taste. But I am well aware that with a good projector one can make one's small troubled light cover the heavens, and one's own spindling sticks can look like the ruggedest of all crosses.

You'll find the book I'm writing now less "tender," "tolerant," etc. When a writer has such feelings, however, it's his business to lead them all into the hottest fire. He must expose them to the most destructive opposites he can find and, if he wishes to be tender, confront the murderer's face. The converse, however, is equally true, for writers who believe there is a Sargasso of vomit into which we must drift are obliged to confront beauty. To deny that, you would have to deny your instincts as a writer.

Well, all right, then. [. . .]

Best,

To Pascal Covici

May 9, 1961   [Rio Piedras]

Dear Pat:

Thanks. I was glad to get your letter, of course, and I re-read the stuff and agree it's not half bad, but it'll need a lot of work yet because it can't decide whether it's funny or grim. It will need a thinning in the places where the thought is concentrated. It's an old problem with me. Maybe I'll get all the philosophy out of my system for good, now. This is the first time I've really shown my hand—my face, if you prefer—in any book. But we'll talk about that next week. I'm packing now and sweating over the papers and tickets and grades. I hear from Susie that you're well and enjoy her cooking.

Give my special love to Dorothy.

As ever,

To Susan Glassman

[n.d.,]   [Rio Piedras]

Now sweetheart, *don't* bring any coats and sweaters, only *ultra*-summery things. Matters like Kosher salami are optional. I'm doing fine. I'm beginning not to be so democratically humble ab't myself. It's me—Bellow!!! I am on loan, or lend-lease, to myself from God. And a rather extraordinary piece of business.

Come, as Shelley said to the night, soon—*soon!*

To Susan Glassman

[n.d.]   [Rio Piedras]

[. . .] I eat very little since you've gone, and I read and write a great deal. Hardly any point in going to Luquillo alone. I read the Old Testament and prophets, and work with *Herzog. He* is doing beautifully and that's some comfort. First I missed you hungrily, and now I'm more peaceful, and in about ten days I'll have gotten every advantage of solitude and I'll have a head full of ache and a void at heart.

[. . .] And I went to see *The Misfits. Oy!* Philosophy, thy name is not Miller.

Love and kisses,

To Susan Glassman

[n.d.]   [Rio Piedras]

My dearest Doll:

Here are twenty pages more, making forty this week since the jet took you from me. Signs of virtue and happiness. I live on broiled meat and salt-pills and my brains and insides go around at high speed. Have you ever visited a clothing factory, heard the sewing machines rrrrh*hhahh*hrrr with the loudness in the middle of the phrase? I feel like that myself, like the operator sliding in the cloth. Only the machinery is internal and the seams never end. Yesterday I went to Luquillo at last, and that was fine, but then the clouds came out and I drove home. In the Studebaker now. The Volks lost six quarts of oil in one week, and I left it in the Botsfords' shop in San Lorenzo. Keith got back early last week. We met for dinner and had some straight talk, which he seems to revel in. He'd rather have me tell him the truth than anyone I ever saw. It isn't always pleasant but then it's about *him* and that's good, glorious. I'm that way myself, as you know.

I didn't like your downcast letter very much, and putting it together with your decision not to go to Chicago I attributed it to the conversation you must have had with home when you got back. Did your mother give you a hard time on the phone? I hope that isn't so, but only the normal swing from excitement and euphoria at coming in safe to New York, and being in your own place, and the friends and the glamour after all of the Big Town, to solitude again, and bitter thoughts. But that's altogether the normal course you should have run. It can't hurt, I hear, to take this Librium. Keith was on it, too. He admits now to having had a little nervous breakdown. Probably his psychiatrist in NYC tells him so. He has a tailor in London and a psychiatrist in NYC on the same standby-footing. Ah, he's a glorious and funny man.

In all the island only I am steadily at work.

Love and good cheer,

To Susan Glassman

Ay Susannah! *Herzog* keeps rippling towards the old estuary, almost to page two hundred. The rapidity frees me somewhat, keeps me from lingering on my favorite themes or poisons. Later, later! Onwards, onwards. I want to end standing on my head like Hippocleides on the banquet table [. . .] The weather is not too keen, to touch on other matters, the cars work worse and worse. I took a lady to dinner who came introduced by my oldest brother. She turned out to be the complete rich neurotic. I mean complete. A woman waits for me, as Walt Whitman started to say; she contains everything, nothing neurotic is lacking. In one respect dinner was rewarding. She is a lobbyist for good causes, and she told me how a Senator tried to lay her in the Capitol during a roll-call vote. She had come to see that he voted, kept his word. His instincts were far better. He wanted to make her drunk in his private office. She said, "Only after the vote." Only the brave deserve the fair! What a world! My only vote, Dolly, I cast for beautiful you, to the tune of *Gaudeamus Igitur* [*]. You are right about these marriage-business alliances, of course, but I suppose this represents the efforts of people who have given up the love-quest to find a reason for continuing together. As such, the love-quest certainly deserves to be tabled, shelved, stored. As romanticism, I mean, or even sexual romanticism of the Reich kind. One swings from shallowness of one sort to shallowness of another, and from misery to misery. But people who see God in one another . . . aren't on the make in NYC.

I kiss you sweetly in the middle,

Bellow, who liked standing on his head, enjoyed Herodotus's tale of Hippocleides, who did so at Cleisthenes's banquet, happily exposing his genitals.

To Josephine Herbst

Dear Josie—

It's wicked to steal a writer's typewriter. It should be punishable by death. I've lost two machines, and I've been angry enough to commit murder, both times. I hope it hasn't held *you* up too badly. Susan tells me that your stay in NYC has not been as happy as it might have been. Certainly, if I'd been

* Latin: Let us therefore rejoice.

there, I wouldn't have allowed it to go off-side. We'd have found a remedy for you—have made a helicopter pilot of you, or something to cheer the winter. The city, when your friends are writers, can be largely awful. One winter at a time, has always been my motto.

P[uerto]R[ico] has been excellent for me. I've no [Alfred] Kazinian complaints to make of it. But my God! When one has been right one has been right. Where does that leave matters? Of course it's barbarous, noisy, undisciplined, etc. And dirty, too, with a great many rats. But there are even more lizards than rats, and more flowers than lizards (I love both) and more perfumes than stinks. And the relation between beauty and garbage strikes me as being right.

The book is going well, too.

Love,

And *The Noble Savage* has you at the top of the list this time—black and green, fresh and handsome, official and new, for spring.

To Susan Glassman

[n.d.]   [Rio Piedras]

Honey, I feel very off this morning, not feverish exactly, but tropical. I am hoping not to burst into hatred of this place between now and departure, but I do feel awfully close and shut in, maybe because I've begun to miss you. I chafe, and I've stopped being obliging. I refused to give a talk to the librarians on Saturday.

What an eye-opener this book is to me now. I seem to have the cure which should only have arrived with the conclusion. It came prematurely.

People have filled up daily conversation with clever and bitter comedy; at the same time, they've tried to behave *responsibly*. And now I've become too big a boy to play on with these secondary things, and *Herzog* shows it. The big, unwieldy, pathetic, and above all unnecessary *responsibility* which has grown larger than principle itself. Ay, ay! Well, I'm sure that, as so often, you find me clear as mud. But the conclusion is clear to me. The Self, as so conceived, is probably the funniest of all human conceptions. This was what I seem to have been after in Bummidge [hero of *The Last Analysis*], and certainly in Henderson (*I* want! *I* want!) So it's farewell with laughter to that darling false self-image. What Herzog does with his memory is to create his darling image. Then he is horrified at, say, his father's renegade desertion of St Dominique St . . . Well, enough of this. What you want to know is, Do I long to hold you in my arms? Yes, I do, greatly. And kiss you on the mouth and elsewhere.

Love,

To Susan Glassman

[n.d.] [Rio Piedras]

Dolly—Today I have aches (*aix les pains,* as J. Joyce said). I reached the dentist at last, and the cavity in that tooth was trifling. What caused the pain was tartar under the gums, which had to be scraped out, and my mouth is limping, now the Novocain has worn off. Life has begun to reach me in PR The day before yesterday, during rush hour on Ave. Ponce, the Studebaker broke down. Four hours later, it was fixed. I had to sit on the curb four hours, waiting for the mechanic. It was all in all rather enjoyable, for I hadn't had so much compulsory peace in quite a while. I'm writing this in Keith's office and he's just come back, and I'll rush to the P.O. so that you may have love's message for the weekend.

Sweetheart!

To Susan Glassman

April 24, 1961 [Rio Piedras]

Dolly, how gladly I'd have crept into your bed last night. I missed you badly. And today, and daily, and especially nightly. I've slept in your bed since you left, but the fragrance has gone out of it by now. My heart is on 68th St. Love, you say? Love.

I had frightful nightmares. I dreamed that Carlos [i.e., Jonas Schwartz] was suing. He's such a hornet, how would he not? And then I woke and the prospect was even worse. It panicked me. And I've involved *Esquire.* Of course I don't really think he'd do anything, it would make him look like a real idiot. He can't afford it professionally. Still. You know. It's dreadful not to be able to write about real matters; it turns all this into child's play while industry and politics etc. do as they like, drive us into the shelters, make our lives foolish horrors and disfigure the whole world. Ay! Anyway, some of the facts have been fiddled with to place the scene in Chicago. And what is life without a few grave anxieties? Incomplete.

This is the second long day of rain, and it's like sharing a green raincoat with a steaming kettle. How I long for the 13th! [. . .]

I feel like Chicken Little after the sky fell.

Love, love, love,

Jonas Schwartz, here referred to as "Carlos," was recognizable in the early excerpt from Herzog *scheduled to appear in* Esquire.

To Susan Glassman

May 1, 1961   [Rio Piedras]

Dolly: Just as you said, I got a raving letter from Pat, foaming with super-latives. One more soul I've made happy. What a terrific record. Only I haven't heard from *Esq.* and it's suspiciously like troubled silence. Oh well, maybe Jonas will sue and it'll be the making of me. They can take my house, etc. and leave me free to say even more. [. . .]

It won't be long now before I shake this green dust from my feet. I wish to look into your blue gray eyes and groan and kiss your fingers and play the beast to your beauty.

With love, love and kisses,

To Susan Glassman

[n.d.]   [Rio Piedras]

Dolly, I haven't heard from you lately. I assume you're busy with your father's visit. And I myself? As you see, slowed up a little, but some of this stuff is new, and it's understandable. The next forty or so pages will be mostly Juli-ana's, and then we pass to Daisy, to Shura's visit, to Mama and Papa and to the conclusion in the country. I had frightening misgivings about the stuff to appear in *Esquire*, and at the last minute I changed Carlos to a crippled war veteran, a hero of Omaha Beach. For the book itself I'll have to consult long with Viking's lawyers. Hate to lose Carlos *comme il est* [*].

Getting off this island is to me identical in feeling with the finishing of this book—two prongs of the same force. You can see I'm not dawdling over it. I want to be free.

Meantime Benitez [chairman of the University of Puerto Rico English Dept.] has asked me to take a permanent appointment here. I said no with thanks. It's flattering. But then I have been good in that course; I can't be modest without distortion, and facts are facts.

[. . .] Last week I read Dr. [Albert] Ellis's *Sex Without Guilt*. It all seems sensible enough, but something—something makes it feel like happiness in a chicken coop. There's a junky sanity about it.

* French: as he is

Yes, I did hear from Greg. He wrote me a wonderful, friendly, familiar, explanatory and excited letter about his visit to Chicago, and his interview for admission, and all his friends. He spent two days with Adam and Sondra and sent me a very full report of everything. So we're perfectly fine. No more crisis.

If you see John McCormick tell him I'd particularly like him to write a response to [Seymour] Krim. "Notes from a Different Cat." We must have a second piece or it'll look as though we sponsor this lunatic. John's going off, I know, but I want to press him very hard to do this. He's the best of all possible answerers.

I miss you, Dolly. I grow hollow at the feet with the sense of incompleteness. I may have to walk into Grand Union on my hands.

Love,

Albert Ellis was a Chicago "sexologist" whom Bellow had consulted in the spring of 1960. Seymour Krim, briefly Bellow's colleague at Minneapolis, was an essayist associated with Kerouac, Ginsberg and others of the Beat movement. His essay "What's This Cat's Story?" had appeared in The Noble Savage.

To Louis Gallo

May 9, 1961   Rio Piedras

Dear Lou:

You'll remember I made no claims whatever. I merely urged you to read *Henderson* because it would reveal more than any letters I might write. You speak of madnesses as though they were all of one color or taste. I came some time ago to think of despair and victimization as being at the service of the ruling class and the whole social edifice. It is the way in which imagination and intelligence eliminate themselves from the contest for power. Not that they are rivals for the same power. There is a difference. But—I have a taste for bluntness, just like yours—the only power they do exercise freely, without interference, is the power to despair. That is the monochromatic madness. Having myself felt it, known it, bathed in it, my native and temperamental impulse is to return to sanity in the form of laughter. This is not an affirmative *policy*. Nor do I expect anything but a disfigured success. But there are other powers from which we have abdicated—powers of gratification, of beauty and strength. When we agree they are gone forever some of us at least are shamefully lying. In my first two books I so agreed, shamefully. Then I realized I was merely doing another conventional thing. Conventionally lying. But I don't want to write you the story of my life. I haven't the time even if I had the inclination. I'm writing a book, and this is my last week on the Island. I'll be back in Tivoli very soon, and perhaps we can meet in NYC one of these days. [. . .]

To Keith Botsford

June 7, 1961   Tivoli

Dear Keith:

[. . .] I went to Ann Arbor to give my lecture, and then to Chicago to see Adam. I saw Sondra, too, for a moment, and I might have seen Jack, I suppose, if I'd cared to look for him. Old Tschacbasov and Sondra are in litigation over Esther's will, and Tschacbasov sent word that he would go to court to witness against Jack and his daughter if I wanted to bring suit for custody of the child. Such a suit doesn't attract me. I want nothing to do with any of them. Through the kid, I'm already involved, but I mean to hold relations with the whole bunch to a sanitary minimum.

I took Adam to the zoo and the aquarium, and picnicking, and shopping for toys. He wears the biggest pistol Marshall Field sells and the most ungunmanlike face in all of Chicago. I couldn't get him off the subject of guns. He's a fiercely singleminded kid. And like Greg he loves jokes. And like his Pa. [. . .]

To Louis Gallo

June 15, 1961   Tivoli, N. Y.

Dear Lou—

I'm back, and a great pleasure it is to be here, too. My mind wasn't my own in Puerto Rico, in the direct rays of the sun. Back, back to the gothic kennel, my stone cellar and dirty rooms. I hope you've seen *The Noble Savage* #3. #4 will contain [your] "Oedipus Schmoedipus" and other good things. Editing has been more than I bargained for. I took it on with the usual good intentions, familiar underfoot en route to hell, and now it has become a full-time unpaid job, with all the troubles and injustices and errors for which executives get high salaries.

Anyway—I'm interested in what you've been writing about the hatred of art among great writers. It's certainly true of Tolstoy. All these men (Tolstoy, Rimbaud, etc.) had the moralist's role to bear. They were Jonahs whose real calling was art. They had to prophesy instead, the higher vocation, and for this reason they were compelled to be severe towards their talents. I haven't thought the matter through as closely as I might but it interests me enormously. If you've written about it I'd like to see what you've done.

Now and then your writing hits the mark with a real clang. You're erratic but you have a true aim. I've lived too long for this to be fooled.

To Keith Botsford

July 24, 1961   Tivoli

Dear Keith,

[. . .] The world, assailed by crisis, is not fighting over *The Noble Savage* at the bookstores. Nor does anyone swoon. Nor do our contributing editors with the exception of Swados and Herb Gold, infighters of old, notice that anything was said about them. I doubt that Ludwig will even look to see whether we have kept him on the masthead, and my annoyance and your point of honor will be equally vain and silly. Nevertheless we must do well, as the world falls sharply through space, and keep the band playing while the *Titanic* sinks in ice water. I am in a mood suitable for gay funerals. [. . .]

In the present state of the world we could do worse. We might also attempt to spend less money, both of us. You, as a Tolstoyan, are even pledged to this. [. . .]

To Ann and Alfred Kazin

July 26, 1961   Tivoli

Dear Ann and Alfred,

I'm terribly pleased with your approval of poor Herzog. I'm here in Tivoli finishing up—or shall I say writing the book? That's more like the truth. *Men makht a leben kam mit tsores* [*]. Now the tomatoes are coming in, I have no pressing economic problem, if the woodchucks will only lay off. It would be wonderful to run up to Wellfleet and visit with you for a day or two. Since that can't be, why don't you come to Tivoli for a long weekend in the fall? Fall and spring are Tivoli's best seasons. Very beautiful. Great deal of room here, woods to walk in, fields, and it would give me very great pleasure. Let's negotiate this when you return from the Cape.

Thanks and love,

* Yiddish: I'm barely getting by.

To Arno Karlen

August 17, 1961 Tivoli, N.Y.

Dear Mr. Karlen:

I'm sincerely sorry if I offended you at the [Wagner College] conference. That I should have failed you was inevitable, since no one ever gives up the belief that there is a "mana," as the Polynesians call it, which must be transferable. I myself have often been indignant with older writers, and I know how you must have felt. But I believe you may have missed something Jewish that passed between us. Whom the Lord loveth he chasteneth, goes the old saying. Your talents were so obvious to me that I fixed at once upon the things that were less satisfactory. Among these were tendencies present in me, and superabundantly present, at your age. In scolding you, was I perhaps correcting myself a long generation ago? "Perhaps" is simply rhetoric. It was positively so, and when you say we are running on parallel tracks you confirm this. I noted at once in your writing the power to cut through superfluities, the hardness of attack that I favor. But the solipsism gets us all. Everyone is writing *Ulysses* all day long, within himself, and when we speak we speak sentences out of an inward context—only the tip of the iceberg appearing above the surface. So that you heard only the clause beginning with "but," and not what preceded it.

What I should have said to you about being a writer would have gone something like this: One has the choice now of coming before the world as a writer or actually being one. The Mailers and the Angries are dissatisfied with what you call the rapping on the cell wall, and they have decided to make a public appearance in the writer's role. I don't take you for a silly man. You are nothing like an Angry; still you were encountering difficulty in the role, and wanted to be acknowledged by the others. It seemed to me a trivial thing for you to be doing. You had it all over most of the people there anyway, and weren't denied publication, and you might therefore have gone a little more softly with them, less gifted and less lucky as they were. An odd tightness or hardness came over you when they criticized you. I saw my own pale tense face twenty years ago, and I spoke and no doubt said the wrong thing. I owed you this explanation then but didn't offer it because I was distracted, annoyed with the whole conference and angry with myself for having gotten into it. To deal with seventeen people within ten days was not easy. And the financial reward was negligible. In ten days of hacking I can easily earn twice as much, three times as much as Wagner paid me, so I was not there certainly for the money. I can't believe that you'd really think there was more to say than, To be a writer one learns to live like one. This I said repeatedly and with variations. The craft one learns oneself. The main business is to find the most appropriate and most stimulating equilibrium. You are a person who writes; the most exacting criticism I could make wouldn't have ten cents' worth of value in the end because your critical principles will come from you. They will appear as you write and rewrite. For this reason I don't feel at all guilty towards the seventeen at the conference. For tactlessness, yes; for failures of instruction, no. I was there to make my own views clear; that's all anyone can do in this enterprise. To the best of my ability I did make them clear. People who write have their own strong conception of how things should go. They tend to be despotic in life, as they often are towards their characters. There were therefore seventeen quite complete versions of how the thing was to go. And I provided the eighteenth.

I frankly and willingly admit that to interrupt the writing of *Herzog* irritated me and possibly made me bearish. I am however always available to you for private conversation. Maybe we can clear some of this up.

Good luck with the Army.

Arno Karlen is the author of, among other works, Napoleon's Glands *(1984),* Man and Microbes *(1996) and* Biography of a Germ *(2000). Wagner College is in Staten Island, New York.*

To Ralph Ross

August 20, 1961   Tivoli

Dear Ralph—

Congratulations to you both. I remember Groucho in some picture, astonished to learn from Margaret Dumont how many children they had, saying, "Let's keep one of each kind and give the rest away." You seem to have achieved the optimum instinctively, without wasted motion.

End of joke. I'm really very happy for you and Alicia.

All best wishes,

To Harvey Swados

September 28, 1961   Tivoli

Dear Harvey:

[. . .] You and I belong to a very tiny group from whom something may be expected. I know what you mean. Malamud's book [*A New Life*] was dead. When he enlarges his scope, or tries to, he comes up with all the middle-class platitudes of love and liberalism. Then you see that the poor guy has been living on some dream of a beautiful and cultured life in Oregon— Lewisohn Stadium floating across the continent with the orchestra playing Tchaikowsky's *Romeo and Juliet*. The thing was mean and humorless. I think you and I have something to be grateful for in the Marxism of our twenties. It made us cantankerous, certainly, but it injected a kind of hardness. I often feel it now as I write *Herzog*. I am no socialist at all, but I have a certain feeling for reality which probably owes a debt to radicalism. I hope *Herzog* will amount to something. As for the magazine, well, I had the fire going and it seemed a shame not to put in another iron. If it doesn't turn out to be another sword we can beat it into a pancake turner.

In January I have to go to Chicago for the winter quarter. I'll be back again in April. Let me know what your plans are. I want to see you. It's been years. We can meet in New York, or at Valley Cottage or at Tivoli, or even Yaddo. We've finally cornered Elizabeth [Ames] and there'll be a swimming pool at Yaddo this coming year.

All best,

To Richard Stern

[n.d.]   [Tivoli]

Cher compagnon:

I take *Herzog* out of this machine in order to write legibly [. . .] I stayed away altogether from the Malamudfest. I liked his book so little I couldn't face the music. So I ate pastrami alone, in grief, while they were drinking champagne cocktails at F[arrar] and S[traus]. Luckily I have been spared the agony of telling anyone so far what I found in the autopsy of that book.

Comrade, on a separate page I am sending a short bibliography for that course. Could you ask the [English] Dept. to make it an afternoon seminar? *Herzog* needs me in the morning. I can argue, like Chaliapin: "Sing? I cannot even spit till lunchtime." And I have no apt. And will Shils be there? The apt. is necessary because of Adam, whom I expect to have on weekends.

Europe, I'm sorry about. It's an amusing book, and that's against it now. The mild comedy in these apocalyptic times is considered middle-class. *Blutwurst und Senf* [*] is what the book-cruds want. Iron punches to the heart and cathodes to make the genitals twitch. Look, it's obvious. Henry Miller and Henry James can't both be winning. Somebody's lying. Henry James is

---

* German: blood sausage and horseradish

in the frontroom by the lace curtains, but in the backrooms—ha! And [your] *Europe* is situated nearer to the old Henry. Well, you will triumph yet. You're doing well against the smaller dragons. Soon you'll be ready for the St. George model. I saw your review of *Catch-22*, and that was what I thought of it too. Candida [Donadio] sent it to me with a stirring cry.

Soon I will be in Chicago, melancholy euphoria following paranoid hypochondria. Alert the clinicians and stand by.

See you soon,

Stayadinovitch

Stern's dissenting review of Joseph Heller's Catch-22 *had appeared in* The New York Times Book Review.

1962

To Susan Glassman Bellow

[Postmarked Chicago, 9 January 1962]

Dolly:

The rounds go on. I'm hardly ever alone, and in a way that rattles me, too. It's too unlike my life. Sunday my sister and my brother M[aurice] and Adam—Adam is simply wonderful. He phoned me this morning and said he had to talk to me. Sondra got on the telephone and said he was afraid of my disappearing like Uncle Lester. It's marvelous to be such a psychologist. Anyway, I'm taking Adam to Lesha's little girl's birthday party on Thursday. That made him happier. He sounded slightly tearful. *Oy*, we with our tears oiling the wheels of the universe. If we had no tears we wouldn't be ourselves, but the mind still finds them an oddity. Anyway . . . M[aurice] gave me a handsome Irish tweed coat, the houndstooth check, which seems to fit. But apparently I insulted him bitterly when he said he couldn't read any of my books, except a few chapters of *Augie*; the rest was nonsense to him and he failed to understand how they could be published profitably. I said after all he was not a trained reader, but devoted himself to business and love. He was offended and said I didn't *respect* him, and that I was a terrible snob. I thought I was being angelically mild, and put my arms about him and said I was his loving brother, wasn't that better than heaping up grievances? Finally I melted him from his touchiness. He freezes when he's offended, and if you think *I'm* vulnerable, I recommend you study him. Shils gave me a long lecture on the touchiness of Jews.

Well, there's a little news. I'm working, I'm well, I'm paid up, I miss you—I miss you in the sack. I'm waiting for the 23rd, and I love you,

Bellow and Susan Glassman had married in November.

To Susan Glassman Bellow

[Postmarked Chicago, 11 January 1962]

Dolly—

I think *Herzog* is about to enter the final stages—two last sections, neither too long, and we're finished.

Not much else gets done, between teaching and writing and check-signing. When you come, perhaps I can catch up on reading as well as fucking. I begin to have erotic dreams about you. And maybe my poor health is nothing but misapplied eroticism (according to St. Norman O. Brown and others of the Freudian church). Had dinner last night (Wed.) at The Coast with Morrie, my brother, and his lady friend and his neighbor Lionel the Knight of the Corridor (Karpel). And now I'm off to fetch Adam, take him to Lesha's party, take him home, come south, lie down and wait for more dreams.

Love,

To Susan Glassman Bellow

January 16, 1962　[Chicago]

Dolly—

Another blizzard, a mere eight inches this time. I was in a snowdrift—night, starless. And chainless. So I had to jack the car again and put on the chains. No fun this time. It was cold, and filthy, and in the dark it took an hour. All the buttons came off the coat my brother gave me, and it's not fit to wear now. Also, I came home exhausted and took to bed (9 P.M.). So I've sworn to lose weight. I feel a million years old. But I got up this A.M. and wrote the nightclub thing in two hours and got it off (the chains were more troublesome). Next, I'm going to move up my Jewish introduction [for the anthology *Great Jewish Short Stories*]. *Faute de mieux on couche avec les manuscrits* [*]. Your letter delighted me this morning. I treated myself like a tired

* French: For want of better company, one goes to bed with manuscripts.

warrior: lunch at the club, a haircut, a slow walk. Now it's about class time, I'm going below. Your ma has invited me to the Epicurean Restaurant Friday. Great relief after the Camelia Room. (The camelias were wax.)

I so miss you, Dolly.

Yours,

To Susan Glassman Bellow

January 17, 1962   [Chicago]

Dolly—

Towers of snow, and we peek out like prairie dogs at Grand Canyon. The air is stale in here, but the windows are stuck with frost. I keep driving (I've lost one chain) in and somehow out of snowdrifts. Could use a little Tivoli, and you on the sofa in my arms breathing peace and love into my arms.

The bureaucratic machine begins to tie me up—official occasions next Mon. and Tues. You're lucky not to be here.

But *Herzog* meanwhile is thriving (p. 194 of the *final* version).

Shils leaves tomorrow morning. I'm taking him to a Chinese dinner tonight, in my opulence. Astonishingly, I wrote that Show Biz piece in two hours and earned two hundred fifty bucks.

There is something that grows for you here under this blue electric blanket.

Kisses and love,

To Susan Glassman Bellow

January 19, 1962   [Chicago]

O Susabella! What a rapid rat-race. These predators of Chicago (U) will leave me no shreds of flesh on my poor bones. I suppose there's a quick way to handle it all: Yoga, or something. Money takes time. I must abandon *The Noble Savage*. Can't handle the mail. And I must ever console Keith and assure him (more superfluous letter writing) that he's a good little Botsford.

I miss you, meantime, Susabella. Thank heavens we can observe next Erev Shabbos together.

The heavens are like a flour-sifter. Six inches more of snow today. Great statuary on campus. Streets impassable. [. . .]

Love from yr. mate,

Herzog has rosy cheeks.

To Susan Glassman Bellow

January 23, 1962   [Chicago]

Dearest Susabreza,

O.K. You're right—I'm wrong. I suppose it's one of my unadmirable *spiels*, and you catch me up very responsibly, and like a good wife.

I've made no dates for the weekend. Maybe I'll pick up Adam on Sunday, but the rest is bed, blanket and you.

A little discouraging last night. Dave Peltz and I took Trilling out slumming. A cold coming we had of it.

Anyway, we'll rub the whole thing off with erasers of love.

To Anne Sexton

[n.d.]   [Minneapolis]

Dear Anne Sexton,

[. . .]

I have both your letters now, the good one, and the contrite one next day. One's best things are always followed by an apologetic seizure. "Monster of Despair" could be *Henderson*'s subtitle. I think you coined this expression. I don't remember it. At this particular point we seem to have entered into each other's minds. A marriage of true minds, or meeting arranged by Agapé. (Where has Eros gotten me?) [. . .]

Your poem ["Old Dwarf Heart"] is genuinely Hendersonian—"breathing in loops like a green hen" is absolutely IT!

Yours in true-minded friendship,

To Susan Glassman Bellow

February 26, 1962   [Chicago]

Dearest Susabousa:

I am seated in my office growling at Life the Tiger. Winter has now turned into a cold fluid—gray. All the old ice looks like Death's protégé. Even the sparrows are *sick* of this. And the elms. Phooey! [. . .]

And I miss you. Your loving *Husband*.

To John Berryman

April 2, 1962   Tivoli

Dear John—

Chicago was colder than the Gold Rush, cliffs of snow and people like Alaskan sourdoughs. I was tempted to fly up to Mpls. but it was even colder there, so I stayed put. [. . .] I am writing on a piece of board over my knees. I await spring. You can hear the bushes marking time.

As ever,

To William Phillips

April 5, 1962 Tivoli

Dear William,

It's true I've written something pretty funny and I see no reason why *Partisan* shouldn't have a look. There's been some professional interest in the play and while I no longer expect to become an American millionaire, still something may come of this interest. I think maybe the thing to do (for me to do) is to have a talk with my agent and see whether there could conceivably be an objection to publishing a few scenes. I would think not. One of these days I will come into the city for a week of civilized happiness and I'd enjoy having a drink with you.

Best,

To Richard Stern

April 26, 1962 Tivoli

Dear Dick—

I am working like a Polish swine, making bratwurst of myself. [. . .] The farce (comedy?) is now entitled *The Upper Depths* and may (n.b. *may*) be produced by Herbert Berghof and Uta Hagen. Or perhaps even by Zero Mostel. We live in hope's eternal purple shade.

Susie and Tivoli are blooming. One wife is becoming enough for me (*O Bellowius senex!*) [*].

Bestow friendly and loving greetings on all.

To John U. Nef

August 10, 1962 Tivoli, N.Y.

Dear Professor Nef,

To be invited to join the faculty of the Committee on Social Thought is a great honor. I gladly accept your offer. I am acquainted with the work of the Committee, and I am happy to know that you think I will be able to contribute something to it.

In my conversations with Edward Shils it was understood that I could not

---

* Latin: old man Bellow

arrange to come for the fall quarter. After some discussion, my wife and I have come to think that we could wind up our affairs in the East by mid-October, and that we could be in Chicago by the end of that month.

I assume it is too late for me to offer a course in the fall quarter. However, I understand that tutoring is also a part of my duties, and I would be happy to make myself available for the balance of the quarter.

I hope you will have no objection to my honoring some previous commitments. They will take me away from the University very seldom, and for brief periods.

I look forward to hearing from you soon, and to seeing you this autumn. Cordially yours,

To Richard Stern

[Postmarked 22 August 1962; postcard of Menemsha Basin, Martha's Vineyard, at evening]

[. . .] Play scheduled for Fall '63 but we're yukking it up already. Hope you have as much trouble reading this as we had reading yours. [. . .] The Vineyard is beautiful—we love it. *Herzog* in final stages—*TNS* put to bed. Freud should have had such a beach—he wouldn't have had so many theories.

Love,

To Sondra Tschacbasov Bellow

September 30, 1962   [Tivoli]

Sondra:

The purpose of your letter is evidently to interfere with my right to see Adam. The provisions for visitation in our divorce agreement were not more clearly specified because I assumed you would deal with me in good faith. But on Labor Day you used the child to bargain for some supposed advantage and refused to let him come with me as we had arranged. Adam was greatly disappointed. The violence of that occasion was provoked by you, perhaps deliberately. You tore my clothing, bruised me, and had to be restrained by Ann Berryman from continuing your attack.

I have no desire whatever to see you. I have no plans to interfere with your privacy. But if you persist in your present course, capriciously changing plans, giving me no opportunity to communicate with someone in a position of responsibility about the child, you will leave me no alternative but to go to court to establish my visitation rights. I have in the past been reluctant to seek legal remedies, but you have created an ugly situation. I have no intention of repeating the mistakes I made in Minneapolis when you forbade me to come to the house, my own house, and threatened me with arrest if I came to see the boy. To keep the peace I stayed in a hotel and the child was brought to me by an intermediary. There will be no repetitions of that situation.

Your pugnacity is a matter of record. Even before the divorce you struck me with your fists. You tried to run me down with the car. On the day when you claim to have been assaulted, I came home with bruises. You have been known to do things you could not remember later. My "violence" is probably another one of your hallucinations.

Since you are working, there ought to be someone looking after the child whom I can call. I tried to find out from you who did take care of him after school, but could get nothing but evasions. You have refused to tell me what provisions, if any, have been made for his daily care. On Saturday September 22, 1962 when I phoned to arrange to see Adam, you told me to phone next day to give you time to make arrangements. On Sunday night when I called again you refused me a visit, alleging for the first time that he had an appointment with the dentist. You also cried out, "You can't see him!" Knowing that I would be leaving soon for Chicago and would be gone for some months, you were simply giving me the runaround. For reasons of your own, you don't want me to see the boy.

I would like Adam to visit with me this coming weekend and I want you to tell me where I can pick him up on Friday October 5th. I am, as I have always been, prepared to agree to anything sensible but I will not accept your arbitrary conditions. A fixed pattern will be set up for these visits. I shall be coming in periodically during my temporary residence in Chicago. You will have ample notice of my visits. I want to have Adam with me on all holidays—Christmas, Easter and part of every summer. If you do not agree to reasonable arrangements I shall have to go to law to try to obtain my rights.

Quarrels and litigation will do him no good. For his sake I have avoided all conflict with you and I suggest that you try to behave reasonably, as I for my part intend to do. I plan to come to Tarrytown next Friday to pick him up, and I expect to hear from you that he will be delivered to me by someone other than yourself. I will not ask anyone to go in my place while I wait in a restaurant like a wrongdoer. I won't send anyone for him. I will insist on my rights, and the thing will be done decently and in good order. I expect a reply from you before Friday. I hope you will not compel me to take legal steps.

To Sondra Tschacbasov Bellow

October 11, 1962   [Tivoli]

Sondra:

The fact that you yourself phoned me last week to make the arrangements for seeing Adam amounts to an acknowledgement of the impossibility of doing these things through the complicated system of intermediaries you wanted to force upon me. I myself want as much as possible to avoid direct contact with you, but I don't want my rights to see Adam questioned, and I won't tolerate any nonsense. I have asked you questions about the boy which are still unanswered. I want to know who takes care of him while you are at work. Please send me the full name and address of the woman you spoke of. I think I should have also a calendar from Adam's school so that I can plan to have the child during holidays. In addition, I think you should send me, or have the doctor send me, an occasional medical report. Adam didn't seem at all well last weekend. He has lost weight and he is not at all cheerful.

I am going to be in New York the weekend of December 7th, and I'd like to pick the boy up on Friday evening and keep him with me for the weekend. If you insist on his attending Sunday School, I can take him there myself and wait for him. With nearly two months' notice, I hope you will not invent any appointments at the last moment. Two weeks ago you told me Adam could not see me because he had to see the dentist. He told me last Saturday that he's never been to the dentist.

I shall send you my new address in Chicago and I expect to hear from you about the weekend of the 7th. I hope we have seen the last of these unnecessary vexations and squabbles.

To Toby Cole

October 28, 1962   Chicago

Dear Toby:

The money's come, and Susie and I have found an apartment on the South Side (address forthcoming; just now the joint's being painted) and everything is highly satisfactory so far. Can't say I miss New York. Chicago with its old associations is oppressive at times and will challenge the flexibility of both of us. But we can always go back to Tivoli, if we're overcome, and spend the rest of our lives in recovering.

Of course I'm highly pleased about the Piccolo Teatro [di Milano]— don't they want to wait till I've rewritten the play? They're welcome to it as is. Or perhaps [Giorgio] Strehler has ideas that might be of use to me? I'd be glad to hear from him (when I've finished my book; all these moves have not advanced it). [. . .]

Since Zero [Mostel] is having temperament (an old-fashioned affliction of artists in the last century) why shouldn't [Jackie] Gleason have a look? Tell Zero from me that what his mood wants is a swift kick in the rear to hasten its departure. We all carry approximately the same load of unwashed plates from life's banquet. On the weak flat feet of the soul. *Henderson* should make things easier, not harder. Well, don't repeat this to him at all. Just give him my regards and say "Bellow's compliments, and please hurry up a little."

Revolutionary greetings,

Toby Cole (1916–2008) was a Los Angeles–based theatrical agent and activist well known for her advocacy of blacklisted talents such as Zero Mostel. In later life, she was a frequent presence on Pacifica Radio. Legendary director Giorgio Strehler (1921–1997) co-founded the Piccolo Teatro in Milan soon after the war and ran it for many years.

To Oscar Tarcov

October 30, 1962   Chicago

Dear Oscar—

Having fled defeated from the scene of my own disorganization, I am here, organizing a new chaos. I can send you the details soon—I'll enjoy doing it. [. . .]

We've found an apartment at 1755 E. 55th St. which is being painted and can be occupied next week. Meantime you (or Zara) can reach me at the University. (It's *very* curious. I am not interfered with at all. My only work has been my own: *Herzog.* I should be finished soon. But Chicago is both depressing—dreadful!—and exhilarating. I am waiting to find out *why* I came here.)

Susie and I could be happy on an ice floe.

It's too early to say how Greg is doing. His first enthusiasm for the school was great but it's wearing off as he settles down to the academic grind. He brings a very *personal* attitude to every class. If he likes his teacher he does well. If the man doesn't meet his personal requirements the results are awful.

We miss you,

To John Leggett

November 12, 1962   Chicago

Dear Jack:

[. . .] My wife read your last note and wanted to know *whom* you had seen me with in Central Park. I don't take girls to Central Park. At my age a man needs steam-heated love. [. . .]

Yours for propriety,

Jack Leggett (born 1917) was an editor at Houghton Mifflin and Harper & Row who left publishing in 1969 to run the Writers' Workshop at the University of Iowa. He has published, among other books, A Daring Young Man: A Biography of William Saroyan *(2002).*

To John Berryman

November 13, 1962   Chicago

Dear John:

Just now in *Poetry* I read four Dream Songs, and wish to say, this being the hour when strength is low, thank you. We keep each other from the poorhouse. If it hadn't been for you there would have been many a night of porridge and a thin quilt, cocoa made with water. I will try to return the favor. With *Herzog.*

Of the eminent names above [on the Committee for Social Thought masthead] I know only half. I love Ed Shils (have you read any of his books?) and David Grene is splendid—rides a horse in the Forest Preserves and teaches Greek and Latin. He also has a farm in Ireland.

Susie and I are settling slowly. Susie is a perfectionist and must have plenty of time. She's an adorable woman.

Greg is on the cross-country team here and takes courses in mathematics and political theory. Life *is* very long.

Greet your wife, and much love,

To Edward Shils

November 21, 1962   Chicago

Dear Edward:

If [Samuel S.] Goldberg did show up, I hope he wasn't too much trouble. He was traveling with my former father-in-law, Tschacbasov the painter, one of the stranger formations of nature in its recent experiments. The thought that they might have appeared together before you in Cambridge [England, where Shils was in residence at King's College] visited me like a nightmare. Not even a student of life like yourself ought to be exposed to so much of it at one time.

As for me—for us—Chicago has opened its arms. I'd like it to stay that way—open arms, not a closed embrace. Susan is very happy here. It would have been unfair and even dangerous to try to keep her on the farm. She has a taste for solitude, like me, but shouldn't be encouraged. Here she has many friends, and isn't dependent on mine as she would be in the East. As for me, I haven't the smallest complaint to make of Chicago; my life here has been altogether pleasant if disordered—but that's normal with me. I've been working very hard, perhaps harder than I should, to finish *Herzog*. I don't know whether the poor fellow can stand as much attention as I've devoted to him. The Committee has been splendid. I float in and out, have a talk with Father Kim. He tells me why he didn't become a Communist; I tell him about modern literature. Then I walk on the Midway for the fresh air, and in the stacks for the stale, gaze at the bare shelves in the office and wonder what books [Friedrich von] Hayek kept. I see his cane, like a prop from Sherlock Holmes, hanging on the wall . . . They say he loved mountain climbing. He has left behind a Schnitzlerian flavor which I very much enjoy. Elsewhere in the city, a certain number of spooks occasionally rise to haunt me. Bitter melancholy—one of my specialties—but sometimes I feel that certain of these old emotions have lost their hold. I realize they no longer have their ancient power. Good idea for a story: the Limbo of terrors which have lost their grip. [. . .]

Yours, as ever,

Edward B. Shils (1910–95), preeminent University of Chicago sociologist and fellow at King's College, Cambridge (1961–70), and Peterhouse, Cambridge (1970–78). His many books include Ideology and Utopia *(1936) and* The Calling of Sociology *(1980). At the Committee on Social Thought, Bellow had moved into the office formerly occupied by Friedrich von Hayek, influential Austrian-born economist and political philosopher, author of* The Road to Serfdom *(1944).*

To Ralph Ross

November 26, 1962   Chicago

Dear Ralph:

I'm afraid John Berryman is overboard again. Monroe Engel just phoned from Cambridge to say that John and his wife came up from Providence, and it's the same sad story—poetry, drink, etc. Nothing for it but to sigh. It's the only way he gets a little rest and comfort, poor John. He came to Tivoli to see us last October, and seemed better than usual. With a child coming, his poise was astonishing. I figured it not to last—safe bet . . . Last year when I talked to the people at Brown I told them he'd be slightly irregular. I hope he'll soon be out. You may want to send him a note. The address is:

McLean Hospital
1075 Pleasant St.
Belmont, Mass.
(It's always Pleasant St., Golden Valley, Lotus Island.)

Meanwhile we sturdier citizens go on. I haven't had a bad fit since I left Mpls. and even then, as you subsequently observed, I wasn't altogether insane. Ludwig and Sondra had really laid a terrible burden on me. [. . .]

Anyway, we've put that behind us. Though it may be dangerous to say it, I'm extremely lucky in my new wife Susan.

Do you ever pass through Chicago? We're at 1755 E. 55th St., Butterfield 8-2530. It's the Committee on Social Thought, the most beautiful of all my employers.

Greetings to Alicia, and to you my warmest and best,

To Edward Shils

December 17, 1962   Chicago

Dear Ed—

I've put myself in the Bulletin for spring with a vague course title. This winter I'm offering something called "Comic Literature from *Rameau's Nephew* to Abram Tertz's 'The Icicle.'"

Susie and I thrive in Chicago, though it has been gloomy. I'm becoming accustomed to the *blitzed* look of Hyde Park. The vast amount of writing I'm able to do makes me immune to the Stygian darkness. There are of course bright beacons here and there, which beckon. Jean Malaquais, Erich Heller and Stephen Spender are at Northwestern, but these beckoning beacons have not tempted me from my desk. [. . .]

Merry Xmas to you and Adam,

1963

To Edward Hoagland

January 7, 1963   Chicago

Dear Ted:

Unfortunately the career of *The Noble Savage* is ended, so I'm sending back your article to Asher in the hope that he may remember the name of your agent. It is gone from my mind. The disappearance of the *Savage* makes it suspiciously easy to say that I would have printed your article—I really would have though, because I agreed with it largely and see that you're a writer, and the magazine existed to print writers. Malamud's book [*A New Life*] soured me; it was mixed up between comedy and earnestness and I suspect he was going by some modern system of critical logarithms and not by his own sort of reckoning. Nor do you prove to my satisfaction that distance from the social issues is more desirable. If there is Baldwin here writing an abominable novel on the issues of the day, Italy provides the example of a Silone who wrote *Bread and Wine* after the outbreak of the Ethiopian War. But of course you recognize yourself that what is wrong is the stridency of writers like Baldwin and their tone of personal injury, at times nothing but an infant cry. The jazz musician in Baldwin's last book sobs to the heavens, "You motherfucker, ain't I your baby too?" He seems to be asking for a nice comfy layette just like the white chilluns have. Perhaps it's the fact that Malamud and Hawthorne have severed themselves from infancy that impresses you. That is significant, in American literature. Hawthorne of course lights out for old age as soon as the bonds are cut, streaking away for palsied eld.

Of myself, no defense. I have done the things I ought not to have done and left undone etc. in the regular Pauline form.

I hope your work is going well. Europe has excited you, and your marriage has made you happy. I am happy for you and send you best wishes,

The "abominable" Baldwin novel was Another Country. *"Palsied eld" is from Shakespeare's* Measure for Measure: *"for all thy blessèd youth / Becomes as agèd, and doth beg the alms / of palsied eld."*

To John Berryman

January 7, 1963   Chicago

Dear John:

Congratulations! How I envy your daughter! If I thought I'd get a similar result I'd start now to persuade Susan; renew the covenant, show our trust in the species (what have I done for it lately?!). What a lucky man you are, for all that comedy about the drained and seedless bag. The biological order lets *us* know ("Don't call me, I'll call you").

Recently there drifted into reach as I rocked in the ocean of life a copy of *Encounter* with more of your poems. Henry is the only prophet left, the last true child of Jeremiah. Texas will not heed him nor learn from him, but we Bible students are in your debt forever.

I have put aside *Herzog* for a while to write a comedy—Old Bummidge is on the threshold of production. Let us hope he will utter some words of truth to the occupants of ten-dollar seats.

Susan is well and joins me in sending love to you both,

To Henry Volkening

February 25, 1963   Chicago

Dear Henry—

If the article in *Perspectives* had been about you, I would have had the same feelings. When I do the mental balance of what people playfully call my "career," I find that my love for H. Volkening is among the biggest of the credits. You can never get into the Freifeld class. He's a sort of brother I must always be prepared to make allowances for, dependably incompetent Sam. He'll *never* understand. You, on the other hand, are always far ahead of me. So we have a good balance.

I see very little here of Sam. I'm still under the curse of busyness. Last week I finished re-writing the play. The experts predicted it would take six months. It took twenty days of very hard work. Since Joe Anthony was pleased with Act I, he won't dislike Act II—they're remarkably consistent. I'm not too busy to brag a bit. This is as sweet a piece of work as I've ever done. What the *team* will do with it we can't foretell, of course, but I've acquitted myself honorably. Now back to Moses [Herzog] and Britannica. I've had what mouse-psychologists call a "closure." The eighth note of the scale has been played at last and I'm enjoying this sense of completion.

It makes me feel stronger.

I've all the money I need, besides, so let's not let Rusty get sassy with us. I suggest you pin him down this week.

Susie and I are driving to Austin, Texas on March 2nd, returning to Chicago about the 12th of the month.

Yours, as ever,

Joseph Anthony (1912–1993) would indeed direct The Last Analysis *on Broadway. "Rusty" was L. Rust Hills (1926–1983), longtime fiction editor at* Esquire.

To Toby Cole

March 21, 1963   Chicago

Dear Toby—

We see eye to eye about *Bummidge*, thank goodness, and I hope for everyone's sake that Zero will put his eye where it belongs. The latest news from Joe Anthony is good but not good enough. He wants to direct the play, thinks I've solved the main problems, but he's a very busy man and has about five large projects for next season. We are simply in his stable, and the hay is very tasty but I'm not a vegetarian. Joe is hoping that Zero will accept. He hopes thereby to gain time since Zero is tied up for some months to come.

Now I can easily understand Zero's position. He may want to continue with [*A Funny Thing Happened on the Way to the Forum*] and I assume that Hal Prince will offer him a fatter contract for the next year. In that case I could never blame Z. for rejecting *Bummidge*. But if Z. isn't going to play with us we must have a new director as well as another star, for it would be absurd to wait for Anthony who may—may!—be able to find time in winter of '64 for us. This is why I must insist on a quick decision by Z. And Z., I know, will grasp the situation quickly. I must ask you to push the matter with impartial zeal—I mean in other words that you must make the thing work for *me*! If this project doesn't advance it will collapse. One beam is buckling already—Joe—and I've told Lyn Austin that I'd like her to find out what Jerome Robbins is up to. Should Joe leave the scene we must be prepared to replace him. But I'd say nothing about this to Zero.

Happy Lent.

Love,

Lyn Austin was the Broadway producer Bellow had been dealing with.

To John Berryman

October 19, 1963   Chicago

Dear John—

My advice is to put nothing in your title to color all the poetry from above. You might as well call it "The Spiritual History of America under the Administration of Dwight D. Eisenhower." Anyway, it's Henry who belongs on the title page and on the spine. I vote for "76: The Lay of Henry." But your own judgment is the only important one.

I can't say that all is well with us. My lifelong friend Oscar Tarcov was carried off by a heart attack on Wednesday. I feel I'd rather die myself than endure these deaths, one after another, of all my dearest friends. It wears out your heart. Eventually survival feels degrading. As long as death is our ultimate reality, it *is* degrading. Only waiting until Cyclops finds us. It is horrible! And it figures that we should be ruled by murderers.

But I know you are pleasantly excited by life—Kate, child. I shall keep the rest of my feelings to myself. All except my love,

Berryman's collection would be called 77 Dream Songs *when it appeared in 1965.*

To Nathan Tarcov

October 22, 1963   [Chicago]

Dear Nathan—

I am deeply, bitterly, sorry that I couldn't attend your father's funeral. Oscar and I had an unbroken friendship for thirty years, and since I was sometimes hasty and bad-tempered it was due to him that there were no breaks. I loved him very much, and I know that no son ever lost such a gentle, thoughtful father as you have lost. This is probably not a consoling thing to tell you but I'm sure it expresses what you feel, as well as my belief and feeling. Oscar's sort of human being is very rare.

My friendship with him and with Isaac Rosenfeld goes back to 1933, when my mother died. I'm sure I brought to these relationships emotions caused by that death. I was seventeen—not much older than you. If I explain this to you, it's not because I want to talk about myself. What I mean to say is that I have a very special feeling about your situation. I experienced something like it. I hope that you will find—perhaps you have found—such friends as I had on Lemoyne St. in 1933. Not in order to "replace" your father, you never will, but to be the sort of human being he was, one who knows the value of another man. He invested his life in relationships. In making such a choice a man sooner or later realizes that to love others is his answer to inevitable death. Other answers we often hear are anger, rebellion, bitterness. Your father, by temperament, could make no other choice. Perhaps you wondered why I was so attached to him. He never turned me away when I needed him. I hope I never failed him, either.

Yours affectionately,

To Toby Cole

December 3, 1963   Chicago

Dear Toby—

What a time . . . I'm confused, myself.

(To begin again.) I've had a conversation or two with Lyn [Austin]. She's just stalling me pleasantly until Joe has time to think about this play. So, I'm still of the same mind ab't Lincoln Center, and I've rather expected to hear from you. Arthur Miller was much interested. Of course you may feel bound by "agent's ethics" not to go into it with Miller or [Harold] Clurman but there's not much to be said against *my* investigating the matter. I've taken a very considerable runaround from Zero first (on Joe's say-so) and then from Joe himself, and I'm a bit fed up.

Love,

"What a time" here means "What times we live in." President Kennedy had been assassinated eleven days earlier.

1964

To Richard Stern

July 21, 1964   Martha's Vineyard

Dear Dick,

After dinner, the Spaniards say, Don't budge! *Ni un sobrescrito leer.* Not even to read a superscription. At the Vineyard, we're in an Irish kind of mist, everything is green. As I recall, the Pacific puts you to sleep, like a blessing. The Atlantic braces. So I go once a day and souse myself, and study eternity. Nice that the organism still can feel keen pleasure.

I thought California would give you the answers you needed. You took your stitch there in time. But be a little careful with California's speciality—the grotesque. Just before I left Chicago, I read the introduction Wright Morris has written for *Windy MacPherson's Son* (in that Chicago novel series at the Press) and he had a lot to say about [Sherwood] Anderson and the grotesque. But he didn't say enough, or rather, loving the grotesque himself, he didn't have it right. I don't either, and I've been pursuing the subject. Maybe it's a taste for Gothic detail (minus cathedrals). But I think it's an important part of the American literary method to EXPOSE the SEEMING. So at bottom it may be Calvinism. "So-and-so *seems* to be one thing but I shall *show* you what he is." The exposed may be Tom in *Gatsby* or marriage in Albee. Or just American "normalcy." Anyway, American novels (this week) are dramas of EXPOSURE! and the grotesque is just one of the methods. It also means the writers accept the challenge to compete with experience by being as grotesque and . . . don't mind my lectures; they're just a sign of affection.

Eager to see you, and the book. When do you come East?

Yours ever,

To Alfred Kazin

July 22, 1964   Martha's Vineyard

Dear Alfred—

Your friends the [Justin] Kaplans received us in splendor with whiskey, wine and lobster, *two* desserts and beautiful views of the Atlantic. I thought they were splendid. She looks like one of Goya's blue-eyed ladies in the Prado (where I put in several *kulturny* weeks in 1947). After dinner we sat eagerly about the TV to listen to Goldwater's acceptance speech, which gave me unpleasant sensations of a blood-pressure sort, toothaches, liberal *leyden* [*]. Then we went home to our sandy beds. Deceptive gains now make life worthwhile—for instance, I have weaned myself from the pills I was taking during the final months of *Herzog*, and this improvement in my nights will set me up metaphysically for at least a year; life is after all simple, decides a complicated mind.

We've seen a bit of Island Society. Styron is our leader, here in little Fitzgeraldville. Then there is Lillian Hellman, in whom I produce symptoms of *shyness*. And Phil Rahv who keeps alive the traditions of Karl Marx. I'm

* Yiddish: pains

very fond of Philip—he's *mishpokhe* [*]—and he gives us a kind of private Chatauqua course in *Hochpolitik* [**] from which I get great pleasure. Why can't we forgive each other before we become harmless?

Much love to you both,

To Alfred Kazin

[n.d.]   [Chicago]

Dear Yevgeny Pavlovitch:

You know me, Yevgeny, and my Russian lack of organization. I am a poor lost woof from the kennel of Fate looking for a dog to belong to. So, do I have that letter from the man? Of course not. And what difference does it make? I will give the same speech anyhow, no matter what they call it. A good speech, but the one for that day, and how do I know in advance what to call it? Pick me a title, like Oliver Twist's name, *und fertig* [***].

How is the beautiful Ann Borisovna? Is her pale beauty as always? I am certain.

I am so bold as to send you my new remark: "Now there are no more frontiers, only borderline cases." This paragraph has nothing to do with the preceding. I yield to no man in my admiration.

You missed a very lively party. For a dull play, no doubt.

Ach, be well. Love and kisses from your crotchety friend,

The Last Analysis *had opened on Broadway on October 1, starring Sam Levene in the role of Bummidge.*

To Dorothy Covici

November 5, 1964   Chicago

Dear Dorothy,

[. . .] Dr. Glassman (Frank, I mean) is recovering from a cerebral aneurysm. He had surgery last week—I won't go into detail—but he's going to be all right, the doctors say. I flew back last night, and Susie and Daniel will come home on Sunday.

* Yiddish: family
** German: politics in the higher sense
*** German: and ready

I have a note on my desk from Keith Botsford, very grieved at the news of Pat's death. He wants to be remembered to you.

Much love,

A baby boy, Daniel, had been born to the Bellows in March. Pascal Covici had died of a heart attack on October 14.

To Leonard Unger

December 4, 1964   Chicago

Dear Leonard—

I've been thinking of you since September, when I got your letter. Evidently there is something in me that insists upon "making something" of suffering. The living, I suppose, can only extend life insofar as they *are* the living. The state is uneven at best, and this last year has not been at all good—some of my dearest friends have died, and I feel not so much spared as stripped. You've been on my mind. I keep thinking of your sister, and your old parents, and asking myself what I might do to express solidarity and friendship at a time when I feel the lines slipping out of *my* fingers. At last I decided simply to be "heard from." I can't make anything of suffering just now.

Say hello to my friends,

1965

To Adam Bellow

[n.d.]   [Chicago]

Dear Adam–

Here are some stamps. Countries sometimes disappear and leave nothing behind but some postage stamps. But Papas and Adams go on and on.

Papa

To Toby Cole

January 23, 1965   Chicago

Dear Toby,

I haven't heard from you in a dog's age, so I assume there's nothing stirring to hear. The Stevenses phone me every few days to tell me how marvelously they attend to my interests, to which I reply uh-huh. It seems that a lady named Nancy Walker has been reading my dramatic works, and wants to direct "The Wen" on Bleecker Street, in a loft. And that is probably where it belongs. I told Annie, however, that she'd have to find excellent actors. The hams I have seen would turn it into an obscenity. It's borderline anyhow. From the Guthrie I got some satisfaction, but have nothing substantial to tell you as yet. Peter Zeisler was here. I like him very much, and he took the play with him and has written me very cheerfully about it. Still I don't know what his intentions are. Nor have I heard anything from the other side of the water. By now I am powerfully convinced that all stories about the British sense of humor are true as far as they go, but that they don't go far enough. British reviews of *Herzog* are solemn to the point of stupidity. I suppose we shall be hearing soon from the French, and from the Wops, my only spiritual brethren. Do drop me a line one of these days. I begin to think that the theater and I will never hit it off, and in all likelihood I shan't be bothering much more with it.

Annie has asked me to write another one-acter to go with "The Wen," and if I can do it carelessly enough, showing my contempt for the medium as it now is in New York, I will scribble something for her.

Yours affectionately always,

To Alfred Kazin

January 28, 1965   Chicago

Dear Alfred—

I enjoyed seeing myself through your eyes in the *Atlantic*. Because I'm accustomed to run the portrait gallery myself, I was taken aback for a moment. Then I grew accustomed to the novelty and thoroughly enjoyed it. You may have been a little too generous. I remember being a very arbitrary, overly assertive type. Maybe there was no other way, in the democratic-immigrant's-son situation, to obtain the required authority of tone. To me, now, the whole thing is a phenomenon; the *personal* element no longer counts for much. You were absolutely right about the Chicago side of things. For some reason neither Isaac nor I could think of ourselves as provincials in N.Y. Possibly the pride of R. M. Hutchins shielded us. For him the U. of C. didn't have to compete with the Ivy League, it was obviously superior. It never entered our minds that we had lost anything in being deprived of Eastern advantages. So we were armored in provincial self-confidence, and came to conquer. Ridiculous boys! And even Isaac was a better realist than I. I think I was altogether *dans la lune* [*]. I had very few social needs, curiously. That saved me from Isaac's gang of Hudson St. insiders.

When will your book be published? I'm eager to read it. I remember that Isaac and I, in our high-court, closed-corporation, solemn Chicago Sanhedrin manner, agreed that *A Walker in the City* was wonderful—your best vein. And now I wait for your portrait of him.

I wonder whether you've seen Jack Ludwig on *Herzog*, in the current *Holiday*. It's a masterpiece in its own way—a great virtuoso performance on the high-wire of self-justification. Ingenious, shrewd, supersubtle, shamanistic, Rasputin-like. I'm really rather proud of the man. His cast-iron effrontery is admirable, somehow. If I ever commission a private Mt. Rushmore I'll stipulate that his head be given plenty of space. Anyway, don't miss this performance. [. . .]

My affectionate best to Annie [Birstein] who defended me against those sophisticated brutes of the *New York Review of Books*.

Yours ever,

Kazin's memoir-essay "My Friend Saul Bellow" had just appeared in Atlantic Monthly. *The book he was readying for publication was* Starting Out in the Thirties.

To Stanley Burnshaw

February 19, 1965   Chicago

Dear Stanley:

In my simplicity I thought the noise of *Herzog* would presently die down, but it seems only to get louder. I can't pretend it's entirely unpleasant. After all, I wanted *something* to happen, and if I find now that I can't control the volume I can always stuff my ears with money. Ridiculously needless to say that I didn't expect it. I sometimes think this prosperity may be the world's way of telling the writer that if his imagination succeeded in one place it failed in another. It did well enough in a book, but now "this is how things really are." After all my talk about "reality instructors" here are reality and instruction for you!

Sometimes I think of the world as impregnated by centuries of fiction and self-fertilized by science swelling out in new forms of consciousness. Anyway,

* French: lit. on the moon; unrealistic, out to lunch

it has gotten well beyond the literary imagination. Novelists (poets too) have so long taken it for granted that they knew how to describe and what to describe and that they were doing all right. What a pathetic error! What overconfidence! The world has beaten and exceeded us all by astronomical miles. One can't hope to catch up. Writers, for instance, can never outdo the political history of the twentieth century in perversity, and it's simply foolish of them to imitate its *Realpolitik* as the Becketts or Burroughses try to do.

In writing *Herzog* I realized how radical it was to be moderate, in our day and age, and, as you guessed, I found a musical form for it, suggested to me by hours of listening to records every day for three years. You are very shrewd to have seen it.

The play was a great disappointment. But instead of making me wretched it only made me obstinate. I've reconstructed it (in my field hospital after the massacre) and Viking is printing the text. I'd root out my desire to write plays if I could; I found theater people to be miserable, untrustworthy creatures.

Susan and I expect to come back to the Vineyard this summer. We have written to real estate agents for a larger place, closer to the water, either Lambert's Cove or South Beach. We expect to see you and Leda. We look forward to it.

Yours,

Stanley Burnshaw (1906–2005) was a poet and the author of a book on poetic creativity, The Seamless Web *(1979), as well as a biography of Robert Frost.*

To Jean Stafford

February 24, 1965   Chicago

Dear Jean:

I liked all the stories, but the one about the old professor and the young know-it-all best. A sign of the times, I suppose. My times, I mean. These days I cross one shadow-line after another.

It's far too long between meetings.

Yours,

Bellow had read Bad Characters, *Stafford's latest story collection.*

To Harvey Swados

June 14, 1965   Washington, D.C.

Dear Harvey:

These quarrels are hateful. I dislike the slap-in-the-face formula and the implied responsibility for death in Vietnam. Let me at the least make clear that the glamour of power means little to me. More, I don't like what J[ohnson] is doing in Vietnam and S. Domingo, though you and I might not agree in our criticisms. But I don't see that holding these positions requires me to treat Johnson like a Hitler. He's not that. He may be a brute in some ways (by no means all) but he is the President, and I haven't yet decided to go in for civil disobedience. Have you? You sound ready to stop paying taxes.

But—no quarrels. My attending a ceremony at the White House doesn't make a fink or criminal of me. Intellectuals, and esp. former Marxists, will really have to decide in the end what they think a government is.

As ever,

To Toby Cole

September 20, 1965   Chicago

Dear Toby—

Yes, I like Shelley Winters. Wasn't she the poor mother in *Lolita*? I liked her better than any of the others. But aren't we low on the scale for the likes of her? (Suppose we admit it's not too horrible for middle-aged men to copulate with small girls, do we then have to make a philosophy of it? I could write a better book from Lolita's point of view.)

Yours equally,

To David Bazelon

October 6, 1965   Chicago

Dear David,

I'm all for getting together, and during the summer I began more than one letter inviting you to the Vineyard, but I wasn't in good shape, and every time I picked up the calendar I got dizzy. I'm dying to know what your fifth career will be—I'm not in a position to tease you about marriages, for perfectly obvious reasons, but I am not opposed to multiples in either field. I think we were both meant to set records. I don't know that survivors always find good company in one another, but it's perfectly clear that we do know a great deal about the past and ought to put our heads together.

I bummed through Buffalo in 1934 with Herb Passin. I continued up into

Canada, and he went to NYC where he borrowed fifteen bucks from Jim Farrell, which he never repaid. So Farrell said, anyway. He would ask me, "When is your pal going to pay up?" About twenty-five years ago I came to Buffalo again to give a speech and was trapped by a blizzard with nobody to talk to except Leslie Fiedler. I wouldn't wish that on anybody.

Let's exchange schedules and try to get together.

All best,

To Edna O'Brien

December 31, 1965   [Chicago]

Dear Edna,

I'm back at my fine bowlegged table in Chicago—in my house—of correction, where I hope to become more nearly myself. There seems to be only one significant thing for me—for the likes of us—and it hasn't a great deal to do with parties.

I took a great liking to you. I think you are a lovely woman.

It's the last day of the year, and I keep saying to people that at least the date on our tombstones won't be 1965. My sort of joke.

Yours affectionately,

1966

To Stanley Burnshaw

January 25, 1966   Chicago

Dear Stanley,

Maybe you recall a series of articles in *Horizon* just after the war called "Where Shall John Go?" Already twenty-five years ago the British felt they were no longer in the middle of things and they were quite right. Sometimes I feel we play medicine ball with the Center. The New Yorkers look towards London and Paris, London looks at New York, and Paris if I'm not mistaken has its eye on Peking. In America of course we are entirely hypnotized by New York with glimpses of Washington and Boston entering at the sides. You ask how I can stand Chicago as a steady diet. Well, it is of course gloomy and ugly, provincial and unsociable, and the worst is that it is unappalled by its own culturelessness— no happenings, no camps, no literary life, and all our celebrities go away and turn into Mike Nichols and Susan Sontag. In plain English, the pleasure Chicago gives is a remission from the pain of New York. As a center New York is a fraud and an abomination. Chicago is something of a frontier city in the sense of not having "caught up" but it is slowly importing, in degenerate form, things degenerate from their inception. Here people have a certain self-conscious naiveté. Often they don't know what to say but they are not full of the knowledge so common in New York of what *not* to say. What I do miss in Chicago is the opportunity, never used in New York, to "go places."

Susan wants to go to the Vineyard again but I am tempting her in this wilderness with visions of Europe. We may eventually find ourselves an acre somewhere near your pond and put up a Bucky Fuller dome, unless the zoning ordinances prevent it. Please give my best to Leda. I was distressed to hear she was ill again and I hope she's better.

All best,

To Edward Shils

January 26, 1966   Chicago

My dear Edward:

The Air India crash gave us a shock. I knew that you were in Cambridge, but you often fly that route and I associate you with it, and I myself am often up in the Boeing 707. Now that Civil Aeronautics has pronounced the 727 dangerous I've stopped using it. Sometimes I feel what a vain numbers-game I'm playing or catch myself applying imaginary brakes in the air. No one has gone into the air traveler's mind, so far as I know. It's waiting for its Dostoyevsky. I have a very distinct impression that sinners derive expiation from jet flights and clear their adulterous consciences by the risk they take, deserving the fair because they are brave. (Not so very brave, but then the fair are not so often very fair.) Then, too, plane travel does something for people in despair. I've seen it happen. Wishers-for-death especially find it soothing. But this is not a good subject—I have tickets to New York Friday night. I'm going to visit Adam, and to look into other less agreeable things. Also, I want to put Mr. Pawlyk aside for a few days. At times I feel very strong and rich, but more often inept and poor with this new subject. I can make a sensible forecast. I'm sure it will be powerful but strange, perhaps too strange. To be really good, among the best, one must get hold of a kind of Tolstoyan normalcy which no one can challenge. I don't believe I can expect that now. I think what I have is relatively good poise in the midst of abnormalities. [. . .]

The most agreeable thing about Chicago is that one doesn't run into many writers, critical *razboiniks* [*] and gangsters of the pen. But then Chicago is also in a state of extraordinary winter nullity, and we haven't seen many people. Winter nights are long. I have an electric blanket and read *War and Peace*. I'm convinced that Leo was a somatological moralist. Eyes, lips and noses, the color of the skin, the knuckles and the feet do not lie. The tone of Speransky's laughter tells you his social ideas are unreliable. It's not a bad system. I seem to have used it myself, most of the time. [. . .]

You were marvelous in England. We shouldn't have taken so much of your time, it made me guilty, but you gave it so willingly and freely and charmingly that I was extremely happy all day. It wasn't just the visit to Cambridge, delightful in itself, it was the love that went into it that made it so extraordinary.

Susan sends her love, too.

"Mr. Pawlyk" was evidently an earlier name for the hero of what would become Mr. Sammler's Planet.

To Alice Adams

February 23, 1966   Chicago

Dear Alice,

It gave me a good deal of pleasure to read your novel [*Careless Love*]. Something like a personal contact. I suppose that disqualifies me somewhat as a critic. I felt it to be about you, I read it as though the woman had been you. But I suppose that's a proof of quality, since you came forward very clearly as a very charming woman, no nonsense, level-headed and clear about everything. It's an excellent portrait within its limits. What I object to (not very strongly since the book was so pleasing to read) are the limits which I would describe as follows: Women like your heroine do seem to live completely in relationships and think of very little apart from their own feminine happiness. This is in its own way attractive—until one strikes what one is always sure to strike, namely, wretchedness, the unreliability of men, the poor human stuff of lovers, the fact that just as in poor Emma Bovary's time they are telling sleazy lies and carrying on their deceptions. What you want to do next, if I may make a recommendation, is to write the last book in the Bovary series. The woman who ends the trend will be gratefully remembered.

* Yiddish: hoodlums, thugs

Having recorded this objection in my solemn and heavy Jewish way I feel free to express the rest, which is gratitude. I much enjoyed reading the book. It made me think of Oregon and that drunken night when you told me that I came on compulsively as a *heymish* [*] type.

Love,

To Margaret Staats

29 March 29, 1966   Chicago

Staats—

Well, I thought that if the plane blew up it would let me out of a good deal of difficulty, and I'd be well ahead, with you as my last recollection. After ten million miles of creeping—a Dutch summit! I see you like that, and I think of you all the time. *All* the time.

Haats.

Bellow had met Maggie Staats at the residence of Harold Taylor, president of Sarah Lawrence College, in the early months of 1966.

To Margaret Staats

[n.d.]   [Chicago]

Now I know what "uneventful" means. It means a noise inside too loud to be affected by ordinary external events. Like airline turkey, gummy brownies, investment-counselors' conversation, etc. I had an uneventful flight.

Next, over the moors of Chicago by yellow cab. Seeing my little boy in a red hood. Dandelions. Then tiresome and strained conversation [with Sondra] covering well-known points about my bad character, mental disorders. In my favor, it is agreed that I have no malice or deadly wickedness. And that is true, so far as I know.

Now and then even a loving heart. Aching at present for you,

To Margaret Staats

April 5, 1966   [Chicago]

I long to see you again. I miss you so much, it's like sickness, or hunger. Childish lovesickness. I tell myself how foolish it is—"A young girl I met in NY . . ." And I remind myself of "my time of life," and of the "offi-

---

* Yiddish: cozy, down-to-earth, unpretentious

cial structure," my responsibilities. But the feelings only come back more strongly.

[. . .]

To Margaret Staats

April 5, 1966   [Chicago]

And what's more, I don't know which way to turn. Every choice, in advance, looks like a mistake. I wouldn't give up the feeling for you that I have if I could. And I couldn't. Although the absurdity of being in love *now* is more than my sense of irony can cope with. I'm fine, somehow, to see *it* overwhelmed.

And don't you think I *know* how different from those women you are? No, I don't need destructive women.

Not to see you makes me suffer. And I don't know what to do.

To Margaret Staats

April 7, 1966   [Chicago]

I didn't believe it possible. Probably I thought I had been damaged, or self-damaged, too badly for this. Whatever the reasons, I didn't expect that my whole soul would go out like this to anyone. That I would lie down and wake up by love instead of clocks.

If I am busy, it's because I need activity and concealment. I should be grateful. And I am. I'm also oppressed and heavy-hearted. It's a case of *amo quia absurdum* [*]—the absurdity is mine, not yours. My age, my situation! It is absurdity.

But what a super-absurdity not to love you. I feel some mystical sort of gratitude for this. I would, even if it turned out that you didn't love me after all.

By and by, I'll write you how I spend my time.

Evidently I cut my finger in NY to have a remembrance. I've got an awfully nice scar.

To Margaret Staats

April 12, 1966   [Chicago]

Well, absurd or not, when I think of you my heart fills up. I love everything I can remember of you. With you I have a feeling I've never had before, that of being infinitely satisfied with another and although I don't know you I

* Latin: I love because it is absurd—a modification of Tertullian's *Credo quia absurdum*, I believe because it is absurd.

believe that going any distance in every direction with you I can never find anything to disappoint me. I expect to love you whatever happens. Even if you should be frightened off by all these grim difficulties. You've made humankind and the world look different. I can never again think about women as I used to, for instance. There's my message this morning. Instead of prayers. Now I can bear to go about my business.

To John Berryman

April 19, 1966   Chicago

Dear Pal:

I'm due in California May 1st, and thought to go earlier but now that I know you're coming I'll wait up until the 30th. My own life-dealings have not been too prosperous—on the spiritual side. Some creatures have it simple. A thorn in the paw removed by a dear young Christian and everybody becomes immortally happy ever after, and exists on a calendar adored by maidens and kiddies.

I'll prepare for our rendezvous by reading a few Dream Songs. Contact in space.

I started some inquiries here for you. They were met with great interest and enthusiasm. If you want to arrange a conversation or two, say the word. This place seems to me better than Mpls. Nice to meet people like [———] if you happen to be on an ice floe, but why live on ice? I don't know how serious you may be about leaving. In any case, it's nice to have options.

Perhaps I am about to write something. ("When may we expect a new work from your pen?" said the late E. Waugh to E. Wilson, like a divil.)

We await you,

To Margaret Staats

April 20, 1966   [Chicago]

In spite of my desire to ease up, I can't let things alone, and I think I'm behaving badly; close to blindness; I sense it. It can't be right to aggravate the disorders at the most disorderly painful stage. And I don't think any good can come of such raw feelings. I think it would be best to force myself to stop, and wait. Only I keep thinking of you.

(Interrupted by ten students.)

Love!

To Margaret Staats

April 21, 1966 [Chicago]

One gets home late afternoon and rages inside till about midnight, falling into bed and sleeping like a stone in the exhaustion of anger and disappointment. So different from our sleep together. In conversation there have been no holds barred but one. To hear and say such things is degrading. But perhaps everything ought to come out.

When I'm not quieter at heart, I can't remember you as I want to remember. That hurts. This afternoon, though, I feel you again, very sweetly inside me.

I'm the one in sole charge, from Sunday evening, for most of the week. Perhaps we could keep Sunday evening for ourselves and the following Monday. You'd lose only one day's work. And I will try to be in NYC earlier in May.

The picture shows you've always had the same dear character as well as the knock-knees. I'll keep it awhile, to absorb the mystery of it. If I may.

Same message.

To Margaret Staats

April 23, 1966 [Chicago]

It was very different, a week ago. A sad difference.

Sometimes I think all these *personal* differences—"I was happy a while ago, now I am sad"—are a sort of joke. (Henderson's "I *want!*")

Why should people, like me, who have won so much freedom, or had it handed to them, feel themselves in jail? Maybe because a week has gone by which might have been full of love but instead was empty. It's not really a very funny joke.

But I'd better not try thinking today. My mind isn't very good. It's like the weather coming over the Lake: foggy. The sparrows are sitting in my tree waiting for spring to start again. I knew their ancestors.

To Margaret Staats

April 28, 1966 [Chicago]

I keep wondering about you—what you must be feeling, what your fears may be. I feel extravagantly protective towards you. It's odd, loving a creature whom I will probably not understand, but only bless without comprehension, and gratefully. I recognize at the same time that it would be better if my protection weren't really needed. My vision of your family makes me anxious, too, and I wonder how much fight is left in me. I used to be quite strong, but it would be only natural to wear out. I don't feel it, but somehow I expect to, having seen vigorous people crack, give out and die—friends and contemporaries. No wonder I think about this. I'd better.

To Margaret Staats

May 31, 1966 [Chicago]

I find it harder and harder to wake up each morning and cling to sleep and dreams. Meantime paper builds up over me like the white cliffs of Dover. Then most of the day I'm drowsy and heartsick and I hear Chicago carrying on its business, like a bad brass band playing all the old tunes. I've been hearing that noise since I was nine years old. Last evening old T[ed] H[offman] gave me a Dutch uncle's lecture about my inability to grasp my own idea except when writing fiction. Almost anybody can profit by my clairvoyance, but I personally can never do it. Maybe that's what it means to be at the edge of the expanding universe. You go forward because everything there is pushes from behind.

I suppose I'm doing my best to come clean, and I listen carefully when I'm told what's wrong with me. But can I understand? I used to have a flourishing literary business to which I could turn but something has gone wrong with that, too.

I miss your voice, eyes, touch and body.

To Margaret Staats

June 2, 1966 [Chicago]

I'd be a lot better if I could put my arms about you and kiss you even once a day, and be kissed—you've never yet accepted a kiss from me without kissing; the fact is important. So my missing you is nothing abstract.

I've been using sleeping pills because, in the night at least, I don't want to know what's going on. In the evening, especially, there are dismal conversations here, and I am put into situations in which hard words (not angry but hurtful) have to be spoken. After which it's better simply to cap out. I've been going to bed at 11:00 and sleeping ten hours or better. You'd think I wouldn't be tired. But it's not sleep I need, it's you.

Today I wrote a few sentences. Then the mail brought the London reviews [of *Under the Weather*, an evening of one-act plays]. Those were all favorable, but since people can't let things alone it was said, here and there, that I am cold and self-centered and that I could never, of course, sustain a full-length play. Which helps to strengthen my opinion that the arts and government attract the worst people. The best are astronomers and geneticists. And pure souls like you.

To Margaret Staats

June 3, 1966 [Chicago]

Here's a change-purse from Paris. Some would call it a *porte-monnaie*, some *une blague*, though strictly speaking a *blague* is for tobacco.

You know, I really don't care for the sort of life that has formed about me in the last few years—accountants, tax-experts, investment counsellors, organizations and fronts, fund-raising, autobiographing, speechifying, mail-answering, lawsuits, interior decorations, spleen and other antipoetic phenomena. I feel it all today. One half hour at my desk. Two at the telephone. And now I'm going to play squash with my friend David Peltz, for relief. I can think of better things to do. With you. As I wish I were now. This separation is very hard.

To Margaret Staats

June 6, 1966 [Chicago]

I suppose I'd better take it easy. It's dreadful how I miss you. All the oldest, worst longings are stirred up—some seem very old, wild, peculiar, something like wrinkled furies along the line of marsh. I see them by the roadside. What I think continually, about you, does not seem to make sense. I can't say that I *know* what I'm doing. What's more, I'm aware that you, too, are an odd one—*must* be odd—and I become afraid of destruction exactly where I feel most certain and most (even biologically) safe.

So today—cloudy, muggy—I go into the street, and I feel a terrible, anxious, devouring bondage, and I try to detach myself, almost by suggestion, from the leaves which stream along in the breeze. One could simply be tranquil and free—like *that*.

It's also like the thought of being with you—all pleasure. Almost all freedom, but only almost. I keep wondering—doubting that you can long accept me. Not that that would stop me, but it is anxious-making.

But it is love. What can one do about that?

To Margaret Staats

[n.d.]

Like a walrus then she kissed him
Wet and whiskered, weighing tons

Pink-and-gray-reticulated
With pale eyes like polar suns
—Frozen yellow polar suns
Spiral of the cosmic floes!
On her violet bristles bright
She blows with weighty daintiness
Her bubble of marine delight
—Frothing with marine delight.
Kisses from a walrus
Wet and croaking, weighing tons
Pinkish gray her belly swelling
And pale eyes like polar suns
—Frozen yellow polar suns
Spirit of the cosmic floes!
Over violet bristles bright
She blows upon deep pillows
Her bubbles of marine delight
—Frothing gaily with delight.

To Sondra Tschacbasov Bellow

June 8, 1966 [Chicago]

Dear Sondra,

I have added thirty dollars to cover Adam's tennis lessons. I shall continue, as in the past, to pay for his needs—within reason. It came as news to me that you were sending him to camp in August. When we discussed his summer plans, you said he would be in Chicago during the month of August, after his visit with me. I think I should be consulted about such arrangements. I am however prepared to pay the camp fee. Please ask Journey's End to bill me directly, as last year.

I understand from [my lawyer] Mr. [Marshall] Holleb that an increase in my monthly payments for Adam is still under consideration.

Sincerely,

To Margaret Staats

June 18, 1966 [Chicago]

For the first time, I feel I've gone out to a dangerous depth with you. Friday P.M. gave me a bad shock. You didn't tell me you were going out with anyone. Your only date was with [————] and his parents on Sat. The Friday man did not seem to me a casual date, but, judging from your changed tone towards me, one that means something to you. You didn't want to express feeling towards me in his presence. I thought, in fact, that you wanted to get rid of me. I've never before felt that you were anything but straight with me; but these last twenty-four hours I've felt it, terribly, wondering whether being in love with you isn't my ticket to destruction.

At the hotel, once, you said "Don't leave me," and had tears in your eyes. Now I'm not sure I can leave. Aren't you doing something with *that*?

When I guessed what the doorbell meant, you sounded guilty. You sounded ashamed.

Maggie—what are you up to?

To Margaret Staats

July 17, 1966   [Chicago]

Today, Sunday, working away in my room, my only refuge, I have such a loving heartache for you I wonder how I bear it. It seems I am only postponing the natural, inevitable, desirable. To obey "advice." It simply doesn't seem right. *What* am I doing here, in this city! If we feel and mean what we say we had better be ready to do what's necessary.

To Margaret Staats

August 3, 1966   [East Hampton]

According to Wm. Blake the road to excess leads to the palace of wisdom. This time it seems to have led elsewhere. We must have missed a turning. I wish I were there to give comfort and love. There's plenty of both here.

To Richard Stern

August 11, 1966   East Hampton

Dear Richard:

Well, it is Louse Point, nothing can be done about it, and a very agreeable place notwithstanding the name. I thought Buffalo would be straight out of Lucian's *Satires*, or Quevedo. I would have gone with chlorate of lime, or whatever it is they put in cesspools. But at least [John] Barth was decent; I would have thought so. It's a pity he has to have the treatment, though. He'll end up ridiculous. The *Times* review was very unfortunate for him, since after the great claims came a quoted paragraph that belonged in the wastepaper basket. All that Shakespearean tupping has a wicked backlash.

Meantime I have been weaving my own modest little fabric of disasters.

Though the surroundings be green and cheerful—white sands, scallop shells—you can hear the spiritual plutonium working up to fusion-heat.

The younger generation is still dreaming of things to come. Lisa is a lovely child. She and Kate were charming together, going into a girl-huddle that lasted hours. As for Daniel, he goes into a corner and says he has found a parking space. Susan is fine. We see a lot of the [Harold] Rosenbergs. Harold now belongs to the Committee [on Social Thought]. Some action, for once.

I get into NYC now and then to look after business and see my friends. Nobody, to quote Berryman, is missing. I asked Candida, but she had little or no information. When may we expect something from your pen? as they used to ask.

I don't know whether what is developing is the strength of the mature or the increased callousness of middle age.

Love to all,

John Barth's novel Giles Goat-Boy *had been favorably received in* The New York Times Book Review *and elsewhere.*

To Richard Stern

[Postmarked East Hampton, N.Y., ? September 1966]

Amigo—

Still on the social barricades of East Hampton—day after Labor Day, the elite remains. Still in a Mexican standoff, as Peltz calls it. Preparing to go abroad two weeks. Have set aside most everything to write a memoir of D. Schwartz. Turns out to be quite a document. We'll be here until Sept 15th. Miss your cheerful being.

Love,

Delmore Schwartz had died of a heart attack in July.

To Margaret Staats

October 11, 1966   [Chicago]

Honey, I'm beginning to feel a little better. I can't tell you how *hurt* I was. And I simply folded and slept a few days. It was convenient too. But I'm awake now. My brother-in-law, Janey's husband, is in the hospital with another coronary. It's doubtful that he'll be able to go on working. I don't know what my sister will do. She hasn't asked for help; refused when I offered it. I suppose they have a bit of money.

Suddenly, after years of complaining, she tells me what a gentle, inoffensive and kind man he's always been. I'm never surprised by what I hear. No more. He *is* long-suffering, that's certainly so. And a simple soul. I've known him since I was twelve, and he's something of a brother. I'm going to the hospital this evening to see him.

Love from Y[our]D[arling]

To Sondra Tschacbasov Bellow

November 2, 1966   Chicago

Dear Sondra:

Thank you for your letter. In answering, I shall try to state the facts as I see them.

Adam is, as you say, nine years old, not thirty. He is in a difficult position and it is inevitable that he should exaggerate and misrepresent. At the time when I am supposed to have told him that I would have no more children, he was no more than five or six. Is it really likely that I would say such a thing to a small boy? I find it odd that you should accept his every report without question. I did not, for instance, tell him that if he were older I would no longer bother to see him; I said that he was not yet of an age to choose between a visit with me and other social engagements.

It is difficult to be always the jolly, uncritical paternal chum. When I think he is going wrong, now and then, I feel that I must correct him. I never do this harshly or angrily. There are certain masculine attitudes the kid can get only from his father. Though he is a gentle, marvelous little boy, he occasionally gives me the Little Prince bit. Generally, I let it pass. This time it was a bit much. It is not for Adam to tell me that he does not wish to continue a discussion.

As for his manners, they are unusually good; they do you credit. But he is beginning to imitate the tone you take with me when I telephone. I don't think he should be allowed to speak to me like that. It's not good for him. The manners only make things worse.

I don't know whether you are aware that Adam is afraid of you. Your temper frightens him. I know that he tries to appease you. He loves you, and he is cowed. It is natural that I should try to strengthen and reassure him. Now and then I am obliged to speak to him about it. It is plain to the boy, besides, that you have no great regard for me. Strong mothers who hold fathers in contempt sometimes make homosexual sons. And I don't think Adam can learn much from you about fathers. I hope you will not be offended by these statements of fact. I have no desire to quarrel. My only interest is Adam's welfare, a topic I am not permitted to discuss with you. I understand that my ideas do not interest you much. You communicate with me in directives. There is no exchange of thoughts. You simply tell me what to do, you send messages by the boy, and you threaten me.

Well, threats at this point are absurd. It is Adam who suffers from these hostilities. I suffer only as he suffers—except through him you haven't much effect on me. The whole thing is a misfortune for him. Knowing how you dislike me, he gains your sympathy and tenderness by complaining about me. It can't be doing him much good to play off one parent against the other. He should have friends, teachers, alternatives. He should be able to turn to someone else. A psychiatrist perhaps.

If I didn't love Adam, the circumstances are such that I would have cut out long ago. I do love the child, and he needs me. Why do I see him? you ask. Because I love him. By presenting the problem to me as *my* problem, the result of *my* misdeeds, you don't help matters much. I am willing to discuss this, willing to listen, and willing to change.

To Margaret Staats

November 15, 1966 [Chicago]

[. . .] I dressed Daniel and we breakfasted on bananas and toast. By 8:00 I was at work, and he wanted to watch me. In the doorway, smearing the door with jam.

Was asked at noon to buy flowers. Funereal-feeling in my fur hat, and very pale. On the street asked myself why I was without you.

One waits for the sun to shine in Chicago. If only it would! Then it shines, you wish it wouldn't. From the inside, disappointed life seems to have sucked at the bricks. That must be why they look so porous in the light, popping with little holes.

Look east, and there's the lake like cold-cream.

I am low. And wouldn't say such things if I didn't love you and understand that you *want* to hear—even such things.

Y. D.

To a Mr. Gillman in London

November 16, 1966   Chicago, Ill.

Dear Mr. Gillman,

It was indeed kind of you to write. The subject you raise is a vast one and I have no great confidence in my power to cope with it. It is true we have a large land mass here and a cultural situation unprecedented in its disorderliness. I cannot help thinking, however, that we are dealing with difficulties that are universal. I refer to the problem of rootlessness and to that of change. It is inevitable that as an Englishman you would see in *Herzog* the Jewish question. On the surface, it is a Jewish book, but the real theme is, to me, far deeper. Like you, I believe one should depend on mutual feelings, on love. But I don't believe that love is a result of civilized roots. If one had to depend on those, injured as they are now or altogether cut off, one would have to wait a very long time.

Yours sincerely,

To Margaret Staats

November 28, 1966   [Chicago]

[. . .] My pleasure in life—to think about you. The white valentine. Face when making love. Hair when hands are raised to comb it. Teeth, lips, eyes, all music for my metronome.

I have enormous good luck!

Y.D.

In early December, Bellow and wife Susan formally separated.

1967

To Margaret Staats

January 11, 1967   [Chicago]

Your pinch-earmuffs were useful this freezing day. What is that Eliot line in "Journey of the Magi"? "A cold coming we had of it." Well! It's all cold and no coming. Like another poet's fellow, Samson Agonistes, I'm grinding the Philistines' corn. Don't mind the complaining—these aren't deep complaints and they seem to relieve me. I'm waiting for the current to light my poor bulb. [. . .]

Much love,

Y.D.

To Barley Alison

Dear Barley:

My meeting with George [Weidenfeld] went off pleasantly and that is very odd because I was vexed with him and came prepared to say no. I shan't say that he wooed and won me, because that's a feminine and inapplicable phrase, but his proposal was too good to refuse. I say this objectively, with the objectivity of prudence, not of greed. He promised a first printing of forty thousand copies for my next book and a uniform edition of all the others. It was awkward because I do rather like [Tom] Maschler [editor in chief at Jonathan Cape]. Actually I could not give George a final answer without telling Maschler the terms of the offer, just as I could not quit George without a final meeting. But I have written Maschler—I tell you this privately; it is a privileged communication—to say that it would be insane of me to turn down George's proposal. I am now waiting to hear from him.

George and I discussed you, of course. It was made quite clear that I would not have stayed with W[eidenfeld] and N[icolson] had you not been there. You may be sure that I betrayed no confidence. George knows nothing of our conversations. I told him that you should have had more influence in the business, and he told me how valuable you were to him. In this I think he was only partly smarmy, for he does value you highly (I am trying to imagine the cavern in which his values are stored). But he did not repeat what you had said in your letter about the three directors of the subsidiary company, and all of that. He said only that he planned to put you at the head of a separate organization. I earnestly hope that you will not let George snow you and that you will consult your family and your lawyers before you go into this.

So there it is. I shall probably be staying with W[eidenfeld] and N[icholson] and, better yet, with you. This last pleases me more than all the rest. I can assure you that the prospect of injuring you by going to Cape did not make me at all happy.

Yours affectionately,

Barley Alison was for many years Bellow's British editor.

To Barley Alison

May 18, 1967   Chicago

Dear Barley,

Your letter is haunting me with Utopian visions. I want very much to come [to Almería, Spain, where Barley had a vacation residence], of course, but I don't know yet whether I can manage it. During the summer I usually have numerous child problems. One of my sons is quite a young man and presents no problems, but the others are still much in need of Papa, and I am, with all my faults, a responsible papa. Still, I may be able to get away for a few weeks. Actually, I'd like nothing in the world better.

People who met you in New York said afterwards that they could easily understand why I have become your partisan and defender. You charmed everyone and I think you ought to have come to New York long ago. You remind me a bit of Hardy's Jude the Obscure, watching the lights of Christminster from his tiny hamlet while the years went by. You must come back often now.

You're sure to have a marvelous summer in that place. If I should turn up, which is not very likely, I shall come alone and curl up in a corner.

Yours affectionately,

To Margaret Staats

June 7, 1967   Athens

When we landed in Rome Monday officials came on board to tell us the war [in the Middle East] had started and that our flight would stop in Athens. Somewhat stunned, I wasn't totally disappointed. Feel a bit scared at the sound of bombs and guns blasting from the radio. But had to go forward and spent Mon. and Tues. fighting for a seat on the plane. I'm going tonight (Thurs. A.M.) and should be in Tel Aviv this hour tomorrow. Couldn't live with myself if I didn't. At US Embassy just now I had my passport validated for the Middle East, signing various documents. It puts one in touch with reality. Otherwise one's decades begin to feel empty like an old amusement park no longer patronized and oneself the caretaker remembering childhood, boyhood-youth as side shows (the fire-eater, the strong man, tunnel-of-love, etc.). This is much better. Though I do love you and my little children and a few other people—but this is all movie-talk! I'll be back on sched. for our holiday. I'll keep in close touch. Please don't bug *Newsday* about me. And don't *worry* so. After all, millions of lives are involved.

Love from Y. D.

On June 3, Bellow had flown from the US to report for Newsday *on the crisis that would lead to the Six-Day War in the Middle East.*

To Margaret Staats

June 10, 1967   Tel Aviv

This bloody thing is simply not to be believed. I ask myself how it would look from News York, but then I can't even say how it looks from here. From the slick Hilton to the battlefields to the Kremlin, etc.—or standing around in an elegant jacket watching armored columns shooting it out, or children being brought up from bomb shelters where parents have kept them for four days under shelling. I don't find it easy to match the pieces. I'm safe and well, and get along perfectly on three hours of sleep. Or none. I found I could wait up all night for a plane, never go to bed at all for forty-eight hours, and feel no fatigue. Only, sometimes, depressed. Today I was up at 4:00 A.M. At 1:00 P.M. I remembered it was my birthday.

Now it's 10:00 at night. I face a large bed which would look far better if it contained you. Write Y loving D here.

To Rosalyn Tureck

September 21, 1967   Chicago

Dear Rosalyn,

Wonderful of you to write. Yours was just the sort of letter I needed at a trying moment. As an admirer of your music, I don't like to miss your concert. The odd fact is, however, that I have at last decided to visit Africa and have accepted an assignment from *Holiday* to go and hover over the sources of the Nile in a helicopter and to write impressions or effusions. I leave just before Thanksgiving and return after Christmas, which lets me out of a couple of trying holidays, but makes it impossible for me to hear you, alas. We shall keep in touch, I hope, and see a good deal of each other yet.

Best wishes,

A classmate of Bellow's at Tuley, Rosalyn Tureck (1914–2003) was an internationally acclaimed interpreter of Bach on piano and harpsichord. (Glenn Gould would name her as his only influence.)

To Benjamin Nelson

October 13, 1967   Chicago

Dear Ben,

You are absolutely right about Brecht and [Eric] Bentley, but I tremble for you or for anyone who is sucked into these theatre quarrels. A most unstable and undesirable crowd; they have inherited all the charlatan traditions of theatre and lost contact with all the good things. Of course it can be argued that no playwright has *any* obligations to historical truth, though if he is writing for a modern, critical and intelligent audience (if such there be), he had better not offend too grossly.

How true to the facts was *Marat-Sade*? Only last night I read in *Encounter* a letter from Leo Labedz on the new [Rolf] Hochhuth play [*Soldiers, Necrology on Geneva*] having to do with Churchill's crimes against the Poles in exile. Churchill is accused of murder, no less, and Hochhuth says he has years of study behind the charge. I doubt that very much and Labedz is furious. I suppose this puts Hochhuth's play in the cold-war propaganda category, and I assume that it's propaganda you oppose and not the disfigurement of facts by a creative person.

Could you send me a copy of the speech you gave in California? I want very much to read it.

Yours affectionately,

Benjamin N. Nelson (1911–77) taught history and sociology at the University of Minnesota, where he met Bellow, and later at the New School for Social Research. His books include Freud and the Twentieth Century *(1957) and a posthumous collection of essays,* On the Roads to Modernity: Conscience, Science, and Civilizations *(1981).*

1968

To Edward Shils

January 20, 1968   Chicago

Dear Ed:

I spoke to your mother yesterday. She complains that she is feeling weak, but she sounded better to me. Her voice seemed stronger. I think it knocked her out to come back from [Dr.] Horner's office on the train. She couldn't get a cab, as I assume she wrote you. Anyway, I think I hear some improvement.

I came back from NY a few days ago with my Gaullist ribbon and medal. Your last letter was on the dining-room table and I re-read it for company. The situation in Chicago is odd and getting odder. It's a peculiarly contactless life, when you're not here. There are lots of people in these buildings. As if the pioneer emptiness were set upright, with indoor plumbing, books, food, but the spirit of the prairies still dominant. [. . .] No one other than David Grene asks me to dinner. If it weren't for my divorce case I would have no social existence whatsoever [. . .] I simply get up in the morning and go to work, and I read at night. Like Abe Lincoln. When I go out there's my city—sodden, mean and boring. [. . .] I tell myself that in any great city I could see as many people as I liked and wonder why I put up with such privation. It gets one. In that same light I saw N[athan] Leites with his bald musclebound skull hurrying through melting slush, moving with ballistic energy from 53rd to 55th, a bottle under his arm—moving with such force, and the muscles of shyness and analytic subtlety (probably pointless) gathered up on his shaven head. [. . .]

Anyway, there it is. I miss you very much. And I may turn up [in England] in mid-May.

Love,

To Meyer Schapiro

March 18, 1968   Oaxaca

Dear Meyer—

I thought you *were* in England. Now that I know you're at home I shall certainly come to see you before you leave.

This is my second morning in Oaxaca. When you wake up in the tropics you understand the horror of your Northern fatigue. And the flowers tell you that you have been around much too long. Unfinished business is my excuse.

Of course I want to contribute to the Delmore fund. And I hope John Berryman will become, and remain, one of the judges. I haven't seen him in two years, and he was in poor condition then, in full alcoholic bloat. I'm very fond of Berryman, and I admire him. I see why these self-destructive lives are led. But I can't convince myself that it is a good tradition.

Did you receive tear-sheets of a longish story ["The Old System"] I published in January? I thought you might be interested in it. *The New Yorker* wanted deletions, so I gave it to *Playboy* in protest—lucrative protest. However, there are no poor but honest magazines. The quarterlies are about as corrupt as the slicks, and Hugh Hefner has pleasanter vices than Wm. Phillips.

My best wishes to you,

To Richard Stern

July 16, 1968   [East Hampton]

Cher Richard—

The summer is hot in East Hampton, and all the artist roses are preening, even the ailing and the possibly dying are drinking their gin in the sun and talking welfare, reform or revolution, anarchy, guerilla warfare, action—building stately mansions on foundations of personal wretchedness.

The swimming is excellent.

I am getting in some good *travail*.

Since you mention weights and measures, I am about ten pounds too heavy and now eat yogurt at lunch. *Toujours poursuivi des femmes, pourtant tracassé. Des circonstances assez marrant. Elles sont* toutes *fachées—au nord, ouest, et ici même. Mais je continue tout de même de faire mes devoirs* [*].

Adam is in excellent condition, only a spot of mother-induced neurosis here and there. *Surtout raisonnable* [**]. One can always *talk* to him, which cannot be said of too many. I realize that this is the last of his childhood, and that we will go forward, towards fuller forms . . . I skip the next comment.

I have death on my mind, today. S. S. Goldberg is ill, John Steinbeck is in the Southampton Hospital, Jean Stafford has just been released from same. So we, here, are feeling the wing. But in this weather it is more cooling than anything else. The Angel of Death, floating over the house, brings air-conditioning.

Much love,

Tape-*moi une lettre.* [***]

---

* French: Still pursued by women; worried nonetheless. An amusing situation.
  They're *all* furious—north, west, and even here, but I continue to do my duty.
** French: Above all, reasonable.
*** French: *Type* me a letter.

To Richard Stern

My dear Richard:

Je m'impatiente de lire ce que t'as écrit [*]. It's a pity because I won't be in Chicago now until October, but perhaps you can send Xerox copies to the Villa Serbelloni, that old Rockefeller château [at Bellagio]. I feel as though I might be more at home in a junkyard, closer to origins, than at Lake Como, but one takes one's junkyard with one.

Anyway, you have probably written something marvelous. I judge by the fact that you are usually so guarded in your opinion of your own work. Your credit is very good with me, you see.

I went to visit Daniel on the Vineyard. Adam and I flew from East Hampton in a chartered bumblebee with short wings through a gale, and we were scared but in heaven. Then we got down on the ground to Daniel's cheers, and spent some time lying on the beaches and having hassles about robins' eggs. [. . .]

I want to thank you for your note on *Mosby*. It encourages me to write more stories. Before the Bartleby silence settles over me. When time's winged chariot gets ahead of you and you can't hear the wheels.

I suppose you'll be back in Chicago before long. Maggie (who sends love and kisses) will be staying on in the country when I leave, using my whirlwind Pontiac. [. . .]

Love,

Mosby's Memoirs and Other Stories *had just appeared.*

To Margaret Staats

September 4, 1968   Villa Serbelloni, Bellagio

Dear Maggie,

It couldn't be better. The very bathroom is situated in a Romanesque tower. Everything is simply beautiful. I am beginning to recover from the flight.

Love,

* French: I'm eager to read what you've written.

To Margaret Staats

September 5, 1968   [Bellagio]

Dearest Maggie—

This is very rough, but you can do it. You have the love of many people—it's not just me. You don't need to go through this alone. I know the doctor gave you a bad scare, but it's about two hundred to one that the tumor is benign. If you badly need me, I can fly back, but I will wait for news on Monday.

But don't isolate yourself from friends—don't lose your head, honey. These will be four grim days. They have to be faced. That's not easy. But don't send people away. You need them. I wish I were there with you, but since we've got the Atlantic between us I'll wait for the results of the biopsy. It should be just that, only that—a biopsy. Harold [Taylor] will advise you. Take his advice. Bless you, honey.

Love,

To Margaret Staats

September 11, 1968   [Bellagio]

Honey, tell me what's happened. I was up all night Tue. praying I would not get a call, but this morning I am still in the dark, really. Send me a wire, at least, saying you're okay, if the thing was harmless. But don't lie to me. If it was not harmless I'll want to fly straight back. Because I didn't hear, I have some hope. I was in despair over you yesterday, and the days before. Have you been getting my mail?

Love,

To Margaret Staats

September 14, 1968   [Bellagio]

Dear Maggie-o:

I'm sorry if I was short on the phone. The reason was that we had just had a phone conversation and I wasn't expecting it to be your call. I thought certainly that something had happened to one of the children, for why would anyone else call. And after thinking it over, though I don't excuse myself, I think you did not do well to call me. I know your need is great, but this is no way to meet it. It's not as though you were calling to reproach me for something or to ask me for something, or to cry. You are in pain, yes, but you have just escaped a horrible operation. You don't have cancer. Instead of relief and gratitude you have—this. It's not good. Not good for you, not good for me. Don't you think, after all this time, that I feel for you, sympathize with you? Waiting here was hellish also. I went to talk to Dr. Bryant, the foundation's doctor here, about your prospects and I sat it out on Tuesday without sleep, or let-up in my panic, waiting for an answer to my wire. And now, at this distance, I can only feel troubled. I can't actually help you. To give the help you want I would have to come back.

And I *have* written, and we have spoken on the phone three times, or is it four, so it's not as if we haven't been in contact. As for your schoolwork, what can I do about it? If you're sick, what can you do? What can anyone do? That's not a thing to phone across the Atlantic about either. Please, Maggie, don't do that anymore, I beg you. You can just leave my stuff, car and all, in East Hampton and I'll look after it later. I've been here now for two weeks, and there are only two more, which I don't want to goof up. I want to get something out of them. It's not your fault that the first two haven't been ideal but now, if only for a bit, I want to turn off the heat. I've had a frightful letter from Sondra—just wicked, a horror. Sometimes I think I should apply to Mao Tse-Tung for asylum.

You know what our relationship is. It's not what you want, but it is a great deal. It is everything that I can make it. When I put my arms around you it is all there. You know I am Y. D. And don't blame the US mails on me. Calm yourself. And honey, lay off the telephone.

Love,

To Sondra Tschacbasov Bellow

[n.d.]   [Bellagio]

Dear Sondra,

The important thing is not to fight. That's important to you, too. If I offended you at the airport, I'm sorry, and I apologize. I shrink from letter-tournaments, long exchanges and all of that. We've been to the wars already and what we want now is the permanent hatchet burial. Margy [Maggie] knows she behaved badly, but she has a good explanation. She needed breast surgery (I didn't know that) and was frantic with worry. The tumor has been removed. It was benign.

She didn't know that I was to repay the twenty-five bucks. *I* knew nothing about it from you. You didn't tell me. When you make loans expecting me to make them good you should communicate with me, not simply assume that I underwrite all of them. I might have overlooked that however, if you hadn't written such a provoking letter. Think what you like, I don't expect miraculous changes, but don't write me such letters. We can get along splendidly, just fine, if we observe the ground rules. I did not observe them at Kennedy, and you knocked them all to hell in two or three sentences. I see a pattern forming and I mean to break it up immediately. I generally pass over this kind of thing in silence, when we chat, but now I think it's best to spell it out for you.

First of all, then: I wrote a successful book. I owe you nothing for that. You damn near killed me. I've put that behind me, but I haven't forgotten the smallest detail. Nothing, I assure you. I made something [in *Herzog*] of the abuses I suffered at your hands. As for the "humiliations" you speak of, I can match you easily. There is another book, isn't there? [*Above Ground*, Jack Ludwig's roman à clef of his friendship with Bellow and affair with Sondra]. It is the product of two minds and two spirits, not one. Kind acquaintances and friends have made sure that I would read it. The letters of the heroine are consciously superior in style, but the book is garbage. It is monstrous to be touched by anything so horribly written. The worst thing about it, to a man who has been faithful to his art for thirty years, is the criminal vulgarity of the thing. I don't worry too much about my reputation, the "image" (I don't think you pay much attention to that, either), but I loathe being even peripherally involved with such shit. Now I've gotten a foot in the cesspool. Enough of that. But suppose the book had been good, successful. Can you see me demanding damages? I don't think you can. So now . . . let the thing stop there. I want you to say nothing more to me about money, and I don't want any hints about damages and indemnities. What I have, what I spend, where I go are no concern of yours. Legally I am obliged to pay three thousand *per annum* for Adam. I give, by my own choice, another three and more. This is a gift and not a commitment. Bailing you out, last year, was also my choice, and it was not dictated by bad conscience, I assure you. In this way something like eight thousand dollars was spent last year, and now you write me an insolent letter about money. You had better not do that again. Keep within bounds, and I will do it too. We will be pleasant to each other, but say nothing to me about your drapes or windowshades or about my trips. Those are no business of yours; your windowshades are nothing to me. I will do everything I can for Adam, whom I love. There will be certain fringe benefits for you. But don't push things.

Now I'm done with that.

I greatly appreciated your bringing Adam to the airport. It was the holiday, and it took four hours to get down from East Hampton, and I'd have had to start at dawn to stop in Great Neck, so I'm grateful. It's not a bad idea though for Adam to begin to take some trouble for his father. It's proper that he should. Among fathers I'm not the world's worst, and he's old enough to develop some feeling for what is due to a father. Gratitude. I've always been a grateful type myself, and he's my child. I'd be sorry to see him grow up devoid of any sense of it.

Always your affectionate friend,

To Margaret Staats

September 16, 1968   [Bellagio]

Dear Maggie:

Thanks for the letters and the clippings. I read them all as soon as they come. I'm not receiving an awful lot of mail. Once in a while Bates sends me a packet of things I wish I'd never seen—bank statements, the disaster of the checks I write, the preposterous correspondence it's my lousy fate to be involved in. It seems that Mr. Bill Cooper accepted [on Bellow's behalf] an invitation, of which I was never told, to speak somewhere in Rinkdink, Penn. tomorrow the 17th, and that people are wringing their hands, demanding explanations from me. Then, too, I'm not awfully well. I have no acute difficulties, only a slight feeling of non-function and dissolution. And there are moments when I am handed a snapshot or pass a mirror and realize that I have not as yet adjusted myself to certain changes, or even grasped them, and that my self-image is about twenty years behind the real object. I don't sleep well, I'm often hazy in the morning, and I haven't been working awfully well. There are mornings when I urge myself to take a long walk over the mountains, and hold up freedom placards to myself. I am, after all, supposed to be Free. That's a very amusing concept and it cheers me up oddly to have thought of it.

The [Arthur] Kopits have been kind to me. We've gotten along extremely well. There have been no other younger folk about, only a lot of singing dowagers. (One lady with a recent degree in Fine Arts from Tucson, Ariz., sixty years if she's a day, sings Viennese café music, with trills. She's a sweet old thing, really.) Last week we had a convention of Taoists. This week medicine and the underdeveloped countries. A bony doctor from a remote province asked me today what my trade was, which grimly gratified me. I haven't been to Milan, yet. Bellagio has one drugstore and a lot of curiosity shops.

The most aged Britishers I've ever seen are here and they make that lady from Oaxaca, you remember her, look like Marilyn Monroe. I've seldom beheld such mummy shanks, such lizard-lapping of tea or heard such Limey discussions of constipation remedies. [Giangiacomo] Feltrinelli, my publisher, is coming on Wednesday to drive me to dinner in Milan. Kopits are leaving on the same day and will arrive (sailing) eight days later with news of me. I'll give them your number. Y.D. at sunset (gorgeous but it makes me blue).

With love,

To David Peltz

September 20, 1968   Villa Serbelloni, Bellagio

Dear Dave:

It's been mighty fine, in some ways, and in others one of my famous exercises in suffering. For one thing, I had only been here a few days when Maggie found she had to have breast surgery, and then there was a spell of waiting for news—fortunately good. After the good news, came hysterics: all kinds of transatlantic telephone oddities. Time out for sobbing. I thought the whales and the winds were talking to me. The Lord sent relief in the form of a wet dream or two. I've had no other. All my ladies seem furious. Not one of them has written, not even Bette [Howland]. She must have done research in my apartment and found sinful evidence. I feel neglected, old and a bit sick. I don't think this is hypochondria. I feel the hook down in my gullet, and I hear that old reel spinning. I think I'd better come back to dreadful Chicago and find out what, if anything, is the matter. In spite of everything I have, as usual, done a certain amount of work. It may turn out all right, but I'm not at my best these days. Maggie's line with me now is that I must mark time while she tries to develop other interests, especially, she says, since she does this out of rejection and therefore I owe her perfect fidelity. Seeing her twice a month is perfectly adequate. I have no more real needs. At my time of life they must be imaginary and delusive. [. . .] Sondra, also, has sent me some record-breaking words. Those I've saved for you, together with my reply, for to try to describe this exchange would be like trying to paint Hell with Daniel's fingerpaints. She claims I made use of her, and of the divorce [in *Herzog*], to make a fortune which I now must share with her. For as things are I treat myself to European trips, etc. while she and Adam have to scrape along on pennies. If Barnum were alive, he and I could make a really great show of this. The great men are gone, though; we have nothing but punks.

I'll see you quite soon—early in October. I've missed you badly. Flee some, lose others, and that's the story.

Love,

To Margaret Staats

September 21, 1968   [Bellagio]

Honey—I played tennis with Prof. Obolensky (Christ Church, Oxford) for nearly two hours yesterday, went to bed at 9:30 with two Gelusil pills and woke up at 8:30, having had no stomach upset. Consequently I feel like a newborn child. Many of my ailments must be caused by my reluctance to sleep nine or ten hours a day. Maybe I should simply give half my life to darkness instead of giving it *all* to confusion.

Maybe you'll get this letter.

Love,

Prince Dimitri Dimitrievich Obolensky was at Villa Serbelloni working on The Byzantine Commonwealth, *his history of eastern Europe in the Middle Ages.*

To Margaret Staats

September 23, 1968   [Bellagio]

Dear Maggie—

[. . .] I think I'd better go and see Louis [Sidran], don't you? What terrible things keep happening. And from here you have no idea how inconceivable the world is. From the peaceful mountains it's all like the plague, down below. [Meanwhile, up here,] only old scholars, old scholars' wives, high cuisine, choice wines, tennis, a peaceful library, Renaissance paintings. Then there are strange events. Last evening after dinner, by the fire, old John Marshall, Harvard '21, told me that I had meant a great deal to him. My books, and myself. Then he began to weep. He's such a decorous Wasp I hardly knew how to interpret this. He simply said that I was one of the people he loved. And he wept. I wept myself, partly at the oddity of human relations. That there should be so much to jump over—so much apparent difference or distance. And then, in people who are *not* old, whose flesh isn't dead, whose hearts aren't dead, one could live a life of Harvard or Chicago (dateless horror, Chicago) until love reclaims one for reality. Well, it all happens. He's a good man.

Mosby came today. To my horror, as I read along p. 5, six lines up from the bottom, "And her and her cowboy . . ." What nitwit let that pass? It's awful! In a house like Viking, and in a short book. I've written to Denver [Lindley] abt it. I was angry, felt nasty, but held it in.

Tell me, how is the new job? I'm afraid you can't answer that. I'll be gone when the answer arrives.

Love,

Bellow's childhood friend Louis Sidran was dying of cancer in Chicago.

To Margaret Staats

September 27, 1968   [Bellagio]

Dear Maggie:

Louie is dead. He went back to the hospital, and there he seemed to give out, his wife says, and he died. I guess he had struggled so long and so hard with the thing that he was used up. I telephoned Winnetka yesterday, and talked to Shirley. I'm very sad and heavy but not grief-sickened. I went about my business, crying some, and thinking now and then of the funeral, yesterday. He was in the ground and the family had gone home. It was his first night there. Shirley kept saying that he was so happy to have come to East Hampton before [he got too ill], and talked of nothing else. He had come to say goodbye to me, and knew it. He got my card from Bellagio and hoped I'd get back before too long. I must have expected to see him again. He died quickly and didn't have to waste away utterly. I feel especially for his mother, who's a fine old woman, and for Ezra [Shirley and Louie's youngest child].

I was glad to get the red leaf. Thank you, honey. And you're right, it's worth a thousand *Timeses*. I keep it with the shells. I think my long celibacy has restored my contemplative eye. I spend more time sitting looking at objects. Much less coming and going at random, helter-skelter but as if I had some purpose. I do a lot of looking at Lake Como.

I am most troubled, when I am troubled, by Daniel. I haven't seen him in nearly three months and I miss him desperately. I may go directly back to see him, and then come to New York some days later to see you. The news from Chicago is not reassuring. I want to see for myself how matters are, and I shan't feel easy until I do. I'll give you plenty of notice. I've missed you. When the fat envelopes of clippings come, I am disappointed when there is no letter, but the term has just begun so you must be over your eyebrows with work.

Saul Bellow: Letters

My German publisher Witsch (wouldn't you know it) has died. Without him the company is floundering and I'm going down to Milan tomorrow to meet Herr Rowohlt of Rowohlt Co. and hear what he has to say. Obolensky, my tennis chum the Prince, has gone back to Oxford. None too soon, probably. I thought the other day that I would keel over on the court. Singles are much too rough for me, especially since I'm a duffer and have to run far more than a real tennis player.

Much love,

Y.D.

To Mark Harris

Dear Mark:

Your letter about *Mosby* set me up for a while in the midst of a disorderly season. I see, looking back at the vanished years, that I wrote few stories and that I seem to have used them as "scale models" for bigger jobs. For that reason I was a bit worried about *Mosby*; I wondered what big job it would lead to. Even now I'm not altogether clear as to what *is* happening. I don't think it's all bad, however. And I hoped that I was not being choppy, only lucid. But all we worshippers of lucidity must be terribly confused to begin with.

The thing at S.F. State was very bad. I'm not too easy to offend, at my age, and I don't think I was personally affronted—that's not my style. The thing was offensive though. Being denounced by [Floyd] Salas as an old shit to an assembly which seemed to find the whole thing deliciously thrilling. [. . .] So I left the platform in defeat. Undefended by the bullied elders of the faculty. While your suck-up-to-the-young colleagues swallowed their joyful saliva. No, it was very poor stuff, I assure you. You don't found universities in order to destroy culture. For that you want a Nazi party.

Enough said. Thanks again and all best,

At San Francisco State University, after delivering a talk entitled "What Are Writers Doing in the Universities?" Bellow had been denounced in the style of the day by boxer-turned-writer Floyd Salas: "You're a fucking square. You're full of shit. You're an old man, Bellow." (Bellow was fifty-two.) The episode would furnish material for a similar scene in Mr. Sammler's Planet, *his novel in progress.*

To Willie Greenberg

December 7, 1968   Chicago

Dear Willie,

It was such a pleasure to see you after so many years. I always remembered you as a very kind boy (to me, at eight, you were a young man, really) and you confirmed the accuracy of my memory by generously giving me those photographs. I was touched by that. Enough to make a middle-aged gent cry.

Thank you, Willie.

Remember me to Molly and Harry. I hope we will meet again before the doors shut.

Love,

Willie Greenberg's family had lived next door to Bellow's in Montreal.

To Margaret Staats

December 9, 1968   [Chicago]

Dearest Maggie—

I am *really* down now, and I must work for an Armistice, a moratorium, some pause. I can't go on like this. I am simply worn out, and I no longer feel natural towards you or anyone else.

I love you, I always will. You are one of the best—probably the best woman I will ever know. I respect you, I wish you every good, but I am trying to save my own sanity just now—probably my very life. I feel it threatened. We must stop. I can't go on without a breather.

To the John Simon Guggenheim Memorial Foundation

December 10, 1968   Chicago, Ill.

CONFIDENTIAL REPORT ON CANDIDATE FOR FELLOWSHIP

Name of Candidate: Louise Glück

Miss Glück has the combination of oddity and verbal power from which something unusually good may result. I am impressed by her poems. She plays no games that I can recognize, she seems entirely independent. I think she should be freed from her stenographic duties.

1969

To Margaret Staats

January 2, 1969   London

Dearest Maggie—

It's all right here. I had night-depressions but really nothing dreadful and I seem to be pulling myself together. I hope you are, too. I was encouraged by your clearer eyes and calmer ways. You'll make it. It's not easy, but you have what it takes—reform, imagination, courage. The courage moves me more than I can say.

To Margaret Staats

[n.d.]   [London]

Dear M—

Good times. I am by myself. From you I have acquired a need for the soul. People without it now are terribly trying. Can't even make them out. There was *only* one way to learn that. It was very chancey. I probably had no choice. So there it is. By now I am probably out on points.

Be back soon—

To Margaret Staats

[Postmark illegible; postcard of King's College, Cambridge]

My dear Maggie—

This is where I am. Some peace, here. A sign on the sundial says, *Sic fugit vita*. Meaning: "Here the sun seldom shines, but we are prepared." Ed [Shils] asks about you.

Love,

To Toby Cole

February 3, 1969   London

Dear Toby

If Eli [Wallach] wants to try [*The Last*] *Analysis* on NET, I have no objection. I'd be willing even to make myself available for consultation (on carefully measured terms).

At 3:55 P.M. I'll be in Paris, and tomorrow I have lunch with my translator, making several additions and corrections in and to the O[range] Soufflé.

I'll keep the notes. Until I finish my novel (half-done; perhaps, at this moment half-baked as well) I'll write no dramas. I do however have in my head two fabulous movie scenarios—one for De Sica, one for Fellini. I'd prefer De Sica for both.

I'll arrive in NY perhaps together with this letter. I'll telephone this time.
Love,

To Barley Alison

February 18, 1969 [Chicago]

My dear Barley,

Greetings.

Here's Chicago, once again. The Lake, seen from this window, is frozen solid and so are a good many other things. Until I got to New York my tour was uneventful enough. Paris was as I thought it would be, largely a waste of time. I did see some old friends. But I did not enjoy my meeting with [Louis] Guilloux and probably I was not highly enjoyable to meet myself. Then on to the US. I was grounded by a blizzard in the East. Fifteen inches of snow. Landing at Idlewild. I telephoned my friend Arlette [Landes] in Chicago. She said she believed we should not see each other anymore. Evidently she couldn't wait until I returned to say this. I assume that she has taken up with someone else. Women generally get the strength for these decisions from other relationships. I don't know that *relationship* is the word for it either. Lord knows that sort of conduct. What kinds of events that poor noun has to subsume! At any rate, I haven't seen my companion, from whom I was inseparable for a month. This is what intimacies seem made of. Of course I'm hurt. I *would* be. But it'll wear off. It generally does.

When I spoke to Pillet, he asked for a thousand dollars in rent. I don't think I will want to pay so much. I've already made plans to take Adam to England on June 23rd. I thought I would, after two weeks, hand him over to his mother in Madrid and then go on to the South to visit you near Almería. If you can put up with me for a week or so from about July 8th or 9th. Adam's mother will continue with him to Italy. I shall probably go back to the US to spend more of the summer with Daniel on or near Martha's Vineyard.

I seem now to be writing still another book. I was thrown from the first by Arlette and had lost the power to concentrate on what I was doing while we were together. Since I loathe and fear idleness I have opened a new project. I can complete this in about two months. It's the *métier* that keeps me sane, bless it.

Love,

To Sylvia Tumin

February 21, 1969   Chicago

Dear Sylvia,

I was in London and didn't get your note in time to wire my congratulations. I know that Mel is sensible enough to be fifty. But I do keep remembering, with enjoyment, his frivolous salad days. Enjoy the following: I telephoned Kappy from London to say that I was coming to Paris to see him. He said that he was just leaving for Switzerland, to ski. I told him that I was flying over primarily to see him. Then he said, "I am desolated." I enjoyed that tremendously. It was worth all the shillings I had dropped into the box.

Blessings on you all.

Love,

To Whit Burnett

April 30, 1969   Chicago

Dear Mr. Burnett:

[. . .] I wrote "Mosby's Memoirs" on six successive mornings in the Mexican town of Oaxaca without the aid of tequila. I seemed to need no stimulants. I was in a state of all but intolerable excitement, or was, as the young now say, "turned on." A young and charming friend [Maggie Staats] typed the manuscript for me. Reading it I found little to change. The words had come readily. I felt as they went into the story that I was striking them with a mallet. I seldom question what I have written in such a state. I simply feel gratitude and let it go at that.

Sincerely,

Whit Burnett (1899–1973), who as editor of Story *had rejected Bellow's early work, was including "Mosby's Memoirs" in his anthology* America's 85 Greatest Living Authors Present *(1970) and had inquired about the circumstances under which the story was composed.*

To Margaret Staats

June 5, 1969   [Bellagio]

Dear Maggie—

Never before on the fifth of June have I seen snow falling. I see it now on the mountaintops, and it is frosty down here in the valley. Not two days has the sun shone in Europe. Have we killed the atmosphere with automobiles? I begin to think the planet is going to hell.

I don't sleep well, I am haggard, I miss you, I miss Daniel, I get no mail from the States, but I manage somehow to look after the main thing. In my chill chalet under the cypress trees. Drinking beer and waiting to creep out into the sun—when it shines again.

It is beautiful here—if you have a nineteenth-century eye. Mine must be of the twenty-first.

Love,

To Margaret Staats

June 8, 1969   [Bellagio]

Dear Maggie-o—

"Writing up a storm," as you call it, thousands of words daily, and not stopping to type because I don't sleep, and if I were to spend the P.M.s at the machine I'd wreck myself and lose the good mornings. What I may do is airmail Xerox copies of the mss. pages to you, just for safekeeping. I'm very cold on [Aaron] Asher. He wants to "hold his own" with me. Sometimes he seems to be pushing himself into the cockpit, but this is a solo flight.

Now: We have a house in London. Three bedrooms not far from the center of things [. . .] Be good. Bless you. See you *soon*.

Love,

Upon Denver Lindley's retirement from Viking, Aaron Asher had become Bellow's editor.

To Richard Stern

August 1, 1969

Dear Dick—

So I'm in Nantucket, ever benevolent, watching pheasants cramming blackberries in the backyard. All is backyard from the window. Good to see American weeds again.

I finished this *Sammler* off properly in Spain, on the Mediterranean coast, Carboneras, very good moon visibility. Maggie caused me *grandes dificultades* [*] in England and in the south but I finished just the same. I am obstinate. I make my own obstacles but jump 'em meself.

I'm delighted to hear that you dare so much. It's excellent—just great, too, that you're rid of Candida [Donadio]. She is to Candor what bangs are to Bangor. She deserves to be whacked about the head by our dear Edward one long evening, that's what she deserves, and may God fall asleep when she reads her apologia before His throne.

[. . .]

Love,

To Margaret Staats

August 4, 1969 [Nantucket]

Dear Maggie—

I'm troubled about your visit—it seems too soon. Europe has left me with still raw hurts, not likely to heal in a short time. I don't want them re-opened, nor do I want you to be hurt again, and my heart tells me to let things ride, to recover first and not to force anything. For the sake of continuing friendship, we ought to keep away from each other.

Love,

To Harvey Swados

August 30, 1969   Nantucket

Dear Harvey:

The novel I have as you say "committed" has kept me busy, and galleys, etc. will continue to keep me busy until October. If it's only advice, mine would be no better than other people's and probably inferior to Candida's. But if you want me to read your book, I can do that in October. I'll be back in Chicago as the nights lengthen. If that does you any good, I am your obedient servant.

As I read your letter I see that we don't share very many basic assumptions. No other two college Trotskyites can have gotten so very far apart. I doubt that I have more use for Nixon and Johnson than you have. My going to the White House [in June 1965] was nonsense, probably. It pleased no one, myself least of all. I wouldn't have gone at all if I had been obliged by my own obstinacy to mark my disagreement with all parties. First I made my views

* Spanish: big problems

on Vietnam and Santo Domingo as clear as possible in the *Times*, and then declared that I would go to show my respect for the President's office—the office of Lincoln. I know about Harding, too, and Chester A. Arthur, but I am not at all prepared to secede. I am not a revolutionary. I have little respect for American revolutionaries as I know them, and I have known them quite well. I don't like the Susan Sontag bit about a doomed America. I had my fill of the funnyhouse in Coney Island.

A reliable source tells me that Johnson's view of the White House culture gala was as follows: "They insult me by comin', they insult me by stayin' away." Could Dwight Macdonald have been more succinct? In fact they have a lot in common.

My best to Bette.

Yrs,

To Philip Roth

December 12, 1969   Chicago

Dear Philip:

Your note did me a lot of good, though I haven't known what or how to answer. Of course the so-called fabricators will be grinding their knives. They have none of that ingenuous, possibly childish love of literature you and I have. They take a sort of Roman engineering view of things: grind everything in rubble and build cultural monuments on this foundation from which to fly the Bullshit flag.

Anyway, it pleases me greatly that you liked *Sammler*. There aren't many people in the trade for whom I have any use. But I knew when I hit Chicago (was it twelve years ago?) and read your stories that you were the real thing. When I was a little kid, there were still blacksmiths around, and I've never forgotten the ring of a real hammer on a real anvil.

Do you like Woodstock? I lived across the river for eight years. *Was* it living? But the place was not to blame. It was beautiful.

Yours,

PART FOUR

1970–1982

———◆•◆•◆———

Y ou know? There's the most extraordinary, unheard-of poetry buried in America, but none of the conventional means known to culture can even begin to extract it. But now this is true of the world as a whole. The agony is too deep, the disorder too big for art enterprises undertaken in the old way. Now I begin to understand what Tolstoi was getting at when he called on mankind to cease the false and unnecessary comedy of history and begin simply to live.

—Humboldt's Gift

1970

To John Berryman

January 19, 1970

Dear John—

Without preliminaries, we have a magazine—Harold Rosenberg, Keith Botsford and I, and of course no magazine involving me can work without you. Poems are essential. Could you also, as with Shakespeare at thirty, think of doing Mozart at twenty, or Bach at forty? [. . .]

I am going to London for three weeks to escape the book reviews.

Love,

The magazine was Anon, *a single issue of which would appear.*

To Margaret Staats

February [?], 1970

[Postcard of "Tippoo's Tiger" at Victoria and Albert Museum]

The sultan had the device wound up, and the British soldier being killed would cry "Help, Mercy." It gave the sultan endless pleasure.

As ever,

To Frances Gendlin

[Postmark illegible; postcard of Debre Berhan Selassie Church, Gondar, Ethiopia]

Dear Fran—

Now Ethiopia. Swept through Kenya and Uganda. Minimum of dysentery. Great fatigue. Bought a mine with Peltz. Feeling grand but I miss you.

To Frances Gendlin

February 9, 1970   New Avenue Hotel, Nairobi, Kenya

Well, the whole mining deal was pure con. Peltz's man w'd not appear. Evidently it was an intercontinental swindle. Hugely funny.

So we are making a safari, and this is written on a bucking plane en route to Kampala, to Murchison Falls. We shall see elephants and crocodiles.

I'd have been very glad if you had joined me, for I do miss you, and no number of elephants and crocodiles can take your place. Nights especially. Forgive me for hoping mildly that the weather is bad in Chicago. African planes *are* hot. I'm sweating. But in Africa one must. Imagine: "He toured Africa without sweating" (said of a cold man, and I am not cold).

Love,

To Frances Gendlin

[Postmark illegible; postcard of two lionesses, Uganda]

Dear Fran—

This, the Upper Nile, is simply astonishing. If the tsetse fly doesn't bite me I shall never forget it. If it does, give away my Mercedes and burn my bills. I sh'd have asked you along.

Love,

To Frances Gendlin

[n.d.]   Hotel Raphael, Rome

I am writing with a ballpoint quill in the lobby of this hotel—an original idea. Why didn't I think of it? The hotel is entirely like that, up-to-date Renaissance. You'd adore it.

I planned to go back to London today, but it's raining fiercely in Rome and I haven't the flying stomach for it after the trips from Addis Ababa to Asmara to Khartoum to Cairo to Athens and here, twelve hours that left me somewhat vacant and pill-bilious (for the troubled gut, for malaria and for sniffles I took a weird mixture of tablets, and Peltz and I drank beer continually, dying of thirst and fearing the water).

This trip I think has met the purpose. I am better, more settled in mind and am willing—no, longing—to come back to 5805 [Dorchester Ave.]. You're a lovely woman, Fran, I've been fortunate, and I've missed you greatly. I'll phone from London in a few days. I expect to depart from Europe about the 26th.

Love,

To Edward Shils

February 25, 1970   Chicago

Dear Ed—

The porter at King's [College] said that you were in the U.S. and that you were expected on Thursday, therefore I was certain I would see you in Chicago but we must have missed each other by a few hours, for on Monday (Feb. 23rd) you were already gone.

I didn't want to spend time in Europe: I was eager to get to Africa. It did not disappoint me. Murchison Falls and the White Nile stunned me. With my "civilized" habit of diminishing or scaling down large impressions in advance, I had thought myself ready for Nature's grandeur (having seen the movies) but all my preparations were (luckily) driven away by the actual sight of the great river.

In Nairobi, Peltz and I seem to have acquired an interest in a beryllium mine. Of course it is mere playfulness for me. I did it in a carnival spirit. Peltz I think is very earnest about it. In any case, it absorbed and amused me for a while and helped to clear my mind of shadows.

I'm sorry we missed each other. When will you come again?

Love,

To Jean Stafford

[n.d.]   [Chicago]

Dear Jean,

Since our little visit and since your kind note was written I have flown to and from Kenya, Uganda, Ethiopia, Texas and Florida, and have just returned from DeKalb, Illinois. Next week I must go—Must? How strange these self-imposed *musts* are!—to Lafayette, Indiana, Cincinnati, Ohio, and St. Cloud, Minnesota. Why I am doing all this I can't easily explain. A golf ball may have gotten in among my genes. I am not one of those monsters of ingratitude of the type you and I have so often met; I was very grateful to you for visiting that cold house with the giddy staircase. I was tempted strongly to buy it but there was only one room that suited me, and it looked out over the swimming pool and all the wild jollity would have assailed me as I tried to finish a sentence. As you perhaps observed in my last book, I have very nearly given up on sentence endings and matters would only have gotten worse in a noisy house. I have not quite given up on East Hampton. Now I am in touch with people in Montauk and Shelter Island and I am sure to turn up soon. I remind myself of those German commandoes who used to come down in parachutes disguised as nuns or dog catchers.

You are going to receive a very long essay in which I attack everyone. I think you will enjoy reading what I had to say about some of our dear old Village pals.

Much love,

Stafford lived in the village of Springs, New York, north of East Hampton. She had done Bellow the favor of going to examine a house he was interested in buying. The all-attacking essay would be "Culture Now: Some Animadversions, Some Laughs," shortly to appear in Philip Rahv's Modern Occasions.

To William Maxwell

March 14, 1970   Chicago

Dear Mr. Maxwell,

I am greatly honored by your invitation. I am also taken aback by it. For two weeks I have been writing a polemical essay—*Contra Tutti*. It is intemperate, and names names. I've worked myself into a bad mood. Your kind letter makes me recognize what I have been up to, and how unfit I have made myself for composing a Blashfield Address. If you had asked for fulminations, for wickedness, I'd have been able to accept.

I remember our meeting at Smith. You were the one speaker in that symposium who did not misbehave. I admired, and envied, your conduct.

Sincerely yours,

Novelist, story writer and editor William Maxwell, at this time president of the American Academy and National Institute of Arts and Letters, had invited Bellow to deliver the organization's annual Blashfield Address.

To Inge Feltrinelli

April 1, 1970   Chicago

Dear Inge,

Of course I am well. I don't know whether I am happy, and can't undertake the necessary research. [. . .] I saw Letizia Ciotti Miller in Rome; she wants to translate *Mr. S.* I have heard also from Sr. Mantovani, who wrote me a passionate letter which I have not been able to answer and which fills me with embarrassment whenever I shuffle through my letters (a most depressing exercise). Paolo Milano prefers Letizia for this job and, since drinking coffee with her, I too favor her. I liked her very much. She is something between a crushed rose and a cabbage—that is to say, large, vegetable, fragrant and damaged. It is up to you to translate my feelings into executive orders, and to satisfy Mantovani, and give the book to Letizia. I suppose, though, that Erich Linder should have something to say about this.

Saul Bellow: Letters

Can't you find a beautiful sanctuary in the Mediterranean for me this summer?

Inge Feltrinelli (born 1931) was president of Giangiacomo Feltrinelli Editore, a position she had assumed after the death of her husband. Erich Linder (1924–1983), the leading literary agent in postwar Italy, represented Bellow there.

To Stanley B. Troup, M.D.

April 1, 1970   Chicago

Dear Dr. Troup:

The title of your symposium intrigues me greatly, and I should certainly attend if I were free. My duties at the University, however, will keep me here in Chicago.

It was Samuel Johnson who said, "Grief, Sir, is a species of idleness." Though I do not quite agree with the old boy, I think he deserves to be taken seriously. It would certainly do many grievers good. I myself have been braced by it.

Sincerely yours,

Dr. Troup was organizing a conference on grief.

To Melvin Tumin

April 11, 1970   Chicago

Dear Mel

I'm delighted! Thanks. As to how I do it—I suppose I do as my mother did, baking strudel.

Roth has been kind about the book, too. It rather set me up.

As for Life—even at best one feels deprived of something. I'm not of the stuff of which Public Figures are made. You don't want to be ignored, but there ought to be a saner mean.

Or, in Yiddish: *Di kale is tzu sheyn?* [*]

Much love,

* The bride is too beautiful? Fig., What am I complaining about?

To Bracha Weingrod

April 24, 1970   Chicago

Dear Mrs. Weingrod:

Your idea is a fine one but I had to decide years ago whether to write in English or in Yiddish, and when I opted for English the Yiddish began to wither. To members of my immediate family (of my own generation) I still speak Yiddish, and I sometimes read a Yiddish book, but I doubt that I could write a play in mother tongue. If I did my mother would not be amused.

Sincerely yours,

To Sara S. Chapman

May 30, 1970   Chicago

Dear Miss Chapman:

You may be right about *Augie March* and the romantic tradition, but I am afraid that I can offer little in the way of support to your theory. When I wrote *Augie* I had of course read *Moby Dick* and the stories of Melville, but I knew nothing then about *Pierre*. I am somewhat ashamed of the dark ignorance that enclosed me then. Though I was in a state of great enthusiasm I was not thinking clearly. I wish I had known more about certain matters. But I became absorbed in the Chicago scene, the social history of the late Twenties and the depression, and I had not the insight to realize that the naiveté of my hero was very unsatisfactory indeed. To my mind he is more like the Sherwood Anderson gee-whiz ingénue than like the gothic and far more interesting romantic hero of Melville's book. As to romanticism, anyone who attended the public schools of Chicago prior to 1932 was immersed in Longfellow, Whittier, Bryant, Fenimore Cooper and the Transcendentalists. We were all infected by this New England moralizing and were weighted down by a certain idealism which, in our surroundings, was comically irrelevant— simply funny. Like Gatsby in love.

Sincerely yours,

To Toby Cole

August 25, 1970

Dear Toby,

[Roman] Polanski has agreed with me about the way to approach *Seize the Day* and I think if he can get Eli Wallach to play Dr. Tamkin and somebody like Alan Arkin for Wilhelm we may have something after all. I have suggested both these names and on that basis I am willing to negotiate the sale. I don't say that I will absolutely insist on the actors but I think both are obtainable and would prefer them above any others I can now think of.

Adam and I will be in Nantucket. I'd like to cross over to the Vineyard for a couple of days, though Adam has a thing about sharing his holiday with his little brother. Under my tactful management he'll probably explode when I suggest it. But I have a concrete bunker, and an asbestos suit from the Father's Department of Brooks Brothers.

Love to all of you,

A film version of Seize the Day *would appear sixteen years later, but directed by Fielder Cook and starring Robin Williams as Tommy and Joseph Wiseman as Tamkin.*

To Benjamin Nelson

September 11, 1970   Chicago

My dear Ben—

Le destin has been against me, using its familiar agents—children, hostages to fortune. I longed to go to Montauk, but Gregory announced that he would be married in August, in San Francisco. He chose the middle of the month, just to make things interesting—a little test of his value to his dear Pa, with a slender golden edge of the Will to Power. To pass this new test I had to spend a large part of August in San Francisco. Next it was the turn of Adam, who is thirteen, to do his stuff. His choice fell on Nantucket. No, it hasn't been one of my better summers. It isn't retirement I dream of, only the majority of my sons. One will keep me going yet, for a long time. I will be seventy when Daniel gets out of college. Something had better be done to rescue me.

[. . .]

I hope you and Marie loved Russia. (Itself, of course; who could love the superstructure?) Please write me a forgiving note.

Ever yours,

To Robert Penn Warren

September 19, 1970   Chicago

Dear Red:

There can't be too much philanthropy in this aging heart of mine but I'm going ahead with the publication of the magazine at my own expense. To borrow a term from crooks, I'm doing it as a public service, for the *Locations* gentlemen have fallen away, welshed out (as they put it in Chicago, which is still basically underworld in its sympathies). I'm going to call the magazine *The Ark* [subsequently *Anon*]. With three sons, I qualify as a Noah. I'm writing a book which will run as a serial and will set some sort of standard for the fiction. You're right absolutely. People will say, After such a squawk what sort of stuff are they giving us. I'm hoping that there will be stuff. No demons of optimism misleading me here. We shall have to wait and see whether good writers will turn up. With few exceptions the people of talent I've known these last thirty years haven't shown much spirit. After an early show of quality there seems little more than a love of status. We could forgive the sins of people who offered us at least *something* to read, but there isn't much of that either, I'm afraid. All right, we'll ship out the *Ark* and wait for Ararat.

I'm delighted that you liked the piece. I thought you might. And of course you're busy; I'm glad of that and hoped you would be. What I really should have explained more clearly is that the magazine will publish all sorts of comment, unsigned. Something of the sort must surely come over you from time to time. You'll be getting the first number soon and will see for yourself what Botsford and I have in mind. Why not have a Menckenian column? It's a fine idea.

Yours most warmly,

To Margaret Staats

September 27, 1970   Chicago

Dear Maggie,

I'm in the state I was in in Oaxaca, writing something while the days speed by as though I were on the safety island in the midst of zooming traffic. What I'm doing may be far less good than it feels to me. Delusion is always possible. Meantime, the hasting days fly by with full career, etc. I wake at five or six. I am afraid of being deluded.

Last year you sent me some pills I didn't take for an ailment I didn't seem to have. I don't know what happened to those tablets. Maybe Daniel played with them. You can try to get a copy of the prescription for me, or another batch of pills. Better yet, two batches, to give me a reserve. I don't like to bother you about this but I haven't the time to fuss with doctors.

In the end Adam condescended—he gave his hand like a princess. I had the inexpressible privilege of bearing him away to Nantucket. I was at work daily at 7:00; he slept until 11:00, very obliging. We had lovely afternoons in the water, and he taught me to hiss like a karate expert. Indispensable in Chicago. Best is to stay in nights.

I was delighted to see you looking so well and talking so sensibly and the affection we felt towards each other was a great improvement over states we've known. Barley wrote a letter of pure praise; she loves you dearly and wants you to come to London.

This is Daniel day—Sunday afternoon, pro football, kid programs, and I'm cooking spaghetti.

As ever,

To Margaret Staats

October 26, 1970   Chicago

Dear Maggie,

Come to think of it, I've never before dictated a letter to you and never imagined that I would. So I apologize right off. It's this siege I'm under, with rocks flying over walls while I crouch down and scheme against my enemies. You were good about the pills, thank you very much. This time I'll make sure that Daniel doesn't play marbles with them. And of course the Ferrers can use me as a reference. I often think how Joe [Ferrer] held out against amputation; for certain dangers of life he has become my model. It occurs to me also—and this has to do with Penny [Ferrer]—that I am wearing my newest suit today which shows me off to splendid advantage and makes me look only half my age which is at the moment a hundred sixty-five. I too have heard from Barley. I read her letters and feel deeply grateful that I am not paying her by the word. When she comes to New York she ought to have a grand party and if she's not planning to visit Chicago I'll come in and of course I'll help you with the tab. She has knocked herself out for me and I'm no ingrate, whatever else. There's plenty else.

As for the rest of the scene, half my dogs are sleeping and lying. The Chicago half however is bowing and wowing in courtrooms and lawyers' offices. It's still a struggle unto the nothing. But Daniel's sweetness only increases and his cleverness too. This cuts my losses by a great deal.

I shan't come to New York without calling you. I haven't been there since September 1st. To which some of my cheerfulness must be ascribed.

Love,

To Hannah Arendt

December 1, 1970   Chicago

Dear Hannah,

Many students have shown great interest in the Kant seminar and David [Grene] and I feel that you would find it worth your while to visit Chicago this winter. Under the circumstances we would not of course wish to press you. I don't know how you feel about leaving New York now. I ran into Hans Morgenthau recently and he said that you don't much enjoy going out. Chicago in winter can be grim but perhaps the students would compensate for the grimness.

In any case we would be delighted to have you.

Sincerely yours,

Arendt's husband, Heinrich Blücher, Bellow's much-admired colleague during the years at Bard, had died in October. Stiff collegial courtesies between Arendt and Bellow evidently continued, despite his attack on her Eichmann in Jerusalem *in* Mr. Sammler's Planet. *He was writing here in his capacity as chairman of the Committee on Social Thought.*

To Nicolas Nabokov

December 19, 1970   Chicago

Dear Mr. Nabokov,

Of course I remember you well. The long years mean nothing—at least certain faculties are not affected by the calendar. The invitation is not merely attractive, it is positively fascinating. It so happens that I know little about the Aspen Institute. I know only the beautiful Mrs. Walter Paepcke whom I used to meet in Chicago's last salon, now closed alas by the death of our aged hostess, Mrs. Epstein, whose walls were hung with paintings by Botticelli, Rembrandt and Goya. No, I've never visited Aspen. At the moment I have only sketchy summer plans and before I can be more definite I must learn what the mothers of my children have in mind for the holidays. I would like to come to the Institute, but what would I be asked to do? I am putting together a singular sort of book and it gives my life a certain oddity; not altogether agreeable, but what can one do? Let me say then that I'd like to come, I may very well be with you in Aspen next July; but I need to know what would be expected of me. With many thanks for your kind letter.

Very sincerely,

Nicolas Nabokov (1903–1978) was for many years resident composer at the Aspen Institute for Humanistic Studies. He is best remembered for his opera based on Shakespeare's Love's Labour's Lost *(libretto by W. H. Auden and Chester Kallman), which premiered in 1973.*

1971

To Norman Podhoretz

March 11, 1971   Chicago

Dear Norman,

Thanks for your note [about "Culture Now: Some Animadversions, Some Laughs"]. It seems that I have a feeling for polemics—evidently I've been holding it down, sitting on it. I've never wanted to become an infighter. Probably this article ought to have appeared in *Commentary* but I wanted Rahv to have it for old times' sake. The old *Partisan* was very generous to Isaac and me when we arrived green and sincere from Chicago. William [Phillips] had no sort of character at all but Philip [Rahv] had a solid Roman-Russian personality, dignified, weighty, and even (there were signs of it) affectionate.

I don't know if I will write anything else like this again, unless provoked. When I was in Paris, I was told that Mary McCarthy was screaming for my blood. Then, at nightfall, in London, who should turn up at a bus stop but Leslie Fiedler, his beard looking rather plucked about the chin. He was very friendly and proposed that we should have a friendly conversation next day. But I said No. And then Katie Carver also materialized and said I was in the wrong. I can never understand why revolutionaries try to hold on to liberal friendly relations with me.

Yours with good wishes,

To Margaret Staats

April 30, 1971   Chicago

Dear Maggie—

Your birthday was not forgotten. On the 16th I was in New York and vainly twenty times dialed your number. Since then I've tried also from Chicago, but you seem no longer to live on 15th St. Wherever you reside now, you are remembered by me.

My own condition isn't too bad, but my sister's husband [Charles Kauffman] has had a stroke again, and this time is partly paralyzed. He lies in the hospital, all the sweetness of his character showing in the new softness of his face. Forgiving everyone. Coming into the intensive-care room, I'm moved by Charlie. And my sister is still pretty, high-school Janey at the eyes—otherwise withered.

So it goes.

And, these weeks, I am on jury-duty and spend many days in a jury-box. Happy birthday and blessings,

To the cast of the Circle in the Square production of The Last Analysis

June 25, 1971   Aspen Institute for Humanistic Studies

To the entire cast:

Bless you all, you've done the thing and done it marvelously! At the first preview, I knew that you could and would make the play go, that you saw life in the thing despite its many faults and that you would surely succeed with it. The blood of the art is still circulating. Not only is the play giving much pleasure to audiences but it is breaking down a stony professional prejudice against novelists in the theater. Six years ago this professionalism broke my back but I hobbled out again for another try [. . .] I can now set my crutch on fire and trade in my wheelchair for a motorcycle.

A lady writing me about *The Last Analysis* says it has to do with "getting it all back from the butchers." That is exactly what the play is about—and for me, personally, you have also redeemed it from the butchers.

I am grateful to you all.

The Last Analysis, *negatively reviewed upon its Broadway premiere in 1964, enjoyed a better reception when Circle in the Square revived it off-Broadway seven years later under the direction of Theodore Mann and starring Joseph Wiseman.*

To Edward Shils

June 26, 1971   Aspen

My dear Edward—

[. . .] Here in the mountains I feel a decided improvement in my state. But there's so much room for improvement. I hope, *just once*, to do the thing which would justify my survival for so many decades. I seem not to be ready just yet, though my spirit is beginning to clear somewhat. Here at least I am not troubled by ladies. No dear creature offers me love or even a stable daily existence. I live alone, now that Adam has gone, in a large house with splendid views. Aspen is fashionable, like the summer place in which Prince Myshkin fell to pieces.

I refused to go to New York for the revival of my revised farce. It seems to be having a *succès fou*. You don't approve of it, I know, but it has a few Aristophanic moments.

Bless you.

Please keep in touch.

Love,

To John and Kate Berryman

June 27, 1971   Aspen

Dear Kate and John—

This is to greet and bless Sarah Berryman on her arrival in this gorgeous wicked world which has puzzled and delighted my poor soul for fifty-six years. I expect the planet will go on a few billion years yet and she will thrive on it.

Love to you all,

1972

To David Holbrook

January 4, 1972   Chicago

Dear Mr. Holbrook:

[. . .] I have an idea that we are all far too susceptible to fashionable ideas and that our power to discriminate has been seriously damaged in this consciousness-explosion of ours. An old Yiddish proverb crops up in my thoughts more and more frequently. It goes like this: A fool throws a stone into the water; then sages knock themselves out trying to recover it. (Very free translation.) The sages evidently are no cleverer than the fool.

There are by now enough fool-cast stones in the water to keep us silly sages going for quite a long time.

I shall try to get a copy of your "Human Hope" book. Sorry I missed you in Chicago.

Sincerely yours,

David Holbrook is the author of many books including Human Hope and the Death Instinct *(1971).*

To Robert Hivnor

January 24, 1972   Chicago

Dear Bob—

I often wondered whether he would. I guessed that he wouldn't. I seldom guess right.

Not many of his sort left, and he was a dear friend.

Thanks for the note. I'll turn up in NY one of these days.

On January 7, 1972, John Berryman had leaped to his death from the Washington Avenue Bridge in Minneapolis.

To Grace Wade

March 7, 1972   Chicago

Dear Mrs. Wade:

In 1956 I spent many months at Pyramid Lake, Nevada, and there I knew several elderly women who lived at mountain sides and in lonely canyons. According to some odd intuitive method of my own I put together *something*. It was a year or two later that I wrote "The Yellow House," moved by my memory of those old women and the Nevada desert. One of the old girls, now dead, was my landlady. From her I rented a shack built of old railroad ties. It was at the water's edge and I dream sometimes of going back for a look. But I am told that the Lake has become a tourist attraction and I'm afraid of returning to cherished memories and finding only Disneyland.

Thank you for writing.

Sincerely yours,

To Nadine Nimier

March 29, 1972   Miami

Dear Nadine,

I'm not moribund. I'm simply as usual—not pulled-together sufficiently. To cure myself, I've come down to Florida with Adam and Daniel and *voilà!*—suddenly I am able to reply to your note. Evidently I come back to life when I voyage. Next month I'm off to Japan. I don't know a word of *le japonais—pas un seul mot.* But I'm fairly good at pantomimes of all sorts. In July I'm going to Aspen, Colorado, and in August I'll be in Europe. Perhaps we shall actually meet in France. I intend to stay until mid-September. I feel sometimes like a novel written by the ghost of Jules Verne and revised by Tutankhamen and Wm. Faulkner—about a Prince of Egypt reincarnated in the twentieth century, fond of southern whiskey and doomed to jet about the earth.

Yours ever,

To Samuel S. Goldberg

[n. d.]

When Mark Twain returned from a visit with Harriet Beecher Stowe and found he had called on her without a necktie, he posted the tie to her and wrote, "Sorry we couldn't both be there at the same time." Thus with this check. On Saturday, I'm off to Tokyo. There I expect to find some excellent second-hand book stores unraided and undespoiled by S. S. Goldberg. I may find something to your liking. Perhaps one of those sexual scrolls to cheer your lonely hours in the office and strengthen you in honorable dealings with Man and Government.

The pickled trout at Max's was better than ever. I left half a buck for the reddish pudgy woman and went back along Fifth Ave. hoping we might meet.

Yours ever,

I'll settle for the [Lawrence] Binyan Dante, volumes I and II. I have the *Paradiso.*

Among Bellow's great friends, Samuel S. Goldberg was a Yiddish-speaking law-yer and bibliophile. The two of them could sometimes be spotted in New York's used bookshops, particularly the Gotham and the Strand.

To Frances Gendlin

May [?], 1972   [Chicago]

Dear Frances:

There are many reasons why I didn't write. For one thing, the jet lag was awful. It took more than ten days to recover. For another, I turned out to be a real or perhaps imaginary celebrity, and immediately began to do seminars, lectures, interviews, radio programs and Japanese semi-state dinners, sitting on the floor, using chopsticks and eating raw fish, or trying to eat it. I drank a good deal of sake to help myself sleep, but I kept waking at four A.M., utterly wretched most of the time. My system is sound enough, for a man of my age, but even it was not able to cope with the terrific time and space changes. After two weeks of this I was allowed to rest in Kyoto, where it was relatively tranquil. Kyoto I thoroughly enjoyed, staying in a Japanese inn, old-style, sleeping on the straw mat and lying on the floors half the day, admiring the little moss garden. Being on the floor was childhood again, and childhood is still the most pleasant part of life. A confession of adult failure. Well, I'd better own up. I haven't done too hot, as the old Chicago phrase runs. For three weeks I didn't hear from you at all, and I was quite put out about it. If you wrote a letter you didn't send, I did, too. And then I was disheartened— *appalled* is a probably more accurate word—to find that I had crab-lice. I felt peculiarly shaky and stupid to make that discovery. I'd had nothing at all to do with women here, except to smile at them over the raw fish held in chopsticks. Going to the doctor was awful. Thinking about it all was awful. Cured now, I feel lousy still. Anti-self, anti-others, but above all the old fool. The world seems to expect that I will do all kinds of good things, and I spite it by doing all kinds of bad ones. They're not terribly *bad*, either. Striking sins are out of reach. I try to break into the next sector, or find the next development, but nothing comes of this except unhappiness for myself and others. The unhappiness to myself I don't much mind. The effect on others is a curse to me night and day. It's true I haven't taken a shot at [George] Wallace, but there isn't much else I can take credit for. At the end of all this, I can say that I think of you a great deal and lovingly.

I'm flying to San Francisco on the 26th. I suppose I'll be there before the letter arrives and back in Chicago about the first of June.

Love,

On May 15, while campaigning in Laurel, Maryland, presidential candidate and Alabama governor George Wallace had been shot and seriously wounded by Arthur Bremer.

To David Grene

June 22, 1972   Chicago

My dear David,

I had thought to find some rest in Japan but it wasn't like that at all—it never is. I found myself running up and down giving lectures and seminars to widely erudite Japanese scholars. Among them there seems to be one of everything under the sun, so that if you call out at Tokyo University for an expert on German armor of the thirteenth century he will appear in a few minutes ready to take sides. Tokyo is a fuming, hissing metropolis, and what God promised Abraham has come to pass in Tokyo, not in Jerusalem. They have what Henry James called "numerosity." There are no small gatherings, only mobs—everywhere mobs of every description. It was desolating to see but often funny, too, and I felt myself something of a Gulliver there. The old temple cities, anyway, were very beautiful and I reached them in the right frame of mind: I was exhausted and cast myself down in the quiet of temple gardens. These were all beautifully arranged, each stone in place and every bamboo leaf quivering on cue. Then I rushed back to San Francisco and came down with some sort of *fever*. They were ten very unpleasant days. Then I had a court confrontation with Susan and then went East and collected degrees from Yale and Harvard—a double-header. Daniel and I were to have spent July in Aspen but my case continues and I am not at all sure that I'll be able to get out of here. However, Adam and I will certainly turn up in Ireland toward the end of August. As yet, I don't know precisely when. [. . .]

Best wishes to everyone,
Yours affectionately,

To John Haffenden

June 27, 1972   Chicago

Dear Mr. Haffenden:

Berryman's last letters to me are still scattered about my flat. I haven't had the heart to gather them into an envelope and put them away. Where would I put them? The relationship is still open, as it were. This may serve to explain why it has been difficult for me to answer your inquiry.

Sincerely yours,

Haffenden was beginning research for The Life of John Berryman, *which would appear in 1982.*

To the Committee on Admissions of the Century Association

September 29, 1972   Chicago

[. . .] I understand that Mr. William Phillips has been nominated for membership in the Century Club. My purpose in this letter is to make clear my very strong reasons for opposing this. I am convinced that Phillips has done great harm to American literature over the last ten or fifteen years. The *Partisan Review* of which he has been an editor from the first was once important and valuable. It continued the cultural line set by *The Dial, Transition* and the best of the little magazines. It published Malraux and T. S. Eliot, Silone and Koestler and George Orwell and Edmund Wilson and Robert Lowell and John Berryman [. . .]. But, the founding editors resigning for one reason or another, William remained in charge, and William lost no time in selling out. He betrayed and, intellectually and artistically, bankrupted the magazine. Over the last ten years *PR* has become trivial, fashionable, mean and harmful. Its trendiness is of the pernicious sort. It despises and, as much as it can, damages literature. The values held by early editors like Philip Rahv and Delmore Schwartz it has repudiated entirely. I think it has become the breeding place of a sort of fashionable extremism, of the hysterical, shallow and ignorant academic "counter-culture." It trades on the reputation of the magazine, and readers who still associate the old names and standards with it are deceived into reading the harmful trash it now prints. In the early days William helped to build the old *Partisan* but he is also responsible for its decay. Standards have become rather soft, I know, but it's nevertheless difficult for me to understand how anyone who has looked into recent numbers of *PR* could think of its editor as a member of the Century Club.

Yours sincerely,

The Century Association, an exclusive Manhattan club, grants members a period in which to support or oppose any candidate standing for membership. Once read by the admissions committee, "red letters" (as negative appraisals are called) are destroyed. Bellow had retained a carbon copy.

To Barnett Singer

November 9, 1972   Chicago

Dear Barney Singer—

[. . .] When I visited Seattle in 1951, I lived in something called the Hotel Meaney and made the rounds with [Theodore] Roethke whom I adored, and Dylan Thomas whom I admired and pitied. I couldn't keep up with them, though, for I'm not a real drinking man.

Thanks for your note.

Barnett Singer (born 1945) has for many years been a professor of history at Brock University, St. Catharines, Ontario. He is the author of, among other works, Maxime Wiegand: A Biography of the French General in Two World Wars *(2008).*

1973

To Nicolas Nabokov

February 20, 1973   Chicago

Dear Nicolas,

Your Stravinsky recollections are delightful. Your mss. gave me nothing but pleasure. To read it *made* my evening.

I have a few remarks to offer, not to be taken as criticisms but only as suggestions for improvement. First, then, let me say that to address Stravinsky in the second person is confusing and unnecessary. There are long passages of exposition during which the device is forgotten, and then one is jolted by the return of the "you." I think it would be far better to say Stravinsky or, for informality, Igor Fyodorovich. What you have to tell us is so lively that it needs no grace notes. A second suggestion is that you cut much of the technical discussion of *Les Noces*. On the whole your musical discussions are rueful and illuminating but this one is too lengthy and unless you could dramatize your meeting with the pedantic musicologists it would be better to cut. About my third and last point you may be rather sensitive—it has to do with Robert Craft, whose image in the end is not entirely clear. One feels how much is left unsaid. Perhaps other people, possibly Auden, would not mind being quoted. But when Craft is mentioned, you fall into psychological diplomacy, ambiguity, etc. This is very different from the free mordant observation which makes the rest of your memoir so delightful. [. . .]

Yours affectionately,

To Louis Lasco

March 5, 1973   [Chicago]

Esteemed Zahar Neoplasmich:

The famous columnist [Sydney J. Harris] appears in my hometown paper. Should I, wishing to glance at the Final Markets or the Obituaries, read a few of his lines by mischance, my feet begin to swell. He gives me edema. Still, I am grateful for your good intentions and your wish to share your delight with me.

You will be interested to hear that when I recently spoke at the University of Missouri in Kansas City, Benny Shapiro's brother Manny turned up with his frau and an elegant young son in a Smith Bros. beard. We reminisced about old times on Cortez St. I mentioned that I had heard from you. We decided that if you were still going to Las Vegas it was a heartening sign of virility, and the fires of life had not been banked in L. Lasco. The young man asked what he should do to become a writer. I said, "Shave!" He was much offended, nettled, and turned away from me.

They said that Benny was selling electrical supplies. Now that capital punishment has ended he's probably selling old electric chairs. There's a story for you, a promoter who tries to peddle old electric chairs to South American dictators. For a small percentage, I give you this idea. I'm always glad to hear from you. I send you fraternal greetings.

S. B. Pamunyitzoff

To Zero Mostel

March 16, 1973   Chicago

Dear Zero,

I can't recall that I was ever able to persuade you to do *anything* but the University of Chicago wants me to try, so here goes: Would you be willing to come to Chicago in May to give a lecture on a subject close to your heart—Painting, for instance? The University has a series called the William Vaughn Moody Series. Only very eminent persons are asked to deliver Moody Lectures (I suppose I mean people like W. H. Auden). The students have a festival of the arts in May and spring has not yet drowned in dust. Harold Rosenberg will be there and you'll have a jolly time, I'm sure.

Yours, with best wishes,

A decade earlier Mostel had declined to star in The Last Analysis, *signing instead to play Tevye in* Fiddler on the Roof.

To Frances Gendlin

April [?], 1973   Monks House, Rodmell, East Sussex
Well, it's beautiful and spooky, the gardens are grand, the house cold, everything creaks but I was not haunted by the ghost of Virginia. I am exhausted, but well. I have no telephone and as yet no car, but I sh'd get the car. The phone is doubtful.

Can you ask Esther to mail me some Committee on Social Thought stationery, *immedjiat?*

I miss you.

Love,

Bellow was at the start of a six-week residency in East Sussex at what had been the country house of Virginia and Leonard Woolf.

To Frances Gendlin

[n.d.]   [Cambridge]
Cara mia Francesca,

To meet you (but on which of two dates?) I can come into London. It means staying overnight at Barley Alison's, but that's feasible. It involves a backgammon tournament, with me rolling disgusting dice. Even worse than in Chicago. I look forward to your arrival (not because of the backgammon). Anyway we can speak on the phone now. This A.M. I am in Peterhouse, Cambridge, black tie unused—an amusing story which I will tell you after more important things (which I have terribly missed).

Lewes is one hour from London. I leave the car and take the train. Then getting to the airport isn't easy, so I'll come a day earlier. Phone me.

Love,

To Frances Gendlin

June 16, 1973   Belgrade
Dear Fran:

Like a Western sheriff with guns drawn, ready to shoot anything that moves—that's [Samuel S.] Goldberg with his dollars. "How much—what is it?" Bang bang. Yesterday he bought four heavy rare volumes of American history. He has them at home in paper, but this edition is worth forty bucks. How will he get them home!? The Serbs have never heard of book-rate postage to the US. So we tote the hilarious bundles while Sam scouts for a Hermès shop. All the old broads in his office have commissioned him to buy perfume, which I daresay they desperately need. Today I'm dragging him off to visit unbuyable monasteries. But we look forward to cheap strawberries.

I'm well but tired, and miss you and my Dorchester [Avenue] comforts. And Daniel. I had my troubles with Adam. I think I told you I was not "received" by his mother—should say not vouchsafed an audience. But soon there will be bills. [. . .]

Much love,

To Ralph Ross

August 14, 1973   Aspen

Dear Ralph:

The subject was painful but your letter was very pleasant. I don't know what we survivors should do with this slaughter-legacy our old friends have made us (I think of Isaac, of Delmore Schwartz). Maybe my little foreword made things too easy. It had the conventional charm for which John himself had a weakness or talent. I was sincere enough, but there were terrible things to say, and I didn't say them. You touched on some of those in your letter. John telling you that he'd never drink again, that he wanted more love affairs. At the same time he knew he was a goner. One moment the post-tomb Lazarus, the next Don Juan, and much of the time someone who merely looked like John, as you put it. I knew that feeling.

Having written a few lines about him I now have the "privilege" of observing the attitudes of people towards the poet and his career. There's something culturally gratifying, apparently, about such heroic self-destruction. It's Good-old-Berryman-he-knew-how-to-wrap-it-up. It's a combination of America, Murderer of Poets, and of This Is the Real Spiritual Condition of Our Times. Perhaps you've seen Boyd Thomes's review of *Recovery*. Maris [Thomes] sent me a copy. It may not have reached you, so I'll quote a few sentences.

"This combination of erudition and progressively more suicidal chaos has become his subject matter, and it was his artistic triumph to create a style sufficiently flexible and powerful to express it . . . John did more to elevate the potential of paranoia than anybody of our generation."

Then he speaks of John as a "poetry-making machine" and so forth. Boyd's all right, one of the Minnesota pals and all of that, but there's something amiss with John's disaster as confirmation of the views on life and society of a sophisticated medical gentleman—"elevating the potential of paranoia." It rather scares me to see how very satisfactory John's life and death can be from a certain point of view.

On this green and sunlit Colorado afternoon, that'll be enough of that.

You're entirely right about these great spaces and the psychic damage they do. Let's repair some of this damage in November. Gregory and his wife are making a grandfather of me then and I shall come out [to California]. Herb and Mitzie will be gone, but the rest of us can, and should, have a grand party. I'll keep in touch.

Yours affectionately,

Bellow had contributed a foreword to Berryman's unfinished, posthumously published novel, Recovery (1973). *Boyd Thomes, M.D., was Berryman's doctor in Minneapolis.*

To Margaret Staats

September 14, 1973   [Chicago]

Where am I? I wish I knew. I'm going to be in New York next week. What about Sat. afternoon? I'll telephone.

I hear that [———] is a women's lib fighter. So is Susan Bellow. I am glad that these poor abused women are fighting back. I am for them a hundred per cent and think their demands should be met in full and at once. In court last week I pleaded for eight hours. I wanted the judge to realize that Susan is a freedom fighter. She belongs to some sort of national women's organization.

Only she doesn't agree with the alimony plank in the platform.

Love and kisses,

To Evelyn [?]

December 14, 1973   Chicago

Dear Evelyn—

I was visiting with cousin Louie Dworkin the other night, and when he spoke of you I found that I could recall you vividly. You had one blue eye and one brown eye, and you were a charming gentle girl in a fur (raccoon?) coat. I thought you might like to know how memorable you were, so I asked cousin Louie (who loves you dearly) for your address, and I take this occasion to send you every good wish.

1974

To **The New York Times**

January 7, 1974   Chicago, Ill.

To the Editor:

Andrei Sakharov and four other Soviet intellectuals have appealed to "decent people throughout the world" to try to protect Aleksandr Solzhenitsyn from persecution.

The word "hero," long in disrepute, has been redeemed by Solzhenitsyn. He has had the courage, the power of mind and the strength of spirit to speak the truth to the entire world. He is a man of perfect intellectual honor and, in his moral strength, he is peculiarly Russian. To the best Russian writers of this hellish century it has been perfectly clear that only the power of the truth is equal to the power of the state.

It is to be hoped that the Brezhnevs and the Kosygins will be capable of grasping what the behavior of such a man means to the civilized world. Persecution of Solzhenitsyn, deportation, confinement in a madhouse or exile will be taken as final evidence of complete moral degeneracy in the Soviet regime.

We cannot expect our diplomats to abandon their policy of *détente* (whatever that may mean) or our great corporations to break their business contracts with Russia, but physicists and mathematicians, biologists, engineers, artists and intellectuals should make it clear that they stand by Solzhenitsyn. It would be the completest betrayal of principle to fail him. Since America is the Soviet Government's partner in *détente,* Americans have a special responsibility in this matter.

What Solzhenitsyn has done in revealing the unchecked brutality of Stalinism, he has done also for us. He has reminded every one of us what we owe to truth.

To Alfred Kazin

March 20, 1974   Chicago

Dear Alfred:

Your letter came on a day when I had a genuine grief, and that helped me to keep matters in perspective. [. . .] I have never met Mr. [Philip] Nobile. I can't remember that I ever wrote to him or spoke to him. Are you sure that I did say the things he attributes to me? Have you any real evidence that I actually said them—whatever they are? By living in Chicago I hoped to avoid all this sort of literary nastiness but there's evidently no way to avoid it. So far as I can see this sort of slander and idiocy is all the literary culture we have left.

It's true that I didn't like your review of *Sammler*. I didn't dislike it more than other pieces of yours, but I disliked it. It appeared more than a year after publication of the book and I had heard that an earlier and more friendly review had been rejected by the editors, but knowing what gossip is I did not take this to be a fact. It was the conclusion of your piece—"God lives!"—that offended me. You meant evidently that I was a megalomaniac. But this didn't seem to me to be literary criticism. About my books you may say what you like. (I seldom reply either to praise or to blame, which is why you heard no "peep" out of me when you wrote the introduction to *Seize the Day*—was an acknowledgment necessary?) For that matter, you may say what you please about my character, too. You haven't much gift for satire and "God lives!" didn't hurt much. What offended me was that you were not reviewing my novel, you were saying that its author was a wickedly deluded lunatic. As for [V. S.] Pritchett, I may not have cared much for his opinion of *Herzog* and perhaps I muttered in my whiskers about it. That again is no great matter. But how do *you* know what I said? And why didn't you ask me, as an old friend, whether I had really expressed myself in that manner? Your complaint is based on nothing but silliness, gossip and slander.

I know my own sins well enough. They distress me, and I struggle with them. You may not believe this but I can, oddly enough, bear to be corrected. Unfortunately, I found nothing very helpful in your letter. Nor does your huffiness at the Century Club contribute much to the improvement of my character or the progress of the species.

"Though He Slay Me . . . ," Kazin's review of Mr. Sammler's Planet, *had appeared in* The New York Review of Books.

To Daniel Fuchs

April 10, 1974   Chicago

Dear Daniel—

What do I think? For one thing you know modern literature; for another you write intelligently; you correctly describe the course I took and my view of modernism; you are right about my Flaubertian and Lawrencian criticism; not quite right about my hostility towards Eliot—Eliot I respect more than you would guess, but on the evidence you are correct.

This having been said, let me add that I don't like to read about myself—I recoil from it, heart and bowels. That is, in its own way, self-criticism. I'm not ready for judgment, the facts aren't in; I know I've done wrong; we haven't gotten to the pith and nucleus yet. We're seeing the limbs, the heart and belly aren't in the picture yet (etc.). Why so slow? I can't say. Maybe it's the situation; maybe a certain timidity or tardiness or sluggishness or laziness—or sleep (Henderson, via Shelley, wants to burst the spirit's sleep). But you should know that I have learned (gathered, inferred) one awful thing from you. This is that I've been arguing too much—debating, infighting, polemicizing. The real thing is unfathomable. You can't get it down to distinct or clear opinion. Sensing this, I have always had intelligence enough (or the intuition) to put humor between myself and final claims. And that hasn't been enough by any means. Hattie in "The Yellow House" and *Henderson* and "The Old System" seem to me my most interesting things because they are not argued. You've made me see this more plainly and I'm much obliged. *Sammler* isn't even a novel. It's a dramatic essay of some sort, wrung from me by the crazy Sixties. The trouble, in these mad times, is that so many adjustments and examinations have to be made for the sake of some balance and nothing else, and the expenditure of mental energy for mere equilibrium is too costly.

Anyway—many thanks and good luck.

Daniel Fuchs's Saul Bellow: Vision and Revision *would appear in 1984. It remains among the best accounts of Bellow's work.*

To Ann Birstein

May 22, 1974   Chicago

Dear Ann—

My correspondence with Alfred was disagreeable, so I didn't associate you with it at all. You and I have never had disagreeable relations. I hope we never shall.

There used to be something like a literary life in this country, but the mad, ferocious Sixties tore it all to bits. Nothing remains but gossip and touchiness and anger. I'm past being distressed by it—I mean merely distressed.

So there it is! Nobody will speak for you to me. One of these days I hope we will have our own private conversation. It's been a long time.

As ever,

To Lionel Trilling

July 7, 1974 [Carboneras, Almería, Spain]

Dear Lionel:

You may think me silly when you read a piece I've written for *Harper's*. I've had regretful second thoughts about it, myself. Such remarks as I make about you are based solely on your *Commentary* essay "Authenticity and the Modern Unconscious" and refer only to the first part and the impossibility of being held "spellbound." It was certainly wrong of me not to read the whole book before sounding off. I feel guilty—no, that won't do—I feel remorseful about it. You do, however, appear to agree with the views of Eliot and Walter Benjamin, and you do say that the narrative past has lost its authenticating power, and perhaps you are too ready to take for permanent what I see to be a mood. What is permanent in this age of upheavals is hard to make out, but I am reluctant to grant moods their second papers. For writers the most important question is simply, What is interesting? I try, inadequately and frivolously, to say something in my article about what it is that intellectuals do or do not find interesting. I've thrown no light on this, and perhaps I've even thickened the darkness a little, but the matter was worth mentioning. I take it we agree, as square old liberals, that without individuals human life ends in a cold glutinous porridge—despite our different opinions as to what makes an "identity." Freudian theory is, to me, another story, albeit a fascinating one. I take the Unconscious to be what we don't know, and don't see that it advances us much to take this unknown psychologically. Why not metaphysically? However, I prefer to remain an amateur in these matters. What I wish to say here is that it was idiotic of me to fix on one chapter of your book. I shall get a copy of it when I come back from Spain later in the month and read it attentively.

Yours apologetically,

Trilling's essay in Commentary *was an excerpt from his Charles Eliot Norton Lectures, published in book form as* Sincerity and Authenticity. *Bellow's essay in* Harper's *was "Machines and Storybooks," to which Trilling would respond angrily, ending all contact between them.*

To David Peltz

July 14, 1974   [Carboneras, Almería, Spain]

Dear David,

I'm sorry you feel hurt. I'm baffled as well. Three years ago Bette [Howland] told you that I was writing about you. You were angry and forbade it. It wasn't *you* who were the subject. People have written about me. Their me is not me. It couldn't matter less. What matters is that good things be written. Dear God, how we need them! [. . .] I promised not to write Your Life. But this was all I *could* promise. We've known each other forty-five years and told each other thousands and thousands of anecdotes. And now, on two bars suggested by one of your anecdotes, I blew a riff. Riffs are irrepressible. Furthermore, no one should repress them. I created two characters and added the toilets and the Playboy Club and the fence and the skyscraper. What harm is there in that? Your facts are unharmed by my version. Writers, artists, friends, are not the Chicago Title and Trust Company or the Material Supply Corp. These aren't questions of property, are they? It might even make you happy that in this world writers still *exist*. And I should think it would touch you that I was moved to put a hand on your shoulder and wanted to remember you as I took off for the moon. For what you think is so major is really quite minor, a small feel taken by your goofy friend to reassure him as he got going. Your facts, three or four of them, got me off the ground. You can't grudge me that and still be Dave Peltz.

Now, David the nice old man who wants his collection of memory-toys to play with in old age is not you! You harm yourself with such fantasies. For the name of the game is not Social Security. What an error! Social Security is an entirely different game. The name of the game is Give All. You are welcome to all my facts. You know them, I give them to you. If you have the strength to pick them up, take them with my blessing. Touch them with your imagination and I will kiss your hands. What, trunk-loads and hoards of raw material? What you fear as the *risk* of friendship, namely that I may take from the wonderful hoard, is really the risk of friendship because I have the power to lift a tuft of wool from a bush and make something of it. I learned,

I paid my tuition most painfully. So I know how to transform common matter. And when I give that transformation, has that no value for you? How many people in Gary, Chicago, the USA, can you look to for that, David? As for me, I long for others to do it. I thirst for it. So should you.

I'll be back from Spain in about ten days. When we talk I will make a particular effort to understand your feelings. When you think about me, remember that we've known each other since about 1929 and make an effort for my sake to understand the inevitability of your appearing among the words I write. And if you think that your friend Bellow, who loves you, is on the whole a good thing, not a bad one, let be. Let be, let be, for God's sake. Let me give what I can, as I can.

Love,

Peltz had been angered by the appearance, in January, of an excerpt from Humboldt's Gift *in* Playboy *that made use of an episode from his life.*

To James Laughlin

August 13, 1974

Dear J.L.—

Monroe Engel is *reminded* of Delmore, perhaps, but [in *Humboldt's Gift*] I am writing of a composite part, inevitably. Sometimes I feel there wasn't a whole man in the lot, and I include myself as a fragment. Life, ourselves assisting, broke everyone up.

I *should* write something about Delmore for the collection you want to publish. I'd like to, but I can't promise anything until I've pried this albatross off my neck.

Yes, I did love Delmore. I believe that you did, too. How comically he loused us all up. It was a privilege to be worked over by him.

When I've read my last galley I'll be free to make promises—and I would like to say a few words about Delmore. I see that you continue to be generous toward him. And I do think he was an important writer.

Anyway, there it is.

All best wishes,

To Louis Lasco

October 1, 1974   [Chicago]

Dear Luigi—

I have noted your new address, and the fact Uncle Benjy had a pet shop. Poor Benjy. If you or I had a pet shop it would be funny. Why is it so sad that Benjy should sell puppies and birds? No gift for life, poor soul.

You ought to subscribe to the *Daily News*. Do you more good than Las Vegas.

Affectionately,
Yakima Canuti

To Philip Roth

October 14, 1974   Chicago

Dear Philip—

Of course, I'm pleased, delighted, honored. Lord! Can this *bello maestro* be me? What a nice thing.

It was obvious to me in 1956 when I came to Chicago and read your stories that you were very good. Over the years, I've muttered words to this effect when your name came up in conversation but (characteristically) I never said it to you.

I was highly entertained by your piece in the *New York Review [of Books]*. I didn't quite agree—that's too much to expect—but I shall slowly think over what you said. My anaconda method. I go into a long digestive stupor. Of course I am not a Freudian. For one fierce interval I was a Reichian. At the moment I have no handle of any sort. I can neither be picked up nor put down.

All best wishes,

Roth had written asking permission to dedicate his essay collection Reading Myself and Others *to Bellow. His essay in* The New York Review of Books *was* "Imagining Jews."

1975

To Meyer Schapiro

January 21, 1975   Chicago

Dear Meyer—

As I read your book, I kept thinking how much better you do your work than I do mine, and how superior your subject is—Moses with his arms held up, and Aaron and Joshua and Rembrandt's Jacob blessing the songs of Joseph. I, by contrast, have such odd people to deal with. Though I don't doubt that I am greatly to blame. Probably there's far more in them than I can see or bring out. Still I do think that I was quite faithful to Von Humboldt Fleisher. I was pleased by your letter, heartened, moved by it. I know that if I satisfy your standards I've done what ought to have been done.

Now I'm wondering what you'll think of the book as a whole. Just now I'm preparing it for the printer and I'm having severe emotional ups and downs as I read it. Lawrence said he cast off his sickness in writing and I understand that thoroughly. On the other hand, looking at what you've set down you see nothing, at times, *except* the sickness.

The letters I've had from readers of the *Esquire* excerpts haven't all been pleasant. Dead-poet cults are quick to form and the cultists are peculiarly psychopathic and offensive. One of them accuses me of doing with Humboldt what Wallace Markfield did with Isaac Rosenfeld in an awful book called *To an Early Grave*—I'd be driven up the wall if I were still agile enough to climb walls.

I hope to see you when I'm in New York next.

Yours most affectionately,

"Burdens of a Lone Survivor," an excerpt from Humboldt's Gift, *had appeared in the December issue of* Esquire.

To Barnett Singer

January 27, 1975   Chicago

Dear Mr. Singer,

If I don't answer all your notes it's only because I'm always in the position of someone without a pilot's license trying to land a Boeing 747. But I will say this of Gore Vidal: He's a specialist in safe scandal. Whenever he steps onto the Senate floor he's already got the necessary votes in his inside pocket. Yes, I am rather fond of him. But I look for no surprises when he rises to speak.

As for me, I'm still there trying.

Sincerely yours,

To Melvin Tumin

[n.d.]   [Chicago]

Dear Mel—

Now *I'm* delinquent. It seems I have too many things going all at once and all keeping me in that essential state of turmoil which, Pascal says, prevents people (*saves* them!) from thinking about salvation. I bump along among unfinished works, promises unkept, things undone, lawsuits without end and the rest of the weak comic furniture of Life, that grand enterprise. Einstein could have used the time to find out more about light. But I must say in my own behalf that I manage to get some pleasing pages written.

I was amused by your conversation with Harold [Rosenberg], the King of the N.Y. intellectuals (old style). He is a grand old man. Sometimes he oddly resembles his late friend Paul Goodman (not one of my favorites). Their views on poetry are similar. It used to annoy Harold when I said that Paul wrote like one of A.S. Neill's Summerhill kids ("creative-writing" for sexually free kiddie cats). Here the paper ends, but not my affection for you.

Love to Sylvia,

To Mark Smith

April 15, 1975   Chicago

Dear Mark,

In great haste—I'm correcting proofs—I want to say that I admired *The Death of the Detective* and that I sent a sub-recommendation to the Guggenheim. I observe that people like Tillie Olsen and Lionel Trilling got fellowships but that your name was not on the list. At least I didn't see you on it and I was disturbed on your behalf and vexed with that obese Gordon Ray whom I sometimes see at the Century Club lowering his four-hundred-pound fanny into a greatly-to-be-pitied chair. His role in the perfect Republic would have been that of third understudy to Laird Cregar (do you remember that fat actor?) in a vile Victorian thriller called *The Lodger*. What can one do? Of course you have got to lose your innocence. It took me six decades to do it.

With indignation towards them and best wishes to you,

Mark Smith (born 1935) is the author also of Smoke Street *(1984) and other novels.*

To Joyce Carol Oates

April 15, 1975   Chicago

Dear Miss Oates,

When I answered your letter of December 20th I said that I would be glad to do the interview-by-mail as soon as I sent off *Humboldt's Gift,* an amusing and probably unsatisfactory novel. Well, it went to the printer a few weeks ago and while I was waiting for the galleys I began to deal with your stimulating questions. Before I could make much progress the galleys began to arrive in batches so I have to put off the project again. When I was younger I used to think that my good intentions were somehow communicated to people by a secret telepathic wig-wag system. It was therefore disappointing to see at last that unless I spelt things out I couldn't hope to get credit for goodwill. I expect to be through with proofs in about two weeks and you should be receiving pages from me in about a month's time.

I'm not sure that you will want a photograph of me in your new journal. It seems that after I have finished a novel, I always want to write an essay to go with it, hitting everyone on the head. I did that when *Henderson the Rain King* appeared, and a very bad idea it was too—guaranteed misinterpretation of my novel. You shouldn't give readers two misinterpretable texts at the same time. And if you do publish my picture I will join the ten most wanted.

Yours most earnestly and sincerely,

Bellow's self-interview would appear that autumn in the inaugural issue of Ontario Review.

To Anthony Godwin

Dear Mr. Godwin:

Is *cosseted* the word? Two days of your proposed program would put me in the hospital, on tranquillizers for a month. When your invitation was conveyed to me by Catharine Carver I thought the visit was to be made British-style, with dignified reticence. But I see you have an American promotional scheme; or go, rather, beyond the wildest promotional fantasies of Madison Ave. I never do the promotion bit here. As Katie can tell you, I shun TV appearances and avoid the speaker's platform. I was willing enough to give a lecture or two, hold one press meeting, tape one BBC program and attend a party. But your lunch parties, trips to Sussex and Edinburgh and "serious" television programs are out of the question. The very thought of them paralyzes me. With half your schedule I could be elected to Congress, and never leave my district. What we need is a compromise. On my terms. I will come for several days and make several appearances, the number to be strictly limited. I don't want my time utilized to the fullest extent. What a terrifying thought!

I am of course delighted to have you publish my books and I appreciate greatly your desire to launch them with flame and thunder. More than once, however, I've seen writers ride bicycles on the high-wire, eat fire, gash themselves open to call attention to their books. They end up with little more than a scorched nose, a broken bone.

Sincerely,

Anthony Godwin was editorial director at Weidenfeld and Nicholson.

To Owen Barfield

June 3, 1975   Chicago

Dear Mr. Barfield:

I've read several of your books—*Saving the Appearances,* the collection of essays on Romanticism, a long dialogue the name of which I can't remember just now and, quite recently, *Unancestral Voice,* a fascinating book. I am not philosopher enough to argue questions of rationality or irrationality, but there are things that seem to me self-evident, so markedly self-evident and felt that the problem of proving or disproving their reality becomes academic. Like you I am tired of all the talk about what matters and avoidance of what *really* matters.

I'd be very grateful for the opportunity to talk to you about the Meggid and about Gabriel and Michael and their antagonists. I'm afraid I don't understand the account you give of the powers of darkness. I am, I assure you, very much in earnest.

Sincerely yours,

P.S. I got your address from Mr. Charles Monteith of Faber.

Owen Barfield (1898–1997), barrister, man of letters, disciple of Rudolf Steiner and expounder of Anthroposophy, Steiner's teaching, published many books including Poetic Diction: A Study in Meaning *(1928) and* What Coleridge Thought *(1971).*

To Harriet Wasserman

July 1, 1975   Casa Alison, Carboneras, Almería, Spain

Dear Harriet:

You'll think it odd that I never wrote to thank you for the magnificent party and the dinner, and it is odd, but I've been oddly tired. This is Sixties Fatigue, and I'm not talking about the last decade. It's only now, after a week in Carboneras, that I'm able to face a piece of paper. Well, it was a significant party that you gave me, with champagne, Chinese food, big surprises and Roman splendor. I was touched. It's seldom that anyone takes so much trouble over me—say, once in sixty years. I'm not used to it (to say the least!). It gave me joy. It also troubled me somewhat because I thought, "So something like this *can* be done by some for others?" I had *heard* about that. And now it becomes a glorious memory. I feel like the small girl in *Little Dorrit* who couldn't forget the hospital—the "*orspital*," I mean.

It appears I have to run to catch the postman with this, so I'll sign off. Write me a letter.

Love,

To David Peltz

July 2, 1975   Casa Alison, Carboneras, Almería, Spain

Dear Dave:

The place is beautiful. I'm not, particularly. I arrived in an exhausted state and have been sleeping, swimming, eating, reading and little else. Let's see if I can get myself flushed out. Life lays a heavy *material* weight on us in the

States—things, cares, money. But I think that the reason why I feel it so much is that I let myself go, here, and let myself feel six decades of trying hard, and of fatigue. My character is like a taste in my mouth. I've tasted better tastes. But it'll pass, and one of these days I'll be able to see that the ocean is beautiful. And the mountains, and the plants, and the birds. Life isn't kind to people who took it on themselves to do something about life. Uh-*unh*!

Adam is here with us—a marvelous young man, surprisingly good-natured for a son of mine. He smiles at his peevish pa and goes on reading science fiction and thrillers. The queen [Bellow's new wife, Alexandra] is good-natured, too. She's in her parlor eating mathematical bread and honey. Even I have an occasional good moment, and when I've slept myself out I may stop being such a bear.

I want to wish you a happy birthday and to ask whether you found time to stop at the Corbins and pick up the trifles I bought for you. I often think about you and wonder how it is to have lost a father at sixty. Sixty alone is hard enough. But I shan't talk to you about death now. God knows there's plenty of that in the book. Oddly enough, I don't think much about *Humboldt*. It's like the end of something. I'm like a fat Sonja Henie—no more fancy figures on the ice. Overweight. That's the end of that. I'm hanging up my skates, retiring. If I ever try it again, it'll be in my own back yard for God's amusement.

Best to Doris, and love,

Bellow had married Romanian-born mathematician Alexandra Ionescu Tulcea the previous autumn.

To Owen Barfield

July 15, 1975   Carboneras, Almería, Spain

Dear Mr. Barfield—

That you should come down to London to answer the ignorant questions of a stranger greatly impressed me. I daresay I found the occasion far more interesting than you could. You were most patient with a beginner trying to learn his A-B-C's. I continue to study your *Unancestral Voice*. It's hard going—some forty years of thought and reading condensed—but I have a strong hunch that you are giving a true account of things. In these matters illumination counts for as much as the sort of "hard proofs" we have been brought up to demand, and lately I have become aware, not of illumination itself, but of a kind of illuminated fringe—a peripheral glimpse of a different state of things. This makes little sense to you perhaps.

Thank you for coming to talk to me.

Sincerely,

To Owen Barfield

July 24, 1975   Carboneras, Almería, Spain

Dear Mr. Barfield:

Your letter was very welcome. I'm glad you saw some merit in *Herzog*. At the Athenaeum [Barfield's London club, where he and Bellow had lunched] I was a totally unknown quantity and felt that I had failed to show why I should be taken seriously. I continue to pore over *Unancestral Voice* and it is most important that you should be willing to discuss it with me. I can readily see why you would take little interest in contemporary fiction. Those who read it and write it are easily satisfied with what your Meggid calls lifeless memory-thoughts. For some time now I have been asking what kind of knowledge a writer has and in what way he deserves to be taken seriously. He has imagination where others have science, etc. But it wasn't until I read your book on Romanticism that I began to understand something about the defeat of imaginative knowledge in modern times! I don't want to labor the point which you yourself have brought to my attention; I only want to communicate something in my own experience that will explain the importance of your books to me. My experience was that the interest of much of life as represented in the books I read (and perhaps some that I wrote) had been exhausted. But how could existence itself become uninteresting. I concluded that the ideas and modes by which it was represented were exhausted, that individuality had been overwhelmed by power or "sociality," by technology and politics. Images or representations *this* side of the mirror have indeed tired us out. All that science did was to make the phenomena technically (mathematically) inaccessible, leaving us with nothing but ignorance and despair. Yes, psychoanalysis directed us to go into the Unconscious. From the dark forest—a sort of preserve of things unknown—painters and poets like good dogs were to bring back truffles . . .

Tomorrow my Spanish holiday ends. My wife and I are returning via London and will be there for about ten days. I hope you will be kind enough to give me a few hours more of your time.

It was very good of you to send me the Steiner book. Will you have lunch with me (as my guest this time) in London? You speak of yourself as the servant of your readers, but this reader, though eager to talk with you, hesitates to impose himself.

Sincerely yrs,

To Philip Roth

August 8, 1975   [Chicago]

Dear Philip,

As your Czechoslovak-writers-aid program was to have run for only one year and, as Mrs. [Esther] Corbin tells me, that year is coming to a close, I should like to know whether you propose to continue. For my part, I'd be glad to go on sending fifty bucks a month.

The party last June was the one and only party in memory that felt to me like a real party. I didn't know what I was saying or doing. It was bliss. I do remember trying to talk to you about The Jewish Writer but I was quite drunk and you were wasting your time. So let's try again.

My wife is going to Jerusalem to give mathematical lectures. I shall be carrying her lecture notes. We will stop in New York en route (about the 8th of November). Shall we try to have a sober conversation or let well enough alone?

Yours sincerely,

To Margaret Staats

September 15, 1975   [Chicago]

On the death matter: With me or without, the preoccupation would have returned. After that night [. . .] I cried with relief but psychically the death (in the shadow-style of the psyche) took place. Many times (Yeats isn't the first to tell us) we die, many times rise again. As for the terror, it drives us to think—it has its function. We don't *go* without that.

I don't know how I ever came to believe that a death-comedy had to be written. Perhaps it was *Measure for Measure* that put it into my head. Charlie [Citrine, narrator-protagonist of *Humboldt's Gift*] himself is in and out of the grave continually. Of course I might have spared you but we were bound together in this comical-death complex, were appalled together and laughed together. We wore the same team cap for a few years. It didn't occur to me that you would be affected so strongly.

But here I am, writing to you on Yom Kippur!

Early this morning Samuel S. Goldberg telephoned and asked whether I had read the review in *The New Yorker* by that "anti-Semitic pornographer." And I remembered that you had mentioned Updike. If I hadn't taken Daniel to see *Jaws* I suppose I might have been upset. *Jaws* gave me perspective. No one has ever accused me of writing bad English—I'm sure I slipped up here and there, in a book of more than five hundred pages that would be inevitable. This morning I'm actually frozen, covered with a thick ice of Jewish inhibitions. Shall I write my next book in Yiddish? But perhaps the grammatical lapses were all Charlie's. Besides, did H. W. Fowler ever write an American novel?

Send me a comforting note. Forgive me for making D[emmie]'s plane crash.

Love,

In Humboldt's Gift, *Demmie Vonghel, a character unmistakably based on Maggie, dies in an airplane crash. In* The New Yorker, *John Updike had criticized* Humboldt *as overwrought and shapeless, comparing it unfavorably to* The Adventures of Augie March.

To Mark Shechner

September 30, 1975   Chicago

Dear Mr. Shechner:

I liked your Rosenfeld lecture very much. I agreed with most of it. Perhaps I wouldn't write to you about Isaac even if I were not running because I am still thinking about his life, his character, his thoughts and his death and am not yet ready to discuss him. But I will say this: He combined all the reticence and shyness of a small sickly Jewish boy from Chicago with heroic ideas about destiny. And after all, history would not have been history without these apparently timid and inconspicuous Jewish children.

May I keep your essay to refer to another time or do you want it returned? I am leaving Chicago for a few months but my secretary, Mrs. Esther Corbin, will return it if you need it.

Many thanks for letting me see it.

Sincerely yours,

Mark Shechner (born 1940) edited Preserving the Hunger: An Isaac Rosenfeld Reader *(1988) and has written numerous books including* The Conversion of the Jews and Other Essays *(1990).*

To Ruth Miller

Dear Ruth:

That was a welcome letter. I haven't forgotten you, either. If I was your first teacher, you were my first pupil, and my heart hasn't altogether turned to stone. I've often reproached myself for my impatience towards you. I mitigate nothing by telling you that I'm like my poor father, first testy then penitent. One must free one's soul from these parental influences. Poor Papa's soul was his, after all, and mine is mine, and it's sheer laziness to borrow his behavior. We all do that, of course. He did it, too. Only he was too busy with life's battles to remove *his* father's thumbprints and cleanse the precious surfaces. We've been luckier. We have the leisure for it.

I read [Louis] Simpson's piece in the *Times* before your letter came, and I didn't quite know how to deal with it. It was cheap, mean, it did me dirt. I had thought Simpson was paying no more attention to me than I've paid to him over the years. One can't look into everything, after all. I was indifferent to his poetry and it was only fair that he should pay no attention to what I wrote. I had no idea that he was in such a rage. But age does do some things for us (nothing comparable to what it takes away) and I have learned to endure such fits. I don't ask myself why the *Times* prints such miserable stuff, why I must be called an ingrate, a mental tyrant, a thief, a philistine enemy of poetry, a narcissist incapable of feeling for others, a failed artist. Nor why this must be done in the Sunday *Magazine* for many millions of readers. Such things are not written about industrialists, or spies, or bankers, or trade-union leaders, or Idi Amin, or Palestinian terrorists, only about the author of a novel who wanted principally to be truthful and to give delight. It doesn't stab me to the heart, however. I know what newspapers are—and what writers are, and know that they can occasionally try to destroy one another. I've never done it myself, but I've seen it done, often enough. [. . .] Louie's hatred and my discomfort are minor matters, comparatively. He can't *kill* me. He's only doing dirt on my heart (by intention—he didn't actually succeed). [. . .]

But I was upset to find you mentioned in his piece, and this is why I say that I didn't quite know how to deal with it. I wondered why *you* should find it necessary to testify against me and say that I was an artist *manqué*. After many years in the trade, I'm well aware that the papers twist people's words and that at times their views are reversed for them by reporters and editors.

But you *were* angry with me, and Stony Brook *isn't* exactly filled with my friends and admirers. Nor do I, from *my* side, think of Stony Brook as a great center of literary power in which a renaissance is about to begin, led by Kazin and Jack Ludwig and Louie. (Not that I've written reviews and articles about *them*.) So I didn't expect you to say kind things about me. But I didn't expect unkind things in print, and I was shocked by the opinion attributed to you that *Humboldt* was my confession of utter failure. Louie I could dismiss. A writer who doesn't know quality when he sees it doesn't have to be taken seriously. A reader who doesn't see that the book is a very funny one can also be disregarded—one can only wonder why the deaf should attend concerts. But you I don't dismiss. And I thought, "I've steered Ruth wrong. What has this girl from Albany Park gained by ending up in Stony Brook? It is *possible* that she should have become one of these killers?"

I began to compose a few Herzog notes in my mind. But I wouldn't have sent any of them. You might *not* have been guilty of any offense. I do *not* defend myself anymore (in the old way). I have other concerns, now. But then your letter arrived. And you are what I always thought you were, and I am still your old loving friend,

Louis Simpson's attack on Bellow in The New York Times Magazine *was "The Ghost of Delmore Schwartz."*

To Edward Shils

December 8, 1975   Mishkenot Sha'ananim, Jerusalem
My dear Ed:
[. . .] The Committee [on Social Thought], though you may not agree, is a very useful thing; it has developed several extraordinary students in recent years. It is no small achievement to turn out Ph.D.s who know how to write English and are at home in several fields—intelligent people who have read Thucydides and Kant and Proust and who are not counterfeits or culture snobs. They will not disgrace the University of Chicago. I've met many graduates from other departments of whom the same cannot be said. I myself have not done all that might have been done for the Committee. I had books to write and problems to face, many of these arising from my own unsatisfactory character, but I have nevertheless taken my duties seriously. Now I think it's the University's turn to be serious and to demonstrate that it considers the

Committee to be something more than a celebrity showpiece. The celebrities are beginning to dodder in any case. Unless new appointments are made the Committee will cease to exist. In about five years it'll be gone.

As for that other dying institution, *Encounter,* I'll contribute five hundred dollars for the coming year, and five hundred more in 1977, if there should be a 1977 in *Encounter*'s destiny. I think Mel Lasky should write to Thomas Guinzburg of Viking Press (Viking and Penguin have just merged) and say that I have told him that I'd be greatly disappointed if Viking didn't make a contribution.

I wish we had the time to stop in Holland en route. I'd love to see you and to talk with you about Israel and other matters. A conversation with you is all-too-rare a pleasure, these days. But my son Gregory is in Chicago for the holidays and we want to see him before he goes back to California.

With most affectionate good wishes for the New Year,

1976

To Owen Barfield

February 25, 1976   Chicago

Dear Mr. Barfield:

It's not a case of out of sight, out of mind. I think often of you and compose quite a few mental letters. But I have no progress to report; much confusion, rather. I mustn't be altogether negative; there are trace-elements of clarity. I continue to read Steiner and to perform certain exercises. I am particularly faithful to the I Am, It Thinks meditation in the Guidance book you so kindly gave me. From this I get a certain daily stability. I don't know what causes so much confusion in me. Perhaps I have too many things going on at once. I had promised myself a holiday after finishing the last book. I think I told you last summer that I was going to Jerusalem with my wife. She gave some lectures at the Hebrew University in Probability Theory. My intention was to wander about the Old City and sit contemplatively in the gardens and churches. But it is impossible in Jerusalem to detach oneself from the frightful political problems of Israel. I found myself "doing something." I read a great many books, talked with scores of people, and before the first month was out I was writing a small book about the endless crisis and immersed in politics. It excites me, it distresses me to be so immersed. I can't mention Lucifer and Ahriman, I don't know enough for that. Neither can I put them out of my mind.

I didn't mention *Humboldt's Gift* to you because I thought you weren't greatly interested in novels. I thought it might even displease you. Besides I tend to think of a book just completed as something that has prepared me to do better next time. You asked me, very properly, how I thought a writer of novels might be affected by esoteric studies. I answered that I was ready for the consequences. That was a nice thing to say, but it wasn't terribly intelligent. It must have struck you as very adolescent. You asked me how old I was. "Sixty," I said. Then you smiled and said, "Sixteen?" It was the one joke you allowed yourself at my expense, and it was entirely justified. It's a very American thing to believe that it's never too late to make a new start in life. Always decades to burn.

As if this weren't enough, we've had to travel a great deal, my wife and I. In the last month we've been to San Francisco, Boston and Miami. We had promises to keep. We'd been away for three months, and couldn't put things off until spring.

I'm a bit ashamed to present such a picture of confusion. You probably knew it wasn't going to be easy to change from one sort of life to another. This is not a very satisfactory letter but I feel that I owe you some account of myself—I feel it because I respect you and because you tried so generously to help me.

Best regards,

The book about Israel that Bellow had set to work on, To Jerusalem and Back, *would appear first in back-to-back issues of* The New Yorker *in July, then in book form in the autumn.*

To Walter Hasenclever

March 3, 1976   Chicago

Dear Walter,

We were delighted to see you in Jerusalem—the best sort of bonus, the unanticipated and undeserved. It isn't altogether true that I had recovered my spirits in Jerusalem—I was still suffering from my concluding efforts with *Humboldt*. Teddy Kollek kept telling me that I must have a holiday. But to have a holiday in Jerusalem is something like consummating a marriage in a laundromat. I'm glad to hear that K[iepenheuer] & W[itsch] approves your translation [of *Humboldt's Gift*]. I'm sure they are right. The yeoman in *Ivanhoe* was right too: "A man can do but his best." It was only Sir Walter who was not doing at all well. Now you had better get a good rest in the Austrian mountains because you will soon be facing a new task, my short book on Jerusalem. I spend half the night boning up on my subject, half the day writing; the rest of my time I'm free to devote to my wife, my children, the University of Chicago and my business affairs and my duties as an unpaid cultural functionary.

Now let me try to answer a few of your questions:

1) Drag racing is the strictly illegal sport of adolescent amateur automobile mechanics who transform an ordinary car into a racer. They hold outlaw matches on back roads, attain speeds of a hundred fifty m.p.h. or better, and are often killed.

2) One can "cock" the wheel of a Thunderbird—that is the driver's wheel can be pushed forward so that the driver may seat himself without inconvenience.

3) I don't remember what I meant by an axle type but I may have been thinking of [Villiers de l'Isle-Adam's] *Axel,* the one about the young man who says, "As for living, our servants can do that for us."

4) Hog belly should really be pork belly. Pork bellies are traded in the commodities market.

5) A pig-in-a-wig is reminiscent of a pig-in-a-poke in the old saying, poke being an old word for sack or bag. Then there is pig-in-a-blanket or ground meat cooked in cabbage leaves. Lastly, we come to the nursery rhyme *Barber, barber, shave a pig, how many hairs to make a wig?* Put this all together and you get the image of a porcine man wearing what looks to be artificial hair.

6) A Roto-Rooter man is an expensive American specialist who unstops clogged drains by inserting a long phallic segmented steel instrument called a "snake." And that is what a Roto-Rooter man is.

7) "Pet" [means here] arbitrary—one's favorite form of obstinacy or crankiness.

8) Vacate the personae simply means to abandon one's favorite masks.

9) To launder money is a well-known Mafia expression. The illest-gotten gains of gangsters cannot legally be declared as income. The underworld has its own ways of making dirty money respectable by sending it through channels, etc.

10) Castro is a manufacturer of folding beds or "hideaway" sofa beds. These generally have dangerously prominent hinges which have been known to injure hasty lovers.

11) What Charlie means on p. 89 is that he believes he can see Cantabile's aura, a personal quality generally invisible.

12) P.102, line 7, "There were a few windbreaks up here on the 50th or 60th floor, and those the wind was storming." These windbreaks, made of stout canvas, protect the workers from the weather. When the wind is high the canvas flaps mightily. On this occasion, the wind was storming, i.e., assaulting the canvas.

13) "Sailing to Byzantium" is a poem by Yeats.

14) Hegel, in his *Philosophy of History*.

15) The "quiet" quote is from Rudolf Steiner and comes, I believe, from a book called *Knowledge of the Higher Worlds and Its Attainment*.

Alexandra and I will be knocking about in June, probably in England. In July and August we will be at Cape Cod or Martha's Vineyard and in September we will return to Chicago. I will tell her what you say about her smile.

As ever,

To Norman Podhoretz

March 8, 1976   Chicago

Dear Norman:

I did give a talk in Miami but I intend to make it part of a longer piece.

And now tell me this: If you were described in someone's magazine as a "burnt-out case" would you be at all inclined to contribute articles to that magazine?

Sincerely yours,

In his unfavorable review of Humboldt's Gift *in* Commentary, *Jack Richardson had wondered whether Bellow was "a burnt-out case."*

To Ben Sidran

May 21, 1976   Chicago

Dear Ben:

You're right about your father [Louis Sidran] and me. And I often feel, when I'm writing, that I'm a composite person. Your father is certainly part of the mixture. It comes over me now and then that I'm trying to do something he wanted done. When, dying, he drove so many hundreds of miles in the station wagon with Ezra from Gettysburg to East Hampton to see me, I got the message quite clearly. I knew what he wanted, whom he loved. I admired and loved him.

I can see why it was hard for you to write to me. The difficulty makes your letter all the more valuable.

Best wishes,

To James Salter

May 26, 1976   [Chicago]

Cher collègue:

I write, as always, in nasty haste, a chronic condition. I am doing what I oughtn't to do, a journalistic job. Dreadful pressure.

Yes, I was miffed by the Graham Greene thing, but not seriously nor for long. Greene didn't find me "difficult"—by "difficult" he meant Jewish. I can't see how any reader of his novels can miss that. American is bad enough [according to Greene]. But to be Jewish as well—well, no combination could be worse.

That's all there was to that.

Alexandra and I are taking off for Dublin and Milan tomorrow. I haven't finished my piece either. I must, tonight.

Yrs. as always,

In an interview Salter conducted for People *magazine, Graham Greene had recalled Bellow as "difficult."*

To Samuel S. Goldberg

July 26, 1976   Chicago

Dear Samuel,

[. . .] A gossip item from the Chicago newspapers announcing the triumph of Susan Bellow greeted me when I returned from Europe. I thought you might like to run your jurist's eye over it. You know, I'm really beginning to think badly of the legal profession. Judges and lawyers simply don't understand how a writer makes his way through life. Page five speaks of the "defendant's misrepresentations." I didn't misrepresent. I simply had no idea what my future income would be. It's true that I took an advance of fifty thousand, but suppose I had been unable to complete the book?

Maybe when you have studied the document you will be able to explain it all to me and especially the murky paragraph at the bottom of page six.

As ever,

The First District Court of Chicago had issued a ruling that Bellow misled former wife Susan Glassman Bellow about his income and directed him to pay increased alimony and child support.

To Owen Barfield

August 13, 1976 Chicago

Dear Mr. Barfield—

By now you will perhaps have written me off as someone who straggled in and then faded out in pursuit of other enthusiasms. The fact is that I continue as well as I can with Steiner and that I am still trying to train myself. I haven't been able to do this steadily. Last autumn I decided—took it as a duty—to write a short book about Israel. I'd never seriously studied Zionism (i.e. the terrible question of the fate of the Jews) but having come to Jerusalem with my wife I "discovered" it; I began to assume a degree of responsibility for it. A solution is beyond anyone's powers, but I wanted at least to state the problem of Israel clearly to the civilized public. For six months I soaked myself in the literature of the subject and spent my nights in reading and my days taking interviews and writing them down. The results have just appeared in *The New Yorker* (July 12 and 19). They aren't satisfactory but they seem to have had a certain effect. I worked very hard at them. I worked myself into such a state of fatigue that I was unable to pull myself together physically, much less write thoughtful letters. The morning meditations, which I continued faithfully, helped somewhat, although there were days in which I could only ramble through them in a promissory way. Later, I would do them properly.

I didn't mind your dismissing *Humboldt*. I expected that. It is a comical and very American examination of the cares and trials of "civilized" people in a civilized country. These cares are by now plainly ludicrous and one can't be truly serious about them. The ultimate absurdity is that it is the spiritual matters, which alone deserve our seriousness, that are held to be absurd. Perhaps it was wrong of me to put this longing for spiritual fruit in a comic setting. I knew that you could never approve and would think it idiotic and perhaps even perverse. But I followed my hunch as a writer, trusting that this eccentric construction would somehow stand steady.

I shall send you the little Jerusalem book when it is published in October. With best wishes,

To Louis Lasco

August 25, 1976   [Chicago]

Highly esteemed Katastrof Efimovitch—my dear school friend:

I thank you for your congratulations. I am afraid I have too many irons in too many fires; letters go unanswered. Like yourself I should be thinking of retirement. I used to flinch from this as a bourgeois idea. Whenever I emerged through the door of a jet plane into California sunshine my first thought was: "Retirement!" And then: "But I am too young!" (Meaning, in fact, that I had not yet satisfied my adolescent ambitions.) But now I think more kindly of people who move gracefully and tranquilly give up, surrender themselves to a quiet and gentle elderliness. Maybe this [long adolescence] is the only maturity I am destined to know.

I don't see Glotzer in Chicago—nor Freifeld, nor Peltz, nor S. J. Harris; none of the Division St. children. Some of them are annoyed with me. I can't say that this causes me much regret. I'm fond of them but nearly fifty years of the same bluffing have worn out my powers of politeness. I seem to have been an extraordinarily polite young person. I sometimes miss Peltz, a good man to have a hearty dinner with. He has some sort of grievance against me. I suppose it will last a decade or so, and we will be reconciled just before the *articulo mortis* [*].

I enjoy hearing from you. "Rosh Hashanah is at our throats again" made my day. Give your dear old mother my warmest regards. I begin to believe that her brother actually was reincarnated in me.

Your affectionate friend,

Bedouin Trofimovitch

* Latin: moment of death

To Teddy Kollek

September 9, 1976   Chicago

Dear Teddy,

Yours was the first of the Israeli reactions [to *To Jerusalem and Back*] and I was understandably apprehensive. The form I adopted obliged me to write quite explicitly about people—and one never knows. There are art historians who explain that two hundred years ago people accepted unfavorable portraits of themselves; warts, harelips, paunches, wrinkles and all. See what Goya did to the Spanish Bourbons. They didn't seem to mind, but our far less noble contemporaries wish to appear without a flaw. One of the paradoxes of democracy.

Your letter pleased me very much and I have received many kind notices from Israel and from America. So I'm encouraged to return to Jerusalem. If you should know of an available apartment, we would be most grateful to have it.

With best wishes for the New Year,

As ever,

To Margaret Shafer

October 15, 1976   [Chicago]

Dear Margaret:

Your note delighted me. There are days, in Chicago, when I think enviously of life in Annandale-on-Hudson, and of intelligent ladies who read and write under the beautiful trees. (Or beautiful ladies and intelligent-looking trees.) I wish I hadn't been so very stupid in Dutchess County—I missed so many things. But then the County was rather dumb about me. I wasn't received in the "best" places. It was funny, at times. Ellison and I would drink martinis together, and then he'd go off in his Chrysler to dinner, leaving me to grill my solitary steak. He and the nobs loved one another. I was amused. Almost no damage to my self-esteem (not easily dented).

My best to you and Fritz,

Canadian-born Margaret Shafer, wife of Fritz Shafer, professor of religion at Bard, taught piano privately and organized music festivals in Annandale-on-Hudson. She and Bellow had been friends from his arrival there in 1953.

To Toby Cole

October 18, 1976   Chicago

Dear Toby,

I am absolutely sure that you are right, and it comforts me to be so well protected by a lady for whom I have so much affection. I think though that everything should be done to protect that ninny [Leon] Kirchner. If he had as many feet as a centipede I know that he would manage somehow to get them all into his mouth. But he has worked long and hard, and I should like to see him produce his opera without interference. Let United Artists do what it will about his expired rights. *We* should not remind those United Artists of their contractual powers. I don't like being on the side of Goliath, Behemoth and Leviathan. The proper course for us is to say nothing and to hope for Leon's sake that the mighty corporation will hear, see and feel nothing. [. . .]

Yours as ever,

Leon Kirchner (1919–2009) was composing Lily, *an opera based on* Henderson the Rain King. *It would have its premiere at New York City Opera in May 1977.*

To John Cheever

November 10, 1976   Chicago

Dear John,

Will I read your book? Would I accept a free trip to Xanadu with Helen of Troy as my valet? I am longing to read the galleys. Since I have to go to New York this weekend, and also to Princeton to see my son Adam playing Antonio, the heavy in *The Tempest*, I shall get Harriet Wasserman at Russell and Volkening to obtain a set of galleys for me from Knopf. I would like to see you too, but I don't know when I will be free from this mixture of glory and horror. But I will write to you pronto about the book, which I'm sure to read with the greatest pleasure.

Yours,

"This mixture of glory and horror" refers to the decision of the Swedish Academy, on October 21, to award the Nobel Prize in Literature to Bellow.

To John Cheever

November 23, 1976   Chicago

Dear John:

Well, I expected the best and that's exactly what I got in *Falconer*. It's splendid. For two days it was my cyclone cellar; I hid out in it. It wasn't without surprises. You generally take a lighter view of the ruins. This is much the toughest book you ever wrote—warlike, nothing softened. But the more decay you got into, the purer the book became. *Falconer* is elegant. You remember what Orwell said about Henry Miller, that Henry had put the spoken language back into literature and gotten rid of the language of protocol. True enough, up to a point, but Henry poured his peculiar cafeteria fruit salad—his "philosophy" and his "poetry"—over everything. You arrange to have the best and the worst live together in high style. But I know you don't go for this literary stuff, and I'm knocking it off now. What I felt all through was an enraged determination to state the basic facts. You stated them, all right, and gave your pal the most intense satisfaction. For which he thanks you from a full heart.

You should sell hundreds of thousands of copies, unless the country is farther gone in depravity than I think. It delighted me that in the *Paris Review* interview you mentioned the pleasant and intelligent people who read the books and write thoughtful letters about them and who have no visible connection with advertising, journalism or the academic world. I love those people. They sustain me, too, as you observed. Your interviewer might have followed up on this important statement.

Ever yours,

Don't you generally go off after you've finished a novel? What you want now is a delicious holiday.

To Teddy Kollek

November 29, 1976   Chicago

Dear Teddy,

I want to get this off to you before I leave for Stockholm—I haven't even prepared the formal lecture. Under this inconceivable barrage I find it hard to concentrate. I did however take great pleasure in the review of the Jerusalem book that you wrote for *The New Republic*—it was clear, it was just, it was intelligent and elegant; I doubt that any other mayor could have written it.

Now as to the requests: People of America have begun to speak of the protection of national resources. I have decided that I am such a national, and even international, resource and am issuing an appeal for protection. Here and now I have a choice to make between becoming a Jewish dervish (the whirling and howling kind) or remaining a writer. Your situation is different, you have a political vocation and you have to deal with all of these outfits. As for Mr. Bernstein, the UJA has contacted me. His letter said that he did not want to use an extract from my Jerusalem book and he urged me to write something "fresh and original" (a wonderful choice of words). The fact is that the Jerusalem book is coming out in France, Italy, England, Germany, etc. and even in Japan, and I feel that it is important that I should maintain a stance of disinterestedness and that it would not be a useful thing for anyone if I were to identify myself with all good Jewish causes indiscriminately. I dread becoming an adjunct, a rubber stamp. I need say no more to you. Less than a word is all you need because you are wiser than most.

Yours with every good wish,

1977

To Adam Bellow

January 31, 1977   [Chicago]

Dear Adam –

I've never been so cold. The weather, making me listless, proves that I have some lizard ancestors, connections with the Mesozoic. You probably suspected it all along. It is five P.M., the temperature is zero, the wind is blowing at twenty m. p. h. And I am about to pour myself a strong drink and rejoin the mammalian order.

Your affectionate Father

To Owen Barfield

February 5, 1977   Chicago

Dear Barfield:

On the contrary, I should have written to you long ago. Nor did I expect you to acknowledge the *Jerusalem* book, which I sent in lieu of a letter, thinking that it would explain why I was so poor a correspondent. I find it most difficult to pull myself together. It is all too bewildering. Steiner makes matters sometimes easier, sometimes much harder. This is not because of the new perspective he gives me; in some ways I am drawn to him because he confirms that a perspective, the rudiments of which I always had, contained the truth. But to reassemble the whole world after a different design isn't easy for a man of sixty. I keep my doubts and questions behind a turnstile and admit them one at a time, but the queue is long and sometimes life is disorderly. Besides I can't put into what I write the faint outlines I am only beginning to see. That would muddle everything, and it would be dishonest, too, in a novice. Writing as a comic novelist, I am capable of anything, mixing desperation and humor just as I like (in my own mind, defining Herbert's "wearie" in "The Pulley" as weary with one's own absurdities). But I was serious in the *Jerusalem* book. It produced a great deal of discussion (to answer your question about its reception) and, in Israel, predictably, many polemics. I don't at all mind being attacked. It rather pleases me, even when the attackers are wicked or idiotic or ideologically muscle-bound. I'd sooner know how things are. Such is my present state of mind, anyway. Perhaps it indicates that I protected myself too well in the past.

I confess that I disliked Mr. [Seymour] Epstein's article in the *Denver Quarterly* and I felt sure that you would ask me about it—I am put off by critics who tell the world with full confidence exactly what you were up to in writing what you wrote, as though they kept a booth at the fair in the middle of your soul. After reading him I thought of your words in *Unancestral Voice* about the work of Ahriman, his chilling of everything in human thinking which depends on a certain warmth and replacing wonder by sophistication, courtesy by vulgarity. Of course one must be careful not to identify every detractor with the powers of darkness, so I shan't say much more about this. I disagreed. I hoped that he was wrong. I found amusement in thinking that many years ago critics were saying does Mr. B. expect us to believe that the spontaneity and verve of his novels are the real thing? And they are followed now by Mr. Epstein, who says, Mr. B.'s spontaneity and verve are gone, and he is a burnt-out case. But the subject can't bear further discussion.

I am looking forward to your collection of essays. Thank you for telling me about René Guénon. I shall inquire at the library about his books.

I passed through London just before Christmas but didn't want to announce myself. I thought it might be inconvenient for you to see me just then. But I will be in England again in April. I'm going back to Jerusalem via

Edinburgh and London. I'm due in London on the 17th or 18th. I very much want to see you, I need hardly say. Eager, is the word.

With many thanks for your letter, and every good wish,

To Marcello Mastroianni

February 16, 1977   Chicago

Dear Mr. Mastroianni,

First of all, let me say that as one of your great admirers I'm delighted to have your letter. The film rights to *Humboldt's Gift* have not been sold. I am sending your inquiry to my representative in New York who will, I am sure, reply promptly.

It is really very good of you to say so many obliging things. It pleases me to think that we could go on saying obliging things to each other for some time.

With perfect sincerity,

Yours very truly,

To Jacques Barzun

March 21, 1977   Chicago

Dear Mr. Barzun:

I'm deeply grateful to you and to the members of the American Academy and Institute of Arts and Letters for this distinguished award. It is a great honor, and my distress at being unable to receive it in person is also great. I am leaving the States soon and on May 18th I will be somewhere in the Middle East. May I ask my publisher to receive the award for me? I shall provide him with a few words to say. Of course I will be glad to send some pages for the manuscript exhibition. You may be sure that I will keep the news under my hat.

Yours with equal parts delight and disappointment,

Sincerely yours,

Barzun had written to inform Bellow that he'd won the Gold Medal for Fiction of the American Academy and Institute of Arts and Letters.

To Ralph Ross

March 22, 1977   Chicago

Dear Ralph:

Years ago (God, what a long time it seems, and how far away Minneapolis is!) you told me something valuable, and it was so unexpected that I couldn't react intelligently on the spot but carried the remark off and worked on it for a couple of decades. You said that Isaac [Rosenfeld] was the most unworldly person you had ever known, with one exception: Compared with me, Isaac was the complete sophisticate. I *felt* the truth of this immediately—being what I was, I couldn't expect to *understand*. And I always made a special point of seeming to be intensely practical and competent because I had no grasp of real life. Isaac was what our French friends call "*faux naïf*," and I saw that all along and understood that he wouldn't have needed such an act if he hadn't been so clever. He was trying to act his way out of (relative) worldliness. I was working in the opposite direction. Was I so innocent? Self-absorbed, rather. Only it was no ordinary form of self-absorption because I *could* understand what I was determined to understand. And if I hadn't sensed so many frightful things I wouldn't have been so intensely unworldly. Evidently I was determined not to understand whatever was deeply threatening—allowed myself to know what conformed to my objectives, and no more. A tall order, to bury so many powers of observation. That sounds immodest; I mean only to be objective. But all the orders have been tall. If you had followed up your shrewd remark you might have saved me some time, but I assume you thought that if I couldn't work out the hint I couldn't be expected to bear a full examination either. I had to go through the whole Sondra-Jack Ludwig business, for instance. I gave them, and others, terrific entertainment. Sondra sent me to the English Department to threaten to resign if they didn't re-appoint Ludwig, whom they had good reason to loathe. It was a barrel of fun. I'm not so keen on this sort of Goldoni comedy as I once was (small wonder), but I can see the humor of it. It gives me great satisfaction to look back in detachment and to think of the wit the gods gave us when they had to reduce our scope. But why didn't they reduce our ambitions correspondingly? Why were we fired up with glorious dreams of achievement leading to such appalling waste? No one could make a true success except a few private persons with limited aims. Some of us, trying hard, were wonderfully unstinting of themselves. I think of John [Berryman], so generous in self-destruction. Or Isaac, who put on every stitch of virtue he had, and got on his horse and jumped into the big hole in the Forum. No one who set out to make the big scene in a big way could, in the nature of the case, get very far.

I don't think the Prize is going to make much difference. It's been very confusing and delusive, but the delusions aren't hard to shake off. Some of the contemporary literary winners have made wonderful comments about Stockholm. Seferis said it allowed him, after long effort, to be *nobody*, to be unnoticed, as Homer said of Ulysses. The noise dies down, and then you find your scale. If you have any sense, you go back to your trade, and the humor is part of my trade.

I'm grateful for what you told me way back when. I should have moved faster but reluctance (or was it torpor?) was part of the problem. You still keep a benevolent eye on me from afar. I feel it and send you my affectionate thanks.

I'm going to be in California next October or November. Let's arrange to meet.

Blessings,

To the American Academy and Institute of Arts and Letters
(Read in Bellow's absence at the Annual Ceremonial, May 18, 1977)
When the honorific rains come, there's no stopping them, and as the honors pelt my humble roof, I sometimes awake in the night and hear a Scriptural warning: "Look unto you when all men shall speak well of you!" But as that can never happen, I whisper "Fat chance!" and I am temporarily comforted. Somerset Maugham says somewhere that becoming famous is like getting a string of pearls. People admire them, but from time to time the owner wonders whether they are real or cultured. Politicians may love a consensus, but writers don't quite trust it, and I sometimes wonder, "Are they giving me all these diplomas, testimonials and medals in order to get rid of me? Am I headed for the waxworks?" The answer to this is: "The Bellow they know may be ready for Madame Tussaud's but the real Bellow has already made his getaway and lighted out for the territory ahead." But in that territory, if I am lucky enough to reach it, I will think of this Gold Medal with particular satisfaction. This one, awarded by my own colleagues, by those who know what it is in these times to write books in the USA, is the most valuable of all. By making the award, my colleagues are telling me, most tactfully and feelingly, that it's okay—that all these honors do not mean that I've gone wrong anywhere, but that I've delivered some of the goods at least. There remain (with luck) about ten years of the threescore and ten to de-

liver the rest. I am most grateful for this vote of confidence, and I shall do everything possible to complete the shipment.

To Adam Bellow

Sept. 25, 1977   Cambridge

Dear Adam:

Your father, used to the decades zipping by, sure that there would always be more where they came from, is now beginning to understand that he is at the shorter end of time. This doesn't bring a sad, bad feeling, but rather a sense that I'd better do the things I haven't done. Not undo the things that I have done—there isn't time for that. And when you write to me about your romances, I have a feeling of comfort (for your sake) seeing that you still have an endless perspective of decades. I shouldn't have used the plural "romances"—excuse me. But if patterns persist, the singular hasn't much of a chance.

I've never lived in Cambridge before, and I'm inspecting rather than relishing the place. I like the joy it gives people to be associated with this town, the big cultural sense they have of themselves and their sublime luck. I watch the young men rowing in the river, and I exercise my muscular Jewish midwestern skepticism indoors.

I agree with Sondra that you oughtn't to travel too much up and down the seacoast but concentrate on your studies; I am, or should be, one of those studies, however, and it would please me greatly if you could find time to visit Boston once or twice this autumn. Three weekends in October are already planned away, out of reach. We'll be in NYC on the weekend of the 14th, but November is fairly open (as yet). You might like to come up to New York on the 15th, and to Boston on a weekend in November or early December. Let me know whether you can manage this.

Love,

Pop

To Margaret Staats

September 24, 1977   Cambridge

Dear Maggie:

One of the penalties of growing older is that my life has so many divisions of old and new, and divisions among the divisions, as my mind is changed and my affections spread (to say nothing of dislikes)—that in the end I can't attend to anyone as I should. And when I get a letter from you, to whom I would have so much to say if we were sitting in the same room, I have to let it lie in my old black satchel until I can pull myself together. Then the whole effort is one of editing out the mountain of chaotic facts so as to get a reasonably coherent message. But the more coherent, the more inexact it becomes. Because I'm in the midst of multiple revisions I'm not really able to do more than express doubts about everything I used to consider stable in life, and transmit my affections, which haven't changed. Not the main ones, and you are one of the permanent objects, or subjects. It upsets me to hear of your operations, comforts me to hear of your marriage, and when you ask me to help with the magazine [*Quest*, where she was then an editor] I won't refuse. The condition I've described doesn't make me a good subject for interviews. I'm all transitions, and this isn't a comfortable age for it. Do you know Emerson's poem "Terminus"? "As the bird trims herself to the gale / I trim myself to the storm of time," the old boy said. But that's only part of the matter. The rest—and the rest is worse than storming time—is that there are almost no people left to whom I speak my mind. And when I say "left" I don't mean that those who might have understood what goes on are dead. No, I couldn't communicate with those either, unless they'd learned something since they died. And when I say this to you, I make no claim to be special. I haven't been at all special. I made all the plainest, most obvious mistakes. But all the large "cultural" trends, and especially the most prestigious ones, are so obviously wrong that I don't have to act to isolate myself. I am passive, registering what's wrong in what this civilization of ours thinks when it speaks of Nature, God, the soul, and it cuts me off from all organized views. It doesn't cut me off at all from the deeper being of people—in fact that's where my reaction against these organized views begins. But I can't manage this new kind of consciousness. I don't know what to do about it.

Always your devoted friend,

To Owen Barfield

September 29, 1977   Cambridge, Mass.

Dear Mr. Barfield:

If you hadn't let me know that you were coming, I wouldn't have thought it in the least churlish. I am old enough to begin to understand how difficult travel is for people of advanced years. Unfortunately, I shan't be in the Midwest. My wife and I are teaching at Brandeis, in Waltham, Massachusetts, this autumn. But I would be most willing, even eager, to fly down to New York if you can spare the time from your schedule at Drew University.

Wesleyan University Press did not send me your book, but I obtained a copy through channels and have read most of it, admiringly. "Read" is not the word for it; I am obliged to study your essays, and I have with a certain amount of difficulty come to understand some of them reasonably well. Writing novels does not prepare one for all this hard work in epistemology. In London I embarrassed myself by asking you several stupid questions. That, unfortunately, is how I learn. I humiliate myself, I grieve, and the point remains permanently with me. I think you will understand how hard this work must be for a man who has led the life that I have led. I count on you to forgive me (as well as you can). The other day I received a letter from a lady who had heard the talk I gave in Edinburgh and who reproached me in the name of what she called all the "anthropops" [disciples of Rudolf Steiner's Anthroposophy] in the front row. They had come to hear a great and stirring message. Instead, I spoke merely of what it had been like to become a novelist in the city of Chicago. What? Waste everyone's time with streets and slums and race and crimes and sex problems (I hadn't mentioned sex, by the way). I must learn to do better, and she appealed to me to take more instruction and draw more inspiration from Owen Barfield. She is, in her way, bang right. But what am I to do? I can't pass myself off for a sage, and it wasn't as a sage that the Arts Council invited me to Edinburgh.

I thought you might be mildly amused by this.

In any case, I would welcome the opportunity to see you in New York, between planes.

With best regards,

To Richard Stern

October 1, 1977   Cambridge

Dear Richard:

[. . .] I strive manfully with life's problems. They will say in the next world, "You certainly went on in good faith, Kid, doing what you were brought up to do. Very responsible. You may have missed a thing or two (of importance) by sticking to these commitments." But there's nothing to be done now. I feel a little weaker than I did in the last decade. I don't recover all my strength in sleep or other forms of rest. I get more and more restless, to less and less purpose. And I can't keep up with all the difficulties. The reason I was slow to write to you was that the court proceedings were hotter and heavier than usual. Just now, for instance, I am in contempt. I am coming to Daniel's bar mitzvah but I may be arrested in front of K[ehilath]

A[nshe] M[a'ariv] next Saturday despite my truce agreement (for the weekend) with Susan. The court held me in contempt because—I will tell it in legal language—pursuant to advice of counsel I refused to comply with the alimony assessment of the court but appealed the decision. Until the appeal is formally filed, I am in comtempt (I can't even spell the damn word, there's so much emotional interference). My lawyers tell me that I won't be handcuffed and dragged away to alimony row. Such a vile shock, or culmination, might actually reverse the emotional tides and bring me peace. Who knows?

So, I go on lecturing on Joseph Conrad, and writing odds and ends, taking absurd telephone messages. For example, this morning: *Fortune* wants to print an article on the earnings of authors. The Franklin Mint Co. wants to put out *Humboldt's Gift* in limp leather, an inscribed edition of fifteen thousand. They will pay me two bucks per signature. If I consent to sign my name fifteen thousand times I will be thirty thousand richer. I mean fifteen, for the govt. would take half. Shall I sign my name fifteen thousand times? My idea is to hire a forger, and pay him two bits per.

If I'm not in County Jail next weekend, I shall give you a ring.

Yours affectionately,

To Richard Stern

[Postmarked Cambridge, Mass., 4 October 1977]

Dear Dick,

Congratulations! Another son. Wordsworth said, "Stern daughter" ("Ode to Duty") but Gay came through with a boy. Well, a son is what the old folks used to call *"a Gan-Eden-schlepper,"* a puller-into Paradise. [. . .] I'm very glad for you, and the kid is fortunate in his parents and siblings. The children must be terribly excited—Chris gets a bigger crew, but poor Andrew, he'll find it hard to swallow at first.

I'm glad to get your kind words about *Herzog*. What am I saying?—I swallow them with joy. That *Herzog* is all right. I hope his luck will last. Though I father interesting characters, it's in the upbringing that they lose out.

I'm a very imperfect and accidental sort of person, a poor over-interrogated witness; you should outstrip me soon. Perhaps even will in any case. I know better than to take any writer's word about his own book. Already in the first pages there was a good deal of strong feeling [in yours].

As for Leeds, I'm sorry for your sake but pleased you'll be in Chicago next winter—*and* Shils. As Edward would say, it's going to be capital.

Try to come out in Sept. Blessings on Gay, and young Nick.

Yours affectionately,

To Edward Shils

November 14, 1977   Cambridge

Dear Edward,

Your call the other morning came when I needed support and I was hoping for just such a sign of affection and solidarity. You told me once that one didn't need many friends; that is perfectly true and it's also just as well since one need not expect to have too many. I am very lucky in having the few that are essential. And you have a friend in me, I assure you. [. . .]

I'm able to fend off my troubles most of the time and get some work done. My anxieties have a way of attacking me at about 3:00 A.M. when my defenses are down and then I think all kinds of nonsensical things and feel agitated. I don't need eight hours of rest, I'm in good health. My mind, though, does require a longer nightly absence from consciousness than it is getting and sometimes feels sere at the edges. Cambridge does not fascinate me. I can take these masses of ivy or leave them. Alexandra, among her mathematicians, is very cheerful but I am beginning to long for vulgar Chicago where facts are facts.

Yours most affectionately,

1978

To Leon Wieseltier

January 18, 1978   Chicago

Dear Leon:

I intended to write at once about your essays but life insists on teaching me a few more lessons. I thought I knew corrupt Chicago, the money world, the legal and accounting professions and all their psychological types and all the political parallels—I did, of course, but it was an intelligent person's closet knowledge and fate decided that I should get a finishing course, that I should feel all the fingers on my skin and have my internal organs well squeezed. In its way this is fair enough. I *said* I wanted to know; I claimed that I already knew; and I held positions in the Higher Life, was its representative in the Midwest. All that has got to be paid for, and I'm in the process of doing that. There is no other way. It's time-consuming, sordid—one is abused, dragged through the *schmutz* [*], publicized. That's one's country, as it is, and that's one's own high-minded self, dedicated to art and wisdom. But then convenience and comfort make us dimwitted, and celebrity threatens to complete one's imbecility. I've seen more than one big figure turn into a cork dummy. It might be nice to have a garden of one's own to cultivate at a time like this and let the preposterous world do its preposterous things. I love rose bushes, but I love objectivity even more, and self-objectivity more than any other type. This makes all the noise, troubling, cheating, vengefulness and money-grabbing tolerable and at times even welcome. When I come home, though, or go to my office, I find the books, journals and letters flooding in. I haven't the time to read, much less comment or answer. No sorcerer arrives to bail the apprentice out. When insomnia permits it, I dream of monasteries or hermit's caves. But I'm a Jew, and married—uxorious.

I tell you these things—for openers—because I found that I could tell you things. It made me happy to see you. It will take you some time to learn that I've a reputation for reticence. A Village painter who did psychiatry as a sideline once called me an "oral miser." He was right, I'm afraid. I couldn't talk to him. There's no one in Chicago to make me freely conversational. Joe Epstein I like and respect but I don't open my heart to him because he doesn't have the impulse—your impulse—to open up. Besides he's more fair-minded than we are, or more circumspect when he discusses our bogus contemporaries. You and I have in common a vivid impatience with jerks which makes us wave our arms and cry out. You won me with your first outburst.

So I galloped at once through the articles you sent and was disappointed only when there was no more to read. They were, as I expected (no, I got more than I expected), comprehensively intelligent, learned, lively, without nonsense, delightful. Some of your views I don't share. I knew [Nicola] Chiaromonte well, liked him, occasionally agreed with him, considered him to be one of the better European intellectuals of the Fifties and Sixties. But Nick was, in many ways, a standard product, often deficient in taste, snobbish. You came closest to the truth in examining his agreement with Hannah

* Yiddish: filth

Arendt, that superior Krautess, on the differences between Platonic and Marxian intellectuals. The reason Nick and Hannah failed to notice the congealment of intellectuals into their own "stratum" (your word) was that they were terribly proud of their own super-eligibility for the highest of all strata. Their American friends could never hope to join them there. We were very nice but not *kulturny* enough to be taken seriously. But I shan't go on about Nick, who was certainly a considerable person. I don't always respect the rule of *de mortuis* [*] but in his case I shall. Even in Hannah's case, though she tempts me more strongly. I used to say unforgivably wicked things about her, and that wickedness should yield to Death. Still it is hard to stop the genius of abuse. If *belles lettres* still existed it would be pleasant to write something about that. I'm sure it's already been done. Probably by Lucian, or someone else I haven't read. But mostly I was in enthusiastic agreement with your views and sent up more than one cheer.

What a pity we had so little time to talk. We have a good deal to tell each other.

All best,

At Bellow's request, Wieseltier had sent a selection of his essays including a review of Chiaromonte's The Worm of Consciousness and Other Essays, *from The New York Review of Books.*

To Sam Wanamaker

March 3, 1978   Chicago

Dear Sam,

I take your proposition [about a film of *Henderson the Rain King*] seriously, and Marlon Brando in the role has a certain charm for me—the charm of the unlikely but feasible. There are any number of reasons why I could not write a screenplay—one is that I am writing a book; no, two books. I don't know what Harriet Wasserman has done about Public Television; we've been out of touch, but I am sending your letter to her and she will be able to give you (I hope) the information you want.

All best to you,

* Latin: *De mortuis (nil nisi bonum dicendum est)*—Speak no ill of the dead.

To Leon Wieseltier

March 9, 1978   Chicago

Dear Leon:

We're taking off for London on one of those diabolical machines that persuade you your journey is necessary. Well, maybe it is. But from my window over Lake Michigan, which is frozen two miles out, bands of spring water begin to show, green, blue and white. The air is the same. You feel it all squeezing and opening like the folds of an accordion. You *are* the accordion, the transparencies are inside. Even if the music is somewhat silly, I don't want to leave. Also, against my will, I have to write a review for the *Times* of Kollek's *Memoirs*. That puts me into the field of diplomacy. First I gather my real opinions together, then I run them through the adapter and hope for a balanced compromise. I like Teddy's kind of character; he is rude, bumptious, but the book is interesting in its way and more candid than most of its kind. The "personal" books of politicians are vexing. How many exceptions are there? De Gaulle, Clemenceau. But if it takes big wars to beget these Clemenceaus we can do without them.

I'm sure your piece ["Auschwitz and Peace," in *The New York Times*] was extremely hard to write. It's a good one, and it will turn discussion in the right direction. You know what to expect from hot controversy over Jewish questions—bangs and blows on the noggin. But it was most important to call attention to the effects of Auschwitz on Israeli leaders, and you were more than tactful in putting it—"saving realism," "accommodation is not surrender," the Jews "never hungered for conquest." I don't see what there is for intelligent people to object to. And one of the encouraging things about the Jews is that they can always come up, as if under warranty, with a number of good heads. The others, too, of course, are always there, and you can count on them to call you a trendy dove. A *dayge* [*]!

You touch some rather deep questions—is anything worth writing that doesn't *graze* these at least? I wonder what this stiffness [. . .] really signifies. Sometimes I think of it as an impossible degree of wakefulness or bolt-uprightness. Supposing the Europeans, and especially the Germans, to have made their wars and their death-camps in a state of possession, nearly a dream state, the effect on the victims and sufferers was one of super wakefulness. Their portion was—reality. At the very least. In this wakefulness they built their society, their army, fought their wars. Perhaps they see the *goyim*

---

* Yiddish and Hebrew: a worry

still ruled by these fatal phantasmagorias of theirs. Is America awake? No kidding! Or France, blundering towards its next elections? And aren't these Jews still spiritually in Europe, together with their dead millions of the war? It's tempting to think whether this reckless game (I wonder whether Begin isn't acting from *fated* motives) may not have its source in some need for critically heightened consciousness.

I've concluded, however, that when people say such things they are often talking about themselves. So I pause to check myself out.

Are you coming to Chicago soon? Give me some notice and I may be able to organize a public lecture at the university. We have little money, but there are a few dollars in the Committee's lecture fund.

All best,

To James Salter

March 29, 1978   Chicago

Dear Jim,

You won't know anything about Jeffrey Harding unless you come here and look at the County Jail. I don't know what sort of movie one could make about it but the jail itself is worth seeing, if Jeff can get you in (and out) safely.

At the moment it seems a more tranquil spot than Asolo [where Salter was vacationing]. What do you want to go to Italy for, and tempt kidnappers and terrorists? I'm having this out with my son Adam who wants to live in Florence next year and study Dante and Petrarch under the auspices of Smith College. I sent him clippings from the papers, which make no impression on him. I had him talk to my agent [Erich] Linder, who sends his own son to a Swiss university. And I don't know whether you noticed a recent dispatch from Rome about the rage of the Mafia against those kidnappers of Aldo Moro. They denounce the terrorists for ruining the rackets in Italy and threaten to have their people inside the prisons execute the terrorists there if Moro is not set free by March 30th.

Seems to me that you and Adam are being pretty old-fashioned about Italy. I know you want to drink wine and breathe the delicious mountain air, but how much breathing do you think they'll let you do? I suggest you come and look at the County Jail. We can go to Gene and Georgetti's and eat our steak in nice quiet *local* Mafia surroundings.

Ciao to you,

Jeffrey Harding, who was making a movie about prison life in Chicago, had been referred to Salter by Bellow.

To John Cheever

May 18, 1978   Chicago

Dear John:

I write to you as a member to the Chairman of the Awards Committee [of the American Academy and Institute of Arts and Letters]. I perish of greed and envy at the sight of all these awards which didn't exist when we were young and mooching around New York. I have no one to recommend for the [American] Academy in Rome—just as well, I wouldn't want any of my friends shot in the legs—but I would like to recommend David Pryce-Jones who wrote the book on the Mitford girls for the E. M. Forster Award. I'd like also to put up a young author named Max Apple who has written a very good book called *The Oranging of America* and also Bette Howland, author of *Blue in Chicago*.

There are no critics I could nominate for anything but crucifixion.

Yours with very sincere affection (this because you signed yourself very sincerely yours),

Love, too,

To Leon Wieseltier

May 19, 1978   Chicago

Dear Leon:

In Chicago when spring comes and the great sun stirs all this great mess and nature begins to produce all its spring phenomena, it's not so much the budding trees and the blooming flowers that come into their own as the machines and the tarnish and the old building materials, and atmospheric lead and carbon are transposed. You get the spring look for lead and sulphuric derivatives. Yesterday we had gorgeous weather, with of course an Ozone Watch and over-heated automobiles with their hoods up blocking expressways. I sat in a stalled car and kept calm by thinking about Rudolf Steiner, and I was perfectly sure that I was taking in deadly carcinogens and would get lung cancer. Today spring is low and gray. No harm in this, I suppose. What you feel is that the world has no elasticity. It's probably un-Jewish of me to yield to external conditions in this way. In Lodz, once, I asked Dr. Marek Edelman, who'd been an adolescent fighting in the last days of the

Warsaw Ghetto and was now a "cardiolog," whether the ugliness of his urban surroundings didn't bother him, and he looked at me with outright contempt. What difference can the *outside* of things make? It's a kind of idolatry or graven-image susceptibility. You can catch an esthetic clap, whoring after these Ruskins, and serve you damn right. Have you heard of Edelman? A remarkable fellow, author of a stirring account of the Ghetto and the Umschlagplatz [deportation point from the Warsaw Ghetto to Treblinka].

I've been on the road to make money to pay taxes and also legal fees, as well as accountants and wives, and children's tuitions and medical expenses. The patriarchal list should go on to include menservants and maidservants and camels and cattle. I'd be lucky to get into the end of the procession, among the asses. When I came back I had to finish writing a short essay on Goethe's *Italian Journey*—a wonderful book—for a German magazine, and so I had no time to go through the letters I'd gotten about our letter [of public protest to the Begin government], but now I've seen most of them, ranging from bouquets to notices of excommunication. You put your name to a document and you get a free bathysphere ride through the oceans of Jewish opinion and emotion. One lady blowfish informed me that the Israelis and the American Jews had problems enough without my acting as any kind of spokesman for them. She could find nothing in my biography or writings that showed any capacity for rational political thinking. Or any other sort. Some of the Israeli papers, I hear from my friend John Auerbach, called me a Russian agent and a Carter stooge. There's nothing I long for less than politics, and I'd be glad to leave political rationality to the Begins and the Weizmanns, if I thought they had it, but Begin was awful on his last trip here, mismanaged everything, demanded the test of strength in the Congress everyone's been dreading and which everything possible should have been done to avoid. He overstates everything, is all emphasis, is pertinacious, hollering—a real Jabotinskyite, and he's going to bring us to a dangerous pitch of fanaticism. It isn't so much that he's wrong on all the issues, he's not; but he doesn't know how to lead the discussion. He's a convulsive sort of man. And imagine the Jews outdone by a Carter. What can explain that but disorder and hysteria in the Jewish ranks. Is there no one in Israel to tell Begin what public relations in the US are all about?

But then there's no one in the US, seemingly, who can tell the Administration what the Saudis, etc. are about. A Bernard Lewis might do it, if anyone would let him get near enough to Jimmy, and if Jimmy were not himself a problem child. And all we private persons can do is think about these matters. They give us *thought* materials. Nor will anyone pay attention to our wisdom, if we should achieve it, what with the Moros and the Cambodias— the crisis-maddened consciousness of intelligent people is what I mean, I suppose. It's because I have a letter from Jean-Paul Sartre asking me to contribute an article to a Big Discussion of the Jewish Question in *Les Temps Modernes* next autumn that this comes up.

Yours ever,

Wieseltier had organized an open letter to protest the Begin government's slowness in answering the peace initiatives of Egyptian president Anwar el-Sadat. Signed by prominent American Jews including Bellow, Irving Howe, Jacob Neusner, Seymour Martin Lipset and Lucy Davidowicz, the letter received front-page coverage in The New York Times.

To Ladislas Farago

May 24, 1978   Chicago

Dear Mr. Farago:

I can return your compliments. I read your Patton book with admiration, so it pains me to contradict you. The letter [to *The New York Times*] I signed was probably too vague because it was too cautiously written but it did not support Carter's Middle East policy and it was only mildly critical of Begin. I can't understand why it should be sinful of American Jews to take positions which are taken also in Israel and expressed in the Knesset. The signers of our letter did not presume to tell the Israelis what they should do. No one expects Israel to commit suicide for the sake of "peace." Why does it undermine Begin to enter a caveat against the dangers of annexation and the dangers of a large Arab population within a Greater Israel? But the last thing I want is to get into political controversies. In the Israeli press I have been called a sellout, a fink, a Carter-stooge and a Moscow agent. I don't think any of these tags does me justice—do you? Well, the right tag is hard to find.

Sincerely yours,

Ladislas Farago (1906–1980) was the author of many World War II histories including Patton: Ordeal and Triumph *(1964) and* Aftermath: The Search for Martin Bormann *(1974).*

To Edward Shils

My dear Edward:

Vicissitudes, yes, or perhaps the increasing contrariness of elderly friends—but it is a friendship and we both know it, and it sustains me in times of trouble. I can bear my difficulties pretty well; I am certainly equal to them mentally. I am not quite in control of them emotionally. I am and for a long time have been ready to do without the money. If the brutal order holds in the Appeals Court, I shall have to borrow to pay my persecutors, and I have no reason to be confident in the judgment of the Court of Appeals. My experience with courts and lawyers leaves no room for optimism. I've been up to the chin in sewage for nearly ten years now. It's time I did whatever I must do to extricate myself.

The whole thing is monstrous—simply monstrous. It has taught me a great deal, though. I don't say this menacingly, or with excessive bitterness. I plan no vengeance. I mean only to say that it has expanded my understanding of human beings very considerably.

However, I did not become a writer in order to make money, nor shall I stop being one because everything is confiscated. I am not quite certain how to go forward. The more I publish, the more vulnerable I am to predators. Perhaps some sort of American *samizdat* is the answer. (My one joke, this sad day.)

I had always thought myself quite sturdy and resistant to knocks, but it often seems that I am not quite so strong as I had believed. I wake in the night, and do not feel very strong. I sometimes find myself praying. Not for favors of any sort, not even for help, but simply for clarification. I am not especially apprehensive about dying. What does distress me is the thought that I may have made a mess where others (never myself) see praiseworthy achievements.

I knew that you would write to me. I told Alexandra before your letter came that I would soon hear from you. Because I do, after all, know what is what (in my own quite limited fashion). And I thank you from a full heart.

And you will forgive my silliness, as you always have.

Affectionately,

An Illinois Court of Appeals would uphold the lower-court ruling that had ordered Bellow to pay Susan half a million dollars in settlement of their long-standing property dispute.

To Owen Barfield

Dear Owen:

I think I better stop waiting for a tranquil moment. There is no tranquil moment.

What I wished to tell you at some length I will tell you briefly. We read *Saving the Appearances* and *Worlds Apart* in a seminar last April and May. It's too soon to say how well I succeeded as your interpreter. The participants were Wayne Booth of the English Department, Professor Wick, a philosopher who specializes in Kant, and a young mathematician named Zable, one of my wife's colleagues who had seen a copy of *Saving the Appearances* on my table and was keen to discuss it with me. There were also two graduate students, one of them interested in Anthroposophy. Booth and the Kantian found the book "interesting but tough," as Huck Finn said of *Pilgrim's Progress*. Booth was extremely sympathetic, keenly interested, Wick was laconic and pulled at his pipe and told us that we didn't really know Kant; we would be hopelessly muddled until we had put in a year or two at the Critiques of This or That. But even he found you an attractive writer. I thought I would get this brief interim report to you while my recollection of the seminar is still fresh. For the rest, the usual difficulties—no, worse than usual. I am being deprived by the courts of all my possessions. This morning I suddenly remembered a touching photograph, taken after his assassination, of Gandhi's possessions: sandals, rice bowl, eyeglasses and dhoti. Can anyone with more property than that resist the powers of darkness? I make light of it, but the threat is serious. Today I was asked for an inventory of my personal belongings, and I wonder whether the court would hesitate to put them on auction. One never knows. I manage nevertheless to concentrate daily on the distinctions between the essential and inessential.

I asked you in London whether you might be willing to look at the manuscript of a novel, or a portion thereof. Are you still of the same mind, or would you rather be spared? As a friend I would advise you to take the easier option. As one of those "writing fellows" (the term used by the indignant old lady in *The Aspern Papers*), you may, I hope, find it in your charitable heart to let me send you a hundred pages or so.

Very best wishes,

To Isaac Bashevis Singer

October 5, 1978   Chicago

Dear Singer:

Rachel [MacKenzie] just called with the news. *Zol es aykh voyl baku-men* [*].

My wife and I happily congratulate you.

On October 5, 1978, I. B. Singer became the first—and, in all probability, last—Yiddish-language writer to receive the Nobel Prize for Literature.

To Julian Behrstock

October 9, 1978   Chicago

Dear Julian:

I didn't see the item in the British paper, so I don't know whether the sum was accurately reported. But it was stupendous, and the legal fees, two hundred thousand, also stupendous. If these judgments hold, I will be where I was in 1937 on the campus, living on an allowance of three bucks a week. I may ask the President to revive the WPA for my sake. When it happened, my lawyer called me and said, "You've got to bite the bullet." So I bit for one, two, three months. Now it's back in my cartridge belt. What's the point of biting bullets? I shall go back to writing books. I may not publish the books, because they will produce money, and the Philistines will be after me again. Samuel was right to be furious with Saul because he did not deliver all the Philistine foreskins on demand. It was wrong of Saul to be so soft-hearted. We are paying for this, now. Come—oddly—to think of it, most of the fellows who have ganged up on me are fully and legitimately circumcised. Well, to hell with it. I'm always happy to hear from you. I'm glad you're feeling pretty good despite the wife-mistress setup. I can say nothing to you today about the Chicago-Jewish sensibilities.

Yours affectionately,

Julian Behrstock (1915–1997), an old friend from Northwestern days, had after the war moved permanently to Paris where he worked at UNESCO.

---

* Yiddish: May you use it well.

To Louis Lasco

October 19, 1978   [Chicago]

Dear Arkady Ivanovich:

I grieve to hear of your diminishing sex drive. Are you really giving up women for art? I remember a time when Chicago was one of the great cultural centers of the world, and elderly Jewish physicians used to announce that they were going to lay down the scalpel and take up the pen. For pen, read Remington. But what are you laying down?

Could I induce you to send a copy of your manuscript here? As one who has admired you for fifty years, I feel I have the right to make such a request.

Yours ever,

Taras Bulba

1979

To Elisabeth Sifton

January 23, 1979   Chicago

Dear Elisabeth:

I, too, am sad at leaving Viking. For thirty years I was a Viking author. It was there that whatever feeling I had for monogamy expressed itself most completely. And I don't want you to think that my decision to move implied any criticism of you. You were in all respects an excellent editor, and certainly the most attractive of them all. I shall miss the good advice and the attractions. After Pat Covici died and Katie Carver entered the spirit world and Denver Lindley retired there came a hiatus during which I went it alone. Then you came along, and I wouldn't for a single instant have you think that you failed me as an editor. You have nothing to do with my decision to go elsewhere. I shall miss you too and I wish you well, and there is no reason why we shouldn't continue to laugh together when we meet.

My affectionate best,

To Barnett Singer

February 12, 1979   Chicago

Dear Barney:

Stone walls may not a prison make but I have enough manuscripts here for a lockup. Today I was presented with three, yours and two others of the same dimensions, all required reading *sous peine d'amende* [*]. When am I supposed to cook curry, wash the dog or examine my toes? I do expect to be in Chicago on the 25th of March and if I have not disappeared under hundreds of reams of paper I'll be glad to talk. In moderation. I don't grudge you the time but I don't want to be discomfited by your hurricane breeziness. You probably don't know what I'm talking about but I will give you a clue: My father, an old European, was incensed when one of my brothers complained to him (my father was then in his seventies) that he had never been a pal to his sons. My father justifiably exploded, "Pal! Has he gone mad? Has he no respect for his father?" I was taught to be deferential to my seniors. If a historian can't understand that, who can?

Yours in candor,

To Bernard Malamud

March 25, 1979   Chicago

Dear Bern,

By direct inheritance from my old man I have the habit of attending to certain necessities before going on a trip—I then find out what I consider most necessary. Alexandra and I are about to leave for Washington to attend the signing of the Egyptian treaty and I can't go without thanking you for *Dubin's Lives*. I was glad to get it, delighted to be moved by good writing, by intelligence, style, into a better articulated and ordered world than the one I've been living in. A first-rate book develops organs in me which I carry about in a state of latency or blindness. I've been *seeing* better since I read *Dubin*. Your Nature-intimacy took me by surprise, glad surprise. You weren't moved to it by the demands of a book. It's something you've done to yourself, you've achieved it. For Jews from Chicago or New York this has to be done later in life. It's not a birthright. *Not* to be cheated of flowers and landscapes, living and dying under subway gratings or elevated trains—that's what it is.

The Lawrence theme didn't do much for me. I read him very closely at one time. Devout admiration, yes; not sainthood though, by a good bit. Anyway, I drove through the Lawrence territory with my dims on. What impressed me very deeply was the nasty winter, the paralyzed writer. That was all too damn real. I've never suffered from the fatal "block." I've been in despair, in hell, but if I'd been asked what was happening it would never occur to me to describe it as "a block."

* French: under threat of penalty

I had great sympathy with the wife, less with Fanny. But I tell you this naively, not critically. How could I be critical? I am too grateful for the pleasure you gave me. Perhaps I've known too much of that sort of sexual sadness to be able to judge it dependably. I am disqualified, therefore; I don't trust myself in this department and I hope you won't take my uneasiness as faultfinding. Your book delighted me.

Affectionately,

To Ann Birstein

April 12, 1979   Chicago

Dear Ann:

So Alfred thought that living with you was like living with me! I can't quite define my reaction, I never took the slightest sexual interest in him. The best I could do was to appreciate his merits. But esteem, you know, is far from attraction.

Hearing that he was at South Bend, I wrote to him in a Christian spirit (what a pity the Christians have a corner on the Christian spirit; isn't there some way to break the monopoly?) and gave him my telephone number and he called me, but we were both too much in demand to make a date, and then we were snowed in for some months, so we haven't seen each other yet. I'm going to try again now that strolling weather is nearly here.

No, I didn't know that you and he had finally separated. Inevitably, I had heard rumors, but gossip can never damage you—I don't mean anybody, I mean you specifically. After three divorces I can't say that I am ever pleased to hear of a divorce. In your case, however (you will forgive me if I tell you this), the delay must have been very damaging. But one can never really regret the course one's life has taken. There are always perfectly sound reasons why it couldn't have gone any other way. It's only my fondness for you (I remember still how Isaac and I were taken with you when you became Alfred's fiancée; I've never changed my mind) that makes me speculate sentimentally.

I take it as a sign of health that you have written a novel. I want to read it when Doubleday begins to send out copies.

Love,

To John Cheever

May 2, 1979   Chicago

Dear John,

Do you realize we haven't seen each other's dear faces in nearly a year? I have seen you in the papers pulling down one award after another and that has given me great satisfaction. I am somewhat sorry for you because you have only the occasional satisfaction of remembering me. We ought to do something about this, especially as it has not been a happy year, and it would do me good to see you. [. . .]

Atop the Hyde Park Bank building in Chicago thirty years ago there was a Russian nightclub called the Troika where they sang "Don't Forget Me," a sentimental *Lied* which applies to us.

Love,

To Hymen Slate

June 28, 1979   West Halifax, Vermont

Dear Hymen,

A note. So that I don't disappear through the trapdoor until September. When we got here, I discovered that I wasn't so well. It is a beautiful place but I was too tired and dejected to like it. I had no idea that I was in such bad shape. You don't know until you begin to relax the tensions and feel the accumulated fatigue. For two weeks I was extremely depressed—depleted. I couldn't even try to pull myself together. If I took a sleeping pill I paid later with insomnia for the night's sleep I got, so I stopped taking the pills. Alexandra went on doing mathematics. She had a paper to prepare for the conference she's attending now in Germany. I was very pleased. The one good thing that was happening. Her youthful vitality, like my own at her age . . . I can remember how quickly I was able to pull myself together after exhausting exertions. Curiously, I seem to have made secret arrangements to enjoy myself through her. In restaurants I ask her to eat desserts I can no longer order for myself.

I miss our Sundays. I hope you're not in the dumps.

Love to you both,

To Allan Bloom

August 10, 1979   West Halifax

Dear Allan,

Splendid, then we'll run a tutorial on any afternoon convenient to you. I refrain from coming to campus in the morning. My habit is to work until noon at whatever I happen to have in hand and then seek refreshment in Hyde Park. We should have a splendid time with Stendhal and Flaubert, against a background of Jean-Jacques. There must be a few students in the Committee who read French. During the winter Alexandra and I will be at Cal Tech, so we're going to have to crowd everything into a single quarter.

We return shortly after Labor Day and there should be plenty of time to lay our schemes. Whenever I taught with David [Grene], there was always a preliminary session for the two of us—at Jimmy's, naturally. You and I can find another suitably grimy spot, if Jimmy's is too much for you. Some people can't take it.

With great expectation,

Ever yours,

Bloom and Bellow would teach seminars together until Bloom's death, in 1992.

To Owen Barfield

August 15, 1979   West Halifax

Dear Owen—

It's been a long time—one thing and then another. It was kind of you to send the C. S. Lewis book, but I've not been able to read it as attentively as I'd like. Shortly after it came we were called to Bucharest. Alexandra's mother was dying. The circumstances—well, I shall spare you the full description, but my wife was allowed to see her mother no more than three times in ten days. Then death, and another mysterious struggle with the bureaucracy about property. Alexandra came back sick with grief. Some three months of illness—and then more difficulties. I know it's not kind of me to speak to you of difficulties. You have so many of your own which, with English restraint, you don't speak of. But I am only trying to tell you why there have been no letters. I continue to read your books and to think about you, and to go on reading Steiner and working at Anthroposophy. I wouldn't like you to think that I am fickle and that I've dropped away. No, it's not at all like that.

I am however bound to tell you that I am troubled by your judgment of the books I've written. I don't ask you to like what you obviously can't help disliking, but I can't easily accept your dismissal of so much investment of soul. It may have come out badly, but none of it was ever false, and although I can tolerate rejection I am uneasy with what I sometimes suspect to be prejudice. And my "heaping of coals," as you expressed it in a letter last year, quite turned me off. I didn't know what to say to that. You don't like novels? Very well. But novels have for forty years been my trade; and if I do acquire some wisdom it will inevitably, so I suppose, take some "novelistic" expression. Why not? A juggler "illuminated" would go on juggling, wouldn't he? I find some support in Steiner: ". . . if a man has no ordinary sense of realities, no interest in the details of others' lives, if he is so 'superior' that he sails through life without troubling about its details, he shows he is not a genuine seer." (*Anthroposophy: An Introduction,* p. 202)

Having gotten that off my chest, I want to tell you that my affection for you is very great, and I am sure you know how much I respect you. For my part, I feel safe with you—i.e., I know you will forgive my idiocies.

Ever yours,

To Hymen Slate

August 19, 1979   West Brattleboro

Dear Hymen:

Don't knock your way of talking, I miss it out here in the green country. I need the green for my mental and bodily health, but it's far from all-sufficient. Someday, when you're inclined to listen, I'll take pleasure in drawing a free-flowing sketch of what gives with me this decade—you ought to be told, and you'd certainly understand. I assume that you'd dispute some of my premises. I assume also, since you're a man of a definite style, that you would listen selectively, with an eye to what seemed to you harmonious. Each of us has his own way of screening esthetically, and the older we grow the fussier we become about the facts we accept. I see that now. It's a lucky man who has a generous style and can accept the wider range of other people's facts. You have a generous style, and that's what makes listening to your talk so agreeable. I've tried some of my facts on you with varying success. You don't really like it when I talk about the cultural void. You insist that there are human characteristics that have nothing at all to do with the cultural void, and to an important extent you're right. The human characteristics have a clear priority. Philistinism is not as important as all that. Still, I have had monstrous encounters with it. My position is peculiar, and there are times when I have a pressing need to tell you what it's like. We are the survivors of a band of boys who were putting something of their own together in cultureless Chicago forty years ago. Now we drink tea together of a Sunday afternoon, and I feel the touch again. It would be merely sentimental if we weren't *really* talking. As you yourself have often observed, we *talk*, the subjects are real. Even when you send an amusing note it has to do with matter and consciousness—a certain arrangement of matter resulting in consciousness. And then I say, yes, but does the arrangement arrange itself by the hit-or-miss method of what the fellows like to call "emergent evolution" or is it a supervised arrangement directed by some power or spirit which uses the physical brain as its instrument? You know which side I favor.

Maybe I'm saying this under the influence of today's thick fog, which cries out for penetration and lucidity. [. . .]

Love to you both,

To Eleanor Clark

October 10, 1979   Chicago

Dear Eleanor,

Reading [your novel] *Gloria Mundi* made my return to Chicago considerably easier, lessened the culture shock. In the summer I am in Vermont, not of it (trees, skies, books, wife—an aesthetic sanctuary). Yours, the real Vermont, put things in perspective. There *are* connections between Wilmington and Chicago.

I admired your book. I took particular pleasure in the speed with which you got over the foothills to reach the necessary altitude, the place where things happen, the stripped-for-action, unencumbered plainness of the narrative. A complex subject presented without awkwardness, complication or rhetorical backing and filling. "Short views, for God's sake!" That's what Sydney Smith said. That's what the art of describing our breakdown demands. I took great satisfaction in your Vermonters, satisfaction of a different sort in the parachuting clergyman and the brat-maniacs. I was happy with your sketch of the Old Man, too. He took such pride in his culture. You remember his Céline essay, I'm sure, and the statements about the future of culture under socialism. Then the common man will be a Goethe, a Beethoven. He had me fooled. Alas for poor him, and poor us.

Alexandra still talks about the evening we spent together. It made [Saul] Steinberg's visit too. Next summer you come and dine with us.

Thanks for the book.

Yours ever,

"The Old Man" was Trotsky, on whose Mexico City staff Clark had served in the later 1930s.

To Owen Barfield

Dear Owen:

With my "meaning to write" I am like a drunkard who says he will re-form: going on the wagon, as drinkers here say, and the wagon is very different from the winged chariot. Your letter moved me by its warmth, kindness and candor. I have too much respect for what you have done, have made of yourself, to answer lightly and easily. Four or five years of reading Steiner have altered me considerably. Some kind of metamorphosis is going on, I think, and I am at a loss for words when I sit down to write to you. You will think it absurd that I should make a judge of you. It *is* absurd, and you must find it disagreeable as well, but the position carries no duties, you owe me nothing. I see you—it came through in your letter—as a man who has learned what to do with the consciousness-soul, has managed to regenerate severed connections and found passages that lead from thought to feeling. I won't embarrass you by going on about this; you may think it bad form. I've observed in your books how you shun all such claims yourself, and that just as the Meggid calls himself the least of Michael's servants you prefer to diminish yourself. The best of us have been destroyed in the wars of this century. Among the survivors there's only the likes of ourselves to go on with. "I am myself indifferent honest, but . . ." Yes, it is like that. I am even more "indifferent honest," myself, so it amused me to be described as a tank surrounded by pea-shooters.

I wanted to see you in Michigan, but it was impossible to go just then. I wouldn't have had much time with you in any case. I have to satisfy myself by re-reading your books. I don't think I shall be coming to England very soon. In Edinburgh two years ago an Anthroposophical lady, admonishing me, said, "Mr. Barfield will have to take you in hand in Kamaloca." But perhaps I will have made some progress by that time and you won't have to be so quite severe with me.

Yours most affectionately,

"Kamaloca" is the first stage of the afterlife, according to Anthroposophy.

1980

To Louis Lasco

January 3, 1980 Pasadena

Dear Luigi—

Peltz loves to tell of a visit to a Polish girl on Iowa St.—third floor. He blew the opportunity—pants down, two bucks gone. The girl was concerned. She said, "Oh, kid, you need practice—practice, practice practice!"

As an old Polish girl, of a sort, I too am a bit concerned. You're a witty writer, but in the mss. you've lost your two bucks. Now, with a little practice you can get, and give, great satisfaction.

Ever yours, with love,

Soolabodoff

To Daniel Bellow

January 31, 1980 Pasadena

Dear Daniel,

Since I haven't heard at all from you I take it that we won't be seeing each other in California either because there is not time between terms or because you did not meet the little condition I set—no need to spell that out. But we often think of you and wonder what's become of you. I mailed off your camp application signed and with a check so your summer is protected. I wish that I could see you more, I often miss you and I think somehow that you have arranged matters so in your own mind that the absence is mine from you and not yours from me. But the move East was after all by your choice. No reproach, I just think you should bear it in mind along with other facts, realities, truths. [. . .]

The other day I saw a set of Parkman in a bookshop. If I thought that you were interested in the early history of North America, the French-Indian wars, I'd send it to you. These are most exciting books. I'd read them myself if I had the time. I did read *The Oregon Trail* once and parts of the book on the Pontiac.

I'd be awfully glad to hear from you.

Love,

To Bobby Markels

Dear Bobby,

I am taking advantage of a crack typist to whirl back a reply. I enjoyed your poem, as I do all your productions. They are so relaxed that they do me good also in the way of détente. I met a lady who lives in your county and she tells me all the young people in Mendocino are in a lovely state of gentle ease. I asked her whether there was any sign of cultivated pot, but she said that she thought everyone there was naturally amiable, lovely and kind. I said this was certainly true of the one person I knew in Mendocino. I didn't at all mind being listed by you. I thought if I could remember the shirt you ironed for me and still had it I would have it mounted and hung in the living room with a sentimental legend. [. . .]

You shouldn't complain too much about being fifty. Fifty doesn't seem much to me, my next birthday will be the sixty-fifth. The fifty years will have been worthwhile however if you have become wise enough to see through Nelson [Algren].

You mustn't be too hard on your own egotism. The Bible says, "I am a worm, and no man." When it comes to being hard on oneself the Bible is way ahead of us. Actually, atheists can never know how really insignificant they are. The same probably goes for agnostics. They only get a rain check.

Ever your affectionate friend,

Bobby Markels (born 1930) is the author of How to Be a Human Bean *(1975) and other works. She lives in Mendocino, California.*

To Albert Glotzer

Dear Al,

To keep you posted on [Ilya] Konstantinovski, he wrote to me from Paris where Gallimard is about to bring out his book. Would I read it, give him a blurb? As the much-esteemed maestro H. L. Mencken used to sign himself "with all the usual hypocrisies," Konstantinovski gave me the usual hypocrisies. I don't mind that, and I suppose by now the book is waiting for me in Chicago. Harper's turned it down. The first reader said it was very good but the second opined that it was the rebellious outburst of a lifelong line-toer, that Konstantinovski, who had no intention ever of returning, was setting himself up in the West as one of the Major Russians of our time and was even recruiting a supporting cast of willing ladies. It seems that when he speaks to ladies he complains that they are unwilling to return his caresses and other acts of kindness. He's not a very attractive man but it can't be as hard as all that. There are ladies in every category, even his. I'll send you a short report when I've read his book. [. . .]

Ever yours,

Ilya Konstantinovski's book was Le Seider de Varsovie. *It has never appeared in English.*

To David Shahar

March 25, 1980   Pasadena

Dear David,

What shocking news! To be mugged in Jerusalem, in your own quiet neighborhood. The police were right, you were lucky to save your eye (I hope you are entirely recovered) from the neo-barbaric assault, as you call it. I take it from your letter that your attackers were not Arabs but North African [i.e., Sephardic] boys, since you speak of their wanting to hit an Ashkenazy. This is your introduction then to the tense watchfulness which has for years been the lot of New Yorkers, Chicagoans, even Londoners, I suppose. Not Muscovites. Theirs is a different system: Crime is a state monopoly. From now on you had better take your Jimmy [Shahar's dog] with you when you go out for cigarettes. I hope he is fiercer than his namesake. Our own Jimmy [Carter] as you probably are aware is an affliction to us and to the rest of the world. I can't say that he is actually the cause of our decline but he has become the foolish, impotent and repulsive symbol. But this is not a political message, rather a note of sympathy. [. . .] We send our love to both of you and to the children.

David Shahar (1926–97), a fifth-generation Jerusalemite and much-honored Israeli writer, was best known for The Palace of Shattered Vessels *(1969–94), his eight-volume series of historical novels.*

To Ralph Ross

June 15, 1980   Chicago

Dear Ralph,

I'm not one of your prompt repliers: rather, a muller over of letters. No, I don't need the Barfield book, I have other copies, also marked. I sometimes wonder what one can get out of Barfield if one hasn't learned the "system." Some of it is very curious, the different view of physics, for certain, the conviction that the law of the conservation of energy is all a mistake (this idea has too many poetic implications to be dismissed). My friends refuse to take any of this seriously. I forgive them as a friend should, and I perform other operations, in confirmation of my right to hold peculiar views. (Or is it a privilege, not a right?) Then I feel that I'm being faithful to Truth, through thick and thin. And it will do them good in the long, *long* run, perhaps after death. [. . .]

Alexandra adds her love to mine.

Yours,

To Walter Hasenclever

June 12, 1980   Chicago

Dear Walter,

Your letter arrives as I am poised for departure, about to launch myself from my wire, too heavy to be a bird, too sinful to be any sort of angel (but somehow I continue to view myself as a flier). Will you come for dinner or for a longer visit? I can tempt you with an unpublished manuscript. Please call us when you arrive. I shan't ask you to bring George Bush when you come—I have nothing really against Mr. Bush, his standing with me improves now that I learn he was one of your pupils, but if he is running on the Reagan ticket as Vice-President he will be too busy to dine with us. The country *does* need a President but where is it to find one? Maybe the office should be abolished for the next four years.

Yours ever,

To Dean Borok

June 17, 1980   West Halifax, Vermont

Dear Mr. Borok—

I at length answer. I always meant to, but my wife and I were in Pasadena until mid-April and then came back only to prepare to leave again. These are (unnecessarily) busy days, and life grows more complex with the years. I had expected it to be simpler.

I took the liberty of showing your letter to my brother Sam, seeing no reason why you should mind. He was moved by it—he, too. (We both found it curious that you should be in Montreal, where we started out; I was born in Lachine.) Neither of us could form a picture of the life you've led. But that's hardly strange when you think that we have no clear picture of our eldest brother's life, either. He sees none of us—brothers, sister, or his two children by his first marriage, nor their children—neither does he telephone or write. He had no need of us. He has no past, no history. His adopted children do not seem to care for him. His present wife? An enigma. He probably has some money—he's thought about little else all his life. But he's old now—seventy-three. And ill; he's had a coronary bypass. I tell you all this to warn you about the genes you seem so proud of. If you've inherited them (it's possible you have) many of them will have to be subdued or lived down. I myself have had some hard going with them.

If you can find the right way to do it, perhaps you should write the story of your life. To get rid of it, as it were. In writing it successfully, you will forgive everyone in the process. Yes, all those who sinned against you will be forgiven. (That's what I would call a successful effort to get one's life down on paper.)

Thank you for writing.

I wish you happiness,

Borok, out-of-wedlock son of Maurice Bellows, wrote to Bellow after he read The Adventures of Augie March, *having realized that a version of his own birth is narrated in the novel.*

To Hymen Slate

Dear Hymen—

I'd be a better correspondent if I weren't writing all the time. You have to be a graphomaniac to spend hours on a manuscript and then turn, for relaxation, to letters. A critic, years ago in Paris, said I had bureaucratic tendencies. He offended me then. Now I'm inclined to see it his way. I learned to organize my daily life for a single purpose. There *was* one other drive, the sexual one, but even that presently gave way. My erotic life was seriously affected, too, in that I diverted myself with a kind of executive indiscriminateness—without a proper interest in women.

(Why is it that as soon as I sit down to write to you I find that I am busily examining my character. In another existence you must have been my confessor.) Vermont is exquisite, and I am doing here what I am supposed to do (or what I intended to do) but I miss our Sunday gabfests. I am glad to discover this. Sometimes I suspect I have too few dependencies. [. . .]

I hope your health is good. I have a small case of arrhythmia or tachycardia. Not serious.

Love,

To William Kennedy

August 22, 1980   West Halifax

Dear Bill—

I'm not what you'd think of as a drifter but I do drift in a real (i.e. barely conscious) sense—a sort of desert rat with a Smith Corona instead of a prospector's mule. Not even the Committee on Social Thought fully remembers me. Just as well.

Your letter, which delighted me, finally reached Vermont where I've been dug in writing (what else?) a small book—something of a cherry bomb or small grenade, I like to think.

I've seen some of your writing. I liked one of your books a lot (I can't recall the title; sclerosis probably gaining on me). I didn't see *Billy Phelan*, but I was stirred by your Upstate outlaws and molls. Did I recommend you for a grant after reading that (which probably you didn't get)? I suspect occasionally that a favorable letter from me is the kiss of death.

And yes, I understand about poor Tom Guinzburg, a poor D.P. with loads of money.

I'd love to see you again and have a talk. We had good talks at Rio Piedras but we were bush-league prophets (or futurologists, not to overload the great word "Prophet"). [. . .]

Very glad to have heard from you.

Yours ever,

To George Sarant

[Postmarked Chicago, Ill., 11 September 1980]

Dear George—

Let's not make too much of this. Quite simply, what happened was that Wm. Phillips, always a devious rat, called me (*most* solicitous and considerate!) to say he was about to publish Isaac's journals. He had said wounding things about me—did I mind? Of course it was weird—a voice from the grave. And of course I said the journals should be printed, uncensored. Canny old William was worried about libel suits. I promised that I would not go to law. Let the dead man have his say.

For me this was a turn of events charged with emotion. I was glad to have so much high feeling over Isaac—a bonus, as I saw it. I was *very* curious. And of course I'm now too old for "hurt feelings." No, it was, Let's hear Isaac's dear voice again. I expected no horrid revelations. I knew quite well what he thought and felt about me—pro and con. I was aware also that his peculiar adaptation of W[ilhelm] Reich was bringing up material from the psychic drainage system—that Isaac felt he owed it to *truth* to bring it to the surface and let it spin and be purified, etc.

Again W. Phillips called—this time to say that fear of libel had made him decide not to publish. He wanted me to know ("act of friendship" etc.—the usual bullshit or, in his case, rat-shit). [. . .]

Isaac's journals made sad reading. He *was* in bad shape, wasn't he? I think he would have recovered. But enough of that. What I didn't like was that you had put the journals into the hands of [————], a nasty opportunist, mean-spirited, a brewer of low-grade troubles and a *shtunk*. As he had taken a cut or two at me in print, to bring me down to size, I did not think well of your handing Isaac's notes over to him. I didn't expect you to consult me, but I had no reason to think you had *inadvertently* given him more ammunition.

But you tell me it was done innocently, and I choose to believe you. I don't want to exaggerate, make swellings and breed stupid disagreements.

Perhaps you'll pay me a visit, one of these days (years).

Remember me to your sister.

Yours ever,

George Sarant (1947–94), a Reichian psychoanalyst, was the son of Isaac Rosenfeld and Vasiliki Sarantakis Rosenfeld; in early manhood he had taken an anglicized version of his mother's family name.

To John Auerbach and Nola Chilton

October 17, 1980   Chicago

Dear John:

A mild gray October morning: We fly to Washington (I'm lecturing to a Brandeis meeting) and instead of making my last will and testament I write to you. We'll post the letter at O'Hare. I miss you greatly. I can't get used to the changed distances, and still move to the telephone to call you in Newton, but in Newton there's only [Milton] Hindus at the other end [whose house John and Nola had rented]. I seldom have occasion to call Hindus. No matter how I squeeze the material he'll never in the real world resemble you.

I was pleased when they put you in charge of the foreign contingent [at Kibbutz S'dot Yam] and very unhappy to hear that you would wash the dishes instead. I have put myself in your place as a mental substitute—I don't mind the dishes, but there's a whole kibbutz to wash for. That is highly undesirable, and I think you ought to resist it, but I know that you won't. I hope the *chaverim* [*] are not being spiteful. But Nola can be depended upon to protect you from excesses. She must be unhappy about your assignment.

But enough of these bad things. I now collect amusing subjects for you in and around Chicago. Here's one of them: A man from the Illinois Arts Council pursued me with messages for several weeks. He wanted to give me a medal for my services to the arts. (One of my services to them was to keep away from him.) I never called. The messages were left with Alexandra at Northwestern—she didn't really pay much attention to them. Then fuller messages and complaints were left. I was to go to Danville, Ill. to be decorated by the Governor himself.

That was different. The Governor when he was the crusading US Attorney had prosecuted my brother [Sam] and sent him to jail for ninety days. For this reason alone the occasion began to seem worthwhile, enjoyable, splendid. I would whisper something outrageous to the Governor as he pinned on the medal. On other occasions he had steered clear of me. Once we were in the same box at the Lyric Opera, guests of the company, and

* Hebrew: friends

he disappeared after the first act, before the lights were on, avoiding embarrassment. But none of this was clear until the very last moment. By now the man from the Council was angry. He told the secretaries at Northwestern that this was the most distinguished award I had ever received. Higher than Pulitzers, greater than Nobels. But Danville is a town two hours away on undistinguished roads. I didn't want to stay overnight. Arrangements should have been made earlier. Alexandra refused to let me take the small plane from Meigs Field. All the usual noise and anxiety. In the end, I had to call the gentleman from the Council and say I couldn't come. Apologies were made—and perhaps even accepted. Someone else would accept the award for me, which turned out to be a book of poems by Illinois poets. I think most of them were in real estate and public relations. In next day's paper the event was reported and the names of the other winners were announced. Among them was Susan [Glassman Bellow]'s longtime lover, a sculptor named Hunt. *He* would have been the top slice of this ironical sandwich. He'd have had more fun at my expense that I could ever have gotten out of the Governor.

I am being called on the house phone. I have just time to address this and send both of you our love.

One of Bellow's most significant correspondents, John Auerbach (1922–2002) was a Warsaw Jew who had survived the war on false papers, working as a stoker on German ships. Arrested while trying to flee to Sweden, he was imprisoned in Stutthof concentration camp. From the summer of 1945 Auerbach worked with Mossad Aliyah B in the transport of Jewish refugees to Palestine. Arrested by British police, he served three years' detention on Cyprus. At the founding of the State of Israel, Auerbach settled in Caesarea at Kibbutz S'dot Yam where he skippered a fishing fleet. Following the death of his son in the 1973 Yom Kippur War, Auerbach retired from the sea and began to write. Twelve books appeared in Israel during his lifetime.

Stanley Elkin,
Amsterdam, 1971

Bernard Malamud

Cynthia Ozick

SB, Richard Stern, Alane Rollings in the garden in Vermont

Teddy Kollek, Jerusalem, 1996

Saul Steinberg

John Auerbach

William Kennedy

Allan Bloom and SB, 1992,
at Robie House, University
of Chicago, on the occasion
of the fiftieth-anniversary
celebration of the Committee
on Social Thought

SB and Janis dancing in Vermont, 1996

Philip Roth and SB on the Connecticut River,
Brattleboro, Vermont, summer 1998

SB and Rosie at the Boston University
Annual Convocation, 2000

SB, Janis and Rosie in Brookline

SB on steps of house
in Vermont

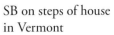

Isabel Fonseca,
Martin Amis, Janis,
Rosie, and SB, East
Hampton, New York,
summer 2001

Rachael Madore

SB in Vermont

SB's studio in Vermont, as he left it

1981

To William Kennedy

January 7, 1981   Chicago

Dear Bill,

There is only one reason why I haven't been replying: I spend my mornings cantering and galloping on the typewriter, the afternoons in revision and my nights in what Shakespeare called the restless ecstasy. We would say threshing about. I got off a corking reference for the Guggenheim. I thought of sending you a copy but it's strictly against the regulations and I didn't feel like Xeroxing forbidden papers. I'm still willing to do an interview. All I need is Time. It keeps getting scanter and scanter. I'm sorry your wife's shop has burned—what a way for me to find out that she *had* a shop.

I didn't take Mark Harris to heart at all. I haven't read his book and I rather enjoy the pummeling he's getting in the press. For once I am a contrast gainer and even getting some sympathy. I don't want that either. I turn my back on it all and wish that I had a back like one of Rodin's burghers of Calais—a big bronze back.

New Year's greetings and all best,

Mark Harris had just published Saul Bellow: Drumlin Woodchuck.

To Allan Bloom

[n.d.]   [Brasenose College, Oxford]

What is there to say? Without you, it's only approximately perfect. Fatigue, passing off in waves, reveals a lump of wicked passions that had been ignored by the work-forces—bypassed. Your observations would be invaluable.

Love,

To Daniel Patrick Moynihan

May 19, 1981   Brasenose College, Oxford

Dear Senator:

Ed Burlingame of Harper & Row tells me that he has asked you to help my wife's aunt, Ana Paonescu, an old woman very dear to her, to get out of

Romania. The aunt is seventy-five and has a bad heart. She has already wound up her affairs, arranged to give up her rooms, distributed the last of the glassware and coffee spoons, and the authorities have her marking time (time is what she hasn't got a lot of). The reason (alleged) is that she hasn't gone through all the formalities (bureaucratic) of giving up a small piece of property in the country. She has *tried* to give it up, has done everything possible to hand it over, but title hasn't actually been transferred, so she gets no passport. Why this is happening I don't know, but her daughter is waiting for her in LA, her niece (my wife) in Chicago. There isn't *too* much time left altogether.

I make this appeal to you, and not to Sen. Percy, because Sen. Percy isn't always attentive to such requests.

But—with malice towards none (Sen. P.) and with gratitude for your generous offer to help, I am yours, as ever,

To Allan Bloom

May 26, 1981 [Brasenose College, Oxford]

Dear Allan—

Well, it was after all a good thing to come here to this stronghold of ruling reptiles. Some of them you can't help liking, and there are sweet smaller lizards and not a few lovable amphibians. You aren't snubbed here as you would have been in the days of Oxford's arrogance. Times are badder and facts are humbler. But it rains *sans cesse*. Of course I had to rewrite everything, and in Sept. I may do it all *da capo*. I am tired and miss Alexandra, and miss talking to you. I have some *new* ideas, more liberating than the old ones. Maybe I should write them in a notebook—yes, I will. I have just the notebook.

Mitterand had wished to invite me to his coronation, and it put me in an awkward position. Barley Alison said that I *must* attend. She drove me up the wall, but I came down from the moulding at last and said no. I had to finish Lecture Two. [. . .]

In London I found a little book about smoking which I will send to you. In Oxford I read a book by [Paul] Morand, *Open All Night*, which I recommend.

Much love,

To Allan Bloom

June 6, 1981   [Carboneras, Almería, Spain]

Dear Allan:

Having someone in Chicago to whom to talk really, I go on the road, for reasons perhaps presently to be understood. I feel I've been inspecting Europe for the last time, taking the concluding view of London and Rome, places now unnecessary. In Rome the victory has gone to Henry Ford. History *is* bunk, and you can't even see it because of the automobiles. Nobody ever imagined that the Gadarene swine would rush around in circles, unable to find the precipice—living it up, meantime, but God how they long for it.

My cultivated old friends are wrecked. The incessant reading of modern books wore them out. Sometimes you watch them trying to put all the puzzle pieces together while Kafka and Proust hover behind them making suggestions. [. . .]

I did well enough in Oxford, although I was very tired, and I met some decent people there. It was intimidating to have Iris Murdoch and [John] Bayley, her husband, in the audience, also Isaiah Berlin and more of the same, but I got through it all. Still I have bad dreams about lecturing and teaching—had one last night. You and I were about to do a class on *Antony & Cleo*, and a graduate student was selling me his (valuable) paper on the play. His price was eight hundred bucks. I had counted out five hundred when it occurred to me that he was just a student, so I stopped putting down dollars and said, "This is unheard of." He was the type that has absolute knowledge of the dollar-value of a product. I have no such knowledge and therefore I give in. So in the end I missed the class altogether, and that was unpleasant. If I were more interested in dreams I'd try to figure it out. However, dream interpretation has given way to an interest probably equally hopeless in clairvoyance. Why be a mere doctor when you can be a seer instead?

Maybe the graduate student stood for the young dons who practiced their snob-judo on me at High Table, and whom I quickly kicked in the pants.

I met lots of dear people in my travels, none clever enough for what we've got to face in Rome. I had one very bad shock. Introduced to an old slovenly woman with bad teeth, I said I was pleased-to-meetcha and so on. She seemed to know me well, reminded me that in 1948 when I was a mere *ragazzo* and before I had written famous books I had often visited her—once in Anacapri. I soldiered it all out with the weapons of social charm. She must have thought me cold and aloof. When she had gone off, bending on her cane, I asked Paolo Milano who she was. Was! It was Elsa Morante, whom I had always liked so much. *That?!* And I remembered how sturdy and handsome she had been, and that in 1948 we would meet every night at the Antico Greco for an aperitif, and tears began to run from my eyes. My friend Milano gave me vast credit for sentiment—gold stars for progress in the cure of my hard heart. Gold stars I didn't feel that I deserved, but it was too much trouble to explain this to poor Milano, who had lived too long by best-accredited modern books to understand without efforts too great to ask a sick old man to make. Besides, I was crying also for him—the *dos courbé* [*], the shuffle, the weak legs, the pacemaker in his chest, the prostate surgery, the faded eyes. He now has a majordomo running his flat with the carefully chosen antiques and the heirlooms. This peasant from the north is small, broad, healthy and gentle, womanly. Cooks the *pasta*, arranges the gladioli, etc. Paolo sleeps in a double bed, left-hand side—the right side is loaded with new books. The wife's side of the bed.

And no—the rest has been, for me, airports, ripoffs (the Roman word for hustlers is *gli abusivi*), anxiety over language, the vertigo of the streets, the lack of desire which defeats my lifelong attraction to shop windows—why deck out the old bod? Etc.

Now I'm in Carboneras on the Mediterranean, the refrains of Barley Alison more persistent than the sea and infinitely less mysterious and beautiful. It was *really* foolish of me to make this trip of final inspection.

I miss you enormously. My eyes come to life when I pick up a can of insecticide named *BLOOM: BLOOM RAPIDE elimine les insects tels que les moustiques, etc. BLOOM RAPIDE se distingue par ses effets rapides et par son parfum agréable.* A message of love,

To Daniel Patrick Moynihan

July 14, 1981   West Halifax, Vermont

Dear Senator—

The old girl has arrived, safe and sound, thanks to your intervention. I should have sent this news sooner, but I was sitting at conference tables in Germany, saving the humanities, and tied in knots. I write you from Vermont (on my wife's stationery). I hope you will allow us to thank you in person, on our next Washington visit. I think Aunt Anna would still be in Romania if you hadn't interceded with the Ambassador.

Yours most gratefully,

* French: bent back

To Allan Bloom

August 15, 1981   West Halifax

Dear Allan:

[. . .] Alexandra is very much afraid, terrified, by the harm my book [*The Dean's December*] may do—friends of the family in Romania persecuted; the most persistent nightmare is that Sanda [Loga] will be refused visas to visit her old parents. It also keeps me up nights. Nothing by halves. I *doubt* that anything so dire will happen, but she astutely points out (and how astute do you need to be for this?) that these people are crazy—wicked fantasists, to put it in my own way.

Hence the plan to make a public noise on publication—be interviewed on CBS and other disagreeable if not hateful places. But that may make matters worse. If I am asked to talk about the regime, I will declare myself an enemy, and it will become nasty if indeed they think me one. Maybe I should be quiet and only talk to people like Moynihan or Scoop Jackson (the former was helpful in getting the old aunt out) about strategies to be adopted if visas are refused. How could I face Sanda if I increase fame and fortune while she . . .

I can use some wise advice. In this world there seems no way to do right except in obscurity and modesty. Doing wrong will cause severe suffering in every way; inwardly; and will Alexandra forgive me?

Romanian-born physicist Sanda Loga was then and remains a close friend of Alexandra's.

To Hymen Slate

August 21, 1981   West Halifax

Dear Hymen:

We traveled and we traveled—in Spain, Italy, France, Germany, Switzerland and England. Why I moved about so much I can't easily explain. Alexandra saw mathematicians in Madrid, Paris and in Germany, but I had no such excuse. I was *going*. Since I was revisiting all these places I had the feeling sometimes that I was giving them the final inspection—never would see them again. I told an old friend in Rome that I'd never return. One can't even see the city for the cars, the Colosseum is fenced up because the tourists have been taking pieces of it as souvenirs, the Romans all look as though they had just gotten up after an adulterous siesta, first-class hotels stink of bad plumbing, everybody is on the make, the exhibitionists don't even zip up between exposures, they walk around on fashionable streets with their genitals in their hands. And that healthy Pole, the Pope, is now an invalid. No more Holy City for me.

I carried my manuscript from country to country, hoping to finish the corrections. In Madrid I was able to do quite a lot in cafés, surrounded by agreeable Spaniards, but I didn't send the book to the printer till last week. Now I get a two-week break while waiting for galley proofs. Not time enough. This is no youthful fatigue. I used to bounce back. Now I drag myself outside mornings to sit under the trees. Late summer, fortunately, is very beautiful. There's only the telephone to fear—news of a new lawsuit by Susan. The wicked never let up. The lawyers learn no kindness. My own are as bad as hers, and the moronic inferno is as hot as ever.

No comfortable conversations with friends of my own age. I need some of your melancholy fun. October looks good to me.

Love,

To John Cheever

December 9, 1981   Chicago

Dear John:

Since we spoke on the phone I've been thinking incessantly about you. Many things might be said, but I won't say them, you can probably do without them. What I would like to tell you is this: We didn't spend much time together but there is a significant attachment between us. I suppose it's in part because we practiced the same self-taught trade. Let me try to say it better—we put our souls to the same kind of schooling, and it's this esoteric training which we had the gall, under the hostile stare of exoteric America to persist in, that brings us together. Yes, there are other, deeper sympathies but I'm too clumsy to get at them. Just now I can offer only what's available. Neither of us had much use for the superficial "given" of social origins. In your origins there were certain advantages; you were too decent to exploit them. Mine, I suppose, were only to be "overcome" and I hadn't the slightest desire to molest myself that way. I was, however, in a position to observe the advantages of the advantaged (the moronic pride of Wasps, Southern traditionalists, etc.). There wasn't a trace of it in you. You were engaged, as a writer should be, in transforming yourself. When I read your collected stories I was moved to see the transformation taking place on the printed page. There's nothing that counts really except this transforming action of the soul. I loved you for this. I loved you anyway, but for this especially.

Up and down on these rough American seas we've navigated for so many decades; we've had our bad trips, too—unavoidable absurdities, dirty weather, but that doesn't count, really. I've been trying to say what does count.

My son Adam, who has been visiting us in Chicago, when I told him that I was writing you wanted me to say that he was charmed by your short book [*Oh What a Paradise It Seems*]. I was, too.

If it isn't possible for you to come to Chicago, I will fly to New York whenever it's convenient for you.

Love,

To Bernard Malamud

December 22, 1981   Chicago

Dear Bern:

Now I see—this book [*God's Grace*] was as much a departure for you as the *Dean* was for me. You told me this one would be different, so I was somewhat prepared but not as prepared as all that. Even the best of readers are like generals in that they are always fighting the last war. Not to keep you in suspense, *God's Grace* excited me and in the end it moved me. Why or how I'm not able to tell you. Maybe the best approach to this mystery is to say what I was thinking as I read you.

First, as to performance: You're always happy when you read a man who has learned his trade, perfected it. He can be trusted. You hand yourself over to him, and that's the first stage of your happiness.

Then you try to identify the species. What sort of book is it? The edge of doom, and over: the destruction of the planet, flood, apocalypse, the voice of God. Cohn is Noah, Cohn is Job, he is even Robinson Crusoe. The world's end can't put an end to Jewish wit. Your God is no humorist, however, and the novel is genuinely apocalyptic. Moreover, it *is* a novel, not the unfolding of an eschatology. It's about our own preparation for the last things, the end. Our minds and feelings, decade by decade, have been forced towards it. It's not a matter of a theme that finds "objective correlatives." We have experienced the correlatives first. These prepared us thoroughly for the worst; we've seen it coming and agreed that we deserved or would deserve it. With approving vengefulness we have endorsed it. This we have done while breathing the air of nihilism and while applying the methods of "science" (the business of this science being to tell us the past, present and future of reality), but also while trying to hang on to decencies of liberalism. All this is in your book. I was intrigued, at times appalled, sometimes irritated, but by the end I found myself moved greatly. Things were as they should be at the end. My doubts passed into the background. There was nothing to doubt in such an emotion, or after-emotion.

It may surprise you to learn how Jewish, Jewish-American, Eastern seaboard and "liberal" I found *God's Grace* to be: Cohn teaching the chimps, the lower primate branch destined perhaps to take its turn at the summit; Cohn deciding to make his human contribution to this development. God rejects this; the laws of animal nature can't be waived in a day, thousands of millennia are needed. Yes, and also Shakespearean grace descending temporarily on Mary M.

After the final disaster Cohn starts over again (like a good Jew, one must keep trying), teaches speech, gives lectures, cultivates minds and morals. I identified myself often with the apes. I too was fascinated (long ago) by the Darwin-Wallace orthodoxy, but later it seemed to me that this materialist orthodoxy could not satisfy deeper questions about the nature of human consciousness. All this gave Cohn's lectures a certain pathos. So did the Ethical Culture spirit of the community he wanted to create. All was to be well. You do treat this with the irony it deserves and see clearly the defeatism implicit in this form of "goodness," but you appear to suggest that no alternative could ever occur to Cohn. The political sense of this is plain to you. Cohn's sentimental will-to-goodness is fatal. It can't anticipate evils, has no force, is unable to defend itself, and is just as unacceptable to God as human wickedness; indeed Cohn must, like the rest of humankind, die. Or should I rather have said "like the West which Cohn so completely represents"? Anyway, Cohn's Isaac sacrifice profoundly moved me. I couldn't say why, or *was alles bedeutet* [*].

I may not be your most representative reader, but I am an admiring one. You may find my reactions odd. For one thing they are unexpectedly political (I myself didn't expect them to be that). But you wrote with a certain openness, and the book is unsettling and I predict that it will invite an unusual diversity of interpretations. For it *is* an unsettling book. In that respect it has much in common with *The Dean's December*. What this may *bedeut* is that as honorable writers we have nothing else in these times to record.

I congratulate you and send you an affectionate embrace.

* German: what it all means

Saul Bellow: Letters

To Philip Roth

December 31, 1981   Chicago

Dear Philip,

Thanks for your generous note. Disappointing that I'm not going to be in Chicago in February. Alexandra and I are clearing out for the winter to British Columbia, which I look forward to as to a sanitarium. I've warned them in the English Department there that if they run me too hard I may have a breakdown. I'm not pretending, I'm ready for a padded cell. *The Dean* took it out of me; I wrote it in a kind of fit and I'm left with the peculiar residue that I don't know how to get rid of. I can't even describe it.

I discovered some time ago that there was nothing to stop me from saying exactly what I thought. I expected flak, and unpleasant results are beginning to come in, but I'm getting support too, which I hadn't looked for.

Your capacity for looking things in the face is not inferior to mine. It's presumptuous of me to go into a senior-citizen routine with you, but I'm being as straight with you as you are with me.

I thank you again for your letter. We'll have dinner some other time.

Yours ever,

1982

To William Kennedy

February 4, 1982   Victoria, B.C.

Dear Bill:

What a delay! But *The Dean*, eighteen months of high excitement, a long spree for a codger, wore me out. To get away from the ensuing noise of battle we made plans to retreat to British Columbia. We were smarter than we could know, because we got away from a disastrous winter, too. Here it rains and rains, but the green moss is delicious to see and there are snowdrops out already. The nervous system was not attuned to this sanctuary. For the first month I suffered acutely from what I called boredom: It *was* boredom but with a wash of deep fatigue, black-and-blue spread over the gray.

By now I've read *Ironweed* (when I saw the heading *Lemonweed*, I preferred it; the novel has as much iron in it as it needs). It's as good as *Billy* [*Phelan*], in my opinion. The key is lower, closer to death at every point. This must be the first human examination of skid row. I never saw another. Of an older American generation, Francis and Helen carried a more respectable, organized humanity with them when they began to sink. My guess is that today people sink from a more prosperous base but also a more disorderly one; they start out more chaotic, without Helen's music or Francis's conscience. Francis, a murderer, is also a traditional champion, the fated man, a type out of Icelandic or Irish epic. To kill is his destiny, and he kills American-style, with techniques learned in play, throwing a stone like a baseball and then swinging a bat in Hooverville. He considers himself a man of sin. No family refuge for him.

All this you do beautifully. Here and there you go a bit too far. The Katrina idyll, for instance, is too idyllic. You ought to reconsider. Not that there were no beautiful pagan ladies, I knew a few myself, but I'm not entirely comfortable with K.

Your *Esquire* article wasn't badly edited, as editing goes. As much as the subject permitted it was slanted towards sensationalism. Your original piece was excellent. If now and then I shrank, it was myself that made me shrink. I *do* say things like "my fucking mouth." All Americans do, but in print it looked out of character.

Tell Cork [Smith] he can count on me, and remember me to Dana.

Yrs, as ever,

Kennedy's article in Esquire *was "If Saul Bellow Doesn't Have a True Word to Say, He Keeps His Mouth Shut." K. Corlies (Cork) Smith was Kennedy's editor at Viking.*

To Alfred Kazin

March 9, 1982   Victoria, B.C.

Dear Alfred—

It made me very unhappy to learn that you were ill. As a member of the class of '15, I have a special concern with your well being; and despite decades of differences and disagreements—misunderstandings—I am attached to you and am distressed when you are sick.

We will discuss my failings (there is such a multitude of them) when you are better.

Yours affectionately,

To Leon Wieseltier

March 12, 1982   Victoria, B.C.

Dear Leon:

I don't think you expected a quick reply to your Arendt articles; the subject (not Hannah but Jewish history) is denser than the Amazon jungle, and even if I were the Paul Bunyan of the machete I could never hack my way through. It would take a long conversation (years, no doubt) to begin to sort out the main problems. Hannah was rash, but she wasn't altogether stupid (unlike her friend Mary McC[arthy]). You do grant her that in your essay. The trouble is that her errors were far more extensive than her judgment. That can be said of us all, but she was monumentally vain, and a rigid *akshente* [*]. Much of her strength went into obstinacy, and she was the compleat intellectual—i.e. she went always and as rapidly as possible for the great synthesis and her human understanding, painfully limited, could not support the might of historical analysis, unacknowledged prejudices, frustrations of her German and European aspirations, etc. She could often think clearly, but to think simply was altogether beyond her, and her imaginative faculty was stunted.

I once asked Alexander Donat, author of *The Holocaust Kingdom*, how it was that the Jews went down so quickly in Poland. He said something like this: "After three days in the ghetto, unable to wash and shave, without clean clothing, deprived of food, all utilities and municipal services cut off, your toilet habits humiliatingly disrupted, you are demoralized, confused, subject to panic. A life of austere discipline would have made it possible for me to keep my head, but how many civilized people lead such a life?" Such simple facts—had Hannah had the imagination to see them—would have lowered the intellectual fever that vitiates her theories. Her standards were those of a "noble" German intelligentsia trained in the classics and in European philosophy—what you call the "tradition of sweet thinking." Hannah not only loved it, she actively disliked those who didn't share it, and she couldn't acknowledge this dislike—which happened to be dislike of those (so inconveniently) martyred by the Nazis. What got her gets us all: attachment to the high cultures of the "diaspora." The Eros of these cultures is irresistible. At the same time assimilation is simply impossible—out of the question to reject one's history. And insofar as the Israelis are secular, they are in it with the rest of us, fascinated and also eaten up by Greece, France, Russia, England.

* Yiddish: impossible woman, ballbuster

It is impossible for advanced minds not to be so affected. At the same time you are precisely where the Jew-hatred of those same cultures has situated you—in Tel Aviv. To complicate matters still more your survival depends upon a technology which . . . but you know more about this than I do. The more complex the problem of armament and the associated problems of diplomacy and of finances become, the more the assumption of a distinct Jewish destiny in Israel dwindles. It is possible to be a mini-superpower without ceasing to be an "excluded" people. (I wouldn't call Israel a "pariah" among the nations.) It is also possible that this mini-superpower, which began as the national home of Zionists and of Jews fleeing destruction, presents itself to America's leaders, some of them, as a convenient package to be traded for this, that or the other. What you call the pornographic strain in Western politics, mingling with supply-side economics, with the State Dep't. Middle Eastern Contingent advising and participating, may not distinguish between diasporas and homelands.

Anyway your Arendt pieces are wonderful, even though the concluding sentence . . . but what else can one conclude but "on course" and "in the dark"? We mustn't surrender the demonic to the demagogic academics. Intellectual sobriety itself may have to take the powers of darkness into account.

All best,

Wieseltier's two-part essay on Arendt had appeared in back-to-back issues of The New Republic, *where he concluded as follows: "There are not anti-Semites because there are Jews, and there are not Jews because there are anti-Semites. There are peoples, and a longing for paradise. The Jews are there for when the longing goes bad, when it ends in tumbrils or in boxcars. But now they have Israel, and America, and the night vision that has always sustained them, that has helped them to believe in the best even as they know the worst, and kept them steady, and on their course, in the dark."*

To Robert Boyers

March 12, 1982   Victoria, B.C.

Dear Boyers:

Well, yes, I suppose I will weather the storm, veteran that I am, although when it's time to founder one simply founders. I was grateful for your letter, for supportive intelligence rather than "emotional" support. I quite clearly understood what I was getting into by writing the *Dean*. Characteristic of those young people at Northwestern to accuse me of distorting the facts—such facts as surround them and may be read daily in the papers, heard daily in the courts (where, however, they never go). The facts themselves shouldn't much matter in a novel, but I went carefully into this particular case, talking to the lawyers and reading the materials in their files. I'm sure the Northwestern kiddies didn't do that, they just told one another over and over that I had misrepresented the facts and out of this repeated telling they made a case and convicted me. Perhaps things have always been done like this but the crisis that surrounds us increases the will-to-lie and the gases given off by intellectual heads cause strange atmospheric distortions and bring down a special sort of acid rain.

The Dean is strange, I don't deny it, and I try to understand what it signifies to have written it and what the reactions of readers and reviewers signify. It's charitable of you to speak of "uncharitable" reviews. [Hugh] Kenner was openly anti-Semitic. He won't set off a wave of Jew-hatred but it's curious that he should decide to come out openly in his Eliot-Pound anti-Semitic regalia. Perhaps he thinks it can be done now. What interests me much more than what he thinks is the effect of the Eliot-Pound phenomenon, the deadly madness at the heart of "tradition" and "culture" as represented by those two. One had to defend poor Pound against philistine, savage America—that was tantamount to protecting art itself. What Pound was actually *saying* didn't so much matter. This was what the literary people defending him assume. A poet might be great despite his obsessions with Usura, Major Douglas, Mussolini, Jews. This was the line taken after the War by literary intellectuals. The inevitable corollary was that the poet's convictions could be separated from his poetry. It was thus possible to segregate the glory from the shame. Then you took possession of the glory in the name of "culture" and kept the malignancies as pets. (In a democracy you can't take away the right to harbor malignancies.) So we now have Mr. K[enner] with all the credit he has inherited from the Modernist Masters, their cultural glamour, crying "Sic 'em" to his Jew-biting dogs and turning them loose on me.

Matters are no better on the left. I anticipated its accusations, too—for which I claim no great credit, it was very easy. I was old, I had gone dry and didactic, I was a neo-conservative, I had abandoned the novel, I was mentally too weak to handle ideas, I had capitulated, I was a fink. No one was willing to face the simple proposition or question: Is this the way we live now or isn't it?

Well, enough of that.

I haven't been able to decide about your invitation. For one thing I can't remember what it was, exactly, and I didn't bring your letter to Canada. For another, I wore out my treads (or threads), I was exhausted by the *Dean*. I expect to feel stronger presently. We're returning to Chicago next week. Will you bear with me a little longer?

Best wishes,

Robert Boyers is the founding editor of Salmagundi *and author of, among other works,* Atrocity and Amnesia *(1985). On a visit to Northwestern in the spring term of 1982, he had encountered students critical of the "factual accuracy" of* The Dean's December. *In the highly publicized court case on which Bellow partly based his novel, a black man and woman were charged with having murdered a white University of Chicago student by pushing him from the window of his third-story apartment. In the course of the trial, which generated support for the defendants among student radicals, an undergraduate was charged with threatening witnesses, one of whom had been shot at. Hugh Kenner's disparaging review of Bellow's novel, "From Lower Bellowvia," had appeared in* Harper's.

To Eileen Simpson

April 10, 1982 Chicago

Dear Eileen:

Your splendid book reached me in Canada and I read it at once. I put off writing to you about it for all kinds of reasons. The Canadian mails are notorious. Letters had been lost. I wanted time to think. There was no hurry, really. The fact was that although I luxuriated in your reconstructed Forties the pleasure was also painful and heavy. Those were not at all the good old days out of which our reputations grew, they were bad times. What was worst about them for me I was reluctant to face, understandably. Then, and later, I declined to examine the phenomena. What were John [Berryman] and Delmore and Cal [Lowell] about, really? I admired their poems, I relished their company; but I was so deeply immersed in my own puzzles, programs, problems that I drove past in my dream-car . . . Something like that. Not without feeling, no; I certainly felt for them but I was a thousand times less attentive than I was capable of being. It came home to me sharply as I read your memoir. I suppose that if John and Delmore hadn't been such entertainers, comic charmers, stylists, if they hadn't had hundreds of intriguing tricks in presenting themselves . . . But really it does no good, this remorse for being so *like* them. Was I to be some singular moral genius, or super-psychologist? Moral geniuses were not in great supply. Your book, then, took me by surprise. I hadn't known, I couldn't have known, what you knew. Besides I hadn't the patience, in my thirties and forties and fifties, to investigate. I can start now. I have started. A project to close out with.

One trifling oddity: I too was interviewed by Whittaker Chambers [for a job at *Time*], introduced to him by [James] Agee. He quarreled with me in the same absurd way. With me the pretext was Wordsworth. I suspect that Agee was aware that he was sending hopeless cases to Chambers who baited and dismissed them. Did those two have an arrangement? Funny that John and I should never have discussed this. Agee was saintly, and Chambers prophetic and both did the work of Henry Luce . . . John and I missed that one. Perhaps he would have disagreed with me, as he did about [Edmund] Wilson and, in some degree, [Allen] Tate. But we needn't go into that here. Sufficient to say (as my paper gives out) that you've written a book of permanent value, a fascinating book. I hope it will have the success it deserves and I send you my affectionate congratulations and thanks (for enlightening me).

Yours ever,

Eileen Simpson had just published Poets in Their Youth, *a memoir about her marriage to Berryman including also portraits of R. P. Blackmur, Randall Jarrell, Delmore Schwartz, Jean Stafford and Robert Lowell.*

To Anthony Hecht

May 20, 1982   Chicago

Dear Tony:

A few years back Red Warren said to me, "Still giving lectures? Bad idea." I fell into a sulk when he said this but as my sixty-seventh birthday approaches (or I approach it in the sense that a fellow jumping from the top of the Empire State approaches the sixty-seventh floor) I better understand his opinion. Write a lecture, board a plane, see one old friend, yes, but also a very large platoon of non-friends, including followers of Lacan and de Man each of whom can be identified by a rictus of jeering rejection. Add to this an incomprehensible failure to agree on the simplest fundamentals not alone of literature but also of politics, sex, drink, nutrition; abrasive seminar rooms; dinners that will not end, etc. I used to wag through all this with puppy vitality, knocking down bricabrac with my tail, but now . . . (why say it?). You and I and your wife will sit down in a nice carpeted and quiet bar and talk of old [Chanler] Chapman and Irma B[randeis].

Yrs fondly,

Irma Brandeis (1905–90) was a colleague of Bellow's and Hecht's at Bard, where she taught Romance languages. Author of The Ladder of Vision: A Study of Dante's Comedy *(1960), she had been in the 1930s the muse and lover of Eugenio Montale, greatest of twentieth-century Italian poets. A gratuitous insult to Brandeis by Bellow in the early 1950s would haunt him for decades until he expiated it in his long comic story* "Him with His Foot in His Mouth," *published in* Atlantic Monthly *in November 1982.*

To Margaret Shafer

May 21, 1982   Chicago

Dear Margaret—

Your note did me much good. *The Dean* made many enemies. The powers of darkness were attracted. I seem to send impulses they readily pick up. Perhaps I should consider more earnestly what *that* signifies.

When C[hanler] Chapman died the *N.Y. Times* tried to get me to certify that he was the original Henderson, and I declined to comment. But I've often thought, half guilty, half amused, that I'd suggested to Chanler how he might emerge from chaos, I'd solved his "identity-problem"; and that although I'd given him some *formal* assistance I hadn't made him more kindly or pleasant. If anything, I'd suggested new forms of hysteria, cunning and aggression. After the book appeared he would come to Tivoli to visit me in his truck. But he was always incoherent—a non-angelic Billy Budd. The purpose of his incoherency was to startle, or frighten. What an oddity he was.

Please remember me to Irma [Brandeis]—I didn't know of her tender attachment to cyclamens. It doesn't surprise me [. . .]

All best,

Mrs. Shafer had remarked in her letter that like Albert Corde, hero of The Dean's December, *Irma Brandeis was a cultivator of cyclamens.*

To Louis Lasco

May 29, 1982   [Chicago]

Dear Polykarp:

Many thanks for the poetical greetings. We missed you at the Tuley reunion. Not all the classmates were well. Bananas Landau didn't seem quite himself, although physically not greatly changed. With many it was, "We meet again—and so farewell." My sharpshooting memory brought down *scores* of targets. The ladies were flattered. "You knew me!" One was from the third grade at Lafayette.

I hope you're happy in retirement, and haven't retired on all fronts.

Yours ever,

Gapon Khoraschevsky

To Eleanor Clark

May 30, 1982   Chicago

Dear Eleanor—

I sh'd think Paolo Milano would answer your questions about [G. G.] Belli. He hasn't answered my letters. The reasons? Ill health, bitterness, general shrinkage. A cook-butler-valet takes care of him, a short peasant, a discreet death-watch kind of man. Paolo is so stooped by now that he has to force his gaze upwards when he wants to look at you. He reads more than ever—i.e. continually—and shares his bed with books. But you don't want all this, only his address.

I think I'll be able to give some money to Yaddo. A man named Brown, in N.Y., says he can sell some of my manuscripts.

We look forward with pleasure to the summer and our annual meetings.

Affectionately,

To Alfred Kazin

June 7, 1982   W. Halifax

Dear Alfred,

A happy birthday to you, and admiration and love and long life—everything. Never mind this and that, this and that don't matter much in the summing up.

Love from your junior by five days,

Your daughter is a charming young woman. We had drinks together in Chicago two weeks ago.

To Marion Meade

June 16, 1982   W. Halifax, Vermont

Dear Ms. Meade,

Dorothy Parker was the nicest of all the participants in the *Esquire* symposium mainly because she was the quietest. Miss Parker was far from young when we first met and seemed depressed when she didn't, more sharply, appear heartbroken. I can't remember that we ever had a personal conversation although I met her on several occasions. We were occasionally invited by Lillian Hellman for tea, and Lillian and Dashiell Hammett did most of the talking. I said little because these great figures were my seniors and Miss Parker said little because she was evidently downcast.

Sincerely,

Biographer Marion Meade was researching Dorothy Parker: What Fresh Hell Is This? *which would be published in 1988.*

To Nathan Gould

August 4, 1982   W. Halifax, Vermont

Dear Natie:

[. . .] I attended the Tuley reunion and it was a depressing affair, on the whole—elderly people nostalgic for youth and the Depression years. There seemed nothing for them (for us) to do but to turn into middle-class Americans, all supplied with the same phrases and thoughts from the same sources. Some came from far away (Rudy Lapp from Oakland, Cal.) and some were crippled and required wheeling. Some, built for stability, appeared not greatly changed, like Bernice Meyer Landau. Her brother [Bananas] who seemed well preserved turned out to have a hereditary disorder affecting his memory so that he was groping, while we talked, and his new wife was deeply uneasy (but behaving well). As for some of the others you name, I haven't seen Passin in some years. We had lunch in Chicago four or five years ago and he was in many respects like a Japanese mask, a bright man but devious. Freifeld a stumbling old chaser and thoroughly undistinguished lawyer. Melancholy. Miserable. George Reedy, whom I used to see in Washington when he was Johnson's press secretary, has remained lively and quite original. He's Dean of the Journalism School at Marquette, in Milwaukee. But my closest friends were Oscar and Isaac, dead for many years. In every decade I try to think what they might have been like had they lived.

As for me, Natie, I have become a sort of public man, which was not at all my intent. I thought, in my adolescent way, that I would write good books (as writing and books were understood in the Thirties) and would have been happy in the middle ranks of my trade. It would have made me wretched to be overlooked, but I wasn't at all prepared for so much notice, and I haven't been good at managing "celebrity." That's a long story and I shan't go into details. I can't do the many things I'm asked to do, answer the huge volume of mail, keep up with books and manuscripts and at the same time write such things as I want and need to write. I write to you because I remember you so vividly and affectionately from the old days, and I would feel alienated from my own history, *false*, if I didn't make time (something like creating a dry spot under this Niagara of mail). I'm delighted to hear from you, I'd be happy to see you, we could talk for many evenings. But to write an introduction for the collection of Mr. [Arthur] Leipzig, clearly a distinguished photographer, I would have to put aside my own manuscripts—give up my frontline defenses against chaos.

A word about Jewish Life: I do my best, but I seldom write anything about Jewish Life that pleases Jewish Opinion. First thing I know there's a brawl, and I come out of it with a shiner.

All the best to you,

To Owen Barfield

August 21, 1982   W. Halifax, Vermont

Dear Owen:

Clifford Monks sent me your review of the *Dean* with the suggestion that I write a reply—take issue with you, perhaps? It would be inappropriate to do such a thing. I wouldn't dream of trying to overturn your opinion. Perhaps your understanding of the book is better than my own. After all, one can never answer fully for what one has written. Besides, the *Dean* is not a "fiction" in the conventional or formal sense. It is, as some people have told me, people whose judgment I value, a very strange piece of work.

I was touched by your close reading of the book and by your interest in (affection for?) its oddball author. It's natural, however, that I should read my reader, criticize the critic, even the friendly and affectionate critic, or try to make out the shape of his thoughts. Besides, I am an apprentice Steiner-reader whereas you are a respected veteran, so I am bound to take an immense interest in your views. Here is a man who has been studying Anthroposophy for fifty years. What effects has this had? What is his vision of the modern world? Etc. And I felt as I read your review that you found me very strange indeed. I was aware from our first meeting that I was far more alien to you than you were to me. American, Jew, novelist, modernist—well of course I am all of those things. And I wouldn't have the shadow of a claim on anybody's attention if I weren't the last, for a novelist who is not contemporary can be nothing at all. Rimbaud's *Il faut être absolument moderne* [*] is self-evidently true, for me. Perhaps for you, too, but you would qualify *moderne* in so many ways that it would no longer be the same thing. In any case, the fact that you find me so alien proves that it is not the same. And why do I say that you are less alien to me than I to you? Well, because you have qualities familiar to me: English, of an earlier generation, educated in classics, saturated in English literature. Your history is clearer to me than mine can ever be to you. I have led an "undescribed life," as it were. Few Europeans really know anything about America. [Denis] Brogan knew a bit, and so does [Luigi] Barzini, but there is something really very different (not in every respect a *good* difference) on this side of the Atlantic. And I hope you won't take offense at this, but in my opinion you failed to find the key, the musical signature without which books like mine can't be read. You won't find anything like it in any of the old manuals. There is nothing arbitrary in this newness. It originates in one's experience of the total human situation. But there is no point in lecturing on the self-consciousness of Americans and how it is to be represented, or why the reflections in the *Dean* are "crowded" into the small corners of sentences. Without the signature the *Dean* is impossible to play. Reading becomes a labor, and then of course one needs frequent rest, and the book has to be put down. And what is this mysterious signature? It is Corde's intense passion. If the reader misses that he has missed everything.

And this is where I think your reading goes wrong, for you see "extremity of self-consciousness" rather than passion, Henry James in shorthand. Not at all. Nothing like it. The *Dean* is a hard, militant and angry book and Corde, far from being a brooding introvert, attacks Chicago (American society) with a boldness that puts him in considerable danger. But he is far more concerned to purge his understanding of false thought than to protect himself. Indeed, what is there to protect when the imagination has succumbed to trivialization and distortion?

Autobiography? Only in the vaguest sense. If I had been writing about

* French: It is necessary to be absolutely modern.

myself I would have recorded that the Dean was reading [Rudolf Steiner's] *Leading Thoughts* and *The Michael Mystery*, and that he saw himself between Lucifer in the East and Ahriman in the West. It's not so much "unwilling-ness to essay the leap beyond" extremity of self-consciousness as it is depend-able and certain knowledge of what the leap will carry you into that is the problem.

I'm quite sure that I haven't changed your mind about anything. I wasn't really trying. I esteem you just as you are.

Yours with best wishes,

About the "leap beyond": "certain knowledge" isn't it either, but it would have to be a leap into a world of which one has had some experience. I have had foreshadowings, very moving adumbrations, but the whole vision of reality must change in every particular and the idols [must be] dismissed. Then one can take flight. It can't be done by fiat, however much one may long for it.

"East, West, and Saul Bellow," Barfield's review of The Dean's December, *had appeared in* Towards.

To Saul Steinberg

December 26, 1982   [Chicago]

Dear Saul:

It's an act of special generosity to send us these Steinbergs. I *need* them in cold Chicago as an aid to survival. As I used to hear them say in Parisian music halls, "*Ça réchauffe un peu.*" [*] I take a particular interest in the Strada Palas because of its vision of childhood—a man-sized boy striding the streets of Bucharest in primordial Romania. The absence of the world-as-represented-by-anybody-else is what I most appreciate. On occasions when I set myself to ponder the "problem of art" I always end up with this. I have my own version of the boy going down the street. If I were to rummage about for technical terms I would say that I had "unmediated percepts" in those days. Life was furnished with objects which hadn't yet been tampered with. These objects were a product of the collaboration of God and Man, with Man contributing

* Warms (the heart) a little.

the shabbiness. I had words of my own for such things when I was a kid, syllables that came to me unsolicited. To this day I have never spoken them aloud. The faces you put in the windows of Strada Palas, the sunflowers, the rain-barrel, the dinosaur-hackled cats on the roof may have come from the same psychic source. I lived on St. Dominique St. in Montreal where orthodox Jews mixed with French Canadians, soldiers from the barracks on Pine Ave., and also cats, many cats, and quite a few nuns. The year was 1920.

I hope we can meet this summer. Alexandra and I have been putting up a house in Vermont. An act of *chutzpah*, at my age (Jewish hubris?).

Many thanks, and blessings,

PART FIVE

1983–1989

───◄•◆•►───

What were we here for, of all strange beings and creatures the strangest? Clear colloid eyes to see with, for a while, and see so finely, and a palpitating universe to see, and so many human messages to give and to receive. And the bony box for thinking and for storage of thoughts, and a cloudy heart for feelings. Ephemerids, grinding up other creatures, flavoring and heating their flesh, devouring this flesh. A kind of being filled with death-knowledge, and also filled with infinite longings.

—"Zetland: By a Character Witness"

1983

To Alfred Kazin

January 24, 1983   Chicago

Dear Alfred:

Sorry you fell down. I am confident though that Martinique will heal your hip and you can leave the walker down there for some old party who really needs it. You say that sleep is tough but sitting up at the desk is possible, which proves that you haven't yet realized how many writers do their sleeping at the desk. I'm glad you enjoyed my story. I don't see that further comment is required. The first criterion is enjoyment, and so are the second and third criteria. The fact that you found it in part puzzling only signifies that you have fallen (temporarily, I hope) into the bad habit of puzzling over such matters. What? You didn't notice how innovative "Him [with His Foot in His Mouth]" was in execution, and failed to notice how different it was from 99.9999 percent of stories recently published (say, past ten years or so)? Well, I forgive you these omissions.

As to your lengthy postscript, I don't like the activists of the Free World Committee (except Midge [Decter] whom I do like for old times' sake), but I belong because the other side smells so bad. Unbearable! And when I read of Gromyko's visit to Bonn and see how effectively the Russians are working to disarm Western Europe unilaterally, then I think frantically of a *No*-blank big enough to accommodate my name. However, I never attend the meetings of such organizations because it interferes with the writing of stories. Enjoy the Plaza.

Yrs. ever,

Kazin attended the neoconservative Committee for the Free World's meeting and would write critically about the organization in "Saving My Soul at the Plaza," in The New York Review of Books. *In February of the following year, Bellow resigned from the Committee for the Free World.*

To Robert Penn Warren

February 4, 1983   Chicago

Dear Red—

Your letter made me so happy that I couldn't think how to answer it. ("The problems of pleasure," a philosopher would say.) Well, thank you for liking the story. When I say that I seem to have found a congenial way to get off a story, I feel like an old prospector with a new hunch. Then it comes to me with amusement and affection that we belong to a small band of old guys mad about writing, wandering in the desert.

I congratulate you on becoming grandparents. One can become a parent simply by fooling around. There's something fortuitous about it: Comedy of Errors, not necessarily a serious thing. But to be a grandparent fits you into the species. You have your place now in the endless list of "begats."

The [new] house [in W. Brattleboro] is almost ready—seven rooms without a chair, a teaspoon or a pillowcase. I'm coming out towards the end of May to buy second-hand furniture from Bolster's Warehouse in Brattleboro. So we'll be seeing you very soon—no small part of the happiness of being in Vermont.

My affectionate greetings to you both.

Yours as ever,

To Jeff Wheelwright

February 4, 1983   Chicago

Dear Mr. Wheelwright:

Many thanks for your letter. Was I really attacking journalism in the *Dean*? It might be nearer the truth to say that I was contemplating a great modern mystery—why, in this age of communication, are we so near the border of total incoherency? The literate masses desire information. A crowd of technicians informs them. Why the information should be haunted by unreality is the great mystery. Some people insist that mass society must kill true meaning. Others (like me) suspect that the confusion may have an epistemological root (of "me," I should add that I occasionally have the metaphysical falling-sickness). The language of science is clear enough, within its limits, but all other important questions are up for grabs. Maybe because for science they have no true meaning. They have been surrendered to an incoherency which assumes various guises, or disguises, of meaning. An interesting variation on "ye have eyes and see not": "ye have words and mean not."

Since we desire nevertheless to be informed we turn on the tube and read the papers but it's all like a strip-tease in which the lights never fail to go out before we can get to the Main Thing. Today, for instance, I tried to read Flora Lewis in the *Times* on the Bulgarian connections of the man who tried to kill the Pope. Flora said that perhaps [Yuri] Andropov was aware that the attempt would be made. We can't afford to know this fact, if it is a fact, because that would bring to us a new, deadlier Sarajevo. If the Russians were provoked by our knowledge of the truth they might be driven to destroy us all (themselves as well) with nuclear weapons. So we had better refrain. I've been reading such items since—oh—1930. The epistemological fits are much more fun. Better than the illusion of communication.

Yrs. sincerely,

Jeff Wheelwright is a science writer for the Los Angeles Times *and the author of* Degrees of Disaster: Prince William Sound: How Nature Reels and Rebounds *(1994) and* The Irritable Heart: The Medical Mystery of the Gulf War *(2001).*

To Teddy Kollek

February 9, 1983   Chicago

Dear Teddy,

I long to get back to Jerusalem and I keep looking for opportunities to get away from Chicago. The problem is always one of coordination—I simply can't get my variety show together so that I write, teach, correspond, fend off lawyers, balance accounts, perform the duties of a father and husband, doctor myself, etc. like a large troupe of trained seals. What all this comes to is that my dream of returning to Jerusalem and your get-together and dialogue [at the Jerusalem Book Fair] cannot find consummation at the same moment. I will add, privately, that I am told you will be entertaining Mr. [V. S.] Naipaul, who does not take a kindly view of me, although I once voted him an award, and have always spoken pleasantly of his books (the better ones). The Latin for all this I believe is *verbum sapienti* [*]. (I think that is the correct dative.) Bless you for your great kindness, and best wishes and regards from the Bellows.

* Latin: A word (is enough) to the wise.

To Anne Doubillon Walter

February 17, 1983   Chicago

Dear Anny,

Unfortunately, there was no time in Paris to look up old friends. Flammarion gave me not a single free hour. [. . .]

When people ask me how I am, I am always inclined to answer like a Roman I once saw knocked down by a Vespa. When people ran toward him to ask how he was, he said, "I was better before." Considering my advanced years, *je me porte assez bien.* [*] You, for your part, sound rather disgruntled and slightly insurrectionary—going to a religious pension and resenting it. Besides, you make me feel that you are watching me from behind a tree like a guerrilla. You won't shoot, but you are armed.

Can you do your next letter on a machine? You are very fond of the last century and its ways but even Tolstoy toward the end owned a typewriter and spoke on the telephone.

Much affection from your old friend,

Anne Doubillon Walter had met Bellow in 1953 at Bard, where she was studying. A writer and filmmaker who worked with Nicholas Ray and Robert Bresson, she lives today in Brittany.

To Allan Bloom

February 28, 1983   [Chicago]

Dear Allan:

They say it's spring-like in Chicago. That means that somewhere beyond the stern gloom intervening, the sky is blue and probably mild and the temperature is moderate. Today I stopped work on my story, feeling neck-weary (my head is too heavy for the stem) and worn, and at about 2:00 P.M. I walked to Dominick's to buy salad oil, as per instructions. On the way to the supermarket I thought of you in Paris, so civilized. [. . .]

I noticed that west of Broadway on Thorndale a little bookshop had opened and stopped to have a look. A West Indian, small beard, outcurved teeth, tried to sell me a paperback *Leviathan*, and then a spiritual guide to rebirth (I am ready but don't expect to do it out of a handbook). He asked me to identify myself. I said I was a professor. This brought him sharply to life, and he wanted to give me his business cards to distribute among friends. He seems to live in

* French: I'm holding up pretty well.

an upright crate at the back of the shop. Now I dragged myself over to the east side of Broadway, and a woman of ninety advanced toward me on a four-pronged cane—tiny, a construction worker's yellow hard hat pulled over her forehead. This apparition passing, there came more: middle-class people, I suppose, but reduced to the status of derelicts, one holding a little boy by the hand while yelling at an acquaintance to get his goddam ass out of her face because she wouldn't submit to suffocation, and then some people affably talking to themselves; and then a nice police dog chained to a parking meter, wearing a cast on his broken leg and barking. He may have been asking to see the humanity in relation to which he was supposed to be a dog. We were at one in this. My tired intelligence found no trace of the hierarchy.

I came up to the iron frames that filter the customers [at the supermarket]. These are small openings, like weirs, just big enough to get through, and some of these openings are sometimes padlocked for reasons of security I haven't yet figured out. I thought, good old Allan is on holiday, leaving me in charge. I was rather pleased than not; glad you were out of this. Taking turns is only fair. After bringing home the bottle of oil, and a box of tandoor spice which wasn't on my list, an impulse purchase, I took off all my clothing and got into bed for an hour of angelic purity and meditation, browsing in [Josef] Pieper's book on the *Phaedrus*. I saw how bad the Sophists were, and it comforted me to be on the right side, faithful to Eros and repudiating spurious sexuality. I am old enough at last to see things in a true light.

To John Auerbach

March 9, 1983   Chicago

Dear John,

I am dictating this on the run, as usual. Last fall I started to write a short story of which there are now about eighty pages with no end in sight, and I find that I haven't the strength to sit down at the typewriter again in the afternoon. I have written only pressing business letters this winter and I plan to take a holiday after the damn story has been finished, and if I haven't by then lost all my best friends I will write a dozen long letters. Adam brought the figurine of Astarte, and I took possession at once, but as is only right and proper since she is the goddess of fertility and sexual love, I surrendered her to my Missus. When the moon is shining I look for her among the math papers (Astarte, I mean). Now John, I was slightly discouraged by your last letter in which you argued that you couldn't leave your dogs long enough to visit Vermont. I suppose it would be foolish for me to say that I would leave my dogs, if I had any, for your sake. I work from a different dog-ethic. If I led a settled life I'd acquire cats and dogs, but Alexandra and I knock about so much that I have to limit myself to houseplants. To which I am devoted. I'll probably be taking them to Brattleboro this summer and I have been trying to argue Alexandra into adopting a cat. The alternative is to buy an ultra-sonic machine advertised in the *Wall Street Journal* as guaranteed to keep away field mice and biting insects. Only, it occurred to me that it would also drive away fertilizing insects from the flowers. I don't want to write you a rambling nonsensical letter. My fixed purpose is to persuade you to fly over in September. [. . .] The dogs are surely generous enough to release you for a few weeks. Let me send you the ticket.

I see that Begin is entertaining Jimmy Carter, who called him psycho when they were quarrelling at Camp David. One would think that he would be far happier to entertain me. He has decided, evidently, not to give me an interview. I can't say that I'm unhappy about it. I would have accepted an invitation from him because it would have given me an excuse to see you.

Love,

To John Auerbach

April 8, 1983   Chicago

Dear John,

Alexandra and I were absolutely delighted with your decision. I would have preferred a June visit, but Alexandra is not able to leave Chicago before the middle of the month. Her childlike conscientiousness—she must give exams, check the grading of papers by her assistants (she really has no use for assistants because she does it all by herself from scratch), record the marks, agonize over the flunks—keeps her in Chicago till the fifteenth, and then she flies to Germany on the twentieth and returns just before Independence Day. [. . .] September is the best month anyway, the trees are turning and the insects have perished. Bear hunters begin operations in mid-September, but two experienced old guys have been given an exclusive franchise and they do their shooting about half a mile away. I think you should come just after Labor Day. [. . .] They tell me that El Al is back in business, unless orthodox rabbis lie down on the runways of Ben Gurion to protect *Shabbat*.

Invitations have been coming from Israel. Not a single one have I been able to accept. The most recent was from Teddy Kollek, who asked me to attend the Jerusalem Book Fair, and the awarding of a literary prize to Naipaul. Since Naipaul dislikes me I saw no reason to be present. I can't think how I offended him, but there doesn't have to be a reason, does there? Anyhow, I declined and told Teddy why it would be awkward. I thought it was idiotic the year before to give medals and money to Graham Greene, that anti-Semite. They criticize Jews in the Diaspora for clinging to their *goyim* and they give prizes to one of the worst, proving that they have more esteem for anti-Semites than for Jews who won't capitulate. There was a charming exchange between Gershom Scholem and Allen Ginsberg some time back. When Scholem asked Ginsberg why he didn't move to Israel, Ginsberg said, "All my life I've been escaping from the Bronx. How can you ask me to live in Tel Aviv?" An answer which pleased Scholem as much as it does me.

I have finished my story—ninety-nine pages of it—and in June I can go to work on it in earnest. For the moment I am diverting myself with some reminiscences of Chicago in the Thirties—my recollections of Roosevelt's first term. I am not doing it of my own free will, but to raise money for furniture in Vermont. Just the other day Harriet [Wasserman] told me that she had received two stories from you. I am fretfully waiting for Xerox copies. She said she hadn't yet had time to read them. She's in a state of fretfulness and distraction, depressed by her father's death and the slump in publishing and who knows what female miseries besides.

I am dictating this letter to Janis [Freedman] because I wear myself out over the typewriter and abuse myself as if I were my own Ayatollah.

Please answer promptly so that I can get the tickets off.

Much love from your friend,

"In the Days of Mr. Roosevelt" would appear in Esquire. *Janis Freedman, a student in the Committee on Social Thought, was at this time Bellow's graduate assistant.*

To Alfred Kazin

[Postmarked Brattleboro, Vt., 17 June 1983]

Dear Alfred:

Once more, a happy birthday, no pangs, no groans. And other congratulations as well.

That I've become an unforthcoming correspondent is perfectly true; I take no pleasure in these silences of mine; rather, I'm trying to discover the reasons why I so seldom reply. It may be that I'm always out with a butterfly net trying to capture my mature and perfected form, which is just about to settle (once and for all) on a flower. It never does settle, it hasn't yet found its flower. That *may* be the full explanation.

The other day I received in the mail the U. of Chicago *Maroon* containing an article on our late friend I. Rosenfeld by a bright undergraduate who fell in love with his essays and his reputation. I was touched by this and all went well until I reached the end. At the end it was Isaac who was true to the high imperative, whereas his corrupt and unworthy friend S.B., by appearing with Dick Cavett, had betrayed the good, the true, the beautiful, Judaism, Wilhelm Reich, Karl Marx, and the legion of sainted Russians from Gogol to Babel who were our spiritual uncles.

The Vermont address is good until mid-September. Will your new book be appearing soon? I am longing to read it.

Yrs. ever,

S.B., Class of '15

To David Shahar

July 15, 1983   West Brattleboro, Vermont

Dear David,

I'm not at all cross. I'm what the French call *ahuri* (bewildered, flurried, confused, giddy-headed), and I had to choose between a letter-block and a writer's block. Naturally I made the right choice. In the fullness of your vigor you are most happily not able to experience a crisis of this sort. My energy diminishing, I have had to lock some of the doors to conserve heat. Nothing else. This year I have written some articles and two stories long enough to be described as novellas; and I have defended myself against the US government and several US (ex-)wives; and dealt with children, and colleagues at the University whose mental powers like my own are failing; to say nothing of an older sister, elder brothers, and the confusions of the age. Now if I had a cork-lined room and a Celeste to wait on me hand and foot, to serve me coffee at the right temperature, and to supply me with handkerchiefs and protect me from all intrusions, I could, as Proust did, keep up with my mail. But the world has been too much with me and I have written very few personal letters. Emergency cases only.

There have been negotiations conducted by the *Atlantic Monthly* for the interviews with Begin and Moshe Arens, and I have been trying to decide whether to accept—whether to stir up the hornets of Jerusalem and the Diaspora with rash and ignorant statements. Israelis now hold a monopoly over all discussions of the Jewish question, which I am not too eager to challenge. I suspect it would be a lapse of judgment to write an article. Still, I may come to Jerusalem next November to do what I probably ought not to do, and one of my rewards will be a visit to the Shahars.

With love and best wishes,

(It would be a mistake not to forgive me.)

To Anne Doubillon Walter

July 16, 1983   West Brattleboro, Vermont

Dear Anny,

You are probably used to my long silences. They aren't a sign of absent-mindedness really or of old-fashioned procrastination ("the thief of time"). I am simply incapable of "keeping up." I have never understood how to manage my time and now I have less strength to invest in attempted management. The days flutter past and this would be entertaining if I could compare them to butterflies, but there's nothing at all picturesque or cheerful about this condition. Rather it makes me heavy-hearted. Not a leaden state, just something permanently regrettable. Thus I hold your letter of March 3rd, which I intended to answer immediately because it contained a request. I wanted to tell you that a book about me *vu par* yourself would please me greatly, and of course you have my permission without restriction.

I thought of looking for you in Paris last September, but Flammarion and Co. left me no time for myself. I had nothing but the use of my eyes for looking past my interlocutors at the Seine. In my "spare" time I was presented to Monsieur Mitterand at the Élysée. He is a pleasant man, but I had some rather sharp exchanges with Mssrs. [Régis] Debray and [Jack] Lang [minister of culture under Mitterand]. I have a friend in Chicago who says that a minister of culture is a fatal clinical symptom. It tells you "culture is more abundant here." And if the French insist on using such American techniques for getting into the papers and onto the television screen, I don't see how they can then have the *toupet* [*] to criticize the Americans. All they can say against the Americans is that they have made more progress in corruption. With a little help M. Lang will outstrip us.

For heaven's sake, Anny, don't worry about returning the loan. You will give me a good dinner one of these days, or send me some French books.

Dear old friend,

* French: nerve or cheek; lit., forelock

Régis Debray, famed veteran of the Che Guevara–led insurrection in Bolivia—sentenced to thirty years' imprisonment there but released after an international appeal led by Jean-Paul Sartre, André Malraux and others—had been appointed special adviser to Mitterand.

1984

To Philip Roth

January 7, 1984   Chicago

Dear Philip:

I thought to do some good by giving an interview to *People*, which was exceedingly foolish of me. I asked Aaron [Asher] to tell you that the Good Intentions Paving Company had fucked up again. The young interviewer turned my opinions inside out, cut out the praises and made it all sound like disavowal, denunciation and excommunication. Well, we're both used to this kind of thing, and beyond shock. In agreeing to take the call and make a statement I was simply muddle-headed. But if I had been interviewed by an angel for the *Seraphim and Cherubim Weekly* I'd have said, as I actually did say to the crooked little slut, that you were one of our very best and most interesting writers. I would have added that I was greatly stimulated and entertained by your last novel, and that of course after three decades I understood perfectly well what you were saying about the writer's trade—how could I *not* understand, or miss suffering the same pains. Still our diagrams are different, and the briefest description of the differences would be that you seem to have accepted the Freudian explanation: A writer is motivated by his desire for fame, money and sexual opportunities. Whereas I have never taken this trinity of motives seriously. But this is an explanatory note and I don't intend to make a rabbinic occasion of it. Please accept my regrets and apologies, also my best wishes. I'm afraid there's nothing we can do about the journalists; we can only hope that they will die off as the deerflies do towards the end of August.

To Leon Botstein

January 18, 1984   Chicago

Dear Leon,

I fiddled all summer like one of the three grasshoppers in the song, but since I returned to Chicago I have been too busy paying rent. (You will recall that the fiddling grasshoppers never paid rent.) My fingertips have lost their calluses. Alexandra's greatly relieved that I have been too furiously busy to fiddle. A shack in the woods is being built for me where I will be able to play the Devil's Trill Sonata to the foxes and the bears.

We've rather given up on visits, they're too great a strain. My social talents, never great, have dried up. I am unable to meet groups, and although I don't dislike gossip, my custom is to file it away for future use. Alexandra feels as I do, and besides she needs graduate students in Ergodic Theory, and without Ergodic Theory she is apt to grow gloomy. So we decline your kind offer, albeit with profuse thanks. [. . .]

Yours quite cheerfully,

To James Salter

January 25, 1984   Chicago

Dear Jim,

That was an illuminating number of *Esquire*. Everybody was more or less as destiny had sketched him out, and people did what they are renowned for doing, e.g., Truman Capote stepping on Katharine Hepburn's feet. If he had bitten her he might have done some serious damage, but of all the harms he is capable of doing, this was certainly the least.

I thought you were perceptive about Eisenhower although you were interested in the military Eisenhower most of all, not in the President. How *weird* those people are in the White House showcase. Now there's a subject one of us should turn his mind to.

I didn't come to the party because I had two or three kinds of Asian flu at the same time. I'm sure I would have liked the party, although I am rarely happy to be the center of attention. Much better to be hidden in a corner looking at everything through a jeweler's glass.

How is Karyl [Roosevelt], and did she get the job I recommended her for? The lady who telephoned from Long Island wanted to make sure that she would be discreet. A confidential secretary? A governess? A stand-in for the wife herself? Southampton has surely seen that kind of thing before. It seemed just the kind of luxury cruise Karyl would adore, on a yacht called the *F. Scott Fitzgerald* (updated, of course).

I think you should stand pat with Mike Strang and John Wix, and if Wix is not a good fellow to be involved with let's not involve ourselves. I am firmly convinced that we will all be able to retire to the Riviera when our Colorado land is sold. (Having read Robin Maugham's memoir of his uncle's last years, I am not attracted by the Riviera. I shouldn't like to die so far from a kosher butcher shop.)

Yours affectionately,

A special issue of Esquire, *"Fifty Who Made a Difference," had included Salter's essay on Eisenhower. In the mid-1970s Bellow, Salter and Walter Pozen had purchased eighty-one acres near Carbondale, Colorado, which they would sell at a loss twenty years later.*

To Karl Shapiro

February 7, 1984   Chicago

Dear Karl,

It *was* great, wasn't it? And you're absolutely right, we've always met heretofore in company (the Freifelds or others), and I was so delighted to have you and your friend all to myself at Les Nomades that I talked my head off. If I say that there is a particular sympathy between you and me I hope that doesn't put you off. I know what it is to go into recoil when affection rises. I should acknowledge also that I was (what the kids call) hyper that night, because I had been banging away day and night for five weeks at a troublesome story. I didn't know it but I was shortly to go down in flames. I am one of those nuts who will go to the zenith just prior to a collapse. But I am perfectly well now and have even sent you a copy of the story that caused the crash. You will see that it runs in the Valentine's Day issue and that I appear with Larry Flynt and other fun personalities.

I hope that you aren't neglecting your memoirs, the reading of which made me even more hyper. Give my best to your delightful lady friend.

Yours ever,

Neglected today, Karl Shapiro (1913–2000) was among the most highly regarded American poets of the Forties and Fifties. His major works include V-Letter and Other Poems, *which won the Pulizer Prize in 1945. In 1969 he shared the*

Bollingen Prize with John Berryman. Shapiro's "delightful lady friend," whom he would shortly marry, was the translator Sophie Wilkins. Her English version, with Eithne Wilkins and Ernest Kaiser, of Robert Musil's The Man Without Qualities *is among the great feats of modern translation. Bellow's long story "What Kind of Day Did You Have?" had just appeared in* Vanity Fair.

To Midge Decter

February 7, 1984   Chicago

Dear Midge:

Inquiries and complaints—mainly complaints—having been made about my participation in or sponsorship of your Special Issue of *Confrontations* ("Winners"), I read the offending number, which I had missed, and although the prize books you attacked seemed squalid enough, your own reviews were in such bad taste that it depressed me to be associated with them. I have for some time been struggling with the growing realization that a problem exists: About Nicaragua we can agree well enough but as soon as you begin to speak of culture you give me the willies. I was on the point of dropping from the Committee when Joseph Epstein last year read a paper in your symposium ascribing to me views I do not hold and pushing me in a direction I wouldn't dream of taking. It was uncomfortable to be misunderstood and misused in a meeting of which I was one of the sponsors and even more uncomfortable to see his speech reprinted in *Commentary*. But where there are politics there are bedfellows, and where there are bedfellows there are likely to be fleas, so I scratched my bites in silence. Your Special Issue, however, is different. I can't allow the editors of *Confrontations* to speak in my name, or with my tacit consent as board-member, about writers and literature. When there are enemies to be made I prefer to make them myself, on my own grounds and in my own language. *Le mauvais goût mène aux crimes* [*], said Stendhal, who was right of course but who didn't realize how many criminals history was about to turn loose.

I am resigning from the board and request that you remove my name from your announcements. Sorry.

Yours sincerely,

* French: Bad taste leads to crimes.

The Committee for the Free World's magazine was in fact Contentions, *not* Confrontations, *though Bellow may have deliberately gotten the name wrong. The essay "Winners" in their Special Issue had mocked a number of the recent recipients of various American book prizes.*

To Mario Vargas Llosa

February 20, 1984   Chicago, Ill.

Dear Mr. Vargas Llosa:

I write to invite you to join us in a meeting I am organizing under the auspices of the Olin Center [of the University of Chicago], to be held in Vermont from August 20th to August 25th, 1984. The participants, in addition to yourself, are to be Alexander Sinyavsky, Leszek Kołakowski, Heinrich Böll, V. S. Naipaul, A. K. Ramanujan, Ruth Prawer Jhabvala, Federico Fellini, Werner Dannhauser, Allan Bloom and myself.

My intention is to bring together a small group of serious writers to discuss our peculiar situation in the world today and to share with one another whatever wisdom and inspiration on the subject we may have. The politics of our century tend to crush imagination—to present us with spectacles and conditions which appear to make art irrelevant. At the same time, in a variety of ways, it is clear that our fragile enterprise remains one of the best hopes of humanity—if we can keep it alive. It is not that I hope to change very much by such a *rencontre* as I propose. But we might hearten one another and have a rare opportunity to reflect together.

The meeting is not intended to beget yet another protest against censorship or a complaint about the unartistic character of "bourgeois" life. Nor is it to be an exercise in flattery of art and the artist. Rather, it is intended to be the broadest kind of consideration of the writer's physical and spiritual dependence on political life and of his responsibility to it—as well as his superiority to it—and of the claims of his art over against it. Lack of clarity about the perennial tension between art and politics may have something to do with the excessive hopes and the overly exposed position of writers in contemporary regimes. The nineteenth century's great expectations for culture made possible the culture ministries of fascist and communist governments of the twentieth century.

I propose a five-day program with one three-hour session per day, tentatively treating the following themes:

Day 1: A philosophic discussion of the problematic relation of art to politics and morals, beginning from Rousseau's *Lettre à d'Alembert sur les spectacles* with its attack on Enlightenment views of the arts and its resuscitation of Plato's criticism of poetry. This would, in addition to its intrinsic merit, serve to take us out of the narrow confines of our time. The paper would be presented by Allan Bloom and commented upon by Leszek Kołakowski.

Day 2: Hitler and Stalin: Writers in the world of totalitarianism. It would be best if this were to be a discussion not only of persecution and the resistance to persecution, but also of writers' involvement with such regimes and especially of the forms art adopts under them. Does art seek only to preserve itself, or does it try to make changes, and what are the effects upon art of either choice? I am asking Alexander Sinyavsky to present the paper at this session and would like you to comment.

Day 3: Weak-Sister Democracy: Is it possible for the writer to be serious— serious as compared to his East European fellows—in soft, easygoing commercial societies? Is he inevitably self-indulgent or does his freedom from killing pressures give him special opportunities for development. I shall give the paper at this session, and ask Federico Fellini to comment on it.

On days two and three some special attention would be given to the writer's audiences in the three worlds.

Day 4: Political Themes: To what extent are political themes necessary to literature? Has the disappearance of the great political figure as the central actor diminished the scope of literature? I hope V. S. Naipaul will give the paper and Ruth Prawer Jhabvala the commentary.

Day 5: The distinction between the Aesthetic and the Moral: Is such a distinction real? Is it, as Nietzsche claims, a sign of decadence? What is the relation of an artist's moral commitment to his art? Heinrich Böll will be asked to deliver the paper and Werner Dannhauser will comment on it.

I would expect that the papers should last from thirty to fifty minutes and the comments from fifteen to twenty. Presumably, these are questions with which all of us have some familiarity. I reiterate that the outline is tentative and open to revision. It is hoped that a small volume would emerge from the proceedings to form a basis for public discussion.

I can offer you the small honorarium of two thousand dollars, in addition to travel and accommodations. Southern Vermont, where I have my summer home, is particularly beautiful at that time of year and would provide an appropriate setting for the individual meetings which would be one of the primary benefits of our gathering. I can assure you that you will be comfortably lodged and well fed.

In addition to the persons mentioned, there will be one or two more writers and a group of about a dozen serious students who would participate in our sessions.

I hope you can join us. It would be personally gratifying to me. Inasmuch as time is getting short, I would appreciate your response as quickly as possible.

Sincerely,

To Joan Ullman Schwartz

April 9, 1984   Chicago

Dear Joan,

I am whirling about at such a rate of speed that to write letters is out of the question, but your last communication was so intelligent and gentle that I am impelled to send a brief note, which will be very much to the point. Not long ago, I remembered what Alexander Pope had written to a lady named Arabella Fermor about "The Rape of the Lock." I looked it up, and there it was. Pope said: "The character of Belinda . . . resembles you in nothing but Beauty." He adds that all the passages in his poem are "fabulous," and that "the Human persons are as fictitious as the Airy ones"—here he refers to the Airy Sylphs by whom Belinda is surrounded. I feel extremely lucky to have found in a great master the total clarification of a diabolically complex problem.

I hope that everything is going well (or better), and that you are more happy than not in New York. On your next visit to Chicago let's have a friendly drink together.

All best,

Joan Schwartz, for many years Harold Rosenberg's mistress, had recognized herself as the original of Katrina Goliger, mistress to the Rosenberg-like Victor Wulpy in "What Kind of Day Did You Have?"

To Sophie Wilkins

April 18, 1984   Chicago

Dear Sophie,

I hope you won't mind my enclosing this note in the same envelope with the one I'm sending to Karl. Your letter did me a world of good, especially the utterance of these great words: *"Yasher Koach!"* [*] You might also have

* Hebrew: "Strength unto you!"

said, "*Khazak!*" [*]—God's first word to Joshua. I am afraid that the gossips have pounced upon Victor and Katrina [in "What Kind of Day Did You Have?"] and that I am besieged by the forces of recrimination and outrage. For this the appropriate Hebrew is "*Gam zeh ya'avor*"—"this too shall pass." But this has to be qualified by a sad piece of incontrovertible French wisdom: "*tout passe*" and also "*tout casse*" [**]. Prudential writes no kind of insurance against any of this, and what the Hebrew fails to tell you is that the ultimate form of "*ya'avor*" is kicking the bucket.

Well, never mind the buckets. That you and Karl feel like twins separated at birth and reunited forty years later is an observable phenomenon, and too marvelous to be envied. Thank God that such things happen.

All the best,

To Karl Shapiro

April 18, 1984   Chicago

Dear Karl,

How nice it was in the days of our youth when, if the fighting writer was decked, he naturally expected to be back on his feet in a matter of minutes, as well as ever, if not better. To age is to understand that the powers of total recovery are gone, are no longer anticipated (except by those who, having lost their marbles, no longer know what to anticipate). So, I am better, but I can't find it in me to assert that I am well and I have begun to think that exaltation is the only possible comeback. Your letter, and also Sophie's, heartened me more than I can say. In return—small compensation—I am asking Harper & Row to send you a copy of *Him with His Foot in His Mouth*. I think you may like the concluding story, "Cousins," written last summer under the trees in Vermont. [. . .]

Do you think we might organize the haters of Hugh Kenner into a club? Fifty years ago, with my friend Isaac Rosenfeld, I used to join clubs of this sort. I remember that we formed a Faerie Queene Club to which nobody could belong who had read *The Faerie Queene*. When I read the first canto I was put on probation, and when I read more I was expelled. But no one could ever dislodge me from a Hate Kenner Society. [. . .]

Yours affectionately,

* Hebrew: "Be strong!"
** French: "Everything passes . . . everything breaks."

To Zipporah Dunsky-Shnay

May 14, 1984   Chicago

Dear Mrs. Dunsky-Shnay,

I wish it were possible for me to accept your very kind invitation, but I am not returning in triumph and delivering speeches in Montreal. I am making a sentimental pilgrimage to old scenes. I shall be seeing elderly cousins and friends of my childhood. To accept an invitation from the Jewish Public Library might give offense to my hosts in Lachine, who have what people in Hollywood call "an exclusive." From 1918 to 1924 I was a child of Saint Dominique Street, and was sent to a basement *cheder* on Milton Street. I have good Jewish credentials in Montreal, which I am happy to acknowledge, but am not free to give lectures.

Sincerely yours,

To Barley Alison

May 25, 1984   Chicago

My dear Barley,

The considerable success of *HWHFM* should make you feel rather good about *Him*'s future in England. Of course one never knows. English book reviewing is even more desolate these days than our own, and professional book reviewers may not be ready to open their stony hearts to emanations of warmth from Chicago. Still, I'm rather inclined to think that they may welcome a change from cold-storage porridge and the awful porno material our two countries have been exporting to each other.

My efforts to get the book out and to please Harper & Row by doing promotional chores have tired me out. There seem to be galvanic batteries under my bed that make me twitch in the night, and although I am not yet like Evelyn Waugh's poor noodle in *The Ordeal of Gilbert Pinfold* who drugs himself with sleeping potions until he hears imaginary voices, I do need to go into dry dock in Vermont. (Alexandra, by the way, has been waiting for you to set the date for your eagerly anticipated descent from the skies.)

Harriet tells me that copies of the English edition are now available, and I should like to ask you to send books to the following: Mr. Andrew Nobile, Mrs. Hildegard Nicholas (wife of the master of Brasenose) and Mr. Rudi Lissau. You will undoubtedly have sent copies to Terry Kilmartin, Richard Mayne, and young Amis. I shan't ask you to send a book for me to Keith Botsford, because I know that you would not oblige me. So I shall have Harriet ship one from New York. But please, do give a copy to Michael and

Susan-Mary [Barley's brother and sister-in-law]. I don't remember now the name of the spirited gloomy gentleman we lunched with who gave me such burning, penetrating glances, and spoke with such taste, care and reticence that I could scarcely understand him. He needs a salutary and friendly shaking up. I liked him actually. Send *him* a copy, too.

Love and kisses from your old friend,

To Margaret Staats

August 6, 1984   W. Brattleboro

Not many opportunities, with a house full of guests, but I wanted to say a few necessary things: I have never been treated with such extraordinary consideration, such feminine generosity. And you are aware that I know how extraordinary you are—that I am one of the few who *can* know what your nature is. And you do need someone to know this, for it is something that demands to be known.

There's the phone, and I'm off. More to come.

Yours ever,

To Margaret Staats

September 16, 1984   Chicago

When you come right down to it, and I am down to it, forced to consider the prospect in detail, going abroad doesn't give me great happiness. In going there I am still dragging here behind me, six thousand miles of melted cheese strung out over the Atlantic. There are things urgently to be done and I'd be better off beginning, somehow, to make a frontal attack on the cheese itself. I have to promise all my friends to have a good time. Everybody's dream of a marvelous holiday pops up when the facts are stated. "Thou hast conquered, O *Holiday Magazine*." But one of my friends tells me, truly, that I am the solitary of solitaries, a combination of a glacier and a volcano, that I have perfected the power to be alone. Well, then, it doesn't matter where one goes. Still, I have powerful connections, known only to me, and to the connections. You are one of the principal ones, as you should know. It seems that I never have accepted my condition. The making of an artist; seven decades of work without being reconciled to the essential facts of my condition. Really, I am a wimp—of considerable distinction, but inarguably wimpy.

My greatest worry is that if I am found out my lady will have a nervous breakdown. I don't exaggerate. That is what most bothers me, I discover, and I owe the discovery to you. It was through you that I became able to pity rather than fight her. And the whole thing is a pity, a pity, a pity! Where a woman's warmest sympathies should be there is a gap, something extracted in the earliest years of life which now is not even felt, not recognized as absent.

Well, I'm not going to change anything now.

She wants us both to visit a shrink. That'll be great fun, you bet. The answer is yes. Of course. I'll go anywhere, do anything. I have a singular advantage in that I can use almost anything that happens. Do you suppose that that's what "Whatever is is right!" really meant?

1985

To Richard Lourie

January 12, 1985   Chicago

Dear Mr. Lourie,

Writers are dilatory, you say so yourself in your novel [*First Loyalty*], so I can hope to be forgiven for being so slow.

I have just read your excellent mixture of thrills and exotic facts about our great enemy the USSR and about the émigrés of the eastern seaboard and I found it vigorous, fresh, sassy, and stirring. It's not for me, a common reader, to say how sound your scientific facts are. I am comfortable and safe with them and don't care whether they are accurate or whether the NYPD will fault you for your portrait of Solly the Detective—these are mere questions of expertise. I was interested in your millenarian or apocalyptic dialogues because they were probably perfectly characteristic and it didn't at all concern me to examine them as historical theses. I didn't care, and neither will other uncaptious readers, to apply a stern test to your account of the present state of civilization. You are located somewhere between James Bond and Heidegger, and the Bond elements, thank God, prevail. [. . .]

Some of the teachings of Master [Andrei] Sinyavsky, against realism and so forth, have been commendably absorbed. It's a lively book and gave me a most enjoyable evening.

All best,

To Margaret Mills

February 21, 1985 Chicago

Dear Ms. Mills,

I must ask you to excuse me from this chore. Singer and I are not the best of friends and while I do not grudge him this award, or any other, my dissimulation apparatus is not strong enough to satisfy your request.

Sincerely yours,

Margaret Mills had requested that Bellow write a short citation endorsing The Penitent *by Isaac Bashevis Singer for the Howells Medal of the American Academy and Institute of Arts and Letters.*

To Robert Hivnor

October 15, 1985 Chicago

Dear Bob,

Months later I come across your note about Mary Manheim and the letter from Katie Carver. I never knew Mary at all well. I did know her psychoanalyst and visited him on the Cape at a time when she (Mary) was being analyzed in his tool-shed. Houseguests were under strict orders to keep out of sight lest we frighten her. Professional ethics did not, however, prevent him from passing on gossip oddments. To this day I've never told a soul what Mary was up to, and even now I don't name the analyst, although he has probably gone to his reward, and might even now be talking his head off in God's tool-shed.

Wish he had been Katie Carver's analyst—a much juicier patient. I'm sorry for them both, poor girls. It's been ten years now since Katie excommunicated me. She used to keep a lightweight typewriter for me in London when she worked for Oxford Press on Dover Street, but I offended her after John Berryman's death by speaking of him while she and I were having a beer, and she said, "How dare you speak of John in a place like this?" As John's death was hastened by alcoholism I didn't see that there was anything improper in reminiscing in the presence of so many bottles. But Katie said in a trembling voice, "Take your typewriter away and never come to see me again." This guarantees that she will not be among my deathbed visitors, and is as close to an insurance policy as I can hope to get.

I can't sign this because my secretary is taking it from [my] dictation [onto a Dictaphone] and I am going to Dublin day after tomorrow.

Janis will verify that I closed with affection and good wishes.

To Teddy Kollek

December 6, 1985   Chicago

Dear Teddy,

It was a real and earnest flu, involving the head and the gastric regions and exorbitant thermometer readings. [. . .]

The World Jewish Congress has invited me to Jerusalem, and I shall be showing myself publicly at a ceremony about which you undoubtedly know all there is to know. I expect to see you on about the 26th of January under, I hope, mild skies. Would you let me give you lunch at the Hyatt Hotel, with perhaps a little tour to see the latest improvements you have made? We can discuss future plans then.

Yours most affectionately,

1986

To the Norwegian Nobel Committee

January 8, 1986   Chicago

I am entering Mayor Teddy Kollek of Jerusalem as a candidate for the next Nobel Peace Prize, confident that he will be seriously considered. The reasons for my confidence in this nomination are self-evident. Mayor Kollek is a very special sort of politician. In Jerusalem he is recognized by all parties, elsewhere in the Middle East waging a furious war, as the embodiment of impartial good will. Arabs in the Old City, Muslims everywhere, are aware that their holy places are respected and protected; Jews, both religious and secular, Christians of all denominations—Catholics, Protestants, Greeks, Armenians, Copts—share the city without conflict. No one is deprived of justice in Jerusalem. Offenses are impartially punished. Old feuds, factional outbursts of violence, are kept under conscientious control. Not another capital in the Middle East can compare with Jerusalem in this respect. Kollek is recognized by traditional enemies as a man who is firm and fair, morally imaginative and humane, whose administration has set an example, has made it possible for antagonists to live together in a peaceful and beautiful city. For contrast, one has only to look at Cairo and its rioters, at turbulent and tragic Beirut bombed and burned by Muslim and Christian armies. Kollek is a statesman who believes that Middle Eastern differences can ultimately be reconciled and has indeed given the region, and the world as well, a practical demonstration that such a belief is not Utopian.

To Edward Burlingame

February 4, 1986   Chicago

Dear Ed,

It's good of you to offer to fly to Chicago. I don't think such a trip would make much difference. Several times I came to discuss *Him with His Foot in His Mouth* with you, and each time I was made to feel that I was entreating Harper & Row to do right by me. It seems that all my suggestions and requests were referred to your marketing people, who simply rejected them. Not once did you do what I asked. I couldn't help feeling that I had placed myself in a humiliating position and I could only conclude that in your view I had written my books for nobody but your marketing experts.

To put the matter at its simplest, I don't care to submit myself to such treatment again.

Yours without rancor,

Following the departure of Harvey Ginsberg in 1980, Burlingame had become Bellow's editor at Harper & Row.

To Karl Shapiro

February 18, 1986   Chicago

Dear Karl,

Mailer mostly wanted a huge media event—that's what he calls living—and I'm sure that we dosed him up for months to come. It boggled my mind to see how greedy the radicals were for excitement "radical-style." I'm speaking of big-time subversives like Ginsberg, Nadine Gordimer, Grace Paley, Doctorow and other representatives of affluent revolution. There was an organization in Montreal when I was a small kid called The Consumer's League, headed by Mrs. Saunders, a cabinet-maker's wife. And when she went out in her corsets to picket the kosher butcher shop she might have been Grace Paley's mother. The comparison will allow you to imagine the political level of PEN. [Günter] Grass listened to nothing that was said by others, and the very idea of reading an American book was inadmissible. I told him privately that if he had skimmed *The Dean's December* he wouldn't have talked such balls about the South Bronx, but even the suggestion that he read one of my books made his mouth drop. I never cared for misanthropy, but I'm being coerced into it.

In your kindness you say, "Be well." But it's not exactly in my power to take your advice and good wishes. After eleven years of marriage and at the age of seventy I find myself evicted on the basis of grievances largely imaginary. But any American has the special gift of making a fresh start in life, so I am girding myself to meet yet one more challenge.

The scene of this unusual effort is Apt. 11E, 5825 S. Dorchester, Chicago, Illinois, 60637, telephone (312) 684-0758. A new group of lawyers is gnawing at my foundations. This brings to mind T. S. Eliot and one of the most hateful poems of this century ("Burbank"). Why send mysterious disturbing communications? Better to state the facts simply.

Yours (both of you) most affectionately,

Bellow refers here to an acrimonious meeting of PEN International in New York at which, attacked by Günter Grass, he had counterattacked by saying, "No intelligent writer is devoid of political feelings. On the other hand, one must not get megalomaniacal notions of the powers of writers." The president of the PEN American Center and host of the event was Norman Mailer. In his anti-Semitic poem "Burbank with a Baedeker: Bleistein with a Cigar," T. S. Eliot wrote: "The rats are underneath the piles, / The jew is underneath the lot. / Money in furs," etc.

To Barley Alison

February 27, 1986 Chicago

Dear Barley,

As you may have read in the papers, I shall be coming over to give a talk at PEN [in London]. I am not altogether on fire with eagerness to travel, but in view of the lamentable changes in my life, it may be constructive to go abroad. It won't cure heartache but it will probably divert me.

My last dinner at The Hungry Horse was so abominable that I shall presume on an old friendship to suggest a small dinner at Harley Gardens. *If* you are up to it, it would be wonderfully agreeable to see Martin Amis and his wife, and one or two other old friends—perhaps Mel Lasky. I'm very fond of him, and haven't seen him in a dog's age. After the guests have gone, you and I can have a chat about Alexandra. Like one of the more forbidding tales in Herodotus, that will be—the one in which the severed head of the defeated prince is plunged into a tub of blood by the barbarian who has killed him. A little will go a long way. I don't want to go back to the Capitol Hotel to be rigid with hateful insomnia all night.

Please don't plan any office parties for me. I am in no mood to face your personnel—all those pretty girls whose reward is to gaze upon celebrities.

I shall be bringing a considerable chunk of manuscript. I view this as a consoling piece of information.

With love from your devoted old friend,

To Philip Roth

February 27, 1986   Chicago

Dear Philip,

This bulletin will inform you that I am arriving on March 20th, and putting up at the Capitol Hotel on Basil Street. I think Harriet Wasserman has accepted a dinner invitation from Heath and Co. (my agent in London, Mark Hamilton) for the 21st. I give my PEN *spiel* on the 22nd, and I should by rights be free for dinner on that evening. Or the next, or the next. I need this trip like a hole in the head, but among the many holes already disfiguring it, one more will never be noticed. Please call me to set a date, I don't think I have your number anywhere—I'll try to get it from my son Adam.

I think I said in my earlier note that I was traveling alone.

All best,

To Rachel E. G. Schultz

March 16, 1986   Chicago

Dear Rache,

My punctilious papa, your great-grandfather B., always paid his bills before taking a trip. A version of the clean-underwear thing for ladies. Shock nobody in the Emergency Room. [. . .]

It was a lovely thing to do for your dad's birthday . . . pleasures that make it possible to go on in what is possibly *not* the best of worlds.

Love to you both,

Rachel E. G. Schultz, M. D. (born 1960), is a granddaughter of Saul Bellow's brother Samuel.

To Philip Roth

April 27, 1986   Chicago

Dear Philip:

Was much moved by your piece on Malamud in the *Times*. It showed me the man's life as I couldn't otherwise have seen it. You saw him at first as an insurance agent. I privately thought of him as a CPA. But I have a secret weakness for the hidden dimensions of agents and CPAs. I never could bring myself to judge by appearances. No faith in the categories (the social categories, I mean). Well, he did make something of the crumbs and gritty bits of impoverished Jewish lives. Then he suffered from not being able to do more. Maybe he couldn't have, but he looked forward to a fine old age in which the impossible became possible. Death took care of that wonderful aspiration. We can all count on it for that.

I want to thank you again for looking after me in London. As you realized, I was in the dumps. The Royal Athletic Club was just the place for me. The Shostakovich quartets did me a world of good. There's almost enough art to cover the deadly griefs with. Not quite, though. There are always gaps.

And also dinner with Edna [O'Brien], the Joan of Arc of Irish sex, armies of horny men behind her. That was lovely. Dick [Stern] says that Claire [Bloom] gives wonderful imitations of her. I hope to see those one day.

Yours ever,

Bernard Malamud had died on March 18.

To John Auerbach

April 28, 1986   Chicago

Dear John,

Not writing many letters because of the hysterical nature of my circumstances. Your letters to me, however, have great value, and I read them with loving attention and store the contents in a locked compartment of my head. So then: I have cancelled my trip to Paris, depending on the stability of your new plans. Since you're going to be in Massachusetts, there will be a room waiting for you in Vermont when you are ready to travel. I am now fairly well settled in new quarters, facing life anew for the thousandth time. Arrangements for the divorce have been agreed to by both parties. Alexandra has arranged compensation for the terrible injuries she received from me at the rate of a thousand dollars per fantasy trauma. Apparently, she suffered one hundred twenty permanently damaging abuses. So, I shall have to earn more money and that need will be an interesting test of my faculties. *I* think I still have all my marbles. So now we'll see about that. [Anthony] Kerrigan came to spend two days here with his new white beard. It makes him look like the Gloucester fisherman from the cod-liver-oil bottle, the smell of which made me hold my nose when my mother poured the oil down my throat. He seems well enough, although flat-broke—one of those flat-broke bohemian millionaire types. Until I published *Herzog*, I was one of those myself, rich enough for anything at all. He lives on Social Security checks and on his GI pension, and apparently supports his son, Elie, as well. They seem to sleep in dresser drawers and eat canned chile con carne. Being on the wagon, Tony has no whiskey bills. Also, he plans to visit Cuba soon, and his fantasy is that Castro will kill him there and solve all his (Tony's) financial worries by making a rich martyr of him. He's as charming as ever and very much like an old, old streetcar transfer, punched full of holes by the conductor but there's always room for one more punch. He earned five hundred bucks here, which will probably buy his ticket to Cuba. More might be done for Tony, but I don't know just what more would be. I do my best to find a few bucks for him here and there.

I am dictating this letter to Janis, one of my aims being to entertain all of us.

It will make me very happy to see you again.

Much love to you both,

Anthony Kerrigan (1919–1991) was noted for his translations of Borges, Neruda, Ortega y Gasset, Cela and others. In 1973 he won a National Book Award for his translation of Unamuno's Tragic Sense of Life in Men and Nations.

To Sigmund Koch

May 1, 1986   Chicago

Dear Professor Koch,

I have a letter from Stephen Toulmin informing me that you were close to Delmore Schwartz at NYU before you became a professional psychologist. A substantial recommendation. Stephen tells me that I would find you congenial, and that I wouldn't be squandering scarce time by talking to you. It's the interviewer himself that matters. Too often he heckles or badgers the poor mousy painter or poet, who then becomes obsessed with crazy plans to escape.

I spend my summers in Vermont, and if I succeed in finishing the small book I'm writing by September, I think I might be able to come to Boston for a day or two. But there is not the slightest chance that I will lay aside an incomplete manuscript to go and chat about aesthetics. The second or third week of September may be possible.

Sincerely yours,

To Barley Alison

July 18, 1986   West Brattleboro

Dear Barley,

Your idea about "Occasional Pieces" looks good on paper, sounds good when read aloud, but I wouldn't dream of molesting Martin Amis who has much more important things to do; it would be a dreadful imposition to ask him to fuss with my old papers. I can see that you don't believe for a single moment that I shall have a book ready to publish by the end of summer. I can always count on you to wave aside my solemnest assurances. *Plus ça change,* etc.

Your last letter is too thick to be used as a bookmark and not thick enough to be wedged under my rickety kitchen table. I am unable to use the advice it contains, and I can't come to greater harm by keeping my own counsel.

Really, Alexandra has done one of her most exquisite snowjobs on you. You are one of a regiment of friends whom she has entirely convinced that *I* wanted to divorce *her.* It all makes excellent sense: Two brothers die, I turn seventy, and then I put myself out on the street. Do you know this anecdote about the Duke of Wellington? He is approached by a gentleman who asks, "Sir, are you Mr. Jones?" Wellington answers, "Sir, if you can believe that, you can believe anything."

Now a brief and simple statement about Alexandra's mathematics: You can have your research assistants at Secker [and Warburg] check this out for you at Cambridge or Oxford. The power of even the ablest mathematicians begins to decline in the third decade. Alexandra is now in her fifties. She may enjoy trotting around to congresses where she is sure of a warm welcome because she is pretty and, thanks to me, well-heeled also. She can stand the young prodigies to lunch, but she has little to contribute to the proceedings. She told me with heavy emphasis not many months ago that for a long time she had not been able to obtain significant results in her researches, and that it was ALL MY FAULT.

There is much much more to be said, but I shan't say it.

Much love from your surviving friend,

To John Auerbach

July 29, 1986   West Brattleboro

Dear John,

One of the peculiarities of rural Vermont is that we have no modern touch telephone here, and all efforts to ring you in S'dot Yam last Sunday failed. Probably these rural operators didn't know that there is a country called Israel. I think this note will arrive before your departure on August 11th. I don't know whether Tony [Kerrigan] has mentioned that we saw something of each other last spring in Chicago, and that he was planning to be parachuted into Cuba, his birthplace. Havana for him, Lachine for me, Warsaw for you, N.Y. for Nola—I say nothing of Bucharest—we make quite a cosmopolitan little family, like the people on your kibbutz. (I re-read two of your stories last week, one of them, "The Witch," a marvelous thing; we must try again to place it.) Finally (I am dictating rapidly), I came across a letter from Ken Moore requesting your address, and I saw no harm in giving it to him, although he and Tony are not on good terms. So he will write to S'dot Yam and you will be in Newton, Mass.

Lots of luck, and love to you both,

To Leon Botstein

September 24, 1986   Chicago

Dear Leon,

Your fiddle is safe in a cupboard in West Brattleboro, Vermont. Had your letter been sent a week earlier I would have brought the instrument to Chicago. Since my house is not far from Marlboro College, it might be brought there if your friend is in a position to come by and claim it. I know of no way to ship it, but the man who takes care of the place when I'm gone might be able to bring it to Bennington or to Greenfield, Mass. or Brattleboro. I was glad to have a violin to play with, but I couldn't really do it justice, so I shut it in the case with reluctance and haven't gone near it for a year or so.

I had intended sending you a note about William Hunt whom I highly and strongly recommend as a poet and teacher, and also as a person. I used to see him often in Chicago, and I still see him as frequently as I can because he is such an illuminating conversationalist that for days after talking to him

I feel elated. He tells me that he has asked you for employment. You've probably made your appointments [at Bard] for the coming year, but if you do have a vacancy you couldn't fill it with a better man.

All best,

To Bobby Markels

November 4, 1986   Chicago

Dear Bobby,

Everything seems to be looking up for you. I thought it could, I thought it would, so I am pleased for your sake. Now that you've got your rose-colored glasses back on your nose I can tell you that I lost two brothers last year, all the brothers I had, and that my wife decided to divorce me and that I am now seventy-one years of age, and have some afflictions that go with high seniority. Putting together all these events, or disasters, you may better understand why it miffed me to receive from you so many self-engrossed communications. It's not altogether bad to be self-engrossed, but it is difficult to receive heaps of requests for encouragement, promotion and what-not-else. Not that I grudge you such things, but to sit down with pieces of paper before a typewriter and pound out letters on request or demand is not always appealing to injured or troubled parties. I found out when the Nobel Prize came my way that I was henceforth to be considered an elder statesman, and a functionary doing good to younger people whose bolt had not yet been shot. If you ever visit my office you will see loads of books to be read, loads of letters to be answered, loads of angels who have no space to fly in and multitudes of inflamed *nudniks* [*] whose mothers told them they were angels, and whose English profs told them that I was a do-gooder: "Send him manuscripts, send him 2,481,526 letters of mounting hysteria demanding replies and ending in vituperations and threats." Well, to hell with all that. I continue to open letters from people I know or like or love, but it does cross my mind from time to time that although they may like or love me still, they haven't said so in ten or fifteen years and either their feelings have dried out or their manners have gone to hell. If you hadn't sent me two nice letters in recent months I wouldn't even be explaining myself. This is a *quid pro quo*. You stopped shaking my tree and you got one peach *gratis*.

Yours affectionately,

* Yiddish: pests, bothersome people

In Memory of Bernard Malamud

(Delivered in Bellow's absence by Howard Nemerov
at the annual luncheon of the American Academy and
Institute of Arts and Letters, New York, December 5, 1986)

Some thirty-five years ago I gave a talk in Oregon, and Bernard and Ann Malamud came down from Corvallis, where he was teaching, to hear me. I don't remember what I said—from time to time one has to talk—but I do remember our meeting. I was struck by his expressive eyes. I didn't of course know what it was that they were expressing. I couldn't know that until, in the course of years, I had read his novels and stories.

Inland Oregon seemed an odd place for a man from New York, and I can recall thinking that it did Corvallis great credit to have imported such an exotic. He was not an exotic to me. We were cats of the same breed. The sons of Eastern European immigrant Jews, we had gone early into the streets of our respective cities, were Americanized by schools, newspapers, subways, streetcars, sandlots. Melting Pot children, we had assumed the American program to be the real thing: no barriers to the freest and fullest American choices. Of course we understood that it was no simple civics-course matter. We knew too much about the slums, we had assimilated too much dark history in our mothers' kitchens to be radiant optimists. Our prospects were sufficiently bright if we set out to become shopkeepers, druggists, accountants, lawyers. Even doctors, if we were able to vault over the quota system. There were, to be sure, higher ambitions. There were Jewish philosophers like Morris R. Cohen, scholars like [Harry] Wolfson at Harvard. At a more heady level there were [Bernard] Berenson types who entered the cosmopolitan art world and associated as equals, or near-equals, with Brahmins and English aristocrats. But if you had no social ambitions of this kind, and no special desire to be rich, to shuffle off emigrant vulgarity and live in an Italian villa, if you set out instead to find a small place for yourself as a writer, you were looking for trouble in uncharted waters, you were asking for it. Of course it was admiration, it was love that drew us to the dazzling company of the great masters, all of them belonging to the Protestant Majority—some of them explicitly anti-Semitic. You had only to think of Henry Adams, or to remember certain pages in Henry James's *The American Scene,* the anguish of his recoil from East Side Jews. But one could not submit to control by such prejudices. My own view was that in religion the Christians had lived with us, had lived in the Bible of the Jews, but when the Jews wished to live Western history with them they were refused. As if that history were not, by now, also ours. Have the Jews no place in (for instance) the German past?

Well, we were here, first-generation Americans, our language was English and a language is a spiritual mansion from which no one can evict us. Malamud in his novels and stories discovered a sort of communicative genius in the impoverished, harsh jargon of immigrant New York. He was a myth-maker, a fabulist, a writer of exquisite parables. The English novelist Anthony Burgess said of him that he "never forgets that he is an American Jew, and he is at his best when posing the situation of a Jew in urban American society." "A remarkably consistent writer," he goes on, "who has never produced a me-diocre novel . . . he is devoid of either conventional piety or sentimentality . . . always profoundly convincing." Let me add on my own behalf that the ac-cent of a hard-won and individual emotional truth is always heard in Malamud's words. He is a rich original of the first rank.

1987

To the Swedish Academy

March 6, 1987   Chicago

Dear Sirs,

I wish to place a nomination for the Nobel Prize in Literature. My candi-date is Robert Penn Warren, America's eldest and most distinguished poet. Mr. Warren had a poetic rebirth in the sixth and seventh decades of his life and has produced some of his most powerful work in old age. He is now in his early eighties and has never been more fertile. In mid-life he was prodi-giously successful (author of *All the King's Men* and other works of fiction). He is also widely known as a critic and scholar. He has written significant studies of Coleridge, Theodore Dreiser and many others. During the Sixties he wrote extensively about the civil-rights struggle. It is not necessary to make an elaborate case for his eligibility and I trust that the Academy will give serious consideration to this nomination.

Sincerely,

To Rachel E. G. Schultz

June 2, 1987   [W. Brattleboro]

Dear Rachel,

When I attended your mother's wedding thirty years ago I knew it was going to be a good thing, with excellent results, and I was dead right. You yourself are one of the best of those results and I send you loving congratulations on your graduation from medical school. It warms my cynical old heart to see that mortal choices sometimes achieve beautiful results. I wish I could come to Cincinnati but I am, to put it succinctly, too beat to travel. Once you finish your residency I will accept anesthetics from nobody but you.

Signed, your Great Uncle.

To Cynthia Ozick

July 19, 1987   West Brattleboro

Dear Cynthia,

At the Academy [of Arts and Letters] I was happy to see you, but then a wave of embarrassment struck me when I was reminded of my neglect and bad manners. You didn't mean to embarrass me when you reminded me that I owed you a letter (there had been a gap of two years). The embarrassment came from within, a check to my giddiness. It excited me to have so many wonderful contacts under the Academy's big top. Too many fast currents, too much turbulence, together with a terrible scratching at the heart—a sense that the pleasures of the day were hopeless, too boundless and wild to be enjoyed. There was such a crowd of dear people to see but I had unsettled accounts with all of them.

I *should* have written you a letter, it was too late to make the deaths of my brothers an excuse. Since they died, I wrote a book; why not a letter? A mysterious but truthful answer is that while I can gear myself up to do a novel, letters, real-life communications, are too much for me. I used to rattle them off easily enough; why is the challenge of writing to friends and acquaintances too much for me now? Because I have become such a solitary, and not in the Aristotelian sense: not a beast, not a god. Rather, a loner troubled by longings, incapable of finding a suitable language and despairing at the impossibility of composing messages in a playable key—as if I no longer understood the codes used by the estimable people who wanted to hear from me and would have so much to reply if only the impediments were taken away. By now I have only the cranky idiom of my books—the letters-in-general of an occult personality, a desperately odd somebody who has, as a last resort, invented a technique of self-representation.

You are the sort of person—and writer—to whom I can say such things, my kind of writer (without sclerosis in the matter of letters). I stop short of saying that you are humanly my sort. I have no grounds for that, I know you through your books, which I always read because they are written by the real thing. There aren't too many real things around. (A fact so well known that I would be tedious to elaborate on it.) You might have been one of the dazzling virtuosi, like [William] Gaddis. I might have done well in that line myself if I hadn't for one reason or another set my heart on being one of the real things. Life might have been easier in the literary concert-hall circuit. But Paganini wasn't Jewish.

You probably see what I am clumsily getting at. I've been wending my way toward your *Messiah* [*of Stockholm*], and I speak as an admirer, not a critic. About Bruno Schulz I feel very much as you do, and although we have never discussed the Jewish question (or any other), and we would be bound to disagree (as Jewish discussants invariably do), it is certain that we would, at any rate, find each other Jewish enough. But I was puzzled by your *Messiah*. I puzzled myself over it. I liked the Hans Christian Andersen charm of your poor earnest young man in a Scandinavian capital, who is quixotic, deluded, fanatical, who lives on a borrowed Jewishness, leads a hydroponic existence and tries so touchingly to design his own selfhood. But when he is challenged by reality, we see the worst of him—nine times nine devils (to go to the other Testament for a moment) rush into him, and in his last state, because he is not the one and only authentic Schulz-interpreter, he becomes a mere literary pro, that is, a non-entity. I read your book on the plane to Israel, and in Haifa gave my copy to A. B. Yehoshua. He wanted it, and I urged him to read it. So in writing you, I haven't got a text to refer to, and must trust my memory or the memory of my impressions. When I read it I was highly pleased. When I thought back on it I felt you might have depended too much on your executive powers, your virtuosity (I've often passed the same judgment on myself) and that you wanted more from your subject than it actually yielded. [. . .]

It's perfectly true that "Jewish Writers in America" (a repulsive category!) missed what should have been for them the central event of their time, the destruction of European Jewry. I can't say how our responsibility can be assessed. We (I speak of Jews now and not merely of writers) should have reckoned more fully, more deeply with it. Nobody in America seriously took this on and only a few Jews elsewhere (like Primo Levi) were able to comprehend it all. The Jews as a people reacted justly to it. So we have Israel, but in the matter of higher comprehension—well, the mental life of the century having been disfigured by the same forces of deformity that produced the Final Solution, there were no minds *fit* to comprehend. And intellectuals [. . .] are trained to expect and demand from art what intellect is unable to do. (Following the foolish conventions of high-mindedness.) All parties then are passing the buck and every honest conscience feels the disgrace of it.

I was too busy becoming a novelist to take note of what was happening in the Forties. I was involved with "literature" and given over to preoccupations with art, with language, with my struggle on the American scene, with claims for recognition of my talent or, like my pals of the *Partisan Review*, with modernism, Marxism, New Criticism, with Eliot, Yeats, Proust, etc.—with anything except the terrible events in Poland. Growing slowly aware of this unspeakable evasion I didn't even know how to begin to admit it into my inner life. Not a particle of this can be denied. And can I really say—can anyone say—what was to be done, how this "thing" *ought* to have been met? Since the late Forties I have been brooding about it and sometimes I imagine I *can* see something. But what such brooding may amount to is probably insignificant. I can't even begin to say what responsibility any of us may bear in such a matter, in a crime so vast that it brings all Being into Judgment. [. . .] "Metaphysical aid," as somebody says in *Macbeth* (God forgive the mind for borrowing from such a source in this connection), would be more like it than "responsibility"; intercession from the spiritual world, assuming that there is anybody here capable of being moved by powers nobody nowadays takes seriously. Everybody is so "enlightened." By ridding myself of a certain amount of enlightenment I can at least have thoughts of this nature. I entertain them at night while rational censorship is sleeping. Revelation is, after all, at the heart of Jewish understanding, and revelation is something you can't send away for. You can't be ordered to procure it. [. . .]

Some paragraphs back I said that you didn't seem to be getting what you really wanted from your *Messiah* novel. I can't think that I would offend you by speaking as I speak to myself. I have often rushed into the writing of a book and after thirty or forty pages, just after taking off, I felt that I had made a crazy jump, that I had yielded to a mad convulsion, and that from this convulsion of madness, absolutely uncalled-for and self-generated, I might never recover. At the start the fast take-off seemed such a wonderful and thrilling exploit. I believed in it still. But could I bring it off, would I land safely or fall into the ocean? I experienced the same anxiety in the middle of your novel (the Mediterranean below). You would be fully justified in calling this a projection and turning it against me. Anyway, I did have the sensation of turbulence, a dangerous air-storm. I felt you were brilliant and brave at the controls. [. . .]

With best wishes,

To Karl Shapiro

July 31, 1987   West Brattleboro

Dear Karl,

Every time I publish a novel it turns out that a test has been administered— no, two tests; in one I am graded by reviewers, while the other is mine, unintentionally given to my fellow Americans. Half of these are totally illiterate, thirty percent more are functionally illiterate, and the rest, while intellectually capable are tremendously unwilling to go along. Democrat that I am, I write for everybody but as you well know not everybody gives a damn. Grateful for what I can get, I absolve one and all. We weren't brought up, you and I, to feel superior. The idea of giving the entire USA a Rorschach test in the arts is horrifying. Still, the fatal facts (for example, that our souls are gasping for oxygen) can't be covered up. Sometimes I see in the entire species a single animal as represented in the paintings of the Northwest Coast Indians. All the parts of the creature—eyes, teeth, belly, tail—have been separated and are arranged in the foreground so that teeth or ears or claws are hypertrophied whereas other important parts are diminutive. Well, everything is *there*, but the parts for whose development I pray are atrophied. One day they will be restored and judgment will occupy its rightful place.

Meantime my hopes are in people—like you and Sophie—who, like me, have devoted their lives to novels, poems, music, painting, religion and philosophy. To most Americans we are respected freaks entitled, like everybody else, to live. They don't have to eliminate curbstones for us, as for the blind. Like spastics whose brains outpace computers, or like those clairvoyants to whom the cops turn to find missing bodies when all police methods are exhausted, we have our place. On TV recently I saw a science prodigy with a strange disease, lecturing an audience of astrophysicists through an interpreter trained to understand him. He used a language only two could speak, and long formulas were written on the blackboard. This has *got* to mean something to you.

But there is nothing to complain about. I am lucky to find a few readers who actually approve. To have even a *minyan* [*] is ecstasy. (Do I catch myself saying, after so many decades of devotion to Anglo-American literature, that the Happy Few resemble the Jews!)

What I intended when I sat down to write was to thank you and Sophie for your assurance that I was indeed on track, doing what I thought I was doing and even directing my attention to things that had escaped me in my frenzy. And then enclosing the poem, which I re-read several times a week, was magnificently symbolic, an act of certification from another initiate; going me one (or more) better. This is a poem Catullus might have written if he had reached your age—"Goodbye to all that." Liberation ladies may be incensed when they read you, but the poem contains history, and history, as Lincoln assured us, we can't escape.

My friend Janis and I will be leaving Vermont toward the end of September, but we can and will entertain you almost as splendidly in Chicago.

Yours ever,

The enclosed poem was, in all likelihood, Shapiro's "Adult Bookstore."

To John Auerbach

August 5, 1987   W. Brattleboro

Dear John,

You haven't heard from me because of my mad obstinacy. I have insisted on reaching you by telephone and after some fifty attempts Janis and I were once or twice rewarded with a ring. There was, however, no answer at your end. So I am writing to say that we're well, thriving, recovering from heavy and fatiguing burdens—convalescing. I begin to have hopes of recovery and one of these days you will hear that I have gone back to my desk. [. . .]

To tell the truth I have felt somewhat waterlogged and half-sunken in the green heat of New England (an unusually stifling summer), and while I have a lively desire to do things I have very little power to act, so I am both agitated and torpid. I have to tell you that I was, however, moved to write a fairly severe letter to Tony [Kerrigan]. He sent a communication to *Commentary* to explain how it was that Borges had been passed over by the Swedish Academy and why it was that so many lesser writers had gotten the prize. I

* Hebrew: the quorum of ten men required for public prayer three times daily

did not feel that Yeats, Eliot, Samuel Beckett, Camus, Churchill, etc. were so very far beneath Borges and I was taken by surprise that Kerrigan should say publicly what I have always thought him to think privately. I went after him for that and if he ever does reply to my letter he will probably take refuge in the usual eccentricities. He may or may not mention this to you, and I think it best to speak about it now. I don't really care whether I stand high or low in Tony's hierarchy but I think that my friends or friendly acquaintances should not surprise me in print with their negative opinions. Only yesterday I recommended Tony to the National Endowment for the Humanities for a translator's grant saying that there was no better interpreter of Borges in English. I mention this to assure you that I am not persecuting him.

Borges declared long ago that contemporary writers ought not to do novels and as Tony is faithful to the master I have a rabbinical problem with him. Every man to his own orthodoxy. Even if I say so myself, *More Die of Heartbreak* is a better read than the Borges story on Raimondo Llull, submitted by Tony with his application for the National Endowment for the Humanities, with its mystical diagrams from the Middle Ages. But I know that a falling out between two of your friends makes you uncomfortable, so I want to tell you simply that I wasn't falling out but only acting from self-respect, drawing the line with Tony. Nor do I intend to quarrel with [A.B.] Yehoshua, for whom I have a genuine liking (with only minimal reservations). I intend to write him a conciliatory epistle this very day.

The flowers around the house come and go and only Janis holds her ground, flower-like but not subject to blossoming and decay like the vegetable kingdom.

Affectionate greetings to Nola.

With much love,

To Wright Morris

August 10, 1987   West Brattleboro

Dear Wright,

I hope you will send me a copy of *The Origin of Sadness* which you say is a meditation on our shared losses. We have had a long friendship and an unusual one, if you bear in mind a certain oddity in our two shapes, a permanent incongruity. I mention it because this time we got out of hailing distance entirely. *More Die of Heartbreak* is a funny book, or was meant to be. Your radar for laughter must have been pointed the wrong way. Your welcome and charming letter compliments me on restoring the word "soul"

Saul Bellow: Letters

to common usage and then you say that I confuse "ego-crack" (a Californian category) with heartbreak. Now it seems to me that people who will not use the word *soul* and are by now unaware that any such thing exists will surely experience a kind of inner suffocation. I have taken the liberty to describe this as heartbreak. Killing sorrow would be an acceptable alternative as in our old friend Chaucer: "Sorrow at hearte killeth full many a manne." With this double invocation of poetic license I send you a comradely embrace.

Nowadays overlooked, Wright Morris (1910–98) was the greatly admired author of The World in the Attic *(1949),* Man and Boy *(1951),* The Works of Love *(1952),* The Field of Vision *(1956),* Ceremony in Lone Tree *(1960) and* Plains Song *(1980). He twice won the National Book Award for Fiction. A native of Nebraska, where most of his novels are set, Morris lived for many years in Mill Valley, California.*

To Ann Malamud

August 30, 1987   West Brattleboro

Dear Ann:

Your note about *More [Die of Heartbreak]* was particularly pleasing because I have come, over the years, to value your opinion. It takes longer to see the wife of another writer clearly, that's the odd truth. It isn't easy to get a direct view of her, especially if you see her not oftener than twice a year. But you bowled me over when you identified Dick Rovere in *The Dean's December*. That was either clairvoyance or genius. I began to listen attentively. True readers are about as small in number as the Apostles. The road is rocky and getting rockier all the time, and all but a few have been bounced off the wagon. (You were lucky to have read only one review—the full picture is appalling.) I think I might have done more to make the meaning of the title clearer: People are now supposed to be dying of *external* causes. Their own souls are of no account, a cause of *nothing*. So human nature, gone underground to a greater depth than ever before, way below Plato's cave, thinks only about biochemistry and lives in total ignorance of itself. To me this naturally seemed a truly comic theme.

I like what you say about the old Jews. Still, I wonder sometimes whether America hasn't been too much for them.

Yours most affectionately,

To Martin Amis

Dear Martin,

I make plans and then have to cancel them, so the pain schedule is fairly steady but the anxiety schedule is always full to overflowing. My own health is none too good and I have a sister who is older and far sicker, in need of care. She is just out of the hospital and has to be looked after until late November when she goes to Florida. It would have made me miserable to have run off to London and its pleasures with only a nurse to look in on her twice weekly.

I'm glad to hear that you are finishing a novel. I desperately need something new to read. Returning from Vermont I found my office stacked with recent books, and when I sized them up I asked what might be in them that I couldn't do without—was there in those heaps a single page containing what is absolutely essential to expansion or survival? Long and bitter experience has jammed the answer into both ears, as definite as doom. Not an ounce of survival in any of *these*.

I already mentioned to two London interviewers that in the younger generation on either side of the Atlantic you stand out like the evening star. So they *will* think that you and I are in cahoots, ganging up on everybody else, conspiring to take the candy away from the other babies. But I am much too old for candy and oddly enough (for a writer of fiction) I have for some years now been saying exactly what I think (whenever I know what that is). The conspiratorial imagination is terrible lively hereabouts. Word has gone out that my friend Allan Bloom is nothing but one of my fictional creations and that I have put him over on the USA, successful book and all. So one does lay oneself open to accusations by being friendly and generous to me, and you *were* generous, when you agreed to do a BBC number. That at least I shall be sparing you by nursing sister Jane in Chicago. [. . .] I'm sorry that we shan't be eating a jolly dinner together. It's still possible that Janis and I might fly over in December, but if that doesn't work out we shall both entertain you handsomely in Vermont next summer.

Yours as ever,

1988

To Todd Grimson

January 27, 1988   Chicago

Dear Mr. Grimson:

This mill grinds slowly, but it does grind. Thank you for your letter of last August. I put it aside with a sense that you are nice not to ask me to do anything. I was then and am now somewhere on that wall to which people refer when they say—"driven up the wall."

I had not heard about George [Sarant]'s heart attack [though by now] old friends of his father's have told me about it. He and I have not been faithful correspondents, so will you tell him for me how very sorry I am? If he is as you say a Reichian or neo-Reichian he will have no use for such sentiments but I am an old friend of the family and remember him as a small boy and I must therefore be allowed to have the feelings of an old friend of the family.

It is hard to keep up with new books especially when you feel continually that time is running out and that one cannot afford to pick up a new novel enthusiastically. Three or four new books arrive daily, to say nothing of letters, magazines, booklets, brochures, appeals, cables and unsolicited manuscripts. I do try, however, to look into all the books. I read a few pages and if I am (the rare case) fascinated I sit down and read the whole thing through. When Oscar Wilde said he could resist anything except temptation he may have meant that he was seldom tempted. Substitute fascination for temptation and my own case is covered. [. . .]

Sincerely yours,

To John Auerbach

March 1, 1988   W. Brattleboro

Dear John,

Janis and I have come to Vermont for ten days and we are now sitting in the kitchen in winter sunshine. Smadar [Auerbach's daughter] and her husband have been very kind, informing us about your surgery which by all reports has been difficult and dangerous, and in our own way we have been going through the whole thing with you from afar—for all the good that may do. The only good we can do is to tell you from a distance of thousands of miles how dear you are to us and how much we want to see you.

I remember that Freud somewhere said that happiness begins when the pain stops, so that our gratifications may be described as one escape after another. If Janis and I are happy here it is as refugees from Chicago. In Vermont we can walk up and down the roads without fear of being overtaken by some drug addict, sex maniac or gunman. We not only walk, we also cross-country ski. Janis has taught me at my advanced age how to keep from falling down. And how once down to rise from my behind to my feet. I get some boyish enjoyment from this. I suppose that age is one of those conditions from which occasional remissions bring some pleasure. Maybe that's what second childhood really means. I have also brought some manuscripts out here, my most dependable opiate, as well as books by the dozen. I haven't yet learned that I can't expect to read them all, but I cling to them as pious Christians do their beads or clergymen their missals. But I do go out of doors and rinse my brains in God's icy air without knowing whether the tears in my eyes come from the cold wind or gratitude to my Creator. The children come: Daniel was here last weekend and Adam and his wife and baby will be here soon. No mail arrives from Chicago, it will all be waiting for us next Monday, stacks of letters and bills. I can't understand how so many insurance companies can have found their way into the list of my dependents.

Tony Kerrigan is spending the winter in Brooklyn with friends or *nafkes* [*] or both. We are on good terms and exchange letters now and then. I sometimes have the feeling that Tony is always suggesting changes to me, hopeful corrections of my character. If it's not too late to learn. I joke with you a bit out of helplessness. All that a friend can do is love you and these small jokes which are love's trimmings. We will try to telephone when you have returned to the kibbutz.

Meanwhile, Janis and I send our love to you and Nola.

Ever your friend,

To Rachel E. G. Schultz

March 11, 1988 Chicago

Dear Rachel,

Bad of me not to have answered your thoughtful and beautiful letter. You will understand though, with a slight allowance for poetic license, that like you I am often up in the night with the sick, both sick characters (fictional)

* Yiddish: whores

Saul Bellow: Letters

and my own ailing neurasthenic self. There are enough sufferers to keep us all busy day and night.

I was touched by what you said about my brother [Sam]—your grandfather—and interested in your observation about his awkwardness and discomfort with women, even with his own granddaughters. Your mother and I have often, since his death, talked about him and I think that my brother, in spite of his considerable charm, was never at ease even with members of his immediate family. In the world he made a great success, but his intimacies were all crippled. I am convinced that he was forever apologizing for his inadequacies. As an adolescent he had a very normal interest in girls, but he also felt menaced by them and took refuge in marital safety. You and your contemporaries would find it hard to grasp the degree of sexual terror that afflicted people of an older generation. It seems to me that my brother's terror took the form eventually of retreat. He shrank into himself and in effect turned himself over to his wife, who offered him a fortress of orthodoxy, in which she could persecute him to her heart's content. About business he was able to think comprehensively and clearly but he had little insight into the people who surrounded him and took him over. His is a case of a man so dominated by self-doubt and fear that he never learned to make any significant human judgments other than business judgments. I saw this, I knew the history of these weaknesses as intimately as only a sibling can, I pitied him for it, and I loved him without any expectation of a return. He forgave me even my numerous and preposterous marriages, by which he must in some way have felt threatened. But I didn't ask him for anything and I knew that he would never understand what I was up to. I learned to love both my brothers and my sister to the extent that they were lovable and even a bit beyond, and it made not the slightest difference to me that I couldn't even begin to talk to them. I had to forgo all communication except what long-standing family love going back to childhood made possible. But that was a great deal. Some four thousand years of Jewish history went into it—I don't mean Talmudic history or anything of that sort. I mean the history of Jewish feeling.

That you should have seen this moves me. A delightful development which I never anticipated: The things that couldn't be said to members of my generation can be said to nieces and great nieces and, here and there, to my own children.

Lots of love,

Your doting G.U.

To Philip Roth

March 15, 1988   Chicago

Dear Philip,

Now that I have decided not to attend Abba Eban's Brussels Conference (my sidekick would have been another friend of Israel, Mr. P. Klutznick of Water Tower Place), I can look forward to seeing you instead and perhaps hearing Claire reading from Virginia Woolf. If you like I will entertain you with an account of my residence at the old Woolf House in Rodmell, about fifteen years ago. I was there for some six weeks. I think the French word would have been *sequestré*. Nothing to compare with the horrors of the Demjanjuk trial. You must tell me about those. As for the little talk, I would like nothing better.

I read of your recent award [National Book Award for *The Counterlife*] with delight. There's so little in the newspapers these days to be pleased about. (I write this on March 15th, Primary Day in Chicago. I don't look forward to the results in the *Tribune* tomorrow morning.)

Yours ever,

Roth had attended the trial of John Demjanjuk, a Detroit autoworker extradited to Jerusalem to stand trial for crimes against humanity. Alleged to be the infamous "Ivan the Terrible" who tortured and murdered tens of thousands at Treblinka and Sobibor, he was in 1988 convicted and sentenced to death. (Ten years later Israel's Supreme Court reversed the verdict. Demjanjuk has subsequently been extradited to stand trial again on the same and additional charges in Germany, where his case continues.)

To John Auerbach

April 15, 1988   Chicago

Dear John,

Dizzy times for me—nobody but nobody gets a break, a reprieve. I can understand why Romantic poets loved rural life. The peasants timed themselves by the sun and had leisure to smell the flowers. In Beethoven's Pastoral Symphony Ludwig started with the fresh fields and then there was a tempest and when the tempest passed you heard the melody of a dear little cuckoo, a capitalist bird sitting in a nest it had not built. So after storms Romantics expected peace, but you and I know better than that and expect no relief after our daily storms. However, I continue to write. I hope you are writing too. I was happy to get a note in your own hand, so I expect you are still able to write stories. As much as possible I ignore health problems and the handicaps that come with age and consider them so many impediments to storytelling—I have just finished a long story called "A Theft." You will have a copy as soon as I can clean it up and impose on Janis to type it.

I don't quite understand what you meant by "moving to the States"— that, from my standpoint, would be the best thing in the world if it were feasible. I go on hearing from Tony, who telephones me for news of your progress and I tell him what I can, which is not much these days, since I hesitate to phone Smadar who will have other things on her mind now. But we are going to be in Philadelphia on the first of May and perhaps by then the baby will have been born. Janis and I are making our Vermont move early this year, at the beginning of May. As peaceful a summer of work as one can arrange in these terrible days of trouble. On the question of Israel I have kept my distance from most factions although I did sign a letter at Teddy Kollek's urging, with co-signers Isaiah Berlin and Isaac Stern. My memory may be suppressing "Boynstein" the conductor. [. . .]

I dictate this note to Janis and it contains love from us both,

To Cynthia Ozick

May 18, 1988   W. Brattleboro

Dear Cynthia,

When I looked around you were gone, and I was greatly disappointed. Our contacts make me think of a billiard game—one light touch and then we're again at opposite ends of the table. Has Providence decided that touches are better than extended contacts? Anyway, I was sad, but during dinner my spirits rose somewhat on your account because you didn't have to listen to the speeches. These got worse and worse with the rank and wealth of the speakers and by the time we got to the most eminent I was in some pain. He [Walter J. Annenberg] made Sartre's void feel like Times Square. Among the other speakers I make an exception for [Chaim] Potok, who gave a very good talk, and gave it in his own words. The others all spoke the synthetic tongue of the media, something far worse than Orwellian double-speak. Double-speak and double-think were, after all, political, whereas with Mr. Annenberg there was no visible reason, it was an *acte gratuit* in the Gide meaning of the term—mental or linguistic murders.

I think that I agreed with a nod when you spoke of the Academy Ceremony, but I have no intention of turning up this year. New York is a ten-hour round trip from Vermont and I can't face that. Not for the privilege of sitting next to John Updike.

It always does me good to see you, and I think it's time we meet face to face for a conversation. Perhaps you and your husband would like to take in a Marlboro concert. If so, we could give you dinner and a night's lodging.

This does not count as an answer to your beautiful letter. I used to be a free and easy correspondent. God knows I never suffered from writer's block, but as I grow older "the mail problem" has become serious. One could write a funny story on this subject, and I may do just that.

(I think the medals they gave us could be used to crack walnuts. Or to subdue *nudniks*. Only nowadays it would be an abuse of some kind.)

Now the hardest part of this letter—an appropriate close: I generally say "best wishes." In your case they really are *the* best,

In Philadelphia, Bellow and Ozick had been among the speakers at the centenary celebration of the Jewish Publication Society of America.

To Harold Brodkey

December 5, 1988   Chicago

Dear H.B.:

Late last summer I told Ann Malamud that I was going to write to you about your stories, which I was reading with pleasure. Now at the beginning of December I am ready to put down some of my impressions—not too long a time, for me. I guess I am slowing down—the gap between intention and performance is getting longer. To go immediately to the point: I see that we agree about human beings as they are represented in fiction, in modern literature. The models irritate or bore us, they are utterly used up; thin but usable for a century, they are coming apart now, a mass of floating threads. Speaking for myself (perhaps for you too) I find that what passes for human in most fiction is not merely inadequate but enraging as well, and in your stories I see a persistent following-up of intuitions that come too often to be passed over. Have I got it right? Take "Hofstedt" (p. 97): "The narrative will be colored like a map, according to the geography of my spirit . . . my lunges at and occasional capture of intelligence, that armored and fatal lizard." (Your note calls me an intelligent writer, but I do understand that intelligence belongs under the lining. Any sane tailor knows that.)

The things I like best have a kind of excited, even passionate vitality breaking out like a profuse nosebleed, a flow of blood, a hemorrhage, as in "Verona: A Young Woman Speaks"—the showpiece child of vain ambitious parents going clean out of herself. It takes the Swiss Alps with their snow to cool her. Or does the snow only make the kid more ecstatic? Each moment is more beautiful than the one before, but she does fall asleep. "This was happiness then."

In the longer stories this is less immediate but then the purpose of all the extended meanders is exploration, leading to the discovery (or surprise and capture) of intuitions. About love. About being.

That's how I interpret "Almost Classical" in your title.

With thanks and best wishes,

Brodkey's book was Stories in an Almost Classical Mode.

1989

To Michael Alison

June 12, 1989   W. Brattleboro

Dear Michael,

Since Barley's death I have been rethinking everything I knew about her. One never does that for the living, somehow; you and Susan-Mary must be going through this too and even more painfully. Barley was physically fragile but she was also proportionately durable in spirit. She had drawn her own line through existence and followed it with extraordinary determination and persistence. What she had ruled out and could not allow herself to wish for was not allowed to interfere or to weaken her purpose. But her generosity was such that she wanted others to have what she had been obliged to relinquish.

I couldn't always understand her reasoning but I know from her bearing that she was receiving signals inaudible to me—probably unintelligible to me, as well. She was a dear and devoted friend and one of the most generous persons I ever knew.

I am not much good at condolences, but I was her affectionate and admiring friend and shall continue to think of her and to feel for her as I have thought and felt for some forty years.

Yours ever,

To Cynthia Ozick

June 15, 1989   W. Brattleboro

Dear Cynthia,

No need for you to make a case, you are entirely in the right about *Tikkun* and the Columbia/PLO/Israeli left. I'd attend your Writers' and Artists' Fair if I were entirely free, and although you will not be terribly interested in the crowded and presidential character of my schedule I can't resist reeling off a sequence of dates representing a) gainful occasions, b) collegial and personal obligations and c) vanity and other mortal frailties. As you know, I shan't be in Chicago next autumn. I agreed without proper forethought to teach at Boston University. I wish I hadn't boxed myself in. I have to be in New York November 9th, back in Boston to teach a class November 10th. I fly to Washington November 30th to honor Malamud's memory. Boston, again, the very next day. Then Tulsa, Oklahoma December 9th. Each of these occasions requires a round trip, your December 3rd conference included. Let me say nevertheless that I am going to try to come. That is, I will come if I can prepare a suitable statement. Being airborne is sometimes illuminating. Flying can stir me up. [. . .]

As for the PEN, my contempt for it is such that I now throw its membership bills into the fireplace. Besides, it gives me something less than pleasure to be listed with the Styrons, Vonneguts, Mailers, to say nothing of the academic specialists, public relations people and promoters whose names fill the membership list. And when you say that I ought to be left in peace to write more sentences I can make the same wish for you. The media experts etc. have it all over us in the field of politics and I am often tempted to take the Nabokov Literature-Only line. Perhaps it was easier for him. The situation of a Russian in exile (a Christian, after all) can't approach that of a Jew with its special complications and singular horrors. The woman who wrote that splendid essay on Primo Levi in your last collection can't possibly stand apart on Literature-Only grounds and keep her self-respect. The only non-fiction book I ever published, and it's not likely to have a successor, was the Jerusalem one. I felt it had to be done, but then it was something I could do on my own terms without conferences, luncheons, speeches and appeals to the press to publicize my position. I can't believe that either alternative (Politics, No Politics) answers the one truly significant question. Because we are Jews we are *scandalized,* and being scandalized sets us apart—i.e. we have to be isolated by "everybody."

I'd like to say since I've mentioned your terrific collection of essays that I thought you were too nice to George Steiner who is, of all pains in the ass, the most unbearable because of his high polish and his snobbery. He is not a good existentialist—Nietzschean-Heideggerian—because the Nietzscheans and Heideggerians made no claims for the Europe that is (or was in the Nineteenth Century) and based all their hopes on a Europe that hadn't yet appeared. They assumed that the old civilization was gone forever and they would not have cared for all this strutting of people dressed in what tatters they could find of the glorious old fabric. The Last Man in *Zarathustra* is not mentioned as an American. I kept thinking of Steiner's opportunistic Old Europe game while I was recently reading Denis Donoghue's piece on [Paul] de Man in *The New York Review of Each Other's Books*. Since the linguistics business interests you, perhaps you too read his back-and-forth article ("Nazism was bad of course and it was wicked of de Man to hate Jews, but let us mitigate our judgment by thinking of the unhappy psychological constitution of the man, etc."). De Man, like his master Heidegger (to whom he was never very faithful), believed that there was nothing further to be said or done for this civilization of ours and that whatever hastened its disintegration was historically justified. [. . .] In doing so, de Man won the admiration of hundreds of intellectuals to whom the decline of the West is just another game.

I never do write you a short letter, do I? Miss M. Kakutani of the *New York Times* said a few weeks ago that I am a garrulous writer. Maybe she meant fluent. Of course no man can know at what point he may have turned into a Polonius.

Yours ever,

To Sophie Wilkins

August 15, 1989   W. Brattleboro

Dear Sophie:

It isn't hard nowadays to count one's blessings, they're well under the number of toes and fingers. It's the scope of those blessings I do enjoy that I'm most gratefully aware of. In this day and age, bringing out a small book or two and hearing from you and from Karl about the one and the other makes me singularly lucky. I'm hardly conscious of anything resembling a "literary life," but as a writer I'm still well above the poverty line. How "my readers" keep their purity and sanity is a profound mystery, given what they

have to absorb in the way of literary journalism and the general *Schlumperei* [*]
of "educated" opinion. To a large sector of that opinion, the heavily ide-
ologized one, I am something of an ogre-reactionary. Besides I am one of the
old-guy heavies who have to be kept in their place. No question but that Karl
too has to put up with this being kept in place. No exceptions are made.

Members of our own dwindling generation who will see the picture as
only those can who have lived as we have—graduates of the same street-
academies, veterans of the same wars, released from the same errors and
prejudices, breathers of the vanishing atmospheres of the Thirties, Forties,
Fifties—are our best judges. When I read, or rather study, one of your letters
I remember the conversation of old friends, the tone of those better days and
the style of thinking and comment of Greenwich Village gatherings. Friends
now dead also come back to enlighten and comfort me and to remind me
that we—the living remnant—are alone now, or all but. The survivors for
the most part are silenter and silenter, reluctant, some of them, to say a single
word. Of those still here a few have become dim, or too cranky to wish to
make themselves intelligible. So you seem to me extraordinarily magnani-
mous. I send you a mere booklet and you answer with a personal letter, a
really valuable communication in the old style. I sometimes think I write
books in lieu of letters and that real letters have more kindness in them,
addressed as they are to one friend. In pleasing you and Karl I have my reward. When you tell me I am more or less on track.

Yours as ever,

To Cynthia Ozick

August 29, 1989   W. Brattleboro

Dear Cynthia:

I can write a small book more easily than a letter—why is that? This is not
so much a question as a mystery, and an idiotic mystery at that. When I am
writing fiction I am *geared up* or fully mobilized (see how I call on mechanical or military figures of speech). I seem to have some difficulty about being
myself, unless it's the fiction-writer that's the real thing. But it's not (thank
God!) an identity problem. The real source of both letters and stories can be
located. Somewhere Kierkegaard has written about the human power to relate everything to everything else. For Jews, it's the *neshama* [**]. Still I find

* German: sloppiness
** Hebrew: soul

letter-writing difficult, a fault which is not trivial, an unpleasant fault. But then what you said about *The Bellarosa Connection* gave me more pleasure than I could handle, and your letter was in every respect so rich and generous that it turned me into a reader, an admiring reader.

And now, as a preface to business, I have something to relate to you: My young friend Martin Amis, whom I love and admire, came to see me last week. He was brought here from Cape Cod by a chum whom I had never met, not even heard of. They stayed overnight. When we sat down to dinner the friend identified himself as a journalist and a regular contributor to the *Nation*. I last looked into the *Nation* when Gore Vidal wrote his piece about the disloyalty of Jews to the USA and their blood-preference for Israel. During the long years of our acquaintance, a dune of salt has grown up to season the preposterous things Gore says. He has a score to settle with the USA. Anywhere else, he might have been both a homosexual *and* a patrician. Here he had to mix with rough trade and also with Negroes and Jews; democracy has made it impossible to be a gentleman invert and wit. Also the very source of his grief has made him famous and rich. But never mind Gore, we can skip him. Let's go on to our dinner guest, Martin's companion. His name is Christopher Hitchens. During dinner he mentioned that he was a great friend of Edward Said. Leon Wieseltier and Noam Chomsky were also great buddies of his. At the mention of Said's name, Janis grumbled. I doubt that this was unexpected, for Hitchens almost certainly thinks of me as a terrible reactionary—the Jewish Right. Brought up to respect and to reject politeness at the same time, the guest wrestled briefly and silently with the *louche* journalist and finally [the latter] spoke up. He said that Said was a great friend and that he must apologize for differing with Janis but loyalty to a friend demanded that he set the record straight. Everybody remained polite. For Amis' sake I didn't want a scene. Fortunately (or not) I had within reach several excerpts from Said's *Critical Inquiry* piece, which I offered in evidence. Jews were (more or less) Nazis. But of course, said Hitchens, it was well known that [Yitzhak] Shamir had approached Hitler during the war to make deals. I objected that Shamir was Shamir, he wasn't the Jews. Besides I didn't trust the evidence. The argument seesawed. Amis took the Said selections to read for himself. He could find nothing to say at the moment but next morning he tried to bring the matter up, and to avoid further embarrassment I said it had all been much ado about nothing.

Hitchens appeals to Amis. This is a temptation I understand. But the sort of people you like to write about aren't always fit company, especially at the dinner table.

Well, these Hitchenses are just Fourth-Estate playboys thriving on agitation, and Jews are so easy to agitate. Sometimes (if only I knew enough to do it right!) I think I'd like to write about the fate of the Jews in the decline of the West—or the long crisis of the West, if decline doesn't suit you. The movement to assimilate coincided with the arrival of nihilism. This nihilism reached its climax with Hitler. The Jewish answer to the Holocaust was the creation of a state. After the camps came politics and these politics are nihilistic. Your Hitchenses, the political press in its silliest disheveled left-wing form, are (if nihilism has a hierarchy) the gnomes. Gnomes don't have to know anything, they are imperious, they appear when your fairy-tale heroine is in big trouble, offer a deal and come to collect her baby later. If you can bear to get to know them you learn about these *Nation*-type gnomes that they drink, drug, lie, cheat, chase, seduce, gossip, libel, borrow money, never pay child support, etc. They're the bohemians who made Marx foam with rage in *The Eighteenth Brumaire*. Well, that's nihilism for you, one of its very minor branches, anyway. Yet to vast numbers of people they are very attractive somehow. That's because those vast numbers are the rank and file of nihilism, and they want to hear from Hitchens and Said, etc., and consume falsehoods as they do fast-food. And it's so easy to make trouble for the Jews. Nothing easier. The networks love it, the big papers let it be made, there's a receptive university population for which Arafat is Good and Israel is Bad, even genocidal.

Now what does one do about all this?

To be more particular, what am I to do about it on Dec. 3rd? I haven't the slightest idea, and there's nothing more depressing than to picture myself spluttering at the podium, making a fool of myself and making your meeting look foolish, too. Nothing would please our own Jewish nihilists more.

What you need, and you've probably thought of this yourself, is a sensible talk by Jeane Kirkpatrick on the PLO.

Ever your admiring and affectionate friend,

Cordial relations would subsequently develop between Hitchens and the Bellows. Edward W. Said's piece in Critical Inquiry *was "Representing the Colonized: Anthropology's Interlocutors."*

To James Atlas

September 20, 1989   Boston

Dear James:

Re-reading your Rosenfeld article this morning, I find it mostly accurate—although I become uncomfortably aware at times that a man I thought I knew well escaped my understanding in the end. At every turn of the spiral everything looks different. But it was a fair, even generous article and I was touched by it. Delmore would sometimes warn me against Isaac, whom he described as monstrously jealous. Perhaps he wanted the place in my affections held by Isaac. One thing they had in common was a belief in the truth of psychological analysis. And by the end of the Fifties I had had it with "psychology," and when I say that Isaac escaped my understanding it's not a psychological understanding that I have in mind. I never gave psychoanalysis so much as a two-year lease. I enjoyed it as a game then being played, and now I see it as trivial pursuit. What saddens me is that we didn't know what we were doing. The cry from the cross, "Father, forgive them," is more true than Freud's complete works.

I don't think you ought to take Lionel Abel's comments seriously. I came across them in *The Intellectual Follies* and they struck me as characteristically and amusingly cockeyed and foolish. Abel didn't drink hard and I doubt he ever took dope; he was on some mind-altering substance of his own (probably he secreted it), and he heard and saw his own inventions and nothing else. To say that the Fourth International was my marriage broker is very funny. I wouldn't have had the wit—at that time—to say it. Lionel must have heard it from someone else, forgot the source and conveniently attributed it to me.

I understand that a book of which I am the subject is about to appear, and I'm thinking of taking sanctuary in a remote part of Madagascar until it has been reviewed, discussed and forgotten.

Best wishes,

"Golden Boy," Atlas's article on Isaac Rosenfeld, had appeared in The New York Review of Books. *The book about Bellow was Ruth Miller's* Saul Bellow: A Biography of the Imagination, *though it would not appear for another two years.*

In Memory of Robert Penn Warren

(Delivered at the Stratton Church, Stratton, Vermont, October 8, 1989)

All the King's Men had just been published when I arrived in Minneapolis in 1946. Red seldom mentioned his novel, nor spoke of its success or his fame. Having written it, he put it behind him—he didn't care to cut a figure. He never spoke of the work he was doing. I had to read his introduction to the Modern Library Edition of *All the King's Men* to learn that he was then finishing his essay on *The Ancient Mariner*.

In Minneapolis, when I was a very junior member of the English Department, I was one of a group of instructors invited by Joseph Warren Beach to meet Sinclair Lewis. When we were ushered into the room Lewis pushed back his chair, stood up, raised his long arms and said, "For God's sake, don't tell me your names."

I give you this as an illuminating contrast. Red wanted to know the names. He took a special interest in your gifts if you had any. He wanted to know what you were writing. He offered to read your manuscript. With me he was especially generous. But he preferred not to be thanked and the lessons he taught me about reserve and silence I couldn't have gotten from anyone else. I never knew a man more free from common prejudices. I hope he didn't find me a hopelessly clumsy pupil.

Two years ago I got one of his rare rebukes. We met every summer in Vermont and in September we said goodbye and I said, "See you next year." It vexed him, and he set me straight. "Don't lie like that," he said. He was right of course to reject my awkward, embarrassed and false words.

But I did see him the next year.

And when we met again some weeks before his death he smiled at me and said, "You didn't expect to see me still alive, did you?"

I said no I hadn't, but that I was glad of course to talk to him again.

The house was filled with small children; it evidently gave him great pleasure to follow them with his eyes.

With him I was especially attentive, because he was a great-souled man. That was very clear to me. A moment ago I said that I hoped he didn't find me a clumsy pupil. Red certainly didn't want disciples, and I am too old now to be formed by anyone. But one doesn't meet many men of Red's stature. They are so phenomenally rare that you find yourself observing them closely, with gratitude and (being in a church emboldens me to use a term not often used nowadays) with reverence.

To John Auerbach

October 23, 1989   Boston

My dear John,

A case of bad timing: When I took this Boston job I assumed you would still be in Newton. If you had been, Janis and I would have spent more time here, but as it is, we shuttle between BU and Vermont. I preach against restlessness but can't do without it, like the rest of my countrymen. This back-and-forth long weekly drive doesn't leave much time for writing, and lack of time comes in the nick of time for I haven't got anything to work on. I wrote one hundred pages of a funny narrative during the summer, but it was like a skyscraper in the desert. I had overlooked the water problem.

Anyway, Janis and I have been flying everywhere—to New York, to Cincinnati, to Chicago—and we have tickets also for Washington and Tulsa, Oklahoma. My typewriter and Janis' computers are idle. But I suppose it will do us no harm to think things over. We are generally working too hard to think at all.

Boston is not so bad. If we could have the trees cut down we could see the Charles from our window; if the trees were down, however, it wouldn't be worth looking at. We are fifteen minutes from the Brookline bakeries and delicatessens, but must avoid stuffing ourselves. In short, every advantage has a long train of attendant problems. Only, thank God, I am not one of Janis' problems, nor is she one of mine. Perhaps this shows that only an odd marriage can be a happy one. Janis speaks of us as an old married couple. I suppose this breaks down as: I am old, we are married. Aside from these facts, social and statistical, we love each other.

I fret with you over the failure of your books to arrive, but I am planning to send you the core of a new library if they don't turn up. Remember you are a dear friend to both of us, and your letters about walking on the shore, swimming in the sea and living among old friends again give us great *nakhes* [*].

With best love from both of us,

Love and greetings to Nola.

Bellow and Janis Freedman had wed on August 25 in the town hall of Wilmington, Vermont.

* Yiddish: joy

To Wright Morris

November 15, 1989   Boston

Dear Wright:

The classic question: What is to be done? The answer is even more classic: A lot of choice we got.

There was no frailty in what you read to me. Only the beholder (listener) was frail, and he drew strength from it.

Years ago I discovered that the reception of a manuscript by an editor or that of a book by the reviewers and the public gave me an index to the cultural condition of the country, one pitiful disaster after another. A psychologist would call this viewing a profile. A reader of entrails (and that's what this calls for) would cry, "Take this goddam chicken out of my sight!" Your agent's phrase about the high expectations of readers is about as terrible a mess of entrails as I've held my nose at this calendar year.

Don't forget that you are Wright Morris and that the books you've given your countrymen are beyond price.

And you need to know that in the last year and a half I have been rejected by the *Atlantic, Esquire* and others.

Since you ask how I am, let me inform you that last summer I married a beautiful young woman. Some would take this as evidence that I am ready for the funny farm but I think much too highly of my wife to take such an opinion seriously.

Yours ever,

To Catherine Lindsay Choate

December 6, 1989   Boston

Dear Catherine:

It was wise of Lakewood College to give you a course to teach. I could be very happy sitting in your class, quasi-invisible, listening to you. You yourself said that you remember I am still in this world, if silent and unseen. Well, I would be silent in your classroom, looking on. It would give me pleasure. To this day, I take pleasure in you, and you're wrong to suggest that your letters are tedious. There is nothing boring about you, there never was.

One of my mistakes, from the first, was to try to draw a line between mad and sane and I can see now, having observed you for so long, that you would accept no such line in your relations with people and that you floated in and out between the lines and over them as your feelings directed. My line-drawing dementia must have made me very perverse. But you seemed to go where your feelings led you, and you put them first even when you were dealing with lunatics. I must have taken my family for normal people. Now that most of them are dead and the survivors very old, the evidence is that they were anything but normal. When my old sister went back to Montreal for a visit, she made a search for a coffee shop she had known sixty-five years ago. It hadn't occurred to her that it wouldn't be there, just as she remembered it. She spent two or three days looking, and of course no one could recall any such place. She had put everything on hold and she was still the pretty and charming girl who used to be taken for treats to this nice place on Sherbrooke. So what *had* happened? Her parents had died, her husband was destroyed, her son committed suicide. But in some respects nothing at all had happened. So when I think of people I have known forever and loved, either more or less or dearly, I see masses of habit possessing the original person and replacing him in the end.

And of course we are creatures of a day, but we don't absolutely believe it.

I've taken some time off from Chicago to spend a few months in Boston, not far from my place in Vermont. I've rather liked Boston; Chicago has been taken over by racial politics—blacks and whites in a contest for control. I find it very disagreeable. On the 15th the Boston holiday ends and we go back.

The botanical garden was nice, wasn't it?

Your friend, as ever,

Catherine Lindsay Choate met Bellow in the early 1950s. They would remain in contact for the rest of his life.

And again out of the flaming of the sun would come to him a secret certainty that the goal set for this earth was that it should be filled with good, saturated with it. After everything preposterous, after dog had eaten dog, after the crocodile death had pulled everyone into his mud.

—"A Silver Dish"

1990

To John Auerbach

February 5, 1990   Chicago

My dear John,

[. . .] For a man approaching the seventy-fifth year of his age I am not doing badly. Janis is a dear woman and she has even overcome some of my more monstrous defects of character.

As more news of deaths arrives (the latest was that of Edith Tarcov, a dear woman whom I think you knew) the less I feel the victory of my survival. There is a strange scratchiness in the viscera when I think matters over.

I will be asking Smadar next week to bear good tidings—your surgery safely behind you.

Much love from your friend,

To John Auerbach

April 5, 1990   Chicago

Dear John:

Your letters sound more cheerful. Think there must be something to the old *Dum spiro spero* [*]. In the worst of times, it comes over you that you are, despite all that sickness and age can do, still inhaling and exhaling.

This is a note to cover a new story, and these stories seem to be the letters we write to each other.

I hope Nola is recovering quickly. Janis and I were sorry to hear of her accident.

Love to you both,

To Martin Amis

June 3, 1990   W. Brattleboro

Dear Martin,

By now you will have heard or read (I can't imagine that Hitchens would have missed an opportunity to convey such news) that on our last day in London Janis and I were received at No. 10 Downing Street and were treated to tea and tittle-tattle by the Prime Minister. Now honestly, can you imagine

* Latin: While I breathe, I hope.

that a pair of US hicks from Chicago would refuse an invitation to see for themselves the seats of the mighty? Like the nursery rhyme pussycats who went to London and frightened a mouse or two under the queen's chair, we have little else to report. It was George Walden [former minister for education in Mrs. Thatcher's government] who arranged this meeting, the same Walden who endeared himself to us by his indignation at your being passed over for the Booker Prize.

Put yourself in our place: Ronald Reagan or George Bush hearing that you are in Washington asks you to tea and you, ever faithful to high principles, return a withering refusal.

American friends have asked me for my impressions: "Well, you're cruising on an interstate highway and a few hundred feet ahead you see a perfectly ordinary automobile like any other GM, Chrysler or Japanese product, and then suddenly it turns on its dangerous blue police lights and you realize that what you took for a perfectly ordinary vehicle is packed with power. It's that unearthly blue flash that makes the difference."

Leaving Heathrow, I opened a London newspaper and there I saw myself exposed to sophisticated ridicule. The writer, with a blue flash of his own, revealed to all the world, and to me, that Clara in *A Theft* was none other than Margaret Thatcher, concealed in the ranks as the prime minister of New York fashions. I now have this to suggest to the pre-Socratic who said you could never twice put your foot in the same river: You are doomed to put your foot in again and again and again.

But ideology is not likely to come between us. We loved seeing you and Antonia. She served us a dinner that made all the other dinners in Europe look sick. Also, Jacob [Amis] immediately recognized that I was a friend which did much to restore my confidence in myself, none too firm these days.

Yours as ever,

And love from Janis.

To Roger Shattuck

June 5, 1990   W. Brattleboro

Dear Roger:

Your letter was entirely reasonable and sensible, and I admit that I was wrong to be so touchy about a trifle. My only defense is that you gave me a hard time at Rosanna [Warren]'s dinner party, beginning with my public address and going on to my rank as a writer—whatever that may mean. I am well used to being put in my place, and I don't really mind when I can feel that I am in the hands of a dependable place-putter.

But these provocations were minor. I don't mind friendly teasing at all. I am however touchy about the language of some of my books, and when I am criticized in a matter of usage I can be a bit crazy. It was unforgivable to burst into your office with a list of references. If we knew each other better I'm sure I'd come to accept the teasing, even to enjoy it, and you might make friendly allowance for an occasional eruption. Of course I knew that you had written a favorable review of *Humboldt,* and you will perhaps remember that I have spoken admiringly of *The Banquet Years,* and of your Proust book. We have no *casus belli.*

The daring of a major move at my time of life sets my teeth on edge but nothing is impossible to unrealistically (perversely?) youthful types like me.

Many thanks for your civilized letter.

Yours,

To Philip Roth

June 24, 1990   W. Brattleboro

Dear Philip:

In you I had a witness of my own kind and a point of balance. Without your support the angry waves would have dashed me on the stern and rock-bound Jewish coast. I am very fond of Cousin Volya who was something of a hero in the Old Country, serving in the Russian cavalry from Leningrad to Berlin. It's easy to mistake him for somebody else. When he explained the difference between Latvia and Lithuania to [Saul] Steinberg, Steinberg said it was a piece of dialogue out of a Marx Brothers' movie. There was however a regiment with machine guns. But I see Steinberg's point of view. With peace, the Marx Brothers return.

Anyway, you were a great comfort to me—representing what it was essential to represent. And I thought you must be enjoying the singing. The *mixture* of a thousand ingredients.

In principle, I'm against such parties but when a surprise turns off the principle I seem to enjoy them quite a lot.

Yours ever,

Your note made Janis happy.

Roth and Claire Bloom had been present in Vermont—along with Bellow's cousin Volya from Riga, Saul Steinberg, Eleanor Clark, Rosanna Warren,

Maggie Staats Simmons, John Auerbach from Israel, Albert Glotzer, Bette How-land, Jonathan Kleinbard, sons Adam and Daniel Bellow and many others—for a surprise seventy-fifth birthday celebration.

To Julian Behrstock

June 26, 1990   W. Brattleboro

Dear Julian:

It never occurred to me to think of myself as the Ancient of Days but there's no getting away from it. What is it that prevents me from realizing that I have grown so old—persistent adolescence? Obstinacy? A refusal to acknowledge what I plainly see in the mirror?

Yesterday I was gardening in front of the house, made a misstep, fell four feet to the ground, landed flat on my back, picked myself up at once and went about my business until Janis ordered me to go upstairs and lie down. No broken bones, no bruises visible, only a stiffness across the hips in the night. My sister Jane, nine years my senior, fell downstairs at the El station on her way to the Loop and kept her appointment nevertheless. She broke no bones either.

I was touched by your birthday message. Janis turns out to be an incredibly gifted organizer. You would have enjoyed the occasion. It was attended by seventy people, two of them greenhorn cousins of my own age just out of the Soviet Union. And children, of course, and grandchildren and old pals, the durable kind like yourself.

Last week I accepted a grant from a foundation, whose intent is not altogether clear. I think they want me to go to Paris in the winter of '91 to teach a course at the Sorbonne. The offer was made and accepted on the telephone, so I'm not altogether clear about the specifics. What is certain is that Janis and I will fly over at the beginning of February and stay until the end of May. Sometimes apartments are exchanged through the university. It's highly unlikely that you might know someone who will be leaving for the Congo in February and returning in May. The perennial adolescent in me insists on believing that anything is possible. My mature purpose is to tell you the news and to say how glad I am at the prospect of seeing you early next year.

Love,

To Jonathan Kleinbard

Dear Jonathan,

Sometimes citizen Bellow has to fight his guilt when he considers what a world this is, and how much he might have done in the public interest if he had put away this idle stuff he insists on calling "art." His books have been a big mistake and it isn't only honest, earnest lawyers, psychologists, engineers, economists, etc.—servants of reality—who believe this, but writers of a different outlook who fault me for ignoring the crisis under our noses and reproach me roughly. I might have been some good as a journalist. But it's too late now to mend and all I can do is to do what I have taught myself. You say, "opening up the heart." People seem to doubt if there *is* such an organ. The advanced view is that there ain't no such thing, and it can find more evidence for this than we can for *our* convictions.

But I'm going to stop here, leaving just enough space to say that the agreement of a man like you outweighs the criticism of thousands of "them."

We have other matters to discuss but they'll have to wait.

With thanks and affection to you and also to Joan,

To Saul Steinberg

Dear Saul:

After the birthday shouting, the silence of Vermont came back. Real life is represented by the cat, who appeared just now to show us the bird he had killed, and to fill Janis' mind with thoughts of vegetarianism.

Your beautiful green diploma is hanging on the bedroom wall, and when I look at it in the morning I think of supernatural places it might get me into. If, that is, I should be in a position to take it with me. Meantime, I have ordered for you a book by one of our friends, Sarah Walden, whose business is restoration. She has, according to the jacket copy, "worked as a restorer on major collections in Europe, including the Louvre: . . . paintings ranging from those of Vermeer to those of Picasso." We found it amusing and instructive. That's what's so nice about ignorance, you can always be instructed, and feel that you need never waste a moment's time.

It was noble of you to fly here, and I hope you found some entertainment in the occasion. Perhaps my Russian cousins made it worth your while.

So much for Bellow's Versailles. What we can offer you now is Bellow's resort or *Kur-Ort* [*]. I promise excellent meals cooked by Janis and conversation only slightly less good.

Love,

To Zita Cogan

July 18, 1990   W. Brattleboro

Dear Zita:

I thank you for your note and for your kind words and also for the color photograph of me in a tennis shirt. I stopped playing tennis some years ago but I have the shirt still, unraveling a little at the cuffs. It's under a pile of junk on the shelf of my clothes closet here in Vermont. I can't remember who took this photograph but one of these cold days when I pull the shirt on and stumble down to the kitchen to light a fire it will remind me of you.

You're kind to Mr. [James] Atlas. I am no more keen about a biography than I am about reserving a plot for myself at 26th and Harlem Avenue. I keep putting it off. I say this in order to make clear that I am not supporting Atlas, nor am I asking my friends to oblige him with recollections of my misconduct.

The Chagall postcard was great. The bridegroom has found a beauty to play piggyback with. The glass of wine is a beautiful afterthought.

Yours with love and kisses,

To Albert Glotzer

August 5, 1990   W. Brattleboro

Dear Al:

We too lived on Augusta Street—then unpaved—between Rockwell and Washtenaw, on the south side of the street. The address I believe was 2629, and we were on the second floor directly above the Polish landlord. I also wore high-top boots and remember the zero-teeth of Chicago eating at my toes. I was then nine years old. Our high-tops had a pen-knife, a bonus, in a sheath. I also remember the Nestor Johnson skates, manufactured on North Avenue near California. One pair of skates had to do for all three boys, two or three sizes too large for me. I did my best on the Humboldt Park lagoon.

I didn't get to Hammersmark's bookshop until I was a high-school student. [Isadore] Bernick brought me there. The year must have been 1930. In

---

* German: old-fashioned thermal spa or cure resort, e.g., Karlsbad, Marienbad, Baden-Baden, etc.

1936 Sam Hammersmark tried to recruit me for the Abraham Lincoln Brigade. But I was an early member of the Spartacus Youth League. Sam and I had a good-natured relationship, by which I mean that we never discussed politics. I can recall borrowing Trotsky's pamphlet on the German question from Freifeld. It knocked me for a loop. But my real interests were literary and I needed Hammersmark to supply me with books otherwise obtainable only in the Loop. Bernick, by the way, introduced me to proletarian art. Hammersmark hung it on his walls. Of a muscular, headless torso, mighty arms crossed, Bernick said that it was "symbolical of the proletariat without leadership." On gloomy days such recollections cheer me up.

I wonder what it is that so fascinates us about the old city. I suppose we had instinctively understood that it filled our need for poetry. Besides, maturity meant work, and work was something dark and blind to which we were sentenced when boyhood ended. It seems to me that we made excellent use of the liberty we enjoyed as schoolboys.

I am in the middle of your Trotsky book. I read it with fascination. I used to think I knew quite a lot about Trotskyism, but what you write shows me to be an amateur. For instance, I had no idea at all that Trotsky was handicapped because he was not a proper old Bolshevik and that he was inhibited in his struggle with Stalin, Zinoviev, etc. because he lacked full credentials. I was stirred also by his unclear answers during the Mexico trials about the seizure of power and the character of the proletarian dictatorship.

Herb Passin and I had an appointment with Trotsky in the summer of 1940, and came up from Taxco only to learn that he had been struck on the head and rushed to the hospital. We went there at once, introducing ourselves as newspapermen, and were led to a room where Trotsky lay dead with a bloody turban of bandages, and his face streaked with iridescent iodine. We turned up again later, after Al Goldman had arrived, and I remember that he was greatly put out by us for some inscrutable reason.

Something remarkable about your book: I have observed that most people are incapable of altering their early beliefs. Most, I've noticed, think of their first education as a sort of investment made during their best, most vital years. Many of the Marxists I've known are unwilling to give up the labor they put into mastering difficult texts. They tend to hang on to the very end. A curious sort of rigidity. In most cases their knowledge became useless long long ago. It's heartening to me to see how willing you are to reconsider your old faith. There are not many people with that kind of intellectual courage.

Thanks for your kind words about my story, and tell Maggie [Marguerite

Horst Glotzer, his wife] that I'm glad it pleased her. Janis is waiting for me to hand over your book, and sends you her best regards.

Affectionately yours,

Glotzer's book was Trotsky: Memoir and Critique.

To Frances Kiernan

August 8, 1990   W. Brattleboro

Dear Mrs. Kiernan:

I knew Mary [McCarthy] quite well, never intimately. She and I never got along. You either had a good relationship with Mary or you had—well, whatever it was that we did have. For a decade or more she hated me, quite frankly. I could not return her feelings with the same intensity but I did what I could. I don't observe the *de mortuis* rule; on the other hand, I see no point in lousing Mary up gratuitously, it doesn't seem right. Then you haven't asked me to louse her up so perhaps we can talk about her on the telephone, though I'd prefer a face-to-face meeting. It could be a brief one, no longer than a fire drill at the *New Yorker*. I did love Rachel [MacKenzie] and I do miss her even now.

Yours, etc.

Frances Kiernan, a former New Yorker *fiction editor, was beginning work on her book* Seeing Mary Plain: A Life of Mary McCarthy. *She had reminded Bellow that it was during a fire drill at the* New Yorker *offices that Rachel MacKenzie introduced the two of them.*

To George Sarant

September 9, 1990   W. Brattleboro

Dear George:

No I don't think Isaac ever met [Wilhelm] Reich. Since I was then in therapy myself he would certainly have told me that he had gone up to Maine. He did in fact say to me that he had had fantasies about being sent for as soon as Reich had news that he, Isaac, was in treatment. In short he was confessing to visions of grandiose importance.

Yes, I did know Paul Goodman. He was friendly with your father, not with me. Isaac believed that Goodman evaded the terrors of therapy by going over to [Gestalt Therapy co-founder] Fritz Perls—taking the easy way out.

Isaac ended by believing that therapy had done him great harm. We had a long conversation a month or two before he died and he declared that he had been out of his mind for a decade and would now try to find some ground to re-establish his sanity. He was an extraordinarily gifted man. Village life, as he interpreted it, was his undoing. I don't entirely blame the Village but his liberation degenerated into personal anarchy. I'm glad to win your good opinion. I hope the record, when all the results are in, won't let us down.

Love from someone who has known you forever,

To Catherine Lindsay Choate

September 17, 1990   W. Brattleboro

Dear Catherine:

Whenever I find a letter from you in my box I brighten up. Yes, I am well, and though I balk a little at admitting it, I am happy too. I can't really explain why I am reluctant to say it—some silliness in character or a superstition, perhaps hereditary. I have no serious diseases and at seventy-five with foolish enthusiasm I pedal a bike up and down the Vermont hills. The neighbors take me for some kind of crazy prodigy. Certain lifelong peculiarities persist. I continue to work at them without believing that I will get anywhere. It's an amusing game that I play. To give an innocent instance, I neglected my Latin sixty years ago and drive myself now to do right by Caesar's *Commentaries*. This is a job I don't do badly but I can't really say that I can explain why I do it at all. However it's the kind of absurdity that amuses me. It occurred to me not long ago that God had probably had an educational motive in putting Adam and Eve between the tree of life and the tree of knowledge. It must have been some sort of educational test. When they flunked he designed a different kind of curriculum for them. It's possible that I've had this idea all my life and that's why I grind away at Caesar and all the ablatives and gerunds.

I'm sorry to say that I have no engagement to speak in San Francisco. I'd love to see you though and I hope you are well.

Yours affectionately,

To John Auerbach

September 17, 1990   W. Brattleboro

Dear John:

Mid-September and Janis and I are getting ready to return to Chicago. Vermont is now at its best. The black flies, deer flies and mosquitoes have perished and it becomes possible to sit on the lawn and read a book, so naturally we'd rather stay. We will miss the country and of course the city will be dreadful—not quite so bad as New York, nothing matches New York, but bad enough. Still we enjoy a certain amount of protection. We have an underground garage and we can go downtown for dinner safely enough although there are people who shun the Outer Drive after dark. Cars that break down and have to be abandoned are stripped by morning. Since you live within reach of Saddam you will see this quite rightly as much ado about nothing.

I'm sorry to say that your *Commentary* subscription can't be canceled. I don't like the magazine; it has decided that I have a bad character and doesn't review my books anymore. Still, it is one of the better journals and although the language of the contributors is something like the kapok that life jackets used to be stuffed with one can always find in it an article or two worth reading. [. . .]

Much love,

To Louis Lasco

October 11, 1990   Chicago

Dear Laibl:

(No patronymics this time.)

Rudy Lapp writes that you have come through a bypass and are better than ever, "a magnificent statue at a hundred seventy." Statues remind me of Rome, and Rome of the Tuley classroom where you read a paper on Roman bath tubs. But archaeology, for us, is no longer a joke. At the Waldheim cemetery [in Forest Park, Illinois] which I recently had occasion to visit I saw the graves of classmates. The family plot is full and the streets are haunted— melancholy pavements where once we wasted life's precious opportunities in horseplay. You never were sentimental (except in your unique manner), nor am I deliberately nostalgic. It's my memory that's the troublemaker. Or perhaps not even my memory but the persistence of certain mental arrangements. The past may be footage of a B-picture directed by me, personally.

[. . .]

I remember that at our rooming house (was it Lord Manor?) fifty years ago you shrugged indifferently when I told you that Harry Lichtenstein was dead. Neither of us will do that when notified of the other's passing.

Fraternal greetings from your old chum—relatively intact,

To Philip Roth

November 15, 1990   Chicago

Dear Philip:

Wish we *were* able to accept. Then I could tell you *viva voce* how much I like your *Patrimony* (which I'm now reading). It gives me just the emotional workout I've been needing, and literary pleasure besides.

We have to see family in NYC. Could we drop in for a drink? We'll call to see whether you have a free hour for us.

All the best,

To John Auerbach

December 3, 1990   Chicago

Dear John:

To raise money for one of my fantasies—and it's the non-literary fantasies which always trap me—I booked myself all over the country to give talks and readings. Experience should have warned me—but then I have a fantasy way of experiencing experience—how dangerously fatiguing this would be. Higher powers of understanding now show me that I *wanted* to be fatigued, that my secret plan was to tire out some of my worst tendencies and escape from them. I hoped that they would be too weak to pursue and overtake me. The results are not yet in. There was also an unforeseeable complication. In September Allan Bloom came down with the Guillain-Barré, a paralyzing disease. Since he has no wife, no children, no one to take care of him but his friends, Janis and I would run back to Chicago from San Antonio, Montreal, Miami, etc. as often as possible. For a while he was in mortal danger. He's better now. His chances for recovery are good. He may be able to walk again.

In the midst of this we heard of your stroke.

Your brain and your circulatory system, anatomy and physiology, have tried everything possible to do you in. Since you've overcome everything they've heaped on you perhaps they'll let you be, withdraw for a decade or two out of admiration for your powers of resistance. The fact that your right hand was spared gives me hope. It may even be that by some secret inner process you preserved your right hand from damage. Imagination can keep you alive and as long as you have tales to tell you may be able to hold death at bay. I'm convinced that unfinished business has kept me alive. Scribbling and survival go together, I think. [. . .]

Go on writing your stories, and we will send waves of love by soul-radio. Love,

To Martin Amis

December 30, 1990   Schomberg, Ontario

Dear Martin,

Janis and I are in Ontario in the top storey of her parents' farmhouse looking into falling snow, trees, fields, a pond, and staring directly into the empty face of a Trojan-helmet chimney emitting smoke from wood chopped by me. We've just come out of the bath and we sit beside a huge white tub-with-a-view, a whirlpool or perhaps even a Jacuzzi into which you pour bubble-bath cream which foams up and makes you into an Olympian, Old Massa Zeus looking down on white Chanel clouds.

Too bad the people I care for are so widely distributed over the face of the earth. But then one tends to think about them all the more. Proximity isn't everything. In this bedroom I have found a volume of Aldous Huxley's letters written during the war years, many of them from Hollywood to correspondents in London and other distant places. His views might have been less kooky if he hadn't left England. But there are such things as inner distances and homegrown or domestic kookiness. I come up with odd ideas on my own Chicago turf and friends in England also send me *their* strange views. Years ago in Greenwich Village I used to say to a particular pal, "There's only me and thee that's sane and I sometimes have my doubts about thee." The occasion for these thoughts is the mention of [Salman] Rushdie's name at the breakfast table, his embrace or re-embrace of Islam. I suggested that he may have believed mistakenly that the civilization of the West had once and for all triumphed over exotic fundamentalism. After all, the Pope didn't excommunicate Joyce for writing *Ulysses* and the Church is even older than Islam. In short, it isn't safe yet to say that such and such a phenomenon has passed into history. Just as we were thinking that *perestroika* and *glasnost* had purified Russia once and for all we read a speech by the chief of the KGB accusing the US of sending radioactive wheat and poisoned foodstuffs to feed the hungry in the Soviet Union.

The likes of us should quit politics and stick to dreams. It gave me pleasure to hear that I recently figured in a dream of yours, positively. I recently dreamt:

Dream I: I identify Tolstoy as the driver of a beat-up white van on the expressway. I ask the old guy at the wheel of this crumbling van what he can do to keep his flapping door from banging against the finish of my car. When he leans over to the right I see that he is none other than Leo Tolstoy, beard and all. He invites me to follow him off the expressway to a tavern and he says, "I want you to have this jar of pickled herring." He adds, "I knew your brother." At the mention of my late brother I burst into tears.

Dream II: A secret remedy for a deadly disease is inscribed in Chinese characters on my penis. For this reason my life is in danger. My son Greg is guarding me in a California hideout from the agents of a pharmaceutical company, etc.

Dream III: I find myself in a library filled with unknown masterpieces by Henry James, Joseph Conrad and others. Titles I have never seen mentioned anywhere. In shock and joy I open a volume by Conrad and read several pages, sentence after sentence after sentence in the old boy's best style, more brilliant than ever. "Why in hell was I never told about this?" I ask. Certain parties have been holding out on us. I am indignant.

I depend on these dream-events to sort me out. Or perhaps to document my disorder more fully.

We may not be going to France after all. Our friend Bloom has for some months been down with the paralyzing Guillain-Barré syndrome and we can make no travel plans till we know whether the paralysis is temporary. Or not. He's making progress but there won't be any holidays until we've seen him through. Somebody at the BBC last year invited me to do a program in May and if the arrangements can be made perhaps we'll fly over and catch you before you leave London.

Best wishes for the New Year to you and Antonia and the kids from Janis and me.

Love,

In an effort to be rid of the fatwa *pronounced on him by Ayatollah Khomeini, Salman Rushdie had issued a tactical statement—later withdrawn—in which he claimed to have turned to Islam.*

1991

To Louis Lasco

January 18, 1991   [Chicago]

Dear Louie:

The old ties it seems are still knotted. When you wrote that you needed more surgery it was hard to take. A good many of my old buddies have gone (also an ex-wife and some brothers). The emotional effects have been variable. I didn't much mourn the Fish. But you turn out to be somebody I won't emotionally relinquish. To get information I phoned Rudy Lapp, and he got in touch with Abe Held. Abe is an American incarnation of the old guys at Cratch-Mandel who used to be sent out to sit with the orthodox dying. You remember him? A left-winger from Humboldt Park. Dark-faced, *simpatico*, an unprominent chin, humane eyes. He reported that you had no listed number. He would stay on the case. However, he had no more information.

So your letter relieved me of immediate anxiety. You've been in my mind quite a lot. My wife took me to see *Cyrano*, which I watched with double vision—or at least a divided mind. Half the interest was in you. Sitting there in the old Fine Arts (S. Michigan Ave.) I fought the sentiments inspired by the death of the lover-warrior-poet. I lost. I had to walk out on my own tears and go down to the men's room to pee.

Now the hard part of this note comes: If a loan would be useful (don't get up on your high horse, remember that in 1929 we pooled our pennies to try to beat the slot machine in Simon's drugstore on Division and Leavitt) I can spare the money.

[. . .] Your old friend hopes to hear from you soon.

To the American Academy and Institute of Arts and Letters

January 23, 1991   Chicago

Nomination for the Gold Medal in Poetry:

In his younger years Karl Shapiro had a reputation for stormy dissent. He dared to attack T. S. Eliot and Ezra Pound. He wrote that Eliot had made ours an age of criticism, and that criticism was the century's substitute for poetry. He was, in short, a maverick dissenter. That America has a particular fondness for its mavericks is a famous fact. But so many mavericks are no more than cranks or posturers, display-figures and mere celebrities. Those philosopher-poets or statesmen who have principles to defend, truths which demand their allegiance, are the real heroes of dissent. *The poet shy and bold as a bullet,* Shapiro has written, characterizing himself in eight words. He is a quiet writer but also a warlike and deep one, a sort of American Jonah, obedient and disobedient at the same time. His controversial book was called *In Defense of Ignorance* but it was poetry not ignorance he was defending. He was a born poet and the irreverent polemic was his declaration of faith. Beyond controversy in his eighth decade, he continues to give us splendidly mature poems to study and admire.

To Stanley Crouch

January 25, 1991   Chicago

Dear Stanley Crouch,

How could I fail to appreciate your book [*Notes of a Hanging Judge*]—how often does one see intelligence, style and courage come together? Your subjects are monopolized by demagogy. The language(s) in which they are discussed prevent thinking, make it simply impossible. The race question (all the questions, the whole complex) is, after war, the single most terrible thing we have to face. *Therefore* very few are able to face it at all. Public discussion of the issues is virtually impossible. Do I say discussion? Real *descriptions* are also prohibited. Even if they weren't prohibited (taboo) there might not be enough intellect and talent around to do the job.

The plain facts are yet to be stated, and it's only men like you who have even begun to state them. So I hope (I pray!) that others will follow your example.

At your urging, I looked up [Meyer] Lansky in the library. Only one book, smart but sketchy, by a man named Hank Messick. I've begun to read it (the first half already read) and promise to think about it.

Many thanks, and best wishes,

To Ruth Wisse

February 12, 1991   Chicago

Dear Ruth,

Since we last dined (so pleasantly) I've been pursuing vain things (writing fiction) and I have (ungraciously and with unbecoming laziness) failed to answer important letters (like yours). I've thought now and then about your suggestion that I publish the talk I gave in Montreal but I can't stop now to revise and edit. Besides, the lecture pleased you, and that's the only sort of "publication" I care about. Where would I print it—in *Harper's* or the *Atlantic*? In *Playboy*? Though you think so, I have no feud with *Commentary*. Norman [Podhoretz] and [Neal] Kozodoy have decided that I don't exist. They review Gore Vidal and they ignore me. And they printed an idiotic story by Joe Epstein of which I am evidently the "protagonist"—a second-rate Jewish writer from Chicago. Gross, moronic, and clumsily written.

I could make those people very unhappy by describing them. *Ober es geyt mir nit in lebn* [*]. And besides, it wouldn't really amuse me.

I think all the better of you for being so loyal to *Commentary* but I don't believe you'll ever bring it off—conciliation, I mean.

But I do read the magazine still and I did read your piece on anti-Semitism. I approved. I liked it. You're right of course and I love you even when you publish in *Commentary*.

Yours affectionately,

To Karl Shapiro

February 23, 1991   Chicago

Dear Karl:

Apprehended while trying to do the right thing!

A conference call [to determine the recipient of the American Academy's Gold Medal in Poetry] was arranged—staged—with [Donald] Hall and [Harold] Bloom, two highly experienced political infighters. I knew Hall once. Never met Bloom. He sounds like one of those new instruments, shaped like a sax and sounding like an oboe—I believe it's called a basset-horn. A voice full of tremors, fluctuating between Oxford and the Bronx. These two conspirators of the East had met and agreed on a list. My additional nomination [of you] took them aback for a moment. One of them said, "Let him be listed but I shan't vote for him." The other said, "Neither will I." Both parties then hung up on me. It's been fifteen years since the Academy invited me to collaborate. They're going to say that I still haven't learned to follow the rules. But who knows—maybe Justice will be done. Let's see what the ballots say. If I were as frivolous as I might be, and perhaps I should be, I could write a tale about the Typhoid Mary of Justice, a carrier of the germ whom the medical police are hunting on both coasts.

Sorry to hear of your phlebitis—I mean your excess of iron. But we need all the iron we can get, in these times. I have no current diseases, if you don't

* Yiddish: But it's not a matter of life or death to me.

count a small hemorrhage in the right eye. It gives me a damn sinister look, and won't go away. For my time of life I'm in good condition. Janis tends me like a plant and now and then is rewarded with a flower.

Love to you and Sophie,

To Roger Kaplan

March 27, 1991   Chicago

Dear Roger,

Sorry, I should have written to tell you what was happening but Janis and I were a long time in the switches, to use a Middle Western expression—something like that Old Jimmy Durante song, "Did you ever have the feeling that you had to go / Started to go / Decided to stay / Started to stay / Decided to go?" That should do it.

For the time being we have decided to stay [in Chicago]. We have also decided to go in the Spring of '92 [to Paris]. '91 as it happens is out of the question. I am supposed to deliver a manuscript to Viking Press in September or October—with a month's grace. Let's hope that all options will still be available next spring. I had sent a letter to M. [Jack] Lang, the Minister of Culture, inquiring whether his Ministry has any accommodations for a visiting Commander of the Legion of Honor. As of now, five months later, no reply. So this whole Commander of the Legion thing has been exposed as a hoax. Another case of How many divisions does the Vatican have? I thought I had *tuyau* [*]. I don't even have a soda-pop straw. [. . .]

Yours most affectionately,

Roger Kaplan, son of Harold "Kappy" Kaplan, is a regular contributor to The American Spectator *and lives in Washington, D.C.*

To Louis Lasco

March 27, 1991   [Chicago]

Dear old chum—

Of course I should have answered you sooner. At this time of life however a couple of months doesn't feel like real procrastination. This is no defense—more like a page from *The Natural History of Septuagenarianism.* Intending to write is *like* writing. Why *do* I "bother" to write at all, as you put it? Because you've figured in my life and I in yours over six decades or so, for the most

* French: pipeline; fig., connections, pull

part affectionately. We see each other at fifteen-year intervals so there's no *practical* involvement of the feelings.

To accuse me of "contempt" is completely cockeyed. I don't see what the things I wrote forty or fifty years ago have to do with subsequent feelings. I always wanted you among my real friends, and I am today as much your friend as it's possible to be. By which I mean that we're far from each other in space and also in time. We have *pictures* of each other. Mine are probably more pleasant than yours. But then I have no reason to be angry with you.

I may indeed have been a *putz*, an asshole deserving no respect—on the other hand there's always been warmth and sympathy between us. Whatever you may think of me, I've always respected you. And when I heard that you were ill my impulse was to be helpful—if help should be needed.

Ever your old friend,

You didn't offend me at all.

To James Atlas

March 29, 1991   Chicago

Dear James,

Are you prepared to consider an alternative?

Suppose that instead of rummaging in grammar-school records devoid of real interest you were to have a tour of the city—a personal conducted tour of Hyde Park, Humboldt Park, and several other locations? I wouldn't at all mind doing this, I might even enjoy it. If you think this is a reasonable proposal I will set aside the time—an afternoon or two. Mull this over a bit. There is no penalty for declining.

Yours with best wishes,

To Louis Lasco

April 9, 1991   [Chicago]

Well, Louie, you're right about one thing—perhaps the only one you are right about: Battles are unnecessary. In the old days I loved you because you didn't resemble anybody I knew. Most important of all you weren't like anybody in my family. Suddenly, in old age (my old age as well as yours), you are like all my relatives rolled into one—accusations, recriminations, denunciations. My poor, ailing, feeble, foolish, vain flesh and blood are fed to the shredder.

Do you happen to remember a kid named Yaddi Oppenheimer? I think he became a member of our club. He was afraid to touch chicken because chicken made him flatulent. This skinny pale little kid came back to me last night, name and all. He put us on notice never to let him eat chicken. But it would never have occurred to us to rebuke anybody for farting. On the contrary; we were pleased because he made us laugh. Chances are, Yaddi is gone as we will all be, shortly. I say to myself as Lady Macbeth did: "Stand not upon the order of your going, but go!" And so I will; when I'm required to.

To change the old song a bit, "With all *my* faults, I love you still."

I remain yours as ever,

To Louis Lasco

May 24, 1991   [Chicago]

Dear Louie—

Okay—I'm not the Bellow of your dreams; you're not the Lasco I *thought* I knew. You think that when I wish you well I do it from self-pity, and I want to infect *you* with pity, blind to the fact that you've had heart surgery twice and that you aren't sure that you're going to make it.

I see it a little differently. We were boyhood friends and I wish you well. Not because I'm trying to undermine your proud determination and independence, not because it's my way of gloating over you. Don't be such a *putz*.

As for who pays for dinner when we next dine together, we can toss a coin.

A few days ago, I was on Division St. Your old block has been razed—both sides of the street. The new hospital (we used to pee in the weeds by the power plant) is monumental. It could be a stadium for the Polish Olympics.

Dope pushers on every corner. We went for cholesterol instead.

Always your affectionate buddy, and good ol' boy,

To Stephen Mitchell

June 22, 1991   W. Brattleboro, Vermont

Dear Mr. Mitchell,

I have the greatest sympathy with what you have done. Let me explain: I was at the age of eight years a patient at the Royal Victoria Hospital, Montreal—dangerously ill in the children's ward.

My people were orthodox Russian Jews. I had a religious upbringing. In those times four-year-old kids were already reading Hebrew, memorizing Genesis and Exodus. Such was my background—the child of a despised people in the Montreal slums.

I had never been separated from the family. It was a hellish winter (1923–24) with heavy snows, fantastic icicles at the windows, the streetcars frosted over. My parents took turns coming to see me—I was allowed one short visit a week. I waited for them. There were three operations. My belly was haggled open—it was draining. I stank. I understood that I might die. I was pretty steady about this, I think. I didn't cry when my mother came and went. I was rather matter of fact about dying. Other children were covered up and wheeled away. In the morning, an empty bed, remade, blank. It was like that.

Then a lady came from some missionary society and gave me a New Testament to read.

Jesus overwhelmed me. I had heard about him, of course—marginal information, unfriendly. (Why should it have been friendly?) But I was moved when I read Gospels. It wasn't a sentimental reaction. I wasn't one for crying. I had to get through this crisis. I had made up my mind about that. But I was moved out of myself by Jesus, by "suffer the little children to come unto me," by the lilies of the field. Jesus moved me beyond all bounds by his deeds and his words. His death was a horror to me. And I had to face the charges made in the Gospels against the Jews, my people, Pharisees and Sadducees. In the ward, too, Jews were hated. My thought was (I tell it as it came to me then): How could it be my fault? I am in the hospital.

But I was beyond myself, moved far out by Jesus (Mark and Matthew). I kept this to myself. No discussions with my father, my mother. It was not *their* Bible. For them there was no *New* Testament. Obviously Jesus was not discussible with them. They had to live, as all Jews must, under a curse, and they were not prepared to interpret this to an eight-year-old child. In their struggle for existence interpretation ought not to be required of them, too. I would have been imposing on them, and it would all too plainly have been disloyal. I also sensed that.

I had never been in a position in which it is necessary to think for myself, without religious authorization, about God. Here at the Royal Victoria I was able, I was *en*abled—I was free to think for myself.

You will understand now why I read you with sympathy. I understand the impulse that led you to make your own translation of the Gospels. But sympathy is not agreement. I am out of sympathy with your generational standpoint. I can't agree that John Lennon stands in the line of the prophets, on a level with Isaiah and the rest. This seems to me a distortion due to fashion, too easy a mingling of the religious and the rock stars. I like rock stars, yes, and I admire gurus (each instance on its separate merits) but I am not so freely ecumenical as you. You and I are Jews whose experiences are roughly similar; we have judged for ourselves. Jesus, yes, but what about two millennia of Jewish history? How do you propose to come to terms with the Jew as the prime enemy of Christianity? You may be interested in a book that has influenced my understanding of these things, Hyam Maccoby's *Revolution in Judea*. It argues that Jesus was anointed, a messiah, a Pharisee who tried to free the Jews from Roman tyranny. The Greek authors of the Gospels named the Jews the enemy race, universally to be hated by the rest of mankind. Love of Jesus could not then be separated from hatred of the Jews. A proposition that must seriously be considered by the likes of you and me.

Sincerely,

Bellow had read Mitchell's newly published The Gospel According to Jesus: A New Translation and Guide to His Essential Teachings for Believers and Unbelievers.

To John Auerbach

July 7, 1991   W. Brattleboro

Dear John,

As civilization declines the interpretation of civilized rules is left in the hands of people like me (self-appointed) and we don't seem to do at all well. Thus I know that I should lift up the tails of my coat, take off my wig and sit down to correspondence like Voltaire. Only Voltaire had a staff of attendants to care for him while he wrote about freedom. I have only Janis, whom I love a thousand times more than Voltaire loved anybody. So I am humanly ahead but losing ground culturally.

Of course I should write to you, my conscience is severely troubled. I think of you continually and I seem to have translated "thinking about" into communication. Which means that civilization has fallen into solipsism. I assume there are two kinds of solipsism—restful and busy. Busyness quickly betrays you to barbarism. What makes me so busy? "My hasting days fly on in full career." (J. Milton, aged twenty-three.) I have X-plus pages to write and I do it under the shadowy threat of "too late." So . . . I am trying to meet a deadline imposed by a contract that I signed in order to spur myself to work more quickly. But I haven't got the energy I once had. Well into my late sixties I could work all day long. Now I fold at one o'clock. Most days I can't do without a siesta. I get out of bed and try to wake up. I ride the bike or swim in the pond. After such activities I have to rest again. It's evening, it's dinnertime. Nine-tenths of what I should have done it now seems too late to do: I protect myself from anxiety by opening some book or other; I catch up on the newspapers. I discover the moose population has increased, and that animals in the road cause more and more fatal accidents. I water the garden and promise myself to do better tomorrow.

I read your story, as I read all your stories. They come straight out of your feelings and go directly into my own. They please me even when I have reservations about them. In your latest it seems to me that you say more than is necessary about Entropy. Your story stands on its own without physics or philosophy. Exceptions to entropy only signify exceptions to death. Life defies entropy as it does the laws of gravity. It wasn't quite clear to me why the Baroness Dinesen-Blixen was in the story. She's always been a bit too trendy for me. I like most of her stories, but dislike the cult that has formed around her. What's high in your story is the human quality, the instant conviction of significance in the writer and the people he associates with. What brings them to life is your warmth.

The Doubleday complete Conrad should be sea-borne cargo by now. Let's hope the books arrive in time for your next birthday. Meanwhile since that good-bad magazine *Encounter* has gone out of business without reimbursement to disappointed subscribers, Janis and I are taking out a subscription to *The Economist* in your name. It's a business magazine, true, but then the planet now is overwhelmingly business. In the latest issue I learned why the Quebecois consider themselves sound enough financially to go it alone. Not the most interesting subject, but simply and sharply described. Good for my mind to see the world handled so neatly week after week. The mental level is high-average and generally dependable. And at least it's not mainly propaganda like *The New Yorker*.

Bostonia, by the way, has survived its crisis and will be published as a quarterly. Good for our side. Your last piece there was terrific. This letter was dictated to Janis and contains love from both of us to a dear friend.

(I promise to write oftener.)

To Florence Rubenfeld

July 15, 1991   W. Brattleboro, Vermont

Dear Ms. Rubenfeld:

My personal connections with Clem[ent Greenberg] were severed during WWII. I reviewed some books for him at *Commentary* and I followed his career, naturally, at two or three removes, when he was Helen Frankenthaler's coach, trainer and spiritual counselor. I last saw him at a luncheon in his honor given by the Arts Club of Chicago. He did not mortally wound me by cutting me dead. Seated at a neighboring table, he turned his back. There was a dish of fruit before me and I got his attention by throwing grapes at him. When he could no longer ignore me (I am a fair shot with a grape) he turned round and declared: "I never did like you." Now Proust or Joyce could have disabled me but Clem simply didn't have the weight. I went home feeling jolly, pleased with myself. [. . .]

Too bad that Sidney Hook has gone to his reward. He held sharp views on Clem's wartime politics.

Sincerely yours,

Florence Rubenfeld was writing Clement Greenberg: A Life, *which would appear in 1998.*

To Florence Rubenfeld

August 18, 1991   W. Brattleboro

Dear Ms. Rubenfeld:

I've never been known to pull practical jokes and have no previous knowledge of the Trilling caper. I can see why Diana might think me to be the perpetrator. Norman [Podhoretz] was Lionel's protégé and Norman had tried to do me in [with a negative review of *Augie March*]. He says as much himself in his autobiography. It did seem that Lionel was playing a double game since he had praised the very same book extravagantly [in *The Griffin*]. He and I had had a sharp exchange about this, but it never occurred to me to make alarming telephone calls.

It's true I am a fairly gifted mimic, and among my friends in the Village I may have spoofed Lionel—no great achievement since he had such conspicuous mannerisms. But it had never crossed my mind to call him or molest Clem. [. . .]

Diana will never replace Agatha Christie.

All best,

Diana Trilling apparently believed that in 1953 Bellow had placed crank calls in which he mimicked her husband's voice.

To Karl Shapiro

August 21, 1991   W. Brattleboro

Dear Karl,

As I write this summer's book, I pray continually that I am not letting Sophie down. She told me that last summer's story, "Something to Remember Me By," would be a hard act to follow. She was right. Now that I draw a diagram of the dilemma it clarifies the difficulty: How to write a novel with the precision necessary to write a short story? She will let me know whether I have done it satisfactorily, but waiting for judgment day naturally makes me anxious. I have to reconcile the habits developed in two different kinds of writing. I have never belonged to any church and Sophie is as close as I have ever come to the idea of papal infallibility.

Otherwise things continue to go on as they have gone on for decades now. In literature the lowing herd is leaving the lea and darkness falls on the enterprise to which you and I have devoted our lives. I feel like somebody who took holy orders about forty years before young Nietzsche showed that God was dead. I still believe we did the right thing, and if we were mistaken we made our mistakes in the best style available and have more class in defeat than any of our enemies. Does this sound a little bit like the noble soldier of the Confederacy reflecting on the doom of the victorious North? [. . .]

Lots of love from your friend,

To Jeff Wheelwright

August 28, 1991   Chicago

Dear Mr. Wheelwright:

In denying that Herzog was a manic depressive I was merely protecting him. I didn't want him pushed into a clinical category. I had known a genuine manic depressive, my dear friend the late Delmore Schwartz. Herzog was not nearly so volcanic and demonic a personality.

Best wishes,

To Virginia Dajani

September 11, 1991   W. Brattleboro, Vermont

Dear Virginia:

In fairness to Isaac Singer I suggest that you ask another member of the Academy for a tribute. Although I admired his work greatly (his character somewhat less), he didn't much care for me and his spirit I think would be more comfortable with a tribute from a writer with whom he enjoyed better relations.

Sincerely yours,

Isaac Bashevis Singer had died on July 24.

To George Sarant

September 21, 1991   W. Brattleboro

Dear George:

A very brief note: Somehow I never find time enough to do what I intend to do. Maybe I'm trying to dope out a way to extend the life span. Not merely "the vegetable span." I need to stay alive in order to get certain things done—and when I am halfway through some essential project I find that something else is even more essential, and then I pursue the more essential, etc.

One of my summer projects was to write you a long letter of the most essential kind, but the right moment never came. I'm sure it will come very soon.

One piece of knowledge about sons and fathers I can share with you now and that is that not all the sons want me to describe their fathers to them. The less they hear from me about Papa—or Mama—the better they like it.

With much love,

1992

To Stanley Elkin

January 27, 1992   Chicago

Dear Stanley—

My dilatory ways.

I've often wanted to write to you to say how much I like your books. We had one sketchy meeting at a silly event in St. Louis. The USA has no expression like "cher maître." And I can't think of any approximate equivalent. What I have to say is simply that you're the real thing—I should have written this to you long ago. But that's how lives are lived—one aimless good intention after another, impulses buried and occasions missed or frittered away.

Yours with best wishes,

To François Furet

February 2, 1992   Chicago

Dear François,

What a pity I couldn't attend the last faculty meeting. I should have liked at least to have been there in spirit, haunting the walls. Nasty Shils the ultimate Dickensian funny monster giving his wickedest performance. Bloom is mad with delight, beside himself when he describes the scene. David Grene once said that Edward was an unlanced boil (*un furoncle*, to you).

I like to have my joke first, that's characteristic of me, but to speak seriously I'm infinitely grateful to you for replying to Edward so simply, so properly. Bloom tells me, and I believe him completely, that you spoke with dignity and severity, and I am doubly grateful not only because you checked him but because you made it clear that the Committee will not tolerate his macabre shenanigans.

A kind friend has sent me *Zazie dans le Métro*. May I ask for your help with the *argot*?

With warm regards to you and Debbie,

François Furet (1927–97), leading French historian, was professor at the École des hautes études and chairman of the Committee on Social Thought at University of Chicago. A member of the Académie Française, he was the author of several important books on the French Revolution as well as Le passé d'une illusion: essai sur l'idée communiste au XXe siècle *(1995).*

To Ruth Wisse

February 20, 1992   Chicago

Dear Ruth,

A belated memo: We were happy to see your daughter in Jerusalem. She seems to have matured, blossomed with tremendous speed. We had seen her only once before, at your dinner, and although she was clearly intelligent and charming, she was very much the college girl and not at all the worldly young person who came to take tea with us at the Mishkenot. I would class her with [Nathan] Sharansky and a handful of other Jerusalemites who made the trip worthwhile. Kollek should be listed in the same category. The more I learn about him the more he intrigues me—a phenomenal personality. And yes, I know all about Teddy the schemer, finagler and arranger. With all his less-than-admirable qualities, he towers over most of the political figures I have known.

Running my eye over the foregoing, I can't understand how I've gotten into so many topics I never meant to bring up. I wasn't entirely myself in December. Janis and I had gone to Italy first. I had to perform before a large audience in Florence. As often happens, I was obliged to rewrite my talk in the hotel room. The whole thing wore me down and we went to Israel to re-cover. Once out of Jerusalem, we had to re-book ourselves directly to Chicago about ten days earlier than planned. When I got back home, I climbed into bed and stayed there for a couple of weeks. Nothing more serious than fatigue, from which I have now recovered. We found your letter waiting.

Abby told us that you were considering a move to Harvard. [. . .] I think you would be happy in Cambridge. And you wouldn't need to be homesick for Montreal. You can buy anything you need in the way of Jewish food on Harvard Street in Brookline.

Janis and I hope to see you again this coming summer.

Yours affectionately,

To John Auerbach

March 2, 1992   Chicago

Dear John—

Returning to Chicago, I took to my bed for some weeks—most of January—with accumulated fatigue. Then there were more weeks of testing—medical knocking and rapping, blood tests and tubes in the esophagus, prostate examinations. From all this I came out relatively clean. An increase in quinine doses and a new prescription for reading glasses. They (the doctors) say, "You're in good condition," and they add, "for a man of your age."

I didn't mind the hospitals, really. I liked the company in the clinics—one gets to *meet* people, instead of *reading* about them. What a freaky lot we are; everybody entertaining everybody else. This has gotten even to the top of the mafia—Gotti clearly behaves at his trial like Marlon Brando. And of course the politicians at this season are all playing "Candidates." In the slums the kids are killing one another with "cheap" handguns. And in the courts, people convicted of murder have filed "abuse" suits against the police. Chicago has a few of these cases going at this hour.

On the air and in the papers the future of the US is debated, some arguing that we will soon belong to the Third World. The Japanese and the Germans are ahead of us. The President is weak and vain, [Pat] Buchanan is not so much a fascist as a parochial pool-parlor punk. And not even the cemeteries are tranquil. A shopping mall has been "developed" near the graves of my parents, and the loudspeakers broadcast rock music day and night.

You mustn't think I'm depressed—I'm only down at the moment. Writing to dear friends whom I would love to see every day makes me a little melancholy.

You ought to do a little more with the pages you recently sent—but of course you're doing what you *can* do, and that little is better than this large output from the dozens, scores, hundreds who fill up the magazines and fight for space on the airport book racks.

Hug Nola for me.

Love,

Janis sends affectionate regards.

To Stanley Elkin

March 12, 1992   Chicago

Dear Stanley:

As pen pals we are released from formalities. Henceforth, first names.

When I was young I used to correspond actively with Isaac Rosenfeld and other friends. He died in 1956, and several more went in the same decade, and somehow I lost the habit of writing long personal letters—a sad fact I only now begin to understand. It wasn't that I ran out of friendships altogether. But habits changed. No more romantic outpourings. We were so *Russian,* as adolescents, and perhaps we were also practicing to be writers. Isaac himself made me conscious of this. When he moved to New York I wrote almost weekly from Chicago. Then, years later, he told me one day, "I hope you don't mind, but when we moved from the West Side" (to the Village, naturally) "I threw away all your letters." And he made it clear that he meant to shock me, implying that I would feel this to be a great loss to literary history. I felt nothing of the sort. I was rid of a future embarrassment.

But it wasn't a good thing to be cured of—the habit of correspondence, I mean. I'm aware that important ground was lost. One way or another it happened to most of the people I knew—a dying back into private consciousness and a kind of miserliness. You begin to work with proxies whom you've appointed yourself.

I suppose the letters in *Herzog* reflect this solipsistic condition: how and why intimacies die and the insanity of "going public" that results. With me, for a long time, it's been fiction or nothing. So is it too late to mend? (A Victorian Christian question.)

Having read you, I'm certain that you're free from this ailment or incapacity. You're able to "say it all." Nobody else is so full, fluent and open. In this department it's you who are the *cher maître*.

To William Kennedy

May 6, 1992   [Chicago]

Dear Bill—

I'm glad you turned again to the family theme—you're always at your best with the Phelans. I'm tempted to speculate that our family-less, out-of-the-void colleagues are anti-family on grounds of ideology (some from the Marxian, some from the Existentialist side). That's okay for people who *really* come out of the void [. . .], but for the majority it's an affectation—a put-on.

For the likes of us, with powerful early connections—well, we *can* say no to those connections. Whether it's yes *or* no we have to live with them openly. Joyce, who was so cold to his Dublin family (perhaps to his Paris family as well), has Bloom pining for his dead little boy, his suicided father. Cruel and kinky-real, but not without curious feelings. If Joyce had been born in the fields, under a cabbage leaf (as Samuel Butler would have preferred to enter life) there w'd have been no *Ulysses*.

With this elaborate preface: I liked *Old Bones* a lot. I read it in one shot, and it did me a world of good.

Yours ever,

To John Auerbach

June 23, 1992   W. Brattleboro

Dear John:

[. . .] At six I watch the news. That doesn't do much for me. I'm as listless as the rest of the country. Bush has nothing to give or say, and neither do I. Indignation gives me a bit of energy—riots in L.A., looting even in Chicago, idiocy on TV, cowardice in the newspapers, stupidity in government. The free-market economic theorists have done too well, they've taught the country that laissez-faire won the Cold War. Furthermore, I believe, people are terrified of the computers that have transformed the supporting structure. They're terrified lest computer error wipe out their savings, their pensions, their insurance—the computerized bureaucracy frightens them to death. Make inquiries when anything goes wrong and you can't get a human response— you get printouts or electronic voices. [Ross] Perot made his billions in government contracts, computerizing Medicare or Medicaid, and this weak-minded little man is believed to be a wizard. Nobody yet has said this publicly—you're getting a special interpretation from me. Perot has proposed to put democracy on an electronic footing. Push a button to make your views known and we won't need a Congress. If the President displeases the majority, an instant plebiscite will force him to step down. Therefore, we won't need a constitution, nor a Supreme Court to interpret it. Only technicians.

All this may pass but no one can be certain that it will.

Meantime the trees grow, the birds sing, the flowers do their stuff, the green is greener than ever. And there's Janis, without whom my blood wouldn't circulate.

And I cling to my friends, as well.

With much love to you and Nola,

To Stanley Elkin

July 22, 1992   W. Brattleboro

Dear Stanley:

Some pen pal you got yourself.

I haven't written to anyone in months, and I puzzle over this, whether it's self-absorption or conceit or what. Not really self-absorption, because I don't take myself as a subject for self-examination, never place myself on the psychological witness stand and am not so much modest as uninterested in studying my motives. I had a father-in-law years ago, a "great painter" in a sort of Stalinist Moulin-Rouge style. He described me to my then-wife as an "oral miser." He didn't take into account my seriousness about language. I don't like babbling. Also I was fascinated by his four-square profundity about art, sex, the Collective Unconscious, his mixture of Marx and Jung, his guile, his swami airs—his commitment to his powers of penetration. The summit of unlikely resemblances: He was like a poet named St.-Jean Perse. Perse would stand on his toes, go rigid, widen his eyes and penetrate you. As in the Eliot line (I see from your last book that you are fond of Eliot) "When I am formulated, wriggling on a pin." They pinned you. Only, I made a phenomenal escape every time.

No it isn't self-absorption. I think continually about people. Because I didn't answer your March letter, perhaps, I've thought about you every day for months and often read your essays [*Pieces of Soap*], agreeing or differing. No, it's another problem, totally other: I haven't got it together, as the children say. It hasn't been together for quite a while now. Maybe there's a profound reason—an enormous and total re-tooling. I'm an old man, after all. I have to rethink, restructure, revise. I'm not even faintly myself when I'm not writing, and won't write as I formerly (in other lives) wrote. That isn't good enough. It isn't deep enough. Not sufficiently comprehensive. Doesn't satisfy the emotional hunger, the ultimate craving. I never had what my old-time Village pals called "Writer's Block." If I'm ever blocked, it's in conversation. Which is why the revolutionary painter father-in-law called me an oral miser. He was right, in a way. I clammed up because he was listenable-to rather than talkable-to.

Maybe the difficulty is due to the season. Strange things happen to the soul in summertime. Rudolf Steiner, whose books I've read by the score, wrote that in summer nature passes out, goes unconscious, lies in a deep sleep. You would think that it slept in winter, which is barren, all its faculties frozen. On the contrary, winter is a season of intense consciousness or wakefulness. It's in the prolific summer that the earth is overtaken by sleep, yielding itself in a swoon to fertility. If the soul had its way it would lie dazed all the summer months.

Like you (in many ways) I agree that writing is writing. I have trouble with thank-you notes or letters of recommendation and so I prefer to think of the pages of fiction that I write as letters to the very best of non-correspondents. The people I love—the great majority of them unknown to me.

Old Tschacbasov wasn't even listenable-to, he was a repulsive old phony and low self-dramatizer, a would-be Father Karamazov but without intelligence or wit. I materialized unwillingly in his studio because I was married to his daughter. She saw me as an "artist" too and held it against me. In the end she fired me because I was her father all over again, in an inferior version.

All best,

To Teddy Kollek

My dear Teddy,

I often think of our visionary conversations at the Mishkenot about a sequel to my Jerusalem book. I sometimes feel that it would be too much for my poor old faculties and that my time-abused frame could never be equal to it. What I need is to hear the summoning Voice to which Samuel answered *"Hineni"*[*]. In your optimism you suggest that I should be lying awake nights—with a hearing aid perhaps. As Mayor of Jerusalem you may have advance notice of the prophetic moment.

Janis and I will be in Chicago in October and although we can't do for you what the multi-million Pritzkers can, we always fall back on the re-sources of the poor, namely, love and respect. Send us your date of arrival and we will round up the *anshey ha'ir* [**] and lay on a memorable evening or two.

A friend of mine, Margaret [Staats] Simmons, editor-in-chief of *Travel Holiday* magazine, will be visiting Jerusalem September 22nd–23rd and has expressed a wish to make an archeological tour. She will be staying at the King David. *Travel Holiday*, owned by *The Reader's Digest Inc.*, has a large circula-tion and Mrs. Simmons is a person of good taste. A little ancient grandeur is all she needs to make her happy. She will write to your office by and by.

Ever yours affectionately,

To Rosanna Warren

October 21, 1992   Chicago

Dear Rosanna,

Pestering? If I were to give out licenses to pester, you'd be near the top of my list. I used to plead lack of time, and now I can add old age in my polite refusals. What's more, I've been hammered flat by the recent death of an old friend [Allan Bloom]. But Bill [Arrowsmith] was an old friend too and it would be more a pleasure than a duty to read his translation of Montale. I promise, even, to get to it as quickly as possible.

In the old days we used to say about people like [John Kenneth] Gal-braith that he was vaccinated with a gramophone needle. But we'll all be in Vermont again next summer and if you come to visit us he'll be sure not to be there.

---

* Hebrew: "Here am I." When called by God in Genesis, Abraham says the same.
** Hebrew and Yiddish: people of the city; here, more specif., dignitaries or worthies

To John Auerbach

November 12, 1992   Chicago

Dear John—

Getting used to a new and none-too-pleasant mode of life—vacancies to fill which are by nature unfillable. I pass Allan's doorway and the great apartment house is like a monument, a pyramid with oneself under it all. I feel and I believe also that I look like someone else these days—perhaps an older member of my own family, but certainly not me, S. Bellow. An uncle or perhaps an aunt. Also I feel a powerful impulse to race away, to escape the constraints which go with being so-and-so, a person for whom (physically) I have no use.

These puzzling differences from what I am accustomed to consider myself must come from mourning, and they may or may not pass. (How can *I* tell?)

I sometimes think that if I were in S'dot Yam we could give each other comfort. If only I could get there by subway! I'd dearly love to walk along the sea with you and watch the water coming in.

I hope this note doesn't depress you. I turn to you when I'm sad, as we will turn to the people we love.

In an effort to "get out from under" I've made myself impossibly busy. I have dozens of jobs to do and drive myself to get them done. A foolish and characteristic measure which only makes things worse. Janis thinks a few days in Vermont catching up on sleep will do us some good, so we'll go off next week. Chicago now has its first taste of winter—you will remember from your pre-Israel days how the seasons trek one up and down.

Our best love to Nola.

Your friend,

To John Silber

December 27, 1992   Chicago

Dear John,

You'll be wondering what became of me. Let me say first, however, how splendid your offer is, and how generous—how pleased I am by it and how grateful.

I can now go on to tell you that it has made my whole life flash before me like the experience of the drowning. We have had to consider, my wife Janis and I, just how life should be lived—i.e. what to make of the future. On the whole, a cheerful thing to do, although there are lurid flashes of an apocalyptic nature on the horizon, and the horizon is furthermore uncomfortably close. Problems of moving and resettlement arise. And then as I grow older I think of reducing the time spent in teaching.

Since Boston and BU have a great many attractions, would it be possible to teach half-time? I could make the public appearances—I don't mind those too much—and it would be agreeable to live in Brookline or the Back Bay. Would it be possible to find a teaching position for Janis? She has just gotten her Ph.D. while studying in the Committee on Social Thought. She taught college courses in political theory and also in literature, and she would be ideally suited for your undergraduate Humanities program.

I'm tremendously grateful for your super invitation, and I hope you will forgive all this elderly fussing about "what to do with my life."

Endless thanks and all the best,

Silber was at the time president of Boston University.

1993

To Jonathan Kleinbard

April 25, 1993   Paris

Dear Jonathan,

[. . .] I can't cope with life in Chicago. A month in Paris has brought back to me the life I knew in the past—free movement, peaceable crowds in parks. I don't expect Boston to be different from Chicago, but there is Vermont close by. I don't feel like breathing my last in the Maginot Line (5825 [Dorchester], Apt 11E).

I shall miss you and Joan and your friendship. Janis will feel being away from Joan as a serious privation.

But it was understood tacitly that we'd have to get out of Chicago. Allan said to me, "You're planning the moves you'll make when I die." That was a bad moment for me, but he was right of course, and I was silent. But after a time I said, "Yes, but I'll be catching up with you soon enough." He agreed with that, and we went back to discussing the Bulls' chances against the Knicks.

So—who was the sports figure that said, "It ain't over till it's over"? He was dead right.

We'll continue to love you both from Boston, Vermont, etc., as well as from the life-to-come.

We'll be back on May 17th, to pack, etc. and we'll have more to say then. Yours ever,

To Philip Roth

July 20, 1993   W. Brattleboro

Dear Philip,

Curious how futile good intentions feel in a case like this. The whole of one's personal morality is on the line—a tug-of-war in which I am out-weighed a million to one by the imponderables. If you were to ask I'd come down to see you, though I've never seen myself as a bearer of remedies. I can't think of a single cure I ever worked. My idea of a *mitzvah* was to tell you a joke, which was like offering to install a Ferris wheel in your basement. Certainly not a useful idea.

This may seem to be a greeting from the horizon but I'm really not all that far. I feel anything but distant.

Affectionately,

Roth had suffered a serious illness, followed by the dissolution of his marriage to Claire Bloom.

To Roger Kaplan

July 20, 1993   W. Brattleboro

Dear Roger,

Don't think we've forgotten you—it isn't forgetfulness, it's the hurly-burly of relocation. There was a thirty-year accumulation of Chicago junk to transport, to say nothing of our cat Moose, without whom no stable domestic life is possible.

I don't know how useful I can be to you, you've done such a job (just as I did at your time of life) of supercomplication. I tried to get this complex operation down in the first pages of *Henderson the Rain King* with a catalogue of burdens, duties and handicaps.

It gave me some feeling of being helpful or useful through our mere presence in Paris. I can't say that I have any grasp whatever of your psychological problems. Psychology (let's be thankful for some things) is not my trade. Nor do I size you up as the sort of person who will tell his shrinker everything. You'd be sure to keep a few capstones or even cornerstones in your pocket. (It slows one up to carry so much rock, but it's the safest strategy.)

Besides, I don't want your foundation stones, only your affection. Reciprocity guaranteed.

Yours ever,

To Nathan Tarcov

August 18, 1993   W. Brattleboro

Dear Nathan,

Your invitation is very kind and I thank you for it. I find it a bit difficult just now, before I have had time to set up a routine for myself at BU, to make plans for this academic year. I'd be more than happy to come in '94–'95. I name these years with a certain hesitancy. At my time of life one becomes somewhat circumspect in the matter of future dates, but the natural thing is to go ahead and make them since I've never had the experience of being prevented by certain powerful forces—often mentioned but not as yet seen (by me)—from keeping an appointment.

It boils down to this: I'd love to come but I am not at this moment able to set a time. I shall be thinking about an appropriate book suitable for discussion at a high-powered seminar.

I was distressed by the Sunday *Times* review of Allan's book. It was not only criminal from an intellectual standpoint but also showed how low the *Times* has sunk. If I were not personally involved I should have written to Max Frankel to ask him how he could allow such stuff to be printed and why it was that he was willing to identify his point of view with that of the *Nation*. This Katha [Pollitt] is the sort of hit-person bred nowadays in the lower depths of New York.

Yours affectionately,

Nathan Tarcov, son of Oscar and Edith, has been for many years a professor of political philosophy in the Committee on Social Thought at the University of Chicago. His books include Locke's Education for Liberty. *Katha Pollitt, a staff writer at* The Nation, *had negatively reviewed Allan Bloom's posthumously published* Love and Friendship *in* The New York Times Book Review.

To John Auerbach

October 18, 1993   W. Brattleboro

Dear John,

We're getting a serious taste of the dying year in Vermont. The leaf-season was brilliant. Now comes cold rain, fog and the trees are dripping. No different from the Polish winters you used to know.

I think of you often, but I seem incapable of writing letters, and the incapacity is symptomatic. I seem to sacrifice everything in order to write a few pages (more often than not, bad ones that have to be thrown away). Loose all over the place—bills and business letters, other peoples' manuscripts accumulating on windowsills and in paper cartons. Everything is on hold. I'm unable to face the fact that I'm not going to catch up. [. . .]

> "Thou hast nor youth nor age,
> But, as it were, an after-dinner's sleep,
> Dreaming on both."
> (*Measure for Measure*)

The only remedy is to come to terms with the biological facts, which I seem to resist bitterly. I do as I learned to do as a sick child (1923, in Montreal) and read books, magazines, papers, clippings, catalogues (L.L. Bean) and even recipes or directions for use on the backs of boxes. I hide in print. All I need to do is acknowledge that I am no longer thirty, nor forty, fifty, sixty, seventy. Old Cousin Louie [Dworkin] used to say when I came to see him— "I'm in the slemonium!"

I suppose I'm trying to find a way of my own—in this as in everything else.

Now tell me—is the *TLS* coming? We took a subscription two months ago.

Greet Nola for me.

Love,

"Slemonium" was evidently Cousin Louie's private word for the stage of life beyond seventy.

1994

To Margaret Staats

January 4, 1994   Boston

Dear Maggie—

We're in Boston now after much hugger-mugger, and trying to live with the aches caused by much property and attendant responsibilities. Just now everything has been shut down by winter storms. I sit facing the Charles, which has been iced over and snowed upon, and it isn't going anywhere either. We'll have to wait for the January thaw—I know it's supposed to arrive—guaranteed by Yankee lore and tradition. And *then* we'll go out and gather impressions of Boston. I have a fair understanding of the Green Line—the other subway colors, not yet.

Janis has found a cake plate for Signora Cinelli-Colombini (you remember *her*) and will send it to Montalcino. You with your bottomless memory are sure to be familiar with the name. Signora C.C. entertained us while I wrote the "Winter in Tuscany" article. You said that we should send a suitable present, and at last we've made a selection.

This morning I was playing whirling dervish—literally. It's one of the Tibetan lamas' exercises for squaring oneself with the *chakras* (vital centers of the spiritual-romantic self). I got dizzy (my first effort) and fell down. A real fall that shook the house. No damages to report.

Yr. indestructible old chum,

"Winter in Tuscany" had been commissioned for Travel Holiday *and had appeared there in November 1992.*

To Martin Amis

July 24, 1994   W. Brattleboro

Dear Martin,

I can generally diagnose my friends' disorders by reading [their stories and novels]. I know from experience that a real comedian is at his best when he's most wretched. I don't like Freud at all but he was on target when he wrote that happiness is the remission of suffering, something he may have swiped from Schopenhauer. You will have guessed that this note is inspired by [Amis's story] "Author, Author" in *Granta*. It's the sort of comic x-ray that sinks the diagnostician's spirits and fills the connoisseur's heart with pure pleasure. I hear an echo here of Brutus after the assassination: We loved Caesar for his greatness but killed him because he was ambitious.

But of course writing well is also a sign of cure and recovery.

Janis who was also knocked flat—"decked" with happiness—sends love.

Yours as ever,

To Julian Behrstock

September 15, 1994   W. Brattleboro

Dear Julian—

As you will have guessed, I am disturbed to hear that you've been ill and had major surgery. When you have bad news your generous impulse is to reassure everyone. That, I've learned, is one of your deepest traits. You could hardly have gone through a course of chemotherapy without deep-fatigue— but the Midi and some rest and musing bring back your *joie de vivre*, and your mood is upbeat.

The other problems—arrhythmia and a runaway heartbeat—one can live with. I've done that for years with large daily doses of quinine. I have other nuisance-ailments associated with age—the medical term is presbyopia. No reason to describe those. "*Edad con sus disgracias*"[*] is the title of one of Goya's etchings. Even reasonable people are taught by life, willy-nilly, to pray, and these days I include you in my stolen prayer sessions. (I like to call them meditations.)

We have hardly budged from Vermont this summer. I watched the summer through the windows while scribbling away at a novel I perhaps should never have started. Life has by now prepared me to write an essay called "How Not to Write a Novel." Lots of critics would say it sh'd be "*Why* Not to Write One." The whole world has accepted biological ("historical") standards. A heart flourishes, then inevitably perishes, and a higher type of the same comes into its own. The new type has a bigger mouth and stronger jaws. You shall hear from me again and soon.

Love,

*Spanish: "Indignities of Old Age": Goya's etching shows an elderly man struggling to rise from his chamber pot.

To Eugene C. Kennedy

November 10, 1994   Grand Case, Saint-Martin

Dear Gene—

The treatment is working. I put it like that because I begin to see how necessary it was for Janis to get me here—I was willing to talk about it, but of my own accord I'd never have gotten here. I just lack the character to do what's necessary. And today I see a parallel between me and the problem drinkers whose doctors send them away to be dried out. Too much festination [*], as Dr. Oliver Sacks would put it. I recommend his book *Awakenings*, and the Parkinsonian case-histories in it. Sarah probably has read it. His account of festination and catatonia went straight to that waiting throbbing target, my heart. The blue of the Caribbean I see from this open door is my form of El Dopa. *Festination!* I had a bad case of it. I suspect that Dr. Sacks believes it's endemic. Civilized people all have it in some form or other. What I do for it is to soak in the ocean twice daily. We have no phone in our small flat (open to the breezes) and no newspapers are available. NO mail is being forwarded. My one daily lapse or cop-out—cheating on the cure—is literary. I work each morning on my *Marbles* book. I may actually get that monkey off my back before X-mas.

A daily greeting in my Village days was "off the couch by X-mas!" It was said of Jim Agee that he *had* to work at *Time* to pay for his analysis. He said it himself—Henry Luce and Sigmund Freud were in cahoots. More than half of the Lucites (or Luciferites) were then in treatment.

Anyway my spirits having risen during these days of submersion in an El Dopa Caribbean, I love you with a fresh impulse. You're a darling man. I wish I could say it in the right brogue.

We return to festinating Boston Nov. 30th. Let's hope we will be able then to live by the good old slogan *Festina Lente* [**].

So, in the same vein—*Excelsior!*

Much love to both of you,

Former priest and dissident Roman Catholic Eugene C. Kennedy is Professor Emeritus of Psychology at Loyola University, Chicago, and the author of many books including The Unhealed Wound: The Church and Human Sexuality

* pathological shortening of the stride and quickening of the gait; more loosely, frenetic activity
** Latin: Make haste slowly!

(2001) and My Brother Joseph *(1998), a memoir of his friendship with Joseph Cardinal Bernardin. Shortly after writing this letter, Bellow fell dangerously ill with ciguatera poisoning. For a month he was unconscious and in intensive care at Boston University Hospital. At the turn of the year he went home to the apartment on Bay State Road, where he slowly recovered.*

1995

In Memory of Ralph Ellison
>*(Delivered in Bellow's absence by Joseph Mitchell at the dinner meeting*
>*of the American Academy of Arts and Letters on April 4, 1995)*

Ralph Ellison, who died last year at the age of eighty, published only one novel in his lifetime. At a Bard College symposium attended by foreign celebrities, Georges Simenon who was at our table asked Ellison how many novels he had written. Hearing that there was only one, he said, "To be a novelist you must produce many novels. You are not a novelist." The author of hundreds of books, writing and speaking at high speed, could not stop to weigh his words. Einstein, a much deeper thinker, had said in reply to a sociable lady's question about quantum theory, "But isn't one a lot, Madame?"

In Ralph's case it certainly was a lot. Simenon remains readable, enjoyable, but Inspector Maigret belongs to a very large family of cops or private eyes or geniuses of detection like Sherlock Holmes or the heroes of Dashiell Hammett, Raymond Chandler *et al.* These honorable and gifted men worked at the writer's trade. Ellison did no such thing. What we witness when we read *Invisible Man* is the discovery by an artist of his true subject matter, and some fifty years after it was published this book holds its own among the best novels of the century. Toward the end of the Fifties, the Ellisons and the Bellows lived together in a spooky Dutchess County house with the Catskills on the western horizon and the Hudson River in between. As writers are natural solitaries, Ralph and I did not seek each other out during the day. A nod in passing was enough. But late in the afternoon Ralph mixed the martinis and we did not always drink in silence. During our long conversations I came to know his views, some of which I shall now transmit in his own words:

"We did not develop as a people in isolation," he told James McPherson in an interview. "We developed within a context of white people. Yes, we have a special awareness, because our experience has in certain ways been different from that of white people; but it was not absolutely different." And, again: "I tell white kids that instead of talking about black men in a white world or black men in a white society they should ask themselves how black they are because black men have been influencing the values of the society and the art forms of the society . . . We did not develop as a people in isolation."

"For me," he said, "some effort was necessary . . . before I could identify the areas of life and personality which claimed my mind beyond any limitations *apparently* imposed by my racial identity." And, again: "This was no matter of sudden insight but of slow and blundering discovery, of a struggle to stare down the deadly and hypnotic temptation to interpret the world and all its devices in terms of race." It took great courage, in a time when racial solidarity was demanded, or exacted, from people in public life, to insist as Ralph did on the priority of art and the independence of the artist. "Fiction," he says, "became the agency of my efforts to answer the questions: Who am I, what am I, how did I come to be? What should I make of the life around me? . . . What does American society mean when regarded out of my *own* eyes, when informed by my *own* sense of the past and viewed by my *own* complex sense of the present? . . . It is quite possible," he adds, "that much potential fiction by Negro Americans fails precisely at this point: through the writer's refusal (often through provincialism or lack of courage or opportunism) to achieve a vision of life and a resourcefulness of craft commensurate with the complexity of their actual situation. Too often they fear to leave the uneasy sanctuary of race to take their chances in the world of art." Ralph did no such thing.

I have let him speak for himself. But there is one thing more, of a personal nature, that I should like to add in closing. Often, when I think of Ralph, a line from E. E. Cummings comes to me: "Jesus, he was a handsome man," Cummings wrote—he was referring to Buffalo Bill. Ralph did not ride a watersmooth stallion, nor was he a famous marksman. But he did have the look of a man from an earlier epoch, one more sane, more serious and more courageous than our own.

To John Hunt

June 18, 1995 Boston

Dear John,

Sorry to have been so very, very long. The reason lies partly in my illness, of which Keith [Botsford] may have told you. I was down, down, down for months. I don't always know what's going on—I've always had a serious focus problem—but this time all reality was pulled away, stored like a carpet. I may or may not have thought that I was in another world—my relations to this one have never been anything but relatively steady. Wherever I may have been, there was no "time" there. I wasn't certifiably unconscious but neither was I in any ordinary sense conscious. After six weeks I was transferred out of intensive care to "recovery." "Recovery" was a euphemism for infantile weakness. I had to learn to walk again, to go to the toilet like an adult, to tell time, etc.

How I (we!) would have loved to be with you in France. But for the time being, I have to stick around the Boston U. Hospital. Life is far from normal. I take huge doses of blood-thinners, and I am warned that to swallow two aspirins may be fatal. I *do* now and then write something, and I can read again, indulge my lifelong vice for books—far too many of them.

To move to the South of France would be infinitely desirable 1.) if we could find someone to buy the Vermont house and 2.) if I hadn't been undermined by pulmonary and cardiac—puzzlingly threatening (and unreal)— disorders. All the granite I depended on has turned into loose sand and gravel. This is the *déreglement de tous les sens* [*] Rimbaud was sold on. Poor Rimbaud, he didn't live very long whereas I, a week ago, "celebrated" my eightieth birthday. People tell me that I look perfectly well. *Sans blague!* [**]

I was *so* grateful for your generous letter. All best to you and to Chantal,

John Hunt (born 1925) is a writer and scientist who during the Fifties and Sixties worked at the Congress for Cultural Freedom in Paris and subsequently at the Salk Institute for Biological Studies in La Jolla, California, the Aspen Institute, and the Institute for Advanced Study in Princeton, New Jersey.

To Herbert Gold

June [?], 1995   Boston

Dear Herb—

Did you ever think we'd live to see the century end? I used to play out the mental arithmetic but never thought I'd finish off the millennium. Maybe I won't. It's not over till it's over, as the great baseball philosopher said.

---

* French: the disordering of all the senses
** French: No kidding!

Your letter dated May 24th reached me about a week ago. I was sorry to read that your brother had died. I know what these deaths are. I had two older brothers. They died ten years ago, within the same week. I find myself thinking of them daily, at odd moments—in an ongoing manner.

I have no case to make against them. I no longer blame them, as I used to do. I am now their senior and one of my responsibilities is to protect them affectionately. For that matter, I am much older than my parents too. I suppose the good do die young. *We* are given more time to re-cobble our virtues and fit ourselves to die.

There does seem to have been a certain estrangement [between you and me], and perhaps the reason is mainly spatial. Separated by an entire continent we've been unable to attend to our friendship. But I've always had warm feelings toward you. There are, perhaps, a few incompatibilities but they aren't, and never were, serious. I value your judgment and your good opinion, and I wish you well.

Herbert Gold (born 1924) is the author of many books including The Man Who Was Not with It *(1956) and* Still Alive! A Temporary Condition *(2008).*

To Saul Steinberg

July 28, 1995   W. Brattleboro

Dear Saul—

When your picture arrived I was again caught in an undertow—one of the drugs I was taking had swollen my tongue and my palate to such an extent that I was unable to swallow.

I was, in short, choking to death. And once more, rallying, I pulled through. I did however have a thoroughly disagreeable week and was unable to call you to say that your picture had been delivered. So it was no *manque de politesse* [*]. Having yet again fought off the forces of assassination I can now look at your harmonious composition with enjoyment. I keep it on the kitchen mantelpiece and study it over my teacup. I badly need the balancing measure and proportion I am enjoying, and feel at certain moments that I am camped in your mind, the source of equilibrium.

Yours gratefully and affectionately,

Janis and I are expecting you one day soon.

* French: want of manners

To John Hunt

September 13, 1995   W. Brattleboro

Dear John,

I might, if I were a more gifted writer, tell you what this year has *really* been like—but I can't transmit the neural creepings and the wing-beating of the spirit, and all the thoughts etc. that use me as a thoroughfare.

It hasn't, all in all, been a sick summer. The strange difficulty is that I have stamina enough to see me through the morning's work, and after that I am *useless*. I take a walk, I lie down at siesta-time, the afternoon expires. I've lost the habit of writing letters. After dark, I can't go back to the desk.

I spent many evenings looking at Faulkner photos in the book you so generously sent me. I should have written to thank you but this morning is the first full one in months. [. . .] For the book, *merci mille fois* [*].

As ever (whatever that is),

To Julian Behrstock

September 13, 1995   W. Brattleboro

Dear Julian—

I hate to think of your chemotherapy, and I do think about it daily. Medicine seems to have made great progress in that department, as in others. More than one doctor has told me that I wouldn't have made it five years ago. And I have the distinct feeling, or intuition, that you and I are meant to go on, for a bit. Actuarial commonsense tells us that a bit is all we can fairly expect. I surround the statistics with prayers and ask the Lord whether he can see his way clear to granting us yet one more breather.

The enclosed story ["By the Saint Lawrence"] is one I wrote when I got out of the hospital in January. Magazines have all become so serious (or seriously pornographic) that they seldom have space for fiction. *The New Yorker* was willing to print me but I was told that the word-rate was lower than for non-fiction—i.e. libelous "exposés" and the trashing of quite inoffensive people. So I accepted *Esquire*'s higher offer. Their fiction editor, Rust Hills, has a sentimental soft spot for me.

With me it's still as it was for Gibbon. When George III met him he said, "Always scribble scribble scribble, eh, Mr. Gibbon?"

Your old and constant pal,

* French: thanks a million

To Martin Amis

September 30, 1995   W. Brattleboro

Dear Martin—

How to explain how it is that I haven't written: I see at once that such a project can only be a dud.

To say that I've been "out of sorts," hung up, convalescent for the better part of a year conveys nothing much. I've been unable to pull myself together. I seem normal enough in the morning—at least until I touch certain tender places, and then I feel nature's spite against the aging when these tender places begin to ail. Then I suspect that I never shall recover—I'm too old to do it. I have cardiac troubles ("atrial fibrillations") and beneath this agitation of the heart muscles there is an unbearable sluggishness, the original sloth of the deadly sin. I have just enough stamina to write for an hour or two, and then I go back to bed for a siesta! At three o'clock I realize that the day has somehow been swallowed up. I take a good many drugs—"beta-blockers"—and these affect the brain weirdly. I am easily depressed. The days fly away, the weeks are uncontrollable, the months and the seasons are like the merry-go-round.

So my only serious effort is to think, or try to think, how to chuck this derangement and drift, and get onto some firm ground.

There are plenty of books around but I don't really *read* them—they go *past* my mind, not into it.

Well, all this is true enough. But it's far from the whole truth. I do take pleasure in Janis's company, and in the weather, the summer blues and greens. I've been too weak to tend the tomato plants, or to dig or prune, but I haven't been completely *hors d'usage* [*]. And I haven't been well enough to see the shoulderless [————]. *That's* an unmixed benefit, a very considerable plus.

Reading your *Augie March* essay was gratifying. You were far too generous, however. I can't read a page of the book without flinching. It seems to me now one of those stormy, formless American phenomena—like Action Painting. It *was* necessary to invent a way to cope with the curious realities of American life, and I did obviously *invent* something. But the book I now find disconcertingly amorphous, sound and fury signifying not too much.

Much love,

* French: out of commission

Saul Bellow: Letters

Amis had contributed an introduction to the new Everyman edition of The Adventures of Augie March.

1996

To Albert Glotzer

January 9, 1996   Brookline

Dear Al,

I thought of you while chatting with Richard Pipes, the Russian historian. He's getting ready to publish a collection of recently released Lenin documents from the early years—1917 to 1923. I wish you had been here when he described some of them. One is an order to find and hang a hundred Kulaks. Just hang them, his instructions were, and leave them hanging as long as possible. A few years ago we in America were calling this consciousness-raising. On the other hand, one still meets people from Harvard with a hear-no-evil fixation on the essential benevolence of the Soviet Union from first to last. But of course now we're talking about character formations of the middle class, not about politics.

I haven't read *Crime and Punishment* in many years—I have it scheduled for the coming winter—but I have a distinct recollection of Raskolnikov's double murder. He waits until the old usurer's sister is out of the way, but just as he hits the money lender on the head with his axe, the door opens and he sees the shocked face of the simpleton sister who has returned. He has no choice but to kill her, too. It is the second killing that plagues his conscience. I can't remember that he ever regrets the first murder. But the innocent sister who unexpectedly comes home is a True Believer and also an intimate friend of the prostitute Sonya whom Raskolnikov eventually marries. Tell Maggie for me that I hope I haven't upset her. I will be reading the book in March and if I'm wrong about the second victim I shall send a dozen American Beauty roses to apologize.

My health improves daily. I say this only to friends. Illness gives me a whole range of marvelous excuses for refusing the thousands of requests that come in the mail.

On Thursday Janis and I are flying down to Coral Gables to attend the wedding of my youngest son, Daniel. Youngest? He'll be thirty-two in March. Nobody is young anymore, except the grandchildren, and even they look a little wrinkled from time to time—my own projection, of course. I must have an ailing cornea. [. . .]

Best wishes,

To Julian Behrstock

January 19, 1996   Brookline

Dear Julian,

Just as I was about to emerge from the woods and to feel approximately normal, the doctors caught up with me and back to the hospital I went for gall-bladder surgery. This imposed a second convalescence on the first, which wasn't quite over. I found myself in the same hospital corridor, only two doorways away from the room I occupied last January. I wouldn't dream of complaining to a non-complainer like you. I'm just chronicling, not bitching. The surgery is about three weeks behind me now. My belly, which must have resembled Picasso's stamp collection, has recovered from the surgical bruises. The only prominent scar goes through my navel. Out of some sheer primitive magical conviction, I felt the navel to be inviolable. I seemed to have believed that it would never be mutilated. Probably some Oedipal residue. Anyway, I am delighted to hear that you are well enough to travel *en famille.*

I have in today's mail a letter from the Ministry of Culture in Paris inviting me to a "Salon du livre" late in March. The national center of this book fair, if you can believe it, is 53 rue de Verneuil. Surely you haven't forgotten the rue de Verneuil.

But this is a pipe dream. I couldn't possibly fly to Paris for three days and bring back a jet lag lasting for weeks.

Janis and I have moved away from Bay State Road and the showpiece apartment belonging to the University is used for visiting firemen. [. . .]

I hope there will be no more medical news at either end. The foregoing explains why you have not been hearing from me.

Yours affectionately,

To Sophie Wilkins

January 19, 1996   Brookline

Dear Sophie,

I seem to be down to notes, even though I long to reply to your delicious letter with a letter equally long.

It took me nearly a year to recover from heart failure, double pneumonia, and a toxic attack on the nervous system, and then, just as I thought I could put it all behind me, the doctors decided that they must remove my gall bladder, and the surgery put me down again for a period of weeks and I am only just beginning to recover. So although I have all sorts of things to tell you, I find that I can't write stories or novels in the morning and long letters in the afternoon. Nor when I look at the shelves in the library can I understand demon correspondents like Voltaire or Alexander Pope. I am too old and bothered to read their books, much less their letters. In my youth I had time for everything. I read scads of books, earned my letter on the track team, chased girls and spoke from a soapbox. I can only think about Voltaire that he must have had an extraordinarily long adolescence. But then Goethe told Eckermann somewhere that whenever he began to write in real earnest the years dropped away and he was once again sixteen and seventeen.

Anyway, I have pulled out of the second nosedive. My youngest son, Daniel, was married last Sunday in Coral Gables, Fla., and Janis and I flew down on Thursday from this gateway to the Arctic to the snowless beauty of the south. We had to wait four hours at Logan for our plane. I had sworn in advance to put up with no long airport ordeal, and I actually had a letter from the doctor certifying that I was too weak to expose myself to fatigue. But I did it all the same. I didn't want the kid accusing me of disappearing on *all* important occasions. So I did it all, including a second trip to the altar with my ex-wife, Daniel's mother. There wouldn't have been a Stoic in all of Rome who wouldn't have congratulated me on my philosophic poise.

Let me add my name to the list of Freud's detractors. If he had been purely a scientist he wouldn't have had nearly so many readers. It was lovers of literature (and not the best kind of those) who made his reputation. His patients were the text and his diagnoses were lit. crit. The gift the great nineteenth-century *nudniks* [*] gave us was the gift of metaphor. Marx with the metaphor of class struggle and Freud with the metaphor of the Oedipus complex. Once you had read Marx it took a private revolution to overthrow the powerful metaphor of class warfare—for an entire decade I couldn't see history in any other light. Freud also subjugated us with powerful metaphors and after a time we couldn't approach relationships in any but a Freudian medical light. Thank God I liberated myself before it was too late.

Anyway, the purpose of the letter is to tell you how much we love you and miss you both. Janis and I will be in New York on April 16th. The reason for

* Yiddish: pests, bothersome people

the visit is a bought-and-paid-for reading at Queens College. Perhaps we will be able to see you then. The trouble is that we must be back in Boston to meet our classes at BU. If the Queens authorities will allow me to fiddle with the dates, we may be able to add a weekend, and thus have time for the really important things.

Yours ever,

In Memory of Eleanor Clark

*(Delivered at the First and Second Unitarian
Universalist Church, Boston, March 9, 1996)*

I met Eleanor Clark in Manhattan in the late Forties. It was Paolo Milano who introduced us. She was then living on the Upper East Side, and he said, "I'm going to call on her—come along." I had read Eleanor in *Partisan Review*. Perhaps she had read me, too. What I recall is that she was a breezy young woman with a fine figure, attractive, a lively conversationalist, a great asker of difficult questions. I think Paolo had been acquainted with her in Rome. I know that in the late Thirties she had been one of Trotsky's staff in Mexico City. I always meant to ask her if she was in the villa when it was attacked—blasted—by an armed band led by Siqueiros the painter. But I never got around to it, somehow.

PR was in its early years strongly flavored by Trotskyist politics. The magazine was in the Thirties what *The Dial* had been in the Twenties, its great days, the days of Marianne Moore—an international journal of literature and the arts. In *Partisan Review* a decade later the arts were mixed with left-wing politics. College students in the Midwest had their eyes opened to the great world by *Partisan Review*. There they could read Malraux, Silone, Gide, Orwell, Auden together with that older generation of American poets and critics—Allen Tate, R. P. Warren, John Crowe Ransom, James Burnham, Sidney Hook, Meyer Schapiro. And suddenly a generation of younger Americans began to appear in this otherwise unattainable company undreamed of in Madison, Wisconsin, or Urbana, Illinois. It was in *PR* that we first read our own gifted contemporaries—Robert Lowell, Delmore Schwartz, John Berryman, Clement Greenberg, Jean Stafford, Harold Rosenberg, James Agee. Eleanor Clark was one of those gifted and, in my view, privileged people—the *avant-garde*, the bohemians—initiates of a sort into all that represented the finest, the deepest, the boldest and the subtlest.

There was something like a literary, painterly and intellectual life in New York in those years. Very brief. It didn't quite make it into the Sixties. Already in the Fifties writers were drifting into teaching positions in the universities. So that when I went to Minnesota in 1946 I became acquainted with Robert Penn Warren. He had not then met Eleanor Clark. I've never been much good at chronologies. In such matters I go, as most of us do, by emotional clocks and affective calendars. The object of these recollections is to turn some lateral or indirect light on Eleanor's life. I can recall driving in winter from Rhinebeck, N.Y., with Fred Dupee and his wife to the Warren house in Connecticut to attend a party they were giving and that Fred, who was driving, had us all swigging whiskey from the bottle Jazz-Age style. The party lasted most of the night, but Eleanor and Red were, unlike most of their guests, unmistakably family people.

Over the years I met the Warrens in a variety of circumstances. I recall that the three of us went together in a car when Eleanor won a National Book Award for *The Oysters of Locmariaquer.* I took the fiction prize in that year, and Red said to the two of us, "Enough of this. You've got your medals. Now get out while the getting's good."

During the last twenty summers we met often in Vermont. Eleanor's eyes were all but gone but she entertained her visitors in style. We sat on the outer deck of the house, drinking. On a conversational roll she barely noticed the chill of the air at sunset or the stinging of the mosquitoes. Like the matriarch she had become she cooked the dinner and, at the head of the table, ladled out the stew and filled the plates of her guests. She often growled at me for my shell-back social views and pounced on my mistakes of grammar or usage. But that was because she loved disputes, sharp answers and social militancy. She was a handsome, brave, big-hearted woman. If you hadn't seen her sweeping aside her handicaps and frailties, coming on like the able-bodied beauty she had been decades ago, you had missed a superb demonstration of gallantry or heroic courage.

To Richard Stern

March 12, 1996   Brookline

Dear Richard—

You are unchallengeably the most generous writer I've ever known. Your firefly friends can be certain when their tails light up with a new color that your innocent heart will respond with joy.

When I got out of the hospital (crawled out) last winter I ran a test or two—naturally—to see whether there was a charge still in the batteries. And of course repetitions—deploying the old troops—wouldn't do.

And . . . I've got at least four or five readers. God has not abandoned me. Why the Lord of hosts has let the ranks become so thin, who can say? *Continuons!* [*]

Much love from your well and grateful friend,

To Martin Amis

March 13, 1996   Brookline

My dear Martin:

I see that I've become a really bad correspondent. It's not that I don't think of you. You come into my thoughts often. But when you do it appears to me that I owe you a particularly grand letter. And so you end in the "warehouse of good intentions":

"Can't do it now."

"Then put it on *hold*."

This is one's strategy for coping with old age, and with death—because one *can't* die with so many obligations in storage. Our clever species, so fertile and resourceful in denying its weaknesses.

I entered the hospital in '94, a man biologically in his forties. Coming out in '95, I was the Ancient Mariner, and the Mariner didn't write novels. He had only one story and delivered it orally. But [I told myself] you *are* a writer still, and perhaps you'd better come to terms with the Ancient.

I may be about to resolve all these difficulties, but for two years they have totally absorbed me.

I've become forgetful, too. Nothing like your father's nominal aphasia. I find I can't remember the names of people I don't care for—in some ways a pleasant disability. I further discover that I would remember people's names because it relieved me from any need to think about them. Their names were enough. Like telling heads.

I can guess how your father must have felt at his typewriter, with a book to finish. My solution is to turn to shorter, finishable things. I have managed to do a few of those. Like learning to walk again—but what if what one wants, really, is to *run*?

I am sure you have thought these things in watching your father's torments.

Last Saturday I attended a memorial service for Eleanor Clark, the widow of R. P. Warren. I found myself saying to her daughter Rosanna that losing a

* French: Let us go on!

parent is something like driving through a plate-glass window. You didn't know it was there until it shattered, and then for years to come you're picking up the pieces—down to the last glassy splinter.

Of course you *are* your father, and he is you. I have often felt this about my own father, whom I half expect to see when I die. But I believe I do know how your father must have felt, sitting at his typewriter with an unfinished novel. Just as I understand your saying that you are your dad. With a fair degree of accuracy I can see this in my own father. He and I never *seemed* to be in rapport: Our basic assumptions were *very* different. But that now looks superficial. I treat my sons much as he treated me: out of breath with impatience, and then a long inhalation of affection.

I willingly take up the slack as a sort of adoptive father. I do have paternal feelings towards you. It's not only language that unites us, or "style." We share more remote but also more important premises.

And I'm not actually at the last gasp. I expect to be around for a while (not a prediction but an expectation). Whilst this machine is to him, Hamlet said.

Yours, with love,

Martin Amis's father, Kingsley Amis, renowned author of Lucky Jim *(1954) and many other works, had died in October of the previous year after a long decline, subsequently chronicled by Martin in his memoir* Experience *(2000).*

To Reinhold Neven du Mont

April 12, 1996   Brookline

Dear Reinhold:

Harriet Wasserman and I have not been able to continue as agent and client. My new agent, as you may have heard, is Andrew Wylie. Harriet has cast me into outer darkness and no longer communicates with me though there is unfinished business to do.

In any case I write to inform you that Mr. Wylie will be representing me and that he has full authority to speak for me. You and I have always had excellent relations and there will be no change in our amicable customs.

I hope that you are well and happy. I have almost recovered from several illnesses and am writing again. I have just finished a novella—something entirely new, I hope.

Yours as ever,

Neven du Mont was an editor at Kiepenheuer & Witsch, Bellow's German publisher.

To Albert Glotzer

April 19, 1996   Brookline

Dear Al,

I spoke with Yetta [Barshevsky Shachtman] and she told me that it was your habit to attend the Boston Marathon and wait at the finish line for your son the runner. I too encourage the oddities of my three sons and my sole grandson, Andrew, who grew up in California where oddities are never in short supply. So I was hoping to see you last Monday, but Yetta said that you were making a quick round trip and would not stay overnight. On last Tuesday I was expected at Queens College—booked for a reading—but the Nervous Nellies of the Queens English Department called on Monday to warn me of bad weather ahead. They urged me to get on the next shuttle. So I was actually in New York City on Monday night. I did my thing on Tuesday. By Wednesday afternoon I was back in Boston. This was my first solo journey and I regretted leaving Janis behind. I am like you in my boyish rejection of elderliness. Antiquity—why not come right out with it? You pack a snowball on a winter day and imagine taking a belly flop on your sled as we all used to do back in the beautiful Twenties—I was ten years old in 1925. All that remains is the freshness of the impulse.

Last Sunday, here in Boston, I spoke at Harvard before Richard Pipes's society [the Shop Club]; its members are Polish intellectuals and Jewish intellectuals (from Poland). The membership was singular, to say the least. Nobody has more intellectual style than these east Europeans. I thought this was a very odd lodge. My subject was anti-Semitism (otherwise known as Jew-hatred) in literature. I concentrated almost entirely on Dostoyevsky and on L.-F. Céline. Afterwards we attended a party at the Pipeses'. Among the guests were many who knew more about my subject than I did, and I wish I could remember their names. The only name that does come back to me is that of the brother of the late James Merrill, a boyish old man, ruddy and blue-eyed, with white curls, who looked as if he might have just left his fielder's mitt on the hall table. For all his billions he was so fresh and engaging that my heart went out to him. He turned out to be an amateur scholar deeply interested in Polish history and literature. But I was monopolized by a mathematician I had known in a former incarnation and by a Polish Céline expert who spoke to me in French about Céline's sick-joke pamphlets recommending the Final Solution.

A house in the country was a great idea, but completely utopian. I love solitude, but I prize it most when plenty of company is available. At this very moment, the roads are swimming in mud in Vermont. How to deal with mud time? Perhaps I might start a new fashion with mud skis. I seem to be one of those natural revolutionists who comes up regularly with million-dollar ideas. [. . .]

I invite you to come and stay with Janis and me when you attend next year's Marathon. This will give both of us something to live for.

Yours,

To John Auerbach and Nola Chilton

May 3, 1996   Brookline

Dear John and Nola—

If I don't write to you, I scarcely write at all. My correspondents have given up on me. Not to write means to be fundamentally out of order, and I suppose that that can be said of me. I am not "drunk" but I am "disorderly"— old before my preparations to be old are completed. I keep thinking what I *shall* be doing *when*—and *when* overcomes me while I'm still considering what to do about it.

A month in intensive care, unconscious, was what did it. At last I was convinced.

It's necessary for me to be in Boston [on account of] its doctors. I have a five-foot shelf of pills. Janis makes sure I take them on schedule, and visit the cardiologist, the neurologist, the dermatologist, the G.U. man, the ophthalmologist, etc. A friendly physician has explained to me that four weeks in intensive care take six months to recover from. I must not expect to be normal again before the end of 1996.

But I have much to be grateful for. Without Janis I'd have joined my ancestors by now. I do think of *them* quite a lot. I'm edging near. But I can't conceive of any sort of life, in any dimension, without her. And, after all, seeing my parents, brothers, friends is by no means a certainty. There's a large cloud of ambiguous promises over all our intimations—a dark atmosphere of hints. This side of death there's nothing definite, about the afterlife, to be found.

The best one can do (the best *I* can do) is to write stories. I've written a novella—sexy but the setting (by and large) is a cemetery. I'll send you a copy when it's fit to be read.

You mustn't think I've forgotten you. I think about you both. But I very seldom send letters. And I can hardly bring myself to read the mail.

I hope you are well, thriving, happy.

Love,

Janis adds *her* love, as well.

The sexy novella would appear next spring as The Actual.

To James Salter

May 20, 1996   Brookline

Dear Jim,

I can't match your chatty insouciance, nobody can. Real insouciance takes character. It's one of the gifts that's been withheld from me. If I were able to take matters lightly I should have come along on this junket. I've had two trips this spring, one to Toronto that knocked me out and another to Queens College that laid me low. A trans-Atlantic trip is something I can't face. Perhaps if I had two or three months to recover in Paris I could do it, but a round trip is out of the question. Also I'm too unforgiving to write *dégagé* [*] anecdotes. To take an example of such skills from your own letter, I loved the Nabokov taxi-cab anecdote but the image of a rose on a hairy chest on which you finish it rubbed me the wrong way. Nabokov was like that—one of the great wrong-way rubbers of all times. Somewhere he said, and said very well, that Borges was a marvelous writer and then he went on to add that Borges's pieces are like beautiful verandas and that after the eighteenth or twentieth porch one says, "Great but where are the houses?" This is Nabokov at his best. At his gruesome worst he pins feminine roses to simian bosoms.

In the old days I used to stay in Gallimard's attic on the Rue Bottin— little bedrooms such as the bedrooms I was used to in Chicago in the Depression: three bucks a week. I'd like nothing better than to follow you around Paris from one thrilling party to another. What a gift you have for filling your days with good company. When your letters come to be collected, you'll be in a class with Samuel Pepys.

All the best,

* French: relaxed, nonchalant

To Julian Behrstock

Dear Julian—

I seem to have become a home-industry of ill news, surrounded by pharmaceuticals (*médicaments*). A text punctuated by pills. The heart turns out to be the problem—I had always suspected that it would end by getting its own back on me. The most sinister of the pills is Coumadin, an anti-coagulant that protects me from a stroke. Born normal enough, I am now a hemophiliac like the Tsarevitch and the other princes descended from Victoria and Albert. (So they tell me.)

I thought of you (thought *particularly*; I often think of you) last month, remembering that we had marched nine years ago in the Northwestern procession [honoring the Class of 1937]. Our sixtieth anniversary comes up next year. It would be a good occasion for both of us, and memorable also for your wife and son.

I've taken two or three domestic flights. Haven't been abroad since the Caribbean holiday that nearly did me in. Janis is keen on going to Paris. We left a tidy sum there at CIC (the bank on Blvd. Raspail) and on three years of interest Janis says we could stay at the Crillon and give the Behrstocks dinner at a four-star joint. It's a brilliant ploy. Janis is not one for small ideas. And I'm on her side. We could spend up a storm at the Crillon *and* march later with the Class of '37.

At this moment we are in Vermont, reading books, writing (on lucky days) and growing flowers.

I don't ask about your health because I don't want to put you to the trouble of replying. But you know I'm pulling for you full strength.

Your old friend,

To Hymen Slate

Dear Hymen—

My son Gregory with his Italian organ-grinder mustachios visited you a few months ago, and said you weren't well—reminding me that we've known each other, you and I, for more than sixty years, and that at this stage of life we experience both the present moment and antiquity. I write to say that I hope you've overcome your illness. Of course, the old expect their surviving friends to be ailing. I had a substantial foretaste of death recently ('94); it's the usual thing for all octogenarians.

Odd how past and present come together in the consciousness of aged men and women. My ninety-year-old sister in Miami Beach goes *every day* to the shopping mall to buy dresses; she exchanges or returns them, and her closets are full of skirts, blouses, shoes. She sees herself, with the help of her Frankenstein's lab of cosmetics, appearing before the world as the smashing beauty she was sixty-five years back.

As for me, you may ask why I write to you now, having dropped from sight about eleven years ago. As a mature observer, you may not see fit to ask at all, only shrug.

But picture the following: In one week my elder brothers had died; I attended both funerals. I turned sixty-nine on June 10th, '84. On that day Alexandra said she was divorcing me. She moved out of the apartment then and there. Not before she had applied circular stickers, big ones, green and white, to her possessions and mine. Even bathrobes and carpet slippers carried these gummed labels, a weird snowfall of large round green and white flakes.

Rather than explain this or discuss it with you, since we had never reached an appropriate stage of intimacy, I simply dropped out. I disappeared. You will certainly understand that there are absurdities or paradoxes that are not and should not be communicable. I found an opening into a new life (the five hundredth one). I left Sheridan Rd. and our friendship, alas, was shelved.

All my best wishes to you and to Evelyn.

Your affectionate pal,

To Martin Amis

August 8, 1996   W. Brattleboro

Dear Martin—

A flying friend picked up *The American Way*, the in-house mag of American Airlines and I read your interview with a special pleasure, because your answers were so short:

Q: *What literary landmarks are important in the city?*
A: Karl Marx's grave. A lot of people go and visit that in Highgate Cemetery.

President Coolidge's wife questioned him one Sunday morning when he returned from Church:

Q: *What was today's sermon about?*

A: Sin.
Q: *What did the minister say about sin?*
A: He was against it.

Funnily enough (my Irish friend David Grene says "funnily enough," and I've picked up the habit) you were garrulous about ethnic foods. You wouldn't dream of going into the West End for dinner. Neither would I. I've had good meals at Turkish restaurants. Odd that you should answer a food question so fully; I've seldom seen you eat a complete dinner, so I took a considerable interest in your opinions.

These days I am eating less, sleeping less. The infirmities of age are coming fast upon me. It's bad form to complain of ill-health. I didn't use to do it—there was no problem; I had vital energy enough to waste on fooleries of every sort. But now I have no strength for the essentials. An hour at the writing table does me in. It troubles me now to write a letter about [your new novel] *The Information*. Page by page the writing gave me pleasure. Your books always do. The words bowl me over. But I find myself resisting your novel and in the end I back away from it.

Very long ago, reading Céline, I recognized the importance of the discovery he had made. He seemed to be saying, in his *Journey to the End of the Night*, that there is always some residue of principle in his nihilists. Thus when Robinson's girlfriend demands that he declare his love for her, he refuses. Outraged, hardly believing her ears, she says, "*Tu ne bandes pas?*"— "Don't you get a hard-on, like everybody else? That's love, ain't it?" But he cannot lie to her. This is his one principle, and she shoots him. He dies for his one belief.

It seems to me that in the "advanced" countries, the Robinsons have become Célines—they think for themselves and they seem to be independently philosophical. This is part of your "bad news" and "terrible information." Writers and characters alike are on "thought trips," squaring themselves one way or another with the prevailing nihilism. When the people one meets and/or writes about seek (and find) ideas it is more or less necessary for writers to cut their connections to the abstractions and to hang on to the phenomena, embrace them for dear life. We have no obligation to justify ourselves intellectually to the ruling philosophy, to be accepted as "authentic."

Of course the mental misery is very great. We don't want to abandon the sufferers. But one does them little good by joining them in their thought-idolatry.

So I come out on Janis's side, more or less. She puts it that "we are invited to stare into the void. But instead of emptiness we find information." My suggestion is that we come to agree—we are pleased to agree—with the leaders of thought, a.k.a. the nihilists. Céline's Robinson still had *one* idea of his own. That was the limit of his independence. We are losing even that.

A cheerless letter. But you did appoint me your spiritual father, and the foregoing is what this s.f. thinks you need.

And of course he sends you his best love,

To Hymen Slate

September 9, 1996   W. Brattleboro

Dear Hymen,

For the life of me I can't remember being unpleasant about your "character." We've known each other for about sixty years (the very idea of such a figure breaks me up). And if anyone had asked me to compare my character to yours, yours would have won hands down. I must confess however that on North Sheridan Road in those years I was having a very bad time. And it may be that what my remark, if I made it, really meant was that one had to have a less than admirable character to be a fiction writer.

Anyway at our age these close encounters with death should make us indulgent with each other. I am glad you explained the Anemia of Chronic Disease. I wouldn't otherwise have known how serious it was. For myself, I am utterly fed up with sickness. This very day I have been waiting for a visiting technician to give me an intravenous antibiotic. Normally (that is to say, formerly) it wouldn't have mattered so much. But after two years of much sickness and much recovery one does become impatient. I suppose the dead would say it is ungrateful of us to complain. But health is either complete or nothing at all. It's not the absence of this fucking technician who has kept me indoors all day, it's the tenacity of my symptoms, that finally drives me around the bend. I can't get rid of them.

So Abe Kaufman has died. Thirty years without a word from him—more like forty, come to think of it—and we still know no more about him than that he has departed. I frequently offered Kaufman friendship in as many ways as I could think of. But he was comically high and mighty with me. When I was at the *Britannica* under Mortimer Adler just before WWII Abe requested or demanded or commanded that I should get him on the payroll. I managed somehow to do just that. Abe then made an illuminating speech: "It is quite natural that you should have done this and it shows that you understand the difference between superior and inferior beings. You are aware that I stand higher in the hierarchy than you and that you therefore have an obligation to me."

It was easier to insult me than to say thanks. Anyway, he didn't want to have to thank me for anything. When last heard from he had just gotten his Ph.D. in philosophy at Harvard. Well, let's hope he will be happier in his next incarnation. It is diverting to think that we may be popping up again and again throughout eternity.

Keeping in touch is a good idea. I have a feeling that your odds on recovery are better than you think.

Affectionately,

To James Wood

September 9, 1996   W. Brattleboro

Dear Mr. Wood,

This is a *pro tem* note, to use congressional slang.

I have meant to write a long and serious letter to thank you for various kindnesses and to express my admiration for any number of reviews in *The New Republic*. Janis and I are especially grateful for the collection of Polish poems in translation.

I had, as a fanatical or *enragé* reader, studied over many decades gallery after gallery of old men in novels and plays and I thought I knew all about them. But to *be* one is full of surprises. Let me see: There is *Oedipus at Colonus*, there is the old sculptor of Ibsen's *When We Dead Awaken*, there is of course King Lear, and also Duncan in *Macbeth* and Polonius in *Hamlet*, and there are Jonathan Swift's Struldbruggs—the repulsive and unkillable old, there is old Prince Bolkonsky in *War and Peace*, there is Father Zossima in *The Brothers K*, there is Gerontion, and Yeats in his final years. But all of this business about crabbed age and youth tells you absolutely nothing about your own self. I shall leave the subject there. I can't even begin to say what it's really like.

I see now what a procrastinator I have always been. I kept my projects in a warehouse (the good-intentions warehouse which I mention all too often) confident that there would be an endless future in which to take care of all business, but a few years ago I began to see at last that I had grown far too old to have so many obligations in the storage bins—on the calendar. When I read your T. S. Eliot piece I began to compose a reply and at odd moments I have mentally worked at it, but you will have forgotten about your essay long before I get my letter on paper. Words shouted into a fierce gale which is anyway blowing in the wrong direction.

I thought I would send you a few lines to explain simply how matters stand. You may expect one of these months to receive a long and serious letter from me.

With best wishes,

To Herbert Mitgang

September 21, 1996   W. Brattleboro, Vermont

Dear Herb,

I'm dictating a few remarks in answer to your letter of September 2nd.

I've always liked Studs [Terkel]. We grew up in the same Chicago neighborhood, the Humboldt Park District. Originally German, this part of the city was by turns Scandinavian, Polish, Ukrainian, Jewish—it is now mainly Puerto Rican. Studs was ambitious to be an actor and could be identified by the copy of *Variety* always sticking out of his back pocket.

Studs's Chicago certainly was not mine. His Chicago was mythical. His myth was common. A convenient way to describe it is to refer you to Carl Sandburg. Sandburg had his gifts as a poet, but he was also a gifted advertising man. I don't think it's too much to say that the image of Chicago they held up to the world was stylized. It was The People, Yes! Populism was the source of their mythology. It was not necessary for them to wonder how to describe any phenomenon because they had ideological ready-mades, cutouts, stereotypes, etc. Poets and street-corner orators can make use of slogans, but slogans will not do for writers. I can readily identify the sources used by Studs Terkel because when I was very young I made use of them too. In the early years of the Depression we were all left-wingers. What I mean to say, as you will quickly recognize, is that as I grew older my left-wing sympathies waned. During the conservative administrations (Eisenhower, etc.)—during the Cold War too—Studs remained steadfast and he faithfully marked time until [in the Sixties] the junior middle-class masses were ready again to line up behind him.

I have always classified you as a good guy and I hope you won't use my candor against me and make me look like a gargoyle. I have learned by now that it is never safe to assume that a good guy is incapable of taking unfair advantage of the unwary and trusting *schnook*.

Best wishes,

In Memory of Yetta Barshevsky Shachtman

*(Printed in the program for Yetta Shachtman's memorial
service in New York City, September 22, 1996)*

Sixty-five years ago in the Humboldt Park District of Chicago, Yetta Barshevsky and I were students at the Tuley High School. Although we were
born in the same year, she was just a bit ahead of me, graduating in 1932.
Yetta was class orator. The title of her speech, a speech I remember very well,
was "The Future Belongs to the Youth." Well, of course it does. Actuarial
statistics make it obvious that, like it or not, youth *will* inherit the future or,
less pleasantly, that it will be thrust if not dumped on them. Al Glotzer tells
me that it was Karl Liebknecht who invented this clumsy slogan. Totalitarianism in the Thirties produced very nasty youth organizations—*Hitlerjugend*
in Germany, Pioneers in Soviet Russia and also the Young Communist
League. Mussolini had his Blackshirt boys. In England and in the USA we
had nothing worse than Baden-Powell's Boy Scout movement. The best that
can be said for the Boy Scouts was that they didn't do the future much harm.

Yetta in her high school days was for a time a member of the YCL. She
left the movement. Perhaps she was expelled. She was far too good, too gentle, too charming to be a hard-faced Third-Period Stalinist. Her mother, as I
remember, was upset when Yetta dropped out of the movement. The mother
was a spectacularly handsome dark-haired woman. I, you see, lived right
around the corner, on Lemoyne Street. The Barshevskys were on Spaulding
Ave. just north of Division Street I was a frequent visitor. I knew her brothers
and also her father. I believe he was a carpenter. The back seat of his jalopy
was filled with saws and sawdust. In those days one didn't have a car and a
truck. If you were a family man you preferred an old touring car to a truck—
the front seat would not accommodate four kids and a wife. Barshevsky was
fairly silent and clearly good-natured and affectionate with his children. I
even came to know Yetta's grandfather, whom I would often see at the syna-
gogue when I came to say Kaddish for my mother. He was an extremely,
primitively orthodox short bent man with a beard that seemed to have rushed
out of him and muffled his face. He wore a bowler hat and elastic-sided
boots. The old women, it seems, were wildly radical Communist sympathiz-
ers. The grandfathers were the pious ones.

The immigrant parents at the graduation ceremonies were delighted with
Yetta's oration. On the platform, this slight, high-voiced young woman was
fearless and formidable. Her manner was militant, urgent. From her you heard
such words as "penury" and "mitigate." I knew "mitigate" only from books. I

had never heard it spoken. It took boldness to say it publicly and with natural confidence. And Yetta was a gentle creature with a fiery irrepressible message for the parents of the graduating class. "We will do right by you," was what she was telling them. "We will give you mitigation." There was a curious earnestness about Yetta.

This, remember, was 1932. The Great Depression was upon us. Hitler and FDR had just spoken their first words on the world's stage.

Yetta introduced me, after a fashion, to world politics. We often crossed Humboldt Park together after school. I was even then "literary," while she was political. She gave me Trotsky's pamphlet on the German question. The view Trotsky developed was, as I remember, that Stalin's policies facilitated Hitler's rise to power. Stalin would not enter into a defensive alliance with the Social Democrats and other Left elements.

In good weather we sat on the steps of the Humboldt Park boathouse, under the huge arches; or in the Rose Garden, where the two bronze bison stood. She lectured me on Leninism, on collectivization, on democratic centralism, on the sins of Stalin and his inferiority to Trotsky. She was engaged, by now, to Nathan Goldstein, and Goldstein had turned from the CP to Trotskyism.

By 1933 Yetta and I had moved on to Crane Junior College, an institution that soon went under for lack of cash—the usual thing, in those years.

Mayor [Anton] Cermak went down to Florida after Roosevelt had won the November election with the aim of getting money to pay the teachers. It was there that an assassin shooting at Roosevelt shot Cermak instead. Cermak was a martyr, therefore, who sacrificed his life for education. With his death the Irish Democrats took over, creating a machine that has ruled Chicago ever since.

I was, at best, a peripheral observer of the political drama. But Yetta loved novels too. She had me reading Romain Rolland's *Jean Christophe*—all three volumes of it. Enormously stirring, this life of a Romantic Titan. When I tried to read it again, decades later, it seemed to me nothing but twaddle.

I suppose I entered into Yetta's enthusiasms for Yetta's sake, for her importance to me was very great. She was one of those persons who draw you into their lives and also install themselves in yours. Even the small genetic accident that made one of her eyes seem oddly placed added warmth and sadness to her look. She always seemed to me to have a significant sort of Jewish beauty. One no more understands these things than the immigrant parents who heard the class orator understood the word "mitigate." There is something radically mysterious in the specificity of another human being which everybody somehow responds to. Love is not a bad word for this response. Today's memorial testifies to Yetta's secret power, the power of being Yetta.

To Hymen Slate

November 25, 1996   W. Brattleboro

Dear Hymen,

I am not going to molest you with my deep thoughts today. I want to say first of all that I greatly enjoyed your letter and have thought of various ways of answering. Since I came down a couple of years ago with a tremendous disease I have learned that people when they ask how you are don't really want a detailed reply. Naturally the sick man has given a great deal of thought to his condition and his disorder and is in a position to tell them something of deep and permanent value. But as you have probably had occasion to observe, their eyes glaze over just as you are getting to the best part. The noblest thing a convalescent can do is to let them off the hook, that is, spare them the consequences of their question. In a way, it's like being old. It's best not to try to tell anybody what it's like.

Janis and I shuttle between Vermont and Brookline. This time of year Vermont turns gloomy and it's also somewhat dangerous. The hunters are out for free meat, a deer for Thanksgiving. We have bought crimson parkas, because the sportsmen get drunk in the woods and fire in all directions. The shooting will be over at the end of the month. Janis taught me how to go cross-country on skis but I doubt that my legs are strong enough these days to do it. I don't think I mentioned that my youngest son, Daniel, a newspaperman, has been working on the *Brattleboro Reformer*, our local paper. One of the attractions of Vermont was that he and his wife lived nearby. They have moved two hours away to the town of Rutland because he has a new job. He has become an editor of the *Rutland Herald*, so we shall be seeing less of him. He has grown up to be literate, bookish, but by now he has seen much more of life than I had seen at his age. My oldest son, who came to visit you last spring, I think, is in California. His daughter, a good-looking young woman of twenty-four, is in New York as is my son Adam. Daniel is the one I see most often.

As for Boston, it's a snooty city that thinks very highly of its cultural opulence. So many art galleries and so much chamber music and so many literary societies and across the river there is Harvard prepared to answer all the questions one can think of. It doesn't have a monopoly on the best minds, but it does have, or claims to have, the biggest concentration of them. There are a few good friends in Brookline where we live, and also two or three at Harvard. We don't see any of them very often. I never was able to do all the things I wanted to do, cover all the bases, but one has to be much younger to have any real gift for relationships. Those we had when we were young remain the best. One of the things that bugged me, grieved me, about living in Hyde Park was to pass the houses where my late friends once lived, and even the windows from which I myself used to look out more than fifty years ago. The daily melancholy of passing these places was among the things that drove me East. Here I have no melancholy past to bug me.

But we did have an agreeable group of pals and rivals, didn't we?

I teach only the spring term at Boston University, so I am free during eight months of the year. We don't do much traveling anymore because I tire so easily. I haven't been to New York in more than a year, but Janis and I are going to be in Chicago next April. This gives us four months to plan a reunion.

Much love from your reasonably intact friend,

1997

To Julian Behrstock

January 14, 1997   Brookline

Dear Julian:

1997—what a date, hey? Long, long ago I used to play the arithmetic game and reckon (born in 1915) how old I would be when the century ended. Eighty-five in the year 2000. A completely unnatural and comical number. That's why my eighty-first year is so unlikely—a laughing matter; except that it's no joke. When I complain about my health it's really about the dwindling of my recuperative powers that I complain. In the past I bounced back after surgeries or pneumonias. Now I lose my footing when I put on my pants. The sense of balance is gone. I lost six pounds in intensive care. I put on about eighty while convalescing, and now I can't get rid of the increment. No matter how I fast I have to hold my breath to fasten the waistband.

Then there is the stamp of old age on the face, head, hands and ankles. These blue-cheese ankles—what a punishment for narcissists! And after a lifetime of dogged realism about oneself and such pride in keeping the record straight! Worst of all, in many ways, is the failure of memory. Yesterday I couldn't recall Muriel Spark. Today I can't pin down the name of a Cambridge prof whose books I liked—Bogan maybe. All the better to appreciate the joke about the old guy who says to the doctor, "There are three things I can't recall: names, faces—and the third I can't remember." This from the fella who knew what your brother Arthur used to call you, back in 1935! So shall I put up a fight to build up this collapsing structure?

All this, because I'm trying to explain why I may have sounded dejected when we spoke. The truth is that I was cheerfully surprised by the strength of your familiar voice. You sounded altogether yourself, and the letter that just arrived was written in a firm hand and perfectly legible.

It's *not* Bogan—the name is Denis *Brogan*, and the book was about nineteenth-century French politics. Brogan was entirely sex-mad. He told me an unforgettable anecdote about one of his girlfriends. They were in a taxi and she said, "Dennis, I want to show you how I feel about you." And she raised her skirt and placed his hand upon her female organ—so gallantly streaming, as our national anthem has it. I tell you this *pour t'égayer, cher vieux copain* [*]. I send you all the finest regards and wishes in the world.

Fight on, and write me soon,

To Philip Roth

May 7, 1997   Brookline

Dear Philip,

Your letter forced me to think my story through again and I admit that I was or am confused about it. I had given some thought to the pain problem. As I followed the characters, they led me to examine their cynicism. They had to be "humorously" cynical and what they possibly hoped was to close out their witty but in the end fatiguing observations of one another. Probably they feel that they can wear their pain out, or attenuate it, or outlive it.

So I concluded that the pain had to be taken for granted.

Harry Trellman is willing—no, happy—to have Amy at last, for no better reason than that she is Amy. She is the ineradicable and irreplaceable actual. So, just as Bodo Heisinger is glad to take back a wife who once put out a contract on him, Harry proposes to Amy though he had heard the sex cries

* French: to cheer you up, old buddy

she uttered under some stranger from New York. He has become aware that he has longed for her and spoken to her (unilaterally) almost daily for decades.

But he gave her no inducement to think of *him*. Still he does see that he has come somehow to belong to Amy. Because she is his actual.

To all this there is a clue, so well hidden that it would have escaped not only Sherlock Holmes but even Sherlock's brother Mycroft, by far the smarter of the two. What is this indispensable hint? It's buried in the conversation between Amy and Mrs. Bodo. Amy tells Mrs. Bodo how Jay prepared his seduction routines. He impressed the ladies with his intellectual powers. He quoted great authors—without attribution, naturally. She repeats verbatim one passage. He had taken it from a book, and she had found the book. The underlined passage speaks of the spiritual character of the human face. Not a single thing in the universe is quite like it. The whole subject is wrapped up in a few sentences: "The face of a man is the most amazing thing in the life of the world. Another world shines through it." A worldly person like Harry, having small use for his worldliness, takes Amy's face for his *actual*. He needs it. He has to have it.

Now, I am not in a position to claim that I made this clear. I felt it. But as somebody coming back (briefly) from the dead I wasn't able to work it out acceptably (to you or me).

You do well to direct me, or connect me, to Eliade. Do you have a copy of [Norman] Manea's article? [. . .]

We'll be in Vermont from the end of May.

Yours ever,

Roth had responded to Bellow's recently published The Actual. *Norman Manea's essay on the historian of religions Mircea Eliade, Bellow's former colleague in the Committee on Social Thought at Chicago, had detailed Eliade's pro-Nazi activities in Romania during the Second World War. The essay appeared first in* The New Republic *and subsequently in Manea's* On Clowns: The Dictator and the Artist *(1993).*

To Richard Stern

[n.d.] W. Brattleboro

Dear Richard—

You did right to send the news of poor Zita [Cogan]'s death. I had heard about it from [Jonathan] Kleinbard, and from her son [Marc Cogan]. The woods grow thinner as the *chênes qu'on abat* [*] fall faster. Zita and I, in our Humboldt Park days, lived on the same street. One of the feats of my youth was to shinny up the front of her house to fetch her from her second-storey room on Sunday mornings and summon her to a picnic. A truckful of high-school students cheered.

Now *there's* a wholesome reminiscence, for a change.

You may be sure that you'd have been on my list of speakers at the Nat'l Portrait Gallery. I wasn't consulted about the arrangements. But it was hand-some of you to fly in from Chicago. In your two-toned shirt *you* looked handsome, too. You were beaming also, and your color was notably high. "Glowing," as young women's gym teachers liked to say. "Not sweating, but *glowing.*"

Give Alane an affectionate greeting.

Ever yours,

Poet Alane Rollings is Richard Stern's wife.

In Memory of Zita Cogan

> *(Read in Bellow's absence in Hyde Park, Illinois, May 16, 1997,*
> *at a memorial tribute organized by Mostly Music,*
> *the organization Zita Cogan founded)*

Many decades ago, on a June morning, we drove up to Zita's house in a truck. Her room was on the second floor and overlooked Humboldt Park. The picnickers honked and shouted. We were bound for the dunes. Her doorbell may have gone dead, or I assumed that it had, so I climbed up the face of the building just as John Barrymore or Douglas Fairbanks would have done, and banged on her bedroom door. I think that this made her very happy. What was said I can't remember. But it was a fine moment.

There was a Russian flavor about Zita. She wore Gypsy blouses and beads and bangles. We were all, in those days, partly Russian. Instead of under-clothes we wore binding and scratchy swim-suits. Our pockets—and our heads as well—were nearly empty in those days of youth and vainglory.

This is one of my favorite recollections of Zita as a young woman. And now as our days on earth are almost used up I cherish this adolescent mo-

---

* French: felled oaks, a phrase from Victor Hugo given currency by *Les chênes qu'on a bat* (1971), André Malraux's account of his final afternoon with de Gaulle.

ment. Showing off? Of course I was. But when I burst in on her she was beautiful, and I was not so full of myself that I couldn't know it.

To Philip Roth

June 17, 1997   W. Brattleboro

Dear Philip,

Just a note: You speak of [Norman] Manea's fantasy of Romania, "the myth he'd been making of it in exile." I haven't talked enough with him to have any notion of this myth and it would be very interesting to hear your account of it. I wonder why his notebook was lost on Lufthansa. You say he left it on the seat beside him when he disembarked? As you must know, I am no Freudian and I never have believed that a man's life is nothing but a front for the operations of his unconscious. Still, there must have been some sound reason for losing the diary of his visit to his native country.

I don't know Orwell's essay on Swift. I shall try to get a copy in the Brattleboro library or from BU. It's true that you hardly realize how deep Orwell goes because he is so clear about what he's doing.

Several years ago Janis and I were invited to a dinner for [Václav] Havel and found a message at our New York hotel to the effect that the dinner had been changed into a public celebration which would be held at the great cathedral (whatever they call it) at Riverside Drive and 120th Street. When we got there there were thousands of people inside the church and crowding to get in, and television crews and everyone was there, a blizzard of celebrities from Hollywood. Arthur Miller, I think, was present, and Paul Newman and a hundred others. Henry Kissinger had come to represent political seriousness, and I had been asked to introduce him. The Czechs didn't know what had hit them. They were sitting all in a row at the front of the cathedral—they were the occasion for this great display by the entertainment industry. Havel and I chatted for about three minutes and were separated as if we were tomato seeds in the digestive tract. Since then I have been several times invited to congresses for this or that in Prague, and I have yet to make my first visit there.

Yours,

To Werner Dannhauser

September 1, 1997   W. Brattleboro

Dear Werner,

This is a good morning for pangs of conscience. The summer is stalled, the day is gray, oppressive, in check, windless—not even a small breeze. I feel that I'm below, in nature's insides, and that she seems to be having a digestive problem.

I haven't written to my correspondents because . . . because, because and because. I haven't added up the deaths of various friends during the last six months. [François] Furet you knew and perhaps you remember Zita Cogan who died a few weeks ago. The others were long-time buddies: a college classmate, in Paris [Julian Behrstock]. In New York, Yetta [Barshevsky] Shachtman, the widow of the US Trotskyite leader. She and I would walk back from school through Humboldt Park (Chicago) discussing Trotsky's latest pamphlet on the German question. We also read the "Communist Manifesto" and "State and Revolution." She was an earnest girl—the dear kind—Comrade Yetta. Her Pa was a carpenter, and his old Nash was filled with tools, shavings and sawdust. And now she has gone—human sawdust and shavings. There was also a clever, clumsy big man named [Hymen] Slate who believed (when we were young) that a sense of humor should be part of every argument about the existence of God. Laughing was proof that there was a God. But God in the end laid two kinds of cancer on him and took him away very quickly. When we were in our late sixties, in East Rogers Park, we met every Thursday to drink tea and consider the question of immortality. Neither of us had read Kant.

Next came the news that David Shahar had died. So many women in his life. When I met him with yet another one on some Jerusalem street he would lay a finger to his lips as he passed. But [his wife] Shula was far too smart to be deceived—even if she had reason to want to be. I thought he must have a large turnover of ladies but evidently he was like a Mafia don. He had a band of Mafiosi girls each with her own turf—Paris, Jerusalem, Tel Aviv, too, or Beersheba. His career would repay close study. I did like him, but my deeper sympathies went to Shula. That too would be worth studying—since so many people devote themselves to these *studies*. What an amazing amount of research is going on around us. But why should I identify with Shula? I suspect that she knew him far better than he could ever know himself. That his afternoons of love were a consolation for his literary failures. Why couldn't he have come to her for consolation?

A stupid question! I really know better than to ask.

I will mention one more death, that of a student from Chicago—very bright and handsome. His dissertation was published and widely reviewed. I argued with him about it. It was a little too fashionable for my taste. I sensed that he saw me as an old fuddy-duddy, but no . . . he ended years later by sharing my opinions. He did well for himself academically and got a tenured appointment in Southern California (Claremont?). He married a Dupont girl from Delaware but they were divorced after a year or two. He was charming, lively, and was strangely loyal to me—came every year to Vermont to talk matters over. He last visited in July and was unusually warm and close. A month later he died in a highway crash, and his tearful parents phoned to tell me what had happened—that they were notifying me because . . . because he had been so close to me and I had seen him through some bad times.

Together with all this I have the feeling that I am in it with him and the others aforementioned. Dying piecemeal. My legs ain't functioning as they ought. Day and night they ache. And I am this, that and the other in many respects, physically. It seems that my tear ducts have dried up, and the eyeballs feel gummy. The details are not worth going into. It's possible that I may never recover from the damage done by cigua toxin. I observe, in writing to you, that you are the last person in the world to complain to, given your "medical history." But at bottom it may be an expression of solidarity. During the war we used to read of the bombing of German "marshalling yards"—the rail centers where freight trains are "made up," organized for their runs.

You must know that for many people you are an elder statesman, venerable, a fighter for the true faith, etc. And I may merely be saying that I am a foot-sore infantry campaigner myself. I'm well aware that you have no need for such declarations of affinity from another *mutilé de la guerre* [*]. I want to feel close to you, just as my late student had sought me out annually.

I think he said that he had been diagnosed with Hodgkin's disease. I'm pretty sure that this was mentioned. I didn't take it up. I saw no way to do it. What good would it have done to discuss it?

This letter I think offers you a road map. It shows where I am at. It's not as bad as it sounds. I just need to get it out of my system today. I won't close with "have fun" but with

Love,

Werner Dannhauser, professor emeritus of political science at Cornell University, is the author of Nietzsche's View of Socrates *(1976). Bellow's student was Brian Stonehill, who taught media studies at Pomona College and whose book was* The Self-Conscious Novel *(1988).*

* French: crippled veteran

To James Wood

Dear Mr. Wood—

It occurred to me last night during an insomniac hour that you might not have received your copy of *News from the Republic of Letters*. I asked Chris Walsh about it today and he said that Botsford had "taken care of it." Now Botsford is a very gifted man but he isn't dependably efficient. He's had a bad year, in and out the hospital with a bad hip. He had been driving too fast on a remote highway in France. French doctors had bungled the surgery. It had to be done again in Boston. And then KB had gone back to the south of France, on a crutch. (He has a house on the Mediterranean coast.) He relies on graduate students to run his Boston "operations," and they do what can humanly be done to carry out his complicated orders.

He and I have done this sort of thing in the past. In the Fifties we brought out a journal called *The Noble Savage*. The idea has always been to show how the needs of writers might be met. *The Noble Savage* was a paperback published by Meridian Books—a company swallowed decades ago by Western Printers, which was devoured by the *LA Times*, etc.

Botsford and I have no publishing house behind us—no corporation, no philanthropical foundations, no patron. We pay for *TROL* ourselves. We do it on the cheap—printing no more than fifteen hundred copies. We tried to get Barnes and Noble to take it but B and N does not deal with magazines directly, only with official distributors. We thought we'd run it for a year in the hope of attracting five or six hundred subscribers. Six or seven hundred good men and true would make it possible for *TROL* to survive.

Nothing like a boyish enterprise to give old guys the shocks they badly need or crave. I feel I owe you this explanation, since you were good enough to let us publish your Ibsen-Chekhov piece. We couldn't afford to pay you properly for it. So you are entitled to a description of what it is that we are doing. Your Chekhov is one of the ornaments of #2. We have money enough for five or six numbers. Then, if we haven't the backing of the subscribers we hope to get, we will fold.

Ten years down the road your copy, or copies, of the paper may be worth a fortune. It'll be a collector's item and a rarity.

Yours with every good wish,

To Albert Glotzer

November 8, 1997   W. Brattleboro

Dear Al:

It seems that nobody gets a break. Whatever it is that deals out the disorders is no respecter of persons. If I had access to him I would say that A. Glotzer was due for a reprieve—a breather—because he has some important things to do, still.

I myself have had arrhythmia for a week straight and can't walk a block without panting. I went last week to visit my old sister in Cincinnati and came back short of breath. My cardiologist is on vacation. My sister is ninety-one years of age. She continues to play the piano although she is quite deaf and can't hear the mistakes she makes—chords with many notes omitted. But she's as proud of her performance as she ever was.

She described how, in Montreal in 1923, she was on her way to a lesson and felt her panties dropping—the rubber was used up. She had so many books in her arms that she couldn't prevent the panties from falling. She stepped out of them and left them on the pavement. I'd heard this dozens of times before. The anecdote has acquired mythic character. In 1923, I was eight years old; she was seventeen. You hadn't yet become a court-reporter, I don't think.

I shall be pulling for you in some remote part of my mind—the mental backwoods where prayers used to be said before we all became so "enlightened."

Your longtime affectionate Chicago chum,

To Herbert McCloskey

December 16, 1997   Brookline

Dear Herb,

A note is just now all that I have signed for. I loved your letter of August. But then I misplaced it. And I was too tired to make a thorough search for it, but yesterday unexpectedly it turned up and I re-read it with sympathy and even a few tears. You write one hell of a letter. I used to be a fair hand at this myself but what with sickness, old age, pharmaceutical lassitude and octogenarian lack of focus, I seem to have lost the knack. Janis, my wife, a godsend if there ever was one, tells me that I should not feel uneasy about the mail. I carry a swollen portfolio of letters from Vermont to Boston and back again to Vermont. But she says that there is no need for me to write letters, I have already written thousands of them, and that people who complain that I don't answer simply don't understand that a morning of writing exhausts me, and that my afternoons should be reserved for oblivion.

Still there is one thing that bothers me. I share your recollections of our trip to Banyuls. Can it be that I was then driving my own car? Or was it your car? I ask because at Banyuls I hitched a ride to Barcelona from a certain Señor Valls, a big-hearted businessman although he didn't say what his business was. [. . .] He took me to a cabaret in Barcelona with several exciting women. And I ate a fine dinner of seafood—to the horror of my ancestors, probably. All those nasty little creatures scraped up from the sea-mud. Next day I took a ferry to the off-shore islands where I chased after a lovely American woman. I'm sorry to say this resulted in a fiasco at the moment of embrace. I am tempted to believe that Anita sent me off under some hex. Anyway, I made my way back chastened. But what really bothers me is that I can't remember where I had left my car.

Anyway your letter was a wonderful letter and had a direct effect on my ice-bound heart. I used to see something of [————] in Chicago, but her gruff husband, a kind of technician-cyclops type, did not encourage our meetings. What a beautiful girl she was, and so appallingly young. And I remember that you entertained us hour after hour by explaining that when you were a kid you couldn't eat graham crackers unless they had been ripened under the pad of the porch swing.

If I had been writing this the effort by now would have worn me out. Luckily, I was able to dictate to my invaluable *simpatico* secretary, name of Chris Walsh, who not only takes letters but also drives me to my frequent hospital appointments. If one of these days I should fail to emerge from the hospital, you can get full details by applying to Chris at my University address. I used to have much confidence in my ability to ward off death. But death is as strong as ever, and I am a much weaker resister.

Lots of love from your old chum,

1998

To Philip Roth

January 1, 1998   Brookline

Dear Philip—

Sorry to be so slow. Janis got to your manuscript first and all her enthusiasm, sympathies and forebodings were then communicated to me. A new Roth book is a big event in these parts. We are, to use the Chicago terms of the Twenties, your rooters and boosters.

When she took off for Canada on X-mas day to see parents and sister, brother, kiddies, she left *I Married a Communist* with me for the Holiday Season. Reading your book consoled me in this empty house. It's a treat to read one of your manuscripts—I say this up-front—but this time the overall effect was not satisfactory. I was particularly aware of the absence of distance—I don't mean that the writer *must* put space between himself and the characters in his book. But there should be a certain detachment from the writer's own passions. I speak as one who in *Herzog* created the same sin. There I hoped that comic effects might protect me. Nevertheless I crossed the border too many times to raid the enemy camp. But then Herzog was a chump, a failed intellectual and at bottom a sentimentalist. In your case, the man who gives us Eve and Sylphid is an *enragé*, a fanatic-for-real.

That's not the outstanding defect of *IMAC*. Your reader, out of respect for your powers, is more than willing to go along with you. He will not, as I was not, be able to go along with your Ira, probably the least attractive of all your characters. I assume that you can no more bear Ira than the reader can. But you stand loyally by this cast-iron klutz—a big strong stupid man who attracts you for reasons invisible to me.

Now there is a real mystery about Communists in the West, to limit myself to those. How were they able to accept Stalin—one of the most monstrous tyrants ever? You would have thought that the Stalin-Hitler division of Poland, the defeat of the French which opened the way to Hitler's invasion of Russia, would have led CP members to reconsider their loyalties. But no. When I landed in Paris in 1948 I found that the intellectual leaders (Sartre, Merleau-Ponty, etc.) remained loyal despite the Stalin sea of blood. Well, every country, every government has *its* sea, or lake, or pond. Still Stalin remained "*the* hope"—despite the clear parallel with Hitler.

But to keep it short—the reason: The reason lay in the hatred of one's own country. Among the French it was the old confrontation of "free spirits," or artists, with the ruling bourgeoisie. In America it was the fight against the McCarthys, the House Committees investigating subversion, etc. that justified the Left, the followers of Henry Wallace, etc. The main enemy was at home (Lenin's WWI slogan). If you opposed the CP you were a McCarthyite, no two ways about it.

Well, it was a deep and perverse stupidity. It didn't require a great mind to see what Stalinism was. But the militants and activists refused to reckon with the simple facts available to everybody.

Enough: You will say that all of that is acknowledged in *IMAC*. Yes, and no. You tell us that Ira is a brute, a murderer. But who else is there? Ira and Eve are at the core of your novel—and what does this pair amount to?

One of your persistent themes is the purgation one can obtain only through rage. The forces of aggression are liberating, etc. And I can see that as a legitimate point of view. Okay if your characters are titans. But Eve is simply a pitiful woman and Sylphid is a pampered, wicked fat girl with a bison hump. These are not titans.

There aren't many people to whom I can be so open. We've always been candid with each other and I hope we will continue, both of us, to say what we think. You'll be sore at me, but I believe that you won't cast me off forever.

Ever yours,

To John Auerbach and Nola Chilton

February 23, 1998   Brookline

Dear John and Nola,

[. . .] Many years ago Bobby Kennedy several times said to me that he was concerned with small dictators who might (easily) produce a nuclear device. One of the things I have always suspected was that aberrant types would somehow find means to realize their mad megalomaniacal dreams. The tendency is, in hundreds of millions of instances, to translate imagination into actualities. You think of blowing up a federal building with a bomb made of cheap components including a sack of fertilizer, and you load your ingredients into a parked truck and it goes off and kills men, women and children. So there's no limit to the possibilities for cranks [. . .] Meantime our president is beset by sex problems. It's a tribute to FDR and even to Jack Kennedy that their sex problems didn't prevent them from governing the country, but I'm not altogether sure that Clinton can carry Monica while conducting foreign affairs. All I can definitely say about this historic episode is that it shows us what a powerful aphrodisiac great politics can be.

Meanwhile most of my contemporaries have gone to the next world, and it's no more than reasonable that I should be preoccupied with the next world, and it is natural also that at my age one should think more often about friends still living.

I hope Chris Walsh has sent you copies of *The Republic of Letters*. We have just published #3.

Much love to both of you,

To Teddy Kollek

April 14, 1998   Brookline

Dear Teddy,

I felt when Isaiah Berlin died that I should send you a note, but then I was too dreary to do it. Instead I recalled the weeks when I was at the Mishkenot and Isaiah and his wife were at the King David just up the street.

Later on I dined with Isaiah several times in Oxford and we reminisced pleasantly about those days in Jerusalem, the Jerusalem you had totally transformed.

I often feel these days that death is a derelict or what Americans nowadays call a street person who has moved into the house with me and whom I can find no way to get rid of. The only solution is to make him a member of the family.

Enough of these gloomy reflections and fantasies. I am trying to express solidarity and exchange sympathies with an old friend who is, I hope, well and happy.

With affection,

To Albert Glotzer

June 3, 1998   W. Brattleboro

Dear Al—

I used to be an eager letter writer, but it fills me with self-disgust now to face the growing pile of unanswered mail. Age is probably to blame—since age is there, I make use of it. Life becomes silenter and silenter. I notice that most of the mental work of the old (the work of this old man, at least) is done in silence. I find myself often talking to the dead (for instance). Others have confessed to me that they do it too. Even rationalist atheists and materialists will admit, if they're old enough, that they expect to meet their mothers in the afterlife.

I marvel at your refusal to give in. I too am a scrapper. Giving in to sickness is inconceivable. It's very strange that after thirty years of heart trouble (fibrillations) I am free from symptoms. I'm rid of the pills. On the other hand, walking has become painful. My arthritic joints find it hard to stand up from a seated position. But I *makh zikh nit visndik*, in Yiddish. The translation is: "Ignore it!" We are forced to do our business, day by day, between narrowing limits and reduced perspectives. Again, it's *makh zikh nit visndik*. [. . .]

Much love to you, and to Maggie,

To Sophie Wilkins

June 17, 1998   W. Brattleboro

Dear Sophie,

[. . .] The delicious chocolates you sent are in the cupboard. Janis makes a point of eating chocolates only on birthdays—excuse me, family birthdays—and anniversaries. I am on my honor never to eat precious candies without permission, but of course I do eat them. I steal them. I am extremely fond of truffles. Of course I shouldn't eat them. I am not desperately sick but neither am I in the best of health. Atrial fibrillation is my chief complaint. Mostly I ignore such troubles. I do bitch from time to time, but at heart I still assume that nothing has changed much since childhood. Maybe this is what psychiatrists mean when they say that a patient is "in denial."

I am very happy to hear that Karl is improving. He has very justifiably taken a long holiday from injustice and idiocy. Maybe he will feel well enough by and by to take up the sword once more. As for Thomas Bernhard, he is a very strange bird indeed. I read him with respect and even admiration but he doesn't reach my warmer feelings. What he does reach is my own bottomless hatred of the Nazis, especially the Austrian ones. He would have you think that virtually all Austrians were and remain Nazis. I see no reason to disagree. When I read Karl's lovely poem about Auden's grave I wondered why Auden should have wished to pass his last years [at Kirchstetten] in the society of such creeps. I seem to recall that he even addressed affectionate lines to some of them. But then Austria was always a monument to bourgeois comforts, and in his declining years Auden too loved pottering in the kitchen and sleeping in bourgeois feather beds.

Janis also sends her love,

To Philip Roth

September 15, 1998   W. Brattleboro

Dear Philip—

So sorry about the delay.

Now that I am in real earnest an old guy, requiring orderliness, I am in circumstances always of disorder—of chaos.

Ever your pal,

To Evelyn Nef

Dear Evvy,

I would much sooner have paid you a visit but as Janis has told you the doctors ordered me to come and have a pacemaker installed. I have had my problems with doctors during this long life of mine. My medical history goes back to 1923 when my appendix was removed in Montreal and I damned near died of peritonitis. After that I was quite sick in Chicago and after that very sick in Boston. And now I am eighty-three years old and still stepping into the batter's box to try for one more hit. So my pacemaker and I will be happy to come and pay a visit and we shall all sit down together in your grand new house. Janis and I—and Walter [Pozen]—are looking forward with anticipated happiness to seeing you again.

Yours with love,

Author, linguist, psychotherapist and philanthropist Evelyn Stefansson Nef (1913–2009) was the widow of John U. Nef, Bellow's longtime colleague in the Committee on Social Thought. Previously, she had been the lover of Buckminster Fuller, the wife of puppeteer Bil Baird, and the wife of explorer Vihjalmur Stefansson.

To Richard Stern

November 15, 1998   Brookline

Dear Richard,

Your notes always give me great comfort.

Am I all right? No, just partly right. My memory, of which I was West-Point proud, keeps disappointing me. Last week I couldn't remember Katharine Hepburn's name and the name of her lover—Somebody Tracy eluded me for several days. And I actually have to go back to reference works, to my great shame. Well, perhaps God is trying to tell me that though I could remember everything, I didn't really understand anything. The pacemaker, however, keeps my heart regular, and I can drink all the wine I like at dinner and thumb my nose at caffeine.

I wouldn't throw in the towel—yet. A little anecdote to illustrate; I dug it up last month in writing a note to Jack Miles (you'll see this for yourself in the next number of *TROL*): An old man lives in the forest alone and gathers winter fuel and finds himself one day unable to lift his burden of sticks. He raises his eyes to heaven and says, "O God, send me Death," and when Death comes

Death says, "Did you send for me, sir?" The old man replies, "Yes, lend me a hand with these sticks. Just put them on my shoulder and I'll do the rest."

You may want that towel one day to wipe your inspired brow.

Say hello to Alane.

Yours ever,

1999

To Edward Simmons

June 3, 1999   W. Brattleboro

Dear Edward:

Your mother tells me how well you're doing. You're off to college now and, inevitably, I think of my own college days back in the Thirties. Those were the Depression years and we were given to understand that our parents were hard-put to raise two dollars for our tuition. Three hundred dollars a year were no trifle, in those lean times, and I was often reminded that idling and drinking were forbidden. A handful of people had money to burn but the immense majority were flat-broke, very nearly down and out. Nevertheless I was often playing pool when I should have been in class. Luckily I was also a smart Jewish kid and read tons of books on my own so that I passed my exams—I squeaked by in my early years. It was only in my junior year that I began to do better, graduating with honors and a fellowship to the University of Wisconsin.

The powers of your own mind will turn against you if you don't master them. They'll cut you down. You seem, to go by your record, to have discovered this for yourself.

But enough of this sententious stuff. I congratulate you. You're doing just fine, and I am pleased for your own sake, and for your parents' as well.

Congratulations.

Your godfather,

To Werner Dannhauser

October 6, 1999   Brookline

Dear Werner:

It's about time you heard from me.

I promised to eliminate what you thought to be objectionable material and I wrote a revised version of *Ravelstein*. It took quite a lot of doing and the doing went against the grain. When I was done the results were highly unsatisfactory; what was lacking was the elasticity provided by sin. In the midst of this lengthy, time-consuming and ultimately sterile procedure I remembered how displeased Bloom had been with *The Dean's December*. He objected to the false characterization of Alexandra and he didn't spare me one bit. But now the shoe is on the other foot and I saw no reason why I should do in *Ravelstein* what Allan himself had so strongly objected to in the earlier novel. After all, I was trying to satisfy Allan's wishes, and I couldn't have it both ways. I couldn't be both truthful and camouflaged. So I did as I think he would have wished me to do. And I know that I am going to alienate most of my Straussian friends. Some of these old friends I can well afford to lose, but you are not in that number. In your case, the loss would be hard to bear. Believe me, none of this is literary frivolity. I've taken the whole matter with great—the greatest—seriousness. And I hope I've made clear to you the sort of bind I found myself in. I *should* expect to lose friends, but I don't expect you to be one of them. I don't think much remains to be said. I often give thought to the Jewish category of *kherem*, which means excommunication. I do hope this novel is not going to estrange us.

Right now I'm taking heat on three fronts: i) Paternity—a fresh start at the age of 84; ii) The messy explosive mixture that James Atlas is preparing for me in the form of a biography; iii) The hue and cry about [*Ravelstein*] against which I must brace myself. Janis occasionally says to me that maybe we should move to Uruguay. I have a remote connection with the family of the dictator and I did get an A in my high school Spanish course . . .

2000

To the Swedish Academy

[n.d.]   [Brookline]

I wish to nominate the American novelist Philip Roth for the Nobel Prize. His books have been so widely examined and praised that it would be superfluous for me to describe, or praise, his gifts.

To Martin Amis

February 7, 2000   Brookline

Dear Martin,

I used to be a ready correspondent but somehow over the years I lost the habit of writing letters. Maybe the death of so many pals was at the bottom of this, a first generation and then a second and even a third dying. I suspect I've lost count. It may even be that the confidences I made to my friends are now offered to my readers. That, if true, is not a good development—but I'm not prepared to go any further in that direction. It's enough to say that I feel like talking to you and that I find myself very often turning to you for relief. It is a kid's game to have imaginary conversations, convinced somehow—as kids are—that the imaginary gets translated reliably into the minds of your friends.

But it's *Ravelstein* I'm thinking of all the while. I'd never written anything like *Ravelstein* before, and the mixture of fact and fiction has gotten out of hand. There are other elements besides, because the facts are so impure. There's fact, and then there is journalistic fact with its usual accents. You can even see the journalists transforming fact into scandal and, towards the top, scandal lapsing over into myth, moving into the medieval territory reserved for plague. I was not prepared to hear a leper's bell ring at the crossroads of affection and eccentric charm.

It seems that many people knew the truth about Allan. If not the pure truth then the bendable, versatile kind that academic politics is familiar with. So I found myself challenged by fanatical people. I discovered very soon that Allan had enemies who were preparing to reveal that he had died of AIDS. At this point I lost my head; when the *New York Times* telephoned to have it out with me I fell apart—I was unable to outsmart the journalists. So here I am, the author of a tribute which has been transformed into one of those civilized disasters no one can be prepared for.

As you well know, the attention of the public and the press is seldom pleasant, and with rare exceptions (the Pope, for instance) it gives no one a break. I tell people that Ravelstein asked me to write a memoir and that it would have been false and wicked to omit the sickness that killed him from the account I gave of his life. With an omniscient wisdom like his it would have been impossible not to predict what would come of this. But I was ready, so I thought, to handle all the embarrassments that were bound to swarm over me. I couldn't have faced myself if I had turned aside from a character of Ravelstein's stature. I long ago understood that what we call the art of fiction was withering because—well, because modern democracies were unheroic.

But I find myself needing to explain unheroic democracy to the journalists and the public and it depresses me beyond all boundaries of former depression. I get what comfort I can get from reflecting that at my age the shop is in any case about to shut its doors. Last week I flew to see my ancient sister in Cincinnati. She's my senior by nine years, and when I heard the news of the crash of an Air Alaska jet off the Pacific coast I thought, "Why not Delta Airlines as well, into the Ohio River?" But no. I landed safely and was driven out to the luxury funny farm where my sister lives. She was glad I had come and wanted to see pictures of the new baby. What we do not discuss is the fact that there's only a single grave left in the family plot.

Janis feels that this is an oppressive letter but it's given me a lift.

To Martin Amis

April 13, 2000   Brookline

Dear Martin,

When your manuscript arrived I was winding up *Ravelstein* and Janis had *Experience* all to herself. That is probably a misleading way to put it—she acts for both of us so she kept me posted while reading, and at lunch, drinks-time and dinner she described what you were up to, praised the stylistic breakthrough you had made. She is an inflammable, excitable and exacting reader. She said you had found a way to digress without appearing to, unloading a heavy freight of information without the slightest appearance of wandering.

I was taken with your asterisk-asides. Altogether, you have come up with a way of writing entirely your own. The unit is no longer a sentence but a characteristic utterance. Can it be that the Amises have somehow developed a consistent way of putting things? If I knew your father's books better I might be able to pin down these characteristics. As it is, there is evidence of an independent expository style. From a variety of angles the book gives an account of the death of your father. Increasingly, I wonder whether these literary accomplishments are traceable to a family way of speaking. I will be interested to see whether Louis and Jacob [Amis's sons] will be tinged by this. My own parents, along with my father's sister, brought me up not in English but in a cognate language spoken by prodigies, wits and wizards. It's possible that your boys, like salamanders, will make themselves at home in the flames. Your father's conduct as well as your own point that way and that's why

Experience doesn't read quite like a written document. I am trying to account for the strong impression your father made on me, his drinking, his womanizing. And his preoccupation with English usage, his absorption, his loyalty—amounting to fanaticism—to the right way with words. I found the man very moving and of course I couldn't help wondering how I would appear to my own sons in my last days.

There is, or was, a Russian thinker named [Vasily] Rozanov who intrigues me. He declared that we wait thousands of years to be born, and then we come in, briefly, to do our stretch (I borrow this term from American-convict lingo). After ages of nonexistence we open our eyes, we see everything for the first time, we *exist*, we come into our intoxicating, dazzling "rights." In our own generation we have glimpses of others, briefly and passionately beginning to see. This is why the murder of your cousin Lucy hits us so hard. Her aim was to live, to perfect herself, to come into her legacy. But she was murdered and buried. I can't help thinking how very different a view of such enormities the media give us. [. . .]

I await your June visit, and I shall bone up on Rozanov. He is certainly worth talking about.

Love,

In 1973 Amis's twenty-one-year-old cousin Lucy Partington vanished. Twenty years later her remains were uncovered beneath the Gloucester house of serial killers Fred and Rosemary West.

To Richard Stern

August 12, 2000   Brookline

Dear Dick,

I don't intend to read [James] Atlas. There is a parallel between his book and the towel with which the bartender cleans the bar. What strikes me uncomfortably about Atlas is that he has great appeal for my detractors. He was born to please them. Another match made in heaven.

Yours ever,

To Philip Roth

[n. d.]   [Brookline]

Dear Philip—

[David] Remnick must know that he struck it rich, this time—no Eng. Lit. Prof. would be capable of doing what you've done with my books. And I too have learned from you. I see now what I was evidently incapable of seeing unaided: that I've done what everybody else does. Everybody takes the cognitive line. Like any sociologist, we understand; like any psychologist, we analyze. No big deal.

What *is* a big deal is that I've had a breakdown and you covered for me. You've concealed my disorder and kept me looking normal—no minor achievement.

Yours,

Roth's essay "Re-Reading Saul Bellow" had been commissioned by David Remnick, editor in chief of The New Yorker. *It appeared there on October 9.*

2001

To Keith Botsford

January 9, 2001   Brookline

Dear Keith,

A few gritty but happily minor details are on my mind this morning: I think it would be advisable to remove my name from the masthead of *The Republic of Letters*, starting with the next issue, and from the stationery when next you order it; also my name should disappear from the joint bank account. (On my tax return, *The Republic of Letters* will be listed as one of my investments, and I shall be claiming a capital loss—or whatever the accountants want it listed as.)

I am sure you won't object to my fading away. On this morning of black and white, snow and tree trunks, some instinct for simplification rises up. I feel like Bismarck when he stepped aside at the request of the young Kaiser. My list of old friends grows shorter and shorter. We, though, shall still be having dinners, drinks, and discussions; and if from time to time I send you some notes, I hope you will view them as coming from a contributor. I hope you will continue to *have* me as a contributor, and if you have suggestions for me in that line, I should be only too glad to have you as my editor.

With every good wish,

2002

To William Kennedy

February 28, 2002   Brookline

Dear Bill,

I don't think it's too late even now to tell you how deeply I loved *Roscoe*. I think it's your most successful novel yet, and I expect that more is to come. Heretofore, I was always concerned about your bringing together your singular and wonderful view of things with the idea of a large fiction always at the back of your mind, and I think you have finally united them both. I have always nagged at you to do just that, and I see that in spite of my nagging you have presented me, and the American public too, with exactly what we have been longing for. I hope you will be able to forgive me for this delay, but it takes me longer than most to catch up with things.

Your gratified reader,

To Karina Gordin

February 28, 2002   Brookline, Mass.

Dear Karina,

Since I am half-Gordin—on my mother's side—I want to say that I was grateful to be in touch with the family again, and that your letter pleased me.

There comes a moment, with increasing frequency, when artists feel that they are hopelessly surrounded by goats and monkeys. I am against falling into despair because of superficial observations such as the foregoing. Actually, I've never stopped looking for the real thing; and often I find the real thing. To fall into despair is just a high-class way of turning into a dope. I choose to laugh, and laugh at myself no less than at others.

Affectionately,

2004

To Eugene Kennedy

February 19, 2004   Brookline

Dear Gene,

I tried to reach you by phone yesterday. *Spurlos*—the word employed by German submarine commanders. It means "without a trace": not so much as an oil slick on the bosom of the Atlantic. (It occurs to me that you must have studied German under the Hollywood German experts.)

I don't do much of anything these days and I spend much of my time indoors. By far my pleasantest diversion is to play with Rosie, now four years old. It seems to me that my parents wanted me to grow up in a hurry and that I resisted, dragging my feet. They (my parents, not my feet) needed all the help they could get. They were forever asking, "What does the man say?" and I would translate for them into heavy-footed English. That didn't help much either. The old people were as ignorant of English as they were of Canadian French. We often stopped before a display of children's shoes. My mother coveted for me a pair of patent-leather sandals with an *elegantissimo* strap. I finally got them—I rubbed them with butter to preserve the leather. This is when I was six or seven years old, a little older than Rosie is now. Amazing how it all boils down to a pair of patent-leather sandals.

I send an all-purpose blessing . . .

EDITOR'S NOTE AND ACKNOWLEDGMENTS

This volume includes about two fifths of Saul Bellow's known output of letters. In some instances, I have emended eccentric punctuation in the interest of clarity, and have silently corrected a handful of spelling errors along with three insignificant factual misstatements. Letters made up of single-sentence paragraphs I have sometimes recast for ease of reading. Deleted material—most of it of doubtful interest, a miniscule portion removed for legal reasons—is indicated throughout by the customary ellipsis between brackets. I have broken with the standard practice of italicizing only published books, as Bellow tended to underline rather than place between quotation marks the titles of works in progress, particularly after an excerpt had appeared; for consistency, I have kept to this in the chronology as well. As to the clarifying or connecting language between brackets: I have sometimes fallen in with the author's voice (e.g., in a letter to Susan Glassman, "Now the CBC has paid me an unexpected three hundred to produce [my one-act play] 'The Wrecker'") and sometimes used third person (e.g., in a letter to John Auerbach, "Smadar [Auerbach's daughter] and her husband have been very kind"). About half the original letters are typewritten and half are by hand. Bellow's cursive comes clear to anyone who perseveres with it. I have been able to decipher every word but one, perhaps blurred by a raindrop or (given the circumstances) a tear.

A letter is a hostage to fortune, as likely to pass into oblivion as posterity. Along with those to Isaac Rosenfeld, one regrets the vanished communications to Sydney J. Harris, Herbert Passin, Harold Kaplan, Delmore Schwartz, Paolo Milano and Rosette Lamont. Still, a great hoard *does* survive. My gratitude to all the individuals who have preserved vulnerable paper is beyond telling. To Sylvia Tumin, widow of Melvin Tumin, I owe a particular debt; she was the first of so many to share letters and photos with me. Professor Nathan Tarcov furnished all of the many communications to Oscar and Edith Tarcov, his father and mother. (I am additionally grateful to Professor Tarcov for inviting me to address the University of Chicago's Committee on Social Thought about my researches.) Katherine Powers provided Bellow's letters to her father, J. F. Powers. I want to thank Eugene Kennedy for his cooperation and friendliness. Monroe Engel gave patiently of his time. Dr. Oliver Sacks recalled swimming in the Bellows' pond in Vermont and kindly made a search of his files. Robert W. Silvers, editor of *The*

New York Review of Books, ran a public call for letters. I am indebted to Cynthia Ozick for her deeply considered reflections on Bellow in several essays over the years. William Hunt provided letters and spoke with me absorbingly and at length. James Salter searched old trunks and was unfailingly helpful. I am much obliged to Professor Daniel Bell for a long and illuminating conversation. I would like to thank Mme. Julian Behrstock and Christie's auction house in New York, where I was allowed to photograph the letters from Bellow to her husband on consignment there. Rosanna Warren helped with several important details pertaining to her parents. Susan Cheever kindly answered queries, as did A. B. Yehoshua and Ian McEwan. Leon Wieseltier clarified backgrounds to several letters and offered pungent English equivalents for Yiddish turns of phrase. Linda Asher and Elisabeth Sifton helped to clarify Bellow's sequence of editors at Viking. David Rieff suggested the solution to an arcane matter pertaining to his father. Maria Campbell reported on Erich Linder. Amanda Vaill told me who Lyn Austin was. Joyce Carol Oates provided context for the letter to her. My dear friend Frances Kiernan decoded an otherwise unintelligible sentence. Professor Henry Hardy, Fellow of Wolfson College, Oxford, and executor of the Estate of Sir Isaiah Berlin, was kindly in touch, as were Tree Swenson, executive director of the Academy of American Poets, Edith Kurzweil, Nicholas Christopher, Debra Romanick Baldwin, Judith Dunford, Ben Sidran, Eugene Goodheart and Leslie Epstein. Robert Boyers, editor of *Salmagundi*, clarified the context of a letter to him. So did Professor Mark Shechner of the State University of New York, Buffalo. Through the generosity of Zachary Leader, who is at work on a biography of Bellow, I was able to include letters to David Peltz and to Herbert and Mitzi McCloskey. I have greatly benefited from frequent exchanges of information with Zach and count him an indispensable friend. Dean Borok journeyed to a storage locker in Brooklyn to retrieve a particularly remarkable letter. Owen Barfield, grandson of the Owen Barfield addressed in these pages, kindly gave access to his grandfather's papers at the Bodleian Library, Oxford. From Kibbutz S'dot Yam, near Caesarea, Nola Chilton dispatched photocopies of the letters to herself and her late husband John Auerbach. Stephen Mitchell furnished the unforgettable document in which Bellow describes his childhood discovery of Jesus, and Professor Martin E. Marty kindly answered my queries about the original, now housed at the University of Chicago Divinity School. Louis Gallo came from Trenton to New York to deliver precious pages and drink a glass of iced coffee. Frances Gendlin was kindly in touch. Daphne Merkin shared her memories of visiting Bellow in Vermont. Joshua Howes, a descendant of Bellow's childhood friend Louis Sidran, clarified the Sidran family tree. Norman Manea reminisced about Margaret Shafer. Barbara Probst Solomon described her long telephonic friendship with Bellow. Dominique Nabokov recalled summers with him at the Aspen Institute. Shirley Hazzard vividly described his visit to Capri in 1984 to receive the Premio Malaparte. And Eleanor Fox Simmons reported on a lost cache of *billets doux* that would, she said, have been the ornament of this book.

I want to thank Gregory, Adam and Daniel Bellow for their swift and friendly response to many queries. Daniel generously gave access to letters to his mother, and Adam puzzled with me over a crux in one of them. Lesha Bellows Greengus and Dr. Rachel Schultz, Bellow's niece and great niece, have been tremendously helpful from the start. Alexandra Ionescu Tulcea Bellow suggested necessary emendations to the chronology for 1973 to 1985. Valiantly generous in her willingness to allow very personal matters into print, Maggie Staats Simmons also solved a chronological mystery and led me to the letters to Samuel S. Goldberg. And Nancy Crampton shared the many photographs of Bellow she took over the years; examples of her marvelous work appear on the hardcover jacket of this book as well as in the inserts.

I thank the Rare Book and Manuscript Library of the University of Pennsylvania for furnishing letters to James T. Farrell. For those to John Berryman, I wish to thank the Manuscripts Division of the Elmer L. Anderson Library of the University of Minnesota, Minneapolis. Harvard's Houghton Library gave access to those to James Laughlin. It is a particular pleasure to thank Timothy Young of Yale's Beinecke Library for his hospitality each time I've worked in that most beautiful of research facilities; Bellow's letters to Edmund Wilson, Dwight MacDonald, Robert Penn Warren, Eleanor Clark, Josephine Herbst and Saul Steinberg are housed there. Professor Iain Topliss of La Trobe University, Melbourne, Australia, who has embarked on a biography of Steinberg, gave crucial advice. The Berg Collection of The New York Public Library made available letters to Alfred Kazin, John Cheever and Louis Lasco. At the Manuscripts Division of the Library of Congress, Dr. Alice Burney bore with my extensive calls on their holdings; Bellow's letters to Ralph Ellison, Hannah Arendt, Norman Podhoretz, Daniel Patrick Moynihan and Philip Roth are there. The Rare Book and Manuscript Division of the University of Delaware houses those to David Bazelon and Mark Harris, which they kindly supplied. William Kennedy directed me to the Special Collections of the State University of New York at Albany for access to the many letters to him. I thank the Howard Gottlieb Archival Research Center of Boston University for access to the papers of William Phillips, Philip Rahv, Leslie Fiedler, Roger Shattuck, Richard Lourie and Rosalyn Tureck. From The Harry Ransom Center of the University of Texas came a particularly rich harvest—letters to Henry Volkening, Pascal and Dorothy Covici, Bernard Malamud, Stanley Burnshaw, Alice Adams, James Salter,

Isaac Bashevis Singer and Keith Botsford. Columbia University's Rare Book and Manuscript Library provided friendly access to the archives of James Henle, Lionel Trilling, Meyer Schapiro, Benjamin Nelson, Richard V. Chase, John Leggett and Herbert Gold. Bellow's congratulatory note to the Circle in the Square cast of *The Last Analysis* I transcribed at Lincoln Center's New York Public Library for the Performing Arts, along with his letter to Zero Mostel. The letter to Theodore Weiss came courtesy of the Department of Rare Books and Special Collections of Princeton University's Firestone Library. Letters to Jean Stafford are preserved in Special Collections of the University of Colorado at Boulder. Those to Anthony Hecht and Edna O'Brien are at Emory University's Special Collections, and those to Toby Cole at Special Collections of the University of California, Davis. Viking Penguin patiently searched their archives and found many remarkable documents including the communications to Monroe Engel, Marshall Best and Elisabeth Sifton. To the Rare Book, Manuscript and Special Collections Library of Duke University go my thanks for opening Harriet Wasserman's archive. I am much obliged to the Rare Book and Manuscripts Collection of the University of Virginia for access to Bellow's vehement letter to William Faulkner. Letters to Stanley Elkin (a great friend to me in younger days and someone with whom I often spoke about Bellow's books) are housed in the Special Collections of The John M. Olin Library, Washington University, St. Louis. From The John Simon Guggenheim Memorial Foundation come those to Henry Allen Moe and Gordon Ray as well as reference letters in behalf of James Baldwin, Grace Paley, Bernard Malamud and Louise Glück; it is a pleasure to record here my gratitude to Edward Hirsch, president of the Foundation, and Andre Bernard, vice president and secretary, for their hospitality. Thanks to the good offices of Rob Cowley, I was able to research Bellow's correspondence with Malcolm Cowley, his father, at Chicago's Newberry Library. The Special Collections and Archives of The W. E. B. Dubois Library, University of Massachusetts, Amherst, provided Bellow's letters to Harvey Swados. And at the American Academy of Arts and Letters, Kathy Kienholtz granted access to the Academy's extensive Bellow file.

All other letters—whether in carbon or photocopy—have come from the Special Collections Research Center of Regenstein Library at the University of Chicago, where David Pavelich in particular made my labors orderly and swift. I owe a particular debt of gratitude to the radiant and phenomenal Esther Corbin, now in her hundredth year; as Bellow's secretary from 1971 to 1976, Mrs. Corbin made and filed hundreds of carbon copies of outgoing mail. I want to thank Michael Z. Yu, executor of the Estate of Allan Bloom, for granting access to Bloom's papers there; Richard Stern, whose archive is also at the Regenstein, and who has been so generous to this project from its inception; and Joseph Epstein, executor of the Estate of Edward Shils. James Atlas, a portion of whose papers are likewise at the Reg, generously gave me access to photocopies of Bellow's letters to Nathan Gould, Frances Gendlin, Willie Greenberg, William Roth, Jonas Schwartz, Leonard Unger, Ralph Ross, Robert Hivnor, Albert Glotzer, William Maxwell, Gertrude Buckman, Ann Birstein, Ladislas Farago, Barnett Singer, Ben Sidran—and Evelyn, the otherwise unidentified girl with one blue and one brown eye. Mr. Atlas's archive at Regenstein will always be a vital basis for Bellow research.

James Wood's chronology in The Library of America's multi-volume edition of Bellow's works served as the foundation for my own. I also made extensive use of Gabriel Josipovici's bibliography—authoritative for 1941 to 1974—in *The Portable Saul Bellow*. And I greatly profited from Norman Manea's inspiring interviews with Bellow for The Jerusalem Literary Project, afterward excerpted in *Salmagundi*; passages from these interviews appear in the chronology. Jacqueline Weld graciously responded to requests for translations of Bellow's unsavory Spanish. Professor Ruth Wisse of Harvard University patiently coped with my endless queries about Yiddish and Hebrew. Catherine Healey answered questions about Bellow's meaty, energetic French; and Anka Mulstein and Louis Begley kindly went to their *Grand Robert* in search of a phrase (nonexistent, it turned out) Bellow thought he had heard while hitchhiking from Banyuls-sur-Mer to Barcelona in the summer of 1947.

My dear friend Stephen Motika traveled with me to Chicago to help with the early stages of research. Brett Hool, Lindsay Alexander and, especially, Patrick "Memphis" Callihan transcribed endlessly and accurately. Patrick has additionally given yeoman service in securing photographic permissions. My freelance editor, Kristin Camp Sperber, was unfailing in precision and insight. Janet Biehl, my copyeditor, saved me from many a blunder. All those at Viking Penguin who have labored long have my thanks: Carolyn Carlson, Beena Kamlani, Amanda Brower, Shannon Twomey and Francesca Belanger. At *The New Yorker*, where an excerpt from this book appeared, I got to know the surpassing professionalism of David Remnick and Katherine Stirling.

Without the ferocious advocacy of Andrew Wylie and Jeffrey Posternak, agents to the Estate of Saul Bellow, this book could not have come to be. I am also grateful to their colleague Alexandra Levenberg, who cheerfully and expertly addressed issue after issue. Walter Pozen, Saul Bellow's lawyer, has been an essential guide and occasional Dutch uncle. Good, wise, sharp-eyed Joel Conarroe read every blessed word of the proofs. To Philip Roth, a godfather to these pages, I owe incalculable debts.

I'd like also to thank Saul Bellow's young daughter Rosie (cat lover, violinist, deep thinker) for her friendship, and for telling me off on one occasion, when I deserved it. To Rosie's mother, the gifted and indefatigable Janis Freedman Bellow, who photocopied all letters leaving Bellow's desk during the last twenty-three years of his life, I am boundlessly grateful: for her scholarly foresight, for the trust she has reposed in me, and for her warmth and wit in fair and foul weather. Were it within my purview to dedicate this book I would do so to J. F. B.

Finally, I want to thank Saul Bellow for the privilege of spending each afternoon of the last three years with him.

INDEX

Page numbers in **bold** indicate correspondence with individuals.

Abel, Lionel, xxii, 77, 81, 82, 457
absurdity, 339–40, 345, 387
The Actual (Bellow), 520
Adams, Alice, **174–76**, **194**, **200**, **256–57**
Adams, J. Donald, 143
adolescence, 340, 468
The Adventures of Augie March (Bellow)
  completion and revisions, 115, 116, 118
  Dean Borok and, 376
  discussions about *Augie March,* 102–3, 122–23, 126–27, 128–29, 210, 298
  enthusiasm for writing, 82, 83, 97, 98
  episodic nature, 101, 102, 103
  excerpt, 95
  publication of chapters, 85, 98, 101
  reviews, xxiv, 110–12, 120–21, 126–27, 487
"The Adventures of Saul Bellow" essay, 177
age and aging
  coping with, 516, 517, 519, 521–22, 524, 529, 530–31
  death and, 535–36, 542, 544–45, 547
  fatigue and, 327–28, 491, 509, 523
  forgetfulness, 516, 531, 544–45
  old friends and, 454, 496, 497
  old men in novels and plays, 525
  thoughts on, 349–50, 408, 465, 468, 501, 503, 542
Agnon, S. Y., xxv, xxviii
agnosticism, 373
Air India plane crash, 255
alchemy of writing, 25, 26
alimony, 213–14, 338–39, 351–52
Alison, Barley, **269–70**, **286–87**, **301**, 313, 382, 384, **422–23**, **428–29**, **432–33**, 451

Alison, Michael, 422–23, **451**
All Marbles Still Accounted For (unfinished novel), xxxiii, 504
All The King's Men (Warren), 44, 436, 458
American Academy and Institute of Arts and Letters, 296, 346, **348–49**, 358, 435, **478–79**, 480
American Communist Party, 5–6, 541
American writing and writers
  Augie March and, 510
  Bernard Malamud and, 242
  discussion of *Invisible Man,* 137–38
  distinct identity of, xxii, xxiv, xxv, 87, 399–401
  Ellison on purpose of fiction, 505–6
  exposing the seeming, 246–47
Ames, Elizabeth, **113**, **115**, 117, **168–69**, 229
Amis, Martin, **444**, **465–66**, **476–77**, **502–3**, **510–11**, **516–17**, **522–24**, **547–49**
Anderson, Sherwood, 247, 298
Anne Bradstreet (Berryman), 156
Anon (journal), 293, 299–300
Anthony, Joseph, 243, 244
anthropology, 7, 8–9, 10–11, 53, 62, 153
anthroposophy, xxix, 327, 351, 362, 368–69, 371–72, 399–400
anti-Semitism
  Christopher Hitchens and, 455–56
  Ezra Pound and, 83–84, 144–45
  Hannah Arendt and, 391–92
  Harvard Shop Club speech, 518–19
  Jerusalem Book Fair and, 411
  Jewish writers finding their place and, 435–36

reviews of *The Dean* and, 393
  Ruth Wisse's article on, 480
Apple, Max, 358
Arendt, Hannah, xxiv, 130, 208, 302, 354–55, 391
Army service, 26, 29, 30
art
  artistic principles, 26
  emergence vs. imposition of positions in, 165
  foundation of, 138
  non-definitive answers of, 28
  power of individual speech and, 119
  "prepared" attitudes and, 165
  value of, 469
  writers as prophets, 225–26
Asher, Aaron, 172, 211, 288, 414
atheism, 373
Atlantic Monthly, 412, 460
Atlas, James, **457**, 470, **482**, 546, 549
Auden, W. H., 65, 303, 311, 312, 543
Auerbach, John
  aging and illnesses, **445–46**, **465**, **491**, **497**, **501**, **519–20**
  Bellow's services to the arts award, **379–80**
  Bellow's seventy-fifth birthday, 468
  Boston University, **459**
  discussion of Borges, **441–42**
  divorce from Alexandra, **430–31**
  each other's writing, **485–86**
  health, writing, and Israel, **448–49**
  Kibbutz S'dot Yam, **379–80**, **433**, **497**
  politics, **492**, **493–94**, **541**
  stroke suffered by, **475–76**
  visits to Vermont, **409–11**, **433**, **474**

Austin, Lyn, 244, 246
avant-garde writing, xxviii,
    78, 131

Baldwin, James, xxii, 130, 242
Bard College, 120, 126, 129–30,
    131, 133–34, 341, 505
Barfield, Owen
    Barfield's judgment of
        Bellow's novels, 335,
        339–40, **368–69**,
        399–401
    Bellow's study of Barfield's
        writings, **326–27**,
        328–30, 350–51, 362
    death of, xxv
    discussions of Israel,
        339–40, 344–46
    discussions of Steiner, 334,
        339, 344, 351, **368–69**,
        371–72
    discussions of writing,
        326–27, 329–30, 334–35
    meetings with, xxix,
        328–29, 399–401
Barshevsky, Yetta, xviii, **3–4**,
    518, 527–29, 535
Barzun, Jacques, **346**
Bazelon, David
    anthropology, 62
    Bellow's advice about
        writing fiction to, **42–43**
    Bellow's plans to meet
        with, **253–54**
    discussion of reviews of
        their writing, **48–49**
    discussion of *The Victim*
        with, **50–51**
    discussions of politics and
        revolution, **35–37, 39**
    mutual friend Margaret,
        86–88, 90–91
    opinion of Bellow's
        writing, 88
    Paris and France, **73–74**,
        80–81
    reading, translating, and
        writing, **53–54**
    remarks on Rome to,
        76–77
    University of Minnesota,
        73, 80, 86
Beach, Joseph Warren, 52, 458
The Beacon, xx, 4–5
Begin, Menachim, 359–60,
    360, 410, 412
Behrstock, Julian, **363, 468**,
    503, 509, 512, 521,
    530–31, 535
Bellevue Hospital, 161, 203

Bellow, Adam (son)
    affection for, 328
    college career of, 357
    conversations with, 230
    correspondence with, **249**,
        344, 349
    custody and parenting
        issues, 198, 201–2, 235–37,
        263, 266–67
    infancy and childhood,
        160, 163, 166, 167, 180,
        183, 189, 190, 195
    visits with, 225, 231, 255,
        274, 275, 279, 286, 299,
        300–301, 306, 342, 387,
        409, 446, 468
Bellow, Alexandra Ionescu
    Tulcea
    career in mathematics, 328,
        353, 367, 410
    divorce from, 428–29,
        430–31, 432
    mentioned, 361, 365, 368,
        371, 375, 379, 380, 415,
        422
    Romanian family of, xxx,
        385
Bellow, Daniel (son)
    affection for, 301
    bar mitzvah of, 351–52
    correspondence with,
        372–73
    marriage of, 511, 513
    mentioned, 248, 265, 267,
        275, 282, 288, 299, 300
    visits with, 301, 306, 446,
        468, 529
Bellow, Gregory (son)
    childhood, 45, 46, 89, 105
    college and, 203, 209,
        224, 238
    letter about alimony to,
        213–14
    marriage of, 299, 315
    mentioned, xxi, 113, 119,
        124, 133, 150, 152, 153, 156,
        173, 195, 521
    visits with, 192, 202, 334
Bellow, Janis Freedman
    doctoral studies of, 498
    marriage to, 459, 465, 468,
        481, 494
    relationship with, 411, 441,
        445–46, 449, 459
Bellow, Maurice (brother),
    xvii, xviii, 105, 230, 231,
    376
Bellow, Naomi Rose
    (daughter), xxxv, xxxvi,
    552

Bellow, Sam (brother), xvii,
    xviii, 8, 159, 243, 376,
    379, 429, 447
Bellow, Susan Glassman
    alimony and child support
        issues, 338–39, 386
    discussions of writing with,
        196–97, 221
    move to Chicago, 237–38,
        240
    relationship with, **194**,
        196–98, 199, 204,
        205–6, 208–9, 218–20,
        222–24, 230–33
    settlement payment, 361,
        362, 363
Belo, Abram (father)
    arguments with, xix, 7–8
    immigration and career of,
        xvii–xix
    money from, 25, 49, 150, 151,
        153, 158, 171
    reaction to death of, xxiv,
        136, 205
    relationship with, 46, 55,
        114, 123, 517
    respect for, 365
Belo, Liza (mother), xvii, xix,
    527
Bentley, Eric, 41, 97, 98, 272
Berghof, Herbert, xxvii
Berlin, Isaiah, 383, 449, 542
Bernick, Isadore, 470, 471
Berryman, John
    alcoholism of, 241, 273,
        314, 425
    Bellow's opinion of, 202,
        347, 394–95
    children of, **305**
    discussions of poetry and
        death, **245**
    discussions of poetry and
        writing, **156–58, 163**,
        164–65, 239, 243
    friendship with, **132**,
        134–35, 151–52, 164–65,
        185, 233–34, 259
    literary magazine work,
        178, 180, 198–99,
        203–4, 293
    suicide of, xxix, 306, 309,
        314–15
Berryman, Kate, **305**
Best, Marshall, 164, **193–94**
bibliophilia, 165, 307, 313–14,
    372–73, 486
Billy Phelan (Kennedy), 377,
    389
Birstein, Ann, 251, **318–19**,
    366

Blackmur, R.P., 53, 204
Blake, William, 182, 215, 264
Bloom, Allan
  death of, xxxiii, 496
  friendship with, **381, 382, 383–84, 385, 408–9,** 444
  illness of, 475, 477
  mentioned, 418, 419, 490
  Ravelstein and, xxxiv, 546
  teaching with, xxxi, **368**
Bloom, Claire, 430, 448, 499
Bloom, Harold, 480
Blücher, Heinrich, xxiv, 129, 130, 134, 302
Böll, Heinrich, 418, 419
Bollingen Prize for poetry, 84, 416–17
bolshevism, 5–6, 87–88
Borok, Dean, **376**
Boston University, xxxiv, xxxvi, 452, 459, 498, 530
Bostonia (journal), 486
Botsford, Keith
  Bellow's divorce from Sondra, **181, 183–84**
  Bellow's opinion of, 219
  hip surgery of, 537
  news of family visits, **225**
  sadness over Covici's death, 248
  staying with in Puerto Rico, 205, 206, 208
  The Republic of Letters and, **550–51**
  work on *Anon* with, 293, 300
  work on *The Noble Savage* with, **200–201,** 211, **226,** 232, 537
Botstein, Leon, **415, 433–34**
Boyers, Robert, **392–94**
Bradley, Mrs. Wm. A., 84–85
Brandeis, Irma, xxiv, 396
Brandeis University, 350, 379
Breit, Harvey, 84, 145
Briggs-Copeland Fellowship, 97, 98
Brodie, Steve, 128, 129
Brodkey, Harold, **450–51**
Brogan, Denis, 400, 531
Browder, Earl, 5–6
Brown, Huntington, 80, 93
Buckman, Gertrude, **154, 203**
Burlingame, Edward, **427**
Burnett, Whit, 27, **287**
Burnshaw, Stanley, **251–52, 254–55**
Bush, George H. W., 375, 466
"By the Rock Wall" (story), xxiii, 66, 101–2

"By the Saint Lawrence" (story), 509

Camus, Albert, xxii, 97
Carter, Jimmy, 359, 360, 374, 410
Carver, Catharine ("Katie") DeFrance, xxvii, 161, 303, 326, 364, 425
Case, James H., Jr., **120,** 129, 134
A Case of Love (unfinished novel), xxxiii
Catton, Bruce, 130, 131
Céline, L.-F., 518, 523, 524
censorship, 24, 78
The Century Association, 310, 317, 324
Cermak, Anton, 528
Chambers, Whittaker, xxi, 395
Chapman, Chanler, xxiv, xxv, 396
Chapman, Sara S., **298**
characters
  in *The Actual,* 531–32
  Allbee in *The Victim,* 50, 61
  basis in real people, 106, 331, 376, 443
  Bummidge in *The Last Analysis,* 243, 244
  Charlie Citrine in *Humboldt's Gift,* 330
  development of, 34, 50, 51
  discussions about *Augie March,* 102–3, 122–23, 126–27, 128–29, 198
  discussions with Keith Opdahl about, **215–16**
  Leventhal in *The Victim,* 50, 61
Chase, Richard V., **177**
Cheever, John, xxiv, xxxii, **342–43, 358, 367, 386–87**
Chiaromonte, Nicola ("Nick"), xxii, 67, 91, 354–55
Chicago
  description of people in, 408–9
  memories of childhood in, 470–71
  opinions of, xxxi, 40, 254–55, 273
  Susan moves to, 237–38, 239, 240
  winter weather, 1, 231, 232, 233, 241, 256, 286, 302, 344
  writers' images of, 526

Chilton, Nola, **379–80, 519–20, 541**
Choate, Catherine Lindsay, **460–61, 473**
Circle in the Square
  production of *The Last Analysis,* 304
citizenship, 16–17
civilization, 65–66, 485
Clark, Eleanor, 118, **370–71, 397,** 467, 514–15, 516–17
Cogan, Zita, xviii, **470,** 532–33, 533–34
cognitive writing, 38, 177
Cole, Toby, **237–38, 244, 246, 249–50, 253, 285–86, 298–99, 342**
Collected Stories (Bellow), xxxv
Colt Press, 29
comedy
  advantages of comedic writing, 345
  as element of *Henderson the Rain King,* 173, 178
  as element of *More Die of Heartbreak,* 442, 443
  intent of *Augie March* and, 124, 126–27, 128–29
  Italian, 137
  The Upper Depths, 234
  wretchedness and comedic writing, 502–3
  writing comedic pieces, 59–60, 79
Commentary (journal), 113, 114–15, 474, 480, 487
Committee for the Free World, 405, 417–18
Committee on Social Thought, 234–35, 239, 240, 302, 333–34, 377, 490, 498
Communist Party, American, 5–6, 541
conferences, dislike of, 227–28
Connolly, Cyril, xxiii, xxvi
Conrad, Joseph, 352, 477, 486
conservatism, 133
Corbin, Esther, 330, 331
Covici, Dorothy, **248–49**
Covici, Pascal ("Pat")
  becomes Bellow's editor, 81
  Bellow's divorce from Sondra, **181–82, 184, 189**
  Bellow's Israel trip, **192**
  Bellow's San Francisco trip, **148–49**
  death of, xxvii, 248–49, 364

Covici, Pascal ("Pat") (*cont.*)
  discussion of writing and
    Ford Foundation grant,
    168, 169–70
  discussions of speaking
    engagements and book
    sales, **165–66, 172–73**
  discussions of writing, **121,
    139, 140–41, 164, 190,
    218**
  mentioned, 52, 116–17, 193
Cowley, Malcolm, **136**
The Crab and the Butterfly
  (Bellow), xxii–xxiii, 59,
  79, 81, 82
craft of writing, 50–51, 227–28
Craft, Robert, 311–12
Crime and Punishment
  (Dostoyevsky), 511
criticism
  Bellow's criticisms of Jack
    Ludwig, 210–12
  Bellow's critique of Elkin's
    writing, **194–95**
  dealing with, 34, 36, 466–67
  of *Jerusalem* book, 323,
    341, 345
  Louis Simpson's attack on
    Bellow, 332–33
  reading about himself and,
    318, 412
  of Whit Burnett, 27
critics
  Bellow's note to Phillips, **177**
  Bellow's thoughts on,
    37–38, 48–49, 53, 154,
    179, 337, 440, 480
  reviews of *Augie March*
    and, 120–21, 124–26
Crouch, Stanley, **479**
cultural understanding, 460
cultural void, 369–70
"Culture Now" essay, 295–96,
  303
Cummings, E. E., 161, 506
cynicism, 531

Dajani, Virginia, **489**
Daley, Richard J., xxvii, xxxiii
Dangling Man (Bellow), xxii,
  27–28, 34, 36
Dannhauser, Werner, 418,
  419, **534–36, 545–46**
darkness as literary theme, 153
The Dean's December (Bellow),
  385, 387, 388–89, 392–94,
  396, 399–401, 406, 427,
  546
death, 159, 330, 496, 497
Debray, Régis, 413, 414

Decter, Midge, 405, **417–18**
"Deep Readers of the World,
  Beware!" article, xxv, 170
Demjanjuk, John, 448
democracy, 341, 419, 494,
  547–48
depression, 367, 492, 510
destiny, 37, 299, 331, 415
distribution of books, 46–48,
  326, 422, 427
diversity in storytelling, 175
divorce, 194, 366, 428–29,
  430–31
dogs, xxi, 207, 409–10
doing things out of sight,
  65–66
Don Quixote (Cervantes), 165
Donadio, Candida, 289
Donat, Alexander, 391
"Dora" (story), xxiii, 41, 44
Dostoyevsky, xxxiv, 511, 518
draft deferments, 16, 17, 21,
  26, 34
dreams, 383, 476–77
"Dr.Pep" (story), 65–66,
  74, 78
Dubin's Lives (Malamud),
  365–66
Dunsky-Shnay, Zipporah, **422**

earnestness, 164, 178
The Economist (journal), 486
egomania, 77
Eisenhower, Dwight, 145, 195,
  415, 416
Eliade, Mircea, 532
Eliot, T. S., xviii, 133, 147, 152,
  310, 318, 319, 393, 428,
  478, 494–95
Elkin, Stanley, **194–95,
  489–90, 492–93,
  494–95**
Ellison, Fanny, **174, 180,** 192
Ellison, Ralph
  Bellow solicits magazine
    submission from, **170–72**
  Bellow's divorce from
    Sondra, **180**
  Bellow's eulogy of, 505–6
  Bellow's memories of, 341
  description of Puerto Rico,
    207–8
  discussions of family and
    writing, **149–50, 160,
    163, 166–67, 192**
  discussions of health, **189**
  Tivoli house and, **152–53,
    176**
Emerson, Ralph Waldo,
  121–22, 350

Encounter (journal), 334, 486
Encyclopedia Britannica, xxi,
  40, 243, 524
enemies, 147–48
Engel, Monroe
  Bellow's Guggenheim
    application and, **98–99,
    100–101, 102–3**
  Bellow's letter from Paris,
    64–65
  discussion of Isaac
    Rosenfeld, **107**
  end of editorial relationship
    with Bellow, 81–82
  mentioned, 63, 199
  reports on writing progress
    to, **85**
entropy, 486
Epstein, Joseph, 354, 417, 480
Epstein, Seymour, 345
Erskine, Albert, 118
Esquire, 222, 223, 390, 398,
  415–16, 460
esthetics, 8, 20, 175, 369–70
Europe (Stern), 229–30
exile, 106, 149
"Expect the Vandals" (Roth),
  162
Experience (Amis), 548–49
exposing the seeming,
  American literature and,
  246–47

Falconer (Cheever), 343
fame, 297, 399
Farago, Ladislas, **360**
Farrell, James T., xx, **5–6,
  40,** 254
father, *see* Belo, Abram
fatigue, 327–28, 339, 389,
  485–86, 491, 509
Faulkner, William, xxvi, 42,
  144–45, 149, 150, 307
Fellini, Federico, 418, 419
Feltrinelli, Giangiacomo, 280
Feltrinelli, Inge, **296–97**
festination, 504
Fiedler, Leslie, 80, 109,
  124–25, 136–37, 161, **165,
  197,** 303
First Loyalty (Lourie), 424
Fitzgerald, F. Scott, fantasy
  story about, 67–72
Flaubert, Gustave, 139, 318
fools, 305
Ford Foundation grant, 168,
  169–70, 193
forgetfulness, 516, 531, 544–45
Fowler, H. W., xxiv, 331
France, 68, 90, 106

Frankel, Max, 500
Freedman, Janis, *see* Bellow,
  Janis Freedman
Freifeld, Rochelle, 28, 46, **64**
Freifeld, Samuel
  discussion of exile, **106**
  family troubles of, 46
  friendship with, 12, 19,
    39–40, **117**, **123–24**,
    127–28, **132–33**, **142**, **159**
  hard work of, 21
  mentioned, 340, 398, 471
  postcards from Bellow, 43,
    64, **77**
  reaction to *Augie March*,
    112, 123
Freud, Sigmund, 197, 235,
  322, 414, 446, 502, 504,
  513, 534
friendships
  appreciation for, 353, 361,
    406, 423, 442–43, 445,
    458, 508, 515–16
  with Barley Alison, 451
  with Catherine Lindsay
    Choate, 460–61, 473
  discussions of with Fiedler,
    165
  forced, 12–13
  with Harriet Wasserman,
    327
  with Henry Volkening,
    140, 243
  loss of, 75, 76, 104, 106, 522
  maintaining, 42, 367, 508,
    519–20, 525
  with Oscar Tarcov, 18–19,
    131, 245
  rift with David Bazelon
    over Margaret, 87–88
Fuchs, Daniel, **318**, **319**
Furet, François, **490**

Gallimard (French publisher),
  85, 373, 520
Gallo, Louis, **209–10**, **217–18**,
  224–25, **225–26**
Gendlin, Frances, **293–94**,
  307–8, **313–14**
Gill, Brendan, 159–60
Gillman, Mr., **268**
Ginsberg, Allen, 411, 427
Ginsberg, Harvey, xxx, xxxi,
  xxxii
Glassman, Susan, *see* Bellow,
  Susan Glassman
Gloria Mundi (Clark), 370–71
Glotzer, Albert, 5–6, 340,
  373–74, 468, **470–72**,
  511–12, **518–19**, 538, 542

Glück, Louise, xxviii, 284
God's Grace (Malamud),
  387–88
Godwin, Anthony, **326**
Gold, Herbert, xxii, 107, 226,
  507–8
Gold Medal for Fiction
  Award, xxx, 346, 348–49
Goldberg, Samuel S.
  Bellow on divorce from
    Susan, **338–39**
  Bellow on *Seize the Day*,
    150–51
  bibliophilia of, 313–14
  friendship with, **307**
  mentioned, 239, 274, 330–31
  owing money to, 213
Goldenweiser, Alexander
  Alexandrovich, 9
Goldknopf, David, **117–18**
Goldstein, Nathan, 4
good intentions, 225, 312, 325,
  414, 499, 516, 525
Goodman, Paul, 324, 472
Gordimer, Nadine, 427
Gordin, Karina, **551**
Goshkin, Anita (wife)
  alimony and, 213–14
  Bellow's divorce from, 119,
    125, 132, 133, 139–40,
    141, 146
  Bellow's quarrels with, 14
  career of, 27, 81
  desire to move to Europe,
    58–59, 61
  family troubles of, 45–46
  Northwestern University
    radicals and, xx, 11
  opinion of Bellow's
    writing, 25
  opinion of Melvin
    Tumin, 24
Goshkin, Catherine, 45–46
Gould, Nathan, xviii, **398–99**
Grass, Günter, 427–28
Great Books Project, 36
Great Jewish Short Stories, 231
Greenberg, Clement, 23, 487
Greenberg, Willie, **284**
Greene, Graham, xxviii, 63,
  338, 411
Greenwich Village, 51, 454,
  473, 476, 487
Grene, David, 239, 273, 302,
  309, 368, 490, 523
grief, 297, 368
Grimson, Todd, **445**
the grotesque, 247
Guggenheim Memorial
  Foundation

Bellow's fellowship
  applications, xxi–xxii,
    40–41, 43, 44, 45,
    52–53, 54
  budget request letters,
    55, **135**
  move to Europe and, **62**,
    63–64
  recommendation of Grace
    Paley, **204–5**
  recommendation of James
    Baldwin, **130**
  recommendation of Louise
    Glück, **284**
  recommendation of others,
    201
  recommendations of
    Bernard Malamud,
    118–19, **162**
  renewal application, 81,
    92, 98
  renewal rejection, 100,
    101, 102
Guinzburg, Harold, 75, 100,
  111, 193
Guinzburg, Tom, 164, 334,
  377

Haffenden, John, **309**
Hall, Donald, 480
Hammersmark, Sam, 471
Hammett, Dashiell, 398
happiness, 164, 198
Hardwick, Elizabeth, 49
Harper & Row, xxx, xxxi,
  xxxii, 381, 421, 422, 427
Harper's Bazaar, 54, 101–2
Harris, Mark, **205**, **283**, 381
Harris, Sydney J., xviii–xix,
  5–6, 312, 340
Harvard University, 75, 92,
  97, 98
Hasenclever, Walter, **335–37**,
  375
Havel, Václav, 534
Hayek, Friedrich von, 240
health issues
  aging and, 503
  ciguatera poisoning, xxxiv,
    505, 506–7, 510, 519
  depression, 367, 492, 510
  during divorce from
    Sondra, 189–90
  eye hemorrhage, 480–81
  of friends, 276–77, 503, 509
  gall-bladder surgery, 512
  heart problems, 377, 503,
    510, 521, 538, 543, 544
  hospital stays, 117
  ignoring, 449

Index

health issues (*cont.*)
  remarks to friends about,
    48, 132, 512–13, 524
  sexually transmitted
    diseases, 190, 308
  sleeping pills, 205, 247, 261,
    281, 300, 301, 521, 542
  weight, 274, 530
  wintertime, 110
Hearst Press, 148
heart of mankind, 114–15
Hebrew, 54
Hecht, Anthony, xxiv, **395–96**
Held, Abe, 478
Hellman, Lillian, xxvii, 168,
  172, 196, 247, 398
Henderson the Rain King
  (Bellow)
  Bellow's reaction to reviews
    of, 179
  Bellow's own assessment
    of, 318
  discussion of with Anne
    Sexton, **233**
  discussion of with Edward
    Hoagland, 216
  discussion of with Leslie
    Fiedler, 165
  excerpt, 187
  expected sales of, 172
  film of, 355
  opera based upon, 342
  reviewing proofs of, 166
  reviews of, 169, 170–71, 173,
    174, 182
  rewriting of, 167
  writing of, 149, 155, 156,
    163, 164
Henle, Jim
  book advances, 44
  complaints about, 49–50,
    59, 62
  correspondence with,
    49–50
  parting ways with, 60, 62
  remarks on pace of Bellow's
    career, 51–52
  The Victim and, 42, 46–48,
    58
Herbst, Josephine, **155,**
  167–68, 169, 178–80,
  220–21
hero figures, 153, 316
Herskovits, Melville J., xix,
  20, 25–26, 53
Herzog (Bellow)
  completion of, 231, 232, 235,
    238, 240
  letters in, 493
  reactions to, 488

reviews of, 250, 317, 352
Bellow's own assessment
  of, 540
success of, 229, 251–52
writing of, 202, 208, 212,
  218, 219, 220, 221, 223, 226
Heschel, Abraham Joshua,
  211–12
Hicks, Granville, 113, **147–48,**
  159–60
"Him With His Foot in His
  Mouth" (story), 396, 405,
  421, 422, 427
Hitchens, Christopher,
  455–56, 465
Hitler, Adolph, 147, 419, 455,
  456, 528, 540
Hivnor, Robert, 45, **97–98,**
  306, 425
Hoagland, Edward, 171,
  216–17, 242
Hoffman, Theodore ("Ted"),
  xxiv, 134, 207, 261
Holbrook, David, **305–6**
Holiday (journal), 142, 149,
  151, 271
Holocaust, 438–39, 456
Hook, Sidney, 487
House Un-American
  Activities Committee, 35
Howe, Irving, 93, 360
Howland, Bette, 280, 320,
  358, 468
Hudson Review monologue, 109
*Human Hope and the Death
  Instinct* (Holbrook), 306
human nature, 387–88
human relations, 281
humanity
  heart as origin and seat of
    importance in mankind,
    114–15
  loss of, 155
  misery and, 209–10
  remarks to Richard Stern
    about, 182
  thoughts on growing older
    and, 349–50
  truth of artistic works
    and, 28
Humboldt's Gift (Bellow)
  completion of, 323, 335
  death and comedy in, 330
  detachment from, 328
  excerpt, 291
  film rights for, 346
  inscribed editions, 352
  Owen Barfield and, 335,
    339–40
  reviews of, 467

Hunt, John, **506–7, 509**
Hunt, William, 433
Hutchins, Robert Maynard,
  36–37, 250
Huxley, Aldous, 476
Hyde Park, xix, xxxii, xxxiv,
  46, 367, 483, 530
hypocrisy, 212

I Married a Communist
  (Roth), 540–41
ideas and writing, 162, 261
"identity," 319
ideology, 136, 165, 175, 182, 466
idleness, 164
Illinois governor, 379–80
"Illinois Journey," 142, 151
illness, *see* health issues
imagination, 51, 118–19, 329,
  475–76
immigration, 16
immodesty, 57
"In the Days of Mr.
  Roosevelt" (essay), 411
inconclusiveness, 177
individuality and technology,
  329
The Information (Amis), 523
The Inmost Leaf (Kazin),
  143–44
Instead (journal), 82–83
integration, 149–50
intellectualism, xxii, xxx, 319,
  324, 354–55, 391–92, 439,
  514–15, 518–19
intelligence, 165, 187, 450
internal work as writing
  theme, 95
Ironweed (Kennedy), 389–90
irony, 36, 41
Israel, 359–60, 391–92, 410–11,
  412–13
Italy, 64, 65, 66, 107

James, Henry, 229, 309, 400,
  435, 477
Japan, 306–9
"The Jefferson Lectures"
  excerpt, 1
Jerusalem, 374–75, 407, 426,
  490–91
Jesus, 484–85
Jewish People's Committee,
  21
Jewishness
  American society and,
    435–36, 443
  Bellow's, 181, 196, 338
  Bellow's critique of Stanley
    Elkin and, **194–95**

Index

in Cynthia Ozick's *Messiah of Stockholm,* 438–40
discussions with Leon Wieseltier, 356–57, 358–60
fellow writers and, 227, 430
the Holocaust and, 438–39
as "marketable," 197
as theme in Bellow's writing, 268, 399
Jhabvala, Ruth Prawer, 418, 419
Johnson, Lyndon, xxvii, 253, 289, 290
Johnson, Samuel, 297
journalism, 19, 343, 406
journalists, 414, 455, 469, 547
Joyce, James, xii, xxiv, xxxi, 143, 222, 476, 487, 493

Kamlani, Beena, xxxiii
Kaplan, Harold ("Kappy"), xxii, 19, 20, 21, 56–57, 287
Kaplan, Justin, 247
Kaplan, Roger, **481, 499–500**
Karlen, Arno, **227–28**
Kauffman, Charles, 265, 303–4
Kauffman, Jane (sister), xvii, xxxvi, 265, 303–4, 444, 468, 522, 538, 548
Kauffman, Lawrence, 167, 168
Kaufman, Abe, xviii, 12–13, 25, 214–15, 524–25
Kazin, Alfred
  discussion of mutual friends, **247–48**
  discussions about writing, **37–38, 60–62, 124, 143–44, 317, 405**
  discussions of family, **137**
  friendship with, 113, **390, 397, 405, 411–12**
  invitation to Tivoli house, **226**
  memoir-essay on Bellow, **250–51**
  opinion of Bellow's early writing, 23, 61
  remarks on Bard College to, **129–30**
  remarks on Paris to, **99–100**
  review of *Seize the Day,* **158**
Kazin, Ann (Birstein), 137, 158, **226**
Kennedy, Eugene C., **504–5, 552**
Kennedy, John F., xxvi, 206, 246

Kennedy, Robert, xxvii, 541
Kennedy, William, **377–78, 381, 389–90, 493, 551**
Kenner, Hugh, 393, 421
Kenyon Review, 78, 79
Kerrigan, Anthony, 431, 433, 441, 446
Kibbutz S'dot Yam, xxxiii, 379–80, 433, 497
Kiepenheuer & Witsch, 335–36, 518
Kiernan, Frances, **472**
Kirchner, Leon, 342
Kleinbard, Jonathan, 468, **469, 498–99,** 532
Klonsky, Milton, 80–81, 87
knowing one's mind, 215
Koch, Sigmund, **431–32**
Koestler, Arthur, xxii, 58
Kołakowski, Leszek, 418, 419
Kollek, Teddy, 335, **341, 343–44,** 356, **407,** 410, **426,** 449, 491, **496, 542**
Konstantinovski, Ilya, 373–74
Kopit, Arthur, 279, 280
Korean War, 108, 112
Krim, Seymour, 42, 224

Landau, Bananas, 397, 398
Landau, Bernice Meyer, 398
Landes, Arlette, 286
Lang, Jack, 413, 481
Lapp, Rudy, 398, 474, 478
Lasco, Louis
  friendship with, xviii, **312, 322, 340, 364, 372, 397, 481–82, 482–83**
  illness of, **474–75, 478**
Lasky, Melvin, 334, 428
The Last Analysis (play), 195, 196, 248, 285, 304
Laughlin, James, 32, **161, 321**
Lawrence, D. H., xx, 87, 174, 198, 318, 323, 365
laziness, 134–35
Leggett, John, **239**
Lehmann, John, xxiii, 67, 82–83, 83, **110–12**
leisure, 164
Leites, Nathan, 273
Leninism, 15
Lennon, John, 484
Les Justes (play), 97–98
letter to Evelyn, **315–16**
letters
  apologies for not writing, 411–12, 413, 437
  difficulty of writing, 152, 454–55, 516, 538

gratefulness for letters from friends, 155
value of, 454
Levi, Primo, 439, 452
Lewis, Sinclair, 458
Lieber, Maxim, xxi, 20–21, 34–35
The Life of John Berryman (Haffenden), 309
light as literary theme, 153
Lily (opera based on *Henderson the Rain King),* 342
Linder, Erich, 296, 297, 357
Lindley, Denver, xxviii, 282, 288, 364
literature
  "literary culture," 92–93
  "literary loyalty," 88, 90–91
  love of, xxiv, 290
  merit of written vs. constructed portions of novels, 138
  polemical, 88
  teaching of, 154–55
living abroad, 75, 76, 77, 106
loneliness, 75, 76, 106
"Looking for Mr. Green" (story), 66, 113
Lourie, Richard, **424**
love
  Bellow's thoughts on, 116, 184–85, 195
  feeling unloved by Anita, 117
  feminine beliefs about, 200
  for friends, 24, 117
  as salvation, 200
  as theme of *Herzog,* 268
  women's ability to make distinctions about, 24
Love and Death in the American Novel (Fiedler), 125
"low seriousness," 124
Lowell, Robert, xxvii, 156, 310
Ludwig, Jack, xxiv, 134, 181, 189, 196, **210–12,** 226, 347

Maccoby, Hyam, 485
Macdonald, Dwight, xxvii, 17, 20, **34–35,** 36, 37, 290
MacKenzie, Rachel, 363, 472
madness as theme in Bellow's writing, 224
Mailer, Norman, 175, 427, 428, 452
Malamud, Ann, **443,** 450

Malamud, Bernard
  Bellow discusses *Augie March* with, **128–29**
  Bellow discusses *God's Grace*, **387–88**
  Bellow on writers' organizations, **176–77**
  Bellow praises *Dubin's Lives*, **365–66**
  Bellow praises *The Natural*, **115**
  Bellow's eulogy of, 435–36
  Bellow's Guggenheim recommendations for, 118–19, 162
  Bellow's opinion of *A New Life*, 228–29, 242
Malraux, André, xxvi, 414
Manea, Norman, 532, 534
Mangan, John Joseph Sherry, **135–36**
Manheim, Mary, 425
Markels, Bobby, **373**, **434**
marketing of Bellow's writing, 46–48, 326, 422, 427
marriage
  as business alliance, 220
  divorce from Alexandra, 428–29, 430–31
  effect on friendships, 12
  quarrels with Anita Goshkin, 14
  thoughts on, 86, 194, 212
Marshall, John, 281
Martin, Jack, 5
Marxism, 11, 137, 229, 253, 354–55, 471, 513
Maschler, Tom, 269
Mastroianni, Marcello, **346**
materialism, 73–74
mature and perfected form of self, 411–12
Maxwell, William, 160, 296
McCarthy, Mary, xxii, xxiv, xxv, 23, 77, 303, 391, 472
McCloskey, Herbert
  discussions of jobs and writing, **92–93**, **109–10**, **112–13**, **195**
  friendship with, **115**, 135, **538–39**
  mentioned, 56, 57, 60, 142, 315
  visits with, **114**, 142
McCloskey, Mitzie, 57, 60, **92–93**, **115**, **195**, 315
McCormick, John, 224
McGehee, Ed, 48, 52
Meade, Marion, **398**
meaning in art, 138

Medal of Freedom, xxxii
meditation, 334, 339
megalomania, 175, 317, 428, 541
Memoirs of a Bootlegger's Son, 134
Mencken, H. L., 373–74
Merchant Marine, xxi, 39–40
Merleau-Ponty, Maurice, xxii, 540
The Messiah of Stockholm (Ozick), 438–40
metamorphosis, personal, 371–72
Milano, Paolo, 61, 62, 64, 66, 97, 113, 296, 383, 384, 397
Miller, Arthur, xxiv, 139, 219, 246
Miller, Henry, 229, 343
Miller, Letizia Ciotti, 296
Miller, Ruth, **137–39**, **141**, **145–46**, **154–55**, **332–33**, 457
Mills, Margaret, **425**
mining deal in Africa, 293, 295
misery and human life, 209–10
The Misfits (movie), 219
misology, 165
Mitchell, Stephen, **483–85**
Mitgang, Herbert, **526**
moderation, 252
modernism, 318
Moe, Henry Allen, **55**, **62**, **63–64**, 75, **98**, **135**
money
  divorce from Anita and, 132, 133
  early book sales, 49–50, 137, 172
  enjoyment of, 166
  Ford Foundation grant, 168, 169–70, 193
  need for, 52, 109–10, 150, 175
  settlement payment to Susan Glassman Bellow, 361, 362, 363
  writing for money, 21, 131, 208–9
Monk, Sam, 45, 73, 80, 109
Monroe, Marilyn, xxiv, 173
Montreal, xvii, 284, 422, 427, 461, 483, 491
Moody Lectures, 312
moral life, 8
Morante, Elsa, 383–84
More Die of Heartbreak (Bellow), 442, 443
Morris, Wright, 137, 147, 171, 247, **442–43**, **460**

Mosby's Memoirs and Other Stories (Bellow), 275, 281–82, 283, 287
Mostel, Zero, 234, 238, 244, 246, **312–13**
Moynihan, Daniel Patrick, **381–82**, **384**, 385
"Mr. Green" (story), 74, 78, 83
Mr. Sammler's Planet (Bellow), 283, 289, 290, 296, 302, 317, 318
Murdoch, Iris, 383
music, 54

Nabokov, Nicolas, **302–3**, **311–12**
Naipaul, V. S., 407, 410–11, 418, 419
Naked Lunch (Burroughs), 196–97
National Book Award, xxiv, xxvii, xxix, 130–31, 172, 515
The Natural (Malamud), 115, 119, 129
natural-resource protection, 343–44
naturalism in writing, 61, 100
Nature-intimacy, 365
Nef, Evelyn, **544**
Nef, John U., **234–35**
negative capability, 156
Nelson, Benjamin, **272**, **299**
nephew's suicide, 167
Nevada, xxiv, 135–36, 139–40, 141, 149–50, 306
Neven du Mont, Reinhold, **517–18**
New Criticism, 120–21
New Directions (publisher), 32, 161
The New Leader article, 53
A New Life (Malamud), 228–29, 242
New Republic, 21, 136
New Writing (journal), 111
New York City, 59, 100–101, 103
The New York Times, 114–15, 143
The New Yorker, 51, 116, 159–60, 273–74, 331
News from the Republic of Letters (journal), 537, 541, 544, 550
Nietzsche, Friedrich, 56, 59, 419, 453, 488
nihilism, 456, 523–24
Nimier, Nadine, **306–7**
Nobel Peace Prize, 426–27

Nobel Prize in Literature, xxx, 342, 348, 363, 434
Nobile, Philip, 317
The Noble Savage literary magazine
  Bellow discusses poetry editing with John Berryman, **178**, 203
  Bellow's opinion of editing for, 225
  continued publication of, 200–201, 203–4, 226, 229
  correspondence with Edward Hoagland about, 216
  correspondence with Louis Gallo about, 209–10
  demise of, 232, 235, 242
  first issue of, 171–72
  praised by Edmund Wilson, 199
  second issue of, 198
  slow publication schedule of, 212
normalcy, 122–23, 165, 247
Northwestern University, xix–xx, xxvi, 160, 241, 379–80, 393, 521
Norwegian Nobel Prize Committee, **426–27**
Notes of a Native Son (Baldwin), 130
Notre Dame Cathedral, 66–67
novels, 138, 147, 488
The Novels of Saul Bellow (Opdahl), 216
New York University, 75, 104, 107, 112

Oates, Joyce Carol, **325**
Oaxaca, 273, 287
objectivity, 354
Obolensky, Prince Dimitri Dimitrievich, 281, 283
O'Brien, Edna, **254**, 430
"The Old System" (story), 273–74, 318
On Native Grounds (Kazin), 100
Ontario Review, 325
Opdahl, Keith, **215–16**
Oppenheimer, Yaddi, 482–83
oppression, 175
oral miserliness, 354, 494, 495
Orwell, George, 310, 343, 534
Orwell, Sonia Brownell, 97
overconfidence of writers, 251–52

Ozick, Cynthia, xxvi, **437–40, 449–50, 452–53, 454–56**

pacifism, 11
Paley, Grace, 201, 427
Paonescu, Ana, 381–82, 384
Paris, 63–64, 67, 68–69, 73–74, 87, 108
Parker, Dorothy, 398
Partington, Lucy, 549
Partisan Review (*PR*)
  announcement of "Dr.Pep" in, 78
  early publications in, 17, 19
  Jean Stafford's writing in, 38
  opinions of, 49, 303, 310, 514
  publication of *Augie March* chapter in, 85, 98
  travel-letter in, 48, 52
Passin, Cora, 22
Passin, Herb
  Anita Goshkin and, 11
  Bellow's friendship with, xviii, xix, 16, 17, 253–54, 471
  conversations with, 19–20
  loss of contact with, 53, 398
  relationships with women, 22–23
  son Thomas, 22
Patrimony (Roth), 475
Peltz, David
  annoyance at Bellow, **320–21**
  friendship with, **208, 280–81, 327–28**
  mentioned, xviii, 233, 262, 265, 293, 294, 295, 340, 372
PEN International Congress, xxvii, 427–28, 429, 452
People, 414
"People to People" Committee, 144–45
Perot, Ross, 494
Pestalozzi-Froebel Teachers' College, xx, 139
pets, 409–10
Phillips, William, xxii, 91, **177, 234**, 274, 310, 378
Piccolo Teatro (Milan), 237, 238
Pipes, Richard, 511, 518
Piscator, Erwin, 44
plane travel, 255, 270–71
plays
  completion of *The Last Analysis*, 195, 243

Lillian Hellman's opinion of *The Last Analysis*, 196
  production of *The Last Analysis*, 244
  reviews of, 261
  The Upper Depths, 234
  writing of, 168, 170, 172, 190
PM (journal), 36–37
Podhoretz, Norman, **303, 337**, 480, 487
poetry
  Bellow's praise of Bobby Markels, 373
  Bellow's "Spring Ode" poem, 105–6
  John Berryman's, 156, 157–58
  Robert Penn Warren's, 116
Poland, 189
polemical literature, 88
politics
  being Jewish and, 452
  Bellow on Stalinism, 540–41
  Bellow's nomination of Teddy Kollek for Nobel Peace Prize, 426–27
  Committee for the Free World and, 405, 417–18
  discussions with David Bazelon about, 35–37, 39
  discussions with Leon Wieseltier about, 356–57, 358–60, 391–92
  Israel and, 334–35
  opinion of office of President, 375
  praise for Stanley Crouch's writing, 479
  racial politics in Chicago, 461
  writers' responsibilities to political life, 418–20
  Yetta Barshevsky and, 527–29
politics (journal), 36
Pollitt, Katha, 500
Positano, 104, 107
postal system, 66, 77, 82, 189, 190
Potok, Chaim, 449
Pound, Ezra, 84, 144–45, 393, 478
Power in America: The Politics of the New Class (Bazelon), 37
Powers, J. F., 58, 62, **66–67, 79–80**, 81
Pozen, Walter, xxxv, 544

PR, see *Partisan Review*
"prepared" attitudes, 165
*Prince of Darkness and Other
    Stories* (Powers), 67, 79
principles, 126–27
Pritchett, V. S., 317
procrastination, 525–26
Progressive Book Club, 47–48
promotion of Bellow's
    writing, 46–48, 326,
    422, 427
prophets, 124, 127, 225–26,
    377–78, 484–85
Proust, Marcel, 138, 383, 487
provincialism, 250–51
Pryce-Jones, David, 358
psychoanalysis, xxviii, 472–73
psychology, 51, 457, 460,
    499–500
Puerto Rico, 205–8, 221
Pulitzer Prize, xxx
"The Pulley" (story), 345
Pyramid Lake, Nevada, 306

Queens College, 75, 98, 514, 518

Rahv, Philip, 58, 59, 74, 78,
    145, 247, 303, 310
Ramanujan, A. K., 418
Ransom, John Crowe, 78, 83
Ravelstein (Bellow), xxxiv,
    xxxv, 546, 547–48
Ray, Gordon, **201**, 324
readers, 124, 343, 443
Reagan, Ronald, xxxii, 375,
    466
reality, 65–66, 154, 469
"reality instructors," 251
Reedy, George, xviii, 398
Reich, Wilhelm, xxiii, 81,
    165, 220, 322, 378, 412,
    445, 472
relationships with women
    Arlette Landes, 286
    escape from feeling
        troubled by ladies, 304–5
    Frances Gendlin, 293–94,
        307–8, 313–14
    letter to Evelyn, **315–16**
    Pearl, 4, 6
    in Poland, 190
    in Tel Aviv, 192
religion, 63, 198
Remnick, David, 550
reviews, *see* criticism; critics
revolution, 35–37, 39, 65–66
Richardson, Jack, 337
Rockefeller Grant application,
    110
Roethke, Theodore, 311

Romania, xxx, 381–82, 384,
    385, 401, 532, 534
Rome, 76–77, 383–84, 385–86,
    474
Roosevelt, Karyl, 415–16
Roscoe (Kennedy), 551–52
Rosenberg, Harold, xxviii,
    265, 293
Rosenfeld, Isaac
    Bellow teaching at NYU
        and, 75, 104, 107
    Bellow's view of, 324, 331,
        347–48
    death of, 154, 156
    doctoral studies of, 6–7,
        8–9, 10
    financial worries of, 113
    friendship with Bellow
        and Tarcov, xviii, 12, 18,
        250–51, 398, 492
    Guggenheim fellowship of,
        52–53, 56, 67
    as irritant, 42
    James Atlas article on, 457
    journals of, 152, 378–79
    Mark Shechner's lecture
        on, 331
    poetry of, 17–18
    psychotherapy and, 472–73
    radio writing for Jewish
        People's Committee, 21
    return to Chicago after
        doctoral studies, 11
    slackening of
        correspondence with, 39,
        98–99
    on volunteering for army
        service, 16
Rosenfeld, Vasiliki, 17–18,
    21, 152
Ross, Ralph, 109, **190–91**,
    207, **228**, **241**, **314–15**,
    347–48, **375**
Roth, Philip
    discussions of writing with,
        162, **414**, **531–32**, **539–41**
    friendship with, **290**, **322**,
        330, **389**, **475**, **499**, **534**,
        543, **550**
    visits with, **429**, **430**, **448**,
        467–68
Roth, William, xxi, **29–33**
Rozanov, Vasily, 549
Ruben Whitfield (lost early
    novel), xx–xxi, 14–15
Rubenfeld, Florence, **487–88**
Rushdie, Salman, 476, 477
Russell & Volkening Literary
    Agency, 42, 342
Russell, Diarmuid, 120

Sacks, Oliver, 504
sages, 305
Said, Edward, 455, 456
Sakharov, Andrei, 316
Salas, Floyd, 283
Salter, James, **338**, **357–58**,
    415–16, **520**
San Francisco, 141, 148, 164
San Francisco Examiner,
    148–49
San Francisco State
    University, 283
Sandburg, Carl, 526
Sarant, George, **378–79**, 445,
    472–73, **489**
Sarda, Jack, 171, 176
Sartre, Jean-Paul, 360, 414,
    449, 540
Sasha, *see* Tschacbasov,
    Sondra
Saturday Review of Literature,
    61, 124, 127
Saul Bellow (Miller), 139, 457
Saving the Appearances
    (Barfield), 362
Schapiro, Meyer, **273–74**, **323**
Scholem, Gershom, 411
Schultz, Rachel E. G.
    (grandniece), **429**, **437**,
    446–47
Schwartz, Delmore
    death of, 265
    friendship with, 132, 457, 488
    mentioned, 138, 273, 310,
        314, 394, 431, 514
    as model for Von
        Humboldt Fleischer,
        154, 321
    paranoid episode of, 161,
        203
Schwartz, Joan Ullman, **420**
Schwartz, Jonas, 190–91,
    201–2, 222, 223
Seager, Allen, 61
seasickness, 63
Seize the Day (Bellow), 139,
    145, 150–51, 155, 159–60,
    298–99, 317
self-absorption, 347–48,
    494–95
self-consciousness, 399–401
self-discovery and
    examination, 6–7, 92,
    183, 377, 423–24
self-image, 279
77 Dream Songs (Berryman),
    245
Sexton, Anne, **233**
sexuality, 377, 409
Shachtman, Max, 4, 15, 110

Index

Shachtman, Yetta Barshevsky, xviii, **3–4**, 518, 527–29, 535
Shafer, Margaret, **341**, **396**
Shahar, David, **374–75**, **412–13**, 535
Shahar, Shula, 535
Shamir, Yitzhak, 455
Shapiro, Benny, 312
Shapiro, Karl, 197, **416–17**, **421**, **427–28**, **440–41**, 478–79, **480–81**, **488**
Shapiro, Manny, 312
Shattuck, Roger, **466–67**
Shechner, Mark, **331**
Shepherd, Elizabeth, 208
Shils, Edward
  Bellow joins faculty of Committee on Social Thought, 234–35
  Bellow on Chicago weather and valued colleagues, **241**
  Bellow on writing and Committee on Social Thought, **239–40**
  correspondence with, 272–73, 294–95, 304–5, 333–34, 353, 361
  discussion of plane crash and traveling, **255–56**
  mentioned, 229, 231, 232, 285
  opinions of, 490
Sidran, Ben, **337–38**
Sidran, Ezra, 282, 338
Sidran, Louis, xviii, 19, 281, 282, **337–38**
Sifton, Elisabeth, **364**
Silber, John, **497–98**
"A Silver Dish" (story), 463
Simenon, Georges, 505
Simmons, Edward, **545**
Simmons, Margaret Staats ("Maggie")
  attraction to, **257–58**, **263–64**
  break with, **284**, **285**, **289**
  discussions of writing with, **288**, **330–31**
  friendship with, **293**, **300–301**, **303–4**, **315**, **349–50**, **423–24**, **502**
  health issues of, **276–77**
  letters from Israel to, **270–71**
  letters from Italy to, **279–80**, **281–83**
  love letters to, **258–59**, **259–63**, **265–66**, 267, **268–69**, 275
Simpson, Eileen, **394–95**

Simpson, Louis, 332–33
Singer, Barnett, **311**, **323–24**, **364–65**
Singer, Isaac Bashevis, xxiii, **363**, 425, 489
Sinyavsky, Alexander, 418, 419, 424
Six-Day War, xxviii, 271
the Sixties, 319, 436
slander, 317
Slate, Hymen, xviii, **214–15**, **367**, **369–70**, **377**, **385–86**, **521–22**, **524–25**, **529–30**, 535
Smith College, 77, 81
Smith, K. Corlies ("Cork"), 390
Smith, Mark, **324–25**
snobbery, 79–80
socialism, 15, 213–14, 229
sociology, 18, 55, 550
Socrates, 26
solitude, 141, 142, 437
Solzhenitsyn, Aleksandr, 316
Sondra, *see* Tschacbasov, Sondra
Sontag, Susan, 255, 290
soul, 285, 369, 458
Soviet Union, xix, 195, 424, 476, 511
Spain, 44, 327–28, 386
Spanish Travelers anthology, 48, 52
speaking engagements
  Blashfield Address, 296
  in Chicago and Pittsburgh, 172
  Columbia University, 165
  fatigue and, 475
  missed, 279
  Moody Lecture at University of Chicago, 312
  Nobel Prize Lecture, 343
  opinion of, 185
  tiring of, 395–96
  verbal attack at San Francisco State, 283
Spender, Stephen, xxiii, xxv, 241
spirituality, 339–40
"Spring Ode" (poem), 105–6
Staats, Margaret, *see* Simmons, Margaret Staats
Stalinism, 5–6, 34–35, 104, 316, 419, 540–41
"The Starched Blue Sky of Spain" (Herbst), 179–80
Steinbeck, John, 144, 274

Steinberg, Saul, xxviii, **401–2**, 467, **469–70**, **508**
Steiner, George, 453
Steiner, Rudolf, xxix, 327, 334, 337, 339, 345, 351, 358, 368, 369, 371, 495
Stendhal, vii, xiii, xx, xxxi, 99, 368, 417
Stern, Gay, 204, 213, 352, 353
Stern, Richard
  Bellow on *Herzog* and *The Noble Savage*, **235**
  Bellow on writing *The Upper Depths*, **234**
  Bellow recommends for Guggenheim, 201
  Bellow's divorce from Sondra, **182–83**
  Bellow's musings on love, **184–85**
  discussions of writing and family, **212–13**, **229–30**, **246–47**, **264–65**, **351–53**, 549
  friendship with, **191**, **202–3**, **204**, **274–75**, **288–89**, **515–16**, **532–33**, **544–45**
  review of *Catch-22*, 230
Stonehill, Brian, 536, 537
Story (journal), 27
Strada Palas, 401–2
Stravinsky memoir, 311–12
Strehler, Giorgio, 237, 238
Styron, William, xxvii, 247, 452
subversiveness and humanism, 165
success, 353–54
suffering, 51, 249, 280
superfluous nature of man, 114–15
Swados, Harvey, 120, **173–74**, 226, **228–29**, **253**, **289–90**
Swedish Academy, **436**, **546**
symposium of writers, 418–20

Tarcov, Edith, 28, **65**, **76**, **104–5**, **126–27**, 465
Tarcov, Miriam, **76**
Tarcov, Nathan, **76**, **245–46**, **500**
Tarcov, Oscar
  anthropology and, 8–9, 10
  apologies to, **6–7**, **65**
  arguments with, 11, 12–13
  Bellow on Susan's move to Chicago, **238**
  Bellow reviews Tarcov's novel, 124, 127

Tarcov, Oscar (*cont.*)
  Bellow's friction with Isaac
    Rosenberg, **104–5**
  Bellow's tentative first novel
    and, 14–15
  congratulates on publication
    of book, 119–20
  correspondence with, **6–20,
    89–91, 119–20, 131**
  death of, 245
  description of life in Paris,
    89–90
  friendship with Bellow
    and Rosenfeld, xviii, 12,
    18–19, 131, 250–51, 398
  health issues of, 117, 119,
    127, 131
  opinion of David Bazelon's
    writing, 36
  postcard from Italy to, **76**
Taylor, Harold, 101, 257, 276
Tel Aviv, 191–92
Les Temps Modernes (journal),
  99
Terkel, Studs, 526
Thatcher, Margaret, xxxiii,
  465–66
theater people, 252
"A Theft" (story), 449, 466
Thomas, Dylan, 311
Thomes, Boyd, 314–15
"The Thoughts of Sgt. George
  Flavin," 83
time, 54, 381, 413, 489
Titoism, 97
Tivoli, New York house, 153,
  154, 171, 176, 192, 194
To Jerusalem and Back
  (Bellow), 334–35, 336,
  339–40, 341
Tolstoy, Leo, 225, 291, 477
totalitarianism, 419
"The Transcendentalist"
  (Emerson), 121–22
transformation as goal of
  writing, 386–87
translations of Bellow titles,
  67, 77
Trilling, Diana, 487, 488
Trilling, Lionel
  Bellow discusses book
    critics with, 114–15
  Bellow discusses Emerson
    and *Augie March* with,
    121–23
  Bellow's opinion of, 147
  correspondence with,
    114–15, 121–23, 319–20
  Guggenheim fellowship
    and, 67

mentioned, 166, 233, 324,
  487
Trotsky, Leon (The Old Man),
  xx–xxi, 6, 15, 370, 471
Trotskyism, xix, 136, 289,
  471, 514
Troup, Stanley B., **297**
truth
  as goal of writing, 332
  obligations to, 272, 316
  study of Barfield's books
    and, 375
  true meaning and
    information, 406–7
  truthfulness as human
    instinct, 178
Tschacbasov, Sondra
  ("Sasha")
  alimony, custody, and
    parenting issues, **235–37,
    263, 266–67, 277–79**
  Bellow's divorce from Anita
    and, 140, 141
  Bellow's relationship with,
    xxiii, 132, 134, 135, 347
  divorce from, 180–84,
    190–91, 193, 194, 198
  dream of Ann (Birstein)
    Kazin, 137
  Jack Ludwig and, 196,
    211–12, 225
  marriage to, 146, 166, 167,
    169–70, 175
  pregnancy of, 152, 154, 156,
    158
Tulcea, Alexandra Ionescu,
  see Bellow, Alexandra
    Ionescu Tulcea
Tuley High School, xviii, xix,
  xxxiii, 91, 215, 397, 398,
  474, 527
Tumin, Melvin Marvin
  advice from Bellow
    regarding women, 23
  apology for not writing
    sooner, 24
  on comedic writing, 59–60
  correspondence with,
    20–29, 45–46, 52–53,
    55–57, 59–60, 297, 324
  loss of contact with, 109
  news of friends from
    Bellow, 21–23
  on possible move to
    Europe, 58–59
  reaction to *Augie March*, 112
  report on Anita's family to,
    45–46
  on writing process and
    Army service with, 25–26

on writing and having an
  agent, 20–21, 23
Tumin, Sylvia, **287**
Tureck, Rosalyn, xviii, **271**
"Two Morning Monologues"
  (story), xxi

Ulysses (Joyce), 227, 476, 493
Unancestral Voice (Barfield),
  326, 328–29, 345
the Unconscious, 319, 329
Unger, Leonard, 45, 93, **249**
unhappiness, 200
University of Chicago, xix, 36,
  203, 209, 333–34, 336
University of Minnesota, xxii,
  42, 47, 52, 76
University of Puerto Rico,
  xxvi
University of Wisconsin-
  Madison, xx, 9, 545
Updike, John, 331, 450
The Upper Depths (working
  title for *The Last
  Analysis*), 234, 235, 237

Vanguard Press, 40, 41, 52, 58,
  59, 116
Vargas Llosa, Mario, **418–20**
Vermont residence, 406, 410,
  433, 474
The Very Dark Trees, xxi, 29,
  30, 32–33
The Victim (Bellow)
  critiques of, 57
  dramatization of, 41, 47
  financial failure of, 59
  Guggenheim fellowship
    application and, 41, 43
  naturalism in, 61
  second draft of, 42
  Bellow's evaluation of,
    xxi–xxii, 50
Vidal, Gore, 324, 455, 480
Vietnam War, 253, 289
Viking Press
  advance installments, 83
  Bellow's correspondence
    with Marshall Best,
    193–94
  Bellow's departure from,
    364
  Bellow's loyalty to, 140, 364
  contracts for novels with,
    79, 83, 481
  Monroe Engel and, 63
  publication of *Augie March*,
    109
Village, Greenwich, 51, 454,
  473, 476, 487

Index

Volkening, Henry
  Augie March discussions,
    101–2, 103–4, 108,
    116–17, 120
  becomes Bellow's agent, xxi
  Bellow's fantasy story about
    F. Scott Fitzgerald, 67–72
  Bellow's love for, 243–44
  Bellow's recommendations
    of to other writers, 146,
    162
  complaints about Henle to,
    44, 46–48, 58, 60
  correspondence with, 51–52,
    62–63, 65–66
  divorce from Anita, 139–40
  dramatization of *The Victim*
    and, 41–42
  editors and censorship of
    writing, 78–79
  progress reports on writing,
    77–79, 81–85
  publication of Bellow's
    short stories, 62
  summer travels, 108
  writing and publication
    discussions, 74–75
Voltaire, 485, 513

Wade, Grace, 306
Wagner College, 227, 228
Walden, George, 466
Walden, Sarah, 469
Walker, Nancy, 250
Wallach, Eli, 285, 298
Walsh, Chris, 539
Walter, Anne Doubillon, 408,
    413–14
Wanamaker, Sam, 355
War and Peace (Tolstoy), 256
Warren, Robert Penn ("Red")
  Bellow's eulogy of, 458
  Bellow's nomination for
    Nobel Prize, 436
  correspondence with,
    43–44, 45, 116, 118,
    130–31, 299–300, 406
  Eleanor Clark and, 515
  living in Manhattan, 113
  news of mutual friends, 45
  opinion of *The Victim*,
    42, 47
Warren, Rosanna, 466, 467,
    496
Warsaw Ghetto, 358–59
Wasserman, Harriet, 327, 342,
    355, 411, 422, 429, 517
Waugh, Evelyn, 79, 259, 422

Weidenfeld and Nicolson,
    269, 326
Weidenfeld, George, xxv, 269
Weingrod, Bracha, 298
Weiss, Theodore, xxiv, 133–34
"The Wen" (play), 250
West, Anthony, 120–21, 123,
    124, 125–26, 159
"What Kind of Day Did You
    Have?" (story), 416–17,
    420, 421
Wheelwright, Jeff, 406–7, 488
White, Katharine Sargent
    Angell, 51, 74, 75,
    120–21, 124, 125–26
Wieseltier, Leon, 353–55,
    356–57, 358–60, 391–92,
    455
Wilde, Oscar, 445
Wilkins, Sophie, 417, 420–21,
    453–54, 512–24, 543
Willingham, Calder, 42–43
Wilson, Edmund, xxi, xxvii,
    xxix, 37–38, 41, 43, 156,
    199, 259, 310, 395
"Winter in Tuscany" (article),
    502
Winters, Shelley, 253
wisdom, 264
Wiseman, Joseph, 299, 304
Wisse, Ruth, 479–80, 490–91
Wolff, Kurt, 57
women's liberation, 315
Wood, James, xxxv, xxxvi,
    525–26, 537
Woolf, Virginia, 313, 448
World Jewish Congress, 426
world view, 345, 347
World War II, 25
"The Wrecker" (play), 208
writers
  Alice Adams, 174–76
  Bernard Malamud, 118–19
  Cynthia Ozick, 438
  Harold Brodkey, 450–51
  imagination and, 118–19
  Jean Stafford, 252
  Martin Amis, 502–3, 523,
    548–49
  Meyer Schapiro, 323
  motivations of, 414
  opinions of, 109–10, 217–18,
    251–52
  Philip Roth, 290
  as prophets, 225–26
  Stanley Elkin, 489–90
  thoughts on being a writer,
    224–25, 227–28, 319

writers' organizations,
    avoidance of, 176–77
writing
  arguments in, 318
  authenticity and, 523–24
  Bellow's evaluation of,
    14–15, 19, 27–28, 37, 57,
    77, 503
  Bellow's views on narrative,
    370
  as business, 32–33, 131
  cognitive writing, 38, 177
  conformity as threat to, 119
  craft of, 50–51, 66, 227–28
  as cure for unhappiness,
    200
  desire to write freely, 50–51,
    216
  "exposing the seeming"
    and, 246–47
  fatigue and, 327–28, 491,
    509, 523
  finding time for, 42, 47,
    54, 501
  growing confidence in, 102
  ideas as palpable element
    in, 162
  Old and New Testaments
    and, 148
  process of, 25, 26, 47, 147,
    372
  reclaiming of unreality, 154
  rejection of, 27, 33
  short stories turning into
    novels, 190
  sources of material for,
    320–21
  Symbolist approach to, 121
  writer's block, 365, 495
Wylie, Andrew, 517

Yaddo (artists' colony),
    113, 115, 117, 153, 168,
    229, 397
Yehoshua, A. B., xxix, xxxii,
    442
"The Yellow House" (story),
    306, 318
Yiddish, xvii, xviii, 298, 305,
    331, 543
Yiddish Courier, 11
Young, Kimball, 9
Yugoslavia, 189

Zeisler, Peter, 250
"Zetland: By a Character
    Witness" (story), 403
Zionism, 339, 392